Lecture Notes in Computer Science 13701

More information about this series at https://link.springer.com/bookseries/558

Tiziana Margaria · Bernhard Steffen (Eds.)

Leveraging Applications of Formal Methods, Verification and Validation

Verification Principles

11th International Symposium, ISoLA 2022
Rhodes, Greece, October 22–30, 2022
Proceedings, Part I

Springer

Editors
Tiziana Margaria ⓘ
University of Limerick, CSIS and Lero
Limerick, Ireland

Bernhard Steffen ⓘ
TU Dortmund
Dortmund, Germany

ISSN 0302-9743   ISSN 1611-3349 (electronic)
Lecture Notes in Computer Science
ISBN 978-3-031-19848-9   ISBN 978-3-031-19849-6 (eBook)
https://doi.org/10.1007/978-3-031-19849-6

Introduction

As General and Program Chairs we would like to welcome you to the proceedings of ISoLA 2022, the 11th International Symposium on Leveraging Applications of Formal Methods, Verification and Validation held in Rhodes (Greece) during October 22–30, 2022, and endorsed by EASST, the European Association of Software Science and Technology.

Returning to the traditional in-person event, ISoLA 2022 provided a forum for developers, users, and researchers to discuss issues related to the adoption and use of rigorous tools and methods for the specification, analysis, verification, certification, construction, testing, and maintenance of systems from the point of view of their different application domains. Thus, since 2004 the ISoLA series of events has served the purpose of bridging the gap between designers and developers of rigorous tools on one side, and users in engineering and in other disciplines on the other side. It fosters and exploits synergetic relationships among scientists, engineers, software developers, decision makers, and other critical thinkers in companies and organizations. By providing a specific, dialogue-oriented venue for the discussion of common problems, requirements, algorithms, methodologies, and practices, ISoLA aims in particular at supporting researchers in their quest to improve the practicality, reliability, flexibility, and efficiency of tools for building systems, and users in their search for adequate solutions to their problems.

The program of ISoLA 2022 consisted of a collection of special tracks devoted to the following hot and emerging topics:

1. Rigorous Engineering of Collective Adaptive Systems
   (Organizers: Rocco De Nicola, Stefan Jähnichen, Martin Wirsing)
2. Programming: What is Next?
   (Organizers: Klaus Havelund, Bernhard Steffen)
3. X-by-Construction meets Runtime Verification
   (Organizers: Maurice H. ter Beek, Loek Cleophas, Martin Leucker, Ina Schaefer)
4. Automated Software Re-Engineering
   (Organizers: Serge Demeyer, Reiner Hähnle, Heiko Mantel)
5. Digital Twin Engineering
   (Organizers: John Fitzgerald, Peter Gorm Larsen, Tiziana Margaria, Jim Woodcock, Claudio Gomes)
6. SpecifyThis - Bridging gaps between program specification paradigms
   (Organizers: Wolfgang Ahrendt, Marieke Huisman, Mattias Ulbrich, Paula Herber)
7. Verification and Validation of Concurrent and Distributed Heterogeneous Systems
   (Organizers: Marieke Huisman, Cristina Seceleanu)
8. Formal Methods Meet Machine Learning
   (Organizers: Kim Larsen, Axel Legay, Bernhard Steffen, Marielle Stoelinga)
9. Formal methods for DIStributed COmputing in future RAILway systems
   (Organizers: Alessandro Fantechi, Stefania Gnesi, Anne Haxthausen)

10. Automated Verification of Embedded Control Software
    (Organizers: Dilian Gurov, Paula Herber, Ina Schaefer)
11. Digital Thread in Smart Manufacturing
    (Organizers: Tiziana Margaria, Dirk Pesch, Alan McGibney)

It also included the following the embedded or co-located events:

- Doctoral Symposium and Poster Session (Sven Jörges, Salim Saay, Steven Smyth)
- Industrial Day (Axel Hessenkämper, Falk Howar, Hardi Hungar, Andreas Rausch)
- DIME Days 2022 (Tiziana Margaria, Bernhard Steffen)

Altogether, the proceedings of ISoLA 2022 comprises contributions collected in four volumes:

- Part 1: Verification Principles
- Part 2: Software Engineering
- Part 3: Adaptation and Learning
- Part 4: Practice

We thank the track organizers, the members of the program committee, and their reviewers for their effort in selecting the papers to be presented, the local Organization Chair, Petros Stratis, and the EasyConferences team for their continuous precious support during the entire period preceding the events, and the Springer for being, as usual, a very reliable partner for the proceedings production. Finally, we are grateful to Christos Therapontos for his continuous support for the Web site and the program, and to Steve Bosselmann for his help with the editorial system EquinOCS.

Special thanks are due to the following organizations for their endorsement: EASST (European Association of Software Science and Technology) and Lero - The Irish Software Research Centre, along with our own institutions - TU Dortmund and the University of Limerick.

We wish you, as an ISoLA participant, lively scientific discussions at this edition, and also later, when reading the proceedings, valuable new insights that contribute to your research and its uptake.

October 2022   Bernhard Steffen
                                                   Tiziana Margaria

Organization

Program Committee Chairs

Margaria, Tiziana   University of Limerick and Lero, Ireland
Steffen, Bernhard   TU Dortmund University, Germany

Program Committee

Ahrendt, Wolfgang	Chalmers University of Technology, Sweden
Cleophas, Loek	Eindhoven University of Technology (TU/e), The Netherlands
De Nicola, Rocco	IMT School for Advanced Studies, Italy
Demeyer, Serge	Universiteit Antwerpen, Belgium
Fantechi, Alessandro	Università di Firenze, Italy
Fitzgerald, John	Newcastle University, UK
Gnesi, Stefania	ISTI-CNR, Italy
Gomes, Claudio	Aarhus University, Denmark
Gurov, Dilian	KTH Royal Institute of Technology, Sweden
Havelund, Klaus	Jet Propulsion Laboratory, USA
Haxthausen, Anne	Technical University of Denmark, Denmark
Herber, Paula	University of Münster, Germany
Hessenkämper, Axel	Schulz Systemtechnik GmbH, Germany
Howar, Falk	TU Dortmund University, Germany
Huisman, Marieke	University of Twente, The Netherlands
Hungar, Hardi	German Aerospace Center, Germany
Hähnle, Reiner	TU Darmstadt, Germany
Jähnichen, Stefan	TU Berlin, Germany
Jörges, Sven	FH Dortmund, Germany
Lamprecht, Anna-Lena	University of Potsdam, Germany
Larsen, Kim	Aalborg University, Denmark
Larsen, Peter Gorm	Aarhus University, Denmark
Legay, Axel	UCLouvain, Belgium
Leucker, Martin	University of Lübeck, Germany
Mantel, Heiko	TU Darmstadt, Germany
Margaria, Tiziana	University of Limerick and Lero, Ireland
McGibney, Alan	Munster Technological University, Ireland
Pesch, Dirk	University College Cork, Ireland
Rausch, Andreas	Clausthal University of Technology, Germany

Saay, Salim	University of Limerick, Ireland
Schaefer, Ina	Karlsruhe Institute of Technology, Germany
Seceleanu, Cristina	Mälardalen University, Sweden
Smyth, Steven	TU Dortmund University, Germany
Steffen, Bernhard	TU Dortmund University, Germany
Stoelinga, Marielle	University of Twente, The Netherlands
Ulbrich, Mattias	Karlsruhe Institute of Technology, Germany
Wirsing, Martin	LMU Munich, Germany
Woodcock, Jim	University of York, UK
ter Beek, Maurice	ISTI-CNR, Italy

Additional Reviewers

Abbas, Houssam	Di Stefano, Luca
Adelt, Julius	Dierl, Simon
Alberts, Elvin	Dubslaff, Clemens
Arbab, Farhad	Duchêne, Fabien
Bainczyk, Alexander	Eldh, Sigrid
Barbanera, Franco	Ernst, Gidon
Beckert, Bernhard	Feng, Hao
Berducci, Luigi	Flammini, Francesco
Beringer, Lennart	Freitas, Leo
Bettini, Lorenzo	Gabor, Thomas
Bhattacharyya, Anirban	Gerastathopoulos, Ilias
Blanchard, Allan	Groote, Jan Friso
Boerger, Egon	Grosu, Radu
Bogomolov, Sergiy	Grunske, Lars
Bonakdarpour, Borzoo	Hallerstede, Stefan
Bortolussi, Luca	Hansen, Simon Thrane
Bourr, Khalid	Hartmanns, Arnd
Brandstätter, Andreas	Hatcliff, John
Breslin, John	Heydari Tabar, Asmae
Broy, Manfred	Hnetynka, Petr
Bubel, Richard	Inverso, Omar
Bures, Tomas	Jakobs, Marie-Christine
Busch, Daniel	John, Jobish
Chaudhary, Hafiz Ahmad Awais	Johnsen, Einar Broch
Chiti, Francesco	Jongmans, Sung-Shik
Ciancia, Vincenzo	Kamburjan, Eduard
Cok, David	Katsaros, Panagiotis
Cordy, Maxime	Kittelmann, Alexander
Damiani, Ferruccio	Knapp, Alexander
De Donato, Lorenzo	Kosmatov, Nikolai
Demrozi, Florenc	Kretinsky, Jan

Kuruppuarachchi, Pasindu
Köhl, Maximilan
König, Christoph
Könighofer, Bettina
Lee, Edward
Lluch Lafuente, Alberto
Loreti, Michele
Madsen, Ole Lehrmann
Massink, Mieke
Mauritz, Malte
Mazzanti, Franco
Merz, Stephan
Micucci, Daniela
Monica, Stefania
Monti, Raul
Morichetta, Andrea
Nardone, Roberto
Naujokat, Stefan
Nayak, Satya Prakash
Neider, Daniel
Niehage, Mathis
Nolte, Gerrit
Ölvecky, Peter
Pace, Gordon
Perez, Guillermo
Petrov, Tatjana
Phan, Thomy
Piterman, Nir
Pugliese, Rosario
Reisig, Wolfgang
Remke, Anne
Riganelli, Oliviero
Ritz, Fabian

Rocha, Henrique
Runge, Tobias
Santen, Thomas
Scaletta, Marco
Schallau, Till
Schiffl, Jonas
Schlatte, Rudolf
Schlüter, Maximilian
Schneider, Gerardo
Schürmann, Jonas
Seisenberger, Monika
Smyth, Steven
Soudjani, Sadegh
Spellini, Stefano
Stankaitis, Paulius
Stewing, Richard
Stolz, Volker
Tapia Tarifa, Silvia Lizeth
Tegeler, Tim
Tiezzi, Francesco
Trubiani, Catia
Tschaikowski, Max
Tuosto, Emilio
Valiani, Serenella
Van Bladel, Brent
van de Pol, Jaco
Vandin, Andrea
Vittorini, Valeria
Weber, Alexandra
Weigl, Alexander
Wright, Thomas
Zambonelli, Franco

Contents – Part I

Verification and Validation of Concurrent and Distributed Heterogeneous Systems

SpecifyThis - Bridging Gaps Between Program Specification Paradigms

SpecifyThis – Bridging Gaps Between Program Specification Paradigms

Wolfgang Ahrendt[1]([⊠]), Paula Herber[4], Marieke Huisman[2],
and Mattias Ulbrich[3]

[1] Chalmers University of Technology, Gothenburg, SE, Sweden
`ahrendt@chalmers.se`
[2] University of Twente, Enschede, NL, The Netherlands
`m.huisman@utwente.nl`
[3] Karlsruhe Institute of Technology, Karlsruhe, DE, Germany
`ulbrich@kit.edu`
[4] University of Münster, Münster, DE, Germany
`paula.herber@uni-muenster.de`

Abstract. We motivate and summarise the track *SpecifyThis – Bridging gaps between program specification paradigms*, taking place at the International Symposium on Leveraging Applications of Formal Methods, ISoLA 2022.

Keywords: Specification · Verification · Formal methods

1 Introduction

The field of program verification has seen considerable successes in recent years. At the same time, both the variety of properties that can be specified and the collection of approaches that solve such program verification challenges have specialised and diversified a lot. Examples include contract-based specification and deductive verification of functional properties, the specification and verification of temporal properties using model checking or static analyses for secure information flow properties. While this diversification enables the formal analyses of ever more kinds of properties, it may leave the impression of isolated solutions that solve different, unrelated problems.

Here lies a great potential that waits to be uncovered: If either of the approaches can be extended to enable the interpretation of specifications used in other approaches and to use them beneficially in its analyses, a considerable extension of the power and reach of formal analyses is achievable. A discipline of "separation and integration of concerns" can be obtained, by, e.g., combining temporal specifications of a protocol with a contract-based specification of its implementation units.

The theme of this track is to investigate and discuss what can be achieved in joint efforts of the communities of different specification and verification techniques. This track is a natural next step following a series of well-structured

T. Margaria and B. Steffen (Eds.): ISoLA 2022, LNCS 13701, pp. 3–6, 2022.
https://doi.org/10.1007/978-3-031-19849-6_1

online discussions within the VerifyThis community during the last year. There, we identified first candidates for the combination/interplay of formal program verification methods. Following that, the ISoLA 2022 track addresses questions such as how specifications which are shared between different approaches should look like, how different abstraction levels can be bridged, how semantical differences can be resolved, which application areas can benefit from which method combinations, what artifacts can be carried forward through different verification technologies, what role user interaction (in form of specifications) plays, and how one can integrate the various techniques into the development processes.

2   Summary of Contributions

Jesper Amilon, Christian Lidström, and Dilian Gurov [1] (*Deductive Verification Based Abstraction for Software Model Checking*) describe a combination of model-checking and deductive verification, where deductive verification is applied to prove local pre-post specifications of source code *units*, and model checking is applied to prove global (temporal) properties of the *system*. The model checker is not applied to the source code, but to the abstractions provided by the pre-post-specifications. The approach is theoretically well founded in abstract contract theory [7], implemented in a combination of Frama-C and TLA+, and demonstrated on an example.

David Cok and Gary Leavens [2] (*Abstraction in Deductive Verification: Model Fields and Model Methods*) report how different abstraction techniques available in the Java Modeling Language JML can be employed to verify Java programs. To this end, the authors describe how model fields and methods can serve as means of abstraction and sketch how existing logical encodings of heap memory can be enriched to accommodate model entities. Abstraction from concrete program states to more abstract notions of state is an important vehicle to cross boundaries between different verification techniques.

Gidon Ernst, Alexander Knapp and Toby Murray [3] (*A Hoare Logic with Regular Behavioral Specifications*) introduce a variant of Hoare logic, which allows to capture trace properties (of terminating programs). In this way, behavioural and state properties can be combined in a single specification. The idea is that a program explicitly emits certain statements, which together form the trace of the program. The Hoare triples specify the assumptions on the trace so far, and capture the trace that will be emitted by the current program fragment. The Hoare logic with traces is proven sound in Isabelle, and the sketch of a completeness argument is given. The approach is implemented in a prototype tool, and illustrated on two case studies.

Klaus Havelund [4] (*Specification-based Monitoring of C++*) proposes an approach for specification-based monitoring of C/C++ applications using a mix of a state machine and rule based language. He presents LogScope, a system for monitoring event streams against formal specifications that are expressed in state-machine style but with expressive rules to describe possible events. LogScope takes such a formal specification together with an application, and translates them into a monitored program. The author illustrates the applicability and expressiveness of the specification language and the overall approach with a number of examples.

Igor Konnov, Markus Kuppe, and Stephan Merz [6] (*Specification and Verification With the TLA$^+$ Trifecta: TLC, Apalache, and TLAPS*) show how different verification paradigms can be applied to models in the same modelling language. The authors use the formalism TLA$^+$ (*temporal logic of actions*) to model a termination detection algorithm for distributed systems. The specifcation, in which operations are defined using before-after-predicates in first-order-logic over set theory, is then subjected to different formal verification approaches, like explicit-state model checking, bounded symbolic model checking, and theorem proving The paper provides insights into how the different formal tools for TLA$^+$ can be used in combination to solve a non-trivial case study.

Gordon Pace and Wolfgang Ahrendt [8] (*Selective Presumed Benevolence in Multi-Party System Verification*) extend an existing sequent calculus for smart contracts with the concept of selective benevolence. To achieve this, they define new proof rules that enable us to assume benevolence of some (specified) parties in smart contract verification, while assuming potentially malevolent (worst-case) behavior from others. The benevolent parties can be defined as a predicate, either statically or dynamically. The authors discuss the benefits of presumed benevolence and its potential uses.

Thomas Santen [9] (*On the Pragmatics of Moving from System Models to Program Contracts*) describes a case study on the VerifyThis Long Term Challenge problem (the Hagrid key server) [5] on how to construct a verified implementation from an abstract system model. It first presents a model for the key server in Alloy. This model consists of a state description, and various transitions that model the key server operations. It then describes how this is transformed into executable code with contracts.

References

1. Amilon, J., Lidström, C., Gurov, D.: Deductive Verification Based Abstraction for Software Model Checking. In: Margaria, T., Steffen, B. (eds.) ISoLA 2022. LNCS, vol. 13701, pp. 7–28. Springer, Cham (2022)
2. Cok, D., Leavens, G.: Abstraction in deductive verification: Model fields and model methods. In: Margaria, T., Steffen, B. (eds.) ISoLA 2022. LNCS, vol. 13701, pp. 29–44. Springer, Cham (2022)
3. Ernst, G., Knapp, A., Murray, T.: A Hoare logic with regular behavioral specifications. In: Margaria, T., Steffen, B. (eds.) ISoLA 2022. LNCS, vol. 13701, pp. 45–64. Springer, Cham (2022)
4. Havelund, K.: Specification-based Monitoring in C++. Margaria, T., Steffen, B. (eds.) ISoLA 2022. LNCS, vol. 13701, pp. 65–87. Springer, Cham (2022)
5. Huisman, M., Monti, R., Ulbrich, M., Weigl, A.: The verifyThis collaborative long term challenge. In: Ahrendt, W., Beckert, B., Bubel, R., Hähnle, R., Ulbrich, M. (eds.) Deductive Software Verification: Future Perspectives. LNCS, vol. 12345, pp. 246–260. Springer, Cham (2020). https://doi.org/10.1007/978-3-030-64354-6_10

6. Konnov, I., Kuppe, M., Merz, S.: Specification and verification with the TLA$^+$ trifecta: TLC, Apalache, and TLAPS. In: Margaria, T., Steffen, B. (eds.) ISoLA 2022. LNCS, vol. 13701, pp. 88–105. Springer, Cham (2022)
7. Lidström, C., Gurov, D.: An abstract contract theory for programs with procedures. In: FASE 2021. LNCS, vol. 12649, pp. 152–171. Springer, Cham (2021). https://doi.org/10.1007/978-3-030-71500-7_8
8. Pace, G., Ahrendt, W.: Selective Presumed Benevolence in Multi-Party System Verification. In: Margaria, T., Steffen, B. (eds.) ISoLA 2022. LNCS, vol. 13701, pp. 106–123. Springer, Cham (2022)
9. Santen, T.: On the pragmatics of moving from system models to program contracts. In: Margaria, T., Steffen, B. (eds.) ISoLA 2022. LNCS, vol. 13701, pp. 124–138. Springer, Cham (2022)

Deductive Verification Based Abstraction
for Software Model Checking

Jesper Amilon, Christian Lidström, and Dilian Gurov[✉]

KTH Royal Institute of Technology, Stockholm, Sweden
{jamilon,clid,dilian}@kth.se

Abstract. The research community working on formal software verification has historically evolved into two main camps, grouped around two verification methods that are typically referred to as Deductive Verification and Model Checking. In this paper, we present an approach that applies deductive verification to formally justify abstract models for model checking in the TLA framework. We present a proof-of-concept tool chain for C programs, based on Frama-C for deductive verification and TLA$^+$ for model checking. As a theoretical foundation, we summarise a previously developed abstract contract theory as a framework for combining these two methods. Since the contract theory adheres to the principles of contract based design, this justifies the use of the approach in a real-world system design setting. We evaluate our approach on two case studies: a simple C program simulating opening and closing of files, as well as a C program based on real software from the automotive industry.

Keywords: Contracts · Deductive verification · Model checking

1 Introduction

The literature on formal software verification can roughly be grouped into two branches, typically referred to as Deductive Verification and Model Checking. Deductive verification historically stems from Floyd-Hoare style logics. Hoare logic contracts in term of pre- and post-conditions (see, e.g., [10]) are meaningful in the context of programs that are understood as *state transformers*, i.e., programs the purpose of which is to transform certain initial values to certain final values, where the intermediate values are just implementation details irrelevant to the computed function. Deductive verification thus focuses on the *transformational behaviour* of programs. Technically, it is typically based on symbolic approaches, such as computing Weakest Preconditions or Symbolic Execution, to convert programs annotated with specifications to formulas in First-Order Logic, and then on (back-end) algorithmic SAT/SMT solving.

This work has been funded by the FFI Programme of the Swedish Governmental Agency for Innovation Systems (VINNOVA) as the AVerT2 project 2021-02519.

T. Margaria and B. Steffen (Eds.): ISoLA 2022, LNCS 13701, pp. 7–28, 2022.
https://doi.org/10.1007/978-3-031-19849-6_2

On the other hand, model checking historically stems from algorithmic approaches to evaluating whether a formula of (some) Temporal Logic holds in a given state of a Kripke structure (see, e.g., [6]). It focuses on the non-terminating, *temporal behaviour* of programs. Technically, it is typically based on property-preserving abstractions of programs (or system descriptions) to finite-state representations, and then on algorithmic state-space exploration.

While this dichotomy of transformational versus temporal behaviour of programs is useful, the two aspects are not mutually exclusive and can be relevant for one and the same software system. For instance, the software embedded in modern vehicles is typically structured in two layers. The lower, infrastructure layer contains a scheduler, which essentially executes an infinite loop that periodically calls, in a predefined order, a fixed set of modules (called applications) in the upper, application layer. The individual applications are of a purely transformational nature: they read certain input values coming from the sensors and set by the infrastructure, and compute, in a finite number of steps, certain output values which are then propagated by the infrastructure software to the actuators. If we have to formally verify the safety of such embedded software, both transformational and temporal properties need to be taken into account. In this particular domain, one can even observe a hierarchy between the two, as a consequence of the hierarchy between the two software layers: one can view the temporal behaviour on top of the transformational one.

In this paper, we propose an approach that can be described as *Deductive Verification Based Abstraction for Software Model Checking*. The essence of our approach is to relativise the verification of the temporal properties of a program on the transformational properties of certain selected program components. The transformational properties are phrased as Hoare logic style contracts, and deductive verification is performed to verify that the components indeed fulfil their contracts. Then, for the purpose of model checking of the temporal properties of the program, the selected components are replaced by their contracts. Since this results in *modular* verification, it has good chances of scaling better than model checking on its own, which is a *monolithic* technique.

Our approach allows the results of deductive verification to be lifted to (and utilised in) the temporal domain. In the context of our embedded software example mentioned above, one would apply deductive verification to verify the transformational properties of the modules in the application layer, and then combine their contracts with the infrastructure software into a model that is model checked against the temporal properties. To combine such heterogeneous approaches to formal verification in a sound and consistent manner, a unifying semantic foundation is needed. In this paper, we summarise a previously developed abstract contract theory [14] as a theoretical framework for combining deductive verification with model checking, and show how our approach can be formalised in this abstract contract theory.

To test our idea, we are currently experimenting with a tool chain for C programs, based on Frama-C for deductive verification and TLA$^+$ for model checking. As preliminary evaluation, we have applied our approach on two example

C-programs, with one being based on a real software module taken from the automotive industry.

Related Work. The idea of combining code with contracts when performing model checking is explored in several previous works.

Sun et al. [20] show how contracts can be used when creating models to be verified with the PAT model checker, by means of a case study where PAT is used to model check itself. The target language is C#, and the approach is to include code and contracts into the models by allowing PAT models to dynamically load C# code (possibly annotated with contracts). This differs from our approach where code and contracts are translated statically into the modelling language. The main focus of their work is, however, the verification of PAT, and they do not evaluate how the use of contracts affects scalability. Their approach also differs from ours in that they perform runtime verification of the contracts.

Beckert et al. [4] use contracts to introduce modularity into the bounded model checker JBMC for Java programs. Their approach differs from ours in that they integrate the program and the contracts by performing transformations on the original Java program, whereas we translate the program and the contracts separately into the modelling language before we integrate them. Similarly, Champion et al. [7] use contracts to achieve modularization for the SMT-based model checker Kind2. They show on an example that their approach improves the scalability of the tool. Contracts are part of the modelling language and specify the behaviour of nodes in the model, as there is no underlying programming language, and thus no translation of programs into models, unlike in our approach.

Closest to our philosophy of using deductive verification for the purposes of formally justifying abstract models of program behaviour, to be then used for model checking, is perhaps the work by Ortwijn et al. [18]. It can be seen as a generalisation of our approach to concurrent programs, where Separation Logic with Fractional Permissions is used for deductive verification, and where the abstraction is into process algebraic muCRL terms. Finally, it should be pointed out that the model of programs proposed here, where certain parts have been abstracted into TLA actions, is very close in spirit to the notion of *flow graph* studied in [19]. The authors consider there the problem of how to compositionally model check flow graphs against temporal properties, but do not address the problem of extracting flow graphs from source code in a provably correct manner, as we do here.

Structure. The paper is organised as follows. In Sect. 2 we present an overview of our approach and the envisaged tool chain. Deductive verification and Frama-C are described in Sect. 3, while model checking and TLA in Sect. 4. Then, Sect. 5 gives a summary of our abstract contract theory from [14], and explains how it serves as a theoretical foundation for our approach. We present a preliminary practical evaluation of our approach in Sect. 6, and conclude with Sect. 7.

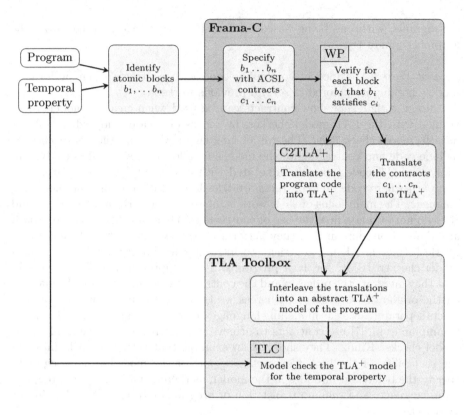

Fig. 1. Flowchart illustrating our verification approach and tool chain

2   Overview of the Verification Approach

The starting point of our approach is a C program and some temporal property, which we want the program to satisfy. Our proposed verification approach and tool chain are illustrated in Fig. 1. As shown, we rely on Frama-C for (abstraction using) deductive verification, and on TLA$^+$ for modelling and model checking.

Illustrating Example. Consider the simple program shown in Fig. 2. The main function of the program repeatedly reads a temperature value, converts it from Kelvin to Celsius, and finally outputs the converted value (the value of the variable **in_kelvin** is expected to be updated between each iteration in the loop). Assume that we want to use the TLC model checker to verify the program against some chosen temporal property (TLA and TLC is described in more detail in Sect. 4.1). Then, the first step of our approach would be to identify sequential blocks in the code that can be recognised as atomic with respect to the chosen temporal property, and then to provide these blocks with *contracts*. For specifying block contracts, we use the (Hoare logic style) ACSL specification language, which is the annotation language supported by Frama-C (described in Sect. 3). For our example program, we have chosen to consider the **convert_temp**

```
1  volatile int in_kelvin;
2  int out_celsius;
3
4  /*@
5    requires k >= 0;
6    assigns \nothing;
7    ensures \result == \old(k) - 273;
8  */
9  void convert_temp(int k) {
10   int res = k;
11   res = res - 273;
12   return res;
13 }
14
15 int main() {
16   int c, k;
17   while (1) {
18     k = in_kelvin;          // read temp (in Kelvin)
19     c = convert_temp(k);    // convert temp
20     out_celsius = c;        // write temp (in Celsius)
21   }
22 }
```

Fig. 2. A simplified temperature converter program

function as an atomic block, which we have annotated with an ACSL function contract (see the text in green preceding the function). Next, we use WP, the Frama-C plugin for deductive verification, to verify that convert_temp satisfies its contract. Then comes the key point of our approach: when creating the TLA$^+$ model of the program, we rely on the (deductively verified) ACSL contract of convert_temp, instead of on its code, to abstract the block into a TLA action. The remaining parts of the main function (i.e., the while loop and the reading/writing) are modelled directly from their code. By using the contract of convert_temp instead of its code, the created model abstracts from the irrelevant implementation details of convert_temp, such as the use of the intermediate variable res, thus decreasing the complexity of the model.

Tool Chain. Figure 1 also shows the envisaged tool chain supporting our approach. On the contract side, we are working with Frama-C, by specifying contracts in ACSL and verifying them using the WP plugin. On the modelling side, we work with the TLA framework by using the TLA toolbox, which allows both for specifying models in TLA$^+$ and performing model checking with TLC over the models. To translate contracts code into TLA$^+$, we use the Frama-C plugin C2TLA+ [15] (see Sect. 4.2).

The steps in Fig. 1 where no specific tool or plugin is specified have, in this work, been carried out manually. There is potential to automate more of the steps. In particular, automating the translation of contracts into TLA$^+$, and interleaving contract and code translations in TLA$^+$, should be straightforward. However, automating some of the steps may be challenging. For instance, automating the (first) step of identifying which code blocks to identify as atomic is problematic. The difficulty stems from the conflicting goals of producing an abstract model of the program that, on one hand, has as a reduced state space as possible, and on the other hand, is faithful with respect to the temporal properties we want to verify. The approach we take in our case study (Sect. 6) is to use functions as atomic blocks. However, this may not always be adequate; in particular, larger functions with side-effects may not be atomic with respect to certain temporal properties.

A further challenge is to automate the (second) step of providing the selected code blocks with contracts. Automated inference of specifications (contracts) is an area of active research showing promising results; see, e.g., [1]. However, automatically generated contracts tend to document the code rather than the intention behind it, and tend thus to be more verbose than contracts provided by humans. Future work is needed to address these challenges. Another possibility is that the code has already been verified against contracts using deductive verification in some other verification context, in which case one can get the contracts for free by reusing the already existing ones.

Abstract Contract Theory. The approach outlined above is compatible with the *contract based design* methodology. This typically entails designing a system in a top-down manner, through refinement and decomposition of contracts, so that low-level components can be independently implemented against their contracts, while ensuring that top-level properties still hold. In Sect. 5 we show that the proposed method of procedure-modular verification can be cast in a previously developed *contract theory* [14]. This provides a strong theoretical foundation for our verification approach, and, since the contract theory supports a contract based design workflow, this translates to the approach presented here.

3   Deductive Verification and Frama-C

Frama-C is a software verification and analysis platform [8] for the C language (specifically, the C99 ISO standard [11]). It follows a modular design, and numerous plugins provide various types of analyses. One of these plugins is WP [3], with which deductive verification (based on Weakest Preconditions) can be performed. Frama-C has its own specification language, called ANSI/ISO C Specification Language (ACSL) [2]. ACSL specifications are written as annotations directly in the source code, as C comments starting with an @ character. A commonly used construct is the *function contract*, which specifies the behaviour of a function and is annotated in the source code. In Fig. 2, an example of an ACSL function contract for convert_temp is shown. The **requires** clause specifies the pre-condition, which is an assertion that must be fulfilled by callers before calling the function. In this case, the original temperature must be at least 0, which is the lowest possible temperature in Kelvin. The **ensures** clause specifies the post-condition, an assertion that should hold after executing the function. Here it specifies that the return value will be the converted temperature. The **assigns** clause specifies the frame condition, i.e., what memory locations may have their values changed during execution. In this case only local variables are updated, so the special keyword \nothing is used to let callers know that no global memory is changed. ACSL also support so-called *ghost* variables and code. Ghost variables are similar to regular variables, except they are only visible in specifications, much like logical variables in standard Hoare logic [10]. Ghost statements, such as ghost variable declarations, are preceded by the **ghost** keyword.

If we take the view of an ACSL contract as separated from the function it specifies, and denote it by $C = (P, Q, L)$, where P is the pre-condition, Q the post-condition, and L all the mutable memory locations per the frame condition, one can give it a denotational semantics as follows:

$$\llbracket C \rrbracket \overset{\text{def}}{=} \{(s, s') \mid \forall \mathcal{I}. (s \models_\mathcal{I} P \Rightarrow s' \models_\mathcal{I} Q) \wedge \forall l \notin L. s'(l) = s(l)\} \qquad (1)$$

where $\mathcal{I}$ ranges over the possible interpretations of logical variables. This is in line with the standard definition of a function satisfying an ACSL contract [2].

4   Model Checking and TLA

This section describes the TLA framework, and how to abstract (deductively verified) contracts into TLA actions, for model checking of programs against temporal properties.

4.1   The TLA Framework

The *Temporal Logic of Actions* (TLA) is a temporal logic for specifying and reasoning about concurrent systems. TLA defines systems and system behaviours using the temporal operators $\square$ (*always*) and $\Diamond$ (*future*) over *actions* as elementary formulas. Below, we summarise the concepts of TLA required for understanding this paper. The formalisation is based on Lamport [12], but adjusted for better integration with our abstract contract theory presented in Sect. 5.1.

Actions. In TLA, an action is a predicate representing transitions between two sets of states. Following the terminology of [12], we say that an action is a predicate over primed and non-primed flexible variables and rigid variables. From a programming perspective, rigid variables act as constants and flexible variables as program variables. Furthermore, a non-primed flexible variable x represents the value of x in the state we are transitioning from, while a primed variable x' represents the value in the state we are transitioning to. Here, we consider states to be mappings from flexible variables to values, and use **State** to denote the set of all states. For example, the action $x' > x$ specifies a transition between any two states s and t such that $t(x) > s(x)$. Semantically, actions are defined, for a given interpretation over rigid variables, as a binary relation on **State**. In Fig. 3, we illustrate, using some example operators, how actions are defined formally, where $\mathcal{I}$ now ranges over all interpretations of rigid variables.

Let A, A_1 and A_2 be actions, s and t states, v a flexible variable, N a rigid variable (constant), e_1 and e_2 integer expressions over flexible and rigid variables. Then, the semantics of a TLA action, denoted $[\![A]\!]_\mathcal{I}$ for a given interpretation $\mathcal{I}$, can be defined as a binary relation on **State**, using the auxiliary function `eval` for evaluating expressions, as follows:

1. $[\![A_1 \wedge A_2]\!]_\mathcal{I} \stackrel{\text{def}}{=} [\![A_1]\!]_\mathcal{I} \cap [\![A_2]\!]_\mathcal{I}$
   $[\![\neg A]\!]_\mathcal{I} \stackrel{\text{def}}{=} (\textbf{State} \times \textbf{State}) \backslash [\![A]\!]_\mathcal{I}$
   $[\![e_1 \geq e_2]\!]_\mathcal{I} \stackrel{\text{def}}{=} \{(s,t) \mid \texttt{eval}(s,t,\mathcal{I},e_1) \geq \texttt{eval}(s,t,\mathcal{I},e_2)\}$

2. $\texttt{eval}(s,t,\mathcal{I},e_1+e_2) \stackrel{\text{def}}{=} \texttt{eval}(s,t,\mathcal{I},e_1) + \texttt{eval}(s,t,\mathcal{I},e_2)$
   $\texttt{eval}(s,t,\mathcal{I},v) \stackrel{\text{def}}{=} s(v)$
   $\texttt{eval}(s,t,\mathcal{I},v') \stackrel{\text{def}}{=} t(v)$
   $\texttt{eval}(s,t,\mathcal{I},N) \stackrel{\text{def}}{=} \mathcal{I}(N)$

Fig. 3. The semantics of actions in TLA

Temporal Formulas. TLA can be lifted to a temporal logic by including the LTL operators $\square$ and $\lozenge$. Formally, we first lift the domain of actions from **State** $\times$ **State** to **State**$^\omega$ (the set of infinite traces), denoted $[\![A]\!]_\mathcal{I}^\omega$, as follows:

$$[\![A]\!]_\mathcal{I}^\omega \stackrel{\text{def}}{=} \{\langle \sigma_1 \sigma_2 \ldots \rangle \mid (\sigma_1, \sigma_2) \in [\![A]\!]_\mathcal{I}\}$$

That is, an action is defined to hold over an infinite trace if it holds when evaluated over the first two states of the trace. With this, we can now treat actions as temporal formulas, and can define the semantics of the temporal operators $\square$ and $\lozenge$ as usual. Let T be a temporal formula, then:

$$[\![\square T]\!]_\mathcal{I}^\omega \stackrel{\text{def}}{=} \{\sigma^\omega = \langle \sigma_1, \sigma_2, \ldots \rangle \mid \forall n \in \mathbb{N}. \ \langle \sigma_n, \sigma_{n+1}, \ldots \rangle \in [\![T]\!]_\mathcal{I}^\omega\}$$

$$[\![\lozenge T]\!]_\mathcal{I}^\omega \stackrel{\text{def}}{=} \{\sigma^\omega = \langle \sigma_1, \sigma_2, \ldots \rangle \mid \exists n \in \mathbb{N}. \ \langle \sigma_n, \sigma_{n+1}, \ldots \rangle \in [\![T]\!]_\mathcal{I}^\omega\}$$

Modelling Programs in TLA. A program is modelled from a triple $(Init, \mathcal{M}, F)$, where $Init$ specifies the constraints on the *initial state*, $\mathcal{M}$ the *next-state* relation describing possible state-transitions in the program, and F defines some *fairness constraints*. From such a triple, a program is defined by a formula:

$$\Phi \stackrel{\text{def}}{=} Init \wedge \square[\mathcal{M}]_{vars} \wedge F,$$

where $vars$ are the program variables in $\mathcal{M}$ and $[\mathcal{M}]_{vars}$ is syntactic sugar for $\mathcal{M} \vee vars' = vars$. This allows "stuttering" steps between (identical) states, which can be useful (in particular) when specifying concurrent systems.

As a simple example, let $\mathcal{M} = (x < 100 \rightarrow x' = x+1) \wedge (x \geq 100 \rightarrow x' = 0)$ and consider the following TLA formula specifying a program that increments the variable x from 0 to 100, and then wraps around to start from 0 again:

$$x = 0 \wedge \Box[\mathcal{M}]_{\langle x \rangle} \wedge \Box\Diamond\langle\mathcal{M}\rangle_{\langle x \rangle} \tag{2}$$

The expression $\langle\mathcal{M}\rangle_x$ is syntactic sugar for $\mathcal{M} \wedge x' \neq x$; thus, the fairness condition simply states that x must always eventually be incremented.

Verifying Temporal Properties (Model Checking). TLA also allows for specifying temporal properties, against which programs can be verified. Since both programs and properties are defined in TLA, verification amounts to showing that the denotation of the temporal property subsumes the denotation of the program: given a temporal property T and an interpretation $\mathcal{I}$, we say that a TLA program Φ satisfies T over $\mathcal{I}$ iff $[\![\Phi]\!]_{\mathcal{I}}^{\omega} \subseteq [\![T]\!]_{\mathcal{I}}^{\omega}$. For example, let Φ be the example program in (2) and T be the formula $\Box(x \geq 0)$. Then, Φ satisfies T since $\sigma^{\omega} \in [\![\Phi]\!] \Rightarrow \sigma^{\omega} \in [\![T]\!]$, thus $[\![\Phi]\!]_{\mathcal{I}}^{\omega} \subseteq [\![T]\!]_{\mathcal{I}}^{\omega}$. In practice, one applies the model checker TLC (see below) to verify that the subset relation between a program Φ and a temporal property T holds.

TLA$^+$ and TLC. TLA$^+$ [13] is a concrete language that implements the TLA framework and allows for specifying models of computer programs. The syntax of TLA$^+$ is intended to resemble mathematical notation: for example, "/\\" and "\\/" denote $\wedge$ and $\vee$, respectively. TLC [21] is an explicit-state model checker, which can be used to model check TLA$^+$ specifications for both safety and liveness properties (which are also specified in TLA$^+$). An example of a TLA$^+$ is shown in Fig. 4. The specification is a translation of the temperature conversion program in Fig. 2 (see Sect. 4.2 for a further description of the translation of the program into the TLA$^+$ specification).

4.2 Translating Code and Contracts into TLA

For contracts, the translation is performed by converting the contract into an action equivalent to the denotation of the contract. Since both contracts and actions are evaluated over **State** × **State**, we can convert the contract into a TLA action by taking its denotation. That is, let A^c denote the action obtained from translating a contract $C = (P, Q, L)$. We then define:

$$A^C \stackrel{\text{def}}{=} \forall\mathcal{I}. \ (P \Rightarrow Q) \wedge \forall l \notin L. \ l' = l$$

The so-defined translation is semantics-preserving, since the definition of the action A^C is equivalent to the definition of the denotation of C.

For the translation of C code into TLA, we do not define a concrete translation function here. Instead, we rely on the C2TLA+ [15] plugin for Frama-C, which automatically translates a program into a TLA$^+$ specification. C2TLA+ translates a given C program into TLA+ by defining, for each statement in the code, an action corresponding to that statement. The control flow of the program is translated by defining a variable in the TLA+ model representing the call stack, program counter, frame pointers, and (global and local) memory. The control flow is then simulated in the model using the program counter and call stack to ensure that, in every reachable state, only one action (statement) is feasible (can be executed).

```
 1 ----------------------MODULE Temperature--------------------------------
 2 EXTENDS Integers
 3
 4 VARIABLES in_kelvin, out_celsius, k, c, result, pc
 5 vars == <<in_kelvin,out_celsius, k, c, result, pc>>
 6
 7 Init == out_celsius = 0 /\ in_kelvin = 273 /\
 8           /\ c = 0 /\ k = 273 /\ result = 0 /\ pc = 1
 9
10 convert_temp(_k) == (_k >= 0) => (result' = (_k - 273))
11                        /\ UNCHANGED(<<in_kelvin, out_celsius, k, c>>)
12
13 M == /\ (pc = 1 /\ in_kelvin' \in 263..283 /\ pc' = 2
14          /\ UNCHANGED(<<out_celsius, k, c, result>>))
15      \/ (pc = 2 /\ k' = in_kelvin /\ pc' = 3
16          /\ UNCHANGED(<<in_kelvin, out_celsius, c, result>>))
17      \/ (pc = 3 /\ convert_temp(k) /\ pc' = 4)
18      \/ (pc = 4 /\ out_celsius' = c /\ pc' = 1
19          /\ UNCHANGED(<<in_kelvin, k, c, result>>))
20
21 Spec == Init /\ [][M]_vars /\ ([]<> <<M>>_vars)
22 ========================================================================
```

Fig. 4. Translation of the temperature conversion program into TLA$^+$

Example. Consider again the temperature conversion program in Fig. 2. In Fig. 4, we show a TLA$^+$ specification created by translating the code in the main function and the contract in the program into TLA$^+$ (following the approach described in Sect. 2). In the model, the control flow of the original C program is simulated using the pc (program counter) variable. Note also that, for each action, we are required to specify variables that are not updated using the built-in UNCHANGED predicate. Here, both the program code and the contract have been translated manually into TLA$^+$. In Sect. 6, we provide more details regarding how to apply the approach and how the C2TLA+ tool can be used to automate the translation of program code into TLA$^+$. Using the model checker TLC, it is possible to verify temporal properties for the specification in Fig. 4. For example, TLC verifies that the specification satisfies the following temporal property stating that if the temperature is always above 273 K, then it will also always be above 0° C:

$$\Box(\text{in\_kelvin} \geq 273) \Rightarrow \Box(\text{out\_celsius} \geq 0) \tag{3}$$

5 Contracts as a Unifying Theory

In this section, we introduce our abstract contract theory and present our work in the setting of this theory. In doing so, we provide a strong theoretical foundation for our work and show that the methodology follows established principles in contract-based design.

5.1   An Abstract Contract Theory

In previous work, we proposed an abstract contract theory [14], which supports the Design-by-Contract methodology developed and advocated by Meyer in [16]. Our theory instantiates the contract meta-theory of Benveniste et al. [5], and thus satisfies several properties considered crucial in system design methodologies, such as *independent implementation*, and *reuse*, of components. The contract theory is developed at the *semantic level*, and can be implemented by means of concrete languages for writing program components and contracts.

As the basic unit of behaviour, we take the abstract notion of a *run*, representing a single execution of a system (or part thereof), and let **Run** denote the set of all runs. In a concrete setting, an example of a run could be an element of **State** × **State**, i.e., a pair of states constituting a possible pre-state and post-state of a procedure call. We focus on procedural, sequential programming languages, and assume some finite universe of procedure names $\mathcal{P}$. For a given set of procedure names $P \subseteq \mathcal{P}$, a *procedure environment* $\mathbf{Env}_P = P \rightarrow 2^{\mathbf{Run}}$ is a mapping from procedure names to their possible runs. Let $\mathbf{Env} \stackrel{\text{def}}{=} \bigcup_{P \subseteq \mathcal{P}} \mathbf{Env}_P$. We define a partial order on procedure environments as follows. For any two procedure environments $\rho \in \mathbf{Env}_P$ and $\rho' \in \mathbf{Env}_{P'}$, we have $\rho \sqsubseteq \rho'$ iff $P \subseteq P'$ and $\forall p \in P.\rho(p) \subseteq \rho'(p)$. The partial order $(\mathbf{Env}, \sqsubseteq)$ forms a complete lattice, since both a greatest lower bound (*glb*), and a least upper bound (*lub*), exists for every subset of **Env**. The *glb* operation on environments is denoted as usual by $\sqcap$, and the *lub* operation by $\sqcup$.

To formally define *components* and *contracts*, we first equip both notions with an *interface* $I = (P^-, P^+)$, where P^- and P^+ are disjoint subsets of $\mathcal{P}$. P^+ is the set of procedures (to be) implemented in a component, and P^- are the procedures called by it, but not implemented within it. Our contract theory is summarised in Fig. 5. We use $\mu x. f(x)$ to denote the least fixed-point of the function f (when it exists), $\rho_P^\top$ to denote the (top) environment mapping every procedure in P to **Run**, and for any mapping $h : A \rightarrow B$ and set $A' \subseteq A$, we use $h_{|A'}$ to denote the *restriction* of h on the sub-domain A'.

Instantiation of the Theory. In our contract theory, we have deliberately left the domain of **Run** unspecified. This allows the domain to be instantiated as needed by the concrete application domain, and even to combine multiple domains. Certain constraints do need to be fulfilled, though. For the theory to be well-defined (e.g., that the involved fixed-points exist), all base components used to build larger components must be monotonic mappings (monotonicity of composed components is then ensured by the composition operator).

In our previous work [14], we argued for the importance of separating contracts from their implementation, and gave contracts a denotational semantics, defining the denotation of a contract C in a way that guarantees that the equation:

$$\llbracket C \rrbracket = \bigcup_{S \models C} \llbracket S \rrbracket \tag{4}$$

1. A *component* m with interface $I_m = (P_m^-, P_m^+)$ is a monotonic mapping of type $m : \mathbf{Env}_{P_m^-} \to \mathbf{Env}_{P_m^+}$.

2. Two components m_1 and m_2 are *composable* iff $P_{m_1}^+ \cap P_{m_2}^+ = \varnothing$.

3. Given two composable components $m_1 : \mathbf{Env}_{P_{m_1}^-} \to \mathbf{Env}_{P_{m_1}^+}$ and $m_2 : \mathbf{Env}_{P_{m_2}^-} \to \mathbf{Env}_{P_{m_2}^+}$, their *composition* is defined as a mapping $m_1 \times m_2 : \mathbf{Env}_{P_{m_1 \times m_2}^-} \to \mathbf{Env}_{P_{m_1 \times m_2}^+}$ such that:

$$P_{m_1 \times m_2}^+ \stackrel{\text{def}}{=} P_{m_1}^+ \cup P_{m_2}^+ \qquad P_{m_1 \times m_2}^- \stackrel{\text{def}}{=} (P_{m_1}^- \cup P_{m_2}^-) \setminus (P_{m_1}^+ \cup P_{m_2}^+)$$

$$m_1 \times m_2 \stackrel{\text{def}}{=} \lambda \rho_{m_1 \times m_2}^- \in \mathbf{Env}_{P_{m_1 \times m_2}^-} \cdot \mu \rho. \; \chi_{m_1 \times m_2}^+(\rho)$$

where $\chi_{m_1 \times m_2}^+ : \mathbf{Env}_{P_{m_1 \times m_2}^+} \to \mathbf{Env}_{P_{m_1 \times m_2}^+}$ is defined, in the context of a given $\rho_{m_1 \times m_2}^- \in \mathbf{Env}_{P_{m_1 \times m_2}^-}$, as follows. Let $\rho_{m_1 \times m_2}^+ \in \mathbf{Env}_{P_{m_1 \times m_2}^+}$, and let $\rho_{m_1}^- \in \mathbf{Env}_{P_{m_1}^-}$ be the environment defined by:

$$\rho_{m_1}^-(p) \stackrel{\text{def}}{=} \begin{cases} \rho_{m_1 \times m_2}^+(p) & \text{if } p \in P_{m_1}^- \cap P_{m_2}^+ \\ \rho_{m_1 \times m_2}^-(p) & \text{if } p \in P_{m_1}^- \setminus P_{m_2}^+ \end{cases}$$

and let $\rho_{m_2}^- \in \mathbf{Env}_{P_{m_2}^-}$ be defined symmetrically. We then define:

$$\chi_{m_1 \times m_2}^+(\rho_{m_1 \times m_2}^+)(p) \stackrel{\text{def}}{=} \begin{cases} m_1(\rho_{m_1}^-)(p) & \text{if } p \in P_{m_1}^+ \\ m_2(\rho_{m_2}^-)(p) & \text{if } p \in P_{m_2}^+ \end{cases}$$

4. A *denotational contract* c with interface $I_c = (P_c^-, P_c^+)$ is a pair (ρ_c^-, ρ_c^+), where $\rho_c^- \in \mathbf{Env}_{P_c^-}$ and $\rho_c^+ \in \mathbf{Env}_{P_c^+}$.

5. A component m with interface $I_m = (P_m^-, P_m^+)$ is an *implementation* for, or *implements*, a contract $c = (\rho_c^-, \rho_c^+)$ with interface $I_c = (P_c^-, P_c^+)$, denoted $m \models c$, iff $P_c^- \subseteq P_m^-$, $P_m^+ \subseteq P_c^+$, and $m(\rho_c^- \sqcup \rho_{P_m^- \setminus P_c^-}^\top) \sqsubseteq \rho_c^+$.

6. A component m is an *environment* for contract c iff, for any implementation m' of c, m and m' are composable, and $\forall \rho_{m \times m'}^- \in \mathbf{Env}_{P_{m \times m'}^-} \cdot \; (m \times m')(\rho_{m \times m'}^-)_{|P_c^+} \sqsubseteq \rho_c^+$.

7. A contract c *refines* contract c', denoted $c \preceq c'$, iff $\rho_{c'}^- \sqsubseteq \rho_c^-$ and $\rho_c^+ \sqsubseteq \rho_{c'}^+$.

8. The *conjunction* of two contracts $c_1 = (\rho_{c_1}^-, \rho_{c_1}^+)$ and $c_2 = (\rho_{c_2}^-, \rho_{c_2}^+)$ is the contract $c_1 \wedge c_2 \stackrel{\text{def}}{=} (\rho_{c_1}^- \sqcup \rho_{c_2}^-, \rho_{c_1}^+ \sqcap \rho_{c_2}^+)$.

9. Two contracts $c_1 = (\rho_{c_1}^-, \rho_{c_1}^+)$ and $c_2 = (\rho_{c_2}^-, \rho_{c_2}^+)$ with interfaces $I_{c_1} = (P_{c_1}^-, P_{c_1}^+)$ and $I_{c_2} = (P_{c_2}^-, P_{c_2}^+)$ are *composable* if: (i) $P_{c_1}^+ \cap P_{c_2}^+ = \varnothing$, (ii) $\forall p \in P_{c_1}^- \cap P_{c_2}^+ \cdot \rho_{c_2}^+(p) \subseteq \rho_{c_1}^-(p)$, and (iii) $\forall p \in P_{c_2}^- \cap P_{c_1}^+ \cdot \rho_{c_1}^+(p) \subseteq \rho_{c_2}^-(p)$.

10. The *composition* of two composable contracts $c_1 = (\rho_{c_1}^-, \rho_{c_1}^+)$ and $c_2 = (\rho_{c_2}^-, \rho_{c_2}^+)$ with interfaces $I_{c_1} = (P_{c_1}^-, P_{c_1}^+)$ and $I_{c_2} = (P_{c_2}^-, P_{c_2}^+)$ is the contract $c_1 \otimes c_2 \stackrel{\text{def}}{=} (\rho_{c_1 \otimes c_2}^-, \rho_{c_1}^+ \sqcup \rho_{c_2}^+)$, where:

$$\rho_{c_1 \otimes c_2}^- \stackrel{\text{def}}{=} (\rho_{c_1}^- \sqcap \rho_{c_2}^-)\big|_{(P_{c_1}^- \cup P_{c_2}^-) \setminus (P_{c_1}^+ \cup P_{c_2}^+)}$$

Fig. 5. Our abstract contract theory

is fulfilled, i.e., that the denotation of a contract is the union of the denotations of all programs that satisfies it. The rationale for this is that we desire programs to satisfy their contracts exactly when $[\![S]\!] \subseteq [\![C]\!]$. Procedure-modular verification is then facilitated by considering a special *contract environment* ρ_c induced by the above equality: let every procedure p be equipped with a contract C_p, we then define $\rho_c(p) \overset{\text{def}}{=} [\![C_p]\!]$. Now, programs are given a *contract-relative* semantics $[\![S]\!]^{cr}$, where the denotations of procedure calls is defined by the denotations of their contracts instead of their bodies. This gives rise to a separate satisfaction relation $S_p \models^{cr} C_p$, based on the contract-relative semantics.

For each domain used to instantiate the contract theory, concrete syntax for implementing and specifying programs is needed. Then, each instantiation requires abstraction functions, which take the concrete syntax and produce components and contracts in the abstract contract theory, as well as a contract-relative satisfaction relation $\models^{cr}$. The abstraction to components and contracts must be such that the following properties hold:

1. For any two disjoint sets of functions P_1^+ and P_2^+, abstracted individually into components m_1 and m_2, respectively, and $P_1^+ \cup P_2^+$ abstracted into component m, we have $m_1 \times m_2 = m$.
2. For any procedure p with procedure contract C_p, abstracted into component m_p with contract c_p, we have $S_p \models^{cr} C_p$ whenever $m_p \models c_p$.

Contracts in Our Approach. In our concrete setting, when working with components in the domain **State** × **State**, contracts and the contract-relative semantics of statements will also be over this domain (by design of the approach, not because of theoretical restrictions). However, when in the domain **State**$^\omega$, we allow certain procedures (which we assume are marked in some way) to have contracts in the domain **State** × **State**, by defining the contract-relative semantics for contracts in both domains. This allows us to verify some components in the setting of pre- and post-states, and then reuse their contracts to verify temporal properties in the domain of infinite traces. Since we are adhering to the contract theory, which follows the axioms of the meta-theory [5], we ensure that the desired properties for proper design-chain management hold. As an example, recall the temperature conversion program in Fig. 2. For this program, we consider the main function to be defined in the domain **State**$^\omega$, while the contract for the conversion function is in **State** × **State**.

5.2 Deductive Verification in the Abstract Contract Theory

In the following paragraph, we provide some intuition for the instantiation of the contract theory with a concrete semantics. We assume that every procedure p is associated with a body S_p. The semantics of statements is defined relative an interface (P^-, P^+) and environments $\rho^- \in \mathbf{Env}_{P^-}$ and $\rho^+ \in \mathbf{Env}_{P^+}$, denoted $[\![S]\!]_{\rho^-}^{\rho^+}$. Specifically, the semantics of a function call is then defined as $\rho^+(p)$ when $p \in P^+$, and as $\rho^-(p)$ when $p \in P^-$. Given $\rho^- \in \mathbf{Env}_{P^-}$, we define the function

$\xi : \mathbf{Env}_{P^+} \to \mathbf{Env}_{P^+}$ by $\xi(\rho^+)(p) \stackrel{\text{def}}{=} [\![S_p]\!]_{\rho^-}^{\rho^+}$ and consider its least fixed point ρ_0^+. This is used as the basis of a *standard denotation* $[\![S]\!]_{\rho^-} \stackrel{\text{def}}{=} [\![S]\!]_{\rho^-}^{\rho_0^+}$. Using this, we can define the contract-relative semantics of statements as $[\![S]\!]^{cr} \stackrel{\text{def}}{=} [\![S]\!]_{\rho_c}$. Details of this formalisation for a simple procedural language can be found in [9].

In this setting, we can now define how to abstract programs and contracts into components and denotational contracts, respectively. For any set of procedures P^+, calling procedures P', we define the component $m : \mathbf{Env}_{P_m^-} \to \mathbf{Env}_{P_m^+}$, where $P_m^- \stackrel{\text{def}}{=} P' \setminus P_m^+$ and $P_m^+ \stackrel{\text{def}}{=} P^+$, so that $\forall \rho_m^- \in \mathbf{Env}_{P_m^-}. \ \forall p \in P_m^+. \ m(\rho_m^-)(p) \stackrel{\text{def}}{=} [\![S_p]\!]_{\rho_m^-}$. For a procedure p with an ACSL contract C_p, calling other procedures P^-, we define the denotational contract $c_p = (\rho_{c_p}^-, \rho_{c_p}^+)$ with interface $P_{c_p}^+ \stackrel{\text{def}}{=} \{p\}$ and $P_{c_p}^- \stackrel{\text{def}}{=} P^-$, so that $\rho_{c_p}^+(p) \stackrel{\text{def}}{=} \rho_c(p)$, and $\forall p' \in P^-. \ \rho_{c_p}^-(p') = \rho_c(p')$.

The full semantics of the concrete languages, C and ACSL, is implicitly defined by Frama-C and will not be expanded upon here. Note that, per the semantics of an ACSL function contract as given in (1), which is the only ACSL construct of concern in the present paper, a function can be verified against its contract, and relative to the contracts of other functions, only if its denotation is subsumed by that of its contract. This is in accordance with condition (4). Thus, the contract-relative satisfaction relation $\models^{cr}$ is such that the two properties of abstraction discussed in Sect. 5.1 hold.

5.3   Procedure-Modular Verification with TLA

Verification in the two domains can now be combined, by abstracting the contracts of the already-verified contracts into actions. This can also be viewed as a form of procedure-modular verification, where temporal properties are checked for a larger program, relative the ACSL contracts of some of the called procedures. To this end, we take the view that a procedure environment $\rho \in \mathbf{Env}_P$ in the domain $\mathbf{State} \times \mathbf{State}$ as discussed in Sect. 3, maps procedure names to actions. We let $\mathbf{Run} = (\mathbf{State} \times \mathbf{State}) \cup \mathbf{State}^\omega$, and as previously explained, assume that certain procedures have been selected to be considered actions. For a TLA program S with interface (P^-, P^+), we can define the denotation $[\![S]\!]_{\rho_c}$ where, for some $p \in P^-$, $\rho_c(p) \in \mathbf{Env}_{P^-}$ are actions, or denotations of type $\mathbf{State} \times \mathbf{State}$ of the called procedure. In this way we get a contract-relative semantics where programs produce infinite state sequences, but depend partially on procedures producing actions, or state pairs. We can then abstract the concrete languages in the same way as in Sect. 5.2.

Note that, while the concrete contract languages are different in the domains (in one case it is ACSL, and in the other TLA$^+$), the concrete language for defining components is the same, namely C, meaning that the abstraction from procedures to components is in reality performed in two steps, first from C code and ACSL contracts to TLA$^+$ specifications and actions, and from there to components. We use TLC to verify programs. From a denotational viewpoint, successful verification in TLC means that there is a subset relation between the denotation of the program and the specification. Hence, the two required properties listed in Sect. 5.1 are fulfilled.

Considering again the example from Fig. 2, the component m_{main} resulting from abstracting the `main` function would map denotations for the called function `convert_temp` in the domain $\textbf{State} \times \textbf{State}$ to denotations of `main` in the domain $\textbf{State}^\omega$. The exact behaviour is obtained from the body of `main` translated to TLA, and parameterised on the behaviour of `convert_temp`. Verification is performed by substituting the contract of `convert_temp` for its behaviour, on the concrete level, which is shown in Fig. 4.

5.4 Contract Based System Design

As we have previously shown [14], our contract theory is an instance of the meta-theory of Benveniste et al. [5], thus establishing a number of properties desired of system design methodologies, such as independent implementation and verification of components. In contract-based design, a system is typically designed in a top-down manner, starting from the desired high-level properties that the system must satisfy, which are then decomposed into contracts for the (sub-)components. The components are then implemented independently, relying only on the contracts of other components.

By casting the approach proposed in the present paper, we have established that it is compatible with the principles of contract-based design. In particular, ensuring correctness of a system as a whole reduces to showing, one the one hand, that the composition of the contracts of the sub-components of the system *refines* the top-level contracts, and, on the other hand, that the concrete procedures satisfy their concrete specifications, according to the contract-relative semantics.

In the example from Fig. 2, we would typically have a top-level contract c specifying the temporal behaviour of the system, without any required procedures. This contract would then be decomposed into contracts c_{conv} and c_{main} for the two procedures, respectively. The former would be defined concretely in ACSL, expressing the possible state pairs resulting from conversion, without needing any assumptions on other procedures. The latter would be defined by a concrete TLA formula, with assumptions on the actions produced by the conversion function. By showing that $c_{conv} \otimes c_{main} \preceq c$, and that the two concrete implementations satisfy their contracts according to the methodology outlined in the preceding sections, it is, by the properties of the contract theory, then established that $m_{conv} \otimes m_{main} \models c$.

6 Preliminary Evaluation

To evaluate our approach, we conducted two experiments, one using a simple toy program simulating some file operation, and the second one using a simplified software module taken from the automotive industry. Both experiments were carried out on a Dell Latitude 7420 using Ubuntu 20.04 running in VirtualBox with 8 GB RAM and on Intel i5 CPU (2 cores).

```
 1 #define OPEN 1
 2 #define CLOSED 0
 3 #define N 32
 4
 5 int file_status;
 6 int input;
 7
 8 /*@ ensures -(N*2) <= input <= N*2; */
 9 void havoc_input(){}
10
11 /*@ assigns \nothing; */
12 int read_file(int i){
13   return i; //Dummy statement
14 }
15
16 /*@ assigns \nothing; */
17 void write_file(int i) {
18   //pass
19 }
20
21 /*@
22   requires 0 <= n < N && file_status == OPEN;
23   ensures file_status == CLOSED;
24   assigns file_status;
25 */
26 void file_operation(int n) {
27   int i; i = 0;
28   int tmp; tmp = 0;
29   int sum; sum = 0;
30   if (file_status == OPEN) {
31     /*@ loop assigns i, tmp, sum; */
32     while (i < n) {
33       tmp = read_file(i);
34       sum += tmp;
35       i += 1;
36     }
37     write_file(sum);
38     file_status = CLOSED;
39   }
40 }
41
42 void main() {
43   while(1) {
44     havoc_input();
45     if (0 < input && input < N) {
46       file_status = OPEN;
47       file_operation(input);
48     }
49   }
50 }
```

Fig. 6. Program imitating behaviours including reading and writing to a file

6.1   Simple File Open-Close Example

The first test case consists of a simple example that simulates a program performing file operations. The program, which is shown in Fig. 6, repeatedly reads from the file, performs some operation and writes to the file. For this program, the temporal property we are interested in verifying (using model checking) is that, whenever the file is open, it will eventually be closed. This property is captured by the following TLA formula:

$$\Box \, (file\_status = OPEN \Rightarrow \Diamond \, (file\_status = CLOSED)) \tag{5}$$

To evaluate our method, we created two TLA$^+$ models: one modelled directly from the program code, and a second abstract model that was created following the approach outlined in Sect. 2. After creating the two models, we compared the size of the state space of the models, and the time required for verifying property (5).

Creating the Models. The first model was translated directly from the C program code using the C2TLA+ tool. Due to limitations in C2TLA+, some manual overhead was required to achieve a correct specification. We also added a fairness constraint to the model (since this is not performed automatically by C2TLA+), stating that the program should never get stuck (i.e., "stutter") indefinitely. Furthermore, we made some abstractions regarding the domain of the variables: input is given the domain $[-2 * N, N]$ and file_status the domain [0,1]. Moreover, in the main function, a call is made to a havoc_input function in each iteration of the loop, which represents non-deterministic assignment of the input variable. In a real setting, input is expected to be assigned by some external component between each iteration of the loop. In the TLA$^+$ model, the havoc effect is achieved by manually inserting an action that simply assigns input non-deterministically within its domain.

The second model is a more abstract version of the first model, achieved by modelling the file_operation function from a contract instead of the program code. The contract used to model file_operation was written in ACSL and is shown as an annotation above the function in Fig. 6. Note that, since the temporal property we are interested in verifying concerns only the open/close property of the file, i.e., the value of the file_status variable, the contract only specifies the behaviour of this variable. Using the WP plugin of Frama-C, we verified that file_operation satisfies its contract. Thereafter, we translated the contract into a TLA action, following the method in Sect. 4.2; that is, it was translated into the action:

$$(0 <= n \wedge n < N \wedge \textit{file\_status} = OPEN) \Rightarrow (\textit{file\_status} = CLOSED)$$

Lastly, we completed the creation of the second abstract model by replacing the parts of the TLA$^+$ model corresponding to file_operation with the translation of the contract. To properly integrate the contract action into the model, we also added a conjunct to handle appropriately the program counters and stack registers of the model.

Table 1. Results of model checking two models for property (5)

	Verified	Total # of states	# of unique states	Verification time
Full model	Yes	832 615	45 574	~51 s
Abstract model	Yes	26 602	841	~5 s

Model Checking. Model checking was performed using TLC on both the full model, created directly from the program code and on the second abstract model including the contract action for file_operation. The results of the model checking are shown in Table 1 and, as expected, the state space of the second abstract model was significantly smaller than the state space of the full model. Moreover, verification time decreased from 51 s to 5 s, showing that the smaller state space, for this example, factored into the time required for verification by TLC. For a fair comparison of the verification time between the two models, one should also add the time required by WP for verifying the contract to the total verification time of the abstract model. However, for this example, the time required by WP was negligible (0.15 s).

```
1  int state[NUM_SIGNALS]; //global vehicle state
2  static int primaryCircuitNoFlowTime = 0; //counter
3
4  void steering() {
5    VEHICLE_INFO veh_info;
6    SENSOR_STATE prim_sensor;
7
8    //read
9    get_system_state(&veh_info);
10
11   //evaluate
12   eval_prim_sensor_state(&veh_info, &prim_sensor);
13   secondary_steering(&veh_info, &prim_sensor);
14
15   //write
16   write(SECONDARY_CIRCUIT_HANDLES_STEERING, veh_info.secondCircHandlesStee);
17   write(ELECTRIC_MOTOR_ACTIVATED, veh_info.electricMotorAct);
18 }
19
20
21 //scheduler
22 void main() {
23   while(1) {
24     steering();
25     havoc_inputs();
26   }
27 }
```

Fig. 7. The steering function from the steering module together with the main function which simulates a scheduler

6.2   Simplified Industrial Example

As a second example, we use a C program based on a real software module taken from the automotive industry. The structure of, and C constructs used in, the case study program follows that of the real module, but the code have been rewritten and to some extent simplified, for proprietary reasons and due to limitations in the current tool-chain. The evaluation method for this example follows exactly that of the previous example. That is, we first created a full model, directly from the program code and then created a second model by abstracting one function using a contract for the function. Then, we model checked both models for a given property and compared the state spaces and verification times.

Description the Software Module. The software module used in this example performs a diagnosis of the status of the primary power steering of a vehicle and, in case of malfunction, activates the secondary (backup) power steering. A power steering is a device that reduces the manual effort required by the driver to rotate the steering wheel of the vehicle. The entry-point function of the module (the `steering` function) and the *scheduler* (the `main` function) of the simplified version are shown in Fig. 7. The full case study module is roughly 120 lines of code. In a real setting, the scheduler would be some external software that repeatedly calls several modules in a given order; here, we encoded the scheduler with the infinite while loop in the main function.

Upon invocation, the `steering` function first reads the current state of the vehicle, then calculates if secondary power steering should be activated and, lastly, writes the result. In a real setting, the reading and writing consist of communicating with a real-time database but, in our simplified version, this is simulated by reading and writing to the global array `state`, which represents the state of the vehicle. Note that, from the perspective of the steering module, the state of the vehicle consists of both inputs and outputs. Similar to our previous example, all (input) variables of the modules are assumed to be assigned by some external component at any time during program execution, which is represented with the call to `havoc_inputs`. The module also contains a counter as the global variable `primaryCircuitNoFlowTime`, the purpose of which is to remember if some property holds over several sequential executions. Specifically, the counter keeps track of the number of sequential iterations (if any) the electric motor of the vehicle has suffered from hydraulic malfunction.

Creating the Models. As for our first example, the first model is created by using the C2TLA+ tool, adding a fairness constraint, and abstracting the domains of certain variables (e.g., variables that are treated as Boolean values in the C programs are assigned the domain $[0, 1]$). The havoc statement in the main function was also treated similarly as in the first example, i.e., by inserting a TLA action in the model that assigns all input variables non-deterministically within their respective domains.

The second model was created by first identifying the `steering` function as a block of code that we consider as atomic and thus should be specified with an ACSL contract. It might appear surprising that we consider almost the entire example program as atomic, but recall that, in a real setting, the steering module will be only one of several modules called by the scheduler. As a contract for the `steering` function, we used an ACSL contract already written in a previous case study [17]. It should be pointed out that since we re-used a contract originally written for deductive verification of the module, no additional manual labour was required for this step in this particular example (and as pointed out above, we indeed advocate such a way of combing deductive verification with model checking). Using WP, we verified that `steering` satisfies the contract. Lastly, we translated the contract into TLA^{+} and integrated it into the first model to create the second abstract model.

Table 2. Results of model checking two models for property (6)

	Verified	Total # of states	# of unique states	Verification time
Full model	Yes	84 720	46 265	~12 s
Abstract model	Yes	35 458	4 552	~10 s

Model Checking. We model checked the two models, using TLC, against the following liveness property:

> *If the electric motor of the engine suffers from hydraulic malfunction,*
> *then the secondary steering should eventually be activated.*

In TLA, this property is captured with the formula:

$$\Box \, (hydraulic\_malfunction \Rightarrow \Diamond \, secondary\_steering) \qquad (6)$$

where *hydraulic_malfunction* represents the condition that the electric motor has suffered from hydraulic malfunction, and *secondary_steering* the condition that the secondary steering is activated.

The results of model checking the two different models are shown in Table 2. As seen, verification was successful for both models. Furthermore, we again see that the state space (number of unique states) was significantly smaller for the abstract model. However, for this example, we did not observe any significant difference in the time required for verification (12 s vs 10 s). Moreover, as with the previous example, one should also consider the time required by WP for verifying the contract (2.150 s) to the total verification time of the abstract model.

7   Conclusion

In this paper, we proposed an approach of how to combine deductive verification with model checking in a natural manner, subordinating the former to the latter. First, deductive verification is used to abstract blocks of code, which can be considered atomic, into Hoare logic style contracts, in a provably correct manner. Then, the program model resulting (conceptually) from replacing the code blocks with their contracts, is model-checked against the temporal properties of interest. The Temporal Logic of Actions was proposed as a framework for representing the resulting program models, since both programs and Hoare logic contracts can be naturally expressed in TLA. We gave a semantic foundation of our modular approach, in terms of an abstract contract theory we developed earlier. Finally, we illustrated our approach on two example programs, using Frama-C for the deductive verification of the selected code blocks, and the TLA$^+$ Toolbox (with TLC) for representing the abstract program models and for their model checking.

Our preliminary experiments are far too few as yet to allow any definitive conclusions to be drawn. Both examples in Sect. 6 showed that our approach led to a significant reduction in the size of the state space of the TLA$^+$ model. Furthermore, the first example indicates that the reduction of the state space may significantly reduce verification time. However, in the second example, no speedup in verification time was observed. A key difference in the two examples is that the contract used in the first example was an *incomplete* specification (in the sense that it does not describe fully the indented behaviour of the program), while the contract used in the second example was a *complete* one (it models fully the intended behaviour of the function). We are as of yet not sure as to why, for the second example, the difference in verification time was not proportionate to the difference in the size of the state space, and it remains to be shown that our approach can improve scalability also when relying on complete specifications for the abstraction.

Another aspect is that the performance of our approach may have been influenced by the particular choice of tools. In particular, the choice of the C2TLA+ plugin and the TLC model checker may not have been optimal as tool support for our approach. One hypothesis is that a symbolic model checker may be a better choice.

Future work includes performing a proper evaluation of our proposed approach, both for complete and incomplete specifications, and to complete and improve the tool chain. Another question that needs investigation is how to adequately choose the granularity of the code blocks to be considered as atomic actions. Lastly, better support for showing decomposition and refinement of contracts is desired, for instance by further developing the contract theory in that direction.

References

1. Alshnakat, A., Gurov, D., Lidström, C., Rümmer, P.: Constraint-based contract inference for deductive verification. In: Ahrendt, W., Beckert, B., Bubel, R., Hähnle, R., Ulbrich, M. (eds.) Deductive Software Verification: Future Perspectives. LNCS, vol. 12345, pp. 149–176. Springer, Cham (2020). https://doi.org/10.1007/978-3-030-64354-6_6

2. Baudin, P., Filliâtre, J.C., Marché, C., Monate, B., Moy, Y., Prevosto, V.: ACSL: ANSI/ISO C Specification Language. https://frama-c.com/acsl.html

3. Baudin, P., Bobot, F., Correnson, L., Dargaye, Z., Blanchard, A.: WP Plug-in Manual - Frama-C 23.1 (Vanadium). CEA LIST. http://frama-c.com/download/frama-c-wp-manual.pdf

4. Beckert, B., Kirsten, M., Klamroth, J., Ulbrich, M.: Modular verification of JML contracts using bounded model checking. In: Margaria, T., Steffen, B. (eds.) ISoLA 2020. LNCS, vol. 12476, pp. 60–80. Springer, Cham (2020). https://doi.org/10.1007/978-3-030-61362-4_4

5. Benveniste, A., et al.: Contracts for System Design, vol. 12. Now Publishers, Norwell (2018). https://doi.org/10.1561/1000000053

6. Burch, J.R., Clarke, E.M., McMillan, K.L., Dill, D.L., Hwang, L.J.: Symbolic model checking: 10²⁰ states and beyond. In: Proceedings of Logic in Computer Science (LICS 1990), pp. 428–439. IEEE Computer Society (1990). https://doi.org/10.1109/LICS.1990.113767

7. Champion, A., Mebsout, A., Sticksel, C., Tinelli, C.: The KIND 2 model checker. In: Chaudhuri, S., Farzan, A. (eds.) CAV 2016. LNCS, vol. 9780, pp. 510–517. Springer, Cham (2016). https://doi.org/10.1007/978-3-319-41540-6_29

8. Cuoq, P., Kirchner, F., Kosmatov, N., Prevosto, V., Signoles, J., Yakobowski, B.: Frama-C. In: Eleftherakis, G., Hinchey, M., Holcombe, M. (eds.) SEFM 2012. LNCS, vol. 7504, pp. 233–247. Springer, Heidelberg (2012). https://doi.org/10.1007/978-3-642-33826-7_16

9. Gurov, D., Westman, J.: A hoare logic contract theory: an exercise in denotational semantics. In: Müller, P., Schaefer, I. (eds.) Principled Software Development, pp. 119–127. Springer, Cham (2018). https://doi.org/10.1007/978-3-319-98047-8_8

10. Hoare, C.A.R.: An axiomatic basis for computer programming. Commun. ACM 12(10), 576–580 (1969). https://doi.org/10.1145/363235.363259

11. ISO: ISO C standard 1999. Technical report, ISO/IEC 9899:1999 draft (1999). https://www.open-std.org/jtc1/sc22/wg14/www/docs/n1256.pdf

12. Lamport, L.: The temporal logic of actions. ACM Trans. Program. Lang. Syst. 16(3), 872–923 (1994). https://doi.org/10.1145/177492.177726

13. Lamport, L.: Specifying Systems, The TLA+ Language and Tools for Hardware and Software Engineers. Addison-Wesley, Boston (2002). https://research.microsoft.com/users/lamport/tla/book.html

14. Lidström, C., Gurov, D.: An abstract contract theory for programs with procedures. In: Guerra, E., Stoelinga, M. (eds.) FASE 2021. LNCS, vol. 12649, pp. 152–171. Springer, Cham (2021). https://doi.org/10.1007/978-3-030-71500-7_8

15. Methni, A., Lemerre, M., Ben Hedia, B., Haddad, S., Barkaoui, K.: Specifying and verifying concurrent C programs with TLA+. In: Artho, C., Ölveczky, P.C. (eds.) FTSCS 2014. CCIS, vol. 476, pp. 206–222. Springer, Cham (2015). https://doi.org/10.1007/978-3-319-17581-2_14

16. Meyer, B.: Applying "design by contract". Computer 25(10), 40–51 (1992). https://doi.org/10.1109/2.161279

17. Nyberg, M., Gurov, D., Lidström, C., Rasmusson, A., Westman, J.: Formal verification in automotive industry: enablers and obstacles. In: Margaria, T., Steffen, B. (eds.) ISoLA 2018. LNCS, vol. 11247, pp. 139–158. Springer, Cham (2018). https://doi.org/10.1007/978-3-030-03427-6_14

18. Oortwijn, W., Gurov, D., Huisman, M.: Practical abstractions for automated verification of shared-memory concurrency. In: Beyer, D., Zufferey, D. (eds.) VMCAI 2020. LNCS, vol. 11990, pp. 401–425. Springer, Cham (2020). https://doi.org/10.1007/978-3-030-39322-9_19

19. Soleimanifard, S., Gurov, D.: Algorithmic verification of procedural programs in the presence of code variability. Sci. Comput. Program. 127, 76–102 (2016)

20. Sun, J., Liu, Y., Cheng, B.: Model checking a model checker: a code contract combined approach. In: Dong, J.S., Zhu, H. (eds.) ICFEM 2010. LNCS, vol. 6447, pp. 518–533. Springer, Heidelberg (2010). https://doi.org/10.1007/978-3-642-16901-4_34

21. Yu, Y., Manolios, P., Lamport, L.: Model checking TLA$^+$ specifications. In: Pierre, L., Kropf, T. (eds.) CHARME 1999. LNCS, vol. 1703, pp. 54–66. Springer, Heidelberg (1999). https://doi.org/10.1007/3-540-48153-2_6

Abstraction in Deductive Verification: Model Fields and Model Methods

David R. Cok[1][(✉)] and Gary T. Leavens[2]

[1] Safer Software Consulting, Rochester, NY, USA
david.r.cok@gmail.com
[2] University of Central Florida, Orlando, FL, USA
Leavens@ucf.edu

Abstract. This Experience report compares using model fields and model methods for specifying abstractions in abstract implementations. Our experience is connected to past discussions of alternatives in modeling heap state changes and the axiomatic basis for deductive verification of programs with uninterpreted, underspecified or recursive methods.

Keywords: Formal methods · SMT solver · Deductive verification · Java Modeling Language · JML · OpenJML

1 Introduction

Deductive verification (DV) of software requires writing specifications in some specification language (SL) to complement an actual program implementation in some programming language (PL). Similarly to writing the implementation, specifications benefit from designs that abstract, clarify and simplify the intent of the program. Good abstractions can make the specification more obviously correct[1] and improve the performance of the underlying DV system in generating the proofs that verify that the specifications and implementation are consistent.

Tools that perform deductive verification of software translate a combination of program source code and specifications into a logical language that can then be submitted to a theorem prover to determine whether the source code and specifications are consistent with each other. The translation process incorporates the semantics of both the PL and the SL. It also must consider which formulation of logical language structure will provide the best proof success, both in proofs succeeding at all and in the time taken to do so.

In the Java Modeling Language (JML) [10,15], as in some other SLs, one has a choice to use *model fields* or *model methods* (or a mixture) in writing specifications.

---

[1] In this paper, as generally in DV, we are concerned to establish that implementations concur with their specifications. But both can be wrong together. Thus a specification that can be written more cleanly and readably is more amenable to human review and can be "more obviously" in agreement with the intent of the software.

© The Author(s), under exclusive license to Springer Nature Switzerland AG 2022
T. Margaria and B. Steffen (Eds.): ISoLA 2022, LNCS 13701, pp. 29–44, 2022.
https://doi.org/10.1007/978-3-031-19849-6_3

In a recent (October 2021–March 2022) specification project for an industrial client, a target example was specified in each way.

The contribution of this Experience Report is to describe how model fields and model methods were used in OpenJML [6, 7] for this example, identify the advantages and disadvantages of each approach, and, in particular, how the logical encoding used by the deductive verification system was affected. To set the stage, early sections of this paper provide a summary of how DV systems encode PL and SL constructs, particularly the heap.

The context of this work is deductive verification for legacy software, in this case software written in Java. Thus we did not have the opportunity to use a system such as Dafny [18, 19] that is designed to verify software as it is written. Rather this project used a specification language (JML) and tool (OpenJML) appropriate to the target language (Java). In this case, OpenJML is translating to SMT-LIB [24], with Z3 [11] as its back-end, automated logical engine.

The examples given below use Java as the PL and JML as the SL; JML embeds specifications in Java code as Java comments beginning with //@. OpenJML was extended to handle reads clauses and recursive model fields and (which are then similar to dynamic frames), both of which were implicit in JML, but without carefully defined semantics. However these techniques and ideas are applicable to other imperative programming languages with heap data storage, such as object-oriented languages, and to other DV tools, particularly SMT-based tools like ACSL [1] and Frama-C [13].

The overall motivation for this project at the outset was to take the work of this report beyond what is reported here, namely to determine (a) which logical encodings of PL features are easier to write and understand (in tool implementations), (b) which encodings show better proof performance and success, and then (c) are the differences significant enough to warrant a substantial refactoring of a DV tool implementation.

2 Logical Encoding of Local Computations

Like other modular DV systems, JML and OpenJML verify a program method by method. Each method's implementation is verified independently against its own specification, using just the specifications of methods on which its implementation and specification depend. The collection of verification proofs of all the methods in the program, together with proofs of termination, constitute a sound verification that the program and its specifications are consistent. A typical DV system translates PL+SL source into logic with a series of steps.

1. Using the semantics of the PL and SL, convert the source into an equivalent form that consists just of a DAG of basic blocks, where each basic block consists only of assignments, assert statements, assume statements and havoc statements. Into each back edge of a loop, where control returns to the loop's beginning, an assertion of the loop's inductive invariant is inserted. In Java, throwing exceptions, try-catch-finally statements, break and continue statements, and the interplay among these can lead to complex flows among many basic blocks. Havoc statements assign to listed variables an arbitrary value consistent with the variable's type; these are used in the representation of loops and method calls.

2. Apply a single-static-assignment (SSA) transformation to all the assignments and variable uses so that each variable has a unique declaration/initialization statement.
3. Transform to a logical form by replacing program variables with logical variables, assignments with assumptions, basic blocks with chains of implications, and the whole DAG of basic blocks as a set of logical block equations. The logical encoding states the property that all the preconditions and other assumptions together imply that all the desired program properties (e.g., not throwing exceptions) and specification assertions hold. This is the property that if proved to always hold verifies that the program implementation and its specifications are consistent.
4. Those logical block equations are then transformed into the input language for a logical solver, such as into SMT-LIB for solvers such as CVC5 [3,4] or Z3 [11].
5. The logical solver then pronounces that set of formulae to be unsatisfiable, satisfiable, or unknown. For SMT solvers, the property to be proved is negated, so that a response of *satisfiable* means that there is a particular, concrete assignment of values to logical variables that satisfies all the preconditions and other assumptions, but also satisfies the negated assertion (that is, falsifies the original assertion), thereby providing a counterexample to a desired proof of consistency. An *unsatisfiable* response means no such assignment exists, and thus the given assertions are entailed by the given assumptions (i.e., the implementation is consistent with the specification). A response of *unknown* means that the solver ran out of time or memory or otherwise could not eliminate all possible satisfying assignments.[2]

Our concern in this paper is principally with the SSA transformation and its interaction with the heap and with method calls. To set the stage for later complications, the following simple example code snippet shows the SSA and logical transformations when only stack variables are used. Stack variables are simple because in languages such as Java that do not permit arbitrary address and pointer calculations, there is no aliasing among stack variables.

Consider this source code snippet (using Java notation for assignments and operators). Here the assert statement can be considered the specification and the other statements the program implementation.

```
x = x + y;
y = x - y;
x = x - y;
//@ assert x == \old(y) && y == \old(x);
```

The \old construct says to evaluate its argument in the context at the beginning of the code snippet. This simple example just has one basic block.

The SSA transformation results in the following.

```
x1 = x0 + y0;
y1 = x1 - y0;
x2 = x1 - y1;
assert x2 == y0 && y1 == x0;
```

---

[2] The presence of quantified expressions often yields a response of *unknown*.

For the transformation to a logical form, we use logical variables that have the same name as the SSA variable, but using subscripts. We obtain the following:

$$(x_1 = x_0 + y_0) \rightarrow (y_1 = x_1 - y_0) \rightarrow (x_2 = x_1 - y_1) \rightarrow (x_2 = y_0 \wedge y_1 = x_0) \quad (1)$$

In (1), $=$ is equality, $\rightarrow$ is right-associative boolean implication, and $\wedge$ is conjunction. Negating formula (1), converting to SMT-LIB, and passing the result to an SMT solver produces `unsat`, i.e., the assertion follows from the program code.

In this example, the $+$ in the program source is addition in Java, the $+$ in the assert statement is addition in the specification language, and the $+$ in the logical formula is addition in the logical language, which in SMT-LIB is addition over the unbounded mathematical integers. Here we mapped the first two into the latter, which is an interpretation of the semantics of the PL addition and SL addition as mathematical addition. However, for Java, addition must be interpreted as 2's-complement addition; addition in JML specifications is by default mathematical addition.

3   Encoding Heap Access and Update—Previous and Related Work

3.1   Notation

The encoding process above becomes more complicated when the PL has references to objects in heap storage. This introduces the possibility of aliasing—different variables can refer to the same object—and objects have substructure in the form of named fields or as array elements. In Java, field names are constants and are not subject to any computation; in C/C++ by contrast, fields can overlap in memory as unions and pointer arithmetic can cause arbitrary aliasing. Java also has arrays, which are essentially objects with computable fields, but in Java array indexes can only refer to elements that are within the bounds of the array. The ensuing discussion will focus on fields, as arrays are handled similarly, with only minor modification.

A heap containing objects with fields is thus a mutable (updatable) structure, indexed by a reference value and a field name, that stores values that have PL types, such as integers of various bit-widths, boolean values and references. The discussion that follows uses the following notation:

- object references are denoted by symbols like o and p in programs with corresponding logical symbols as o and p
- references to arrays are denoted by variations on a in PL and SL and a in logic
- variations on i, j, k are PL and SL variables of various integer-like types; corresponding logical variables are i, j, and k
- field names use letters like f and g; the logical equivalents are variations of f and g, as constants, or of F and G as maps
- letters like v and v indicate values of various types stored in PL fields or in logical maps
- the heap is implicit in programs, but is represented as variations on h (as an index) or H (as a map) in logical equations

– brackets, as in $f[o]$ or $\mathscr{L}[h, o, f]$, denote map lookup; the notation $f[o := v]$ and $\mathscr{L}[h, o, f := v]$ is map update: $f[o := v]$ denotes a new map f' that is the same as f except that $f'[o] = v$. That is, these two operations satisfy the axioms

$$\forall f, o, v : f[o := v][o] = v \text{ and } \forall f, o, p, v : p \neq o \rightarrow f[o := v][p] = f[p]$$

and similarly for maps with other types and numbers of indices.

3.2   Heaps as Maps

Most generally then, we can represent a heap access as a lookup $\mathscr{L}$ in a map h, where $\mathscr{L}[h, o, f]$ returns a value v corresponding to object o and field f in heap h, and $\mathscr{L}[h, o, f := v]$ returns a new heap value h' in which the value v is now associated with o and f, but otherwise h' is the same as h. One complication is that the type of v must match the type of f, for a typed PL like Java.

In 2011, Böhme and Moskal [5] published an assessment of a variety of heap encodings and measured their performance on a set of bespoke benchmarks when implemented for a number of logical engines. The encoding variations stem from treating the heap as an index in $\mathscr{L}$ or as a map itself; similarly, fields can be represented as either constant values that are indices into a map or as maps themselves. That gives a number of options, as presented and named in [5]:

synchronous heap   the heap H is an updateable 2-dimensional map indexed on object and field, with lookup $H[o, f]$. (Standard SMT-LIB does not support explicitly two-dimensional arrays, though some SMT solvers, such as Z3, do.)

two-dimensional heap   the heap H is a nested map of maps, where either the object or the field may be the first index, with lookup $H[o][f]$ or $H[f][o]$. These nested maps make update more complicated: instead of $H[o, f := v]$, there is either $H[o := H[o][f := v]]$ or $H[f := H[f][o := v]]$.

field heap   the heap is separated into a number of heaps by field, so each field f is represented by a map $F[o]$. This corresponds to currying the map $H[f]$ into a map F (for each field) from references to values, which is possible because field names are pure constants.

The fact that the heap is implicit in the field heap encoding, whereas in all other encodings it is explicit, makes the field heap categorically different than the other encodings. In some ways the field heap encoding is simpler to use, particularly in the absence of method calls. However, it does lose the ability to quantify over fields, which can be useful in modeling features such as frame conditions. Thus axiomatization with non-field heaps can be more succinct, whereas with field heaps those axioms may need to be re-instantiated whenever the heap changes.

For C or C++ another option is needed to model pointer arithmetic:

linear heap   lookup is $H[dot(o, f)]$, which uses an operation, dot, that combines a pointer and a field.

Böhme and Moskal measured performance of these options, axiomatizing each encoding option for a variety of logical solvers. Variations of orders of magnitude in performance were measured. They reported several interesting observations:

- The field heap encoding was by far the most efficient in most cases; the two-dimensional heap of the form $H[p][f]$ was comparable in time performance for Z3, but solved many fewer problems.
- Performance on other heap encodings varied considerably across solvers and across encodings.
- In the case of Z3, the performance varied significantly depending on the set of tool parameters used. It also varied significantly with the use of patterns to guide the instantiation of quantified formulas.
- SMT-based solvers (e.g., Z3, CVC3, Yices) performed overall better on this benchmark set than did ATP solvers (e.g., E, SPASS, Vampire).
- Breaking up a large verification formula can produce some performance improvement.

An overall observation is the importance of design choices (heap encoding, tool, tool parameters) to the performance of the DV system. However, the systems involved in this study were measured more than a decade ago; they have been significantly improved since then, as evidenced by the results of the annual SMTCOMP competition [8,23,25], but as the measurements have not been repeated, we are building, cautiously, on the original conclusions.

The reasons for differences in performance for different heap encodings are a matter of speculation. However, a reasonable hypothesis is that in the field heap the solver spends less time doing alias determination than in the two-dimensional heap mappings, since in $H[f][p]$, some reasoning steps are needed to determine whether two field identifiers f and f' are the same or different.

3.3   Arrays

Arrays are encoded like fields, but with an integer index. Like fields, there are a variety of ways to encode arrays. In Java, these must take account of the property that Java arrays are aliasable; that is, the assignment b = a; means that b now refers to the same array as a, not to a copy of it. Element i of array-typed field a of an object o, that is, o.a[i], might be encoded as $\mathscr{A}[\mathscr{L}[h, o, a], i]$ or $H_A[H[o, a], i]$ or $E[A[o]][i]$, where $\mathscr{A}$, H_A, E, and A are maps for the portion of the heap containing arrays. Type considerations add complexity because $\mathscr{L}[h, o, a]$ and $A[o]$ are now an array type. There are now two layers of heap lookup, but otherwise the kinds of axioms and reasoning needed are similar to those for regular fields. It is also possible to consider integer indices (of arrays) to be just another kind of field identifier, further unifying the treatment of fields and arrays. We ignore arrays in the following discussion.

3.4   Embedding in SMT

If we use SMT-LIB [24] as the logical language, then we need to consider to what extent SMT-LIB supports these encoding models. (Even if a tool uses Boogie [17] as an intermediate language, the encoding will eventually be mapped into SMT-LIB.)

There is a design choice in how SMT-LIB is used to encode mappings with a single index: one can use either SMT-LIB's uninterpreted functions or its maps with single-index but with arbitrary index and value types.

- The advantage of using SMT-LIB's built-in maps is that then the solver can use the solver's built-in, highly engineered decision procedures for read-over-write maps, which includes extensionality.[3] However, SMT-LIB is also strictly typed, which means that different map types are needed for different field types.
- Objects can be treated more uniformly if the model uses generically axiomatized uninterpreted functions; e.g., heap values that are arrays can be treated the same as heap values that are other references. The types of different field values can be handled by defining injective functions that wrap values into a generic container and unwrap them into specified types.[4] One disadvantage of this approach is that the solver then needs to reason its way through these wrapping and unwrapping functions.

Also, SMT-LIB does not support maps with more than one index (though Z3 does), so $H[o, f]$ must necessarily be either axiomatized as uninterpreted functions or embedded in standard SMT-LIB as either $H[o][f]$ or $H[f][o]$.

In addition to Böhme and Moskal [5], other authors have discussed the use of these encodings in specific systems.

- Leino and Rümmer [20] present how these encodings are accommodated in the design of Boogie [17].
- Weiss [26] recaps Böhme and Moskal's discussion of heap encodings in the context of the KeY tool [14] and its JavaDL logic.
- *The KeY Book* [2] also gives axioms for heap encoding in the KeY tool.
- Mostowski and Ulbrich [21] also discuss the semantics and implementation of JML model methods in the context of dynamic dispatch.
- Müller [22] discusses extensively the problems in verifying abstractions, though without detailed discussions of logical heap encodings.

OpenJML currently uses the field heap encoding, inheriting it from its predecessors ESC/Java2 [9] and ESC/Java [12]. Part of the goal of this project was to determine whether a change in heap encoding would be worth the refactoring effort.

4   Model Fields and Model Methods

As will be illustrated in the next section and discussed in more detail in Sect. 7, abstract properties of a class can be represented by either model fields or model methods.

A *model field* is a field that is only present in the specification. It may be completely uninterpreted, with its properties determined by axioms, invariants and pre- and post-conditions. Or it can be set equal to an expression using JML's `represents` clause, in which case that equality results in an axiom or assumption about the value of the model field. In other respects, a model field is encoded just like other fields—as an array lookup as described in Sect. 3.2.

A *model method* is a pure (i.e. side-effect-free) method that is part of the specification but can be used with specification expressions. A model method typically has pre-

---

[3] Private communication with Clark Barrett regarding CVC5. April 2022.

[4] Private communication. Rustan Leino regarding encoding in Dafny and Boogie. April 2022.

and postconditions that stipulate when it is well-defined and what its value is. Generally speaking, method calls used in implementations or specifications are replaced by assertions of preconditions and assumptions of postconditions. But there are circumstances in which a matching logical function is defined that mirrors the definition of the model method. This helps with ensuring that underspecified model methods are deterministic and is also necessary for recursive methods.

5 Simple Example

Consider the simple example shown in Fig. 1. The interface Shape has properties sides and perimeter, which are model fields. JML allows interfaces to have instance fields for this purpose. The Java methods sides() and perimeter() report these properties. In Java these are abstract methods with no implementation, but in JML we can give specifications telling their values in terms of the model fields. Another method twice() doubles the linear dimensions of the Shape. Consequently it is specified as assigning to (potentially modifying) perimeter, but not to sides.

The class Square is one implementation of Shape. The notable item here is the use of the represents clauses to associate expressions with the interfaces's model fields. One can easily imagine another class Triangle that also implements Shape.

Figure 2 shows a test program. With the addition of features to avoid arithmetic overflow,[5] this combination of program and specification verifies. Keep in mind that verification in JML is modular: the verification of test() refers only to the specifications of methods it calls, that is, only to methods in Shape and not to anything in Square. Similarly, Shape knows nothing about Square.

The key question is this: the call of twice() in test() modifies the heap, and test() only knows that it has a Shape object, so how does the verifier know that the value of perimeter() has changed but the value of sides() has not? The answer combines information from two parts of Shape's specification:

(a) The frame condition (i.e., the assigns clause) of Shape.twice() states that the method might change the value of the model field perimeter but not sides. (OpenJML enforces the rules that two model fields with different names have disjoint data groups. In derived classes, a field may not be added to two data groups unless one is explicitly a member of the other.)
(b) The postcondition of Shape.twice() uses the new value of perimeter but the call to sides() only uses the not-changed value of sides.

That is, to verify the test program in Fig. 2, the verifier uses the frame condition (assigns perimeter;) and the specifications of the model methods from Shape. The specifications of the model methods are effectively inlined in the logical representation of the source and specifications for verification.

---

[5] The full program is available from the author, but not included for reasons of space.

```
1  public interface Shape {
2    //@ public model instance int sides;
3    //@ public model instance int perimeter;
4
5    //@ assigns perimeter;
6    //@ ensures perimeter == 2*\old(perimeter);
7    public void twice();
8
9    //@ ensures \result == sides;
10   //@ pure
11   public int sides();
12
13   //@ ensures \result == perimeter;
14   //@ pure
15   public int perimeter();
16 }
17 public class Square implements Shape {
18   public int side; //@ in perimeter;
19
20   //@ represents sides = 4;
21   //@ represents perimeter = 4*side;
22
23   //@ ensures side == s && sides == 4;
24   public Square(int s) { side = s; }
25
26   // specification inherited
27   public void twice() { side = 2*side; }
28
29   // specification inherited; cf the represents clause for sides
30   //@ pure
31   public int sides() { return 4; }
32
33   // specification inherited; cf the represents clause for perimeter
34   public int perimeter() { return 4*side; }
35 }
```

Fig. 1. Simple example specified with model fields

```
1  public class Test {
2    public void test(Shape shape) {
3      int s = shape.sides();
4      int p = shape.perimeter();
5      shape.twice();
6      int ss = shape.sides();
7      int pp = shape.perimeter();
8      //@ assert s == ss;
9      //@ assert 2*p == pp;
10   }
11 }
```

Fig. 2. A test program for Shape

6   Using Model Methods

Now why are the model fields even needed? Could we not simply use the methods size() and perimeter() to model the properties of the Shape? Note that in JML one can model the behavior of a system using mathematical types and operations, such as mathematical integers and reals, sequences, sets and maps. These mathematical functions do not interact with the heap; thus, one could declare model fields with such mathematical types and connect them to the implementation through represents clauses. However, doing so would require significant duplication of concepts and implementation: the actual implementation and a parallel structure, perhaps more abstract, in the specification. It is often more convenient and more concise, especially in simple situations, to use Java methods themselves (either ones in the actual Java implementation or ones added as model methods in the JML specification) as modeling elements. JML allows some Java methods (those that are declared pure, do not have side-effects, do not throw exceptions, and always terminate) to be used as such modeling functions.

For example we could write, in interface Shape,

```
1 //@ old int oldSides = sides();
2 //@ old int oldPerimeter = perimeter();
3 //@ ensures sides() == oldSides;
4 //@ ensures perimeter() == 2*oldPerimeter;
5 void twice();
```

(Here the old clause captures a value computed in the pre-state as a local variable available in the post-conditions. It is used to simplify reading or to extract common subexpressions.) However, verification along these lines does not work without further modification. The first problem is that twice() does not indicate what it might alter. We still need a frame condition, which can be specified using a *datagroup* that limits the changes that twice() may perform.[6] The second problem is that because there is no concrete field in which to ground the values of sides() and perimeter(), we need to implement in the encoded logic that the methods are *deterministic*. This determinism ensures that two successive calls of, say sides(), with no intervening change in the heap produce the same result.

The standard encoding for method calls is that the preconditions are asserted, the frame conditions are translated into havoc statements, and the postconditions (giving the relationships of new values of the havoced variables to old ones) are assumed. In the absence of postconditions, the havoced variables are unconstrained. To encode that the method is deterministic, OpenJML adds an assumption of the form $result ==$ $f(args)$, where $result$ is a logical variable representing the result of the method call and f is a logical function that represents the method being called. The encoding of such functions is discussed below; the effect of this assumption is that, within the same heap state, a given (pure) method always gives the same result, even if that result is underspecified.

A third problem, is that the postcondition of Shape.twice() must include statements about how twice() affects both sides() and perimeter(). Given this postcondition, the implementation of test() can be verified. But if there are 20 methods instead of two, all 20 would have to be listed. The reason? There is no specification of what these methods depend on. Even if we add the datagroup mentioned above, we have no indication about whether these methods depend on memory locations in that datagroup. Without knowing that sides() does not depend on side, the system cannot conclude that its value does not change when twice() is called. The solution to this problem is to add *reads* (a.k.a. accessible) clauses to the specifications of functions that list the memory locations on which the functions depend.

---

[6] There is not space here to explain the use of datagroups; see [16] for a justification of the datagroup approach used in JML.

```
1  interface Shape {
2
3    //@ model instance JMLDataGroup _state;
4    //@ model instance JMLDataGroup _sides;
5
6    //@ public normal_behavior
7    //@    old int oldPerimeter = perimeter();
8    //@    reads _state;
9    //@    assigns _state;
10   //@    ensures perimeter() == 2*oldPerimeter;
11   public void twice();
12
13   //@ public normal_behavior
14   //@    reads _sides;
15   //@ pure
16   public int sides();
17
18   //@ public normal_behavior
19   //@    reads _state;
20   //@ pure
21   public int perimeter();
22 }
23
24 class Square implements Shape {
25   //@ public normal_behavior
26   //@    ensures side == s ;
27   public Square(int s) { side = s; }
28   public int side; //@ in _state;
29
30   //@ also public normal_behavior
31   //@    old int oldSides = sides();
32   //@    old int oldPerimeter = perimeter();
33   //@    reads side, _state;
34   //@    assigns side, _state;
35   //@    ensures sides() == oldSides;
36   //@    ensures perimeter() == 2*oldPerimeter;
37   public void twice() { side = 2*side; }
38
39   //@ also public normal_behavior
40   //@    reads _sides;
41   //@    ensures \result == 4;
42   //@ pure
43   public int sides() { return 4; }
44
45   //@ also public normal_behavior
46   //@ reads _state;
47   //@ ensures \result == 4*side;
48   //@ pure
49   public int perimeter() { return 4*side; }
50 }
```

Fig. 3. Specification using model methods

The adjusted specification is shown in Fig. 3 (the code for Test is unchanged) and verifies without problem.

The important conclusions to draw from this example are these:

- In Shape, the model methods perimeter() and sides() are uninterpreted functions. They may have some properties that can be axiomatized, such as having non-negative values, but they are very underspecified.
- Reasoning about repeated invocations of such model methods within the same program state (i.e., with reference to the same heap) relies on these methods being deterministic—always producing the same values for the same arguments and eval-

uation context. Axioms relying on a definition of a corresponding logical function in the encoding must be added to the translation of a method call to ensure this determinism.

– Reasoning about invocations of a model method in different heaps relies on knowing that the memory locations that might have been changed in altering the heap are disjoint from the memory locations that are read by the model method.

The issues here concern underspecified functions—functions with insufficient specification to enable their results to be computed from their specification. It is worth noting that the same problems arise with recursive functions, even fully defined ones, because logical reasoning engines do not do induction on their own and do not unroll recursive definitions. Recursive functions are also essentially underspecified, axiomatized, uninterpreted functions.

Invariants pose one additional difficulty for model methods. With model fields one can easily state an invariant like `0 <= perimeter` in `Shape`. With model fields one would write `0 <= perimeter()`. But in JML, invariants must hold when methods are called; so in this case, `0 <= perimeter()` must hold before `perimeter()` is called. A circular invocation of `perimeter()` results. The usual way to fix this is to declare `perimeter()` as a `helper` method for which invariants are neither required nor guaranteed. But then in the call of `Square.perimeter()` the invariant cannot be assumed and an arithmetic overflow might occur. In such situations a model field might be needed in any case.

7 Encoding Model Methods

This section describes logical encodings for model methods, that is, methods that are used in specifications and so need a logical representation.

One can translate a method like `perimeter` into a corresponding logical function that has formal parameters for every entity on which the value of the method depends. In this case that is the `Shape` reference itself and the heap; functions that represent Java methods with additional parameters will also need logical equivalents of those additional parameters.

There are variations on this theme that depend on the heap encoding. To explain these we use the logical type REF as the type of all Java objects and $Heap$ as the logical type of heaps in the encoding.

– If heaps are encoded as *synchronous* or *two-dimensional* heaps, then a model method is encoded as a logical function that takes a heap parameter; e.g., `perimeter()` is encoded as the logical function $perimeter(h, p)$ where h has type $Heap$ and p has type REF.

– If the *field heaps* encoding (see Sect. 3.2) is used, then the heap parameter is replaced by a list of the specific field heaps needed in the evaluation of the function's specification. However, such a list might be long.

– The heap parameter can also be made implicit by currying $perimeter(h, p)$ into $perimeter_h(p)$, where there is a different logical function for `perimeter` for each heap (i.e., for each program state). With this option neither the heap nor any field maps need be listed as parameters.

The last option works best with field heaps, for which the heap is already an implicit parameter. For other heap encodings the first option works best, because there is an explicit heap that can be passed as an argument; with some theorem provers, this is a rationale for preferring encodings other than field heaps. However, when working with underspecified methods, both alternatives suffer equally from the problem described next.

For underspecified methods, the reasoning problem is the lack of sufficient information about such methods. We can contrast this with completely specified methods, such as Square's method perimeter, which is specified to return a value of $4 \times \mathscr{L}[h, p, \#side]$, where $\#side$ is a constant corresponding to the field side. By contrast, for an underspecified method, such as Shape's model method perimeter, a call may have different results in different program states; because the heap h is a parameter to the encoding $perimeter(h, p)$. For reasoning about such calls, the reads clause is crucial. Consider two heap states, h and h', where h' is derived from h by some sequence of heap-changing operations. Let $\Delta(h, h')$ be the set of memory locations which are changed between the two heaps; the prover knows that $\Delta(h, h')$ is at most the union of the frame location sets for each heap-changing operation in the sequence going from h to h'. In general, for a method m with receiver p, arguments $args$, and reads footprint $f_{reads}(h, p, args)$, if $f_{reads}(h, p, args)$ is disjoint from $\Delta(h, h')$, then $m(h, p, args) = m(h', p, args)$. (Note that in general a reads footprint depends on the function's arguments and the current heap.)

There are a couple design options that encode such reasoning. On the one hand we can state the above relationship between heap-change footprints and function reads footprints as a general property of heaps, footprints, and functions. But this requires encoding heaps, frame footprints for heap changing methods, reads footprints of functions, and functions themselves as first-class elements in the logical encoding. Such an encoding adds to the reasoning load for the theorem prover.

On the other hand, we can introduce axioms stating under which conditions $m(h, p, args) = m(h', p, args)$ for each pair of heaps and each function as needed, but only as needed. This adds many more axioms, but they are tailored for specific situations in the program encoding; in addition the axioms can often be instantiated for the method arguments that are actually used, avoiding the need for the logic engine to figure out when to instantiate the quantified axiom.

Our experience in actual practice is that this latter approach works acceptably. It was implemented because it was the smaller step from the existing implementation, though an experiment contrasting this approach with the approach of using general axioms is still needed. We say "working acceptably" due to the smallish scale of our test examples and target system. The number of axioms and states was manageable because the size of methods was moderate and the numbers of methods used for modeling within a given method was not large.

8   Contrast and Conclusion

The goal of this work was to make a comparison between specifying using model fields vs. using model methods. To summarize the differences in practice of these two abstraction mechanisms,

a model field

- is a possibly-uninterpreted abstract specification-only field
- may be given an interpretation using a `represents` clause
- has an associated datagroup that, in combination with the frame conditions of heap-changing operations, implies when the model field (for a given object) is unchanged and when it might be changed by those heap-changing operations

a model method

- is a possibly uninterpreted abstract specification-only method
- may be given an interpretation using postconditions
- has an associated `reads` clause that, in combination with the frame conditions of heap-changing operations, implies when the value of the model method (for a given object and set of arguments) is unchanged and when it might be changed by those heap-changing operations

Summarized in this way, model fields and model methods are quite similar: model fields are like model methods that depend only on the heap and the receiver object; model methods can describe properties that have more parameters than just the receiver object.

Here are our experience-generated informal observations on using both mechanisms.

- Both means of modeling were overall successful in specifying the target example.
- Where both mechanisms were applicable, model fields were easier to use because:
  - They can precisely specify a method's result for an otherwise underspecified abstract method.
  - They rely on a heap encoding that is already implemented in the tool.
- Model methods are necessary to specify properties that need arguments or that are not simple values characteristic of an object (e.g., a model method is needed to describe the value of a list element at some index, whereas the length of a list can be a model field).
- Reasoning about underspecified model methods in the presence of heap changes required implementing additional axioms that enabled reasoning about changes in those methods (or lack thereof) when the program's state changed. This included implementing `reads` clauses and the infrastructure for comparing locations sets from `assigns` clauses and `reads` clauses.
- The interaction between invariants and model methods, particularly uninterpreted model methods in interfaces or abstract classes, typically makes it easier to write specifications using model fields (when invariants are involved).
- The simplest and most successful specifications were those that consisted of model fields that were values of some mathematical type. Those values and their operations are not part of the heap and so reasoning about them bypasses the issues noted in this paper; the model fields themselves are part of the program state and are part of `assigns` sets of memory locations.

These (informal) observations are from a single project's experience and on a relatively small project. It will take future work on larger projects to determine how well they generalize.

Acknowledgements. Work on JML and OpenJML has benefited from various NSF research grants. OpenJML has also benefited from sponsorship by various industrial clients, including AWS and Goldman Sachs. Thanks also to Rustan Leino and Mattias Ulbrich for private conversations regarding heap encodings in their various tools.

References

1. ACSL. ANSI-C Specification Language (2021). https://github.com/acsl-language/acsl/
2. Ahrendt, W., Beckert, B., Bubel, R., Hähnle, R., Schmitt, P.H., Ulbrich, M.: Deductive software verification - The KeY Book. In: LNCS, Springer, Cham (2016). https://doi.org/10.1007/978-3-319-49812-6
3. Barbosa, H., et al.: CVC5: a versatile and industrial-strength SMT solver. In: TACAS 2022. LNCS, vol. 13243, pp. 415–442. Springer, Cham (2022). https://doi.org/10.1007/978-3-030-99524-9_24
4. Barrett, C., et al.: CVC5 web site (2022). https://cvc5.github.io/
5. Böhme, S., Moskal, M.: Heaps and data structures: a challenge for automated provers. In: Bjørner, N., Sofronie-Stokkermans, V. (eds.) CADE 2011. LNCS (LNAI), vol. 6803, pp. 177–191. Springer, Heidelberg (2011). https://doi.org/10.1007/978-3-642-22438-6_15
6. Cok, D.R.: (2021)
7. Cok, D.R.: JML and OpenJML for Java 16. In: Proceedings of the 23rd ACM International Workshop on Formal Techniques for Java-like Programs (FTfJP 2021), pp. 65–67. Association for Computing Machinery, NY (2021). https://www.openjml.org
8. Cok, D.R., Déharbe, D., Weber, T.: The 2014 SMT competition. J. Satisfiability Boolean Model. Comput. **9**, 207–242 (2014)
9. Cok, D.R., Kiniry, J.R.: ESC/Java2: Uniting ESC/Java and JML. In: Barthe, G., Burdy, L., Huisman, M., Lanet, J.-L., Muntean, T. (eds.) CASSIS 2004. LNCS, vol. 3362, pp. 108–128. Springer, Heidelberg (2005). https://doi.org/10.1007/978-3-540-30569-9_6
10. Cok, D.R., Leavens, G.T., Ulbrich, M.: Java Modeling Language (JML) Reference Manual, 2nd edn (2022). www.openjml.org/documentation/JML_Reference_Manual.pdf
11. de Moura, L., Bjørner, N.: Z3: an efficient SMT solver. In: Ramakrishnan, C.R., Rehof, J. (eds.) TACAS 2008. LNCS, vol. 4963, pp. 337–340. Springer, Heidelberg (2008). https://doi.org/10.1007/978-3-540-78800-3_24
12. Flanagan, C., Leino, K.R.M., Lillibridge, M., Nelson, G., Saxe, J.B., Stata, R.: Extended static checking for Java. In: Proceedings of the ACM SIGPLAN 2002 Conference on Programming Language Design and Implementation (PLDI 2002), vol. 37(5), pp. 234–245. SIGPLAN, NY. ACM (2002)
13. Frama-C: (2021). https://frama-c.com
14. KeY: The KeY project (2021). www.key-project.org
15. Leavens, G.T., Baker, A.L., Ruby, C.: Preliminary design of JML: a behavioral interface specification language for Java. Technical Report 98-06-rev29, Iowa State University, Department of Computer Science (2006). Also ACM SIGSOFT Softw. Eng. Notes **31**(3), 1–38 (2006)
16. Leino, K.R.M.: Data groups: specifying the modification of extended state. SIGPLAN Not. **33**(10), 144–153 (1998)
17. Leino, K.R.M.: This is boogie 2 (2008)
18. Leino, K.R.M., et al.: Dafny github site (2021). https://github.com/dafny-lang/dafny. Accessed Sept 2021
19. Leino, K.R.M., Ford, R.L., Cok, D.R.: Dafny reference manual. https://github.com/dafny-lang/dafny/blob/master/docs/DafnyRef/out/DafnyRef.pdf. Accessed Jul 2021

20. Leino, K.R.M., Rümmer, P.: A polymorphic intermediate verification language: design and logical encoding. In: Esparza, J., Majumdar, R. (eds.) TACAS 2010. LNCS, vol. 6015, pp. 312–327. Springer, Heidelberg (2010). https://doi.org/10.1007/978-3-642-12002-2_26
21. Mostowski, W., Ulbrich, M.: Dynamic dispatch for method contracts through abstract predicates. In: Proceedings of the 14th International Conference on Modularity (MODULARITY 2015), pp. 109–116. Association for Computing Machinery, NY (2015)
22. Müller, P.: Modular Specification and Verification of Object-Oriented Programs, pp. 143–194. Springer-Verlag, Heidelberg (2002). https://doi.org/10.1007/3-540-45651-1_5
23. SMTCOMP: Smtcomp competition (2022). https://smt-comp.github.io/2022/
24. Tinelli, C., et al.: SMT-LIB web site (2003). https://smtlib.cs.uiowa.edu/
25. Weber, T., Conchon, S., Déharbe, D., Heizmann, M., Niemetz, A., Reger, G.: The SMT competition 2015–2018. J. Satisf. Boolean Model. Comput. 11(1), 221–259 (2019)
26. Weiß, B.: Deductive verification of object-oriented software: dynamic frames, dynamic logic and predicate abstraction. PhD thesis, KIT (2011)

A Hoare Logic with Regular Behavioral Specifications

Gidon Ernst[1(✉)], Alexander Knapp[2], and Toby Murray[3]

[1] LMU Munich, Munich, Germany
gidon.ernst@lmu.de
[2] Augsburg University, Augsburg, Germany
knapp@informatik.uni-augsburg.de
[3] University of Melbourne, Melbourne, Australia
toby.murray@unimelb.edu.au

Abstract. We present a Hoare logic that extends program specifications with regular expressions that capture behaviors in terms of sequences of events that arise during the execution, akin session types and process-like behavioral contracts. In comparison, the approach presented here strikes a particular balance between expressiveness and proof automation. The approach is modular and integrates well with auto-active verification tools. We describe and demonstrate our prototype implementation in SecC using two case studies: A matcher for E-Mail addresses and a specification of the game steps in the VerifyThis Casino challenge.

Keywords: Hoare logic · Behavioral specification · Regular expressions

1 Introduction

Context of this work is the aim to declaratively specify the state machine logic of programs that have a control state and in which the sequence of events matters. A typical example are stateful protocols (e.g. the TCP handshake) and device drivers. One motivation for this paper in particular is the Casino case study from the ongoing VerifyThis discussion series since 2021.[1] Goal of these discussions is to bring different communities together and bridge specifications using contract-based mechanisms typically found in deductive verification tools and the automata-based approaches of model-checking. Of particular interest was the integration of automata-like specifications and models with deductive program verification tools. Attributing and verifying temporal behavior of systems has a long history, e.g. [2,17,26]. Contemporary approaches include an embedding of a highly expressive process-calculus language into the Separation Logic assertions [4,23,24,30], tackling highly complex protocols and low-level implementations at the same time at the cost of manual annotation and proof

---

[1] https://verifythis.github.io/casino/.

© The Author(s), under exclusive license to Springer Nature Switzerland AG 2022
T. Margaria and B. Steffen (Eds.): ISoLA 2022, LNCS 13701, pp. 45–64, 2022.
https://doi.org/10.1007/978-3-031-19849-6_4

burden. At the other end of the spectrum are approaches for temporal logic model checking of C programs [8, 29, 33], which achieve full automation by abstraction, bounded search, or by restricting the properties that can be verified.

Goal: Here, we aim to explore a particular point in the design space of embedding declarative behavioral specification of event traces into the pre- and postconditions of a Hoare-like logic. The approach combines strong reasoning about the *functional correctness* of programs with a light-weight integration of *behavioral aspects* into contracts. We strive for an as-simple-as-possible extension of Hoare logic with such behavioral specifications; and by restricting ourselves to behaviors described by regular expressions the additional proof obligations can be decided automatically with little additional effort in the verification.

We illustrate these ideas with an example in Sect. 2, which will uncover that an entirely naive approach does not work and that behavioral specifications need to take some form of dependence on the state to capture interesting behavior.

Contribution: In Sect. 3, we develop a Hoare-like logic with judgements $\{P \mid U\}\ c\ \{Q \mid V\}$, where in addition to the ordinary pre-/postcondition pair P, Q for command c, we have two regular trace specifications U and V that record the *history* [4] of events emitted so far and after termination of c, respectively. The logic is proved sound in the Isabelle/HOL proof assistant and we suggest a corresponding completeness result. We have implemented the approach in the deductive verification tool SecC [11], as discussed with details on this automation in Sect. 4. We illustrate and discuss in depth the approach with two case studies in Sect. 5: A matcher for E-Mail addresses and the Casino challenge. We discuss related work in Sect. 6, where in addition to the approach taken here, a dual view has been proposed on the role of trace specifications U and V that are part of the judgements. We clarify how this affects properties of the resulting logics.

2   Motivation

We clarify the minimal ingredients that are needed for the construction of the logic using an example. Consider a loop that generates a sequence of alternating events even and odd, where the loop test nondeterministically terminates the loop but only in a state when b is false, expressed as pseudocode:

```
b := false
while nondet() ∨ b do
    if b then emit odd
        else emit even
    b := ¬b
end
```

Fig. 1. Event alternation

The specification command emit a demarks the occurrence of an event during program execution, and we are interested in specifying the behavior of programs in terms of the event traces that can occur at runtime. Events are sometimes attributed to certain steps of the program's semantics, but here we just keep them abstract and assume that the right events have been placed at appropriate locations in the source code in terms of emit statements.

The behavior of the above program is captured nicely by a regular expression:

$$\textbf{program specification} \qquad (\text{even}\cdot\text{odd})^* \qquad\qquad (1)$$

where $\cdot$ denotes concatenation and $*$ denotes repetition. The program is indeed correct with respect to this specification, informally because the loop body is executed for the first time with $\neg b$, thus emitting an even event first, the loop alternates between the two events, and terminates never, only after no event or after an odd event has been emitted.

A straightforward idea to specify the traces of a while loop is to repeat whatever the body produces, using the star operator. In the example above, the behavior of the loop body can be abstracted by the regular expression $(\text{even}+\text{odd})$ from which we can conclude that the loop adheres to $(\text{even}+\text{odd})^*$. However, this naive approach cannot capture the alternation of even and odd events as produced by the loop. This insight coincides with the fact that the finite automaton that accepts the same language as (1) has *two* states, thus, we need *two* regular expressions to describe traces with respect to the current value of b.

Just as with the functional component of loop specifications, we can choose whether we want to describe the events observed so far (analogously to an invariant), or alternatively whether we want to specify the traces that are still permitted to occur (analogously to a loop postcondition or summary [10,12,32]). For this example, the two alternative loop specifications are:

loop invariant	$(\text{even}\cdot\text{odd})^*$ if $\neg b$	$(\text{even}\cdot\text{odd})^*\cdot\text{even}$ if b
loop summary	$(\text{even}\cdot\text{odd})^*$ if $\neg b$	$\text{odd}\cdot(\text{even}\cdot\text{odd})^*$ if b

The regular expressions are conditioned upon a formula which depends on the value of b in some arbitrary intermediate state encountered at the loop head. If b is currently true, then the invariant expresses that this current state has been reached by a trace prefix that ends in an even event, such that the subsequent iteration *concatenating* an odd to the end of this regular expression will again give (1). Conversely, the loop summary in this case makes it explicit that the next event expected is an odd event. For now we will focus on the invariant approach as it is easier to present and more familiar (cf. [10, Rule LoopContract]).

3   Approach

We present an extension of Hoare logic that integrates trace specifications in terms of regular expressions with deductive proofs, where program correctness is expressed as judgements of the form $\{\,P \mid U\,\}\ c\ \{\,Q \mid V\,\}$ with respect to pre-/postconditions P, Q and a command c. In addition, there are two conditional regular expressions U and V, subsequently called regular behavioral specifications, denoting the trace prefix and resulting trace, respectively.

3.1 Preliminaries and Notation

Conditions P, Q and ϕ are represented syntactically as formulas. Semantically, formulas can be evaluated over states $s \in S$, written P_s for instance, to result in a semantic truth value. We occasionally make use of primed variables, e.g., in rule SPEC. Within the standard non-relational evaluation wrt. a single state s, these are treated as any other variable (i.e., the prime is part of the name). States map variables to values, the updated state $s' = s(x \mapsto v)$ has $s'(x) = v$ and $s'(y) = s(x)$ for all $x \neq y$. Syntactic substitutions σ are written with square brackets in comparison, e.g., $P' \equiv P\sigma \equiv P[\vec{x} \mapsto \vec{x}']$ for $\sigma = [\vec{x} \mapsto \vec{x}']$ is understood to replace variables $\vec{x}$ by their primed counterparts $\vec{x}'$.

In the semantic description of the specification statement in Sect. 3.3, we use the relational semantics of R, written as $R_{s,s'}$. Only here, primed variables have a special meaning to be evaluated in s' instead, whereas all unprimed variables are evaluated in s as usual. For example, an action that increases x nondeterministically could be written as a relation $x < x'$.

3.2 Regular Behavioral Specifications

Plain regular expressions u, v, w consist of the empty language, the empty word, symbols of an alphabet $a \in A$, sequential composition, choice,[2] and repetition:

$$u ::= \varnothing \mid \epsilon \mid a \mid u{\cdot}v \mid u + v \mid u^*$$

The language $\mathcal{L}(u)$ of an expression u is defined as usual as a set of words which are finite sequences of symbols, representing behavioral traces $\tau = \langle a_1, \ldots, a_n \rangle$ here. A regular expression u is called *nullable* if its language contains the empty word, i.e., $\langle \, \rangle \in \mathcal{L}(u)$; and u is called *empty* if its language is the empty set, i.e., $\mathcal{L}(u) = \varnothing$. Language inclusion and equivalence are defined as follows

$$u \sqsubseteq v \iff \mathcal{L}(u) \subseteq \mathcal{L}(v) \qquad u \equiv v \iff \mathcal{L}(u) = \mathcal{L}(v)$$

such that u is nullable if and only if $\epsilon \sqsubseteq u$, and u is empty if $u \equiv \varnothing$. Nullability and emptiness can be checked efficiently by a simple recursion over the syntax.

Definition 1 (Regular Behavioral Specification). A regular behavioral specification U, V, W is a state-dependent choice between plain regular expressions u_i:

$$U ::= \quad u_1 \text{ if } \phi_1 \ + \ \cdots \ + \ u_n \text{ if } \phi_n$$

We tacitly interpret a plain regular expression u if *true* with a trivial guard as such a specification. Syntactic substitutions $U\sigma$ propagate to the conditionals:

$$(u_1 \text{ if } \phi_1 + \ \cdots \ + u_n \text{ if } \phi_n)\sigma = (u_1 \text{ if } \phi_1\sigma + \ \cdots \ + u_n \text{ if } \phi_n\sigma)$$

---

[2] Denoted by + here instead of | to avoid syntactic confusion with EBNF.

Similarly, the language $\mathcal{L}_s(U)$ of such a specification relative to a state s picks those cases that are satisfied in s and discards the others:

$$\mathcal{L}_s(u_1 \text{ if } \phi_1 + \cdots + u_n \text{ if } \phi_n) = (u_1 \text{ if } \phi_1)_s \cup \cdots \cup (u_n \text{ if } \phi_n)_s$$

$$\text{where} \quad \mathcal{L}_s(u \text{ if } \phi) = \mathcal{L}(u) \text{ if } \phi_s \quad \text{and} \quad \mathcal{L}_s(u \text{ if } \phi) = \varnothing \text{ otherwise}$$

Later, for rule FRAME in Sect. 3.4, we refer to sequential composition of such specifications which semantically obeys $\mathcal{L}_s(U \cdot V) = \mathcal{L}_s(U) \cdot \mathcal{L}_s(V)$ but we refrain here from giving a general syntactic account for brevity, and because this construct may be somewhat misleading as U and V are evaluated in the *same* state, even though sequential composition suggests that V might occur *after* U, and maybe after a state change in the program. However, we can freely move state-independent regular expression fragments in and out of this composition as in $\mathcal{L}_s(u \cdot V) = u \cdot \mathcal{L}_s(V)$, which will be the use case in the implementation (Sect. 4). We reflect language inclusion and equivalence as predicates over states, too

$$(U \sqsubseteq V)_s \iff \mathcal{L}_s(U) \subseteq \mathcal{L}_s(V) \qquad (U \equiv V)_s \iff \mathcal{L}_s(U) = \mathcal{L}_s(V)$$

such that, e.g., $P \implies U \sqsubseteq V$ can be regarded as a logical formula. This will be useful in particular to express a strong consequence rule in Sect. 3.4.

3.3   Programs and Behavioral Correctness

Imperative commands c are formed by the grammar shown below, comprising specification statements [19] and the usual composition constructs:

$$c ::= \vec{x} \colon [G \rightsquigarrow R \,\mathbin{|}\, U] \mid p(\vec{e}; \vec{z}) \mid c_1; c_2 \mid \text{if } t \text{ then } c_1 \text{ else } c_2 \mid \text{while } t \text{ do } c \mid \cdots$$

Atomic commands like skip and assignments are subsumed by specification statements [19] extended by a regular behavior, written $\vec{x} \colon [G \rightsquigarrow R \,\mathbin{|}\, U]$. Provided that guard G holds in a given state, the specification command takes a nondeterministic transition by modifying the variables $\vec{x}$ according to a transition relation R, and by emitting a trace of the language of U. Emission of single events can be encoded as emit $a \equiv - \colon [\text{true} \rightsquigarrow \text{true} \,\mathbin{|}\, a]$ with no modified variables and no constraints on the transition. We also include procedure calls $p(\vec{e}; \vec{z})$ with input arguments given by expressions $\vec{e}$ and results assigned to variables $\vec{z}$.

The natural big-step semantics describes executions of commands $c \; k \xrightarrow{\tau}{}^* k'$ from an initial configuration (**run** $s \colon c$) with state s to a final configuration that is either (**stop** s') (regular termination in final state s') or **abort** (subsuming runtime errors). The sequence of events that have happened during this particular execution is annotated as a trace τ. The definition of the rules governing $k \xrightarrow{\tau}{}^* k'$ are entirely standard, except perhaps for the specification statement:

$$(\textbf{run } s \colon \vec{x} \colon [G \rightsquigarrow R \,\mathbin{|}\, U]) \xrightarrow{\tau}{}^* \textbf{abort} \qquad \text{if not } G_s \text{ and } \tau \text{ arbitrary}$$

$$(\textbf{run } s \colon \vec{x} \colon [G \rightsquigarrow R \,\mathbin{|}\, U]) \xrightarrow{\tau}{}^* (\textbf{stop } s') \qquad \text{if } G_s \wedge R_{s,s'} \wedge \tau \in U_{s,s'}$$

where $s' = s(\vec{x} \mapsto \vec{v})$ denotes the modified state in which the variables $\vec{x}$ have been updated to some arbitrary new values $\vec{v}$, leaving all other variables unchanged. The arbitrary trace τ reflects that a diverging program could have any effect. The derived command emit a behaves as expected

$$(\textbf{run } s\colon \texttt{emit } a) \xrightarrow{\langle a \rangle}{}^* (\textbf{stop } s)$$

For a given procedure declaration $p(\vec{x}; \vec{y}) \, \{\, c \,\}$, a call unfolds to the body c:

$$(\textbf{run } s\colon p(\vec{e}, \vec{z})) \xrightarrow{\tau}{}^* k \qquad\qquad \text{if } (\textbf{run } s'\colon c') \xrightarrow{\tau}{}^* k$$

where $c' = c[\vec{x}, \vec{y} \mapsto \vec{x}', \vec{z}]$ refreshes all formal input parameters $\vec{x}$ to ensure they are treated as local variables, whereas the formal output parameters $\vec{y}$ (typically just one, denoted \result in JML) are replaced by the actual variables $\vec{z}$ such that the body c' computes over these instead. Accordingly, the modified state $s' = s(\vec{x}' \mapsto \vec{e}_s)$ assigns to $\vec{x}'$ the evaluation of the arguments $\vec{e}$ in s.

Judgements $\{\, P \mid U \,\} \, c \, \{\, Q \mid V \,\}$ comprise the usual constituents, precondition P, command c, and postcondition Q, as well as the (state-dependent) regular expressions specification U over the alphabet A collecting possible trace prefixes seen so far, and V constraining how these may be extended by executing c.

Definition 2 (Valid Hoare Triples). A Hoare triple $\{\, P \mid U \,\} \, c \, \{\, Q \mid V \,\}$ is *valid*, if for all $s \in S$ with traces τ, and for all configurations k'

$$P_s \text{ and } (\textbf{run } s\colon c) \xrightarrow{\tau}{}^* k' \text{ implies}$$
$$\text{there is } s' \text{ with } k' = (\textbf{stop } s') \text{ and } Q_{s'} \text{ and } \mathcal{L}(U_s \cdot \tau) \subseteq L(V_{s'})$$

Note that P and U are evaluated in the pre-state s, whereas Q and V are evaluated in the post-state s', and that $k' \neq \textbf{abort}$.

The judgement as defined above is based on *histories* [4] of completed executions. As such, it cannot reason about event traces of nonterminating executions, as diverging runs are simply not generated by the semantics by design. We discuss a dual view of Hoare triples in Sect. 6, which is based on traces allowed in the *future* instead [23,24]. However, our implementation described in Sect. 4 relies on the best *forwards* trace transformer for dispatching procedure calls modularly, which is unavailable in the future-based setting that has a best backwards transformer instead, cf. Sect. 6.

3.4   Hoare Logic Proof Rules

The proof rules are standard with respect to the functional correctness aspects captured by the pre-/postcondition. Regarding the trace specifications, there are some aspects that are worth discussing. Typically, traces that occur during execution are simply added to the regular expression specification in the precondition. For example the derived rule for the emit command is just

$$\frac{}{\{\, P \mid U \,\} \text{ emit } a \, \{\, P \mid U \cdot a \,\}} \text{ EMIT}$$

The more general specification statement can be executed whenever its guard G follows from the current precondition P. Given then that binary relation R

between unprimed and primed variables holds, we establish Q in that successor state and that the extension of pre-traces U by any trace of W is covered by V:

$$\frac{P \implies G \qquad P \wedge R \implies Q\sigma \wedge (U{\cdot}W \sqsubseteq V\sigma)}{\{P{\mid}U\}\; x{:}\; [G \rightsquigarrow R{\mid}W]\; \{Q{\mid}V\}}\;\; \text{Spec}$$

where $\sigma = [\vec{x} \mapsto \vec{x}']$ takes care of shifting the modified variables into the successor state within Q and V, where the primed variables are constrained by R as described in Sect. 3.1. Rule EMIT is then an instance of SPEC for $G, R \equiv \text{true}$, $\vec{x} = \langle\rangle$, and $W = a$ (cf. Sect. 3.3), such that the second premise collapses to $U{\cdot}a \sqsubseteq V\sigma$ for the empty substitution σ and $V = U{\cdot}a$.

Example 1. We can represent the loop body of our motivating example in Fig. 1 by a single specification statement for demonstration purposes here

$$b\colon [\text{true} \rightsquigarrow b' = \neg b \mid a] \quad \text{where } a = \begin{cases} \text{even}, & \text{if } \neg b \\ \text{odd}, & \text{otherwise} \end{cases}$$

Recall the invariant-like characterization of traces from Sect. 2, formalized as a regular expression specification $U(b)$ over program variable b:

$$U(b) \quad\equiv\quad (\text{even}{\cdot}\text{odd})^* \text{ if } \neg b\; +\; (\text{even}{\cdot}\text{odd})^*{\cdot}\text{even if } b$$

The part of the instantiated precondition of rule SPEC that relates the pre-traces to the post-traces takes $V = U$ to re-establish the invariant after executing the body, which leads to the following proof obligation

$$b' = \neg b \implies U(b){\cdot}a \sqsubseteq U(b')$$

This can be reduced by case analysis where $U(b)$ and $U(b')$ pick the the opposite regular expression, respectively, underlining the most recently emitted event a.

$$(\text{even}{\cdot}\text{odd})^*{\cdot}\underline{\text{even}} \sqsubseteq (\text{even}{\cdot}\text{odd})^*{\cdot}\text{even} \qquad\qquad \text{if } \neg b$$
$$(\text{even}{\cdot}\text{odd})^*{\cdot}\text{even}{\cdot}\underline{\text{odd}} \sqsubseteq (\text{even}{\cdot}\text{odd})^* \qquad\qquad \text{otherwise}$$

Clearly, both conditions are satisfied. $\qquad\qquad\qquad\qquad\qquad\qquad\qquad\qquad\quad\heartsuit$

The following framing rule allows one to put a subpart of the execution into the context of a prefix W that captures the past up to that point. This rule encodes that the program execution itself cannot depend on past events, because traces have no manifestation at runtime:

$$\frac{P \wedge Q\sigma \implies W \equiv W\sigma \qquad \{P{\mid}U\}\; c\; \{R{\mid}V\}}{\{P{\mid}W{\cdot}U\}\; c\; \{Q{\mid}W{\cdot}V\}}\;\; \text{FRAME}$$

for $\sigma = [\vec{x} \mapsto \vec{x}']$ wher $\vec{x}$ are the variables modified in c. Just as with the frame rule in Separation Logic [27] there is a side-condition that the frame W is independent of the program execution, which we can express by an additional premise as shown. This premise is trivially satisfied for state-independent regular expressions and our implementation uses this heavily as explained in Sect. 4.

The frame rule expresses, intuitively, that execution of code fragments cannot depend on the trace prefix, which means that in principle, we could avoid the presence of the prefix U in the judgements alltogether. However, as we have seen for example with $U \cdot W \sqsubseteq V\sigma$ in the premises of SPEC we have to be careful to which state we relate the respective trace specifications. Having both a prefix U and result V symmetrically in the judgements therefore admits the usual and straight-forward treatment of sequential composition:

$$\frac{\{\,P \mid U\,\}\ c_1\ \{\,Q \mid V\,\} \qquad \{\,Q \mid V\,\}\ c_2\ \{\,R \mid W\,\}}{\{\,P \mid U\,\}\ c_1; c_2\ \{\,R \mid W\,\}}\ \text{SEQ}$$

In contrast to judgements but like specification statements, modular specifications of procedure contracts can and should not mention a trace prefix at all and just specify the trace fragment produced, in relation to the state upon procedure call. A contract for a procedure $p(\vec{x}; \vec{y})$ therefore encompasses precondition G, postcondition R, and trace annotation W, with the corresponding call rule:

$$\frac{\{\,P \mid U\,\}\ \vec{z}\colon [G\sigma \rightsquigarrow R\sigma' \mid W\sigma']\ \{\,Q \mid V\,\} \qquad \{\,G \mid \epsilon\,\}\ c\ \{\,R \mid W\,\}}{\{\,P \mid U\,\}\ p(\vec{e}; \vec{z})\ \{\,Q \mid V\,\}}\ \text{CALL}$$

where substitutions $\sigma = [\vec{x} \mapsto \vec{e}]$ and $\sigma' = [\vec{x}, \vec{y} \mapsto \vec{e}, \vec{z}\,']$ instantiate the procedure's contract with the actual arguments in the first premise. The second premise ensures that the procedure satisfies its contract, assuming for simplicity that the body c does not modify the inputs $\vec{x}$ such that these in R and W still refer to the values in the state at the call. This is expressed by a Hoare triple that starts from the empty trace ϵ, such that the correctness of p wrt. its contract needs to be verified once only, independtly of calling contexts.

The consequence rule exhibits the usual co-/contravariance duality: We may wish to conduct the proof with a weaker precondition P_2 and a larger set of traces seen so far U_2 to establish a stronger postcondition Q_2 than necessary together with a more precise set of extended traces V_2.

$$\frac{P_1 \implies P_2 \land (U_1 \sqsubseteq U_2) \quad \{\,P_2 \mid U_2\,\}\ c\ \{\,Q_2 \mid V_2\,\} \quad Q_2 \implies Q_1 \land (V_2 \sqsubseteq V_1)}{\{\,P_1 \mid U_1\,\}\ c\ \{\,Q_1 \mid V_1\,\}}$$
$$\text{CONSEQ}$$

This rule feeds contextual information from predicate logic formulas into the inclusion conditions of regular language specification, just as we have seen for the SPEC rule in Ex. 1. Note that this rule makes up for not having defined sequential concatenation of trace specifications: We can manually re-arrange regular expressions with respect to their outer conditionals.

The rule for conditional statements is entirely standard:

$$\frac{\{\,P \land t \mid U\,\}\ c_1\ \{\,Q \mid V\,\} \qquad \{\,P \land \neg t \mid U\,\}\ c_2\ \{\,Q \mid V\,\}}{\{\,P \mid U\,\}\ \text{if } t \text{ then } c_1 \text{ else } c_2\ \{\,Q \mid V\,\}}\ \text{IF}$$

However, we can use the consequence rule to feed information about the positive or negative outcome of test t into the respective occurrences of U in the two premises to rewrite them as desired (e.g. by dropping infeasible choices).

As we have motivated by the examples above, the rule for while loops employs in addition to an ordinary invariant I a regular expression specification U that characterizes the traces observed when executing the loop.

$$\frac{\{t \wedge I \mathbin{\vert} U\} \; c \; \{I \mathbin{\vert} U\}}{\{I \mathbin{\vert} U\} \; \text{while } t \text{ do } c \; \{\neg t \wedge I \mathbin{\vert} U\}} \; \text{WHILE}$$

The same U occurs for all traces in the rule in four places. This reflects the fact that the loop specification must already be given in a closed form that is generalized with respect to an arbitrary number of iterations. The evaluation of U is still relative to the context for that occurrence, specifically, with the postcondition $\neg t \wedge I$ in the conclusion we can narrow down U to those cases that actually match the exit state.

Example 2. In Sect. 2, we had specified that the loop must not exit when b is true, such that $U(b)$ simplifies to the desired *overall* behavior of the program with properly paired even and odd events $(\text{even·odd})^*$. $\qquad\qquad\heartsuit$

With the help of this rule, we can justify the naive approach to loops that just repeats any observation that can be made about the executions of the loop body without taking any sequencing constraints into account, given here by a plain regular expression v to simplify the presentation.

$$\frac{\{t \wedge I \mathbin{\vert} \epsilon\} \; B \; \{I \mathbin{\vert} v\}}{\{I \mathbin{\vert} \epsilon\} \; \text{while } t \text{ do } B \; \{\neg t \wedge I \mathbin{\vert} v^*\}} \; \text{WHILE*}$$

It follows from rule WHILE for invariant $U = v^*$, and we use the frame rule for $W = v^*$ to justify the needed intermediate condition $\{t \wedge I \mathbin{\vert} v^* \cdot \epsilon\} \; B \; \{I \mathbin{\vert} v^* \cdot v\}$ from the given premise of rule WHILE*. The rest is stitched together by rule CONSEQ and the algebraic laws of the repetition operator.

As an example, taking $v = (\text{even} + \text{odd})$ we can derive the weaker characterization of the loop's behavior that was mentioned in Sect. 2.

Theorem 1 (Soundness). *The rules presented in this paper are sound: if the premises are valid according to Defintion 2 then the respective conclusion is also valid.*

Proof. Mechanized in Isabelle/HOL, available online. [3]
https://gist.github.com/gernst/6a156facbe402f6d7f8db8b6520c7d70 $\qquad\qquad\square$
We remark that the soundness proof does not in any way depend on the fact that the trace specifications are regular or finitely representable.

Conjecture 1 (Completeness of Trace Annotations). If there is an ordinary regular expression v that describes the traces of a given program c, i.e., the triple $\{P \mathbin{\vert} \epsilon\} \; c \; \{Q \mathbin{\vert} v\}$ is valid, then we can find regular expression specifications to compose this fact using the proof rules, including trace invariants for loops.

Proof (Main Idea). Partition the actual state space of the program into equivalence classes with respect to their trace prefixes at each program location. Since the automaton corresponding to v has finitely many states, we can describe them by a finite number of regular expressions that are conditional upon a predicate logic formula characterizing the respective equivalence class. $\qquad\qquad\square$

---

[3] The mechanization will be made available permanently at a later date, e.g., as an entry to the Archive of Formal Proofs at https://www.isa-afp.org/.

4 Tool Support in SecC

We have implemented support for trace specifications in SecC, which is an autoactive deductive program verifier for low-level concurrent C code with expressive security specifications. It is based on the logic SecCSL [11], which for the purposes of this paper is analogous to standard concurrent separation logic. The tool and case studies are publicly available at https://bitbucket.org/covern/secc.

The tool follows the classical design of most deductive tools, in which all C functions are specified modularly in terms of user-supplied contracts, such that they can be verified in isolation to avoid the combinatorial path explosion of interprocedural verification. To that end, SecC supports program annotations for function contracts, loop invariants, auxiliary statements such as intermediate assertions and other proof hints. It is possible, too, to specify logical functions and separation logic predicates, as well as to encode mathematical proofs (e.g. by induction) as lemmas and lemma functions, see e.g. [16].

4.1 Specification Syntax

For this work, we extended the specification language by trace annotations. We use the example from Sect. 2 as shown in Fig. 2 to explain the specification syntax in general as well as for the traces.

```
int nondet();

void even_odd()
  _(trace (even odd)*)
{
  int b = 0;

  while(nondet() || b)
    _(trace (even odd)*      if !b)
    _(trace (even odd)* even if  b)
  {
    if(!b) { _(emit even) }
    else   { _(emit odd)  }

    b = !b;
  }
}
```

Fig. 2. Even/odd example in SecC

In SecC, auxiliary code is wrapped inside _(...), an idiom taken from VCC. This is used here for different purposes, foremost, in the contract of function even_odd() to specify its behavior. An annotation _(trace U) for a function with body c corresponds to a Hoare triple $\{ \_ \ \vdots\ \epsilon \} \, c \, \{ \_ \ \vdots\ U \}$ (pre-/postconditions P and Q are absent in the example). Inside the loop, the specification statement _(emit a) generates the respective events. It is the proof engineer's task to place these at the program locations of their interest—in the future we may support events that are implicitly generated, e.g., by function calls as in [9]. There is also a trace annotation for the loop, which showcases the concrete syntax for conditionals, analogous to the presentation earlier in this paper albeit in SecC each choice is listed separately. By convention, absence of a trace annotation, even for just a particular case, enforces that no events may be emitted at all.[4]

4.2   Verification Engine

In contrast to the Hoare-style rules of Sect. 3, which mirror those of the logic SecCSL behind the tool, SecC operationalizes the proof rules by a forward symbolic execution algorithm, first described in [3], similarly to VeriFast [15] or the Silicon backend of Viper [20]. The engine traverses the program using execution states, consisting of a store of symbolic variables, a path constraint, a symbolic representation of the heap, and for this work a trace prefix. The design of the logic necessitates being careful about branching not just for case distinctions in the program but also in the logic itself. To address this, SecC always takes apart relevant case distinctions and follows the branches individually, pruning those with an unsatisfiable path constraint. The same principle is applied to the regular trace specifications, which are broken apart into plain regular expressions eagerly, such that SecC can make use of the rule FRAME, e.g., to concatenate the possible trace extensions after a while-loop is dispatched modularly. However, one has to be careful not to discard any execution branch vacuously just because there is no trace specified for it. Therefore, SecC always completes behavioral annotations with an empty trace that is the negation of the disjunction of all other cases (which might of course be unsatisfiable).

At the end of each execution path, SecC needs to check that the trace produced up to this point is covered by the behavioral specification annotated to the surrounding context (a C function or a loop). The inclusion check is implemented for plain regular expressions by an approach similar to the one shown in [1]. It is based on the derivative $\delta_a u$ of u with respect to symbol a that captures the language of suffixes of u after a leading occurrence of a, i.e., $\mathcal{L}(\delta_a u) = \{\tau \mid a{\cdot}\tau \in \mathcal{L}(u)\}$. The algorithmic check $\Gamma \vdash u \sqsubseteq v$ for language inclusion exploits this idea. It maintains in Γ pairs of expressions seen already and proceeds recursively as shown below. Effectively, Γ is a simulation relation between u and v from the transitions that are possible over u via the derivative.

$$\Gamma \vdash u \sqsubseteq v \iff \begin{cases} true, & \text{if } (u, v) \in \Gamma \\ u \text{ empty}, & \text{if } v = \varnothing \\ \Gamma \cup \{(u, v)\} \vdash \delta_a u \sqsubseteq \delta_a v, \forall\, a \in \mathit{first}(u), \\ \quad \text{and } u \text{ nullable} \implies v \text{ nullable} & \text{otherwise} \end{cases}$$

Here, $\mathit{first}(u) \subseteq A$ is an overapproximation of the set of first symbols of words in $\mathcal{L}(u)$, which can be computed recursively from the syntax. Termination is ensured by unfolding each pair of expressions once only (first line).[5] The second

---

[4] We have omitted some annotations related to SecC's enforcement of absence of timing side-channels, which requires an invariant that b never contains any secret such that we can branch on it, similarly for the return value of function nondet(), shown at the top of the code listing, that models nondeterministic choice.

[5] Note that it is crucial that the check whether a given pair of expressions is contained in Γ already considers equivalence modulo reordering and duplicates of the choice operator, otherwise, one may keep accumulating larger and larger expressions.

case catches when $\delta_a v$ has become empty, which corresponds to an event a of u that is not covered by the specification. Conversely, in the last case when u is nullable but v is not, some required events were missed.

5 Case Studies

We present two case studies, a regular expression matcher in Sect. 5.1, and the Casino in Sect. 5.2, followed by a discussion in Sect. 5.3.

5.1 Case Study: Regular Expression Matching

A canonical case study for the specification approach of this paper is to verify the state machine of a matcher that checks whether some input adheres to a given concrete regular expression. Here, we match E-Mail addresses in a much simplified format [a-z]+[@][a-z]+[.][a-z]+ which expects a name part and domain part with a single dot, where both parts are separated by an @ sign.

```
void lex()
  _(trace letter+ at letter+ dot letter+ eof)
{
  int state = 0;

  while(0 <= state && state <= 5)
    _(invariant 0 <= state && state <= 6)
    // _(trace ...) see running text
  {
    char c = next();
    check(c);

    if(state == 0) {
      if('a' <= c && c <= 'z') state = 1;
      else                     abort();
    } else if(state == 1) {
      if('a' <= c && c <= 'z') state = 1;
      else if(c == '@')        state = 2;
      else                     abort();
    } // states 2 to 4 omitted
    ...
    } else if(state == 5) {
      if('a' <= c && c <= 'z') state = 5;
      else if(c == -1)         state = 6;
      else                     abort();
    }
  }
}
```

Fig. 3. E-Mail address matcher in SecC

Often, such matchers are implemented as a library in programming languages, which at runtime translates textual representations of regular expressions into some internal automaton. For high-performance code, however, the preferred alternative is to compile this automaton upfront into source code, e.g., using the popular tool re2c [5]. Possible translation schemes make use of language features like loops/gotos and switch/conditionals, representing the automaton either implicitly via control flow, or with an outer loop and an explicit state variable, as shown in the example in Fig. 3. We will show how to verify this code with respect to the declarative specification of the expected matches in terms of the trace annotation at the top.[6]

The input is read by repeated calls to some external function next() which returns the next

---

[6] Available in the SecC bitbucket repository at examples/case-studies/matcher.c.

input character. The switching logic of the state machine is implemented via variable `state` which is modified according to transitions encoded in the nested chain of conditionals. For example, state 0 expects a first letter symbol as the repetition is non-empty, whereas state 1 may subsequently transition over an occurrence of the symbol `@`. The loop terminates in state 6 after the input becomes empty, encoded by `c == -1`. To simplify matters further, the code calls `abort()` when an unexpected input character is encountered, which exposes nontermination via a postconditon `_(ensures false)`, i.e., a call to this function will vacuously verify that branch of the computation.

The function `check()`, shown in Fig. 4, denotes the events that are emitted in relation to the respective input characters, and also includes an `error` event for all other characters. This additional event does not occur in the top-level specification of `lex()`, such that clearly the only way to satisfy the trace constraints when such an `error` is encountered is to reject the match via a call `abort()`. Function `check()` is a specification artifact that separates out the *interpretation* of inputs in terms of the four abstract events `letter`, `at`, `dot`, and `eof`. While it may appear somewhat cumbersome to draw this connection explicitly, we emphasize that this just reflects the prototypical nature of the design that does not ascribe any meaning to events upfront. Of course one may provide support for certain kinds of events out-of-the-box, perhaps complemented by character class definitions as abbreviations for finite enumerations.

```
void check(char c);
  _(trace letter if 'a' <= c && c <= 'z')
  _(trace at     if c == '@')
  _(trace dot    if c == '.')
  _(trace eof    if c == -1)
  _(trace error  otherwise)
```

Fig. 4. Specifying the correspondence between inputs and abstract events

The verification consists of two parts: Annotating the `while` loop with conditional trace invariants that must jointly be preserved over the loop body, and ensuring that this annotation implies correctness of the outer procedure. The possible trace prefixes in the respective states are captured as follows.

```
_(trace ()                                     if state == 0)
_(trace letter+                                if state == 1)
_(trace letter+ at                             if state == 2)
  ...
_(trace letter+ at letter+ dot letter+ eof     if state == 6)
```

They reflect the part of the input that has been matched already, starting with the empty trace, written as `()` in SecC in state 0, up to the final trace in state 6. Given the negated loop test at exit together with the invariant, the last line is the only one with a satisfiable guard, which is precisely the guarantee we need to satisfy the contract of `lex()`. Preservation over a single iteration over the loop body is briefly discussed with respect to state 1. Its corresponding trace `letter+` is initially established from a single `letter` event in the incoming transition from state 0. Reading the next character in the range `[a-z]` in state 1 extends the trace to `letter+ letter` by another `letter` event from `check()`, which is subsumed by `letter+` in state 1 again as required. On the other hand, reading an `@` symbol produces the trace specified for state 2, which is the one transitioned to at the end of this iteration. All other transitions work analogously.

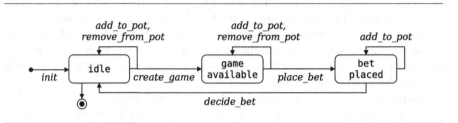

Fig. 5. Automaton specification (adapted from a model by Mattias Ulbrich, https://verifythis.github.io/casino/spec/)

5.2   Case-Study: VerifyThis Casino Challenge

The Casino case study fueled a series of online discussions in the context of the VerifyThis competition. The case study deals with a Casino that was originally implemented as a smart contract on the Ethereum blockchain, but which has since been specified, modeled, and verified in a number of different approaches.

The Casino game is offered by an operator to a player who can bet on the outcome of a coin toss, which is decided upfront but remains hidden in an envelope, until after the player has placed their bet and the operator decides to resolve. Cheating by the operator is prevented by encoding the sealed envelope by publishing the cryptographic hash of a secret number whose last bit determines the winning side of the coin. If the player wins, they receive double the amount of money that they bet, otherwise it goes to the operator. After that, the game can be played again. For a very nice graphical exposition of the rules by Wolfgang Ahrendt we refer the reader to https://verifythis.github.io/casino/.

As mentioned in the introduction, a particular goal of the efforts around this challenge was to bridge between different verification approaches, such as finite state models, contract-based models, and hybrid solutions. An aspect in focus is the *pot* of money associated with the game, which is supplied by the operator and which needs to cover the prize of the player, causing an invariant that encodes this requirement. Figure 5 shows a high-level description that avoids draining the pot by simply restricting the operator to reduce the amount in the pot as long as an unresolved bet has been placed.

SecC models this game as follows:[7] Data on the blockchain is treated as memory that has public visibility, a feature that is supported by the logic. All data passed in and out of the operations that encode the moves in the game are likewise specified to be public. Ownership, e.g., of a wallet or a payment that has been sent but not received yet, naturally maps to resources in Separation Logic, encoded into abstract predicates that cannot be duplicated.

---

[7] Available in the SecC bitbucket repository at examples/case-studies/casino.c.

The game itself is specified as a main function with a top-level loop that nondeterministically chooses among the next possible moves and then calls the function that implements the respective transition. Each of these functions emits one of the events shown in Fig. 5. The corresponding behavior of the game is captured by the regular expression shown below. It declaratively specifies all traces through the automaton in Fig. 5. We point out the inclusion of some trailing changes to the pot. Moreover, it is noteworthy that after a place_bet event no further remove_from_pot can happen until the game is decided.

```
_(trace init
    ((add_to_pot | remove_from_pot)* create_game
     (add_to_pot | remove_from_pot)* place_bet
      add_to_pot*                    decide_bet)*)
    (add_to_pot | remove_from_pot)*
```

Since the game can be in one of three states (idle, game available, bet placed), the trace invariant for the loop has three parts, that analogously to those of the matcher in Sect. 5.1 reflect the different stages of the game. Like with the even/odd example, the trace invariant duplicates as a prefix the entire specification in order to be inductive, which results in a somewhat large, but structurally straight-forward annotation, for example that right before deciding the bet we have seen everything *apart* from the event decide_bet.

```
_(trace (...)
    ((add_to_pot | remove_from_pot)* create_game
     (add_to_pot | remove_from_pot)* place_bet
      add_to_pot*)  if state == BET_PLACED)
```

where (...) here omits the entire game specification as shown above.

We have experimented further with simplified variants that just include the functionality directly related to the trace behaviors.[8] The approach taken for the full case study is complemented by the naive approach with rule WHILE*. Furthermore, we formulate the game as a set of several mutually tail-recursive procedures, each corresponding to one state. This affects the annotations in two ways: First, each function on its own can specify its contribution to the observable behaviors, and second, we are effectively encoding the summary-based approach from Sect. 2, which in comparison to an invariant reasons about the trace suffixes that are yet to be fulfilled, which in comparison to the corresponding part of the loop annotation, specifies possible additions to the pot and includes a final decide_bet before the game repeats recursively (where again (...) omits the game but without init).

```
void game_placed()
_(trace (add_to_pot* decide_bet) // <-- behavior of just game_placed
      (...))
```

---

[8] Available in repository at examples/case-studies/casino-statemachine.c.

5.3 Discussion

The two case studies demonstrate how behavioral specifications in terms of regular expressions can capture declaratively properties of C functions as part of their top-level modular contracts. However, loop annotations become quite involved, and in the approach taken the user has to come up with the equivalence classes of regular expressions corresponding to the control states of the loop.

Moreover, these expressions are typically larger than the original annotation, and are repeated in significant parts for the many different cases. We think that this can be addressed for example by allowing the user to abbreviate expressions as it is possible for example in typical scanner generators like flex. Another idea is to infer such specifications automatically, e.g., by having the user annotate the *conditions* that partition the state space, but not the regular expressions themselves. We think that this is feasible but we leave this idea for future work.

SecC verifies both case studies in less than 5s on a Thinkpad T470p. We do not think that these numbers are particularly meaningful, as they were done with a cold-cache JVM and they include many calls to an external SMT solver. The overhead introduced by the regular expression inclusion check contributes noticeably to the time to verify functions which have many paths, like the main loops of the case studies. Nevertheless, this was never a limiting factor here, on the contrary, thanks to the decidability of the inclusion check once the conditionals are settled, there is no additional manual effort involved to help out the verifier with additional proof hints, as it is often typical with expressive functional contracts. Perhaps, when scaling up to regular expressions as they may occur in practice, an efficient automata-based implementation may be preferable.

Finally, as hinted at already in Sect. 5.1, built-in support for certain kinds of domain-specific events can help streamline the verification process. For example, related work has considered opening and closing of file handles [6], as well as function calls and returns [9]. These applications, however, would strongly benefit from a context-free specification language, instead of a regular one, to pair each open with a close for instance. Similarly, attaching data drawn from finite sets or even symbolic data like file handles to events is useful. However, such extensions reflect different trade-offs wrt. automation as the inclusion check may become undecidable. This opens up a research space in between the work presented here and the highly expressive approaches, in which one can experiment with practical heuristics supported by domain-specific proof hints when needed.

6 Related and Alternative Approaches

Session types [13] capture the interactions between software components as part of the type system. Similarly, interface automata [7] capture possible interactions at the system level. Temporal contracts have been proposed for a functional language in [9], but considering runtime checking only, and giving completeness to ease the specification burden. Temporal contracts for an object-oriented language are described in [29], and for smart contracts in [25]. Our regular behaviors are of course closely related to session types, and we complement this area of work with a different view and presentation of such ideas as a classic Hoare-style logic. Moreover, the state-dependence of conditionals here gives additional expressive power comparable to "dependent" session types, cf. [31].

Deductive verification tools like Dafny [18] and vanilla SecC [11] without the extensions from Sect. 4 come with strong support for logical specifications, which would in principle enable to encode regular traces into lists explicitly. A common strategy is to encode behaviors into abstract permission-based predicates, which integrates event histories with expressive logical data types and to some extent first-class reasoning over such behaviors. For example, VeriFast supports such I/O-specifications and has support not just for safety properties but also for liveness [14,24]. VerCors has a highly elaborate mechanism to capture behaviors as process models [23], which can then be given to a model checker to verify system-wide properties. Another work that cuts into this direction is Igloo [30], in which modularity and composition is a key concern. The latter two [23,30] demonstrate how the behavioral processes can be semantically embedded as part of an enriched heap. This bridges the gap between process calculi and the style of local reasoning that is already supported by backend verifiers like Viper [20].

In our semantics of triples $\{\,P\,\flat\,U\,\}\,c\,\{\,Q\,\flat\,V\,\}$ as presented, both U and V are *histories* of events arising from program executions, similarly to [4] but avoiding the complexity of an embedding into separation logic formulas. In contrast, [14, 23,24,30] are *future*-based, i.e., the precondition specifies which traces are still allowed. The advantage of this formulation is that it can reason about infinite behaviors, and it is therefore based on a coinductive semantics, cf. Nakata and Uustalu [21]. In follow-up work [34], the same authors propose a Hoare logic with expressive specifications in which traces are characterized by a composition of state-formulas (instead of just events). Similarly, temporal program logics like [28] expand the scope of properties that can be verified at the expense of proof automation for the temporal behavior.

The proof systems for history-based and future-based specifications have much in common, e.g., all rules for compound commands if and while from Sect. 3.4 are as expected. However, trace annotations in rules SPEC, FRAME, and CONSEQ change the order of concatenation as well as swap the order of trace inclusion (e.g., $\sqsupseteq$ instead of $\sqsubseteq$ in the premise of CONSEQ). This notably affects reasoning about event-nondeterminism: Let $traces(c)$ denote the (finite) traces that a program c can emit, ignoring any reference to states and to pre-/postconditions here, with $traces(\text{emit } w) = w$ nondeterministically emitting some trace $\tau \in w$. Then, let $\lceil u \rceil\, c\, \lfloor v \rfloor = u \cdot traces(c) \subseteq v$ coincide with $\{\,\_\,\flat\,u\,\}\,c\,\{\,\_\,\flat\,v\,\}$ and conversely $\lfloor u \rfloor\, c\, \lceil v \rceil = traces(c) \cdot v \subseteq u$, for some sets of traces u and v. Mnemonically, $\lceil . \rceil$ denotes a set of traces that cannot just be enlarged and $\lfloor . \rfloor$ denotes a set that cannot be made smaller without invalidating a judgement. We have:

$$\frac{}{\lceil u \rceil\ \text{emit}\ w\ \lfloor u \cdot w \rfloor}\ \text{EMIT}^{\rightarrow} \qquad\qquad \frac{}{\lfloor w \cdot u \rfloor\ \text{emit}\ w\ \lceil u \rceil}\ \text{EMIT}^{\leftarrow}$$

where the history-based version on the left denotes the most precise (smallest) post-set when started from u (cf. [4, Rule ACTION in Fig. 5]) and the future-based version instead computes the most precise pre-set of traces that must be allowed upfront (cf. [23, Rule HT-PROC-UPDATE in Fig. 5]).

However, in the presence of nondeterministic emits, the two converse transformers cannot be formulated in this logic. Consider $\lfloor (aa)+(bb) \rfloor$ emit $(a+b) \lceil v \rceil$ where v should capture which traces are still allowed after emitting either an a or a b: Clearly, $v = a + b$ is too weak, because it would allow subsequent program steps to emit either an a or a b *regardless* of the first event observed, such that the overall set of traces becomes $(a+b) \cdot (a+b)$ instead. This is analogous to the lack of best backwards transformer for Incorrectness Logic as observed by O'Hearn [22, Sec. 5.2], albeit, that both formulations of the logic presented here are definitely *overapproximative* with respect to the allowed traces.

On the other hand, asking for the best v in $\lfloor (aa) + (bb) \rfloor$ emit $(a+b) \lceil v \rceil$ may be somewhat meaningless in practice, since a subsequent program fragment cannot actually determine whether to emit a second a or b in the absence of further information—we cannot build a correct program around the shown triple. Therefore, we argue that useful trace specifications always need to resolve such nondeterminism explicitly, e.g., as in emit $(a \text{ if } \phi + b \text{ if } \neg\phi)$ with a formula ϕ explaining the choice in reference to the current state. This is typically done in the examples and case-studies in [23,30] and Sect. 5 anyway.

7   Conclusion

We have presented a Hoare logic that integrates external behaviors as regular expressions into deductive verification systems. This can be used to declaratively specify sequences of events occurring during the execution. The approach supports loops with control states via conditions in the specification, such that interesting sequential behavior across multiple iterations can be captured. There is much room for experimentation with different trade-offs between automation, ease of specification, and expressiveness, to be explored in the future.

Acknowledgement. We thank the reviewers for their detailed comments and suggestions to improve the presentation.

References

1. Almeida, R., Broda, S., Moreira, N.: Deciding KAT and Hoare logic with derivatives. arXiv preprint arXiv:1210.2456 (2012)
2. Alur, R., Chaudhuri, S.: Temporal reasoning for procedural programs. In: Barthe, G., Hermenegildo, M. (eds.) VMCAI 2010. LNCS, vol. 5944, pp. 45–60. Springer, Heidelberg (2010). https://doi.org/10.1007/978-3-642-11319-2_7
3. Berdine, J., Calcagno, C., O'Hearn, P.W.: Symbolic execution with separation logic. In: Yi, K. (ed.) APLAS 2005. LNCS, vol. 3780, pp. 52–68. Springer, Heidelberg (2005). https://doi.org/10.1007/11575467_5
4. Blom, S., Huisman, M., Zaharieva-Stojanovski, M.: History-Based Verification of Functional Behaviour of Concurrent Programs. In: Calinescu, R., Rumpe, B. (eds.) SEFM 2015. LNCS, vol. 9276, pp. 84–98. Springer, Cham (2015). https://doi.org/10.1007/978-3-319-22969-0_6

5. Bumbulis, P., Cowan, D.D.: RE2C: a more versatile scanner generator. ACM Lett. Program. Lang. Syst. (LOPLAS) **2**(1–4), 70–84 (1993)
6. Das, M., Lerner, S., Seigle, M.: ESP: Path-sensitive program verification in polynomial time. In: Proceedings of the ACM SIGPLAN 2002 Conference on Programming language design and implementation, pp. 57–68 (2002)
7. De Alfaro, L., Henzinger, T.A.: Interface automata. ACM SIGSOFT Softw. Eng. Notes **26**(5), 109–120 (2001)
8. Dietsch, D., Heizmann, M., Langenfeld, V., Podelski, A.: Fairness modulo theory: a new approach to LTL software model checking. In: Kroening, D., Păsăreanu, C.S. (eds.) CAV 2015. LNCS, vol. 9206, pp. 49–66. Springer, Cham (2015). https://doi.org/10.1007/978-3-319-21690-4_4
9. Disney, T., Flanagan, C., McCarthy, J.: Temporal higher-order contracts. In: Proceedings of the 16th ACM SIGPLAN international conference on Functional programming, pp. 176–188 (2011)
10. Ernst, G.: Loop verification with invariants and contracts. In: Finkbeiner, B., Wies, T. (eds.) VMCAI 2022. LNCS, vol. 13182, pp. 69–92. Springer, Cham (2022). https://doi.org/10.1007/978-3-030-94583-1_4
11. Ernst, G., Murray, T.: SecCSL: Security Concurrent Separation Logic. In: Dillig, I., Tasiran, S. (eds.) CAV 2019. LNCS, vol. 11562, pp. 208–230. Springer, Cham (2019). https://doi.org/10.1007/978-3-030-25543-5_13
12. Hehner, E.C.R.: Specified Blocks. In: Meyer, B., Woodcock, J. (eds.) VSTTE 2005. LNCS, vol. 4171, pp. 384–391. Springer, Heidelberg (2008). https://doi.org/10.1007/978-3-540-69149-5_41
13. Hüttel, H., et al.: Foundations of session types and behavioural contracts. ACM Comput. Surv. (CSUR) **49**(1), 1–36 (2016)
14. Jacobs, B.: Modular verification of liveness properties of the I/O behavior of imperative programs. In: Margaria, T., Steffen, B. (eds.) ISoLA 2020. LNCS, vol. 12476, pp. 509–524. Springer, Cham (2020). https://doi.org/10.1007/978-3-030-61362-4_29
15. Jacobs, B., Smans, J., Philippaerts, P., Vogels, F., Penninckx, W., Piessens, F.: VeriFast: a powerful, sound, predictable, fast verifier for C and Java. In: Bobaru, M., Havelund, K., Holzmann, G.J., Joshi, R. (eds.) NFM 2011. LNCS, vol. 6617, pp. 41–55. Springer, Heidelberg (2011). https://doi.org/10.1007/978-3-642-20398-5_4
16. Jacobs, B., Smans, J., Piessens, F.: VeriFast: Imperative programs as proofs. In: VSTTE workshop on Tools & Experiments (2010)
17. Lamport, L.: The temporal logic of actions. ACM Trans. Program. Lang. Syst. (TOPLAS) **16**(3), 872–923 (1994)
18. Leino, K.R.M.: Dafny: an automatic program verifier for functional correctness. In: Clarke, E.M., Voronkov, A. (eds.) LPAR 2010. LNCS (LNAI), vol. 6355, pp. 348–370. Springer, Heidelberg (2010). https://doi.org/10.1007/978-3-642-17511-4_20
19. Morgan, C.: The specification statement. ACM Trans. Program. Lang. Syst. (TOPLAS) **10**(3), 403–419 (1988)
20. Müller, P., Schwerhoff, M., Summers, A.J.: Viper: a verification infrastructure for permission-based reasoning. In: Jobstmann, B., Leino, K.R.M. (eds.) VMCAI 2016. LNCS, vol. 9583, pp. 41–62. Springer, Heidelberg (2016). https://doi.org/10.1007/978-3-662-49122-5_2
21. Nakata, K., Uustalu, T.: Trace-based coinductive operational semantics for while. In: Berghofer, S., Nipkow, T., Urban, C., Wenzel, M. (eds.) TPHOLs 2009. LNCS,

vol. 5674, pp. 375–390. Springer, Heidelberg (2009). https://doi.org/10.1007/978-3-642-03359-9_26

22. O'Hearn, P.W.: Incorrectness logic. In: Proceedings of the ACM on Programming Languages 4(POPL), 1–32 (2019)

23. Oortwijn, W., Gurov, D., Huisman, M.: An abstraction technique for verifying shared-memory concurrency. Appl. Sci. **10**(11), 3928 (2020)

24. Penninckx, W., Timany, A., Jacobs, B.: Specifying I/O using abstract nested Hoare triples in separation logic. In: Proceedings of the 21st Workshop on Formal Techniques for Java-like Programs, pp. 1–7 (2019)

25. Permenev, A., Dimitrov, D., Tsankov, P., Drachsler-Cohen, D., Vechev, M.: Verx: Safety verification of smart contracts. In: 2020 IEEE symposium on security and privacy (SP), pp. 1661–1677, IEEE (2020)

26. Pnueli, A.: The temporal logic of programs. In: 18th Annual Symposium on Foundations of Computer Science (sfcs 1977), pp. 46–57, ieee (1977)

27. Reynolds, J.C.: Separation logic: A logic for shared mutable data structures. In: Proc. of Logic in Computer Science (LICS), pp. 55–74, IEEE (2002)

28. Schellhorn, G., Tofan, B., Ernst, G., Pfähler, J., Reif, W.: Rgitl: A temporal logic framework for compositional reasoning about interleaved programs. Ann. Math. Artif. Intell. **71**(1), 131–174 (2014)

29. Soleimanifard, S., Gurov, D., Huisman, M.: Procedure-modular specification and verification of temporal safety properties. Softw. Syst. Modeling **14**(1), 83–100 (2013). https://doi.org/10.1007/s10270-013-0321-0

30. Sprenger, C., et al.: Igloo: Soundly linking compositional refinement and separation logic for distributed system verification. In: Proceedings of the ACM on Programming Languages 4(OOPSLA), 1–31 (2020)

31. Toninho, B., Caires, L., Pfenning, F.: A decade of dependent session types. In: 23rd International Symposium on Principles and Practice of Declarative Programming, pp. 1–3 (2021)

32. Tuerk, T.: Local reasoning about while-loops. Proc. of Verified Software: Theory, Tools, and Experiments (VSTTE) 2010, 29 (2010)

33. Urban, C., Ueltschi, S., Müller, P.: Abstract interpretation of CTL properties. In: Podelski, A. (ed.) SAS 2018. LNCS, vol. 11002, pp. 402–422. Springer, Cham (2018). https://doi.org/10.1007/978-3-319-99725-4_24

34. Uustalu, T., Nakata, K.: A hoare logic for the coinductive trace-based big-step semantics of while. Logical Methods Comput. Sci. **11**(1), 488–506 (2015)

Specification-Based Monitoring in C++

Klaus Havelund$^{(\boxtimes)}$

Jet Propulsion Laboratory, California Institute of Technology,
Pasadena, CA, USA
klaus.havelund@jpl.nasa.gov

Abstract. Software systems cannot in general be assumed proven correct before deployment. Testing is still the most common approach to demonstrate a satisfactory level of correctness. However, some errors will survive verification efforts, and it is therefore reasonable to monitor a system after deployment, to determine whether it executes correctly. Both for testing and post-deployment monitoring, it may be desirable to be able to formalize correctness properties that can be monitored against program executions. This is also referred to as runtime verification. We present a specification language and a monitoring system for monitoring such specifications against event streams. The monitoring engine front-end, written in Scala, translates the specification to C++, whereas the back-end (the monitoring engine), written in C++, interprets the generated C++ monitor on an event stream. This makes it feasible to monitor the execution of C and C++ programs online.

1 Introduction

The correctness of software is usually demonstrated through extensive testing. A test suite usually consists of test cases, where each test case consists of a test input vector and a *test oracle*, which determines whether the test case executes properly. Since testing does not provide 100% coverage of all execution paths, there is also a need after deployment to monitor the software as it executes. For this the concept of *monitors* is needed. We present LOGSCOPE (available at [24]), a system for monitoring event streams (traces) against formal specifications, also referred in literature as Runtime Verification (RV). A formal specification, written by a user, is translated into a monitor in C++, which can be used both as a test oracle before deployment, or for monitoring the system as it executes after deployment. A monitor generated from a formal specification is event-driven. It receives events, one by one, modifying its internal state for each observed event, and emitting an error message or calling a callback function in case a violation of the specification is encountered. Such a system can be used *offline*, analyzing log files, or *online*, monitoring the system real-time as it executes. The system solves the following problem:

The research performed was carried out at Jet Propulsion Laboratory, California Institute of Technology, under a contract with the National Aeronautics and Space Administration.

Given a sequence of events emitted from a software application, how can we assure that the event stream satisfies a set of desired properties?

The *frontend*, written in the SCALA programming language, parses a specification and translates it to an Abstract Syntax Tree (AST) in C++. The *backend*, the monitoring engine itself, written in C++, imports the C++ AST generated by the frontend, and interprets it over a sequence of events emitted to it. The fact that the backend is implemented in C++ makes it possible to monitor applications online that themselves are written in C or C++, which is important for embedded systems. It is for example unthinkable to call a monitor in JAVA or PYTHON from a C/C++ program in an embedded application, unless monitoring is performed remotely and asynchronously. Numerous RV systems have been developed in the past, as discussed in Sect. 2, but most are implemented in high-level languages such as JAVA. In most cases there will be a need to convert events generated by the software to the event format of LOGSCOPE. This is, however, a straightforward task.

The specification language allows to state properties about events that can carry data, e.g. relating data occurring in events at different positions in the trace. We refer to this as *parametric monitoring*. What makes the specification language stand out compared to most related work is that it combines a rule-based language and a state machine language. A rule-based system consists of a set of rules operating on a set of facts in a memory, where a fact is a named data record. Each rule has a condition and an action. The condition of a rule can refer to the memory and query whether certain facts are present or not, including the data they carry, which is used to support parametric monitoring. The action of a rule can add facts to or delete facts from the memory. As such several facts can be active at any moment in time. The ability to refer to the presence/absence of facts can be used to model past time temporal properties by letting facts be generated when certain events occur that need to be remembered in the future. LOGSCOPE is fundamentally a rule-based system but its specification language has a state machine look and feel by supporting the definition of event triggered transitions as part of fact definitions.

The paper is organized as follows. Section 2 discusses related work. Section 3 provides an overview of the tool. Section 4 explains the notation through a series of examples. Section 5 outlines how to use the tool. Section 6 briefly outlines aspects of the implementation. Section 7 describes experimentation performed. Finally, Sect. 8 concludes the paper. Appendix A contains visualizations of the monitors presented throughout the paper, generated by LOGSCOPE.

2   Related Work

LOGSCOPE's concepts can be traced back to the early RULER system [2], where the idea of merging rule-based programming with state machine notation was first explored, and implemented in JAVA. That work was followed by the first version of LOGSCOPE[1] [4,23], implemented and executing monitors in PYTHON, in contrast to the here presented system where monitors are generated in the higher performing C++. The algorithmic approach, however, was the same, namely parsing a monitor specification into an Abstract Syntax Tree (AST) and then *interpreting* it over the trace, as we shall discuss later on. The earlier system did not allow to query the fact memory for presence/absence of facts. It was, however, richer in a number of other ways, including providing a temporal logic layer translated to the automaton layer, and allowing PYTHON code to be written as part of monitors, such as in e.g. conditions and actions. The here presented version does not yet offer similar capabilities for including C++ code in monitor specifications.

We have developed other runtime verification systems based on the same idea of merging rule-based programming with state machines, including DAUT [10,17] (in SCALA) and PYCONTRACT [8,27] (in PYTHON). Both are so-called *internal* DSLs, in contrast to LOGSCOPE, which is an *external* DSL with its own grammar and parser. In an internal DSL monitors are written directly in the host language, which we in Sect. 7 shall see can have important impact on performance. We also developed the purely rule-based runtime verification system LOGFIRE [18,22], also an internal SCALA DSL, based on the RETE algorithm [12,13] traditionally used in expert systems, in order to explore the applicability of this algorithm for runtime verification. The RMOR monitoring framework for C [16] generates C code from an external state machine DSL that includes aspect-oriented programming for instrumenting code to be monitored.

Numerous other RV systems have been developed over time providing external DSLs. Many are written in high-level application programming languages, such as e.g. JAVA, SCALA, and OCAML, which makes them less suited for online monitoring of embedded systems. JAVA-MAC [21] was an early system supporting a past time temporal logic, allowing for a clear separation between the definition of the primitive events of a system and the system properties. It enables automatic instrumentation of JAVA code to generate events for the monitor. JAVA-MAC does not support parametric monitoring, however.

A number of systems support efficient parametric monitoring through slicing: the idea of splitting the trace of events carrying data into several subtraces of propositional events, each of which is then submitted to a propositional monitor. MOP [25] offers several data parametric specification formalisms as separate plugins, including state machines, past and future temporal logics, regular expressions, grammars, etc. The logics are separated in the sense that any property is expressed in one of the logics. The parameterization is based on slicing, which is very efficient, but which offers a somewhat limited expressiveness. MOP supports automated code instrumentation using aspect-oriented programming (via ASPECTJ). The QEA system [28] is based on extended finite state machines, and improves the expressiveness of the slicing approach compared to MOP by

---

[1] The original system was focused on Log analysis, hence the name LogScope (scope as in telescope).

allowing so-called free variables that can be updated in the monitors. LARVA [6] offers a specification language for writing Dynamic Automata with Timers and Events (DATEs), also a form of extended finite state machines, and similar to timed automata enriched with stopwatches. It supports a basic form of parametric monitoring with slicing. Various other specification formalisms are translated into DATEs. DATEs can communicate via channels and global variables. The system also supports automated code instrumentation using aspect-oriented programming (via ASPECTJ).

A different branch of formalisms include those supported in stream-based systems. LOLA [9] is a synchronous stream-based language which allows the user to specify the properties of a program in past and future linear time temporal logic. The language guarantees bounded memory to perform online monitoring, but differs from most other synchronous languages in that it is able to refer to future values in a stream. It allows the user to collect statistics at runtime and to express numerical queries. The COPILOT specification language [26] is an internal HASKELL DSL from which monitors in C are generated for monitoring hard real-time reactive systems. It supports a past time temporal logic and a bounded future time temporal logic, both mapped into stream expressions. It supports data parameterization, which is bounded due to the real-time constraints requiring statically bounded execution time and memory usage.

Closely related are systems resembling variants of the linear μ-calculus, using recursion. EAGLE [3] implements a recursive data parametric calculus with past and future time operators. HAWK [7] extends EAGLE with constructs for capturing parameterized program events such as method calls and method returns. Parameters can be executing thread, the objects that methods are called upon, arguments to methods, and return values. The tool automates program instrumentation of JAVA programs (via ASPECTJ). DETECTER [1] implements a future time data parametric Hennessy-Milner logic with recursion for monitoring ERLANG programs.

Several systems have been developed specifically supporting forms of first-order linear time temporal logic as the core logic. MONPOLY [5] supports a first-order linear time temporal logic with future and past time temporal operators. The logic also supports aggregation operators (e.g., sum and average), increasing the expressiveness of the logic. BEEPBEEP [15] permits writing first-order linear time temporal logic properties over the data in a trace of XML messages. In [11] is presented a framework that lifts monitor synthesis procedures for propositional temporal logics to a temporal logic over structures within a given first-order theory. To evaluate such specifications, SMT solving and classical monitoring of propositional temporal properties are combined. DEJAVU [19] supports a first-order past linear time temporal logic and represents data occurring in events with BDDs. In [20] is described an extension that augments that logic with rules.

3   Overview

LOGSCOPE supports formal analysis of event (telemetry) streams. The tool takes as input:

– a formal specification in the SCOPE language, expressing the properties that the event stream has to satisfy. The specification consists of a collection of monitor specifications.
– an event stream.

LOGSCOPE produces on standard output a report describing where (if at all) the event stream violates the specification. The results of monitoring can also be accessed as a data structure for further processing. The SCOPE specification language merges rule-based programming with state machines. An example of a monitor specification in the SCOPE language is the following, formalizing the property that: *"Every command (with some apriori unknown name, bound to the variable 'x') must eventually succeed, without a failure before"* (the language will be explained in detail in subsequent sections):

```
monitor CommandsMustSucceed {
  always {
    COMMAND( name : x) ⇒ RequireSuccess(x)
  }

  hot RequireSuccess(cmdName) {
    FAIL ( name : cmdName) ⇒ error
    SUCCESS ( name : cmdName) ⇒ ok
  }
}
```

Figure 1 illustrates the architecture of LOGSCOPE. A monitor specification, written in the SCOPE specification language by a user, is by the **frontend** (written in the SCALA programming language) translated to an AST in C++, representing the structure of the specification, and stored in the file `contract.cpp`. The **backend** compiles with the `contract.cpp` file, as well as with a main program in the `main.cpp` file, also written by a user. This main program is responsible for obtaining events $E_1, E_2, \ldots$ from the *System Under Observation*, referred to as SUO, and forwarding them to the backend, which then monitors them using the contract in `contract.cpp`.

For each monitor in `contract.cpp` is maintained an internal memory, called the *frontier*, which is a set of active *states* $S_1, S_2, \ldots, S_k$. States in LOGSCOPE are similar to those of state machines, however, in contrast to traditional state machines the frontier can contain more than one state, each parameterized with its own data. As we shall see, a state can have transitions out of the state, which can delete states, create new states, and/or issue error messages to a report. For each incoming event E_i, a monitor conceptually applies the event to each state $S_1, S_2, \ldots, S_k$ in the frontier[2], causing states to be removed, states to be added, and/or error messages to be issued.

---

[2] Optimizations similar to slicing can avoid examining all states.

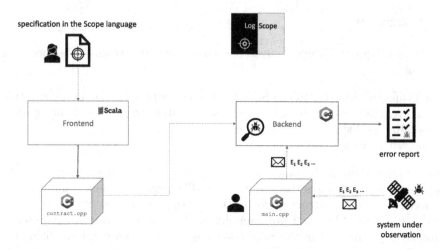

Fig. 1. The LOGSCOPE architecture.

In *online* monitoring, where the monitor continuously monitors the SUO as it executes, there is conceptually no end to the monitoring, it theoretically continues "forever". However, in *offline* monitoring, analyzing e.g. a log file, monitoring terminates after the last event in the log file has been processed. The specification language contains language constructs, which only have meaning when/if end of monitoring occurs. Specifically it is checked that there are no remaining unfulfilled obligations: events that should occur but did not.

In the following we first present the SCOPE specification language, and subsequently the tool itself in terms of the frontend and backend.

4   The Specification Language

A *specification* consists of one or more files, each containing zero or more *monitor specifications*. From each monitor specification is generated a *monitor* AST (in C++). When there is no confusion possible, we shall use the term *monitor* instead of *monitor specification*. Each monitor specification represents a *property* that must hold on an event sequence. We shall illustrate the LOGSCOPE specification language through a sequence of examples, that combined cover the different aspects of the language. All the examples concern the commanding of a planetary rover. We start with examples where events do not carry data, and then move on to the more interesting case where events carry data.

4.1   Events

Conceptually, an event is a named record, with a *name* and a *mapping* from fields to values, where both fields and values are strings. We can think of an event to have the following form:

$$name(field_1 : value_1, \ldots, field_n : value_n)$$

In case the map is empty we just refer to the *name*. Some examples are:

– *reboot*
– *command*(*name* : *"TURN"*, *kind* : *"FSW"*, *sol* : *"125"*)

This description suffices to understand the specification language. Later, in Sect. 5, we shall see how such events are concretely created with the backend C++ API.

4.2 A Simple State Machine

Let us assume that the SUO repeatedly emits two events:

– command : command being issued to, and received by, rover
– succeed : successful termination of command execution on rover

Note that for this first example we do not care about the fact that there are different kinds of commands. We also do not care about the data that events carry. We want to monitor the following property:

Property P_1:
After submission of a command, a success of the command must follow, and no other command can be submitted in between.

The monitor for this property is shown in Fig. 2. The monitor, named M1, first declares which events it will monitor, namely command and succeed. Declaring such events has the main purpose of reducing the risk of making specification mistakes by e.g. misspelling event names when defining the states. Then two states are defined: Command and Succeed. The state Command is the initial state of the state machine, indicated by the *state modifier* **init**. The state contains one transition: command ⇒ Succeed, expressing that if a command event is observed, then we leave (remove from the frontier) the Command state and enter (add to the frontier) the Succeed state. The Succeed state is annotated with a **hot** modifier, with the meaning that this state must be left (removed) before *end of monitoring* occurs (if it occurs). Leaving the Succeed state can happen in one of two ways. Either a succeed event occurs, in which case we return to the Command state, or another command event occurs, in which case we report an **error**.

Textual monitors are visualized by LogScope using GraphViz's dot-format, see Appendix A. This can help in convincing the specification writer that the specification expresses the intended property.

```
monitor M1 {
  event command, succeed

  init Command {
    command ⇒  Succeed
  }

  hot Succeed {
    succeed ⇒  Command
    command ⇒  error
  }
}
```

Fig. 2. Monitor M1 for property P_1.

4.3   Some Alternative Monitors

Figure 3 shows some alternative monitors for property P_1, illustrating different aspects of the language. In the monitor M1a, instead of alternating between the states Command and Succeed, whenever a command event is observed in the Command state, in addition to creating a Succeed state, we immediately re-create the Command state. This is done by listing the Command state on the right-hand side of the transition arrow ⇒ , in addition to the Succeed state, separated by a comma. In the Succeed state itself, instead of creating a Command state on observing a succeed event, the **ok** state is entered, which effectively means that we are leaving the Succeed state successfully. This approach is, however, semantically slightly different in the sense that this monitor will keep looking for successes of commands, even after a failure due to a command being issued while waiting for a success. In the monitor M1, such an extra command will cause the frontier to become empty. Note that we have not annotated the Command state with the modifier **init**. In case no states are annotated with **init**, the first state is by default initial (unless the monitor contains *anonymous states* as shown in monitor M1c).

Monitor M1b shows how we can annotate a state with the modifier **always** to obtain the same effect as the transition in the Command state in the M1a monitor. The **always** modifier causes the state to always persist, even when transitions out of the state are taken. It is common for such **always** states to be anonymous, by not giving them a name. This is shown in the monitor M1c, which is the recommended (most convenient) way to write this monitor. If there are anonymous states in a monitor they become initial states in addition to states explicitly annotated with the modifier **init**. Only if there are no states annotated with **init** and there are no anonymous states, the first state becomes the initial state.

4.4   Monitoring Events that Carry Data

We shall now monitor events that carry data, represented as maps from fields to string values. This is where LOGSCOPE distinguishes itself from traditional state machines. In our next example along the same theme, we shall specifically distinguish between different commands identified by name and kind. That is, our events have the form:

```
monitor M1a {
   event command, succeed

   Command {
      command ⇒
         Succeed , Command
   }

   hot Succeed {
      succeed ⇒ ok
      command ⇒ error
   }
}
```

(a) Monitor M1a.

```
monitor M1b {
   event command, succeed

   always Command {
      command ⇒
         Succeed
   }

   hot Succeed {
      succeed ⇒ ok
      command ⇒ error
   }
}
```

(b) Monitor M1b.

```
monitor M1c {
   event command, succeed

   always {
      command ⇒
         Succeed
   }

   hot Succeed {
      succeed ⇒ ok
      command ⇒ error
   }
}
```

(c) Monitor M1c.

Fig. 3. Alternative monitors M1a, M1b, and M1c for property P_1.

```
− command(name : c, kind : k)  :  command being issued
− succeed(name : c)            :  successful termination
```

The kind k can for example be the string "FSW" (Flight Software, in contrast to Flight Hardware). We shall now modify the property P_1 slightly. The property stated that *"After submission of a command, a success of the command must follow, and no other command can be submitted in between"*. We shall now distinguish between different commands, identified by their names, and relax the property to:

Property P_2:
After submission of a flight software command with a name x, a success of the command named x must follow (with the same name), and that command x cannot be re-submitted in between.

Note that x is a variable representing any command name observed. This means that in between a command named x and its success, another command named y can be submitted as long as $x \neq y$. A monitor for this property is shown in Fig. 4. Now the events are declared to carry maps (data). The event command carries a map defining two fields, name, a string denoting the name of the command, and kind, the kind of the command. The succeed command carries its name. Note that all data are strings[3]. The anonymous initial **always** state contains a single transition, which on the left-hand side of the arrow ⇒ matches any command event where the kind field is the string "FSW". On such a match the command name itself is *bound* to the variable x. This x is then referred to on the right-hand side state, where it is bound to the c field of the created Succeed state. So, e.g. if the command $command(name : "TURN", kind : "FSW")$ is observed, then a $Succeed(c : "TURN")$ state is created.

The Succeed state itself is parameterized with a map with a single field c. This field is referred to in the transitions. For example, the first transition states that if a succeed event is observed with a map, which maps the field name to the value of c that was passed as parameter, then we successfully leave the Succeed state by creating an **ok** state. On the other hand, if a command event is observed where the name is c, it is an **error**.

---

[3] An extension of the language can allow different types of values.

The general rule for when a variable name in a transition is *bound* versus *matched against* is the following. A variable, such as x in the **always** state, is *bound* to an incoming value of an event if x is not occurring as parameter to the state. A variable, such as c in the Succeed state, is *matched against* if occurs as parameter to the state.

Note that we do not refer to the kind field of the command event in the second transition of the Succeed state (even though all commands monitored by this monitor defines a kind field in their associated maps). The intent is that we do not want any command of any kind with the name c to occur while waiting for a success. We could alternatively have narrowed it down to flight software commands by adding a kind : "FSW". Note that the order of arguments are not important since we are dealing with maps. The format of monitor M2 is typical, many properties will have this form.

```
monitor M2 {
  event command(cmd,kind), succeed(cmd)

  always {
    command(cmd : x, kind : "FSW") ⇒ Succeed(c : x)
  }

  hot Succeed(c) {
    succeed(cmd : c) ⇒ ok
    command(cmd : c) ⇒ error
  }
}
```

Fig. 4. Monitor M2 for property P_2.

4.5   Referring to the Past

The properties we have seen so far are what we call a *future time* properties. They have the general form: *"if some event occurs, then some other events have to occur in the future and/or other events should not occur in the future"*. It is, however, also useful sometimes to refer to things that happened in the past, and specifically to things that did not happen. Let us add a constraint to property P_2, namely that *a command is only allowed to succeed, if it has been commanded in the past and not yet succeeded*. The added constraint refers to the past. That is, our property now becomes:

Property P_3:
After submission of a flight software command with a name x, a success of the command named x must follow (with the same name), and that command x cannot be re-submitted in between. Furthermore, a command is only allowed to succeed if it has been commanded in the past and not yet succeeded.

The monitor M3 in Fig. 5 monitors this property. The monitor is the same as in Fig. 4 except that in the initial **always** state we have added an extra transition:

```
succeed(name : x) @ !Succeed(c : x) ⇒ error
```

In addition to the event pattern succeed(name : x), after the symbol @ follows a condition !Succeed(c : x) stating that there does not (! is negation) exist a state in the *frontier* with a map that maps the field c to the value x bound in the event on the left-hand side of the @ symbol. If there is no such state, hence the command x is not expected to succeed, then an error is reported. In general, after the @ symbol, a comma separated list of conditions can occur (negated or not), which each have to be true for the transition to be taken. The conditions can bind variables, exactly as does our event here. Bindings can be seen in patterns occurring to the right of the bindings.

```
monitor M3 {
  event command(cmd,kind), succeed(cmd)

  always {
    command(cmd : x, kind : "FSW") ⇒ Succeed(c : x)
    succeed(cmd : x) @ !Succeed(c : x) ⇒ error
  }

  hot Succeed(c) {
    succeed(cmd : c) ⇒ ok
    command(cmd : c) ⇒ error
  }
}
```

Fig. 5. Monitor M3 for property P_3.

4.6   A Complex Property

The following final example does not introduce essential new language features (except a less essential one), but illustrates how a more complex monitor can look like. We expand the scenario with additional events. We here assume that when a command is received on the rover, it is not immediately executed, but rather it is stored in a queue. While in the queue the command can be cancelled. If not cancelled it is then eventually dispatched for execution. The execution can fail or it can succeed. After successful execution, the command has to be closed (e.g. cleaning up). Each command, in addition to having a name, is now also associated with a command number, increased by 1 for each submitted command. We consider the following events:

- command(name : c, nr : n, kind : k)
- cancel(name : c, nr : n)
- dispatch(name : c, nr : n)
- fail(name : c, nr : n)
- succeed(name : c, nr : n)
- close(name : c, nr : n)

We shall refer to the combination of a command name and its number as a *command instance*. Our new property is as follows.

P4:

After submission of a flight software command instance, a dispatch of the command instance must follow, unless it is cancelled first. Once dispatched, it must succeed, without any failure occurring before. In between the dispatch and the success of a command instance, we should observe no resubmission of that command (any command instance with that name). A command instance is not allowed to succeed unless it has been dispatched. Once a command instance has succeeded, it must be closed, and it is not allowed to succeed again.

The monitor for property P_4 is shown in Fig. 6. The second transition in the initial **always** state uses a condition to catch command successes that are not expected. The first transition in the Succeed state creates two new states, a NoMoreSuccess state and a Close state. The second transition in the Succeed state uses a wildcard symbol _ to indicate that any flight software command instance with the name sc will cause an error in this state, we don't care what the command number is. In this monitor, the transition has the same meaning as the following transition where we do not mention the nr field at all:

command (cmd : sc , kind : "FSW") ⇒ **error**

Whether we use a don't care symbol _ or not does, however, have an effect in case we do not declare our events at the beginning of the monitor: using a don't care symbol, as in **nr : _**, does require that there is an nr field in the command's data map. If not an error is issued.

```
monitor M4 {
   event command(cmd,nr,kind),  cancel(cmd,nr),  dispatch(cmd,nr),
         fail(cmd,nr),  succeed(cmd,nr),  close(cmd,nr)

   always {
      command(cmd  :  c,  nr  :  n,  kind  :  "FSW")  ⇒  Dispatch(dc  :  c,  dn  :  n)
      succeed(cmd  :  c,  nr  :  n) @ !Succeed(sc  :  c,  sn  :  n)  ⇒  error
   }

   hot Dispatch(dc,dn) {
      cancel(cmd  :  dc,  nr  :  dn)  ⇒  ok
      dispatch(cmd  :  dc,  nr  :  dn)  ⇒  Succeed(sc  :  dc,  sn  :  dn)
   }

   hot Succeed(sc,sn) {
      succeed(cmd  :  sc,  nr  :  sn)  ⇒
         NoMoreSuccess(nc  :  sc,  nn  :  sn),
         Close(cc  :  sc,  cn  :  sn)
      command(cmd  :  sc,  nr  :  _,  kind  :  "FSW")  ⇒  error
      fail(cmd  :  sc,  nr  :  sn)  ⇒  error
   }

   NoMoreSuccess(nc,nn) {
      succeed(cmd  :  nc,  nr  :  nn)  ⇒  error
   }

   hot Close(cc,cn) {
      close(cmd  :  cc,  nr  :  cn)  ⇒  ok
   }
}
```

Fig. 6. Monitor M4 for property P_4.

4.7   The Complete Grammar

The complete grammar for the SCOPE language is defined in Fig. 7. In addition to traditional grammar notation we also use $A,^*$ denoting A zero or more times, separated by commas, and likewise for $A,^+$ denoting A one or more times, separated by commas.

Note that one does not need to define events. In that case the events are inferred from the state transitions. Providing event definitions, however, serves two purposes: (1) to offer an additional well-formedness check on the state transitions, that they refer to events declared, and (2) if no events are declared, then only events used in the state transitions are submitted to the monitor, otherwise all declared events are submitted. This can make a difference when using **step** and **next** modifiers explained below.

The non-terminal 'Modifier' introduces two modifiers we have not explained before. A **step** state will be deleted from the frontier at the next event if none of its transitions fire. A **next** state will cause an error at the next event if none of its transitions fire. In the definition of the non-terminal 'Trans' (transition), if a pattern on the right-hand side of $\Rightarrow$ is negated, the corresponding state is removed. Such patterns must be grounded with no undefined identifiers. Note that when taking a transition, the source state containing the transition is removed from the frontier, unless the state is annotated with the **always** modifier.

```
Specification ::= Monitor*
Monitor ::= monitor Id '{' EventDef* State* '}'
EventDef ::= event Event,+
Event ::= Id [ '(' Id,+ ')' ]
State ::= Modifier+ '{' Trans+ '}' | Modifier* Id [ '(' Id,* ')' ] [ '{' Trans+ '}' ]
Modifier ::= init | always | hot | step | next
Trans ::= Pat [ '@' Pat,+ ] '⇒' Pat,*
Pat ::= [ '!' ] Id [ '(' Constraint,* ')' ]
Constraint ::= Id ':' Range
Range ::= Value | Id | '_'
Value ::= String | Number
Id   ::= Letter (Letter | Digit | '_')*
Letter ::= 'a' - 'z' | 'A' - 'Z'
Digit ::= '0' - '9'
Number ::= Digit Digit*
String ::= text between double quotes
```

Fig. 7. Grammar for the LOGSCOPE language.

5   Usage

The front-end is delivered as a jar-file and a script referring to the jar-file. The logscope script is applied as follows to n files (for $n \geq 1$) containing monitor specifications in the SCOPE language:

$$\text{logscope } \langle file_1 \rangle \text{ .... } \langle file_n \rangle$$

LOGSCOPE will merge the monitor specifications in the different files into one specification and translate it to C++. It does not matter in which order the files are provided, or how monitors are distributed over the files. In case the input specification passes the parsing and type checking, LOGSCOPE will generate a directory `tool-generated`, containing the file `contract.cpp` with the generated C++ AST (which will be used to monitor the specified monitors) and visualizations of monitors in `.png` format, one for each monitor.

The user writes a program, say `main.cpp`, which is compiled with the generated `contract.cpp` file, and which instantiates the specification in `contract.cpp` and feeds it events. Figure 8 shows a program, `main.cpp`, using the `contract.cpp` file (by importing `contract.h`) that is generated by the frontend from the monitor specification in Fig. 5.

In line 4 we create a `SpecObject` object via a call of the `makeContract` function, that the generated file `contract.cpp` defines. The `SpecObject` contains the AST of the specification as a C++ object tree. We then create a trace, a list of four events, in lines 5–10. In our case, the specification in Fig. 5 processes the events: command(cmd,kind) and succeed(cmd). Here command and succeed are the names, and cmd and kind are the fields. If we look at the first event in line 6, it represents a command at time 10, with the "cmd" field having the value "TURN" and the "kind" field having the value "FSW". The for-loop in lines 11–13 iterates through each event e in the trace, and feeds it to the contract via a call of the eval method. Finally, in line 14, we end the monitoring. This can cause additional error messages to be produced in case any hot states remain in the frontier of monitor. Note that during online monitoring this method may never be called. As shown in this example, the monitor must be fed events e via calls of the form contract.eval(e). For the purpose of a simple presentation we created an explicit trace. When monitoring an application in *online* mode (as it executes) it is up to the implementer of the application to invoke these calls. When monitoring an application in *offline* mode, it us up to the implementer of the application to write events to a file, which can then later be processed.

```
1    #include "contract.h"
2
3    int main() {
4        SpecObject contract = makeContract();
5        list<Event> events = {
6            Event(10,"command",{{"cmd","TURN"},{"kind","FSW"}}),
7            Event(20,"command",{{"cmd","TRACK"},{"kind","FSW"}}),
8            Event(30,"succeed",{{"cmd","TURN"}}),
9            Event(40,"succeed",{{"cmd","SEND"}}),
10       };
11       for (Event &e : events) {
12           contract.eval(e);
13       };
14       contract.end();
15   }
```

Fig. 8. The main program in `main.cpp`.

Monitoring the above trace causes two errors to be detected, the first due to the 4th event (line 9 in Fig. 8), which is a success of a command that has not been issued. At the end of monitoring (at the call contract.end() in line 14), an additional error is detected, indicating that the monitor M3 ends in the **hot** Succeed state, since the TRACK command has not succeeded.

6   Implementation

The front-end, implemented in SCALA, parses the SCOPE specification using SCALA's parser combinator library and produces an AST in SCALA. The AST is type checked, and then written out as an AST in C++ to the file contract.cpp. Monitors are visualized with GRAPHVIZ [14]. The backend is implemented in C++14 (the 2014 version).

The monitoring engine can be conceived as operating with objects of three main classes. An object of the SpecObject class represents the specification, which is a collection of monitors, each of which is represented by an object of the MonitorObject class. Each such monitor, at any moment in time during monitoring, contains a set of active states, each represented by an object of the StateObject class. Each of these three classes defines an eval(Event &e) method, evaluating a single event, as shown in Fig. 9.

```cpp
void SpecObject::eval(Event &e) {
    for (MonitorObject *m : monitors) m->eval(e);
}

void MonitorObject::eval(Event e) {
    if (isRelevant(e)) {
        event = e;
        statesToDelete.clear();
        statesToAdd.clear();
        for (auto state: states) state.eval();
        for (auto &state: statesToDelete) states.erase(state);
        for (auto &state: statesToAdd) states.insert(state);
    }
}

void StateObject::eval() {
    bool fired = false;
    for (ast::Transition *trans : stateAST->transitions) {
        TransitionResult result = evalTransition(trans);
        if (result == TransitionResult::FAILED) error();
        fired = fired || (result != TransitionResult::SILENT);
    };
    if (stateAST->isNext && !fired) error();
    if (!stateAST->isAlways &&
        (stateAST->isNext || stateAST->isStep || fired)) {
        monitor->recordStateToDelete(*this);
    }
}
```

Fig. 9. Evaluation methods.

The SpecObject::eval method calls the eval method on each of its monitors. The method MonitorObject::eval only handles events relevant to the monitor (either declared, or if no event declarations: used). It calls the eval method on each of its states. It operates on two variables storing states to be deleted and states to be added due to the effect of the transitions in the monitor. Finally, the StateObject::eval method walks through the transitions. Next-states must fire. The state is removed if it is not an always state, and it is a next or step state, or a transition fired.

7 Experiment

7.1 Setting Up the Experiment

In order to evaluate LOGSCOPE's performance, we compared it to two other monitoring systems: DAUT [10,17] and PYCONTRACT [8,27]. As previously mentioned, while the LOGSCOPE specification language is an external DSL – a stand-alone language, where a monitor specification is *translated* to an AST (in C++) and then interpreted; both DAUT and PYCONTRACT are internal DSLs, in respectively SCALA and PYTHON, implementing automata concepts very similar to the one of LOGSCOPE. An internal DSL is effectively a library in the host language. A user is therefore not limited to the expressiveness of the DSL, but can use the entire host language for writing monitors if needed. This can e.g. be useful for performing computations on the data appearing in events. Generally, high-level languages such as PYTHON, and especially SCALA, are well suited for defining internal DSLs. Both internal DSLs use the host language's pattern matching to match events against transition left hand sides. This turns out to be a crucial difference from the C++ implementation of LOGSCOPE, where this pattern matching had to be implemented. The aging earlier version of LOGSCOPE [4,23], implemented in PYTHON, and executing in PYTHON, was not performing well, and has for this reason been eliminated from the numeric comparison.

We monitored a slight modification of property M4 in Fig. 6, shown in Fig. 10, which requires less memory, avoiding the accumulating memory needed by the NoMoreSuccess state for example. The DAUT version of this property is shown in Fig. 11 and the PYCONTRACT version is shown in Fig. 12. We applied each monitor to 8 logs (traces) with varying length and shape. Table 1 shows the execution times in seconds and milliseconds. Each log is generated by an artificial log generator developed specifically for the experiment, parameterized with a shape $S = (P, R)$ of positive integers, where P denotes how many commands are active in parallel, from issuing the command, dispatching, succeeding, and closing (four events), and R indicates how many times such a parallel execution is repeated.

7.2 Result and Interpretation

The surprise here is that LOGSCOPE, with a backend implemented in C++, is slower than the other two systems implemented in SCALA and PYTHON. The SCALA version has the best performance, which in part likely can be contributed to the JVM's just-in-time compilation. We believe the reason for LOGSCOPE's weaker performance to be the following. LOGSCOPE supports an external DSL, where a monitor specification is translated (by the SCALA frontend) into an AST (in C++). This AST is subsequently during monitoring *interpreted* on the stream of input events. The interpreter includes our own implementation of *pattern matching* of events against transition left-hand sides. In contrast, both DAUT and PYCONTRACT are internal shallow DSLs, where monitors are written directly in the host language, and specifically using the pattern matching provided by the host languages, yielding an advantage wrt. Performance. Note that this performance advantage of internal shallow DSLs also holds when compared to interpretation of *internal deep* DSLs, which are similar to external DSLs, in that a program/specification in the DSL is represented as a data structure (AST). Note finally that the C++ implementation uses dynamic memory allocation (as do DAUT and PYCONTRACT). This should in a revised version for embedded software monitoring be replaced by a static memory pool, potentially providing efficiency improvements wrt. Time and memory.

The presented C++ version of LOGSCOPE, however, performs better than the earlier version described in [4,23]. This is perhaps not so surprising since they both use fundamentally the same technique of interpreting the monitor specification AST over the trace, and C++ is a high performance programming language compared to Python.

```
monitor M4_modified {
    event command(cmd,nr,kind), cancel(cmd,nr), dispatch(cmd,nr),
        fail(cmd,nr), succeed(cmd,nr), close(cmd,nr)

    always {
        command(cmd : c, nr : n, kind : "FSW") ⇒ Dispatch(dc : c, dn : n)
    }

    hot Dispatch(dc,dn) {
        cancel(cmd : dc, nr : dn) ⇒ ok
        dispatch(cmd : dc, nr : dn) ⇒ Succeed(sc : dc, sn : dn)
    }

    hot Succeed(sc,sn) {
        succeed(cmd : sc, nr : sn) ⇒ Close(cc : sc, cn : sn)
        command(cmd : sc, nr : _, kind : "FSW") ⇒ error
        fail(cmd : sc, nr : sn) ⇒ error
    }

    hot Close(cc,cn) {
        succeed(cmd : cc, nr : cn) ⇒ error
        close(cmd : cc, nr : cn) ⇒ ok
    }
}
```

Fig. 10. Monitor M4 modified, used in experiment.

```
class M4_modified extends Monitor[Event] {
    always {
        case Com(c, n, "FSW") ⇒ Dispatch(c, n)
    }

    case class Dispatch(cmd:String, nr:String) extends state {
        hot {
            case Can('cmd', 'nr') ⇒ ok
            case Dis('cmd', 'nr') ⇒ Succeed(cmd, nr)
        }
    }

    case class Succeed(cmd:String, nr:String) extends state {
        hot {
            case Suc('cmd', 'nr') ⇒ Close(cmd, nr)
            case Com('cmd', _, "FSW") ⇒ error()
            case Fai('cmd', 'nr') ⇒ error()
        }
    }

    case class Close(cmd:String, nr:String) extends state {
        hot {
            case Suc('cmd', 'nr') ⇒ error()
            case Clo('cmd', 'nr') ⇒ ok
        }
    }
}
```

Fig. 11. Monitor M4 modified, in the SCALA DSL DAUT.

Table 1. Result of experiment. For each log is shown shape S of the log: a pair (P, R) of constants, where P denotes how many commands are active in parallel, from issuing the command, dispatching, succeeding, and closing (four events), and R indicates how many times such a parallel execution is repeated. The number of events in a log is $4 * P * R$.

log nr	1	2	3	4	5	6	7	8
$S = (P,R)$	(1,12500)	(50,250)	(1,50000)	(5,10000)	(10,5000)	(20,2500)	(1,125000)	(5,25000)
nr. of events	50,000	50,000	200,000	200,000	200,000	200,000	500,000	500,000
LogScope	5.172 s	42.974 s	20.571 s	14.884 s	21.857 s	35.537 s	23.471 s	37.256
PyContract	0.373 s	4.600 s	1.567 s	3.425 s	5.120 s	8.811 s	4.511 s	9.483 s
Daut	0.595 s	0.733 s	0.927 s	0.938 s	1.000 s	1.221 s	1.482 s	1.431 s

```
class M4_modified(Monitor):
    def transition(self, event):
        match event:
            case {'name': 'command', 'cmd': c, 'nr': n, 'kind': "FSW"}:
                return self.Dispatch(c, n)

@data
class Dispatch(HotState):
    cmd: str
    nr: str

    def transition(self, event):
        match event:
            case {'name': 'cancel', 'cmd': self.cmd, 'nr': self.nr}:
                return ok
            case {'name': 'dispatch', 'cmd': self.cmd, 'nr': self.nr}:
                return self.Succeed(self.cmd, self.nr)

@data
class Succeed(HotState):
    cmd: str
    nr: str

    def transition(self, event):
        match event:
            case {'name': 'succeed', 'cmd': self.cmd, 'nr': self.nr}:
                return self.Close(self.cmd, self.nr)
            case {'name': 'command', 'cmd': self.cmd, 'nr': _, 'kind': "FSW"}:
                return error()
            case {'name': 'fail', 'cmd': self.cmd, 'nr': self.nr}:
                return error()

@data
class Close(HotState):
    cmd: str
    nr: str

    def transition(self, event):
        match event:
            case {'name': 'succeed', 'cmd': self.cmd, 'nr': self.nr}:
                return error()
            case {'name': 'close', 'cmd': self.cmd, 'nr': self.nr}:
                return ok
```

Fig. 12. Monitor M4 modified, in the Python DSL PyContract.

8   Conclusion

We have presented a framework in C++ for monitoring event streams, with a frontend written in Scala supporting an external DSL. We compared the implementation with two other monitoring systems implemented in respectively Scala and Python. It turns out that those systems perform better, likely due to the fact that they are internal DSLs benefiting from the host language's pattern matching constructs.

The current version of the tool is a prototype. A continuation of this work would include the following activities. There is a need to obtain a better understanding of the performance differences. In general, there is a need to modify the backend C++ code to match embedded programming practices. This includes most importantly to avoid dynamic memory allocation, using instead statically sized object pools. The backend monitoring engine can be further optimized. One can e.g. use indexing to quickly identify what states an event is relevant for. Various extensions to the specification language can be considered, such as e.g. allowing the use of C++ code as part of specifications. Currently arguments to a state are passed by referring to the formal parameter names. Allowing positional arguments without referring to the formal parameter names might be desirable. Finally, a more optimal way to translate a monitoring specification is to translate it to a C++ program that is specialized for the monitor (rather than translating it to an AST in C++). Partial evaluation could be considered as an approach to achieve this, partially evaluating the interpreter given a specification, yielding a program that now only takes the event trace as input.

A   Visualization of Monitors

Textual monitors are automatically visualized using GRAPHVIZ's dot-format [14]. This appendix shows the visualization of the textual monitors presented in Sect. 4.

Monitor M1. The monitor M1 in Fig. 2 is visualized in Fig. 13. Hot states (annotated in text with the modifier **hot**) are visualized as orange arrow shaped pentagons. Orange means danger: this state has to be left eventually. Non-hot states are visualized as green rectangles, we can stay in those "forever" (terminating monitoring in such a state is ok). The initial state Command is pointed to by an arrow leaving a black point. Transitions are labelled with events (and additional *conditions* as we shall see later). The color red in general indicates error. For example a command issued in the Succeed state causes an error, symbolized with a red cross on a horizontal line.

Fig. 13. Monitor M1 visualized.

Monitors M1a, M1b, and M1c. The three monitors M1a, M1b, and M1c in Fig. 3 are visualized in Figure 14. Figure 14a, the visualization of M1a, shows how multiple target states are visualized: the transition of the Command state triggered by a command event creates a Succeed and a Command state. This is visualized with a black triangle (symbolizing a Boolean 'and': ∧) with dashed lines leading to the target states. Note how in the Succeed state, a succeed event leads to **ok** which in the visualization is shown as a green dot. The visualization of monitor M1b in Fig. 14b illustrates how an **always** state is visualized: with an unlabelled self loop. The difference between the visualization of this monitor and of M1c in Fig. 14c is only that the initial state in Fig. 14c has no name.

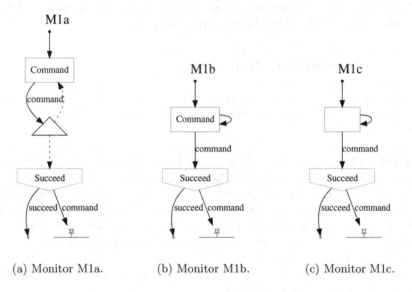

(a) Monitor M1a.   (b) Monitor M1b.   (c) Monitor M1c.

Fig. 14. Monitors M1a, M1b, and M1c visualized.

Monitor M2. Monitor M2 in Fig. 4 is visualized in Fig. 15. The difference from previous visualizations is that now events carry data maps, which is shown. It is also shown how bindings to fields in target state maps are created. Specifically, the transition 'command(name : x, kind :"FSW") ⇒ Succeed(c : x)' from the initial **always** state is shown as an edge labelled with command(cmd : x, kind : "FSW"), and below it the binding of the c field of the Succeed state (see its definition) to the x that was bound on the left of the ⇒ symbol.

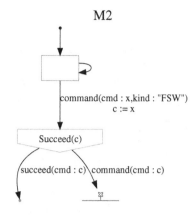

Fig. 15. Monitor M2 visualized.

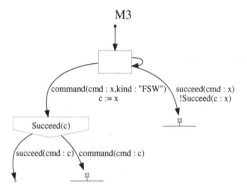

Fig. 16. Monitor M3 visualized.

Monitor M3. Monitor M3 in Fig. 5 is visualized in Fig. 16. The only new visualization concept here is that the transition from the initial **always** state to the error state is now labelled not only with the event pattern succeed(name : x) but also with the condition pattern !Succeed(c : x) underneath.

Monitor M4. Monitor M4 in Fig. 6 is visualized in Fig. 17. Recall that by observing the color scheme one can from the graph quickly understand the violations being checked for: orange means terminating here is a violation, and red means an occurred violation.

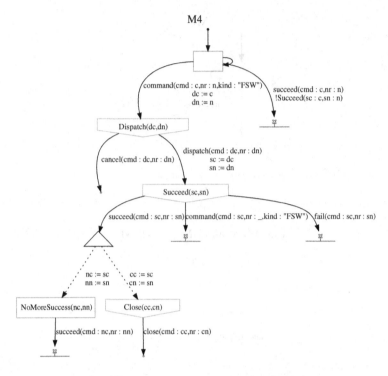

Fig. 17. Monitor M4 visualized.

References

1. Attard, D.P., Cassar, I., Francalanza, A., Aceto, L., Ingólfsdóttir, A.: A runtime monitoring tool for actor-based systems. In: Gay, S., Ravara, A. (eds.) Behavioural Types: from Theory to Tools, chapter 3, pp. 49–76. River Publishers (2017)
2. Barringer, H., Rydeheard, D., Havelund, K.: Rule systems for run-time monitoring: from EAGLE to RULER. In: Sokolsky, O., Taşıran, S. (eds.) RV 2007. LNCS, vol. 4839, pp. 111–125. Springer, Heidelberg (2007). https://doi.org/10.1007/978-3-540-77395-5_10
3. Barringer, H., Goldberg, A., Havelund, K., Sen, K.: Rule-based runtime verification. In: Steffen, B., Levi, G. (eds.) VMCAI 2004. LNCS, vol. 2937, pp. 44–57. Springer, Heidelberg (2004). https://doi.org/10.1007/978-3-540-24622-0_5
4. Barringer, H., Groce, A., Havelund, K., Smith, M.: Formal analysis of log files. J. Aerosp. Comput. Inf. Commun. **7**(11), 365–390 (2010)
5. Basin, D.A., Klaedtke, F., Marinovic, S., Zălinescu, E.: Monitoring of temporal first-order properties with aggregations. Formal Methods Syst. Design **46**(3), 262–285 (2015)
6. Colombo, C., Pace, G.J., Schneider, G.: LARVA – safer monitoring of real-time Java programs (tool paper). In: Proceedings of the 2009 Seventh IEEE International Conference on Software Engineering and Formal Methods, SEFM '09, pp. 33–37, Washington, DC, USA, IEEE Computer Society (2009)

7. d'Amorim, M., Havelund, K.: Event-based runtime verification of Java programs. In: Proceedings of the Third International Workshop on Dynamic Analysis, WODA '05, pp. 1–7, New York, NY, USA, Association for Computing Machinery (2005)
8. Dams, D., Havelund, K., Kauffman, S.: Python library for trace analysis. In: Dang, T., Stolz, V. (eds) Runtime Verification. Tbilisi, Georgia, September 28–30, Springer, Cham, LNCS (2022). https://doi.org/10.1007/978-3-031-17196-3_15
9. D'Angelo, B., et al.: LOLA: Runtime monitoring of synchronous systems. In: Proceedings of TIME 2005: the 12th International Symposium on Temporal Representation and Reasoning, pp. 166–174, IEEE (2005)
10. Daut. https://github.com/havelund/daut (2022)
11. Decker, N., Leucker, M., Thoma, D.: Monitoring modulo theories. Softw. Tools Technol. Transf. (STTT) **18**(2), 205–225 (2016)
12. Robert, B.: Doorenbos. Production Matching for Large Learning Systems. PhD thesis, Carnegie Mellon University, Pittsburgh, PA (1995)
13. Forgy, C.: Rete: a fast algorithm for the many pattern/many object pattern match problem. Artif. Intell. **19**, 17–37 (1982)
14. Graphviz. https://graphviz.org (2022)
15. Hallé, S., Villemaire, R.: Runtime enforcement of web service message contracts with data. IEEE Trans. Serv. Comput. **5**(2), 192–206 (2012)
16. Havelund, K.: Runtime verification of C programs. In: Suzuki, K., Higashino, T., Ulrich, A., Hasegawa, T. (eds.) FATES/TestCom -2008. LNCS, vol. 5047, pp. 7–22. Springer, Heidelberg (2008). https://doi.org/10.1007/978-3-540-68524-1_3
17. Havelund, K.: Data automata in Scala. In: 2014 Theoretical Aspects of Software Engineering Conference, TASE 2014, Changsha, China, September 1–3, pp. 1–9. IEEE Computer Society (2014)
18. Havelund, K.: Rule-based runtime verification revisited. Softw. Tools Technol. Transf. (STTT) **17**(2), 143–170 (2015)
19. Havelund, K., Peled, D.: Runtime verification: from propositional to first-order temporal logic. In: Colombo, C., Leucker, M. (eds.) RV 2018. LNCS, vol. 11237, pp. 90–112. Springer, Cham (2018). https://doi.org/10.1007/978-3-030-03769-7_7
20. Havelund, K., Peled, D.: An extension of LTL with rules and its application to runtime verification. In: Finkbeiner, B., Mariani, L. (eds.) RV 2019. LNCS, vol. 11757, pp. 239–255. Springer, Cham (2019). https://doi.org/10.1007/978-3-030-32079-9_14
21. Kim, M., Kannan, S., Lee, I., Sokolsky, O.: Java-MaC: a run-time assurance tool for Java. In: Proceedings of the 1st International Workshop on Runtime Verification (RV'01), vol.55(2) of ENTCS. Elsevier (2001)
22. LogFire. https://github.com/havelund/logfire
23. LogScope in Python. https://github.com/havelund/logscope (2022)
24. LogScope in Scala/C++. https://github.com/logscope (2022)
25. Meredith, P.O.N., Jin, D., Griffith, D., Chen, F., Roşu, G.: An overview of the MOP runtime verification framework. Int. J. Softw. Tech. Technol. Transf (STTT) **14**249–289 (2011)
26. Pike, L., Wegmann, N., Niller, S., Goodloe, A.: Copilot: Monitoring embedded systems. Innov. Syst. Softw. Eng. **9**(4), 235–255 (2013)
27. PyContract. https://github.com/pyrv/pycontract (2022)
28. Reger, G., Cruz, H.C., Rydeheard, D.: MARQ: monitoring at runtime with QEA. In: Baier, C., Tinelli, C. (eds.) TACAS 2015. LNCS, vol. 9035, pp. 596–610. Springer, Heidelberg (2015). https://doi.org/10.1007/978-3-662-46681-0_55

Specification and Verification with the TLA+ Trifecta: TLC, Apalache, and TLAPS

Igor Konnov[1], Markus Kuppe[2], and Stephan Merz[3(✉)]

[1] Informal Systems, Vienna, Austria
[2] Microsoft Research, Redmond, USA
[3] University of Lorraine, CNRS, Inria, LORIA, Nancy, France
stephan.merz@loria.fr

Abstract. Using an algorithm due to Safra for distributed termination detection as a running example, we present the main tools for verifying specifications written in TLA+. Examining their complementary strengths and weaknesses, we suggest a workflow that supports different types of analysis and that can be adapted to the desired degree of confidence.

Keywords: Specification · TLA+ · Model checking · Theorem proving

1 Introduction

TLA+ [13] is a formal language for specifying systems, in particular concurrent and distributed algorithms, at a high level of abstraction. The foundations of TLA+ are classical Zermelo-Fraenkel set theory with choice for representing the data structures on which the algorithm operates, and the Temporal Logic of Actions (TLA), a variant of linear-time temporal logic, for describing executions of the algorithm.

Most users write TLA+ specifications using one of the two existing IDEs (integrated development environments): the TLA+ Toolbox [11], a standalone Eclipse application, and a Visual Studio Code Extension, which can be run in a standard Web browser. To different degrees, both IDEs also integrate the three main tools for verifying TLA+ specifications: the explicit-state model checker TLC [16], the symbolic SMT-based model checker APALACHE [8], and the TLA+ Proof System TLAPS [2], an interactive proof assistant.

In this paper, we use a non-trivial algorithm for detecting termination of an asynchronous distributed system [5] as a running example for presenting the three tools. Based on their complementary strengths and weaknesses, we suggest a workflow that can serve as a guideline for analyzing different kinds of properties of a TLA+ specification, to different degrees of confidence. This is the

Support by the Inria-Microsoft Research Joint Centre and Interchain Foundation, Switzerland is gratefully acknowledged.

T. Margaria and B. Steffen (Eds.): ISoLA 2022, LNCS 13701, pp. 88–105, 2022.
https://doi.org/10.1007/978-3-031-19849-6_6

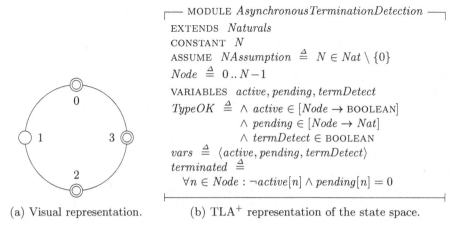

(a) Visual representation.   (b) TLA$^+$ representation of the state space.

Fig. 1. The ring of nodes and its TLA$^+$ representation.

first paper that applies all three tools to a common specification and identifies their complementary qualities. We hope that future TLA$^+$ users will find our presentation useful for applying these tools to their own specifications. All of our TLA$^+$ modules and ancillary files for running the tools are available online [9].

Outline of the Paper. Section 2 presents a high-level specification of the problem of termination detection written as a TLA$^+$ state machine, whose properties are verified in Sect. 3. Safra's algorithm is informally presented in Sect. 4. Section 5 describes different approaches for verifying the properties of the algorithm using model checking and theorem proving, including checking that the algorithm refines the high-level specification introduced earlier. Finally, Sect. 6 concludes the paper and outlines ideas for future work.

2 Specifying Termination Detection

Before presenting Safra's algorithm for detecting termination of processes on a ring, we formally state the problem to be solved. Although this is not strictly required for using TLA$^+$, it will allow us to succinctly state correctness of the algorithm in terms of refinement, and to introduce the TLA$^+$ tools on a small specification.

As illustrated in Fig. 1a, we assume N nodes that perform some distributed computation. Each node can be active (indicated by a double circle) or inactive (single circle). When a node is active, it may perform some local computation, and it can send messages to other nodes. Messages can be understood as carrying tasks to be performed by the receiver: an inactive node can still receive messages and will then become active. The purpose of the algorithm is to detect whether all nodes are inactive. Note that the ring structure indicated in Fig. 1a is unimportant for the statement of the problem: it will become relevant for the termination detection algorithm to be introduced later.

Figure 1b contains the initial part of a TLA$^+$ specification that formally states the problem of termination detection. Specifications appear in TLA$^+$ modules that contain declarations of constant and variable parameters, statements of assumptions and theorems, but mainly contain operator definitions of the form $Op(args) \triangleq expr$; if the operator does not take arguments, the empty pair of brackets is omitted.

Whereas constant parameters are interpreted by fixed (state-independent) values, variable parameters correspond to state variables that represent the evolution of a system: a *state* assigns values to variables. TLA$^+$ expressions are classified in four levels: *constant formulas*[1] do not contain any variables, thus their value is the same at all states during the execution of a system. *State formulas* may contain constants and unprimed variables, and such formulas are evaluated at individual states. *Action formulas* may additionally contain primed variables; they are evaluated over pairs (s, t) of states: an unprimed variable v denotes the value of v in s whereas the primed variable v' denotes the value of v in t. Finally, *temporal formulas* involve operators of temporal logic such as $\Box$ (*always*) and $\Diamond$ (*eventually*), and they are evaluated over (infinite) sequences of states. By abuse of language, we will sometimes say that a module defines a state predicate rather than that it defines an operator representing a Boolean state formula, and similarly for the other levels.

TLA$^+$ modules form a hierarchy by extending and instantiating other modules. Module *AsynchronousTerminationDetection* extends module *Naturals* from the standard library in order to import the definition of the set *Nat* of natural numbers and standard arithmetic operations. It declares a constant parameter N and defines the constant *Node* as the interval of integers between 0 and $N - 1$. It also declares variable parameters *active*, *pending*, and *termDetect*, intended to represent the status of each node (active or inactive), the number of pending messages at each node, and whether termination has been detected or not. TLA$^+$ is untyped, but it is good engineering practice to document the expected types of constants and variables using a formula of the shape $v \in S$ where S is a set that denotes the type of v. Thus, assumption *NAssumption* states that N must be a non-zero natural number, and the state predicate *TypeOK* indicates the expected types of the variables:[2] *active* and *pending* are Boolean and natural-number valued functions over *Node*, whereas *termDetect* is a Boolean value. The formal status of the two typing predicates is quite different: an instance of the module that does not satisfy *NAssumption* is considered illegal, whereas *TypeOK* just defines a predicate. (We will later check that the predicate indeed holds at every state during any execution.) Finally, the module declares a predicate *terminated* that is true at states in which the system has globally terminated: all nodes are inactive, and no message is pending at any node.

The part of the specification shown in Fig. 1b corresponds to the static model of the system. Module *AsynchronousTerminationDetection* continues as shown

---

[1] In TLA$^+$ jargon, the term "formula" denotes any expression, not necessarily Boolean.

[2] In TLA$^+$, long conjunctions and disjunctions are conventionally written as lists whose "bullets" are the logical operator, with nesting indicated by indentation.

$Init \overset{\Delta}{=}$
$\quad \wedge\ active \in [Node \rightarrow \text{BOOLEAN}]$
$\quad \wedge\ pending = [n \in Node \mapsto 0]$
$\quad \wedge\ termDetect \in \{\text{FALSE}, terminated\}$
$Terminate(i) \overset{\Delta}{=}$
$\quad \wedge\ active[i]$
$\quad \wedge\ active' = [active \text{ EXCEPT } ![i] = \text{FALSE}]$
$\quad \wedge\ pending' = pending$
$\quad \wedge\ termDetect' \in \{termDetect, terminated'\}$
$SendMsg(i,j) \overset{\Delta}{=}$
$\quad \wedge\ active[i]$
$\quad \wedge\ pending' = [pending \text{ EXCEPT } ![j] = @ + 1]$
$\quad \wedge\ \text{UNCHANGED } \langle active, termDetect \rangle$
$RcvMsg(i) \overset{\Delta}{=}$
$\quad \wedge\ pending[i] > 0$
$\quad \wedge\ active' = [active \text{ EXCEPT } ![i] = \text{TRUE}]$
$\quad \wedge\ pending' = [pending \text{ EXCEPT } ![i] = @ - 1]$
$\quad \wedge\ \text{UNCHANGED } termDetect$

$DetectTermination \overset{\Delta}{=}$
$\quad \wedge\ terminated$
$\quad \wedge\ termDetect' = \text{TRUE}$
$\quad \wedge\ \text{UNCHANGED } \langle active, pending \rangle$
$Next \overset{\Delta}{=}$
$\quad \vee\ \exists i \in Node : RcvMsg(i)$
$\quad \vee\ \exists i \in Node : Terminate(i)$
$\quad \vee\ \exists i,j \in Node : SendMsg(i,j)$
$\quad \vee\ DetectTermination$
$Spec \overset{\Delta}{=}$
$\quad \wedge\ Init \wedge \Box[Next]_{vars}$
$\quad \wedge\ WF_{vars}(DetectTermination)$

Fig. 2. End of module *AsynchronousTerminationDetection*.

in Fig. 2 with the specification of a transition system that abstractly represents the problem of distributed termination detection. The initial condition *Init* expresses that the variable *active* can take any type-correct value and that no messages are pending. As for *termDetect*, it will usually be FALSE initially, but it could be TRUE in case the predicate *terminated* holds.[3] The transition formulas *Terminate(i)*, *SendMsg(i,j)*, *RcvMsg(i)*, and *DetectTermination* describe the allowed transitions. For example, *Terminate(i)* describes local termination of node *i*. The action is possible if node *i* is active, the value of variable *active* after the transition is similar to its previous value, except that *active[i]* is FALSE, and variable *pending* is left unchanged. The variable *termDetect* may also remain unchanged, but a clever termination algorithm may set it to TRUE provided the predicate *terminated* has become true with the termination of node *i*. Note that updates of function-valued variables are expressed using EXCEPT clauses, which describe for which arguments the function is set to a new value. On the right-hand side of such a clause, the symbol @ refers to the old value of the function at the argument that is updated. The definitions of the remaining actions are similar.

The action *Next* is defined as the disjunction of the actions introduced before, and the temporal formula *Spec* corresponds to the overall specification of the system behavior. It has the standard form

$$Init \wedge \Box[Next]_{vars} \wedge L$$

---

[3] Remember that the purpose of this specification is not to describe a specific termination detection algorithm, but rather an abstract transition system meant to represent any such algorithm.

of a TLA$^+$ specification, asserting that executions must start in a state satisfying the initial condition and that all transitions must either correspond to a system transition (described by formula $Next$) or leave the variables $vars$ unchanged. The supplementary condition L is usually a conjunction of fairness conditions; in our example, we require that termination detection should eventually occur provided that it remains enabled. Indeed, the formula $\mathrm{WF}_v(A)$ is defined in TLA$^+$ as

$$\Box((\Box \text{ENABLED} \langle A \rangle_v) \Rightarrow \Diamond \langle A \rangle_v)$$

which asserts that the action $\langle A \rangle_v$, defined as $A \wedge v' \neq v$, must eventually occur if it ever remains enabled. Enabledness of an action is defined as

$$\text{ENABLED } A \triangleq \exists v' : A$$

where v is the tuple of variables that have (free) primed occurrences in A.

One may consider assuming stronger fairness conditions for this specification, such as that any pending message should eventually be received. However, weak fairness of the action $DetectTermination$ is all that is required to ensure that global termination will be detected.

3   Verification by Model Checking and Theorem Proving

Module $AsynchronousTerminationDetection$ provides a high-level specification of termination detection; it does not describe a mechanism for solving the problem. Nevertheless, we can already use the TLA$^+$ tools in order to verify some correctness properties, including type correctness, safety, and liveness.

The safety property asserts that termination is not detected unless the system has indeed terminated, while liveness asserts that termination will eventually be detected. These properties can be expressed as the temporal formulas

$$Safe \triangleq \Box SafeInv, \text{ where } SafeInv \triangleq termDetect \Rightarrow terminated,$$
$$Live \triangleq terminated \rightsquigarrow termDetect.$$

The formula $F \rightsquigarrow G$ is shorthand for $\Box(F \Rightarrow \Diamond G)$, and it asserts that whenever F is true, G must eventually become true. Correctness of the specification means proving the theorems that $Spec$ implies the above properties. We may also want to verify that once the system has terminated, it will remain quiescent, expressed as

$$Quiescence \triangleq \Box(terminated \Rightarrow \Box terminated).$$

Note that the two properties $Safe$ and $Quiescence$ imply the derived property

$$\Box(termDetect \Rightarrow \Box terminated)$$

asserting that once termination has been detected, the system will remain globally inactive.

```
INIT Init              CONSTANT   N = 4
NEXT Next              INVARIANTS TypeOK Safe
```

Fig. 3. A TLC configuration file: It fixes N as 4, the initial and transition predicates as *Init* and *Next*, and the invariants to be verified as *TypeOK* and *Safe*.

3.1   Finite-State Model Checking Using TLC

TLC is an explicit-state model checker for checking safety and liveness of finite instances of TLA+ specifications [16]. In order to describe the finite instance and to indicate the properties to be checked, TLC requires, in addition to the TLA+ specification, a *configuration file*. In our example, we have to provide a value for the constant parameter N representing the number of nodes. For example, the configuration file in Fig. 3 instructs TLC to check the invariants *TypeOK* and *Safe* against the instance of four nodes. TLC is integrated into both IDEs for TLA+, the TLA+ Toolbox and the Visual Studio code extension. Both IDEs generate TLC configuration files in the background.

Since in our specification, nodes may send arbitrarily many messages, the state space is infinite even for a fixed number of nodes. We therefore add a state constraint bounding the number of pending messages to K messages per node.[4] TLC quickly verifies all four properties introduced earlier and reports that the system has 4,097 distinct reachable states for $N = 4$ and $K = 3$. For $N = 6$ and $K = 3$, we obtain 262,145 states, illustrating the well-known problem of state-space explosion.

It is instructive to observe what happens when a specification contains an error. For example, let us assume that we forgot the conjunct *active[i]* in the definition of action *SendMsg(i)*. Running TLC on the modified specification indicates that the invariant *Safe* is violated.[5] TLC produces a counter-example containing a step where all processes are inactive and termination has been detected, but where a message is sent. In the successor state, *terminated* is therefore false, while the variable *termDetect* is still true, violating the asserted invariant.

Besides checking the invariants *TypeOK* and *Safe*, TLC can also check properties of specifications expressed as temporal formulas, including *Quiescence* and *Live*. For the latter, it is important to include the fairness assumption in the specification of the instance to be verified by replacing the INIT and Next entries in the configuration file by SPECIFICATION Spec.

3.2   Bounded Model Checking with Apalache

APALACHE [8] is a symbolic model checker that leverages the SMT (satisfiability modulo theories) solver Z3 [4] for checking TLA+ executions of bounded lengths

---

[4] More precisely, TLC will not compute any successors of states at which the constraint does not hold.

[5] Property *Quiescence* is also violated, but invariant violations are found earlier.

```
CONSTANT
    \* @type: Int;
    N
VARIABLES
    \* @type: Int -> Bool;
    active,
    \* @type: Int -> Int;
    pending,
    \* @type: Bool;
    termDetect
```

Fig. 4. Type annotations for APALACHE.

as well as proving inductive invariants. Similar to TLC, APALACHE can check instances of specifications where the size of data structures remains bounded. Reusing the configuration file shown in Fig. 3, APALACHE does not actually require a bound K for the number of pending messages, as it can reason about unbounded integers.

Whereas TLC enumerates the reachable states one by one, APALACHE encodes bounded symbolic executions as a set of constraints, which are either proven to be unsatisfiable or solved by an SMT solver. APALACHE uses the standard many-sorted first-order logic of SMT, and it infers types of expressions in a TLA$^+$ specification based on an annotation of constants and variables with types, as shown in Fig. 4. Its type checker ensures that these annotations are consistent with the use of the constants and variables in the expressions that appear in the specification.

Similar to the foundational paper on bounded model checking [1], we write

$$Spec \models_k \Box Inv$$

to denote that a state formula Inv holds true in all states of all bounded executions of specification $Spec$ that perform at most k transitions. By abuse of notation, we also allow Inv to be an action formula, which must then be true for all pairs of subsequent states within these bounded executions, and we call Inv an *action invariant*.

APALACHE can check that the state invariants $TypeOK$ and $SafeInv$ hold of an instance of our specification where $N = 4$ and $k \leq 10$, in less than a minute. Figure 5a shows the performance of APALACHE when checking the combined invariant $TypeOK \wedge SafeInv$, for $N \in 3..6$ and execution length k up to 20 steps. As can be seen, APALACHE suffers from considerable slowdown when the parameters N and k are increased. This is caused by combinatorial explosion of the underlying SMT problem, similar to state explosion of state enumeration in TLC.

We can also direct APALACHE to check that the invariant

$$IndInv \triangleq TypeOK \wedge SafeInv$$

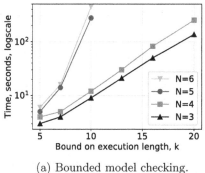
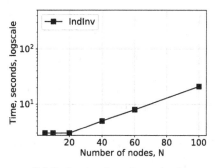

(a) Bounded model checking.   (b) Inductive invariant checking.

Fig. 5. Checking $TypeOK \wedge SafeInv$ using APALACHE.

is inductive and therefore holds for executions of arbitrary length. Informally, this means that $IndInv$ holds true for the initial states specified with $Init$, and that it is preserved by all transitions specified with $Next$.

Using the notation introduced above, we frame these two properties as the APALACHE queries (1) and (2) below. The first query establishes that $IndInv$ is a state invariant of the original specification for all executions of length 0, and therefore it must hold in all states that satisfy $Init$. The second query confirms that $IndInv$ is a state invariant for all executions of length 1 when using $IndInv$ as the initialization predicate instead of $Init$. Therefore, any step of an execution starting in a state in which $IndInv$ holds preserves the invariant.

$$Init \wedge \Box[Next]_{vars} \models_0 \Box IndInv \tag{1}$$
$$IndInv \wedge \Box[Next]_{vars} \models_1 \Box IndInv \tag{2}$$

Both of these runs take only a second on a standard laptop for $N = 4$. In fact, we can show the inductiveness of $IndInv$ for $N = 100$ in 20 s. Figure 5b shows the performance of APALACHE when checking property (2) for various values of N. Comparing Figs. 5a and 5b, it becomes apparent that we can prove inductive invariants of instances of specifications that have astronomically larger state spaces than those for which standard bounded model checking is feasible. Moreover, inductive invariants guarantee that the property holds for executions of arbitrary length. However, as we will see in Sect. 5, finding useful inductive invariants is not always as easy as it was in this example.

We cannot directly check the property $Quiescence$ with APALACHE, as it is written as a temporal property. One way of doing so would be to introduce a history variable that records the sequence of states seen so far and formulate the property as a state invariant over this history. APALACHE offers support for this approach in the form of checking so-called trace invariants.

However, we can avoid the encoding as a trace invariant by observing that the property $Quiescence$ can be verified by checking that the action invariant $terminated \Rightarrow terminated'$ holds for all transitions taken from the reachable states. Since we have shown that *IndInv* is an inductive invariant, it suffices to use APALACHE to check the following:

$$IndInv \land \Box[Next]_{vars} \models_1 \Box(terminated \Rightarrow terminated') \tag{3}$$

It takes APALACHE 3 s and 11 s to show that property (3) holds for $N = 4$ and $N = 100$, respectively.

3.3 Theorem Proving Using TLAPS

Model checking is invaluable for finding errors, and the counter-examples computed in the case of property violations help designers understand their root cause. However, it is restricted to the verification of finite instances, and it suffers from combinatorial explosion. The TLA$^+$ Proof System (TLAPS) [2] can be used to prove properties of arbitrary instances of a specification. The effort is independent of the size of the state space, but it requires the user to write a proof, which is then checked by the system.

TLAPS does not implement a foundational proof calculus for TLA$^+$, but relies on automatic back-end provers to establish individual proof steps. Correspondingly, TLA$^+$ proofs are written as a collection of steps that together entail the overall theorem. A proof step may be discharged directly by a back-end, or it may recursively be proved as the consequence of lower-level steps, leading to a hierarchical proof format [12]. The proof of an inductive invariant such as *TypeOK* is written as follows.

THEOREM $TypeCorrect \triangleq Spec \Rightarrow \Box TypeOK$
$\langle 1 \rangle 1.\ Init \Rightarrow TypeOK$
$\langle 1 \rangle 2.\ TypeOK \land [Next]_{vars} \Rightarrow TypeOK'$
$\langle 1 \rangle 3.$ QED   BY $\langle 1 \rangle 1,\ \langle 1 \rangle 2,$ PTL DEF $Spec$

It consists of three top-level steps $\langle 1 \rangle 1 - \langle 1 \rangle 3.$[6] The first two steps assert that the initial condition implies the invariant, and that the invariant is preserved by any transition allowed by $[Next]_{vars}$. The final QED step corresponds to proving the theorem, assuming the preceding steps could be proved. The BY clause directs TLAPS to check the proof of this step by invoking the PTL back-end (for "propositional temporal logic"), assuming steps $\langle 1 \rangle 1$ and $\langle 1 \rangle 2$, and expanding the definition of formula *Spec*. PTL can discharge this proof obligation, which essentially corresponds to an application of the proof rule

$$\frac{I \Rightarrow J \qquad J \land [N]_v \Rightarrow J'}{I \land \Box[N]_v \Rightarrow \Box J}$$

of temporal logic. By relying on the PTL back-end, which implements a decision procedure for linear-time temporal logic, the user does not have to indicate a specific proof rule, and TLAPS can discharge more complex steps involving temporal logic.

---

[6] Steps are named $\langle l \rangle n$ where l indicates the nesting level of the step and n is arbitrary.

In order to complete the proof of the theorem, we must provide proofs for steps $\langle 1 \rangle 1$ and $\langle 1 \rangle 2$. These steps assert (the validity of) a state and an action formula, respectively, and therefore do not require temporal logic.[7] The first step can be proved by invoking the assumption *NAssumption* and expanding the definitions of *Init*, *TypeOK*, and the defined operators used therein. The second step requires some more interaction and is decomposed into one sub-proof per disjunct in the definition of *Next*. The TLA+ Toolbox provides an assistant for such syntactic decompositions. The proofs of the invariant *Safe* and of the safety property *Quiescence* are similar, but they also use theorem *TypeCorrect* in order to introduce predicate *TypeOK* as an assumption.

The proof of the liveness property makes use of the fairness hypothesis that appears as part of the specification. Since the fairness formula is defined in terms of ENABLED (cf. Sect. 2), we first prove a lemma that reduces the relevant enabledness condition to a simple state predicate.

> LEMMA $EnabledDT \triangleq$
> ASSUME $TypeOK$
> PROVE $(\text{ENABLED } \langle DetectTermination \rangle_{vars})$
> $\Leftrightarrow (terminated \wedge \neg termDetect)$

The proof of this lemma makes use of specific directives for reasoning about ENABLED provided by TLAPS. The proof of the liveness property is then finished in a few lines of interaction:

> THEOREM $Liveness \triangleq Spec \Rightarrow Live$
> $\langle 1 \rangle$. DEFINE $P \triangleq terminated \wedge \neg termDetect$
> $\langle 1 \rangle 1$. $TypeOK \wedge P \wedge [Next]_{vars} \Rightarrow P' \vee termDetect'$
> $\langle 1 \rangle 2$. $TypeOK \wedge P \wedge \langle DetectTermination \rangle_{vars} \Rightarrow termDetect'$
> $\langle 1 \rangle 3$. $TypeOK \wedge P \Rightarrow \text{ENABLED } \langle DetectTermination \rangle_{vars}$
> $\langle 1 \rangle 4$. QED   BY $\langle 1 \rangle 1$, $\langle 1 \rangle 2$, $\langle 1 \rangle 3$, $TypeCorrect$, PTL DEF $Spec$, $Live$

The first two steps are proved by expanding the required definitions, the third step is a consequence of lemma *EnabledDT*, and the final step follows from the preceding ones, and theorem *TypeCorrect*, by propositional temporal reasoning. More complex cases would typically require induction over a well-founded ordering, which is supported by a standard library of TLA+ lemmas.

4   Safra's Algorithm for Termination Detection

In his note EWD 998 [5], Dijkstra describes an algorithm due to Safra for detecting termination on a ring of processes. Safra's algorithm extends a simpler algorithm due to Dijkstra, described in note EWD 840 [6], which assumes that message passing between processes is instantaneous. In both algorithms, node 0 plays the role of a master node that will detect global termination.

---

[7] TLAPS replaces primed variables occurring in action formulas by fresh variables, unrelated to their unprimed counterparts.

In addition to the activation status and message counter represented by the variables *active* and *pending* introduced for the state machine of Sect. 2, each node now has a color (white or black) and maintains an integer counter that represents the difference between the numbers of messages it has sent and received during the execution. In addition, a token circulates on the ring whose attributes are its color *token.c*, its position *token.p* (i.e., the number of the node that the token is currently at), and an integer counter *token.q* that represents the sum of the counter values of the nodes visited so far. Safra's algorithm does not have the variable *termDetect*.

Informally, the algorithm relies on the idea that when the system has globally terminated, each node is locally inactive and the sum of the differences between sent and received messages is 0. By visiting each node, checking its activation status and accumulating the counter values, the token reports these conditions to the master node. Colors are used in order to rule out false positives: nodes color themselves black at message reception (i.e., when they may have become active again), and the token becomes black when it passes a black node. A round in which a black token returns to node 0 is deemed inconclusive.

Formally, the algorithm is described by a state machine. The initial values of each node's activation status and color are arbitrary, all node counters are 0, and there are no pending messages. The token is initially black (ensuring that it will perform at least one full round of the ring), and its initial counter value is 0. The token can be located at any of the nodes. The transitions of the algorithm are as follows.

InitiateProbe. Node 0 may initiate a new round of the token when it holds the token (i.e., $token.p = 0$) and when the previous round did not detect termination: either the token is black, node 0 is black, or the sum of the counter of node 0 and *token.q* is positive. Node 0 transfers a fresh white token to its neighbor node (i.e., $token.p = N − 1$, $token.c = white$, and $token.q = 0$) and repaints itself white.

PassToken. A non-zero node i may pass the token to its neighbor when it holds the token (i.e., $token.p = i$) and when it is inactive. After the transition, $token.p$ will be $i − 1$, *token.q* is augmented by node i's counter value, and the token will be black if node i is black or if it was already black, whereas node i becomes white.

SendMsg. This action is similar to the corresponding action of the abstract state machine, except that the sender's counter value is incremented by 1.

RcvMsg. Again, this action is similar to the corresponding action of the abstract state machine. However, the receiver's counter value is decremented by 1, and the receiver becomes black.

Terminate. This action is analogous to the corresponding action of the abstract state machine.

Node 0 declares global termination when it is inactive, has no pending messages, holds a white token, its color is white, and the sum of *token.q* and its own counter value is 0. A TLA$^+$ specification of the algorithm is available online [9].

5 Analyzing Safra's Algorithm

As for the high-level specification of Sect. 2, we use the model checkers TLC and APALACHE to gain confidence in the correctness of the algorithm by checking its properties for small instances, and then start writing a full correctness proof using TLAPS. Instead of rechecking the elementary correctness properties introduced in Sect. 3, an attractive way of verifying the correctness of the algorithm in TLA$^+$ is to formally relate it to the high-level algorithm by establishing refinement.

5.1 Model Checking Correctness Properties

We start by writing a type-correctness invariant for the TLA$^+$ specification of Safra's algorithm and define the predicate of termination detection as follows:

$$
\begin{aligned}
termDetect \ \triangleq \ &\wedge token.p = 0 \wedge token.c = \text{"white"} \\
&\wedge color[0] = \text{"white"} \wedge \neg active[0] \wedge pending[0] = 0 \\
&\wedge token.q + counter[0] = 0
\end{aligned}
$$

We use TLC to verify type correctness, as well as the properties *Safe*, *Live*, and *Quiescence* introduced in Sect. 3, for fixed values of N. Again, we need a state constraint for bounding the number K of pending messages at each node, but also the maximum counter values C and token counter Q. The state space of this specification is significantly larger than that of the higher-level model: fixing $N = 3$, $K = C = 3$ and $Q = 9$, TLC finds 1.3 million distinct states and requires 42 s on a desktop-class machine. For $N = 4$ and the same bounds for the other parameters, we obtain 219 million distinct states, and TLC requires about 50 min. While TLC scales to multiple cores and can, e.g., verify safety of EWD998 for $N = 4$ on a machine with 32 cores and 64 GB of memory in around 10 min, it would be hopeless to model check the specification for larger values such as $N = 6$ in reasonable time.

Experience indicates that by exhaustively checking all reachable states, including corner cases that would arise very rarely in actual executions of the algorithm, model checking finds errors in small instances of a specification. Choosing suitable parameter values is a matter of engineering judgment. For example, an error introduced into the definition of action *PassToken* such that the token adopts the color of the visited node, independently of the current token color, is found by TLC when $N \geq 4$, but the definition is correct for $N \leq 3$.

If exhaustive model-checking is infeasible due to the size of the state space, TLC can verify safety and liveness properties on randomly generated behaviors. Since randomized state exploration has no notion of state-space coverage, TLC runs until either it finds a violation, is manually stopped, or up to a given resource limit. Because randomized state exploration is an embarrassingly parallel problem, it scales with the number of available cores.

To illustrate the effectiveness of randomized state exploration with TLC, we separately introduced six bugs in the specification of Safra's algorithm that we observed while teaching TLA$^+$ classes. Beyond the previously mentioned bug of not taking into account the token color when non-initiator nodes pass the token, we initialize the token to white, allow an active node to pass the token, omit to whiten a node that passes the token, or prevent the initiator from initiating a new token round when its color is black. Half of these bugs violate property Inv, while the other half violate $TD!Spec$ (see below). With the parameter value fixed to $N = 7$ and no state constraint, randomized state exploration, with a resource limit of 2 to 3 s and for behaviors of length up to 100 states, finds violations of Inv and $TD!Spec$ in the majority of runs for any of the six bugs. Thus, the minimal resource usage makes it feasible, and the high likelihood of findings bugs makes it desirable to automatically run randomized state exploration repeatedly in the background while writing specifications. Users can run randomized state exploration with the Visual Studio Code Extension whenever its editors are saved. Once a spec has matured and randomized state exploration stops finding bugs, users can switch to exhaustive model-checking.

For more complex specifications, the likelihood of finding bugs with repeated, brief randomized state exploration can usually be increased further. If a candidate inductive invariant $IndInv$ is known, using it as the initial condition makes TLC explore states that are located at arbitrary depths in the state space. Should the set of all states defined by $IndInv$ be too large or even infinite, TLC can randomly select a subset from that set with the help of operators defined in the standard *Randomization* module. This technique is described in more detail as part of a note on validating candidates for inductive invariants with TLC [14].

APALACHE again is particularly useful when it comes to checking inductive invariants. Dijkstra's note [5] introduces the following inductive invariant Inv (written in TLA$^+$):

$$
\begin{aligned}
Sum(f, S) &\triangleq FoldFunctionOnSet(+, 0, f, S) \\
Rng(a, b) &\triangleq \{i \in Node : a \le i \wedge i \le b\} \\
Inv &\triangleq \wedge Sum(pending, Node) = Sum(counter, Node) \\
&\quad \wedge \vee \wedge \forall i \in Rng(token.p + 1, N - 1) : active[i] = \text{FALSE} \\
&\quad\quad\quad \wedge token.q = Sum(counter, Rng(token.p + 1, N - 1)) \\
&\quad\quad \vee Sum(counter, Rng(0, token.p)) + token.q > 0 \\
&\quad\quad \vee \exists i \in Rng(0, token.p) : color[i] = \text{"black"} \\
&\quad\quad \vee token.c = \text{"black"}
\end{aligned}
$$

The expression $Sum(f, S)$ represents the sum of $f[x]$ for all $x \in S$; it is defined in terms of the operator $FoldFunctionOnSet$ from the TLA$^+$ Community Modules [10], a collection of useful libraries for use with TLA$^+$.

As explained in Sect. 3.2, we can use APALACHE to check that Inv is indeed an inductive invariant for finite instances of the specification. For $N = 4$, this takes 11 s. It is not hard to see that Inv, together with predicate $termDetect$, implies *terminated*. Indeed, *termDetect* implies that the three final disjuncts of the invariant are false, hence the first disjunct must be true. Thus, all nodes are inactive, and *token.q* equals the sum of the counter values of nodes $1 .. N - 1$. By *termDetect*, it follows that the sum of the counter values of all nodes must be 0, and by the first conjunct of *Inv* it follows that there are no pending messages at any node, hence *terminated* is true.

5.2 Safra's Algorithm Implements Termination Detection

Instead of verifying the TLA+ specification of Safra's algorithm against correctness properties such as *Safe* and *Live*, we can show that it implements the high-level state machine of Sect. 2. It then follows that the properties verified for that state machine are "inherited" by the low-level specification. Since in TLA+, refinement is implication, this assertion can be stated by inserting the following lines in the module representing Safra's algorithm:

$$TD \triangleq \text{INSTANCE } AsynchronousTerminationDetection$$
$$\text{THEOREM } Refinement \triangleq Spec \Rightarrow TD!Spec$$

The first line declares an instance TD of the high-level specification in which the constant parameter N and the variable parameters *active*, *pending* and *termDetect* are instantiated by the expressions of the same name in the specification of Safra's algorithm.[8] Theorem *Refinement* asserts that every run of *Spec* (the specification of Safra's algorithm) also satisfies $TD!Spec$, defined in Fig. 2.

TLC can reasonably verify refinement for values of $N < 5$, and with a similar state constraint as before, simply by indicating $TD!Spec$ as the temporal property to be checked. APALACHE cannot handle the fairness condition that is part of $TD!Spec$, but it can verify initialization and step simulation. Technically, this is done by checking one state invariant and one action invariant with APALACHE:

$$Init \wedge \square[Next]_{vars} \models_0 \square TD!Init \tag{4}$$

$$TypeOK \wedge Inv \wedge \square[Next]_{vars} \models_1 \square[TD!Next]_{TD!vars} \tag{5}$$

Checking condition (4) with the APALACHE machinery is equivalent to showing $Init \Rightarrow TD!Init$, which is needed to show the initialization property of refinement. To prove step simulation, we have to show that any transition described by $[Next]_{vars}$, starting in any reachable state of the low-level specification, simulates a high-level transition according to $[TD!Next]_{TD!vars}$. As expressed in condition (5), the previously established inductive invariants $TypeOK$ and Inv are sufficient for proving step simulation.

The TLA+ specification of Safra's algorithm as described in Sect. 4 can be refined further by introducing explicit message channels and node addresses. We refer readers to the modules $EWD998Chan$ and $EWD998ChanID$ [9] that contain corresponding TLA+ specifications for which refinement can be checked using the TLA+ tools.

---

[8] In general, INSTANCE allows constant and variable parameters to be instantiated by expressions defined in terms of the operators defined in the current context.

5.3 Proving Correctness Using TLAPS

After gaining confidence in the validity of our specification of Safra's algorithm, we again use TLAPS for proving its correctness for arbitrary instances. The type correctness proof is quite similar to that of the high-level specification described in Sect. 3.3. We also used TLAPS for proving the inductive invariant Inv introduced in Sect. 5.1. However, at the time of writing, no theorem libraries exist in TLAPS for operators such as $FoldFunctionOnSet$, and we therefore stated elementary properties without proof, and specialized them for the derived operator Sum such as

> LEMMA $SumIterate \triangleq$
> ASSUME NEW $fun \in [Node \rightarrow Int]$,
>   NEW $inds \in$ SUBSET $Node$, NEW $e \in inds$
> PROVE $Sum(fun, inds) = fun[e] + Sum(fun, inds \setminus \{e\})$

The invariance proof itself was written in one person-day and required about 230 lines in the proof language of TLA$^+$. The hierarchical proof style helps to focus on individual steps without having to remember the overall proof.

Based on the inductive invariant and the following lemma

> LEMMA $Safety \triangleq TypeOK \wedge Inv \wedge termDetect \Rightarrow Termination$

that formalizes the argument presented at the end of Sect. 5.1, it is not hard to use TLAPS for proving the safety part of the refinement relation, i.e. the implications expressed by properties (4) and (5), for arbitrary instances of the specification. The proofs of the lemma and the safety part of the refinement theorem require about 110 lines of TLA$^+$ proof and were written in half a person-day.

In order to prove liveness of the algorithm, we first reduce the enabledness condition of the action for which fairness is assumed, to a simple state predicate, as we did in Sect. 3.3. We must then show that any state satisfying predicate $terminated$ must be followed by one where $termDetect$ holds. Relying on the already proved invariants, we set up a proof by contradiction and define

$$BSpec \triangleq \Box TypeOK \wedge \Box Inv \wedge \Box \neg termDetect \wedge \Box [Next]_{vars} \wedge \mathrm{WF}_{vars}(System)$$

where the last conjunct corresponds to the fairness assumption of the specification, in which $System$ represents the disjunction of the token-passing transitions. Informally, detecting termination may require three rounds of the token:

1. The first round brings the token back to node 0, while $terminated$ remains true.
2. After the second round, the token is back at node 0, all nodes are white (since no messages could be received), and $terminated$ is still true.
3. At the end of the third round, the same conditions hold, and additionally the token is white and the token counter holds the sum of the counters of the nodes in the interval $1 .. N - 1$.

We prove a lemma corresponding to each of the rounds. For example, for the first round we assert

LEMMA $Round1 \triangleq BSpec \Rightarrow (terminated \leadsto (terminated \wedge token.p = 0))$

The proof proceeds by induction on the current position k of the node: if $k = 0$, the assertion is trivial. For the case $k+1$, any step of the system either leaves the token at node $k+1$ or brings it to node k. Moreover, the token-passing transition from node $k + 1$ is enabled, and it takes the token to node k.

The statements and proofs of the two other lemmas are similar. Finally, the post-condition of the third round, together with Inv, implies $termDetect$, concluding the proof. As a corollary, we can finish the refinement proof: we showed in Sect. 3.3 that the enabledness condition of $TD.DetectTermination$ corresponds to the conjunction $terminated \wedge \neg termDetect$, and we just proved that this predicate cannot hold forever, implying the fairness condition. The TLA$^+$ proof takes 245 lines and was written in less than one person-day, aided by the fact that the three main lemmas and their proofs are quite similar.

6 Conclusion

TLA$^+$ is a language for the formal and unambiguous description of algorithms and systems. In this paper, we presented the three main tools for verifying properties of TLA$^+$ specifications: the explicit-state model checker TLC, the symbolic model checker APALACHE, and the interactive proof assistant TLAPS, at the hand of a formal specification of a non-trivial distributed algorithm. The ProB model checker can also verify TLA$^+$ specifications through a translation to B [7], but we did not evaluate its use on the case study presented here. The three tools that we considered have complementary strengths and weaknesses. They offer various degrees of proof power in exchange for manual effort or computational resources. Whereas TLC is essentially a push-button tool, TLAPS requires significant user effort for inventing a proof. Likewise, APALACHE can sometimes prove invariants of specifications that have significantly larger (or even infinite) state spaces than TLC can handle, but it requires human ingenuity to find an inductive invariant. Hence, we advocate the following basic workflow.

Since errors in specifications are usually found for small instances, it is easiest to start by using TLC for checking basic invariant properties. The same properties can also be checked using APALACHE for short execution prefixes. However, APALACHE really shines for checking inductive (state and action) invariants since doing so only requires considering a single transition. Once reasonable confidence has been obtained for safety properties, liveness properties can be verified using TLC. One potential pitfall here is that the use of a state constraint may mask non-progress cycles in which some variable value exceeds the admissible bounds. Both model checkers suffer from combinatorial explosion; for APALACHE the length of the execution prefixes that need to be examined tends to be the limiting factor. For very large state spaces, TLC provides support for randomized state exploration, which empirically tends to find bugs with good success when exhaustive exploration fails. When model checking finds no more errors and even more confidence is required, one can start writing a proof and check it using TLAPS. In this way, properties of arbitrary instances can be verified, at the expense of human effort that can become substantial in the presence of complex formulas.

All three tools accept the same input language TLA$^+$. Whereas APALACHE requires writing typing annotations for state variables and certain operator definitions, these are usually not very difficult to come up with. Not surprisingly, the tools pose additional restrictions on the input specifications. For example:

1. TLC rejects action formulas of the form $x' \in S$ when S is an infinite set, and no unique value has been determined for the variable x' by an earlier conjunct: in this case, the formula would require TLC to enumerate an infinite set. However, the user can override operator definitions such as S during model-checking without modifying the original specification.
2. APALACHE has recently dropped support for recursive operators and functions in favor of fold operations, e.g., *FoldSet* and *FoldFunction*. Folding a set S of bounded cardinality, that is, $|S| \leq n$, for some n, needs up to n iterations, which is easy to encode in SMT as opposed to general recursion.
3. TLAPS currently does not handle recursive operator definitions, and support for proving liveness properties has only recently been added. In practice, reasoning about operators that are not supported natively by its backends requires well-developed theorem libraries.

Despite these limitations, all three tools share a large common fragment of TLA$^+$. This ability to use different tools for the same specification is extremely valuable in practice, for example for using the model checkers to verify a putative inductive invariant in the middle of writing an interactive proof.

Future work should focus on improving the capabilities of each tool. Although TLC is quite mature, it could benefit from better parallelization of liveness checking. Recent work has focused on improved presentation of counter-examples, including their visualization and animation [15], and on randomized exploration of state spaces. For APALACHE, alternative encodings of bounded verification problems as SMT problems could help with performance degradation when considering longer execution prefixes. It would also be useful to lift the current restriction to the verification of safety properties and consider bounded verification of liveness properties. TLAPS users would appreciate better automation, such as the tool being able to indicate which operator definitions should be expanded, better support for higher-order problems, and for verifying liveness properties. The IDEs could help with using the tools synergistically, such as starting an exploratory model checking run that corresponds to a given step in a proof.

Besides the work on verifying properties of formal specifications, there is interest in relating TLA$^+$ specifications to system implementations. The two main lines of research are model-based test case generation from formal specifications and trace validation, in which the specification serves as a monitor for supervising an implementation. Davis et al. [3] present an interesting real-life case study, in which trace validation was found to be particularly successful.

References

1. Biere, A., Cimatti, A., Clarke, E., Zhu, Y.: Symbolic model checking without BDDs. In: Cleaveland, W.R. (ed.) TACAS 1999. LNCS, vol. 1579, pp. 193–207. Springer, Heidelberg (1999). https://doi.org/10.1007/3-540-49059-0_14
2. Cousineau, D., Doligez, D., Lamport, L., Merz, S., Ricketts, D., Vanzetto, H.: TLA+ proofs. In: Giannakopoulou, D., Méry, D. (eds.) FM 2012. LNCS, vol. 7436, pp. 147–154. Springer, Heidelberg (2012). https://doi.org/10.1007/978-3-642-32759-9_14
3. Davis, A.J.J., Hirschhorn, M., Schvimer, J.: Extreme modelling in practice. Proc. VLDB Endow. **13**(9), 1346–1358 (2020)
4. de Moura, L., Bjørner, N.: Z3: an efficient SMT solver. In: Ramakrishnan, C.R., Rehof, J. (eds.) TACAS 2008. LNCS, vol. 4963, pp. 337–340. Springer, Heidelberg (2008). https://doi.org/10.1007/978-3-540-78800-3_24
5. Dijkstra, E.W.: Shmuel Safra's version of termination detection (1987). https://www.cs.utexas.edu/users/EWD/ewd09xx/EWD998.PDF
6. Dijkstra, E.W., Feijen, W.H.J., van Gasteren, A.: Derivation of a termination detection algorithm for distributed computations. Inf. Proc. Lett. **16**, 217–219 (1983)
7. Hansen, D., Leuschel, M.: Translating TLA+ to B for validation with PROB. In: Derrick, J., Gnesi, S., Latella, D., Treharne, H. (eds.) IFM 2012. LNCS, vol. 7321, pp. 24–38. Springer, Heidelberg (2012). https://doi.org/10.1007/978-3-642-30729-4_3
8. Konnov, I., Kukovec, J., Tran, T.: TLA+ model checking made symbolic. Proc. ACM Program. Lang. **3**(OOPSLA), 123:1–123:30 (2019)
9. Konnov, I., Kuppe, M., Merz, S.: TLA+ specifications of EWD998 (2021). https://github.com/tlaplus/Examples/tree/ISoLA2022/specifications/ewd998
10. Kuppe, M.A., et al.: TLA+ community modules. https://github.com/tlaplus/CommunityModules
11. Kuppe, M.A., Lamport, L., Ricketts, D.: The TLA+ toolbox. In: Monahan, R., Prevosto, V., Proença, J. (eds.) Fifth Workshop on Formal Integrated Development Environment (F-IDE). EPTCS, vol. 310, pp. 50–62. Porto, Portugal (2019)
12. Lamport, L.: How to write a proof. Amer. Math. Monthly **102**(7), 600–608 (1995)
13. Lamport, L.: Specifying Systems. Addison-Wesley, Boston (2002)
14. Lamport, L.: Using TLC to check inductive invariance (2018). https://lamport.azurewebsites.net/tla/inductive-invariant.pdf
15. Schultz, W.: An animation module for TLA+ (2018). https://easychair.org/smart-slide/slide/8V76
16. Yu, Y., Manolios, P., Lamport, L.: Model checking TLA+ specifications. In: Pierre, L., Kropf, T. (eds.) CHARME 1999. LNCS, vol. 1703, pp. 54–66. Springer, Heidelberg (1999). https://doi.org/10.1007/3-540-48153-2_6

Selective Presumed Benevolence in Multi-party System Verification

Wolfgang Ahrendt[1] and Gordon J. Pace[2]

[1] Chalmers University of Technology, Gothenburg, Sweden
ahrendt@chalmers.se
[2] University of Malta, Msida, Malta
gordon.pace@um.edu.mt

Abstract. The functional correctness of particular components in a multi-party system may be dependent on the behaviour of other components and parties. Assumptions about how the other parties will act would thus have to be reflected in the specifications. In fact, one can find a substantial body of work on assume-guarantee reasoning with respect to the functional aspects of the component under scrutiny and those of other components. In this paper, we turn to look at non-functional assumptions about the behaviour of other parties. In particular, we look at smart contract verification under assumptions about presumed benevolence of particular parties and focusing on reentrancy issues—a class of bugs which, in the past few years, has led to huge financial losses. We make a case for allowing, in the specification, fine-grained assumptions on benevolence of certain parties, and show how these assumptions can be exploited in the verification process.

Keywords: Smart contracts · Interactive systems · Non-functional specifications

1 Introduction

Verification of a component in a distributed system which brings together multiple actors comes with the need for assumptions about how the other parties will interact with the component under scrutiny. In a setting where the other components are processes designed to work well with our code (whether its another method we wrote, a library we trust or a service we rely on), we would typically assume their well-behaviour, effectively presuming their benevolence. In an open-world setting, however, when a component interacts with external parties on whom we have no control, we may have to assume these parties to be malicious. Design of such systems and their verification typically takes one of these two extreme views.

Now consider smart contracts—essentially executable code running on a decentralised platform [12,13] regulating the behaviour of multiple parties. The correctness of such code is, indeed, of high importance to a user of such a system. Bugs may affect functionality, interfering with the user (and other parties)

© The Author(s), under exclusive license to Springer Nature Switzerland AG 2022
T. Margaria and B. Steffen (Eds.): ISoLA 2022, LNCS 13701, pp. 106–123, 2022.
https://doi.org/10.1007/978-3-031-19849-6_7

and hindering them from interacting through the smart contract in the originally intended manner. Take, for instance, a smart contract allowing parties to purchase, sell and transfer tokens, and a bug which may occasionally create a new token with a new owner but reusing an existing id, effectively stopping the current user from exercising their rights on their token. Other bugs may be better described as vulnerabilities, not deviating from expected behaviour when used normally, but allow a malicious party to capitalise on them to carry out logic not as originally (hopefully) intended by the smart contract developer. Many such types of vulnerabilities are known in the smart contract world: integer over- and underflow, transaction order dependency, reentrancy, gas-limit attacks, unexpected reverts, etc., with some being easier to avoid than others. Although there is no line, fine or otherwise, to draw between these two types of bugs, the main difference between the two would lie in the *intention* of the party triggering the bug.

Take reentrancy, which we discuss in more detail later on in this paper, and which we will use as an illustrative use case for our contribution. Informally, a smart contract is vulnerable to reentrancy bugs if it exhibits wrong behaviour when the smart contract invokes another party, which unexpectedly calls back the original smart contract.[1] This was the cause of various high-profile instances of bugs, the exploitation of which led to huge financial losses [5]. A verification engineer would not be fazed by such bugs, reasoning that having identified a class of such undesirable behaviour, we can write an anti-specification to capture instances of such bugs. But it is not as simple as this. Sometimes (albeit rarely), reentrancy may be a desirable feature, and in others it may not lead to any undesirable behaviour, making such blanket analyses undesirable.

Furthermore, such a vulnerability may not necessarily be a show-stopper for a particular party. For instance, if we know that there is such a vulnerability which only we can exploit, we may still decide to participate as part of the smart contract (which may already be in place, and cannot be updated). After all, we trust ourselves not to exploit the loophole if the otherwise normal behaviour of the smart contract is what we are after. Consider a smart contract which allows a party to send funds to another party with an intermediary performing due diligence checks on the two parties. If such a contract has a reentrancy vulnerability exploitable only by the receiver resulting in the loss of the funds, and someone is willing to send us funds through the smart contract, we can simply accept and use the contract in the expected way, not exploiting the bug.

This notion can be extended to situations in which we may assume certain other parties not to be malicious.[2] Consider a smart contract which handles the

---

[1] The design of the execution platform on blockchains such as Ethereum, even transferring funds from one smart contract to another involves a call to the recipient's code, providing potential for reentrant calls.

[2] We are sorely tempted to simply say that we *trust* those other parties. However, in the blockchain world, the word *trust* has been heavily used and comes with much baggage—trustless computation, trusted oracles, trusted parties, etc. We thus chose to avoid the use of the term in order to avoid confusion and talk about *benevolence* and *trust that a particular party will not perform a reentrancy attack*.

sale of a property, involving the seller and their spouse, the real-estate agent, and the buyer. The smart contract to be used may have reentrancy issues which only the seller and/or their spouse may exploit. This may certainly be an issue for the buyer and for the real-estate agent, but from the seller's point-of-view, if they are happy to assume that neither they nor their spouse will exploit the vulnerability they would not object to the use the smart contract and enabling the transaction to go through. Similar situations may arise in which the parties who may exploit such code would have other incentives, economic, social or otherwise, outweighing their gains from exploiting the smart contract, in which case another party may choose to presume that they will not carry out malicious actions. We propose verification techniques verifying a multi-party system against a specification whilst selectively presuming benevolence of certain parties.

These are the sort of scenarios we will explore in this paper, essentially proposing a language semantics which allows for proving the correctness of specifications annotated by the set of parties presumed to be benevolent—essentially having such *presumptions becoming an element of the specification*. This paper is driven by the idea that the distinction of who we will presume will act in good faith should be made explicit in the specification, and capitalised in the verification. In particular, we will illustrate these notions by focusing on verification of smart contracts written in Solidity [6], explicitly making assumptions about party-benevolence with regards to reentrancy attacks.

Related Work. Different variations of relative correctness have been studied extensively in the literature (even if 'relative correctness' is not regularly used as a term). In particular, assume-guarantee reasoning has been invented [7,10] to allow compositional verification of component based software. The approach typically taken is to specify functional-correctness properties by writing specifications that make explicit both the assumptions that the component can make about its environment, and the guarantees that it provides. In contrast, in our approach we talk about the *functional guarantees* made by a component, but against *non-functional assumptions* about other components. The use of such compositional verification for smart contracts has not, to our knowledge, been explored, despite the fact that smart contracts are typically multi-party systems. If one focuses on vulnerability due to reentrancy attacks, the literature is rife with techniques and tools to identify them e.g. [8,9,11]. However, all these techniques simply identify the possible reentrancy, and are not concerned with which parties may (or may not) initiate the according attack. Ironically, based on our experience in the sector, it is not uncommon that when faced with such a potential vulnerability, a domain expert may dismiss the concern due to the fact that the only party that can trigger the 'attack' is a trusted party, e.g., the sole owner of a wallet contract, or generally some party that has no interest in running the attack.

The paper is organised as follows. In Sect. 2 we provide the necessary background about smart contract programming and reentrancy required for the rest of the paper. In Sect. 3 we present previous work on proof rules for Solidity taking a best or worst case approach to reentrancy (i.e. either trusting everyone not to perform a reentrancy attack, or not trusting anyone). Based on this, in Sect. 4 we present a new proof rules parametrised by presumed party-benevolence, and we finally conclude in Sect. 6.

2   Smart Contracts, Solidity and Reentrancy

Agreements between autonomous agents identify obligations and rights of those agents. Automation of the actions regulated by the agreement partially addresses this concern, in that if actions (and the lack thereof) are enforced by the execution engine, the original agreement is guaranteed to be adhered to. We say that this only *partially* addresses the problem, since a party which can exercise control over the execution platform can still interfere with adherence to the contract. With the development of blockchain and other decentralised ledger technologies, the technology was adapted to provide trustless decentralised execution platforms on which smart contracts can be hosted. On public blockchains such as Ethereum [13], miners validate and carry out transactions initiated by users of the blockchain, recording them in a *block* in return for a mining reward. It is up to the other nodes on the network to ensure that only valid blocks are accepted. The initialisation and execution of smart contracts take the form of special transactions, also executed by a miner writing that transaction in a block, and checked to be a faithful execution by the others. However, unlike a transaction consisting solely of a transfer of funds, executing arbitrary code is not a constant cost operation. The solution typically used is to providing the miner with a reward proportionate to the cost of the computation. This is done by associating each virtual machine instruction with a number of *gas* units, and having the initiator of the call pay a fee to cover the gas required to execute the code. The miner takes funds to cover the total number of gas units consumed by the execution of the call. If the fee does not cover the whole call, it is reverted, but the miner still gets to keep the fee.

Solidity [6] is an imperative programming language (with a sprinkle of object-oriented features) designed and developed to write smart contracts, originally for the Ethereum [13] blockchain. A Solidity smart contract consists of a set of functions each of which can be invoked by parties through a blockchain transaction.

```
1 contract MultiWallet {
2     private mapping (address => uint) balances;
3
4     function depositTo(address receiver) payable public {
5         balances[receiver] += msg.value;
6     }
7
8     function withdraw(uint amount) public {
9         require (balances[msg.sender] >= amount);
10        msg.sender.transfer(amount);
11        balances[msg.sender] -= amount;
12    }
13 }
```

Listing 1. A multi-user wallet written in Solidity.

Listing 1 shows a simple multi-user wallet programmed as a smart contract, which allows multiple users to keep cryptocurrency (in the smart contract) and pay other parties (directly from the smart contract), with a separate account held per user. The state of the smart contract is a mapping from addresses of owners to balances—crypto value is represented as an unsigned integer in Solidity. Two functions are provided, depositTo() to allow depositing funds into an individual's account, and withdraw() to send funds from a user's account in that smart contract to their address on the blockchain.

At a glance, one may see no features distinguishing the language from the myriad of other imperative or object-oriented languages computer scientists are familiar with. There are, however, certain features which particularly characterise smart contract programming languages:

- Firstly, smart contracts typically handle cryptocurrency (or some form of digital assets), and programming languages for smart contracts provide native functionality to receive and send funds. It is worth noting that smart contracts can own cryptocurrency themselves, which is how the MultiWallet contract works. Any funds received are kept in the smart contract and any payment is done by sending funds from the smart contract to the recipient. Solidity provides a payable keyword to annotate functions, such as depositTo() which, when called, may also receive funds (unless a function is annotated to be payable, calls made to the function carrying funds would fail at runtime). For instance, depositTo() which is used to put crypto in a user's account, will update the mapping for the identified user by the amount of funds sent upon calling the function. Note that in Solidity, information about the call is stored in the msg structure which includes, amongst others, the field value which provides the amount of funds sent with the call. To send funds *out* of the smart contract, Solidity uses a method transfer() called on the recipient's address.

- The other feature of smart contracts is that they (usually) act as multi-party computation, and thus have an inherent notion of parties. On Ethereum, these parties are identified by their address which corresponds to where a smart contract is located, or to a personal address at which a user can accumulate and control funds. In the MultiWallet smart contract, the addresses are used as the key of the mapping to keep track how much of the funds kept in the smart contract are owned by each user.[3] They are also used in the require statement (in the withdraw() function), which checks that the caller of the function (identified by another field in the msg structure—msg.sender) has enough funds accumulated in the smart contract to send on.[4]

---

[3] Note that this allows both humans and other smart contracts to use this smart contract, the former through transactions and the latter through direct calls to the MultiWallet smart contract.

[4] If the condition appearing in the require statement is not satisfied, the whole computation is aborted and reverted, i.e., any changes to the state are reversed and only a record that a reverted call was made is kept on the blockchain.

We have kept this example simple in order to illustrate the language, but one could have additional logic, for instance releasing the funds only once a trusted third party has checked the identity of the sender or the receiver of the funds.

One distinguishing feature of how smart contracts on Ethereum, and indeed most other Distributed Ledger Technologies (DLTs), work is that a transaction is performed in isolation of others. In other words, if a user sends a transaction to `MultiWallet.depositTo()`, and another user sends one to `MultiWallet.withdraw()`, one of the two transactions is executed to completion before the other can be started. This ensures a degree of atomicity of computation in that function executions do not overlap. However, if a smart contract performs a call to another smart contract, that smart contract may call back the original smart contract, violating this illusion of atomicity. The original transaction will still have been executed to completion, but halfway through, the smart contract was reentered, thus executing another call, possibly even to the same function, within that transaction (on a different level of the call-stack). Such external calls thus require additional care in order to ensure smart contract correctness.

The snag is that when the `transfer` command is used to send funds to another smart contract, this performs an external call to the `receive()` function on the receiver's smart contract,[5] thus ceding control to the other party, who may call back the original smart contract. The simple and innocent-looking code shown in the `MultiWallet` smart contract, in fact, does not take this into account.

Consider a situation in which `depositTo()` is called with Alice's address, sending 1 Ether[6] in the process, and once again with Bob's address, also with 1 Ether. This results in the smart contract storing a total of 2 Ether with the table of balances showing that Alice and Bob own 1 Ether each. If `MultiWallet` is correct, neither Alice nor Bob should be able to use more than 1 Ether from the smart contract. Now consider a call to `withdraw(1 Ether)` coming from Bob's address. Since Bob's balance is 1 Ether, the `require` statement succeeds, allowing the transfer to be called. Recall that if Bob's address points at a smart contract, this is a call to the `transfer` function in that smart contract, which may, apart from receiving the funds, maliciously call `MutliWallet.withdraw(1 Ether)` again. Note that Bob's balance is still recorded as 1 Ether, thus allowing the sending of 1 more Ether to Bob. If Bob's transfer function now just accepts the funds, the calls terminate successfully with Bob having taken 2 Ether out of the `MultiWallet` smart contract, even though he owned only 1 Ether. This class of bugs, called *reentrancy bugs*, have been the cause of many high profile major cryptocurrency losses due to incorrect code, perhaps the most notorious being The DAO[7] hack [5].

---

[5] In older versions of Solidity, it was the (nameless) fallback function which was executed on the receiver side of a transfer.

[6] Ether is the unit of cryptocurrency on the Ethereum blockchain.

[7] *The DAO* was a smart contract implementing a venture capital fund in a decentralised manner (hence the name DAO referring to Decentralised Autonomous Organisation).

In this case (and as typically recommended in most Solidity developers' guidelines), one solution is to update the balance *before* the transfer is performed, thus avoiding reentrant calls abusing of the balance not yet being reduced. The following example shows that this rule-of-thumb is not a foolproof one.

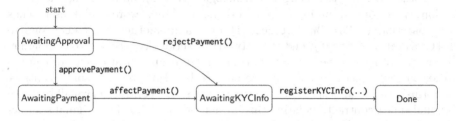

Fig. 1. Process flow of a one-shot KYC-approved transfer.

Example 1. Consider a smart contract to handle a one-shot payment which depends on an intermediary oracle to perform checks on the proposed receiver of the funds. In practice, such know-your-customer (KYC) checks are required for regulatory purposes, and this contract enables compliance to such requirements by having the sender identify a KYC oracle whose responsibility is to approve or reject the transfer based on background checks they may perform. In return, the oracle smart contract gets paid a commission. The abstract process flow of the smart contract is shown in Fig. 1.[8] The smart contract allows the processing of a single transaction, the details of which are assumed to be given in the constructor. Once initialised, the KYC oracle can approve and affect the payment (along the transitions labelled with calls to `approvePayment()` and `affectPayment()` in sequence), or reject it (along the transition labelled with `rejectPayment()`). Whether the oracle approves or rejects the transaction, they are then expected to register the KYC information (along the transition labelled `registerKYCInfo(..)`. These calls (and transitions) implicitly carry information and transfer of funds not shown in the diagram: (i) upon contract setup, the *sender* sends funds into the smart contract by calling the (payable) constructor, providing the *receiver*, the *intermediary* (the KYC checker), the amount to be paid to the receiver, and the amount due as commission to the intermediary; (ii) the intermediary can then approve (using `approvePayment()`) or reject (using `rejectPayment()`) the payment, getting half of their commission; (iii) in case of a rejection the sender gets their funds back immediately, whilst in the case of an approval, the receiver can then withdraw their funds using `affectPayment()`; (iv) at the end of the process, the intermediary can record (a hash of) the KYC information to prove that they really did perform background checks using `registerKYCInfo(..)` receiving the rest of their commission.[9] List-

---

[8] The full code of the smart contracts used in this paper can be found in the public repository https://github.com/gordonpace/reentrancy-bugs.

[9] In practice, we would also need functionality to deal with the case of the intermediary or the receiver not performing their part, introducing timeouts after which the other party can force the logic of the smart contract forward.

ing 2 shows select parts of the code. Note that in order to keep track of the state of the smart contract, a variable mode is used, ranging over an enumerated type. Also note the constructor which is called when the smart contract is set up.

The contract uses the generally accepted rule-of-thumb of performing transfer of funds at the end of functions, after all variables have been updated. So can anything go wrong due to reentrancy? Upon rejecting a payment using rejectPayment(), the intermediary and the sender receive some funds, but upon inspection, one can see that the intermediary can use the fact that the mode of the contract has already been updated, and when their transfer function is called, they immediately call registerKYCInfo(..) to steal *all* the remaining funds including those of the sender. Therefore, in this example, doing all assignments before the transfers does not prevent the possibility of a harmful reentrance attack!

```
1  contract KYCTransfer {
2    constructor (
3      address payable _receiver, uint _payment_amount,
4      address payable _intermediary, uint _commission_amount
5    ) payable { ... }
6
7    function approvePayment() public byIntermediary { ... }
8
9    function rejectPayment() public byIntermediary {
10     // Make sure that we are in the right mode and move
11     // on to the mode awaiting KYC information to be recorded
12     require (mode == Mode.AwaitingApproval);
13     mode = Mode.AwaitingKYCInfo;
14
15     // The intermediary gets 50% of their commission (rounded
16     // down if necessary)
17     intermediary.transfer(commission_amount / 2);
18
19     // The payer gets his money back
20     payer.transfer(payment_amount);
21   }
22
23   function affectPayment() public byReceiver { ... }
24
25   function registerKYCInfo(bytes32 _KYC_information) public byIntermediary {
26     // Check that the contract is in the right mode and move
27     // on to the final mode where no other action is possible
28     require (mode == Mode.AwaitingKYCInfo);
29     mode = Mode.Done;
30
31     ...
32     // Reset payment and commission amounts for safety
33     payment_amount = 0;
34     commission_amount = 0;
35
36     // Send the remaining commission funds to the intermediary
37     // (avoiding rounding calculations)
38     intermediary.transfer(address(this).balance);
39   }
40 }
```

Listing 2. Code of a smart contract implementing a one-shot KYC-approved transfer.

An interesting observation can be made here, one that is at the heart of this paper: from the point-of-view of the sender the contract is unsafe, but from the intermediary's point-of-view it can be considered safe. Obviously, it depends on what we mean by safe. In this case, we can specify an invariant which states what funds are expected to be sent and received to and from which party. For instance, one part of the invariant could be that the intermediary will never receive more funds than the amount specified in the constructor. Taking a worst-case scenario (i.e. allowing all parties to perform reentrant calls) this invariant does not hold, although it holds if we take a best-case scenario view (i.e. we assume that no party will perform reentrant calls). However, we can also look at what happens if we only assume that certain parties will not perform a reentrant call. If we only trust the intermediary not to perform such call (either because we are the intermediary or perhaps because the intermediary has too much at stake to perform such attacks), the invariant can be proved to hold no matter what other parties do. Trusting the sender and receiver not to perform reentrant calls, however, does not suffice to enable the invariant to be proved.

So Why Does It Really Matter? The root problem indicated by the above examples is that both the developer and the reader of a contract's implementation often focus on the main purpose of `transfer`, which is the passing of crypto funds to some receiver. They may not consider the possibility of the receiver calling back the sending contract during the execution of `transfer`.[10]

The fact that this feature led to a number of high-profile losses on Ethereum, resulted in a change in the way the blockchain execution engine handles smart contract fund transfers—there is a cap on the amount of gas which calls to `transfer` can use. The notion of *gas* as a resource to be paid for to execute code is the most common way through which public blockchains motivate miners (the nodes in the decentralised network which process transactions and record them on the blockchain) to execute and record execution of smart contract code. The execution of every operation of the (compiled) smart contract code uses gas, to be paid by the caller. Since many versions of the Ethereum protocol (the latest is called Arrow Glacier at the time of writing), the gas fee of `transfer` is lower than the fee of a call. Thereby, the gas passed to the receiver of `transfer` is not sufficient for the receiver to call any other contract. Any such call would result in the whole call reverting. In particular, this means that it cannot call back.

There are, however, various arguments why one still should consider potential callbacks during `transfer`. One is that the current protection against callbacks depends entirely on the fees for `transfer` and for calls. For instance, a well established Ethereum community blog [1], emphasises that gas fees can and will change, and that *"smart contracts should be robust to this fact"*. But even with stable gas fees, the concern would not go away. The `transfer` operation is actually only one way to pass crypto funds. Another is to explicitly use the `call` operation. For instance, instead of `c.transfer(1 Ether)`, one can write `c.call{value: 1 Ether}("")`. This passes the same 1 `Ether` to c, but with the difference that all remaining gas is passed on, which makes callbacks possible. Although less safe, this is widely used, even in the standard Solidity library collection *openzeppelin* (e.g., in `utils/Address.sol`). Moreover, a blog [1] from

---

[10] Some are even unaware that any code at all is executed on the receiver side during execution of `transfer`, in case the receiver is a contract address.

Consensys Diligence, an important player in the Ethereum community, heavily advocates the use `call` instead of `transfer`.[11]

Even if one trusts the call-back protection induced by the gas fee of `transfer`, one just has to replace every `transfer` in this paper by a `call`, and the callback protection is gone. The main reason why we use `transfer` in this paper rather than `call`, is one of simplicity of presentation.

Although we have focused on the reentrancy in smart contracts, we note that the problem is just one instance of a much more general issue. In all computational contexts where we have a multi-party code base, and where interacting parties may have potentially conflicting interests, there is the question of what can and cannot be assumed of other parties' behavior, and what the consequences of such assumptions are on the safety of one's own code.

3   Semantics of Solidity and Handling of Callbacks

There are many reasons why smart contracts are a killer application for formal verification [4]: potentially conflicting interests between participating parties, the immutable nature of the code, the handling of digital assets of value, etc. In [3], a program logic calculus was presented for a core fragment of Solidity. The calculus is implemented in the (currently prototypical) program verification system SolidiKeY, a version of the KeY system [2] dedicated to Solidity verification.

In this section, we will briefly present the calculus rules for `transfer` (with minor adaptions for presentation) in two different versions: (i) a version allowing for the possibility of callbacks during the call to `transfer`; and (ii) a version which assumes no such callbacks. In the previous work [3], the two rules served as a means of performing a best case or worst case scenario verification. Such an upfront decision can be motivated by technical arguments (like the aforementioned gas fees) or as a choice between trusting *everyone*, or *no one* to not call back during a transfer. We will use this as a baseline on which we will later on build rules for handling presumption of *selective* benevolence in later sections.

The KeY approach is based on *dynamic logic* (DL), an extension of first-order logic (FOL) by a *multi-modality* that is parameterised by programs. DL formulae are defined inductively, with FOL connectives as the base forms. The additional form in DL is the *box* modality: $[\pi]$post, which takes a program π (in our context Solidity code), and another DL formula post. The formula means: *if* π terminates successfully (i.e., it does not revert), then the property post holds in the reached final state. Due to this inductive definition, DL formulas are closed under the usual propositional and first-order connectives. A frequently encountered DL formula pattern using these operators is pre $\rightarrow$ $[\pi]$post, which corresponds to the Hoare triple: {pre}π{post}. DL formulas are evaluated in

---

[11] The rationale behind their advice is that by not having the safety net of a gas limit, developers are bound to design smart contracts more carefully. The authors disagree. This is akin to saying that one should not wear a helmet on a motorbike, because that would mean that you will drive more carefully.

states, which are essentially a mapping from program variables to values. A DL formula is valid if it evaluates to true in all states.

In KeY, DL is further extended with *updates* for symbolic execution. An update $v_1 := t_1 \parallel \ldots \parallel v_n := t_n$ consists of program variables $v_1, \ldots, v_n$ and terms $t_1, \ldots, t_n$ (where n can be 1), and represents a state change in the form of explicit substitutions. If u is an update and ϕ is a DL formula, then $\{u\}\phi$ is also a DL formula, with $\{v_1 := t_1 \parallel \ldots \parallel v_n := t_n\}\phi$ evaluated in state s being equivalent to ϕ evaluated in a state s', where s' coincides with s except that each v_i is mapped to the value of t_i in s. In a proof construction, a DL formula of the form $\{u\}[\pi]$post represents the status of symbolic execution where the a prefix of a program (path) has already been turned into update u, and the remaining program π is still to be executed (symbolically). At intermediate proof steps, we can have DL formulae with nested updates like in $\{u_1\}\{u_2\}[\pi]$post, which will be merged to a single update by further proof steps. See [2,3] for details.

To reason about the validity of formulae, we use a *sequent calculus*, which we present here in a simplified fashion. A *sequent* $\phi_1, \ldots, \phi_n \Longrightarrow \psi$ has a set of formulas $\phi_1, \ldots, \phi_n$ on the left and a single formula ψ on the right[12] and whose meaning is equivalent to $(\bigwedge_{i=1..n} \phi_i) \to \psi$. Calculus rules are denoted as rule schemata of the form:

$$
\text{name} \quad
\overbrace{\Gamma_1 \Longrightarrow \phi_1 \quad \ldots \quad \Gamma_n \Longrightarrow \phi_n}^{premises}
$$
$$
\underbrace{\Gamma \Longrightarrow \phi}_{conclusion}
$$

where $\Gamma, \Gamma_i, \phi, \phi_i$ denote sets of formulas or just formulas, respectively.

Since one important feature of smart contracts is that they can receive, store and send crypto assets, in specifications and proofs it is frequently required to express properties about the asset flow. In order to do so, Solidity DL as presented in [3] has the notion of financial *net*—the difference between incoming and outgoing payments which a contract has with another address. Solidity DL uses the built-in function net : address $\to \mathbb{Z}$ to keep track of the asset flow between this contract and other addresses, with:

$$\text{net}(a) = \text{money received from } a - \text{money sent to } a$$

The verification methodology is based on contract invariants relating the external flow of money with the persistent internal data of the contract (which we call *storage*). These contract invariants are expected to hold whenever control is outside the contract. For instance, in the setting of an auction contract where every user can make bids, increase bids, and withdraw bids, the contract invariant I may look something like:

$$I \quad \equiv \quad \forall a \in \text{address. } \text{bids}[a] = \text{net}(a)$$

---

[12] The implemented calculus allows for more than one formula on the right-hand side of a sequent, but here we limit ourselves to one formula for simplicity of presentation.

This invariant states that bids is a mapping with the current effective bid of an address a, equivalent to the financial net of the contract with address a.

With this notation, we are now in a position to present the proof rules for the symbolic execution of the transfer function in the code of the sending contract.

Rule for transfer with Callback. We start by looking at the version which allows for callback, making no assumption about the receiving contract. Since the transfer may result in callbacks, we must ensure that the smart contract invariant holds before the transfer is made in order to ensure that any callback will find that the invariant holds, and thus also allows us to assume that the invariant will still hold when control is returned after the transfer:

transfer (with callback)

$$\frac{\Gamma, \mathsf{c} \neq \mathsf{this} \implies \{u\}\{\mathsf{net}(\mathsf{c}) := \mathsf{net}(\mathsf{c}) - \mathsf{v}\}I \qquad \Gamma, \mathsf{c} \neq \mathsf{this} \implies \{u\}\{\mathsf{storage} := st \parallel \mathsf{net} := n\}(I \to [\omega]\phi)}{\Gamma, \mathsf{c} \neq \mathsf{this} \implies \{u\}[\mathsf{c}.\mathsf{transfer}(\mathsf{v}); \omega]\phi}$$

The rule handles a transfer to the destination address c other than this same contract this, and allows us to reach a conclusion that ϕ will hold after executing c.transfer(v);ω, if we start with u as the result of symbolic execution so far. The rule splits the proof into two branches establishing that: (i) after sending the requested amount to c (i.e., after subtracting v from the financial net this contract has with c), invariant I of contract this holds, thus ensuring that the contract is in a consistent state when control is handed over to c; and (ii) if the invariant holds, but making no assumption about the storage and net variables[13] (since callbacks may have changed these values in the meantime), then executing ω will ensure that ϕ will hold upon termination.

Rule for transfer Without Callback. For the second version of the rule, which assumes that the receiver of the transfer will not perform a callback, we know that this contract will not be accessed and therefore we need not prove the invariant but simply that ϕ will finally hold. This makes the rule substantially simpler:

transfer (without callback)

$$\frac{\Gamma, \mathsf{c} \neq \mathsf{this} \implies \{u\}\{\mathsf{net}(\mathsf{c}) := \mathsf{net}(\mathsf{c}) - \mathsf{v}\}[\omega]\phi}{\Gamma, \mathsf{c} \neq \mathsf{this} \implies \{u\}[\mathsf{c}.\mathsf{transfer}(\mathsf{v}); \omega]\phi}$$

In this case, we simply need to prove that, after updating the net of the receiving address, executing ω to completion will ensure that ϕ holds at the end.

In SolidiKeY, the user can configure which rule to use for a proof as a whole, thus deciding *upfront* to either allow potential callbacks from *all* contracts (with callback), or from *none* (without callback). Examples which were verified using either of the rule settings are discussed in [3].

---

[13] The variable storage and the mapping net are assigned newly generated constants st and n, about which no knowledge can be inferred. After that update, the invariant I is assumed, meaning the invariant is all we know about storage and net when continuing symbolic execution of ω.

4   Presumption of Benevolence

The original motivation for having two different rules was to allow the user of SolidiKeY control whether to trust gas fee-based callback prevention. However, as we have already discussed, the choice can also be made with regards to assumptions about the benevolence of certain parties, where benevolence of a receiver c of a transfer c.transfer(v) is taken to mean that c will not call back into the sender (directly or indirectly) during execution of the transfer.

Presumption of benevolence can be either *static*, where a fixed set of addresses are presumed to be consistently benevolent, or *dynamic*, where the addresses to be trusted is determined at runtime and may change throughout the execution. In all cases, the specification has to clearly state the assumption under which a property is expected to hold, hence giving rise to different guarantees under different assumptions.

4.1   Presuming Benevolence of Oneself

When a smart contract provides a service which a user may want to access, and with no knowledge about other parties involved in the contract, one may try to prove correctness of a specification using a worst case scenario, in which we allow any transfer to perform callbacks. However, although a particular user may not be able to make any assumption about the behaviour of others, they can make them of themselves (or of a smart contract they control). If it is in the user's interest that the smart contract works as per the given specification, they can attempt to prove correctness by assuming no callbacks from transfers to their address—effectively presuming benevolence of themselves.

The following proof rule allows for the differential treatment between a trusted address s (oneself) and that of others:

transferBenevolentOneself

$$\frac{\begin{array}{l} \Gamma, \mathsf{c} \neq \mathtt{this}, \mathsf{c} = s \Longrightarrow \{u\}\{\mathsf{net}(\mathsf{c}) := \mathsf{net}(\mathsf{c}) - \mathsf{v}\}[\omega]\phi \\ \Gamma, \mathsf{c} \neq \mathtt{this}, \mathsf{c} \neq s \Longrightarrow \{u\}\{\mathsf{net}(\mathsf{c}) := \mathsf{net}(\mathsf{c}) - \mathsf{v}\}I \\ \Gamma, \mathsf{c} \neq \mathtt{this}, \mathsf{c} \neq s \Longrightarrow \{u\}\{\mathsf{storage} := st \parallel \mathsf{net} := n\}(I \rightarrow [\omega]\phi) \end{array}}{\Gamma, \mathsf{c} \neq \mathtt{this} \Longrightarrow \{u\}[\mathsf{c}.\mathtt{transfer(v)}; \omega]\phi}$$

The rule effectively combines the two rules given in Sect. 3, branching over whether the receiver's address is the trusted caller i.e. $\mathsf{c} = s$—if it is, the premise from the no-callback rule applies[14] (appearing as the first antecedent of the rule above), and if not, the two premises of the possible-callback rule apply (appearing as the second and third antecedents in the rule above).

Assuming benevolence of oneself, whoever the caller of a function, we only rely on the fact that if a transfer is made to the trusted address s, there will be no callback into the contract, and symbolic execution proceeds accordingly, with no need to show the invariant at that moment.

---

[14] By 'premise applies', we mean that the branches produced by the other premises close trivially, as their left sides are false.

4.2   Presuming Benevolence of a Static Group

As a generalisation of this rule, it may be reasonable to presume benevolence of several parties. For instance, when buying a house together with your siblings, you may choose to trust the behaviour of yourself and your siblings, but not that of the ones selling the house or that of the estate agent. This is an example of a statically determined trusted group and can be encoded as the following rule:

transferBenevolent(S)
$$\frac{\begin{array}{l} \Gamma, \mathtt{c} \neq \mathtt{this}, \mathtt{c} \in S \Longrightarrow \{u\}\{\mathtt{net(c)} := \mathtt{net(c)} - \mathtt{v}\}[\omega]\phi \\ \Gamma, \mathtt{c} \neq \mathtt{this}, \mathtt{c} \notin S \Longrightarrow \{u\}\{\mathtt{net(c)} := \mathtt{net(c)} - \mathtt{v}\}I \\ \Gamma, \mathtt{c} \neq \mathtt{this}, \mathtt{c} \notin S \Longrightarrow \{u\}\{\mathtt{storage} := st \parallel \mathtt{net} := n\}(I \to [\omega]\phi) \end{array}}{\Gamma, \mathtt{c} \neq \mathtt{this} \Longrightarrow \{u\}[\mathtt{c.transfer(v)}; \omega]\phi}$$

The rule is almost identical to the previous one, but trusts a receiver if they appear in a (constant) set S i.e. $\mathtt{c} \in S$.

4.3   Presuming Benevolence of a Dynamic Group

The two rules we have just seen require the parties to be trusted to be decided statically a priori, and remain unchanged throughout the execution of the smart contract. In practice, this may be too much of a constraint. For instance, one may want to trust a party which is only known at runtime or which may change e.g. in an auction smart contract, one may trust that the current top bidder has no interest in breaking the smart contract's invariant, but the top bidder is not known before the smart contract starts executing, nor does it remain constant throughout the execution.

If we use a predicate **ben** to characterise which addresses are trusted at any point during execution i.e. an address $\mathtt{c}$ is trusted if $\mathtt{ben(c)}$, we can encode such dynamic presumed benevolence using the following rule:

transferBenevolencePredicate
$$\frac{\Gamma, \mathtt{c} \neq \mathtt{this} \\ \Longrightarrow \\ \{u\} \left(\begin{array}{l} \mathtt{ben(c)} \to \{\mathtt{net(c)} := \mathtt{net(c)} - \mathtt{v}\}[\omega]\phi \\ \wedge \neg\mathtt{ben(c)} \to \{\mathtt{net(c)} := \mathtt{net(c)} - \mathtt{v}\}I \\ \wedge \neg\mathtt{ben(c)} \to \{\mathtt{storage} := st \parallel \mathtt{net} := n\}(I \to [\omega]\phi) \end{array} \right)}{\Gamma, \mathtt{c} \neq \mathtt{this} \Longrightarrow \{u\}[\mathtt{c.transfer(v)}; \omega]\phi}$$

Compared to the earlier rules, this one makes a case distinction over the predicate **ben**, which may depend on the state. Thereby, the set of trusted parties is not statically fixed. The rule thus has only one premise, meaning it does not cause an immediate branching of the proof since the code which was (symbolically) executed before the transfer, and which is captured in the update u, can potentially influence the validity of $\mathtt{ben(c)}$. The rule will still, indirectly, cause a branching of the proof, which is however delayed to after applying u to the conjunction in further proof steps.

The predicate **ben** will be defined in the specification of the contract. For instance, the contract at hand may have a mapping `trustworthy` from addresses to **bool** to indicate which parties may be trusted. The specification of the contract could define **ben** as follows:

$$\text{ben}(a) \ \equiv \ (\text{trustworthy}[a] = \text{true})$$

As another example, one may trust all addresses which have invested more than 2 Ether into the contract, in which case **ben** would be defined as follows:

$$\text{ben}(a) \ \equiv \ (\text{net}(a) \ \text{>=} \ 2 \ \text{ether})$$

As a final example, we may return to trusting the current top bidder in an auction smart contract by defining **ben** to be:

$$\text{ben}(a) \ \equiv \ (a = \text{top\_bidder})$$

5   Collaborative Malicious Behaviour

One important property of these semantics is that they are monotonic under presumed benevolence. In other words, an invariant which can be proved when trusting a set of parties would still hold if we trust even more parties. For instance, if we write $C \vdash_B I$ to indicate that smart contract C satisfies invariant I if parties B are presumed to be benevolent, we should be able to show that:

> *Program invariants are monotonic with respect to the set of presumed benevolent parties. Given sets of parties B and B', smart contract C and invariant I, if $B \subseteq B'$ and $C \vdash_B I$, then it follows that $C \vdash_{B'} I$.*

A natural question is whether we can also use proofs with different sets of parties to require trust in less parties. For instance, if we know that $C \vdash_{B_1} I$ and that $C \vdash_{B_2} I$, can we argue that we do not need to presume benevolence of $B_1 \setminus B_2$ since they are not presumed to be benevolent in the second assumption, nor that of $B_2 \setminus B_1$ since they are not presumed to be benevolent in the first assumption. In other words, does it follow that $C \vdash_{B_1 \cap B_2} I$? We show that this is not the case by counter-example, showing a system and an invariant which holds if we presume benevolence either of party p_1 or of party p_2. However, we show that the invariant will not hold if we cannot presume benevolence of anyone i.e. $\{p_1\} \cap \{p_2\}$.

Example 2. Consider a two-party token system, in which token ownership by one party indicates certain rights of that party, impinging on the other party e.g. use of a single parking space exclusive to the two parties. An implementation of this as a smart contract is shown in Listing 3, and cycles across three phases (i) the first in which anyone may load the smart contract with funds using `loadAndLaunchTokens()` (e.g. the funds could be jointly contributed to by the two parties, or by their employer); (ii) the second phase in which the parties may acquire the tokens using `acquireToken1()` and `acquireToken2()`, and implemented in such a manner that whenever one party takes a token, the other is compensated in funds; (iii) the third phase in which owners may use the tokens.

```
1   contract TwoUtilityToken {
2       /*@ contract_invariant
3           !(tokens_owned1 == 2 && tokens_owned2 == 2) &&
4           tokens_owned1 <= 2 && tokens_owned2 <= 2
5       */
6       ...
7
8       function loadAndLaunchTokens() public payable { ... }
9
10      function acquireToken1() public {
11          // Only user1 may invoke this
12          require (msg.sender == user1);
13          // The contract must be in token acquisition mode
14          require (mode == Mode.TokenAcquisition);
15
16          // User 1 acquires one token
17          tokens_owned1++;
18          // Pay user 2 compensation
19          user2.transfer(1 ether);
20
21          // Move on to the token usage mode if enough tokens have been acquired
22          if (tokens_owned1 + tokens_owned2 >= 2)
23              mode = Mode.TokenUsage;
24      }
25
26      function acquireToken2() public { ... }
27
28      function useToken() public { ... }
29  }
```

Listing 3. Code of a two user utility token.

The smart contract invariant will ensure that the supply of tokens is limited—it will never be the case that any one of the users owns more than two tokens, or that both users own two tokens each. The implementation takes a safer route, and switches to token usage mode (phase 3) as soon as the sum of tokens owned reaches two as can be seen in the code shown for function `acquireToken1()`. It is worth noting that the state of the smart contract is encoded in the variable `mode`, which is updated at the *end* of `acquireToken1()` i.e. after transferring funds, because of reentrancy. Since control is temporarily given to user 2 during the transfer of funds, if we would have already updated the mode, that party would have the opportunity to use any token they own *before* user 1 can, thus giving them an undesirable advantage.

The question is whether anything can go wrong. Verifying the invariant using the no-reentrancy semantics allows us to prove that the contract is safe, indicating that if anything can go wrong, it would have do so due to reentrancy. The invariant can also be proved if we assume that the first user will not attempt reentrancy, and similarly for the second party. Good, both primary stakeholders have the power to ensure that the smart contract does not violate the invariant. But does that suffice? Consider the following execution pattern: (i) user 1 acquires one token using `acquireToken1()`; (ii) user 1 calls `acquireToken1()` again to acquire a second token, but when user 2 is given control through the call to transfer (on line 19), (iii) user 2 calls acquireToken2()[15] to (hurriedly) acquire a token, but as user 1 gains control when their compensation is being transferred, (iv) user 1 will call acquireToken1() again. Since the mode is only changed at the *end* of the functions,[16] all tokens will be successfully acquired, resulting in user 1 owning 1 token, and user 2 owning 3 tokens, thus violating the invariant. Furthermore, if gas were not a concern, the two parties can nest this attack to any depth, acquiring even more tokens.

Verifying the smart contract allowing both parties to use reentrancy would, in fact, identify this vulnerability. But is the contract safe to use if violation can only occur through collaboration? It largely depends on other parties involved in the contract. If a third party e.g. the employer of the two users is the one loading the smart contract with funds to pay compensation, then the parties might collaborate together to take more funds than originally envisaged. However, if the parties are the only ones involved (they are also the ones who would load funds into the smart contract), then the contract is safe in that either party can play clean to ensure that the invariant is not violated. This illustrates an interesting game theoretic situation in which we would be able to reason about conditional contract safety with respect to an invariant as long as we have a notion of user benefits and gains.

6   Conclusions

We have looked at a particularly thorny issue of reentrancy in smart contracts— a vulnerability that has led to huge financial losses in the past few years. In fact, the problem is a much more general one, that of reasoning about systems which perform synchronous external calls and may thus have to handle callbacks when ceding control to these other parties. Typically, such systems are designed with their specifications holding only when they can trust certain other parties never to perform such callbacks, which raises the issue of how to deal with specifications whose correctness may be conditional on other parties. In a way, it is a problem akin to assume-guarantee, but with the assumptions being non-functional ones i.e. not about what properties hold of the results that the external party will give us, but rather about how that party will compute that result. Combining such functional and non-functional aspects of a specification in order to enable formal proof is not straightforward, as we have seen in this paper.

One aspect of smart contracts which we have alluded to multiple times in this paper is that of parties' interest. Since smart contracts explicitly encode the notion of parties and of digital asset migration, one can typically encode some form of utilitarian interpretation to a particular smart contract state change being to the benefit of a particular party but possibly not to that of another. Such an interpretation would allow for economics-based reasoning of whether

---

[15] The code of acquireToken2() is identical to acquireToken1() but with the parties switched.

[16] As already discussed, moving it forward in the code will open another vulnerability.

a particular party stands to gain or lose from a callback. This would enable a more refined version of callback-freedom semantic analysis: assuming rational agents, and thus that a party would never engage in callbacks if they stand to lose if they do so, does a smart contract satisfy a particular specification under such an assumption? The notion of a party's interest in a contract is not always straightforward to encode (e.g. is the value of gaining 10 tokens alone any different from that of yourself and another party gaining 10 tokens each?) and we leave this as future work.

References

1. Consensys Diligence: Stop Using Solidity's transfer() Now. https://consensys.net/diligence/blog/2019/09/stop-using-soliditys-transfer-now/
2. Ahrendt, W., Beckert, B., Bubel, R., Hähnle, R., Schmitt, P.H., Ulbrich, M. (eds.): Deductive Software Verification - The KeY Book. From Theory to Practice, vol. 10001. Springer, Cham (2016). https://doi.org/10.1007/978-3-319-49812-6
3. Ahrendt, W., Bubel, R.: Functional verification of smart contracts via strong data integrity. In: Margaria, T., Steffen, B. (eds.) ISoLA 2020. LNCS, vol. 12478, pp. 9–24. Springer, Cham (2020). https://doi.org/10.1007/978-3-030-61467-6_2
4. Ahrendt, W., Pace, G.J., Schneider, G.: Smart contracts: a killer application for deductive source code verification. In: Principled Software Development, pp. 1–18. Springer, Cham (2018). https://doi.org/10.1007/978-3-319-98047-8_1
5. Atzei, N., Bartoletti, M., Cimoli, T.: A survey of attacks on Ethereum smart contracts (SoK). In: Maffei, M., Ryan, M. (eds.) POST 2017. LNCS, vol. 10204, pp. 164–186. Springer, Heidelberg (2017). https://doi.org/10.1007/978-3-662-54455-6_8
6. Ethereum: Solidity. Online Documentation (2016). https://solidity.readthedocs.io/en/develop/introduction-to-smart-contracts.html
7. Jones, C.B.: Development methods for computer programs including a notion of interference. Ph.D. thesis, Oxford University, UK (1981)
8. Li, B., Pan, Z., Hu, T.: Redefender: detecting reentrancy vulnerabilities in smart contracts automatically. IEEE Trans. Reliab. **71**(2), 984–999 (2022). https://doi.org/10.1109/TR.2022.3161634
9. Liu, C., Liu, H., Cao, Z., Chen, Z., Chen, B., Roscoe, B.: Reguard: finding reentrancy bugs in smart contracts. In: 2018 IEEE/ACM 40th International Conference on Software Engineering: Companion (ICSE-Companion), pp. 65–68 (2018)
10. Misra, J., Chandy, K.: Proofs of networks and processes. IEEE Trans. Softw. Eng. **7**(7), 417–426 (1981)
11. Mueller, B.: Smashing Ethereum smart contracts for fun and real profit. In: HITB SECCONF Amsterdam (2018)
12. Nakamoto, S.: Bitcoin: a peer-to-peer electronic cash system. White Paper (2009). https://bitcoin.org/bitcoin.pdf
13. Wood, G., et al.: Ethereum: a secure decentralised generalised transaction ledger. Ethereum Project Yellow Paper **151**(2014), 1–32 (2014)

On the Pragmatics of Moving from System Models to Program Contracts

Thomas Santen[✉]

Formal Assurance, Aachen, Germany
santen@formalassurance.com
http://www.formalassurance.com

Abstract. Consider a software development process supported by Formal Methods that includes an abstract system model and contract-based program verification. Relative to the total size of the formal system model and the information captured in program contracts, the interface between those two levels of abstraction is relatively small. This encourages a clear separation of concerns between the two and a well-structured transition from system model to program contracts even if they are expressed in different formalisms. The paper discusses the implications of such a development process, and illustrates it by way of the Hagrid key server, with Alloy as a system modeling language and VCC's annotated C as a contract language.

Keywords: Formal modeling · Program contracts · Program verification

1 Introduction

The transition from a formal model describing the data and behavior of a system independently of a particular implementation structure to a contract-based specification, including pre- and postconditions and data invariants of actual program code, is a crucial step in a software development process that is supported by Formal Methods. Informed by customer projects, this paper provides a pragmatic view on some challenges in that transition and promising ways to address them. It is guided by the following observations:

Formal modeling and specification languages, and their supporting tools, are usually designed to address a certain goal at a certain level of abstraction, such as verifying crucial properties of the information processed in a system or the protocols used to communicate with the system environment. While specification languages may provide features to express different views of the system, e.g., data and behavior, the levels of abstraction that they can most adequately capture are usually limited. For example, a system modeling language will not provide native features to talk about the program heap, whereas it may be necessary

© The Author(s), under exclusive license to Springer Nature Switzerland AG 2022
T. Margaria and B. Steffen (Eds.): ISoLA 2022, LNCS 13701, pp. 124–138, 2022.
https://doi.org/10.1007/978-3-031-19849-6_8

to address properties of the heap in program contracts. Attempting to bridge a broader range of abstractions within a single language may be possible but often leads to unnecessarily complex specifications that are hard to comprehend and maintain, and push support tools to their limits. For example, a system modeling language will not provide native features to talk about the program heap, whereas it may be necessary to address properties of the heap in program contracts.

Transitioning from one language to another that describes the aspects of the system at a significantly different level of abstraction offers the opportunity to establish a clear separation of concerns between the different system specifications. While a contract-based specification will necessarily rephrase some of the information contained in an abstract system model, it will augment that information in the contracts with other information that specifically relates to the code in a particular programming language with a specific execution and memory model, such as aliasing of data, framing of changes to memory, or controlling access to specific chunks of memory. Devising contracts with special attention to that additional information provides structure and guidance to the development process.

In the development of a larger system, not all developer roles have access to all development artifacts, in particular if different organizations are involved. For example, the team constructing a formal model of the system under development to obtain a Common Criteria EAL-6 certification [5] needs to understand the (informal) specification of the system but will not necessarily have access to the actual implementation. A set of Formal Methods to be applied in a development process with limited sharing of artifacts must be chosen carefully to support such an access control regime.

These observations suggest a development process that clearly distinguishes a system modeling activity from a software design and implementation activity, in which both activities are supported by specific Formal Methods. In this process, system modeling produces a formal description of the system to be built and its operations. Software design and implementation produce contract-based specifications of system interface operations and abstract data structures, as a basis for further implementation steps producing executable code. Large parts of these activities will be conducted by developers because they require human creativity. Automated tools may be used to verify desired properties of the system model or the software contracts. They may also help to keep the system model and the software contracts consistent.

The transition from a system model to contracts consists of three major tasks: first, an initial step preparing the actual translation; second, the translation of the relevant parts of the system model to partial contracts; and third, the augmentation of the contracts with assertions specific to the targeted programming model and language.

It turns out that the link between the system model and the contract-based specification is smaller than one might expect. A considerable part of the system model does not contribute information to construct software contracts, while that information is by no means sufficient to construct a complete contract-based specification at the code level.

This setting also suggests that heterogeneous specifications in different specification languages can strongly support a clear separation of concerns in a formal development process and, in particular, provide structure to the transition from implementation-independent system models to contract-based specifications of code.

To illustrate the impact of those observations, the following presentation uses Alloy [9] in its latest Version 6 [1] as a system modeling language, and annotated C as used by VCC [4] as the contract language. The VerifyThis long term challenge Hagrid [8] provides a running example.

Section 2 introduces the running example. Section 3 sketches an Alloy model and some critical system-level properties that can be verified with the Alloy analyzer. Different aspects of the transition from Alloy to annotated C are described in Sect. 4. Generalizing the technical considerations of the previous sections, the final Sect. 5 reviews the pragmatics of applying Formal Methods in real-life customer projects and suggests some directions of future research.

2   The PGP Server Hagrid

The VerifyThis long term challenge of a PGP key server [8] is inspired by the actual PGP key server implementation *Hagrid* [7], which is running on https://keys.openpgp.org/. The functionality of the key server presented here is simplified for illustration purposes. It is not intended to be a basis for a practically useful system.

The Hagrid system consists of three major components. First, the frontend *server* provides a number of operations, which in a real system would be presented through a web server. Second, the *key database* stores PGP keys indexed by email addresses. Third, the *mailer* sends confirmation codes to user email addresses.

The key server system provides the following operations:

$get(e)$ returns the key k that is associated with the email address e, if any.

$add(e, k)$ requests the server to associate the key k with the email address e. The server keeps this request in a set of pending requests and produces a unique confirmation code c, which is forwarded to the mailer to send it to the email address e.

$del(e, k)$ requests the server to delete the key k that is supposed to be associated with the email address e. If k is indeed associated with e, the server keeps the deletion request in a set of pending requests and produces a unique confirmation code c, which is forwarded to the mailer to send it to the email address e.

$addConf(c)$ confirms a previous add request for the confirmation code c, if such a request is pending. Then, the pair (e, k) associated with c is added to the key database and the operation returns success. Otherwise, the operation returns a failure result and the key database remains unchanged.

Listing 1. Alloy signature *Server*

```
1   abstract sig Server {
2     mail : Mailer,
3     var kdb : set DBEntry,
4     var addReq : set Request,
5     var delReq : set Request,
6     var used : set ConfCode
7   }{
8     // active ConfCodes have not been used before
9     let active = (addReq + delReq).rc | {
10      no (active & used)
11    }
12    // delete requests refer to existing db entries
13    delReq.rdb in kdb
14    // requests respect ConfCode types
15    addReq.rc in AddConfCode
16    delReq.rc in DelConfCode
17  }
18  abstract sig ConfCode {}
19  sig AddConfCode, DelConfCode extends ConfCode {}
```

$delConf(c)$ confirms a previous deletion request for the confirmation code c, if such a request is pending. Then, the pair (e, k) associated with c is removed from the key database and the operation returns success. Otherwise, the operation returns with a failure result and the key database remains unchanged.

Both, *add* and *del* re-send a previously generated confirmation code if they are called with parameters for which a request is pending.

3   The Alloy Model

Alloy [9] is a temporal first-order relational logic. The Alloy analyzer uses the Kodkod relational model finder and a number of SAT solvers to explore Alloy models and verify assertions about them. The latest Version 6 of the Alloy language and analyzer [1] comes with new features allowing one to specify and assess behavioral models natively. It allows one to mark the mutable parts of a system state, specify the transition relation, and assert temporal properties of the resulting set of system traces. In addition to checking bounded traces with SAT solving, standard model checkers like NuSMV can be used to verify temporal properties for unbounded traces.

Listing 1 shows the Alloy signature Server describing the state of the Hagrid server. The mailer mail is used to send confirmation messages. The key database kdb is modeled as a set of database entries DBEntry, which in turn contain keys and associated email addresses (not shown in the listing). Similarly, the sets addReq and delReq model the pending add or delete requests, respectively.

Listing 2. Transition predicate for *add*

```
1  pred add [ s : Server , e : Email , k : Key , c" : ConfCode ]{
2    c" in AddConfCode
3    some req : Request | {
4      req.rdb.ek = k
5      req.rdb.ee = e
6      req.rc = c"
7      { // re-issue same request
8          req in s.addReq
9      } || {
10         // issue new request
11         req.rc !in s.addReq.rc + s.delReq.rc + s.used
12     }
13     // update server
14     s.addReq' = s.addReq + req
15   }
16   sendConfirmation[s.mail,e,c"]
17   // framing
18   s.kdb' = s.kdb
19   s.delReq' = s.delReq
20   s.used' = s.used                                        }
```

The field rc of a Request holds the confirmation code issued for that request. Lines 15 and 16 require that rc is a member of the signatures AddConfCode or DelConfCode, respectively, which partition the abstract signature ConfCode. The set used of confirmation codes keeps track of the confirmation codes that the server has previously used. The keyword **var**, newly introduced in Alloy 6, declares all fields of Server except mail to be mutable in a state transition.

The signature invariants of Server show the elegance of the relational calculus in Alloy. The expression defining the set of active requests in Line 9 of Listing 1 projects the union of addReq and delReq to the field rc of Request, which is the confirmation code associated with a request. Thus, active is the set of confirmation codes used in pending requests.

The Hagrid operations are modeled as transition predicates in Alloy. For example, the predicate add in Listing 2 requires that there exists a request req for the given email address e and key k that is either in the set of pending add requests or uses a fresh confirmation code c". We use the convention to mark "output" parameters of transition predicates by double quotation marks, so c" is supposed to be an output of add.

The equality s.addReq' = s.addReq + req in Line 14 of Listing 2 describes the state change of the server s. In Alloy 6, the "primed" field name s.addReq' denotes the value of that field in the post state of the transition. Similarly, Lines 18 to 20 state that the other mutable components of s remain unchanged. The predicate sendConfirmation models the mailer operation that enqueues a message containing a confirmation code to be sent to the given email address.

Listing 3. Transition predicate for *addConf*

```
1   pred addConf [ s : Server , c : ConfCode , r" : Result ]{
2     c in AddConfCode
3     some req : s.addReq | {
4       req.rc = c
5       r" = Success
6       s.kdb' = s.kdb + req.rdb
7       s.addReq' = s.addReq - req
8       s.delReq' = s.delReq
9       s.used' = s.used + req.rc
10    } || {
11      c !in s.addReq.rc
12      r" = Fail
13      frameServer[s]
14    }
15    frameMailer[s.mail]                                    }
```

The other operations of the Hagrid system are modeled as transition predicates in a similar way, e.g., Listing 3 shows the one for *addConf*. The predicate initSystem describes the valid initial system configurations. The transition relation systemStep of the Hagrid system is an existentially closed disjunction of the operation transition predicates. Thus, the axiom initSystem && **always** systemStep requires the model to exhibit all valid traces of the system.

Alloy has been designed to allow for easy validation of the specified system behavior and assessment of critical system requirements. Alloy **run** commands allow one to explore system behavior by incremental model finding. For scenarios of limited size, the visualizer is a valuable tool to inspect system traces graphically, e.g., to validate how the system processes a pending *add* request. For more complex scenarios, query evaluation on the generated models often provides insight into possible defects of the model. Inspecting specific system traces in this way is a good means to validate an Alloy specification against informal requirements.

Critical system requirements can be formalized as assertions and then verified either for bounded traces using the SAT solvers that come with the Alloy analyzer or with a standard model checker like NuSMV for unbounded traces. An example is the assertion in Listing 4. It states that *addConf* can only be successful for a confirmation code that has resulted from a previous *add*, i.e., if *addConf* returns *Success* for some confirmation code *c*, then *c* was generated by an *add* operation in some previous state and has been in the set of confirmation codes of pending add requests in all states since the *add* operation was performed.

Interestingly, the mailer need not send a confirmation code for a pending request before *addConf* can be successful, because the environment could just guess the right confirmation code. An attempt to check the corresponding assertion produces a concise counterexample illustrating such a situation.

Listing 4. Temporal assertion relating *add* and *addConf*

```
assert  addConfOnlyAfterAdd {
  all  c :  ConfCode |
    always (
      addConf[System.s,c,Success]
      implies
        c in  System.s.addReq.rc
        since
        some e :  Email, k :  Key |  add[System.s,e,k,c]) }
```

4   From Alloy to VCC Contracts

When proceeding from a system model like the one presented in Sect. 3 to a piece of executable code that is specified by contracts, a number of design decisions need to be taken that will eventually relate the abstract mathematical concepts of the system model to the specific data structures and algorithms used in the implementation. At one point during this process, a transition from the language of the system model, Alloy in our case, to the annotated programming language, such as annotated C, needs to be made. We propose to decompose that transition into three steps: first, precondition and framing analysis; second, translation of Alloy signatures and predicates to annotated data structures and partial contracts; and third, augmentation of the resulting annotated C with assertions addressing ownership domains and resource limitations.

The tool VCC [4] is an industrially viable verifier for concurrent C. It supports function- and thread-modular verification of highly-optimized product-quality C code. VCC has been used to verify a large part of the kernel of Microsoft's Hyper-V [11]. VCC uses first-order predicate logic as a specification language. Primary features of the annotation language include pre-/post-condition function contracts with heap frames, data invariants for C structs with an ownership discipline, and ghost data and code. VCC uses Z3 [12] to support fully-automatic verification of annotated C.

4.1   Precondition and Framing Analysis

The Alloy language does not offer constructs specific to programming. Therefore, it makes sense to move from the system model to contract-based program annotations without much "refinement" of the Alloy system model. Only a precondition analysis on the transition predicates specifying the system operations (c.f., Listing 2), and a framing analysis prepares the transition to VCC contracts.

The precondition analysis is done in the standard way proposed, e.g., in the VDM [10] and Z [13] methodologies, by existentially quantifying a transition predicate over the post-state and result parameters. For example, the precondition of add in Listing 2 is obtained by eliminating the existential quantifier the following definition of addPREex. The resulting predicate addPRE conjoins Lines 3 to 15 but Lines 6 and 14, which address the effect of the operation.

Listing 5. C struct for Alloy signature Server: fields

```
 1  typedef struct _Server {
 2    Mailer *mail;
 3    _(ghost \objset kdb;)
 4    _(invariant \forall \object o;
 5      o \in kdb ==> \typeof(o) == \typeof((DBEntry*)NULL))
 6    Ptrset* kdbl;
 7    _(invariant \forall void* o;
 8      o \in kdbl->abs <==> (DBEntry*)o \in kdb)
 9    [...] // similar for: addReq, delReq, used
10    // distinctness of implementation sets
11    _(invariant kdbl != addReql && [...] && delReql != usedl)

12    [cont. in Listing 7]
```

```
pred addPREex [ s : Server , e : Email , k : Key]{
  some s.mail.mailqueue',
    s.kdb', s.addReq', s.delReq', s.used', c" | {
    add[s,e,k,c"]                                   }}
```

The framing analysis identifies the parts of the system state that a system operation will keep unchanged under all circumstances, i.e., for a transition predicate op, all state variables x must be identified for which op **implies** x' = x holds. The resulting framing predicate conjoins the equations thus found. For add, these are Lines 18 to 20 of Listing 2.

Finally, the parts of the transition predicate not covered by the precondition and framing predicates form the postcondition predicate that talks about actual change of the system state. As a result of this preparatory step, the specification of add is re-written to the equivalent form

addPRE[s,e,k] && addPOST[s,e,k,c"] && addFRAME[s]

where addPRE, addPOST, and addFRAME are the precondition, postcondition, and framing predicates derived from the original transition predicate in Listing 2.

While some automation support is conceivable to find that decomposition of a transition predicate, it will still remain a manual step to ensure comprehensibility and allow developers to work productively with those predicates in the following development steps. Eventually the automated verification that the decomposition is equivalent to the original transition predicate ensures the soundness of the decomposition step.

4.2   Translation to Annotated C

Although we will not provide a rigorous justification of the transition from Alloy to VCC annotations, a comparison of the semantics of those two formalisms motivates our approach. In particular, we consider the translation of Alloy signatures to C structs, in which pointers represent atoms; we identify an appropriate

Listing 6. Generic pointer set

```
typedef struct _Ptrset
{
  _(ghost \objset abs;)
  void* buf[SETSIZE];
  unsigned size;
  _(invariant size <= SETSIZE)

  [...] // coupling invariant buf to abs
} Ptrset;
```

representation of Alloy sets as VCC ghost data; and we address the translation of relational calculus to first-order predicate logic, which is used in VCC.

Signatures to Structs, Atoms to Pointers. Similar to an Alloy signature, a C struct talks about fields that have values associated with the particular struct. Thus, C structs are a natural target for representing Alloy signatures.

The semantics of an Alloy signature is a type, which is a finite set of unstructured "atoms". The semantics of a field of a signature is a (globally visible) relation between the type of the signature and the type mentioned in the declaration of the field. For example, the declaration mail : Mailer in Server of Listing 1 semantically maps to a relation between the types of Server and Mailer, which is further constrained to be a total function: each server maps to exactly one mailer. For fields marked as **var**, the relation between signature and field value evolves with each transition in a system trace.

This matches well with the ghost type \object in VCC, which is the type of all C pointers to structs. Each \object has an associated type, which is the type of struct that the pointer references.

Furthermore, the dereferencing access s−>f to the field f of a struct pointer s resembles the semantics of the relational composition s.f accessing a field f of a single Alloy signature s.

Therefore, we map Alloy signatures to C structs, Alloy atoms to pointers to the respective struct types, and (for singletons s of signature types) the relational composition s.f to a dereferencing access s−>f.

Listing 5 shows the representation of the Alloy signature Server as an annotated C struct. Line 2 represents the field mail as pointer to the struct type Mailer, which in turn represents the Alloy signature of the same name.

Sets. In VCC, the ghost set \objset is the type of sets of all pointers, independent of their target types. Representing Alloy signatures as struct pointers, it appears natural to represent Alloy sets as VCC object sets. Thus an Alloy declaration kdb : **set** DBEntry would be represented by the ghost declaration _(**ghost** \objset kdb;). The typing information about kdb, namely that it is a subset of DBEntry, can be covered by an invariant requiring that all members of the object set kdb are pointers to DBEntry, see Line 4 of Listing 5.

Listing 7. C struct for Alloy signature Server: invariants

```
18    // active ConfCodes have not been used before
19    _(invariant \forall Request* r;
20       (r \in addReq || r \in delReq)
21       ==> ! (r->rc \in used))
22    // delete requests refer to existing db entries
23    _(invariant \forall Request* dl;
24       dl \in delReq ==> dl->rdb \in kdb)
25    // requests respect ConfCode types
26    _(invariant \forall Request* ar;
27       ar \in addReq ==> AddConfCode(ar->rc))
28    _(invariant \forall Request* dr;
29       dr \in delReq ==> DelConfCode(dr->rc))
30    [cont. in Listing 9]
```

The field kdbl in Line 6 of Listing 5 provides an implementation of the object set kdb. A common idiom in C is to implement "generic" pointers by the type **void***. Upon use, such a pointer is cast to the actual pointer type. The type definition of Ptrset sketched in Listing 6 makes use of this idiom to provide a very simple implementation of a generic finite pointer set by an array of a fixed size. The ghost set abs contains the members of the set. The implementation is an array buf of pointers to **void**. The field size is the cardinality of the set, which must be less than the size SETSIZE of buf. A coupling invariant (not shown) ensures that buf holds exactly the members of abs. The invariant in Line 7 of Listing 5 ensures that kdbl holds exactly the data base entries in kdb.

Similarly, the other set-valued fields addReq, delReq, and used of the Alloy signature Server are mapped to the fields addReq and addReql, etc. in Listing 5. As those sets are distinct, Line 11 requires that their implementations do not alias.

Predicate Logic and Relational Calculus. Alloy is a temporal first-order relational logic. VCC uses first-order predicate logic. In Alloy, we confine the use of temporal operators to the description of the system transition relation and assertions about the system behavior. This is justified because temporal operators are hardly needed to describe signature invariants or transition predicates. As a consequence, the translation of the relevant Alloy logic operators to their VCC counterparts is straight-forward.

VCC provides the usual set operations, such as union, intersection, and membership, for **\objset**. However, there is no counterpart for the more powerful operations of relational calculus. In particular, the translation of Alloy's general relational composition R.S, which joins the relations R and S on their co-domain and domain, respectively, needs more consideration. Unless one of the relations is a singleton, a systematic translation involves existential quantification, which imposes considerable burden on analysis tools.

Listing 8. C function for add

```
1   ConfCode* add(Server *s, Email *e, Key *k)
2   _(writes s,e,k)
3   _(maintains \wrapped(s))
4   _(requires \wrapped(e))
5   _(requires \wrapped(k))
6   _(requires s->addReql->size < SETSIZE)
7   _(requires s->mail->mailqueuel->size < SETSIZE)
8   _(requires addPRE(s,e,k))
9   _(ensures addPOST(s,e,k,\result))
10  _(ensures addFRAME(s));
11  _(ensures e \in \domain(s))
12  _(ensures k \in \domain(s))
```

Consider the definition of active in Line 9 of Listing 1. Semantically, addReq and delReq are sets of atoms of type Request, and rc is a relation mapping requests to confirmation codes. Thus, the relational composition (addReq+DelReq).rc evaluates to the relational image of that set union under the relation rc, which is a set of confirmation codes.

A systematic translation of Alloy's relational calculus to VCC in the style of a denotational semantics would result in quite complex formulas with many nested existential quantifiers. The resulting VCC assertions would be quite hard to comprehend, and they would put a considerable burden on the SMT solver Z3 to find witnesses for the existential propositions. We therefore choose to manually translate expressions of relational calculus to propositions explicitly referring to the members of the involved sets. For increased assurance, this transformation could be carried out in Alloy as a preparatory step like the precondition and framing analyses. Then, the Alloy analyzer could check the equivalence of the transformed assertion to the original formulation.

For the Hagrid specification, the invariant in Line 9 of Listing 1 translates to the struct invariant in Line 19 of Listing 7. Similarly, the invariant stating that pending delete requests refer to existing data base entries in Line 13 of Listing 1 translates to the struct invariant in Line 23 of Listing 7. The last two invariants of Listing 7 are further examples of this way of translating formulas involving relational composition.

System Operations to C Functions. We map system operations to C functions. VCC function specifications come in the form of contracts consisting of three major parts: preconditions, postconditions, and framing.

Listing 8 shows the declaration and contract of the C function corresponding to the transition predicate of add in Listing 2. The output parameter c" of the Alloy predicate becomes the result of the function. The precondition addPRE(s,e,k), and the postconditions addPOST(s,e,k,\result) and addFRAME(s) are obtained by the analysis described in Sect. 4.1. The parameter \result refers to the return value of the function.

Listing 9. C struct for Alloy signature Server: ownership

```
34    _(invariant \mine(mail))
35    // ownership for kdb and its implementation kdbl
36    _(invariant \mine(kdbl))
37    _(invariant \forall DBEntry* o;
38        o \in kdb ==> \mine(o))
39    [...] // similar ownership for: addReq, delReq, used
40  } Server;
```

4.3 Contract Augmentation

The remaining parts of the contract of add in Listing 8 specify properties of the C function that cannot be derived from the Alloy specification, but are specific to the target contract language or the chosen implementation. For the case study, they specifically relate to object ownership and resource limitations.

Ownership and Framing. VCC uses a variant of object ownership [6] to control the effect of updates to the C heap in the presence of pointer aliasing and concurrency. Struct invariants allow one to define *ownership domains* that basically describe sets of struct instances whose invariants depend on one another, such that modifying one member of the ownership domain may require checking the invariants of other members of the ownership domain. The *admissibility* of invariants [3] ensures that the validity of the invariants of all objects outside that ownership domain is not affected by that modification.

Listing 9 sketches the ownership invariants of the struct Server. They require that the mailer and all members of the sets kdb, addReq, delReq, and used, as well as their implementations are owned by the server.

The contract of add reflects this design of the ownership domain. Lines 3 to 5 of Listing 8 require that the function receives three input parameters which are \wrapped. For the server s, this state is also ensured as a postcondition. A \wrapped object is *closed* and owned by the currently executing thread. If an object is *closed*, its invariants hold and it cannot be changed. The ghost operation **unwrap** makes a \wrapped object \mutable such that subsequent statements can change it. The ghost operation **wrap** transfers a \mutable object to the \wrapped state. Its precondition requires that the invariants of the object hold. In this way, code can be annotated to explicitly mark the parts of the code that are supposed to change certain parts of the heap while invariants can be assumed to hold of all objects that are not \mutable.

The *writes frame* in Line 2 of Listing 8 restricts possible modifications of the heap to the ownership domains of the three parameters. It is obvious that add needs to modify s to store an add request for (e,k). By the construction of the ownership domain of Server and the structs it refers to, this means that both, e and k, become members of the ownership domain of s. The last two postconditions of add make this explicit. As the owners of e and k change, their state is modified by the function. Therefore, they need to be members of the writes frame as well.

The struct invariants and the parts of function contracts that relate to ownership describe genuine properties of the code design. They cannot be inferred from the system model but developers need to carefully design them to allow the verification of the entire code to succeed. For example, the decision to transfer the new email address and key to the ownership of the addReq field of the server implies that the mailer cannot own that same email address, which it needs to store in a set of messages to send.

Resource Limitations. Two additional preconditions in Lines 6 and 7 of Listing 8 relate to the fixed capacity of the set implementation used (c.f., Listing 6). Both, the number of pending add requests and messages in the mail queue must be less than the set capacity. Otherwise, adding a new request or sending the respective confirmation code might fail.

The need to make those preconditions explicit in the contract, in addition to the ones derived from the Alloy system model, points to a more general issue that needs to be addressed in the transition from a system model to a contract-based specification of implementation code: how to deal with resource limitations, or exceptions, that must be handled in the code but may or may not be addressed in the system model. Whether or not a formal treatment of resource limitations is necessary in the transition from system model to program contracts depends on their possible impact on system level requirements. If it is, the restrictions may be propagated from the contracts to the system model, or the concept of retrenchment [2] may be useful to represent them formally.

5   Discussion

The case study presented in the previous sections highlights some aspects of the pragmatics of applying Formal Methods that manifest themselves much more prominently in real-life projects.

Loose Coupling. The coupling of system model and software contracts that we see in the case study resembles the shape of an hourglass, where the bottleneck consists of the shared properties of system model and contracts. These are the invariants of the abstract data and the transition predicates of the system operations, in the decomposed form of preconditions, postconditions, and framing predicates. The larger parts of both, system model and annotated program code, do not contribute to that connection between the two.

Approximately half of the Alloy code in the case study describes the system data and operations. The other half constructs the state transition relation of the system and some assertions providing a rudimentary analysis of the system behavior. In a real-life project, an adequate validation of the model with respect to informal requirements would require substantially more Alloy code, further reducing the relative size of the behavior description proper. Similarly, a substantial part of the C annotations contribute to the contract augmentation discussed in Sect. 4.3, which would considerably grow if the code was extended to a full, executable implementation.

Considering the formal specification as a piece of software, the coupling between system model and software contracts is less strong than one might expect. Consequently, it may be advantageous to use *different* languages for the system model and the code contracts to come up with elegant specifications and make good use of their respective support tools. The advantage gained in comprehensibility of the specifications and performance of the tools may easily outweigh the redundancy and additional effort introduced by translating "the bottleneck" between the two languages.

Well-Structured Transition. As the case study illustrates, the transition from system model to software contracts can be clearly structured into a number of development activities, such as the precondition analysis, the actual translation between languages, or the design of ownership domains. Proof obligations, such as the equivalence between the decomposed form and the original formulation of a transition relation predicate, help establish the soundness of the development steps. Considering the transition as part of a software development process with clearly defined steps involving human creativity offers guidance to developers.

Automation. The degree of automation that can be achieved to support the translation between the system modeling and the contract languages obviously depends on the specific languages. As the contracts resulting from the translation build the basis of further coding and verification steps, they must be well accessible and comprehensible by developers. The case study shows that it may not be desirable to generate partial contracts directly from the system model. However, tool support can help to verify proof obligations, or in a more heuristic sense support manual activities, e.g., by systematically searching for state components that provably do not change under a transition relation and should therefore be included in the framing predicate.

Future Work. Languages can always be improved, and there never is sufficient tool support. This is true for Alloy and VCC as well. As a learning from the specific case study, however, a feature allowing one to mark and track the different specification parts involved in the transition from system model to annotated C would be instrumental. This could be implemented as meta-data managed by an IDE, rather than an extension of the two languages and their specific tools.

The selection of specific features to implement should be well informed by experience from substantial application projects, because some deficiencies or limitations only become visible "at scale". Unfortunately, many such projects need to remain confidential. It would be desirable to see the experience gained in those projects more often re-cast into academic, publicly available case studies highlighting successes but also deficiencies that academia can learn from and address in future research.

Acknowledgment. Thanks to my customers for allowing me to learn from real-world applications of Formal Methods, to the anonymous reviewers for insightful and constructive criticism, and to Maritta Heisel for comments on an earlier draft of this paper.

References

1. Alloy analyzer version 6 (2021). https://allytools.org/alloy6.html
2. Banach, R., Jeske, C.: Retrenchment and refinement interworking: the tower theorems. Math. Struct. Comput. Sci. **25**(1), 135–202 (2015). https://doi.org/10.1017/S0960129514000061
3. Cohen, E., et al.: Invariants, modularity, and rights. In: Pnueli, A., Virbitskaite, I., Voronkov, A. (eds.) PSI 2009. LNCS, vol. 5947, pp. 43–55. Springer, Heidelberg (2010). https://doi.org/10.1007/978-3-642-11486-1_4
4. Cohen, E., et al.: VCC: a practical system for verifying concurrent C. In: Berghofer, S., Nipkow, T., Urban, C., Wenzel, M. (eds.) TPHOLs 2009. LNCS, vol. 5674, pp. 23–42. Springer, Heidelberg (2009). https://doi.org/10.1007/978-3-642-03359-9_2
5. Common Criteria for Information Technology Security Evaluation (CC), version 3.1 revision 5 edn. (2017)
6. Dietl, W., Müller, P.: Object ownership in program verification. In: Clarke, D., Noble, J., Wrigstad, T. (eds.) Aliasing in Object-Oriented Programming. Types, Analysis and Verification. LNCS, vol. 7850, pp. 289–318. Springer, Heidelberg (2013). https://doi.org/10.1007/978-3-642-36946-9_11
7. The hagrid verifying OpenPGP server. https://gitlab.com/hagrid-keyserver/hagrid
8. Huisman, M., Monti, R., Ulbrich, M., Weigl, A.: The VerifyThis collaborative long term challenge. In: Ahrendt, W., Beckert, B., Bubel, R., Hähnle, R., Ulbrich, M. (eds.) Deductive Software Verification: Future Perspectives. LNCS, vol. 12345, pp. 246–260. Springer, Cham (2020). https://doi.org/10.1007/978-3-030-64354-6_10
9. Jackson, D.: Software Abstractions: Logic, Language, and Analysis. Revised edition. MIT Press, Cambridge (2011)
10. Jones, C.B.: Systematic Software Development using VDM, 2nd edn. Prentice Hall, Hoboken (1990)
11. Leinenbach, D., Santen, T.: Verifying the Microsoft Hyper-V hypervisor with VCC. In: Cavalcanti, A., Dams, D.R. (eds.) FM 2009. LNCS, vol. 5850, pp. 806–809. Springer, Heidelberg (2009). https://doi.org/10.1007/978-3-642-05089-3_51
12. de Moura, L., Bjørner, N.: Z3: an efficient SMT solver. In: Ramakrishnan, C.R., Rehof, J. (eds.) TACAS 2008. LNCS, vol. 4963, pp. 337–340. Springer, Heidelberg (2008). https://doi.org/10.1007/978-3-540-78800-3_24
13. Spivey, J.M.: The Z Notation - A Reference Manual, 2nd edn. Prentice Hall, Hoboken (1992)

X-by-Construction Meets Runtime Verification

X-by-Construction Meets Runtime Verification

Maurice H. ter Beek[1]([✉])[iD], Loek Cleophas[2,3]([✉])[iD], Martin Leucker[4][iD],
and Ina Schaefer[5]

[1] ISTI–CNR, Pisa, Italy
m.terbeek@isti.cnr.it
[2] Eindhoven University of Technology, Eindhoven, The Netherlands
l.g.w.a.cleophas@tue.nl
[3] Stellenbosch University, Stellenbosch, Republic of South Africa
[4] University of Lübeck, Lubeck, Germany
leucker@isp.uni-luebeck.de
[5] KIT, Karlsruhe, Germany
ina.schaefer@kit.edu

Abstract. In recent years, researchers have started to investigate X-by-Construction (XbC)—beyond correctness as considered by the more traditional Correctness-by-Construction (CbC) paradigm—as a refinement approach to engineer systems that by-construction satisfy certain non-functional properties—also, and in particular, in the setting of probabilistic systems and properties. In line with the need to join forces with concepts from runtime verification (RV), this track brings together researchers and practitioners working to share their views on the many possible synergies between CbC/XbC at design time and RV at runtime.

1 Motivation

Correctness-by-Construction (CbC) sees the development of software (systems) as a step-wise refinement process from specification to code, ideally by CbC design tools that automatically generate error-free software (system) implementations from rigorous and unambiguous requirement specifications. Afterwards, testing only serves to validate the CbC process rather than to find bugs.

A lot of progress has been made on CbC, and after a successful track on the combination of CbC with post-hoc verification at ISoLA 2016 [7], at ISoLA 2018 it was time to look further than correctness by investigating a move from CbC to *X-by-Construction* (XbC), i.e., by considering also non-functional properties [6]. XbC is thus concerned with a step-wise refinement process from specification to code that automatically generates software (system) implementations that by construction satisfy specific non-functional properties (i.e., concerning security, dependability, reliability, resource or energy consumption, and the like). In line with the growing attention to fault tolerance and the increasing use of machine-learning techniques in modern software systems, which make it hard to establish guaranteed properties [22], as witnessed in other tracks at ISoLA 2022 [16,20],

T. Margaria and B. Steffen (Eds.): ISoLA 2022, LNCS 13701, pp. 141–148, 2022.
https://doi.org/10.1007/978-3-031-19849-6_9

a third track in this series, at ISoLA 2020/2021, focussed on XbC in the setting of probabilistic systems and properties [5].

Runtime verification (RV) is concerned with monitoring and analysing actual software (and hardware) system behaviour [17]. RV is of paramount importance to system correctness, reliability, and robustness by providing an additional level of rigour and effectiveness when compared to testing, and improved practical applicability when compared to exhaustive formal verification. RV can be used prior to deployment, for testing, verification, and debugging purposes, as well as after deployment, for ensuring reliability, safety, and security—and for providing fault containment and recovery or online system repair, possibly paired with a digital twin acting as the virtual counterpart of the actual real-time (software and/or hardware) system behaviour [9].

2 Aim

Building on the highly successful ISoLA tracks mentioned above, the aim of this track is to bring together researchers and practitioners who are interested in CbC/XbC, and who acknowledge the need to join forces with concepts from RV. We believe this is important since (1) achieving correctness starting at design time is difficult—if not impossible—with the current proliferation of systems with data-driven AI components, while (2) a system failure detected by RV may possibly be repaired, but how can it be ensured that the corrected system is indeed better than before?

Given this specific topic, this ISoLA 2022 track fits perfectly as fourth track in the aforementioned series of ISoLA tracks:

ISoLA 2016   Correctness-by-Construction and Post-hoc Verification:
                       Friends or Foes?
ISoLA 2018   X-by-Construction
ISoLA 2020/2021   X-by-Construction: Correctness Meets Probability
ISoLA 2022   X-by-Construction Meets Runtime Verification

We have therefore invited both researchers and practitioners working in the following communities to participate in this track and share their views on the many possible synergies between CbC/XbC at design time and RV at runtime:

- People working on system-of-systems, who address modelling and analysis (considering correctness, but also non-functional properties concerning security, reliability, resilience, energy consumption, performance, sustainability, and the like) of networks of interacting legacy and new software systems, and who are interested in applying CbC/XbC or RV techniques in this domain in order to provide guarantees for system-of-systems.
- People working on quantitative modelling and analysis, for instance through probabilistic/real-time systems and probabilistic/statistical model checking, in particular in the specific setting of dynamic, adaptive or (runtime) reconfigurable systems with variability. These people typically work on lifting successful formal methods and (runtime) verification tools from single systems to

families of systems, i.e., design and (runtime) verification techniques that need to cope with the complexity of systems stemming from behaviour, variability, and randomness—and which focus not only on correctness but also on non-functional properties concerning safety, security, performance, dependability, and the like. As such, they may be interested in applying CbC/XbC or RV techniques in this domain to provide proper guarantees for families of systems.

– People working on systems involving components that employ machine-learning (ML) or other artificial intelligence (AI) approaches. In these settings, models and behaviour are typically dependent on what is learned from large data sets, and may change dynamically based on yet more data being processed. As a result, guaranteeing properties (whether correctness or non-functional ones) becomes hard, and probabilistic reasoning needs to be applied instead with respect to such properties for the components employing AI approaches. As a consequence, people working in this domain may be interested in applying CbC/XbC or RV techniques to provide guarantess for such AI-based systems.

3   Contributions

We briefly describe the contributions of this track and group them thematically.

3.1   CbC: Robustness, Co-piloting, and Digital Twinning

In [18], Nayak et al. consider *correctness-by-construction* in the light of robustness. While an optimal strategy may meet the correctness criteria under the given model of the environment, small deviations of the environment's behaviour may render the strategy non-optimal or even incorrect. Especially, if the environment is non-antagonistic, strategies could be improved. Based on robust specifications in so-called robust Linear Temporal Logic (rLTL), the authors study the problem of monitoring the behaviour of the environment and adapting strategies accordingly to achieve *robustness-by-construction.*

In [3], Ahrendt et al. suggest a novel approach to development of safety-critical software, combining learning-based *co-piloting* with formal methods in order to assist agile, simultaneous development of (1) implementation, (2) specification, and (3) tests. The vision is that an IDE supporting this approach would assist users by suggesting necessary changes to the other elements if one of the three were changed. Controlled by the user, such changes could be used to reestablish consistency, possibly in an iterative fashion. The authors describe the approach, and argue that the community is in a good position to realise this vision, covering challenges and possible solutions.

In [14], Kamburjan et al. address the problem of reestablishing the twinning property between a digital twin and a physical twin when the latter changes over time due to adaptation and reconfiguration. To this aim, the authors propose to combine feedback loops from the well-known MAPE-K (Monitor-Analyze-Plan-Execute over a shared Knowledge) reference control model for organising autonomous and self-adaptive systems with semantic reflection to automatically ensure that digital artefacts twine correctly with physical systems, i.e., that the resulting system is *twinned-by-construction*.

In [10], Coto et al. explore the impact that the introduction of syntactic or semantic restrictions to rule out models that could lead to communication glitches like message loss or deadlocks have on the usability of formal modelling. To this aim, the authors benchmark the use of a formal choreographic modelling language designed to support the *correctness-by-construction* principle of message-passing systems for the modelling of real business processes taken from the official documentation of European customs business process models. As such, the current paper provides an initial comparison between modelling with the Business Process Modelling Notation (BPMN), widely used in practice, and formal choreographic approaches, deeply investigated theoretically.

3.2   CbC and RV: Configurable and Cyber-Physical Systems

In [12], Dubslaff and Köhl coin *configurable-by-construction* runtime monitoring inspired by automata-theoretic *runtime verification*, featured transition systems from software product lines, and stream-based runtime monitoring. The authors consider runtime monitoring with variability in the system being monitored as well as in the monitor itself. The need for configurable monitors is motivated with an example of real driving emissions tests. In this running example, both the system being monitored as well as the monitor itself are configurable as they depend on the sensor configuration of the car. Considering monitors to be themselves configurable opens many new challenges, several of which are discussed in the current paper. The authors introduce an automata-based framework for configurable monitors and their synthesis from featured LTL specifications, and they present an extension of the stream-based specification language Lola to the setting of *configurable systems*.

In [15], Kittelmann et al. introduce a method to refine hybrid automata representing verified (safety-critical) *cyber-physical systems* into corresponding executable source code amenable to *runtime verification*. Their approach employs ArchiCorC, a component-based architecture-level tool incorporating the *correctness-by-construction* paradigm, to generate code. As a case study, the authors consider the context of driving maneuvers, and apply ArchiCorC in this context. Subsequent simulation of executable and verified maneuvers allows requirement validation for various scenarios.

In [1], Abbas and Bonakdarpour address the setting of a hybrid (continuous or discrete) distributed system (model). They analyse the opportunities and challenges concerning the exploitation of various kinds of knowledge for the benefit of more effective, or more efficient, *runtime verification* in the context of *cyber-physical systems*. The current paper describes cutting-edge problem space, provides ideas and directions for solutions, and points out numerous directions for further research.

3.3   XbC: Security, Resilience, and Consumption Properties

In [11], Dam et al. present a proof of concept combining fault localisation techniques and automated program repair methods for *security* errors in C programs. The approach is to exploit program traces using statistical model checking and to apply patch candidates that are identified by a genetic algorithm. For this purpose, the authors evaluate populations of patches using a novel Q-function, which indicates the probability to choose patches at a certain validation state. They demonstrate the effectiveness of their approach for memory usage-related errors using benchmarks from the automotive domain.

In [2], Adelt et al. discuss the analysis of safety and *resilience* of intelligent hybrid systems. In contrast to purely deductive verification methods, which mostly focus on worst-case behaviour based on pessimistic assumptions, they propose a novel methodology that combines deductive verification of hybrid systems with statistical model checking. This enables (1) to construct provably safe and resilient systems, but also (2) to achieve certain performance levels with a statistical guarantee. The authors demonstrate applicability on an intelligent water distribution system, whose behaviour was learned through reinforcement learning. Based on the proposed approach, the water distribution system is proven to be safe and resilient towards pump failures with respect to failure probability and repair time, while guaranteeing low energy costs.

In [19], Riganelli et al. present the test tool Test4Enforcers that is able to validate the correctness of software enforcers for both functional and non-functional properties. The functional correctness part was presented in prior work. The current paper focusses on the *non-functional properties* of *power consumption, memory consumption, launch time,* and *responsiveness*. To this aim, Test4Enforcers generates a test suite and executes this suite on apps with and without enforcers. By comparing the performance measurements, degradation introduced by faulty enforcers is detected.

3.4   CbC and RV: Reinforcement Learning and Synthesis

In [21], Tappler et al. present a way to avoid safety violations during *reinforcement automata learning* using *shield synthesis*. The unknown environments are modelled as Markov Decision Processes (MDPs) with associated cost/reward functions. Shields are constructed from recorded traces, and subsequently serve as runtime guards/monitors that block actions that introduce a too high risk of safety violations within the next k steps of the automaton. Iteratively, the collected data is used to learn new MDPs with higher accuracy, resulting in shields able to prevent more safety violations. An implementation and application to a case study of a Q-learning agent show that while the agent explores the environment during training, the improved learned models lead to shields that are able to prevent many safety violations.

In [8], Berducci and Grosu present a pipeline for solving Constrained Markov Decision Processes (MDPs), starting from formal requirements, in a *correct-by-construction* style. A *reinforcement learning*-based iterative approach to the *synthesis* of control policies has to balance target, safety, and comfort in its objective. The model-based reinforcement-learning algorithm presented by the authors ensures with high probability that policy updates only occur when safety performance stays the same or improves. To improve on previous approaches, the authors propose to combine model-based and model-free approaches for more data-efficient algorithms. The authors suggest that the resulting dynamics model fit to the data can be used to validate the obtained policy before deployment.

In [4], Azzopardi et al. study the potential of combining *controller synthesis* and *runtime verification*. Controller synthesis is a general technique to ensure *correctness-by-construction*: given a controllable system (and environment) description and a specification of the system behaviour to achieve, controller synthesis allows to obtain a controlled version of the system meeting the specification. However, this promise is only met if the environment in which the system is running is modelled correctly, and the computational resources allow the synthesis of a corresponding strategy. Runtime verification considers the actual behaviour of the system and its environment may be used in combination with controller synthesis in several ways. The authors identify and discuss three different patterns: (1) monitors that identify when control is needed and what needs to be controlled; (2) monitors that identify violation of environment assumptions; and (3) monitors that mediate between different controllers and other agents.

In [13], Gorostiaga et al. elaborate on a concrete combination of *correctness-by-construction* and *runtime verification* in the setting of controlling Unmanned Aerial Vehicles (UAVs). In this setting, often temporal planning is used as a method for getting an a priori correct plan to steer the UAVs. Again, assumptions about the environment as well as simplifications have to be made to obtain a plan. In the current paper, it is shown how stream runtime verification can be integrated with the temporal planning to monitor the assumptions about the environment and to mitigate deficiencies of the current plan.

References

1. Abbas, H., Bonakdarpour, B.: Leveraging system dynamics in runtime verification of cyber-physical systems. In: Margaria, T., Steffen, B. (eds.) ISoLA 2022, LNCS 13701, pp. 264–278. Springer, Heidelberg (2022)
2. Adelt, J., Herber, P., Niehage, M., Remke, A.: Towards safe and resilient hybrid systems in the presence of learning and uncertainty. In: Margaria, T., Steffen, B. (eds.) ISoLA 2022, LNCS 13701, pp. 299–319. Springer, Heidelberg (2022)
3. Ahrendt, W., Gurov, D., Johansson, M., Rümmer, P.: TriCo – triple co-piloting of implementation, specification and tests. In: Margaria, T., Steffen, B. (eds.) ISoLA 2022, LNCS 13701, pp. 174–187. Springer, Heidelberg (2022)
4. Azzopardi, S., Piterman, N., Schneider, G.: Runtime verification meets controller synthesis. In: Margaria, T., Steffen, B. (eds.) ISoLA 2022, LNCS 13701, pp. 382–396. Springer, Heidelberg (2022)
5. ter Beek, M.H., Cleophas, L., Legay, A., Schaefer, I., Watson, B.W.: X-by-construction: correctness meets probability. In: Margaria, T., Steffen, B. (eds.)

ISoLA 2020. LNCS, vol. 12476, pp. 211–215. Springer, Cham (2020). https://doi.org/10.1007/978-3-030-61362-4_11

6. ter Beek, M.H., Cleophas, L., Schaefer, I., Watson, B.W.: X-by-construction. In: Margaria, T., Steffen, B. (eds.) ISoLA 2018. LNCS, vol. 11244, pp. 359–364. Springer, Cham (2018). https://doi.org/10.1007/978-3-030-03418-4_21

7. ter Beek, M.H., Hähnle, R., Schaefer, I.: Correctness-by-construction and post-hoc verification: friends or foes? In: Margaria, T., Steffen, B. (eds.) ISoLA 2016. LNCS, vol. 9952, pp. 723–729. Springer, Cham (2016). https://doi.org/10.1007/978-3-319-47166-2_51

8. Berducci, L., Grosu, R.: Safe policy improvement in constrained Markov decision processes. In: Margaria, T., Steffen, B. (eds.) ISoLA 2022, LNCS 13701, pp. 360–381. Springer, Heidelberg (2022)

9. Colombo, C., et al.: COST action IC1402 runtime verification beyond monitoring. In: Colombo, C., Leucker, M. (eds.) RV 2018. LNCS, vol. 11237, pp. 18–26. Springer, Cham (2018). https://doi.org/10.1007/978-3-030-03769-7_2

10. Coto, A., Barbanera, F., Lanese, I., Rossi, D., Tuosto, E.: On formal choreographic modelling: a case study in EU business processes. In: Margaria, T., Steffen, B. (eds.) ISoLA 2022, LNCS 13701, pp. 205–219. Springer, Heidelberg (2022)

11. Dam, K.H.T., Duchêne, F., Given-Wilson, T., Cordy, M., Legay, A.: Automated repair of security errors in C programs via statistical model checking: a proof of concept. In: Margaria, T., Steffen, B. (eds.) ISoLA 2022, LNCS 13701, pp. 279–298. Springer, Heidelberg (2022)

12. Dubslaff, C., Köhl, M.A.: Configurable-by-construction runtime monitoring. In: Margaria, T., Steffen, B. (eds.) ISoLA 2022, LNCS 13701, pp. 220–241. Springer, Heidelberg (2022)

13. Gorostiaga, F., Zudaire, S., Sánchez, C., Schneider, G., Uchitel, S.: Assumption monitoring of temporal task planning using stream runtime verification. In: Margaria, T., Steffen, B. (eds.) ISoLA 2022, LNCS 13701, pp. 397–414. Springer, Heidelberg (2022)

14. Kamburjan, E., Din, C.C., Schlatte, R., Tapia Tarifa, S.L., Johnsen, E.B.: Twinning-by-construction: ensuring correctness for self-adaptive digital twins. In: Margaria, T., Steffen, B. (eds.) ISoLA 2022, LNCS 13701, pp. 188–204. Springer, Heidelberg (2022)

15. Kittelmann, A., Runge, T., Bordis, T., Schaefer, I.: Runtime verification of correct-by-construction driving maneuvers. In: Margaria, T., Steffen, B. (eds.) ISoLA 2022, LNCS 13701, pp. 242–263. Springer, Heidelberg (2022)

16. Larsen, K.G., Legay, A., Nolte, G., Schlüter, M., Stoelinga, M., Steffen, B.: Introduction to formal methods meet machine learning (F3ML). In: Margaria, T., Steffen, B. (eds.) ISoLA 2022. LNCS, vol. 13703, pp. 393–405. Springer, Heidelberg (2022)

17. Leucker, M., Schallhart, C.: A brief account of runtime verification. J. Log. Algebraic Methods Program. **78**(5), 293–303 (2009). https://doi.org/10.1016/j.jlap.2008.08.004

18. Nayak, S.P., Neider, D., Zimmermann, M.: Robustness-by-construction synthesis: adapting to the environment at runtime. In: Margaria, T., Steffen, B. (eds.) ISoLA 2022, LNCS 13701, pp. 149–173. Springer, Heidelberg (2022)

19. Riganelli, O., Micucci, D., Mariani, L.: Non-functional testing of runtime enforcers in Android. In: Margaria, T., Steffen, B. (eds.) ISoLA 2022, LNCS 13701, pp. 320–334. Springer, Heidelberg (2022)

20. Seisenberger, M., et al.: Safe and secure future AI-driven railway technologies: challenges for formal methods in railway. In: Margaria, T., Steffen, B. (eds.) ISoLA 2022. LNCS, vol. 13704, pp. 246–268. Springer, Heidelberg (2022)
21. Tappler, M., Pranger, S., Könighofer, B., Muškardin, E., Bloem, R., Larsen, K.: Automata learning meets shielding. In: Margaria, T., Steffen, B. (eds.) ISoLA 2022, LNCS 13701, pp. 335–359. Springer, Heidelberg (2022)
22. Wing, J.M.: Trustworthy AI. Commun. ACM **64**(10), 64–71 (2021). https://doi.org/10.1145/3448248

Robustness-by-Construction Synthesis: Adapting to the Environment at Runtime

Satya Prakash Nayak[1]($\boxtimes$) (iD), Daniel Neider[2] (iD), and Martin Zimmermann[3] (iD)

[1] Max Planck Institute for Software Systems, Kaiserslautern, Germany
`sanayak@mpi-sws.org`
[2] Safety and Explainability of Learning Systems Group, Carl von Ossietzky
Universität Oldenburg, Oldenburg, Germany
`daniel.neider@uni-oldenburg.de`
[3] Aalborg University, Aalborg, Denmark
`mzi@cs.aau.dk`

Abstract. While most of the current synthesis algorithms only focus on correctness-by-construction, ensuring robustness has remained a challenge. Hence, in this paper, we address the robust-by-construction synthesis problem by considering the specifications to be expressed by a robust version of Linear Temporal Logic (LTL), called robust LTL (rLTL). rLTL has a many-valued semantics to capture different degrees of satisfaction of a specification, i.e., satisfaction is a quantitative notion.

We argue that the current algorithms for rLTL synthesis do not compute optimal strategies in a non-antagonistic setting. So, a natural question is whether there is a way of satisfying the specification "better" if the environment is indeed not antagonistic. We address this question by developing two new notions of strategies. The first notion is that of adaptive strategies, which, in response to the opponent's non-antagonistic moves, maximize the degree of satisfaction. The idea is to monitor non-optimal moves of the opponent at runtime using multiple parity automata and adaptively change the system strategy to ensure optimality. The second notion is that of strongly adaptive strategies, which is a further refinement of the first notion. These strategies also maximize the opportunities for the opponent to make non-optimal moves. We show that computing such strategies for rLTL specifications is not harder than the standard synthesis problem, e.g., computing strategies with LTL specifications, and takes doubly-exponential time.

1 Introduction

Formal methods have focused on the paradigm of correctness-by-construction, i.e., ensuring that systems are guaranteed to meet their design specifications. While correctness is necessary, it has widely been acknowledged that this property alone is insufficient for a good design when a reactive system interacts with an ever-changing, uncontrolled environment. To illustrate this point, consider a typical correctness specification $\varphi \Rightarrow \psi$ of a reactive system, where φ is

T. Margaria and B. Steffen (Eds.): ISoLA 2022, LNCS 13701, pp. 149–173, 2022.
https://doi.org/10.1007/978-3-031-19849-6_10

an environment assumption and ψ the system's desired guarantee. Thus, if the environment violates φ, the entire implication becomes vacuously true, regardless of whether the system satisfies ψ. In other words, if the assumption about the environment is violated, the system may behave arbitrarily. This behavior is clearly undesirable as modeling any reasonably complex environment accurately and exhaustively is exceptionally challenging, if not impossible.

The example above shows that reactive systems must not only be correct but should also be *robust* to unexpected environment behavior. The notion of robustness we use in this paper is inspired by concepts from control theory [20,32, 33,35] and requires that deviations from the environment assumptions result in at most proportional violations of the system guarantee. More precisely, "minor" violations of the environment assumption should only cause "minor" violations of the system guarantee, while "major" violations of the environment assumption allow for "major"violations of the system guarantee.

To capture different degrees of violation (or satisfaction) of a specification, we rely on a many-valued extension of Linear Temporal Logic (LTL) [28], named *robust Linear Temporal Logic (rLTL)*, which has recently been introduced by Tabuada and Neider [36]. The basic idea of this logic can best be illustrated by considering the prototypical environment assumption $\varphi := \Box p$ ("always p"), which demands that the environment ensures that an atomic proposition p holds at every step during its interaction with the system. Clearly, φ is violated even if p does not hold at a single step, which is a "minor" violation. However, the classical Boolean semantics of LTL cannot distinguish between this case and the case where p does not hold at any position, which is a "major" violation. To distinguish these (and more) degrees of violations, rLTL adopts a five-valued semantics with truth values $\mathbb{B}_4 = \{1111, 0111, 0011, 0001, 0000\}$. The set $\mathbb{B}_4$ is ordered according to $1111 > 0111 > 0011 > 0001 > 0000$, where 1111 is interpreted as *true* and all other values as increasing shades of *false*. In case of the formula φ, for instance, the interpretation of these five truth values is as follows: φ evaluates to 1111 if the environment ensures p at every step of the interaction, φ evaluates to 0111 if p holds almost always, φ evaluates to 0011 if p holds infinitely often, φ evaluates to 0001 if p holds at least once, and φ evaluates to 0000 if p never holds. The semantics of rLTL is then set up so that $\varphi \Rightarrow \psi$ evaluates to 1111 if any violation of the environment assumption φ causes at most a proportional violation of the system guarantee ψ (i.e., if φ evaluates to truth value $b \in \mathbb{B}_4$, then ψ must evaluate to a truth value $b' \geq b$).

Here, we are interested in the synthesis problem for rLTL specifications. As usual, we model such a synthesis problem as an infinite-duration two-player game. Since we study rLTL synthesis, we consider games with rLTL winning conditions, so-called rLTL games.

rLTL games with a Boolean notion of winning strategy for the system player have already been studied by Tabuada and Neider [36]. In their setting, the objective for the system player is as follows: given a truth value $b \in \mathbb{B}_4$, he must react to the actions of the environment player in such a way that the specification is satisfied with a value of at least b. As for ω-regular games, a winning strategy for the system player can immediately be implemented in hardware or software. This implementation then results in a reactive system that is guaranteed to satisfy the given specification with at least a given truth value $b \in \mathbb{B}_4$, regardless of how the environment acts.

While rLTL games provide an elegant approach to robustness-by-construction synthesis, the Boolean notion of winning strategies that Tabuada and Neider adopt has a substantial drawback: it does not incentivize the system player to satisfy the specification with a value better than b, even if the environment player allows this. Of course, one can (and should) statically search for the largest $b \in \mathbb{B}_4$ such that the system player can win the game. However, this traditional worst-case view does not account for many practical situations where the environment is not antagonistic, e.g., in the presence of intermittent disturbances or noise, or when the environment cannot be modeled entirely [15,16,25,26,37]. In such situations, the system player should exploit the environment's "bad" moves, i.e., actions that permit the system player to achieve a value greater than b, and adapt its strategy at runtime.

We present two novel synthesis algorithms for rLTL specifications that ensure that the resulting systems are *robust by construction* (in addition to being correct by construction). These are based on two refined non-Boolean notions of winning strategies for rLTL games which both optimize the satisfaction of the specification.

The first notion, named *adaptive strategies*, uses automata-based runtime verification techniques [6] to monitor plays, detect bad moves of the environment, and adapt the actions of the system player to optimize the satisfaction of the winning condition. The second notion, named *strongly adaptive strategies*, is an extension of the first one that, in addition to being adaptive, also seeks to maximize the opportunity for the environment player to make bad moves. We show that both types of strategies can be computed using methods from automata theory and result in effective synthesis algorithms for reactive systems that are robust by construction and adapt to the environment at runtime.

After recapitulating rLTL in Sect. 2, we introduce adaptive strategies in Sect. 3 and show that one can compute such strategies in rLTL games in doubly-exponential time by reducing the problem to solving parity games [10]. In Sect. 4, we then turn to strongly adaptive strategies. It turns out that this type of strategy does not always exist, which we demonstrate through an example. Nevertheless, we give a doubly-exponential time algorithm that decides whether a strongly adaptive strategy exists, and, if this is the case, computes one. Our algorithm is based on reductions to a series of parity and obliging games [14]. As the LTL synthesis problem is 2EXPTIME-complete [29], which is a special case of the problems we consider here, computing both types of adaptive strategies is 2EXPTIME-complete as well. Furthermore, the size of the (strongly) adaptive strategies our algorithms compute is at most doubly exponential, matching the corresponding lower bound for LTL games, demonstrating that this bound is tight. Thus, our results show that adaptive robust-by-construction synthesis is asymptotically not harder than classical LTL synthesis.

All proofs omitted due to space restrictions can be found in the full version [24].

Related Work. Robustness in reactive synthesis has been addressed in various forms. A prominent example is work by Bloem et al. [7], which considers the synthesis of robust reactive systems from GR(1)-specifications. In subsequent work, Bloem et al. [9] have surveyed a large body of work on robustness in reactive synthesis and distilled three general categories: (i) "fulfill the guarantee as often as possible even if the environment assumption is violated", (ii) "if it is impossible to fulfill the guarantee, try to fulfill it whenever possible" and (iii) "help the environment to fulfill the assumption if possible".

Prototypical examples include the work by Topcu et al. [37], Ehlers and Topcu [16], Chatterjee and Henzinger [12], Chatterjee et al. [14], and Bloem et al. [8].

However, our notion of adaptive strategies is more closely related to the notion of subgame perfect equilibrium [19]. A strategy profile is a subgame perfect equilibrium if it represents a Nash equilibrium of every subgame of the original game, i.e., the strategies are not only required to be optimal for the initial vertex but for every possible initial history of the game. Subgame perfect equilibria have been well studied in the context of graph games with LTL objectives [19, 38]. Our results on adaptive strategies can be used to extend this concept to games with rLTL objectives. In particular, a pair of adaptive strategies for both players in such games forms a subgame perfect equilibrium and vice versa. Moreover, a subgame perfect equilibrium in such games is more fine-grained than subgame perfect equilibria in games with LTL objectives due to the many-valued semantics of rLTL. On the other hand, our notion of strongly adaptive strategies is more general than subgame perfect equilibria.

Also, the work of Almagor and Kupferman [1] is very similar to our notion of adaptive strategies. They introduced the notion of good-enough synthesis that is considered over a multi-valued semantics where the goal is to compute a strategy that achieves the highest possible satisfaction value. While some of the methods mentioned above do adapt to non-antagonistic behavior of the environment, we are not aware of any approach that would additionally optimize for the opportunities of the environment to act non-antagonistically, as our notion of strongly adaptive strategies does.

Quantitative objectives in graph-based games (and their combination with qualitative ones) have a rich history. Among the most prominent examples are mean-payoff parity games [13] and energy parity games [11]. The former type of game combines a parity winning condition (as the canonical representation for ω-regular properties) with a real-valued payout whose mean is to be maximized, while the latter type seeks to satisfy an ω-regular winning condition with the quantitative requirement that the level of energy during a play must remain positive. However, to the best of our knowledge, research in this field has focused on worst-case analyses with antagonistic environments.

Our notion of (strongly) adaptive strategies relies on central concepts introduced in the logic rLTL [36], a robust, many-valued extension of LTL. One of rLTL's key features is its syntactic similarity to LTL, which allows for a seamless and transparent transition from specifications expressed in LTL to specifications expressed in rLTL. Moreover, it is worth mentioning that rLTL has spawned numerous follow-up works, including rLTL model checking [2–4], rLTL runtime monitoring [21], and robust extensions of prompt LTL and Linear Dynamic Logic [27], as well as CTL [22].

Finally, let us highlight that preliminary results on adaptive strategies have been presented as a poster at the 24th ACM International Conference on Hybrid Systems: Computation and Control [23].

2   Preliminaries

In this section, we describe the syntax and semantics of Robust LTL and how it is different from classical LTL. Moreover, we discuss some important results on rLTL and introduce games with rLTL specifications.

Robust Linear Temporal Logic. We assume that the reader is familiar with Linear Temporal Logic [28]. We fix a finite non-empty set $\mathcal{P}$ of atomic propositions. The syntax of rLTL is similar to that of LTL with the only difference being the use of dotted temporal operators in order to distinguish them from LTL operators. More precisely, rLTL formulas are inductively defined as follows:

- each $p \in \mathcal{P}$ is an rLTL formula, and
- if φ and ψ are rLTL formulas, so are $\neg\varphi$, $\varphi \vee \psi$, $\varphi \wedge \psi$, $\varphi \Rightarrow \psi$, $\odot\varphi$ ("next"), $\boxdot\varphi$ ("always"), $\diamondsuit\varphi$ ("eventually"), $\varphi \mathbf{R} \psi$ ("release") and $\varphi \mathbf{U} \psi$ ("until").

As already discussed, rLTL uses the set $\mathbb{B}_4 = \{1111, 0111, 0011, 0001, 0000\}$ of truth values, which are ordered as follows:

$$1111 > 0111 > 0011 > 0001 > 0000.$$

Intuitively, 1111 corresponds to "true", and the other four values correspond to different degrees of "false".

The rLTL semantics is a mapping $\mathcal{V}$, called *valuation*, that maps an infinite word $\alpha \in (2^{\mathcal{P}})^\omega$ and an rLTL formula φ to an element of $\mathbb{B}_4$. Before we define the semantics, we need to introduce some useful notation. Let $\alpha = \alpha_0\alpha_1 \cdots \in (2^{\mathcal{P}})^\omega$ be an infinite word. For $i \in \mathbb{N}$, let $\alpha_{i...} = \alpha_i\alpha_{i+1} \cdots$ be the (infinite) suffix of α starting at position i. Also, for $1 \le k \le 4$, we let $V_k(\alpha, \varphi)$ denote the k-th entry of $\mathcal{V}(\alpha, \varphi)$, i.e., $\mathcal{V}(\alpha, \varphi) = V_1(\alpha, \varphi)V_2(\alpha, \varphi)V_3(\alpha, \varphi)V_4(\alpha, \varphi)$. Now, V is defined inductively as follows, where the semantics of Boolean connectives relies on *da Costa algebras* [31]:

$$\mathcal{V}(\alpha, p) = \begin{cases} 0000 & \text{if } p \notin \alpha_0 \\ 1111 & \text{if } p \in \alpha_0 \end{cases} \qquad\qquad \mathcal{V}(\alpha, \neg\varphi) = \begin{cases} 0000 & \text{if } \mathcal{V}(\alpha, \varphi) = 1111 \\ 1111 & \text{otherwise} \end{cases}$$

$$\mathcal{V}(\alpha, \varphi \vee \psi) = \max\{\mathcal{V}(\alpha, \varphi), \mathcal{V}(\alpha, \psi)\} \quad \mathcal{V}(\alpha, \varphi \Rightarrow \psi) = \begin{cases} 1111 & \text{if } \mathcal{V}(\alpha, \varphi) \le \mathcal{V}(\alpha, \psi) \\ \mathcal{V}(\alpha, \psi) & \text{otherwise} \end{cases}$$

$$\mathcal{V}(\alpha, \varphi \wedge \psi) = \min\{\mathcal{V}(\alpha, \varphi), \mathcal{V}(\alpha, \psi)\} \qquad \mathcal{V}(\alpha, \odot\varphi) = \mathcal{V}(\alpha_{1...}, \varphi)$$

$$\mathcal{V}(\alpha, \boxdot\varphi) = \left(\inf_{i \ge 0} V_1(\alpha_{i...}, \varphi), \sup_{j \ge 0} \inf_{i \ge j} V_2(\alpha_{i...}, \varphi), \inf_{j \ge 0} \sup_{i \ge j} V_3(\alpha_{i...}, \varphi), \sup_{i \ge 0} V_4(\alpha_{i...}, \varphi) \right)$$

$$\mathcal{V}(\alpha, \diamondsuit\varphi) = \left(\sup_{i \ge 0} V_1(\alpha_{i...}, \varphi), \sup_{i \ge 0} V_2(\alpha_{i...}, \varphi), \sup_{i \ge 0} V_3(\alpha_{i...}, \varphi), \sup_{i \ge 0} V_4(\alpha_{i...}, \varphi) \right)$$

The semantics for the temporal operators **U** and **R** can be generalized similarly. We refer the reader to Tabuada and Neider [36] for more details.

Example 1. We can see that for the formula $\boxdot p$, the valuation $\mathcal{V}(\alpha, \boxdot p)$ can be expressed in terms of the LTL valuation function W by

$$\mathcal{V}(\alpha, \boxdot p) = W(\alpha, \boxdot p) W(\alpha, \diamondsuit\boxdot p) W(\alpha, \boxdot\diamondsuit p) W(\alpha, \diamondsuit p).$$

This evaluates to different values in $\mathbb{B}_4$ distinguishing various degrees of violations as seen in Sect. 1.

Example 2. Now let us see how the rLTL semantics for a specification of the form $\varphi \Rightarrow \psi$ captures robustness. Consider an instance where the environment assumption φ is $\boxdot p$ and the system guarantee ψ is $\boxdot q$ and assume the specification $\boxdot p \Rightarrow \boxdot q$ evaluates to 1111 for some infinite word. Let us see how the system behaves in response to various degrees of violation of the environment assumption.

- If p holds at all positions, then $\boxdot p$ evaluates to 1111. Hence, by the semantics of implication, $\boxdot q$ also evaluates to 1111, which means q holds at all positions. Therefore, the desired behavior of the system is retained when the environment assumption holds with no violation.
- If p holds eventually always but not always (a minor violation of $\boxdot p$), then $\boxdot p$ evaluates to 0111. Hence, $\boxdot q$ evaluates to 0111 or higher, meaning that q also needs to hold eventually always.
- Similarly, if p holds at infinitely (finitely) many positions, then q needs to hold at infinitely (finitely) many positions.

Hence, the semantics of $\boxdot p \Rightarrow \boxdot q$ captures the robustness property as desired. Furthermore, if $\boxdot p \Rightarrow \boxdot q$ evaluates to $b < 1111$, then $\boxdot p$ evaluates to a higher value than b, whereas $\boxdot q$ evaluates to b. So, the desired system guarantee is not satisfied. However, the value of $\boxdot p \Rightarrow \boxdot q$ still describes which weakened guarantee follows from the environment assumption.

From rLTL to Büchi Automata. Given an LTL formula φ, a generalized Büchi automaton (see [34] for a definition) with $O(2^{|\varphi|})$ states and $O(|\varphi|)$ accepting sets can be constructed that recognizes the infinite words satisfying φ [5], where $|\varphi|$ denotes the number of subformulas of φ. Using a similar method, Tabuada and Neider obtained the following result.

Theorem 1 ([36]). *Given an* rLTL *formula φ and a set of truth values $B \subseteq \mathbb{B}_4$, one can construct a generalized Büchi automaton $\mathcal{A}$ with $2^{O(|\varphi|)}$ states and $O(|\varphi|)$ accepting sets that recognizes the infinite words on which the value of φ belongs to B, i.e., $L(\mathcal{A}) = \{w \in (2^P)^\omega \mid \mathcal{V}(\alpha, \varphi) \in B\}$.*

rLTL Games. We consider infinite-duration two-player games over finite graphs with rLTL specifications. Here, we assume basic familiarity with games on graphs. Formally, an rLTL game $\mathcal{G} = (\mathcal{A}, \varphi)$ consists of (i) a finite, directed, labelled arena $\mathcal{A} = (V, E, \lambda)$ with $V = V_0 \uplus V_1$, an edge relation $E \subseteq V \times V$, and a labelling function $\lambda \colon V \to 2^P$, and (ii) an rLTL formula φ over P. The game is played by two players, Player 0 and Player 1, who construct a *play* $\rho = v_0 v_1 \cdots \in V^\omega$ by moving a token along the edges of the arena. A play $\rho = v_0 v_1 \cdots$ induces an infinite word $\lambda(\rho) = \lambda(v_0)\lambda(v_1) \cdots \in (2^P)^\omega$, and the *value* of the play, denoted by $\mathcal{V}(\rho)$, is the value of the formula φ on $\lambda(\rho)$. Player 0's objective is to maximize this value, while Player 1's objective is to minimize it.

Strategies. A *play prefix* is a finite, nonempty path $\mathbf{p} \in V^*$ in the arena. Then, a *strategy* for Player i, $i \in \{0, 1\}$, is a function $\sigma \colon V^* V_i \to V$ mapping each play prefix $\mathbf{p}$ ending in a vertex in V_i to one of its successors. Intuitively, a strategy prescribes Player i's next move depending on the play prefix constructed so far.

A strategy σ is *memoryless* if it only depends on the last vertex, i.e., for every prefix $\mathbf{p}$ ending in vertex v, it holds that $\sigma(\mathbf{p}) = \sigma(v)$. Moreover, we say a strategy has *memory size m* if there exists a finite state machine with output with m states computing the strategy (see Grädel et al. [18] for more details).

Next we define the plays that are consistent with a given strategy for Player i. Typically, this means that the token is placed at some initial vertex and then, whenever a vertex of Player i is reached, then Player i uses the move prescribed by the strategy for the current play prefix to extend this prefix. Note that the strategy does not have control over the initial placement of the token.

Here we will use a more general notion, inspired by previous work in optimal strategies for Muller games [17] and in subgame perfect equilibria in graph games [19,38]: the initial prefix over which the strategy does not have control over might be longer than just the initial vertex. This means strategies are also applicable to prefixes that where not constructed according to the strategy. However, crucially, the strategy still gets access to that prefix and therefore can base its decisions on the prefix it had no control over. This generality will turn out to be useful both when defining adaptive strategies and when combining strategies to obtain adaptive strategies.

Formally, for a play prefix $\mathbf{p} = v_0 v_1 \cdots v_n$ and a strategy σ for Player i, a play ρ is a $(\sigma, \mathbf{p})$-play if $\rho = \mathbf{p} v_{n+1} v_{n+2} \cdots$ with $v_{k+1} = \sigma(v_0 v_1 \cdots v_k)$ for all

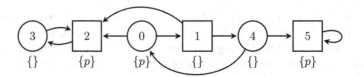

Fig. 1. First motivating example for adaptive strategies

$v_k \in V_i$ with $k \geq n$. Note that the prefix p is arbitrary here, i.e., it might not have been constructed following the strategy σ. Moreover, a (σ, p)-play prefix pp' is a prefix of a (σ, p)-play. We say that a play ρ starting in some vertex v is consistent with σ, if it is a (σ, v)-play (which is the classical notion of consistency). Finally, a play prefix p is consistent with σ if it is the prefix of some play that is consistent with σ.

In the paper introducing rLTL [36], Tabuada and Neider gave a doubly-exponential time algorithm that solves the classical rLTL synthesis problem, which is equivalent to solving the following problem.

Problem 1. Given an rLTL game $\mathcal{G}$, an initial vertex v_0 and a truth value $b \in \mathbb{B}_4$, compute a strategy σ (if one exists at all) for Player 0 such that every (σ, v_0)-play has value at least b.

Note that Tabuada and Neider were interested in strategies for Player 0 that enforce the value b from v_0, i.e., strategies such that every consistent play starting in the given initial vertex has at least value b. In contrast, we will compute strategies that are improvements in two dimensions: (i) they enforce the optimal value rather than a given one, and (ii) they do so from every possible play prefix, even if they did not have control over the prefix.

3   Adaptive Strategies

In this section, we start by presenting a motivating example, a game in which classical strategies for Player 0 are not necessarily optimal (in an intuitive sense). We then formalize this intuition by introducing adaptive strategies and give a doubly-exponential time algorithm to compute such strategies.

Motivating Example. Consider the arena given in Fig. 1 (where Player 0's vertices are shown as circles and Player 1's vertices are shown as squares) with the rLTL specification $\varphi = \boxdot p$.

Suppose the token is initially placed at vertex 0. Considering Player 1 plays optimally, the token would eventually reach vertex 2, from which the best possible scenario for Player 0 is to enforce a play where p holds at infinitely many positions. As the classical problem only considers the worst-case analysis, a classical strategy for Player 0 is to try to visit vertex 2 infinitely often. That can be done by moving the token along one of the following edges every time the token reaches Player 0's vertices: $\{0 \rightarrow 1; 3 \rightarrow 2; 4 \rightarrow 0\}$. Note that the move $4 \rightarrow 0$

is irrelevant in this worst-case analysis, as vertex 4 is never reached if Player 1 plays optimally.

Suppose Player 1 makes a bad move by moving along $1 \rightarrow 4$. Then, Player 0 can force the play to eventually just stay at vertex 5, and hence, p holds almost always. However, the above classical strategy for Player 0 moves the play back to vertex 0, from which p might not hold almost always. Therefore, a better strategy for Player 0 is to move along $4 \rightarrow 5$ if the token reaches vertex 4 to get a play where p holds almost always; otherwise, enforce a play where p holds at infinitely many positions as earlier by moving along $0 \rightarrow 1$ and then $3 \rightarrow 2$ repeatedly.

In the worst case, i.e., if Player 1 does not make a bad move by reaching vertex 4, both strategies yield value 0011. However, if Player 1 does make a bad move by reaching vertex 4, the second strategy achieves value 0111 on some plays, while the second one does not. So, in the worst case analysis, both strategies are equally good, but if we assume that Player 1 is not necessarily antagonistic, then the second strategy is better as it is able to exploit the bad move by Player 1. We call such a strategy *adaptive* as it adapts its moves to achieve the best possible outcome after each bad move of the opponent. We will formalize this shortly.

To further illustrate the notion of adaptive strategies, consider another game with the arena shown in Fig. 2 and with rLTL specification $\varphi' = (\ominus \neg q \Rightarrow \Box p) \wedge (\ominus q \Rightarrow \Box r)$. In this example, Player 1 has only two strategies starting from vertex 0: one moving the token along $0 \rightarrow 1$ and one moving the token along $0 \rightarrow 2$.

The best truth value Player 0 can enforce in this game is 0011. This is because Player 1 can move along the edge $0 \rightarrow 2$, which satisfies the second implication with value 1111 (as q does not occur), but also satisfies the premise of the first implication with value 1111. Hence, the value of the whole formula is the value of the subformula $\Box p$. The best value Player 0 can achieve for it is indeed 0011 by looping between vertices 3 and 2. His only other choice, i.e., to move to 4 eventually, only results in the value 0001.

However, if Player 1 does not take the edge $0 \rightarrow 2$ but instead moves to vertex 2 via vertex 1, Player 0 can gain from this *bad move* by instead moving to vertex 4. In that case, the formula is satisfied with truth value 1111. Thus, a strategy that adapts to the bad move by the opponent can achieve a better value than one that does not, if they do make a bad move.

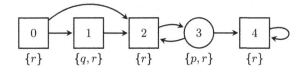

Fig. 2. Second motivating example for adaptive strategies

3.1 Definitions

Recall that a $(\sigma, \mathbf{p})$-play for a strategy σ for Player i and a play prefix $\mathbf{p}$ (not necessarily consistent with σ) is an extension of $\mathbf{p}$ by σ, i.e., Player i uses the strategy σ to extend the play prefix p they had not control over, while still taking the prefix $\mathbf{p}$ into account when making the decisions. We say that a strategy σ for Player 0 *enforces* a truth value of b from a play prefix $\mathbf{p}$, if we have $\mathcal{V}(\rho) \geq b$ for every $(\sigma, \mathbf{p})$-play ρ. Similarly, we say a strategy τ for Player 1 enforces a truth value of b from a play prefix $\mathbf{p}$, if we have $\mathcal{V}(\rho) \leq b$ for every $(\tau, \mathbf{p})$-play ρ. This conforms to our intuition that Player 0 tries to maximize the truth value while Player 1 tries to minimize it. Moreover, we say Player i can enforce a value b from some prefix $\mathbf{p}$ if they have a strategy that enforces b from $\mathbf{p}$.

Remark 1. Let $\mathbf{p}$ be a play prefix. If Player 0 can enforce value b_0 from $\mathbf{p}$ and Player 1 can enforce value b_1 from $\mathbf{p}$ then $b_0 \leq b_1$.

For example, consider the game given in Fig. 1 with the rLTL specification $\boxdot p$. Using the analysis given in Sect. 3, we can see that Player 0 can enforce 0111 and 0011 from prefixes 014 and 012, respectively, by moving the token along $\{0 \rightarrow 1; 4 \rightarrow 5; 3 \rightarrow 2\}$. It is easy to check that these are the best values Player 0 can enforce from those prefixes as Player 1 can enforce the same values from these prefixes.

We are interested in a strategy that enforces the best possible value from each play prefix. This is formalized as follows.

Definition 1 (Adaptive Strategies). *In an* rLTL *game, a strategy σ_0 for Player 0 is adaptive if from every play prefix $\mathbf{p}$, no strategy for Player 0 enforces a better truth value than σ_0, that is, if some strategy σ for Player 0 enforces a truth value of b from $\mathbf{p}$, then σ_0 also enforces the value b from $\mathbf{p}$.*

Note that $\mathbf{p}$ is not required to be consistent with σ_0 in the above definition, i.e., an adaptive strategy achieves the best possible outcome from every possible play prefix (even for those it had no control over when they are constructed). Also, let us mention that a dual notion can be defined for Player 1.

As mentioned earlier, one can notice that the concept of adaptive strategies is similar to the concept of subgame perfect equilibrium [19]. Furthermore, adaptive strategies can be used to extend the notion of subgame perfect equilibrium to rLTL games as in the following remark.

Remark 2. Given an rLTL game, a pair of adaptive strategies for both players forms a subgame perfect equilibrium for the game, and vice versa.

Here, we prefer the notion of adaptive strategies over the notion of subgame perfect equilibria, as we focus on strategies for Player 0 and generally disregard strategies of Player 1.

3.2 Computing Adaptive Strategies

Now, to synthesize an adaptive strategy, we need to monitor the bad moves of the opponent at runtime by keeping track of the best value that can be enforced from the current play prefix. To do that, using the idea of automata-based runtime verification [6], we construct multiple parity automata to monitor the bad moves of the opponent and then we synthesize adaptive strategies by using a reduction to parity games (see [18] for definitions).

Given an rLTL game $\mathcal{G} = (\mathcal{A}, \varphi)$ with $\mathcal{A} = (V, E, \lambda)$, we proceed as follows:

1. We construct generalized (non-deterministic) Büchi automata $\mathcal{A}^b$ such that $L(\mathcal{A}^b) = \{w \in (2^{\mathcal{P}})^\omega \mid \mathcal{V}(w, \varphi) \geq b\}$ for all $b \in \mathbb{B}_4$.
2. We determinize each $\mathcal{A}^b$ to obtain a deterministic parity automaton $\mathcal{C}^b$ with the same language.
3. For each b, we construct a parity game $\mathcal{G}^b$ by taking the product of the arena $\mathcal{A}$ and the parity automaton $\mathcal{C}^b$.
4. We solve the above parity games $\mathcal{G}^b$ [10], yielding, for each truth value b, a finite-state winning strategy for the original game $\mathcal{G}$ with value b (if one exists).
5. We combine all these winning strategies for Player 0 computed in the last step to obtain an adaptive strategy σ for Player 0.

Let us now explain each step in more detail.

Step 1. We construct the generalized non-deterministic Büchi automata $\mathcal{A}^b$ such that $L(\mathcal{A}^b) = \{w \in (2^{\mathcal{P}})^\omega \mid \mathcal{V}(w, \varphi) \geq b\}$ for all $b \in \mathbb{B}_4$. By Theorem 1, the automaton $\mathcal{A}^b$ has $2^{O(|\varphi|)}$ states and $O(|\varphi|)$ accepting sets.

Step 2. We determinize each $\mathcal{A}^b$ to get a deterministic parity automaton $\mathcal{C}^b = (Q^b, 2^{\mathcal{P}}, q_0^b, \delta^b, \Omega^b)$ with $2^{2^{O(|\varphi|)}}$ states and $2^{O(|\varphi|)}$ colors [34].

Step 3. We construct the (unlabelled) product arena $\mathcal{A}^b = (V^b, E^b)$ of the arena $\mathcal{A} = (V, E, \lambda)$ and the parity automaton $\mathcal{C}^b$ such that $V^b = V \times Q^b$, $V_i^b = V_i \times Q^b$ for $i \in \{0, 1\}$, and

$$((v, q), (v', q')) \in E^b \text{ if and only if } (v, v') \in E \text{ and } \delta^b(q, \lambda(v)) = q'.$$

The function $\bar{\Omega}^b$ assigns colors to the vertices such that $\bar{\Omega}^b(v, q) = \Omega^b(q)$. The desired parity games are the $\mathcal{G}^b = (\mathcal{A}^b, \bar{\Omega}^b)$ with $b \in \mathbb{B}_4$.

It is easy to verify that Player 0 wins a play $\rho' = (v_0, q_0^b)(v_1, q_1^b) \cdots$ in $\mathcal{G}^b$ if and only if the value of the play $\rho = v_0 v_1 \cdots$ in $\mathcal{G}$ is at least b. Furthermore, given a path $\rho = v_0 v_1 \cdots v_k$ in $\mathcal{A}$, there is a unique path of the form $\rho' = (v_0, q_0^b)(v_1, q_1^b) \cdots (v_k, q_k^b)$ in $\mathcal{A}^b$, that is when $q_{i+1}^b = \delta^b(q_i^b, v_i)$ for all $0 \leq i \leq k-1$.

Since winning a play in $\mathcal{G}^b$ is equivalent to the corresponding play in $\mathcal{G}$ satisfying φ with truth value b or greater, we can characterize the enforcement of b in $\mathcal{G}$ by the winning region of Player 0 in $\mathcal{G}^b$, i.e., the set of vertices from which Player 0 has a winning strategy. This can easily be shown by simulating a winning strategy from (v, q) to extend the play prefix p and vice versa.

Remark 3. Fix a play prefix p in the rLTL game $\mathcal{G}$, and let (v, q^b) be the last vertex of the corresponding play in the parity game $\mathcal{G}^b$ for some b. Then, Player 0 can enforce b from p if and only if (v, q^b) is in his winning region of $\mathcal{G}^b$.

Step 4. We solve the resulting parity games $\mathcal{G}^b$ and determine the winning regions $\mathrm{Win}(\mathcal{G}^b)$ of Player 0 and uniform memoryless winning strategies σ^b for Player 0 that are winning from every vertex in the corresponding winning region. The parity games have $n = |V| \cdot 2^{2^{O(|\varphi|)}}$ vertices and $k = 2^{O(|\varphi|)}$ colors. Since $k < \lg(n)$, these can be solved in time $O(n^5) = |V|^5 \cdot 2^{2^{O(|\varphi|)}}$ [10].

Step 5. Consider the extended rLTL game $\mathcal{G}' = (\mathcal{A}', \varphi)$, where $\mathcal{A}' = (V', E', \lambda')$ with $V' = V \times Q^{0000} \times \cdots \times Q^{1111}$,

$$E' = \{((v_1, q_1^{0000}, \ldots, q_1^{1111}), (v_2, q_2^{0000}, \ldots, q_2^{1111})) \mid$$
$$(v_1, v_2) \in E \text{ and } \delta^b(q_1^b, \lambda(v)) = q_2^b \text{ for all } b \in \mathbb{B}_4\},$$

and λ' such that $\lambda'(v, q^{0000}, \ldots, q^{1111}) = \lambda(v)$ for all $v \in V$ and $q^b \in Q^b$.

It is easy to see that there is a one to one correspondence between the plays in both games $\mathcal{G}$ and $\mathcal{G}'$. Besides that, the rLTL specification is also the same in both games. Therefore, computing an adaptive strategy in the game $\mathcal{G}$ is equivalent to computing one in the game $\mathcal{G}'$. Now using the analysis given in Step 3, we have the following in the rLTL game $\mathcal{G}'$:

- A vertex v' is in $\mathrm{E}_{\geq b} = \{(v, q^{0000}, \ldots, q^{1111}) \in V' \mid (v, q^b) \in \mathrm{Win}(\mathcal{G}^b)\}$ if and only if Player 0 can enforce b from every play prefix in $\mathcal{G}'$ ending in v'.
- Using these sets, we now define the set $\mathrm{E}_{=b}$ of vertices from which the maximum value Player 0 can enforce is b. Formally, this set is given by

$$\mathrm{E}_{=b} = \begin{cases} \mathrm{E}_{\geq 1111} & \text{if } b = 1111, \\ \mathrm{E}_{\geq b} \setminus \mathrm{E}_{\geq b+1} & \text{if } b < 1111, \end{cases}$$

where $b+1$ is the smallest value bigger than $b < 1111$. Note that the sets $\mathrm{E}_{=b}$ form a partition of the vertex set of $\mathcal{G}'$.

Furthermore, it is easy to see that if a play ρ satisfies a parity objective then every play sharing a suffix with ρ also satisfies the parity objective. Since the game $\mathcal{G}'$ is a product of parity games and since we have characterized the enforcement of truth values via the membership in the winning regions of the parity games (see Remark 3), the next remark follows.

Remark 4. In the rLTL game $\mathcal{G}'$, for two play prefixes $\mathsf{p}_1, \mathsf{p}_2$ ending in the same vertex, the following holds: if a memoryless strategy σ for Player 0 enforces a truth value b from p_1, then it also enforces the value b from p_2.

Then, we can see that if the token stays in $\mathrm{E}_{=b}$ for some b, then Player 0 can simulate the strategy σ^b for $\mathcal{G}^b$ to enforce the value b in $\mathcal{G}'$. Therefore, we obtain a memoryless adaptive strategy σ for Player 0 in the game $\mathcal{G}'$ as follows: for every vertex $(v, q^{0000}, \ldots, q^{1111})$ in $\mathrm{E}_{=b}$, we define $\sigma(v, q^{0000}, \ldots, q^{1111})$ to be the unique successor of $(v, q^{0000}, \ldots, q^{1111})$ in $\mathcal{G}'$ that corresponds to the successor $\sigma^b(v, q^b)$ of (v, q^b) in $\mathcal{G}^b$. Thus, σ simulates the strategy σ^b for the largest b such that the value b can be enforced (which is exactly what σ^b does from such a prefix). Hence, it is an adaptive strategy for Player 0 in $\mathcal{G}'$.

Finally, using the strategy σ, one can compute a corresponding strategy in the game $\mathcal{G}$ with memory $Q^{0000} \times Q^{0001} \times \cdots \times Q^{1111}$, which is used to simulate the positional strategy σ. The resulting finite-state strategy is an adaptive strategy for Player 0 in $\mathcal{G}$.

Note that the adaptive strategy in $\mathcal{G}$ is of doubly-exponential size in $|V|$ and $|\varphi|$. This upper bound is tight, since there is a doubly-exponential lower bound on the size of winning strategies for LTL games [30], which can be lifted to rLTL games.

Similarly, one can compute an adaptive strategy for Player 1. Hence, an adaptive strategy for both players in an rLTL game can be computed in time doubly-exponential in the size of the formula.

Theorem 2. *Given an* rLTL *game, an adaptive strategy of a player can be computed in doubly-exponential time. Moreover, each player has an adaptive strategy with doubly-exponential memory size.*

Note that adaptive strategies enforce the best possible value from the given prefix. This value can be obtained at runtime as follows: Given a play prefix $\mathbf{p}$ ending in some vertex v, let $(q^{0000}, \ldots, q^{1111})$ be the state of the automaton implementing the adaptive finite-state strategy computed above is in after the prefix $\mathbf{p}$. Note that this state has to be tracked to determine the next move the strategy prescribes at prefix $\mathbf{p}$ (in case $v \in V_0$). Then, there is a unique b such that $(v, q^{0000}, \ldots, q^{1111}) \in \mathrm{E}_{=b}$. Then, the value currently enforced by the adaptive strategy is b, which, by construction, is the maximal one that can be enforced from $\mathbf{p}$.

4 Strongly Adaptive Strategies

In the previous section, we have argued the importance of adaptive strategies and proved that in every rLTL game both players have an adaptive strategy. Intuitively, such a strategy exploits bad moves of the opponent to always enforce the best truth value possible after a given prefix. However, such a strategy does not necessarily seek out opportunities for the opponent to make bad moves. We argue that this property implies that some adaptive strategies are more desirable than others, which leads us to the notion of strongly adaptive strategies.

In this section, we define strongly adaptive strategies, which are based on a fine-grained analysis of the possibilities a strategy gives the opponent to make bad moves and the resulting outcomes of such bad moves. We show that strongly adaptive strategies do not exist in every rLTL game. This is in stark contrast to adaptive strategies, which always exists. Nevertheless, we give a doubly-exponential time algorithm that decides whether a strongly adaptive strategy exists and, if yes, computes one.

4.1   Bad Moves

We already have used the notion of bad moves in Sect. 3 in an intuitive, but informal, way. Formally, we say a play $\rho = v_0 v_1 \cdots$ contains a bad move of Player i at position $j > 0$ if the player can enforce some value b from the prefix $v_0 \cdots v_{j-1}$ but can no longer enforce the value b from the prefix $v_0 \cdots v_j$. Note that the position j is the target of the bad move. Moreover, note that moving from $v_0 \cdots v_{j-1}$ to v_j can only be a bad move for Player i if it is Player i's turn at v_{j-1}. Also, there must be some other edge from v_{j-1} to a vertex $v \neq v_j$ so that they can still enforce b from $v_0 \cdots v_{j-1} v$.

For the example given in Fig. 1, we know that Player 1 can enforce the value 0011 from 01 (by moving the token from 01 to 2). Suppose she moves the token from 01 to 4 instead. Then, Player 0 can enforce 0111 by visiting vertex 5. Hence Player 1 can no longer enforce 0011 from 014. Therefore, the move from prefix 01 to vertex 4 made by Player 1 is bad.

Note that if Player 1 makes a bad move from a play prefix $\mathbf{p}$ to vertex v, then the maximum value Player 0 can enforce from $\mathbf{p}v$ is strictly larger than the maximum value he can enforce from $\mathbf{p}$. Hence, if the maximum value Player 0 can enforce from a play prefix is 1111, then Player 1 can not make any bad move from that prefix. Moreover, assuming Player 0 does not make any bad move, the maximum value Player 0 can enforce from any play prefix can increase at most four times during a play. Thus, Player 1 can make at most four bad moves against an adaptive strategy, because such a strategy does not make any bad moves.

Remark 5. Let σ be an adaptive strategy and $\mathbf{p}$ a play prefix (not necessarily consistent with σ). Then, every $(\sigma, \mathbf{p})$-play $\rho = v_0 v_1 \cdots$ contains at most four bad moves of Player 1 after $\mathbf{p}$. Also, if there is no bad move by Player 1 at positions $j_0, j_0 + 1, \ldots, j_1$ in ρ, then σ enforces the same truth values from every prefix of the form $v_0 \cdots v_j$ with $j_0 - 1 \leq j < j_1$.

Our next example shows that an adaptive strategy does not actively seek out opportunities for the opponent to make bad moves, it just exploits those made.

4.2   Motivating Example

Recall the example given in Fig. 1. The strategy for Player 0 given by $\{0 \rightarrow 1; 3 \rightarrow 2; 4 \rightarrow 5\}$ is adaptive: if Player 1 makes a bad move by moving from 1 to 4, then moving from 4 to 5 improves the value of the play to 0111. Such an improvement can only be enforced after the bad move.

Another adaptive strategy for Player 0 is to move along $0 \rightarrow 2$ directly in his first move and then move along $3 \rightarrow 2$ every time. Then, the token can never reach vertex 1. Hence, Player 1 can never make a bad move. However, it also means that there can not be a play with value 0111. By contrast, if Player 0 moves along $0 \rightarrow 1$, there is a chance of getting such plays (when Player 1 makes a bad move of $1 \rightarrow 4$). Therefore, using the earlier strategy of moving the token along $0 \to 1$, Player 0 might be able to enforce 0111 at some point, but he can never achieve the value 0111 when moving directly to vertex 2.

Similarly, in many games, a player may have two (or more) optimal choices to move the token from some prefix. In such situations, that player should compare the bad moves their opponent can make in both choices and determine the choice in which they can enforce the best value after a bad move has been made by the opponent. To capture this, we refine the notion of adaptive strategies by introducing strongly adaptive strategies, which are, in a sense to be formalized below, the best adaptive strategies.

4.3 Definitions

In this section, we introduce the necessary machinery to define strongly adaptive strategies for Player 0. Throughout this section, we are concerned with ranking adaptive strategies according to the number of bad moves they allow Player 1 to make, and on the effect these moves have. For the sake of conciseness, unless stated otherwise, from now on a bad move always refers to a bad move by Player 1.

We begin by introducing a ranking of plays and then lift this to strategies. As the number of bad moves in one play is bounded by four, this results in at most five truth values that can be enforced from prefixes of the play, i.e., the one that is enforced before the first bad move, and the ones after each bad move. If Player 1 makes less than four bad moves during a play, we use the symbol $\perp \notin \mathbb{B}_4$ to signify this.

We collect this information in a summary, a five-tuple $(b_0, \ldots, b_k, \perp, \ldots, \perp) \in (\mathbb{B}_4 \cup \{\perp\})^5$ such that $\perp \neq b_0 < b_1 < \cdots < b_k$. The set of all summaries is denoted by $\mathcal{S}$.

Fix an adaptive strategy σ for Player 0, a play prefix $\mathbf{p}$ not necessarily consistent with σ, and a $(\sigma, \mathbf{p})$-play ρ, and let $0 \leq k \leq 4$ be the number of bad moves by Player 1 after $\mathbf{p}$. Define $\mathbf{p}_0 = \mathbf{p}$ and let $\mathbf{p}_j$, for $1 \leq j \leq k$, be the prefix of ρ ending at the position of the j-th bad move. Due to Remark 5, these prefixes contain information about all possible truth vales that are enforced by Player 0 from prefixes of ρ. We employ summaries to capture the values a given *strategy* σ enforces from these prefixes. Formally, for $0 \leq j \leq k$, let b_j be the maximal value that σ enforces from $\mathbf{p}_j$. As σ is adaptive, these values are strictly increasing. So, we can define the summary $\mathrm{smry}(\sigma, \mathbf{p}, \rho) = (b_0, \ldots, b_k, \perp, \ldots, \perp)$. Intuitively, the summary collects all information about which truth values the strategy σ enforces after each bad move has been made. If there are less than four bad moves in ρ after $\mathbf{p}$, then we fill the summary with $\perp$'s to obtain a vector of length five.

We will use such summaries to compare strategies. To do so, we compare summaries in lexicographic order $\leq_{\mathrm{lex}}$ with $\perp$ being the smallest element. In other words, we prefer larger truth values of smaller ones and prefer the opportunity for a bad move over the impossibility of a bad move.

Example 3. Consider again the game in Fig. 1. Let σ_1 be the memoryless Player 0 strategy always making the moves $\{0 \to 1; 3 \to 2; 4 \to 5\}$. Then,

$$\text{smry}(\sigma_1, 0, 0145^\omega) = \text{smry}(\sigma_1, 01, 0145^\omega) = (0011, 0111, \bot, \bot, \bot)$$

and $\text{smry}(\sigma_1, 014, 0145^\omega) = (0111, \bot, \bot, \bot, \bot)$ because the play 0145^ω does not contain a bad move of Player 1 after 014. In addition, $\text{smry}(\sigma_1, \text{p}, 01(23)^\omega) = (0011, \bot, \bot, \bot, \bot)$ for every prefix p of $01(23)^\omega$, as the play does not contain any bad move of Player 1.

Let σ_2 now be the memoryless Player 0 strategy given by $\{0 \to 2; 3 \to 2; 4 \to 5\}$. Then, we have $\text{smry}(\sigma_2, \text{p}, 0(23)^\omega) = (0011, \bot, \bot, \bot, \bot)$ for every prefix p of $0(23)^\omega$ because the play does not contain bad moves of Player 1.

We continue by listing some simple properties of summaries that are useful later on. Consider the prefixes 0, 01, 014 of 0145^ω in Example 3. The former two have the same summary s, while the summary of the latter is obtained by shifting s to the left. Note that moving from 01 to 4 is a bad move of Player 1, while moving from 0 to 1 is not. By inspecting the definition of play summaries, it is clear that extending plays by bad moves corresponds to a left shift, while Remark 5 implies that the absence of bad moves keeps summaries stable.

To formalize this, we use the following notation: for $s = (b_0, \ldots, b_k, \bot, \ldots, \bot) \in \mathcal{S}$ with $k > 0$ let $\text{lft}(s) = (b_1, \ldots, b_k, \bot, \ldots, \bot) \in \mathcal{S}$, i.e., we shift s to the left and fill the last entry with a $\bot$. As entries in summaries are strictly increasing, we have $\text{lft}(s) >_{\text{lex}} s$ for every s with at least two non-$\bot$ entries.

Remark 6. Let σ be an adaptive strategy for Player 0, let p be a play prefix, and let $\rho = v_0 v_1 \cdots$ be a (σ, p)-play. Further, let $n = |\text{p}|$, i.e., v_{n-1} is the last vertex of p, and note that ρ is also a $(\sigma, \text{p}v_n)$-play.

If ρ has a bad move at position n, then $\text{smry}(\sigma, \text{p}v_n, \rho) = \text{lft}(\text{smry}(\sigma, \text{p}, \rho))$ (reflecting the fact that ρ has one bad move less after $\text{p}v_n$ than after p), otherwise we have $\text{smry}(\sigma, \text{p}v_n, \rho) = \text{smry}(\sigma, \text{p}, \rho)$. Note that we have kept σ and ρ fixed and just added a vertex to the prefix we consider.

As seen above, a bad move shifts the summary to the left. The following remark shows a dual result, allowing us to determine the summary of a play prefix of length one from the summary of play prefix up to the first bad move. In Example 3, note that the strategy σ_1 (using the edges $\{0 \to 1; 3 \to 2; 4 \to 5\}$) enforces value 0011 from 0, i.e., the first entry of $\text{smry}(\sigma_1, 0, 0145^\omega)$ is 0011. The play 0145^ω has its first bad move of Player 1 at position 2, and the corresponding summary is $\text{smry}(\sigma_1, 014, 0145^\omega) = (0111, \bot, \bot, \bot, \bot)$. Hence, $\text{smry}(\sigma_1, 0, 0145^\omega)$ must be the "concatenation" $(0011, 0111, \bot, \bot, \bot)$ of 0011 and $(0111, \bot, \bot, \bot, \bot)$ (with the last $\bot$ removed). In general, we have the following property.

Remark 7. Let $s = (b_0, \ldots, b_k, \bot, \ldots, \bot) \in \mathcal{S}$ with $k > 0$ and let v be a vertex. Let σ be an adaptive strategy such that b_0 is the maximal value that σ enforces from v and let ρ be a (σ, v)-play with at least one bad move, and let p be the prefix of ρ ending at the position of the first bad move. Then, $\text{smry}(\sigma, \text{p}, \rho) = \text{lft}(s)$ if and only if $\text{smry}(\sigma, v, \rho) = s$.

Again, recall Example 3, and consider the plays $\rho_b = 0145^\omega$ (with a bad move by Player 1) and $\rho_n = 01(23)^\omega$ (without a bad move), which are both $(\sigma_1, 0)$-plays. We have $\mathrm{smry}(\sigma_1, 0, \rho_b) = (0011, 0111, \bot, \bot, \bot)$ and $\mathrm{smry}(\sigma_1, 0, \rho_n) = (0011, \bot, \bot, \bot, \bot)$. Disregarding the $\bot$'s the summary of ρ_n can be seen as a strict prefix of the summary of ρ_b. Note that $(0011, \bot, \bot, \bot, \bot) <_{\mathrm{lex}} (0011, 0111, \bot, \bot, \bot)$.

In general, fix a strategy σ, a play prefix $\mathbf{p}$, and a $(\sigma, \mathbf{p})$-play ρ with $\mathrm{smry}(\sigma, \mathbf{p}, \rho) = (b_0, \ldots, b_k, \bot, \ldots, \bot)$. Then, for every $k' < k$ there is a $(\sigma, \mathbf{p})$-play ρ' with $\mathrm{smry}(\sigma, \mathbf{p}, \rho') = (b_0, \ldots, b_{k'}, \bot, \ldots, \bot)$, i.e., any play where Player 1 stops making bad moves after the first k' ones (recall that making bad moves is a choice).

To formalize this, we say that a summary $(b_0, \ldots, b_k, \bot, \ldots, \bot)$ is a strict prefix of a summary $(b'_0, \ldots, b'_{k'}, \bot, \ldots, \bot)$ if $k < k'$ and $b_j = b'_j$ for all $0 \leq j \leq k$, i.e., we only consider non-$\bot$ entries. Now, fix $(\sigma, \mathbf{p})$-plays ρ, ρ'. We say that ρ is $(\sigma, \mathbf{p})$-covered by ρ' if $\mathrm{smry}(\sigma, \mathbf{p}, \rho)$ is a strict prefix of $\mathrm{smry}(\sigma, \mathbf{p}, \rho')$. Also, we say that ρ is a $(\sigma, \mathbf{p})$-uncovered play if there is no $(\sigma, \mathbf{p})$-play ρ' that covers it. When σ and $\mathbf{p}$ are clear from context, we drop them and say that a play is uncovered. In the example, ρ_n is $(\sigma_1, 0)$-covered by ρ_b, which is $(\sigma_1, 0)$-uncovered.

Now, we lift summaries from plays to strategies by defining $\mathrm{smry}(\sigma, \mathbf{p})$ as the lexicographical minimum over all $\mathrm{smry}(\sigma, \mathbf{p}, \rho)$ where ρ ranges over $(\sigma, \mathbf{p})$-uncovered plays. Note that if ρ $(\sigma, \mathbf{p})$-covers ρ', then the summary of ρ is a strict prefix of the summary of ρ' and, therefore, strictly smaller. Our definition of $\mathrm{smry}(\sigma, \mathbf{p})$ discards such plays when computing the minimum, but the information is not lost as it appears as a prefix of a covering play.

In the running example, we have $\mathrm{smry}(\sigma_1, 0) = (0011, 0111, \bot, \bot, \bot)$ and $\mathrm{smry}(\sigma_2, 0) = (0011, \bot, \bot, \bot, \bot)$.

Remark 8. Let σ be an adaptive strategy for Player 0 and let $\mathbf{p}$ be a play prefix. If $\mathrm{smry}(\sigma, \mathbf{p}) = s$ for some $s \in \mathcal{S}$, then there exists a $(\sigma, \mathbf{p})$-uncovered play ρ such that $\mathrm{smry}(\sigma, \mathbf{p}, \rho) = s$.

Finally, we are ready to formalize our intuitive notion of strongly adaptive strategies, i.e., adaptive strategies that seek out opportunities for the opponent to make bad moves. Recall that summaries record the possibility, and the effect, of Player 1 making bad moves. So, we intuitively say a strategy is strongly adaptive if it maximizes the summaries globally.

Recall that a strategy is adaptive if the value it enforces from any possible play prefix is as large as the value any other strategy enforces from that prefix. Analogously, a strategy is strongly adaptive if its summary for every play prefix is as good as the summary from the play prefix for any other strategy.

Definition 2. *An adaptive strategy σ_0 is strongly adaptive if $\mathrm{smry}(\sigma_0, \mathbf{p}) \geq_{\mathrm{lex}} \mathrm{smry}(\sigma, \mathbf{p})$ for every adaptive strategy σ and every play prefix $\mathbf{p}$.*

Before we start our proof, let us introduce one more useful bit of notation. For every play prefix $\mathbf{p}$, let $\mathrm{smry}(\mathbf{p})$ denote the lexicographical maximum of $\mathrm{smry}(\sigma, \mathbf{p})$ over all adaptive strategies σ for Player 0 in the game $\mathcal{G}$, i.e.,

$$\text{smry}(\mathbf{p}) = \max_{\sigma} \text{smry}(\sigma, \mathbf{p}),$$

where σ ranges over all adaptive strategies for Player 0.

Note that every strongly adaptive strategy is adaptive by definition, and the first entry of $\text{smry}(\mathbf{p})$ is equal to the maximal value that can be enforced from $\mathbf{p}$. However, as argued above, not every adaptive strategy is strongly adaptive, so in particular a strongly adaptive strategy for Player 0 never makes a bad move (of Player 0).

4.4 Existence of Strongly Adaptive Strategies

While strongly adaptive strategies generalize adaptive strategies, there is a catch in the definition: The former may not always exist, whereas the latter always do. To show this, consider the graph given in Fig. 3 with initial vertex 0 and the formula $\varphi = \square p$. It is clear that Player 0 can enforce 0011 from every play prefix in $0(10)^*$ by eventually moving to vertex 3. And if at some point, Player 1 makes the bad move $1 \rightarrow 2$, then Player 0 enforces 0111 as the token stays at vertex 2 forever. However, every adaptive strategy for Player 0 has to eventually visit vertex 3, unless Player 1 makes a bad move prior.

Note that Player 1 can only make a bad move at vertex 1, so visiting 1 once more when at vertex 0 instead of moving to vertex 3 gives her another chance to make a bad move. So, to optimize the enforced value under one bad move, Player 1 should stay in the loop between 0 and 1 forever. However, this is not the optimal behavior if no bad move occurs, as looping yields a value of 0000, which is smaller than the value 0011 that is achieved by eventually moving to 3.

Formally, for $n \geq 0$, let σ_n be the strategy such that $\sigma_n(0(10)^{n'}) = 1$ for all $n' < n$ and $\sigma_n(0(10)^{n'}) = 3$ for all $n' \geq n$, i.e., σ_n gives Player 1 n chances to make a bad move and then moves to 3, thereby preventing her from making a bad move. Note that each of the σ_n is adaptive, but σ_{n+1} gives Player 1 more opportunities to make a bad move than σ_n, namely for the prefix $0(10)^n$.

Fix some n. There are only two $(\sigma_{n+1}, 0(10)^n)$-plays, i.e., $0(10)^n 10(34)^\omega$ (Player 1 does not make a bad move) and $0(10)^n 12^\omega$ (Player 1 makes a bad move). Then, $\text{smry}(\sigma_{n+1}, 0(10)^n, 0(10)^n 10(34)^\omega) = (0011, \perp, \perp, \perp, \perp)$ as well as $\text{smry}(\sigma_{n+1}, 0(10)^n, 0(10)^n 12^\omega) = (0011, 0111, \perp, \perp, \perp)$. Hence, we conclude $\text{smry}(\sigma_{n+1}, 0(10)^n) = (0011, 0111, \perp, \perp, \perp)$, as the former is covered by the latter.

Towards a contradiction assume there is a strongly adaptive strategy σ. By definition, we have

$$\text{smry}(\sigma, 0(10)^n) \geq_{\text{lex}} \text{smry}(\sigma_{n+1}, 0(10)^n) = (0011, 0111, \perp, \perp, \perp) \qquad (1)$$

for every n. As we have $\text{smry}(\sigma, 0(10)^n) <_{\text{lex}} (1111, \perp, \perp, \perp, \perp)$ (p does not hold at vertex 0), σ must give Player 1 the chance to make at least one bad move after the prefix $0(10)^n$. So, we must have $\sigma(0(10)^n) = 1$, as Player 1 can only make a bad move at vertex 1.

Thus, the play $(01)^\omega$ (with value 0000) is a $(\sigma, 0(10)^n)$-play for every n, i.e., σ only enforces 0000 from every such prefix. Hence, the first entry of

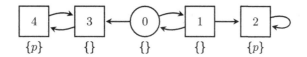

Fig. 3. An rLTL game with no strongly adaptive strategy

smry$(\sigma, 0(10)^n)$ is 0000 for every n. This contradicts Inequality (1). Therefore, σ is not strongly adaptive, i.e., Player 0 does not have a strongly adaptive strategy in the game.

As strongly adaptive strategies do not necessarily exist, we are interested in the following problem.

Problem 2. Given an rLTL game, determine whether a strongly adaptive strategy for Player 0 exists and, if yes, compute one.

4.5 Computing Strongly Adaptive Strategies

We solve Problem 2 for an rLTL game $\mathcal{G} = (\mathcal{A}, \varphi)$ by constructing the parity games $\mathcal{G}^b$ for each b and the extended game $\mathcal{G}' = (\mathcal{A}', \varphi)$ as in the algorithm given in Sect. 3.2. Recall that Player 0 wins $\mathcal{G}^b$ if and only if he can enforce b in $\mathcal{G}$ and that $\mathcal{G}'$ is the product of the $\mathcal{G}^b$. As we have described in Step 5 of that algorithm, it is easy to see that solving Problem 2 for the game $\mathcal{G}$ is equivalent to solving the problem for game $\mathcal{G}'$. Hence, from now on, we only consider $\mathcal{G}'$ and show properties for the game $\mathcal{G}'$, which we can use later to compute a strongly adaptive strategy in $\mathcal{G}$. This strategy can then be transformed into a strongly adaptive strategy for $\mathcal{G}$. In the following, it is often useful to focus on one truth value by equipping $\mathcal{G}'$ with the parity condition of $\mathcal{C}_b$ for some b: a vertex $(v, q_{1111}, \ldots, q_{0000})$ has the color that q_b has in $\mathcal{C}_b$. Thus, $\mathcal{G}'$ equipped with the parity condition of $\mathcal{G}^b$ is equivalent to $\mathcal{G}^b$.

To decide whether a strongly adaptive strategy exists, we proceed as follows:

1. We first give a characterization of the vertices v of $\mathcal{G}'$ with smry$(v) = s$ that only uses summaries that are larger than s. This allows us to compute smry(v) for every vertex v by induction over the summaries.
2. Using the decomposition of $\mathcal{G}'$ into regions with the same summary and the characterization we construct a series of obliging games [14]. In an obliging game, Player 0 has a strong winning condition that has to be satisfied on every play and a weak winning condition that must be satisfiable if Player 1 cooperates. In our case, the strong winning condition requires Player 0 to always enforce the best value that is currently possible and the weak condition requires Player 1 to have a chance to make a bad move (if the summary encodes that this is still possible), i.e., whenever possible, Player 1 is given the chance to make a bad move.
3. Finally, if Player 1 has in all obliging games a strategy satisfying both the strong and the weak condition, then these can be turned effectively into a strongly adaptive strategy, otherwise there is no such strategy.

We first provide a useful lemma showing that a strategy in $\mathcal{G}'$ is strongly adaptive if and only if its summary is history independent, i.e., only depends on the last vertex.

Lemma 1. *A strategy σ for Player 0 in $\mathcal{G}'$ is strongly adaptive if and only if for every play prefix $\mathbf{p}$ ending in vertex v, it holds that $\mathrm{smry}(\sigma, \mathbf{p})) = \mathrm{smry}(v)$.*

As computed in Sect. 3.2, let $\mathrm{E}_{=b}$ be the set of vertices in $\mathcal{G}'$ from which the maximum value Player 0 can enforce is b. Furthermore, for a summary $s \in \mathcal{S}$, let $\mathrm{V}_{\geq s}$ denote the set of vertices v in $\mathcal{G}'$ for which $\mathrm{smry}(v) \geq_{\mathrm{lex}} s$. Let $\mathrm{V}_{=s}$, $\mathrm{V}_{>s}$, and $\mathrm{V}_{<s}$ be defined similarly.

Remark 9. Let $s = (b_0, \ldots, b_k, \bot, \ldots, \bot)$. Then, $\mathrm{V}_{=s} \subseteq \mathrm{E}_{=b_0}$.

For a vertex set F, let $\mathrm{pre}(F)$ denote the set of vertices from which there is an edge to F. Maybe surprisingly, we do not distinguish between vertices of Player 0 and Player 1, but we will only apply $\mathrm{pre}(F)$ when it is Player 1's turn.

Next, we characterize the sets $\mathrm{V}_{=s}$ in terms of the existence of strategies that witness summaries. The key aspects of this characterization is that it only refers to summaries $s' >_{\mathrm{lex}} s$, which will later allow us to compute these sets inductively.

Given a strategy σ for Player 0 in $\mathcal{G}'$ and a play prefix $\mathbf{p}$, let $\Pi(\sigma, \mathbf{p})$ denote the set of $(\sigma, \mathbf{p})$-plays that do not contain a bad move by Player 1 after $\mathbf{p}$.

Definition 3. *Let σ be a strategy for Player 0, $\mathbf{p}$ be a play prefix, and $s = (b_0, \ldots, b_k, \bot, \ldots, \bot)$ a summary. We say that σ is an s-witness from $\mathbf{p}$ if and only if it satisfies the following three properties:*

> ***Enforcing*** *Every play in $\Pi(\sigma, \mathbf{p})$ satisfies the parity condition of the game $\mathcal{G}^{b_0}$. Thus, a witness has to enforce b_0 unless Player 1 makes a bad move.*
> ***Enabling*** *If $k \geq 1$, there exists a play in $\Pi(\sigma, \mathbf{p})$ that visits $\mathrm{pre}\big(\mathrm{V}_{=\mathrm{lft}(s)}\big)$. Thus, if there is the chance to reach a vertex where Player 1 can make a bad move, then a witness has to visit such a vertex. Note that we require that the bad move leads to a vertex with summary $\mathrm{lft}(s)$, which is the largest summary that can be guaranteed to be reached from $\mathbf{p}$ after a bad move.*
> ***Evading*** *If $k \geq 1$, then let us define $\mathrm{Ev}(s)$ to be the set of summaries $s' = (b'_0, \ldots, b'_{k'}, \bot, \ldots, \bot)$ with $b'_0 > b_0$, $s' <_{\mathrm{lex}} \mathrm{lft}(s)$, and such that s' is not a strict prefix of $\mathrm{lft}(s)$. Then, no play in $\Pi(\sigma, \mathbf{p})$ visits $\mathrm{pre}\big(\mathrm{V}_{=s'}\big)$ for any $s' \in \mathrm{Ev}(s)$. Thus, a witness can never reach a vertex where Player 1 can make a bad move to reach a summary that is worse than $\mathrm{lft}(s)$.*

Recall that $\mathrm{lft}(s) >_{\mathrm{lex}} s$ and that $s' \in \mathrm{Ev}(s)$ implies $s' >_{\mathrm{lex}} s$.

Our next lemma shows that witnesses do indeed witness the summaries of vertices.

Lemma 2. *In the game $\mathcal{G}'$, for some summary s and for some vertex v, we have $v \in \mathrm{V}_{=s}$ if and only if $v \notin \mathrm{V}_{>s}$ and there is an s-witness from v.*

We now give a method to compute $V_{=s}$ for each summary $s \in \mathcal{S}$ by induction from the largest to the smallest summary. Since truth values in a summary are strictly increasing, $(1111, \bot, \ldots, \bot)$ is the maximal summary. We have $V_{=(1111,\bot,\ldots,\bot)} = E_{=1111}$, which we can compute using Tabuada and Neider's result for classical rLTL games (see Sect. 2). For the inductive step, assume that for a summary $s = (b_0, \ldots, b_k, \bot, \ldots, \bot)$ the sets $V_{=s'}$ are already computed for every $s' >_{\text{lex}} s$. The set $V_{=s}$ can then be computed using the following algorithm:

1. If $k = 0$, then return $E_{\geq b_0} \setminus V_{>s}$. Here, $E_{\geq b_0}$ can again be computed using Tabuada and Neider's result for classical rLTL games.
2. Now assume $k > 0$. Let $\mathcal{A}_s$ be the subgraph of $\mathcal{A}'$ restricted to the vertex set

$$E_{\geq b_0} \setminus \left(V_{>s} \cup \bigcup_{s' \in \text{Ev}(s)} \text{Reach}_1(V_{=s'}) \right),$$

where $\text{Reach}_1(F)$ denotes the set of vertices of $\mathcal{A}'$ from which Player 1 can force the token to reach F. This set can be computed in linear time (in the number of edges of $\mathcal{A}'$) using standard methods to solve reachability games (see [18] for more details). In the proof of correctness of the algorithm (see Lemma 3) we show that $\mathcal{A}_s$ does not have any terminal vertices. Also, the sets $V_{=s'}$ for $s' \in \text{Ev}(s)$ are already computed, because the summaries $s' \in \text{Ev}(s)$ are all greater than s.
3. Let $\text{Win}(s)$ be the winning region for Player 0 in the parity game with arena $\mathcal{A}_s$ and coloring as in the game $\mathcal{G}^{b_0}$. Return the set of vertices in Player 0's winning region $\text{Win}(s)$ from which $\text{pre}(V_{=\text{lft}(s)})$ is reachable in the subgraph of $\mathcal{A}'$ restricted to $\text{Win}(s)$.

Lemma 3. *The algorithm described above computes the sets $V_{=s}$ for $s \in \mathcal{S}$.*

Now, we give a characterization of strongly adaptive strategies in terms of summary witnesses.

Lemma 4. *In the game $\mathcal{G}'$, a strategy σ is strongly adaptive if and only if it is a $\text{smry}(p)$-witness from every play prefix p.*

Now, we show how to decide whether a strategy satisfying the condition given in Lemma 4 exists, i.e., a strategy that is a $\text{smry}(p)$-witness from every play prefix p. Furthermore, if such a strategy exists, we compute one. To do so, we present a reduction to another type of game, called *obliging games*. So, before describing the details of the reduction, let us recapitulate the definitions and useful results on obliging games.

Obliging games are two-player games introduced by Chatterjee et al. [14]. They have two winning conditions, S and W, called strong and weak conditions. The objective of Player 0 is to ensure the strong winning condition while allowing Player 1 to cooperate with him to additionally fulfil the weak winning condition. Formally, a strategy σ for Player 0 is *uniformly gracious* if it satisfies the following:

- for every vertex v, every (σ, v)-play is S-winning, and
- for every play prefix p consistent with σ, there is a W-winning (σ, p)-play.

We are only interested in parity/Büchi obliging games (i.e., the strong condition is a parity condition, and the weak one is a Büchi condition). The next theorem follows directly from the results by Chatterjee et al. [14].

Theorem 3. *A parity/Büchi obliging game with n vertices and a parity condition with k colors can be reduced to a parity game with $O(n)$ vertices and $O(k)$ colors. Moreover, if Player 0 has a uniformly gracious strategy in such an obliging game, he has a uniformly gracious strategy with a memory of size at most $O(k)$.*

Now, coming back to our problem, we define obliging games $\mathcal{G}_s$ (for each $s \in \mathcal{S}$), which are subgames of $\mathcal{G}'$, such that a uniformly gracious strategy in $\mathcal{G}_s$ satisfies the properties of an s-witness locally. In particular, the games are defined in way such that the strong condition resembles the Enforcing property, the weak condition resembles the Enabling property, and the restricted vertex set ensures that the Evading property is satisfied.

Definition 4. *Given a summary $s = (b_0, \ldots, b_k, \bot, \ldots, \bot) \in \mathcal{S}$, let $\mathcal{G}_s$ be the obliging game obtained from $\mathcal{G}'$ as follows:*

- *The set of vertices $V(\mathcal{G}_s)$ is the set $V_{=s} \cup \{v_{new}\}$, where v_{new} is a new vertex that does not belong to V'.*
- *The set of edges $E(\mathcal{G}_s)$ contains the following edges:*
  - *The edges of the game $\mathcal{G}'$ restricted to the vertex set $V_{=s}$.*
  - *All edges of the form (v, v_{new}) where v is a terminal vertex in the game $\mathcal{G}'$ restricted to $V_{=s}$.*
  - *A self loop on v_{new}.*
- *The strong condition S_s is a min-parity condition such that the color of v_{new} is 0 and the color of any other vertex is the same as in $\mathcal{G}^{b_0}$.*
- *If $k = 0$, then there is no weak condition, i.e., W_s is a Büchi condition with $F = V(\mathcal{G}_s)$. If $k > 0$, then the weak condition W_s is a Büchi condition with $F = \mathrm{pre}(\mathrm{lft}(s)) \cup \{v_{new}\}$.*

The following lemma formalizes the connection between uniformly gracious strategies in the obliging games $\mathcal{G}_s$ and strongly adaptive strategies in $\mathcal{G}'$.

Lemma 5. *There exists a strongly adaptive strategy in $\mathcal{G}'$ if and only if there exists a uniformly gracious strategy in every obliging game $\mathcal{G}_s$. Given a uniformly gracious strategy with finite memory in each obliging game $\mathcal{G}_s$, one can effectively combine these into a strongly adaptive strategy with finite memory in $\mathcal{G}'$.*

Since the game $\mathcal{G}'$ has doubly-exponential size, using Theorem 3, the parity/Büchi obliging games $\mathcal{G}_s$ can be reduced to doubly-exponential-sized parity games. Once we computed a strongly adaptive strategy for $\mathcal{G}'$, it can then be reduced to a strongly adaptive strategy for the original game $\mathcal{G}$.

Moreover, note that strongly adaptive strategies also have doubly-exponential memory since the obliging games we constructed have doubly-exponential size. By Theorem 3, uniformly gracious strategies in such obliging games require memory of linear size, leading to the following result.

Theorem 4. *Given an rLTL game, one can decide in doubly-exponential time whether Player 0 has a strongly adaptive strategy. If yes, one can compute one with doubly-exponential memory in doubly-exponential time.*

Note that by dualizing the definitions and the constructions, an analogous result for Player 1 can also be obtained.

5 Conclusion

We argued that in a reactive system, in addition to correctness, we also need to ensure robustness. To this end, we introduced adaptive strategies for rLTL games that satisfy the specification to a higher degree when the environment is not antagonistic. We also presented a stronger version of adaptive strategies that additionally maximizes the opportunities for the opponent to make bad choices. Finally, we showed that both adaptive and strongly adaptive strategies can be computed in doubly-exponential time. As we know that the classical LTL and rLTL synthesis algorithms also take doubly-exponential time, we conclude that adaptive and strongly adaptive strategies are not harder to compute.

In future work, we aim to investigate even more general notions of adaption to the behavior of a not necessarily antagonistic environment. Possible approaches include observing the environment's behavior and trying to compare that to optimal strategies for the environment.

References

1. Almagor, S., Kupferman, O.: Good-enough synthesis. In: Lahiri, S.K., Wang, C. (eds.) CAV 2020, Part II. LNCS, vol. 12225, pp. 541–563. Springer, Cham (2020). https://doi.org/10.1007/978-3-030-53291-8_28
2. Anevlavis, T., Neider, D., Phillipe, M., Tabuada, P.: Evrostos: the rLTL verifier. In: ACM International Conference on Hybrid Systems: Computation and Control, HSCC 2019, pp. 218–223. ACM (2019). https://doi.org/10.1145/3302504.3311812
3. Anevlavis, T., Philippe, M., Neider, D., Tabuada, P.: Verifying rLTL formulas: now faster than ever before! In: IEEE Conference on Decision and Control, CDC 2018, pp. 1556–1561. IEEE (2018). https://doi.org/10.1109/CDC.2018.8619014
4. Anevlavis, T., Philippe, M., Neider, D., Tabuada, P.: Being correct is not enough: efficient verification using Robust Linear Temporal Logic. ACM Trans. Comput. Log. **23**(2), 8:1–8:39 (2022). https://doi.org/10.1145/3491216
5. Baier, C., Katoen, J.: Principles of Model Checking. MIT Press, Cambridge (2008)
6. Bauer, A., Leucker, M., Schallhart, C.: Runtime verification for LTL and TLTL. ACM Trans. Softw. Eng. Methodol. **20**(4), 1–64 (2011). https://doi.org/10.1145/2000799.2000800
7. Bloem, R., et al.: Synthesizing robust systems. Acta Informatica **51**(3–4), 193–220 (2014). https://doi.org/10.1007/s00236-013-0191-5
8. Bloem, R., Chatterjee, K., Henzinger, T.A., Jobstmann, B.: Better quality in synthesis through quantitative objectives. In: Bouajjani, A., Maler, O. (eds.) CAV 2009. LNCS, vol. 5643, pp. 140–156. Springer, Heidelberg (2009). https://doi.org/10.1007/978-3-642-02658-4_14

9. Bloem, R., Ehlers, R., Jacobs, S., Könighofer, R.: How to handle assumptions in synthesis. In: Workshop on Synthesis, SYNT 2014. EPTCS, vol. 157, pp. 34–50 (2014). https://doi.org/10.4204/EPTCS.157.7

10. Calude, C.S., Jain, S., Khoussainov, B., Li, W., Stephan, F.: Deciding parity games in quasipolynomial time. In: ACM SIGACT Symposium on Theory of Computing, STOC 2017, pp. 252–263. ACM (2017). https://doi.org/10.1145/3055399.3055409

11. Chatterjee, K., Doyen, L.: Energy parity games. Theor. Comput. Sci. **458**, 49–60 (2012). https://doi.org/10.1016/j.tcs.2012.07.038

12. Chatterjee, K., Henzinger, T.A.: Assume-guarantee synthesis. In: Grumberg, O., Huth, M. (eds.) TACAS 2007. LNCS, vol. 4424, pp. 261–275. Springer, Heidelberg (2007). https://doi.org/10.1007/978-3-540-71209-1_21

13. Chatterjee, K., Henzinger, T.A., Jurdzinski, M.: Mean-payoff parity games. In: IEEE Symposium on Logic in Computer Science (LICS 2005), pp. 178–187. IEEE Computer Society (2005). https://doi.org/10.1109/LICS.2005.26

14. Chatterjee, K., Horn, F., Löding, C.: Obliging games. In: Gastin, P., Laroussinie, F. (eds.) CONCUR 2010. LNCS, vol. 6269, pp. 284–296. Springer, Heidelberg (2010). https://doi.org/10.1007/978-3-642-15375-4_20

15. Dallal, E., Neider, D., Tabuada, P.: Synthesis of safety controllers robust to unmodeled intermittent disturbances. In: IEEE Conference on Decision and Control, CDC 2016, pp. 7425–7430. IEEE (2016). https://doi.org/10.1109/CDC.2016.7799416

16. Ehlers, R., Topcu, U.: Resilience to intermittent assumption violations in reactive synthesis. In: International Conference on Hybrid Systems: Computation and Control, HSCC 2014, pp. 203–212. ACM (2014). https://doi.org/10.1145/2562059.2562128

17. Fearnley, J., Zimmermann, M.: Playing Muller games in a hurry. Int. J. Found. Comput. Sci. **23**(3), 649–668 (2012). https://doi.org/10.1142/S0129054112400321

18. Grädel, E., Thomas, W., Wilke, T. (eds.): Automata, Logics, and Infinite Games: A Guide to Current Research. LNCS, vol. 2500. Springer, Heidelberg (2002). https://doi.org/10.1007/3-540-36387-4

19. Kuhn, H.W.: Extensive Games and the Problem of Information. Princeton University Press, Princeton (1953)

20. Majumdar, R., Render, E., Tabuada, P.: A theory of robust omega-regular software synthesis. ACM Trans. Embed. Comput. Syst. **13**(3), 48:1–48:27 (2013). https://doi.org/10.1145/2539036.2539044

21. Mascle, C., Neider, D., Schwenger, M., Tabuada, P., Weinert, A., Zimmermann, M.: From LTL to rLTL monitoring: improved monitorability through robust semantics. In: HSCC 2020: 23rd ACM International Conference on Hybrid Systems: Computation and Control, pp. 7:1–7:12. ACM (2020). https://doi.org/10.1145/3365365.3382197

22. Nayak, S.P., Neider, D., Roy, R., Zimmermann, M.: Robust computation tree logic. In: Deshmukh, J.V., Havelund, K., Perez, I. (eds.) NASA Formal Methods. LNCS, vol. 13260, pp. 538–556. Springer, Cham (2022). https://doi.org/10.1007/978-3-031-06773-0_29

23. Nayak, S.P., Neider, D., Zimmermann, M.: Adaptive strategies for rLTL games. In: HSCC 2021: ACM International Conference on Hybrid Systems: Computation and Control, pp. 32:1–32:2. ACM (2021). https://doi.org/10.1145/3447928.3457210

24. Nayak, S.P., Neider, D., Zimmermann, M.: Robustness-by-construction synthesis: adapting to the environment at runtime. CoRR abs/2204.10912 (2022). https://doi.org/10.48550/arXiv.2204.10912

25. Neider, D., Totzke, P., Zimmermann, M.: Optimally resilient strategies in push-down safety games. In: International Symposium on Mathematical Foundations of Computer Science, MFCS 2020. LIPIcs, vol. 170, pp. 74:1–74:15. Schloss Dagstuhl - Leibniz-Zentrum für Informatik (2020). https://doi.org/10.4230/LIPIcs.MFCS.2020.74

26. Neider, D., Weinert, A., Zimmermann, M.: Synthesizing optimally resilient controllers. In: EACSL Annual Conference on Computer Science Logic, CSL 2018. LIPIcs, vol. 119, pp. 34:1–34:17. Schloss Dagstuhl - Leibniz-Zentrum für Informatik (2018). https://doi.org/10.4230/LIPIcs.CSL.2018.34

27. Neider, D., Weinert, A., Zimmermann, M.: Robust, expressive, and quantitative linear temporal logics: pick any two for free. Inf. Comput. 104810 (2021). https://doi.org/10.1016/j.ic.2021.104810

28. Pnueli, A.: The temporal logic of programs. In: Symposium on Foundations of Computer Science, 1977, pp. 46–57. IEEE Computer Society (1977). https://doi.org/10.1109/SFCS.1977.32

29. Pnueli, A., Rosner, R.: On the synthesis of a reactive module. In: ACM Symposium on Principles of Programming Languages, 1989, pp. 179–190. ACM Press (1989). https://doi.org/10.1145/75277.75293

30. Pnueli, A., Rosner, R.: On the synthesis of an asynchronous reactive module. In: Ausiello, G., Dezani-Ciancaglini, M., Della Rocca, S.R. (eds.) ICALP 1989. LNCS, vol. 372, pp. 652–671. Springer, Heidelberg (1989). https://doi.org/10.1007/BFb0035790

31. Priest, G.: Dualising intuitionictic negation. Principia Int. J. Epistemol. **13**(2), 165–184 (2009). https://doi.org/10.5007/1808-1711.2009v13n2p165

32. Samuel, S., Mallik, K., Schmuck, A., Neider, D.: Resilient abstraction-based controller design. In: HSCC 2020: ACM International Conference on Hybrid Systems: Computation and Control, pp. 33:1–33:2. ACM (2020). https://doi.org/10.1145/3365365.3383467

33. Samuel, S., Mallik, K., Schmuck, A., Neider, D.: Resilient abstraction-based controller design. In: IEEE Conference on Decision and Control, CDC 2020, pp. 2123–2129. IEEE (2020). https://doi.org/10.1109/CDC42340.2020.9303932

34. Schewe, S., Varghese, T.: Tight bounds for the determinisation and complementation of generalised Büchi automata. In: Chakraborty, S., Mukund, M. (eds.) ATVA 2012. LNCS, pp. 42–56. Springer, Heidelberg (2012). https://doi.org/10.1007/978-3-642-33386-6_5

35. Tabuada, P., Caliskan, S.Y., Rungger, M., Majumdar, R.: Towards robustness for cyber-physical systems. IEEE Trans. Autom. Control **59**(12), 3151–3163 (2014). https://doi.org/10.1109/TAC.2014.2351632

36. Tabuada, P., Neider, D.: Robust linear temporal logic. In: Conference on Computer Science Logic, CSL 2016. LIPIcs, vol. 62, pp. 10:1–10:21. Schloss Dagstuhl - Leibniz-Zentrum für Informatik (2016). https://doi.org/10.4230/LIPIcs.CSL.2016.10

37. Topcu, U., Ozay, N., Liu, J., Murray, R.M.: On synthesizing robust discrete controllers under modeling uncertainty. In: Hybrid Systems: Computation and Control, HSCC 2012, pp. 85–94. ACM (2012). https://doi.org/10.1145/2185632.2185648

38. Ummels, M.: Rational behaviour and strategy construction in infinite multiplayer games. In: Arun-Kumar, S., Garg, N. (eds.) FSTTCS 2006. LNCS, vol. 4337, pp. 212–223. Springer, Heidelberg (2006). https://doi.org/10.1007/11944836_21

TriCo—Triple Co-piloting of Implementation, Specification and Tests

Wolfgang Ahrendt[1]([⊠])[iD], Dilian Gurov[2][iD], Moa Johansson[1][iD], and Philipp Rümmer[3,4][iD]

[1] Chalmers University of Technology, Gothenburg, Sweden
{ahrendt,moa.johansson}@chalmers.se
[2] KTH Royal Institute of Technology, Stockholm, Sweden
dilian@kth.se
[3] University of Regensburg, Regensburg, Germany
philipp.ruemmer@ur.de
[4] Uppsala University, Uppsala, Sweden

Abstract. This white paper presents the vision of a novel methodology for developing safety-critical software, which is inspired by late developments in learning based co-piloting of implementations. The methodology, called TriCo, integrates formal methods with learning based approaches to co-pilot the agile, simultaneous development of three artefacts: implementation, specification, and tests. Whenever the user changes any of these, a TriCo empowered IDE would suggest changes to the other two artefacts in such a way that the three are kept consistent. The user has the final word on whether the changes are accepted, rejected, or modified. In the latter case, consistency will be checked again and re-established. We discuss the emerging trends which put the community in a good position to realise this vision, describe the methodology and workflow, as well as challenges and possible solutions for the realisation of TriCo.

1 Introduction

In this white paper, we present the vision of a software methodology, called *TriCo* (Triple Co-Piloting), which targets in particular, but not exclusively, the development of safety-critical software, where defects can incur high financial or reputational costs, or can compromise human safety.

The latest safety standards in the avionics (DO-178C) and automotive (ISO 26262) areas now require or recommend the use of formal methods for ensuring the robustness of safety-critical embedded software, as conventional methods such as testing alone do not provide the required safety guarantees. However, traditional formal methods are not a good match for the current state-of-practice. The threshold to apply formal methods is high, as their application requires significant expertise, and formal methods are not well integrated into development

© The Author(s), under exclusive license to Springer Nature Switzerland AG 2022
T. Margaria and B. Steffen (Eds.): ISoLA 2022, LNCS 13701, pp. 174–187, 2022.
https://doi.org/10.1007/978-3-031-19849-6_11

processes. Tackling this challenge, TriCo aims to formulate a new approach to develop robust software cost-efficiently. TriCo builds on the enormous progress that has recently been made in a number of relevant fields: in automated reasoning and constraint solving, which have in the last years produced tools that are significantly more scalable than the techniques available before; in verification and model checking, where new algorithms have been found to fully automatically analyse software programs of substantial complexity; and in machine learning, which is today able to automatically solve problems that were long thought to be beyond the reach of computers. Leveraging those advances, TriCo represents a new co-development paradigm that treats specifications as first-class objects, to be developed *simultaneously* with implementations and tests, and proposes the use of co-piloting to intelligently assist software developers in this process.

In this paper, we outline our vision of how efficient development of robust software will be conducted in the near future, with the help of novel tools, acting as the developer's co-pilot, which integrate recent advances in automated reasoning, machine learning, and synthesis.

1.1   Triple Co-piloting at a Glance

There are two main reasons why the adoption of traditional formal methods in industrial practice has been slow. Firstly, formal specifications are in general difficult to create and maintain, and require a considerable level of expertise and training. Secondly, formal techniques do not always scale well with the size of software, and their application often lacks the necessary efficiency. Both of these issues are particularly problematic when formal methods are applied a posteriori, i.e., after the software code has been produced. On the other hand, developing good specifications first, to only then start coding, has not either been a workable approach in software development practice.

The TriCo methodology aims to address these problems, using a novel method for co-development of code, tests and specifications, by means of a software development *co-pilot* integrated seamlessly into development environments. The purpose of the co-pilot is to enable the developer to create *code*, *tests* and *specifications simultaneously*, from the very beginning, and to guide the developer in this process by suggesting human-understandable modifications in the respective other artefacts whenever the developer changed one of them, such that *the three are kept consistent*. Figure 1 illustrates our approach, which is based on exact, logic-based techniques, boosted by machine learning. It can be seen as a generalisation of the well-known *correctness-by-construction* paradigm, in that all three types of artefacts are treated as citizens with equal rights when it comes to them being correct.

Recent advances in AI, and in particular in machine learning (ML), have made the latter a powerful tool to efficiently solve problems in many areas, such as computer vision, pattern recognition, and natural language processing, which have hitherto been solved only inefficiently with algorithmic approaches.

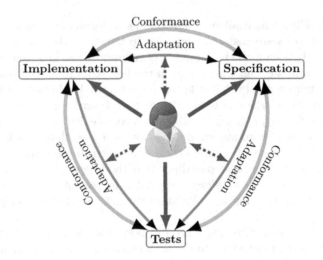

Fig. 1. Co-development and co-piloting of implementations, tests, and specifications.

The TriCo methodology aims to use ML to enhance exact techniques in a number of ways, for example, to enable the co-pilot to learn suggesting human-understandable specifications based on test-cases and implementations. ML will be used to train the co-pilot, before and during its use, learning when and what suggestions to give to the developer in different situations.

The method should be supported by IDEs, providing automated co-piloting to the developer, facilitating the agile development and maintenance of the implementation-tests-specification triangle. The system would constantly analyse formal consistency of the three artefacts when one of them has changed, and provide suggestions for adaptation of the other two, to be *accepted or rejected by the developer*. The system should feed the user decisions into a common training set, thereby achieving a *federated learning* of appropriate artefact adaptions. By combining the complementary strengths of *machine learning* on the one hand and *logic based automated reasoning* on the other, the TriCo methodology forms a novel, seamlessly integrated method for developing *robust software efficiently*.

2   Emerging Trends in Software Technology

Our approach of co-development of code, tests and specifications in the spirit of co-piloting is well suited for encompassing many emerging technologies, and thus support human developers in different ways. We note that our methodology does not aim at automated *decisions* about any of the artefacts. Rather, it aims at automated *suggestions* for adapting the artefacts to each other. The suggestions are *triggered* by the user, who changed one of the artefacts, and they have to be *accepted* (and possibly modified) by the user, to bring all three artefacts in sync again in a way which matches the intentions. In the following, we review emerging trends which this endeavour can build on.

2.1   Code Synthesis Through Large Language Models

With the current development of large language models with billions of parameters, trained on open source code from, e.g., GitHub, code synthesis co-pilots seem set to soon becoming an everyday tool for programmer's integrated in common IDEs [6,10,11]. The user may type in some code or a description in natural language, and the system automatically provides a suggestion. Other tasks include translating between different programming languages, or suggesting fixes for broken code, given a compiler error message. In many cases the code is perfectly sensible, but it should be noted that no guarantees whatsoever can be given about actual correctness, and sometimes nothing useful will be generated at all. Furthermore, the large language models make no claims about understanding how the generated programs function, but they are very good at picking up common patterns seen in the vast training data, making them suitable for generation of boiler-plate code for frequently used programming languages and applications, such as web programming. The authors of Google's recent PaLM system summarise some of the limitations and risks [11], p. 26:

> *"When deploying LM-based systems within software development, a key risk is that the generated code could be incorrect, or introduce subtle bugs.[...] Developers should review suggested code before adding it to a program, but they may not always find subtle bugs in suggested code.[...] Functional correctness is only one aspect of source code quality; LM-produced suggestions must also be readable, robust, fast, and secure"*

The authors further point out that there is little work on software testing and verification methods for systems including code synthesis from large language models.

Our proposed methodology can cover also software development including this kind of "untrusted" synthesis components. Suggestions from, e.g., a large language model are harnessed in a larger environment which complements it with test-cases and specifications. The latter may be written by a human, but an alternative is to allow automated generation of (suggested) test cases and specifications, which we survey next.

2.2   Automated Test Case Generation

For TriCo, a particularly relevant automated test generation technique is *property-based random test-case generation*, which manifests itself in the QuickCheck family of tools [16]. It features strong requirements coverage and very effective test-case minimisation. Here, the programmer writes down specific properties that are desired by the system, commonly as quite compact statements. One can envision a user typing in such properties for testing, which perhaps may also be used by the kind of code synthesis system we describe above as cues. The synthesised code can then be tested automatically. *Symbolic execution*-based techniques [3,24], on the other hand, feature instead high code coverage (e.g., MC/DC, full feasible branch coverage). Further, there are advances in enhancing coverage-directed test generation by machine-learning techniques [17]. Our proposed co-piloting methodology is meant to exploit automated test generation of a variety of styles, to exploit the complementary strengths of the techniques. However, as far as the test oracle is concerned, the user shall have the final word on whether or not an oracle matches the intended behaviour.

2.3   Specification Synthesis

Formal specifications serve several purposes. They provide a compact and precise description of the functions and properties of software, and can be used as input to formal verification systems for proving correctness, or to test-case generation systems. Our co-pilot will need to perform specification synthesis to produce suggestions of specification updates when code has been changed, or to provide a compact description of code that has been synthesised. Even without passing it to a verification system, it can be helpful for the user to spot an error in generated code if complemented by a suggested specification of its functionality. Does the code do what the specification says? If not, which of them matches the intention?

Due to the effort required to write specifications by hand, specification synthesis has been recognised as a problem of increasing importance, and received attention in several communities. Specifications in the form of contracts can, for instance, be computed using the classical weakest-precondition calculus, symbolic execution [15], counterexample-guided abstraction refinement [23], or through model checking [5]. The concept of Maximal Specification Inference [4] generalises the inference of weakest pre-conditions and considers the specifications of multiple functions simultaneously. Specifications can also be derived using dynamic analysis, as for instance in the Daikon tool [12].

Theory exploration [27] is another emerging method. Given a (functional) program, it invents a concise formal description of the program behaviour as a set of equational statements. Generation is interleaved with automated testing or symbolic evaluation [26]. These properties may then be inspected by the programmer, and passed to a theorem prover to verify that the code satisfies the statements. Naturally, if given a buggy program, a specification generation tool will generate a corresponding "buggy" specification. In our co-piloting setting, the human user will still have the task of checking that the generated specification is in accordance with the users intentions, but we argue that this task can be easier than spotting a bug in the source code itself.

2.4   Formal Software Verification

Reasoning about conformance is one of the principal tasks underlying the TriCo methodology. Any change in the three considered artefacts—implementation, tests, specification—implies that the three conformance relations have to be reevaluated, so that possible mismatches are identified and can be corrected. The conformance *Implementation* ↔ *Specification* is known as the formal software verification problem, and has been studied for a long time and in a variety of fields. For us, in particular two styles of verification are relevant, namely *deductive verification* (e.g., [2,7,19]) in which automated tools are applied to check fully-annotated programs; and *software model checking* [18], which attempts to handle also programs that are only partially annotated in an automated way. A recent direction of research that combines concepts from deductive verification with model checking algorithms are approaches based on *Constraint Horn Clauses* [9,13], which form an intermediate verification language in software model checking, but more generally can provide automation for a wide range of program logics.

Machine Learning for Verification. ML for automatic verification can largely be split into three different areas: (i) methods that see each verification instance as a separate learning task, e.g., the task of learning a loop invariant from observed program behaviour; (ii) methods that see each verification instance as one data point, which are then used to train a verification system; and (iii) methods for parameter learning. An overview of (i) is given in the recent tutorial [21]; the approach has seen increasing adoption over the last years, and uses algorithms like decision-tree learning, syntax-guided synthesis, or reinforcement learning [25] to solve verification problems. Approach (ii) has turned out much less successful, up to this point, given the big gap between the approximate reasoning of statistical inference and the exact nature of program verification. Approach (iii) is significantly easier to implement, and is today used, for example, to choose the right verification back-end for each verification task (e.g., [22]).

3   The TriCo Methodology

The ambition of the TriCo methodology is to take test-driven agile development [20] to a higher robustness level. In addition to the developer eagerly writing unit tests which describe the behaviour for a set of selected input cases, the methodology advocates that formal specifications covering all inputs and prestates are co-developed along with tests and implementation. The workflow is an extension of test-driven development, but gives much stronger robustness guarantees. The methodology aims in the first place at sequential correctness of programs, i.e., the absence of errors which already manifest in sequential execution.

Consider the productive use of *redundancy* in existing development processes. Typically, the latter make extensive use of *testing* to validate software behaviour: two artefacts, implementations and tests, are written that both describe intended program behaviour. Unit/regression tests are written early during the process, and are re-executed and augmented whenever new functionality is introduced, or defects are corrected. Development maintains the invariant that, at any commit point, implementations and test cases are consistent, i.e., the implementation will pass all tests. Inconsistencies between the implementation and the tests constitute a bug (in the implementation, in the tests, or in both), and today's development infrastructure will enforce the immediate correction of such bugs.

It is the process of keeping implementations and tests consistent that leads to higher quality of *both* artefacts.

Test cases, however, only describe the behaviour of the implementation on selected inputs and prestates. Assurance of code behaviour beyond specific test cases can only be provided by *formal, mathematical methods*. Formal specifications describe the intended behaviour of a program (unit) for *all* inputs and prestates in a precise, unambiguous, and machine-readable format. Specifications can, for instance, include data-consistency invariants of classes and data structures, loop invariants, procedure contracts, or assumptions and guarantees between caller and callee units. Most formal verification methods require formal specifications. Unfortunately, formal specifications are hard to produce. Furthermore, in the way formal methods are used today, their benefits during the software lifetime are long-term and hard to quantify [14]. As a consequence, most software projects do not work with formal specifications.

3.1 Envisaged Workflow

The TriCo methodology provides a software development method and the necessary tool support for efficient, agile software development, while achieving a high level of robustness. Our approach is based on three main principles, as illustrated on Fig. 1: (a) *co-development* of three artefacts: implementation, test cases, and specification, (b) *co-piloting* of adaptions made necessary by changes in any of the artefacts, and (c) *combining learning-* and *logic*-based methods to achieve (b). To achieve scalability, the method is *compositional* w.r.t. code units, in the sense that each unit gives rise to a separate triple of artefacts, to be co-developed by the user with help of the co-pilot.

With the three artefacts come three conformance relations:

1. Conformance of an *implementation* unit and the associated unit *test cases* means foremost that the implementation makes the oracle of each test case pass successfully. But other aspects can also be included into this conformance relation, such as code coverage criteria.
2. Conformance of an *implementation* unit and its *specification*, on the other hand, means that the behaviour of *every possible run* of the unit's code satisfies the specification. This can be determined by numerous formal verification methods. In TriCo, the analysis of this conformance shall be provided in an integrated manner, in the background, without the user having to choose, install, or learn about the various methods and backend-tools which collaboratively solve this task under the hood.
3. Finally, conformance of a unit's *test cases* and the corresponding *specification* means that the specification is strictly a generalisation of all the unit's test cases (each consisting of a concrete input/prestate plus an oracle on the output/poststate). In turn, this means that each of the test cases can be understood as a very concrete 'lemma' implied by the specification. Also here, the according analysis methods execute in the background.

A basic principle of the TriCo methodology is that *mutual conformance* of implementation, tests, and specification is an *invariant that is intact in between different work passes* of code development and maintenance. When the user changes any one of the three artefacts (blue solid arrow in Fig. 1), this will typically break the conformance invariant. For instance, a new test case may not be satisfied by the implementation, and/or require a generalisation of the specification. Or a change in the implementation may invalidate a property from the specification, and/or make some test cases fail. To address these arising inconsistencies, a TriCo empowered IDE shall analyse in the background whether conformance to any of the other two artefacts is broken. If that is indeed the case, the system computes an *adaption* of the affected artefact(s) that re-establishes mutual conformance. Computing such adaptions is based on a combination of *machine learning* with *exact, formal methods*. The adaption is presented as a suggestion to the user, who has to accept or reject it (blue dotted arrow in Fig. 1). *Only after the user has accepted a suggested adaption, it will take effect.* It is this very point which makes the method very *user-centered.* We argue that this will lead to higher-quality software than automated adaption decisions, in particular because a mismatch between two artefacts can indicate an error on either of them, and the user should decide which side meets the intention of the software unit. Finally, the user's decisions to accept or reject suggested adaptions are used to *train* the learning facilities, which will generate ever better adaption suggestions over time.

3.2 Use Cases

To be more concrete, let us consider the use case where, starting from mutually conforming implementation, test cases, and specification, the user changes the implementation. This may lead to a violation of the specification (among others), to be detected by formal methods operating in the background. Once a violation is diagnosed, the co-pilot will suggest an adaption of the specification. The adaption is produced by the trained machine learning facility, but validated with exact methods, to be finally accepted or rejected by the user, thereby training the co-pilot in turn. In case the user decides to reject an adaption of the specification, numerous proceedings can come into play, such as reverting the latest change of implementation, or hand-editing the rejected suggestion (to be re-checked), or letting the co-pilot suggest a finer modification on the latest implementation.

As a second use case, let us consider a code unit which was developed with (pure) *test driven development*, so far without any formal specifications. The user can then ask the co-pilot to incrementally suggest *specifications, obtained by generalisation from the test cases*, against which (if accepted by the user) the implementation will be verified. As a variation of this use case, a code unit may be developed from the start with the co-pilot, but by developers initially unfamiliar with formal specifications. Continuous generalisation of the incrementally developed test cases, and the corresponding verification, will make the development of formally verified software a side-product of agile test driven development, thereby offering a smooth learning curve into using the TriCo methodology.

As a third use case, let us consider the integration of legacy code into the TriCo process. When connecting actively developed code with legacy code, what is needed most for further analysis are interface specifications of the legacy units. TriCo shall support intelligent editing of such interface specifications, empowered by machine learning. Moreover, the caller-side use of legacy functionality can be employed to infer contract specifications, and corresponding test cases to validate the contract specifications. Another approach to the same problem is to provide data generators, run the legacy code on the generated data, and generalise the observed output to synthesise specifications, following a theory exploration approach.

3.3 Envisaged Technology

Achieving the goal of integrated co-piloting of implementation, test cases, and specification requires a hybrid, highly integrated set of functionalities. For that, the TriCo methodology envisages to employ, expand on, and combine numerous techniques, such as machine learning (neural networks, reinforcement learning), formal software verification, symbolic execution, symbolic debugging, specification/contract inference, specification mining, theory exploration, test automation, automated test case generation, runtime verification, code refactoring, and combinations thereof.

We envisage a tool chain which provides to users an environment where they can co-develop, in an agile way, the three aforementioned artefacts with continuous co-piloting support. The architecture of the tool chain would be such that the core functionalities are provided in a web-service, paired with a user side web-interface. The server architecture also enables *federated training* of the learning facilities.

4   Research Efforts Required for TriCo

While much of what is presented in this paper is a vision still waiting to be turned into reality, we believe that the time is right to start a research programme that will provide the required components for TriCo. This research can build on the enormous progress that has recently been made in a number of relevant fields: in automated reasoning and constraint solving, which have in the last years produced tools that are significantly more scalable than the techniques available before; in verification and model checking, where new algorithms have been found to fully automatically analyse software programs of substantial complexity; and in machine learning, which is today able to automatically solve problems that were long thought to be beyond the reach of computers. This section discusses some of the remaining research challenges in the different fields.

Challenge 1: Representation and Transformation of Artefacts

The Challenge: Formal methods have to handle the complexity of real-world programming and specification languages, e.g., of languages like C, Java, ACSL, or JML. In TriCo, this complexity is amplified by the multitude of modifications and transformations taking place between the three different artefacts (Fig. 1): all three artefacts can be edited by the developer, at any point; all three artefacts can also be synthesised or adapted by the co-pilot to (re-)establish the conformance relations. Changes computed by the co-pilot must not destroy the cues the developer depends on (e.g., formatting, naming, or comments), and editing by the developer must not compromise meta-data maintained by the co-pilot.

A Possible Solution: This challenge could be addressed by defining a uniform intermediate language to represent all three artefacts, implementations, specifications, and test cases. This intermediate language is not intended for direct human editing, but is connected through meta-data to multiple real-world presentation languages (e.g., C and ACSL). The developer works with the presentation languages, and any changes made are automatically and incrementally mapped to the intermediate representation. The co-pilot primarily operates on the intermediate language, and changes on this layer are reflected by carefully updating the presentation layer.

As one suitable intermediate language, we consider the use of extended versions of *Constraint Horn Clauses (CHC)* [9,13]. CHCs have been adopted in software model checking as a common interface between programming language front-ends and verification back-ends, since CHCs are general enough to capture many programming language features (including control structure, procedure calls, various concurrency models, heap models), provide simple and unambiguous semantics in terms of the SMT-LIB theories [8], and can easily be connected to various automatic verification approaches.

Challenge 2: Efficient Automatic Conformance Analysis

The Challenge: In TriCo, any change in the three artefacts (implementation, tests, specification, Fig. 1) requires a co-pilot to reevaluate the three conformance relations, so that possible mismatches are identified and can be corrected. The existing methods for conformance checking, which are formal software verification, software testing, and checking specification refinement, are all algorithmically hard, and often limited in terms of scalability.

A Possible Solution: Given the existing huge body of research on the different kind of conformance checking, no step-changes are to be expected in the near future, but we believe that the right application and combination of existing methods can carry TriCo a long way. A co-pilot can be based on (i) a bespoke combination of static and dynamic methods, utilising their complementary strengths, so that rapid feedback can be provided to the developer after each change; (ii) incrementality in checking, which is achieved, e.g., by the caching of conformance certificates in the form of rich program annotations (e.g., computed loop invariants); and (ii) the use of machine learning to boost checking, for instance to predict likely cases of conformance violations, or along the lines described in Sect. 2.4.

Challenge 3: Defect Diagnosis and Suggestion of Adaptations

The Challenge: At the core of TriCo is the ability to identify and suggest adaptations of any of the artefacts—implementations, specifications, tests—when any of the other artefacts change. This is largely a new direction of research, since not all of the six possible combinations of artefacts have been considered in prior research. Closely related areas include *program repair,* which can be used to compute updates of an implementation when the specification is modified, and *model-based diagnosis* to explore the space of possible explanations for observed inconsistencies.

A Possible Solution: Diagnosis is triggered by conformance violations detected by the methods from Challenge 2, and aims at inferring plausible explanations for which part or feature of an artefact is responsible for the non-conformance. For this, as well as for computing adaptations, a combination of techniques from different fields is needed: *formal methods,* to exactly model the relationship between the artefacts, based on results of conformance checking; *constraint solving and optimisation,* which ensure minimality of the provided explanation or adaptation, and can be provided through modern techniques from the Satisfiability Modulo Theories (SMT) field; and *machine learning,* which is able to rank explanations and adaptations in a way that is consistent with the expectations of the user.

An important aspect is that techniques should reflect existing software development practices: a co-pilot has the purpose of supporting the developer, not to enforce a coding style the developer is unfamiliar or uncomfortable with. One line of thought towards this goal is the concept of *transformation models,* which are abstract characterisations of typical artefact modifications; covering, for instance, notions of refactoring, but also other typical steps in code editing. By learning how transformations of one artefact induce corresponding transformations of the other artefacts, a co-pilot will be able to compute and rank adaptations in a way that is consistent with developer expectations and habits. This ambitious goal of the methodology requires research in several directions: (i) an effective, domain-specific language to express transformation models has to be defined; (ii) algorithms to mine transformation models from recorded editing sequences of developers; and (iii) methods for pairing, on-the-fly matching, and instantiation of transformation models.

5　Turning Vision into Reality

What are the concrete steps to turn the TriCo vision into reality? As a first step towards implementing a full-fledged co-pilot, we envisage the development of a TriCo demonstrator in the form of an advanced integrated development environment (IDE) that includes the co-piloting functionality proposed in Sect. 3. The IDE could for instance be designed as a web application, to be gradually extended over time. The implementation could proceed as follows:

1. Initially, the IDE would mainly be an *editor* for implementations, specifications, and tests. This editor can be built on top of existing JavaScript frameworks, for instance the CodeMirror system [1]. It can already offer opt-in functionality to record the editing steps done by a developer, and automatically collect this data, which can later serve as training data for machine learning.
2. A second version of the IDE could include *conformance checking*, and thus initial support for co-editing all three artefacts.
3. Next, support for *diagnosis* and *adaptation* could be added to the co-pilot. Again, the IDE shall be able to record and collect developer interaction sequences, so that data becomes available to further improve the co-pilot.
4. Further extensions could include support for *collaborative development*, the integration with version control (GitHub), and support for standard continuous integration systems.

All this would lay the ground for plugging in, and closely integrate, a glowing variety of techniques, reasoning based and learning based, analytic and synthetic, to keep the three artefacts mutually in sync, in a co-piloting fashion, when the user evolves any of them.

Co-development and co-piloting have to be constantly evaluated in the light of the original objectives: to enable *efficient* production of *robust* software. Further, data has to be produced as input for training the verification and adaptation methods, using the data collection functionality, and guidelines to be developed for the integration of the TriCo approach into industrial development practices, including Agile development [20] in general and, for instance, Scrum [28]. For evaluation purposes, case studies can be formulated and carried out in different contexts: with industrial collaborators, covering development tasks that are close to the industrial practice; and within course projects at universities, providing a setup in which comparative studies between different development practices carrying out the same development task are possible. To evaluate efficiency and robustness, one could monitor the development effort in the projects and assess the quality of developed implementations and specifications through code review and independent testing, and by interviews with the developers.

We strongly believe that co-development of implementations, specifications, and tests is the future of software development. Triple co-piloting is our vision of how this future can materialise. We now invite the community to join us in discussing and further developing this vision, and to participate in its realisation.

References

1. Codemirror. https://codemirror.net
2. Ahrendt, W., Beckert, B., Bubel, R., Hähnle, R., Schmitt, P.H., Ulbrich, M. (eds.): Deductive Software Verification-The KeY Book. LNCS, vol. 10001. Springer, Cham (2016). https://doi.org/10.1007/978-3-319-49812-6

3. Ahrendt, W., Gladisch, C., Herda, M.: Proof-based test case generation. In: Ahrendt, W., Beckert, B., Bubel, R., Hähnle, R., Schmitt, P., Ulbrich, M. (eds.) Deductive Software Verification – The KeY Book. LNCS, vol. 10001, pp. 415–451. Springer, Cham (2016). https://doi.org/10.1007/978-3-319-49812-6_12

4. Albarghouthi, A., Dillig, I., Gurfinkel, A.: Maximal specification synthesis. In: Proceedings of POPL, vol. 51. ACM (2016)

5. Alshnakat, A., Gurov, D., Lidström, C., Rümmer, P.: Constraint-based contract inference for deductive verification. In: Ahrendt, W., Beckert, B., Bubel, R., Hähnle, R., Ulbrich, M. (eds.) Deductive Software Verification: Future Perspectives. LNCS, vol. 12345, pp. 149–176. Springer, Cham (2020). https://doi.org/10.1007/978-3-030-64354-6_6

6. Austin, J., et al.: Program synthesis with large language models (2021). arXiv:2108.07732

7. Barnett, M., Fähndrich, M., Leino, K.R.M., Müller, P., Schulte, W., Venter, H.: Specification and verification: the Spec# experience. Commun. ACM **54**(6), 81–91 (2011)

8. Barrett, C., Fontaine, P., Tinelli, C.: The SMT-LIB Standard: Version 2.6. Technical report, Department of Computer Science, The University of Iowa (2017). http://www.smt-lib.org/

9. Bjørner, N., Gurfinkel, A., McMillan, K., Rybalchenko, A.: Horn clause solvers for program verification. In: Beklemishev, L.D., Blass, A., Dershowitz, N., Finkbeiner, B., Schulte, W. (eds.) Fields of Logic and Computation II. LNCS, vol. 9300, pp. 24–51. Springer, Cham (2015). https://doi.org/10.1007/978-3-319-23534-9_2

10. Chen, M., et al.: Evaluating large language models trained on code, arxiv:2107.03374 (2021). arXiv:2107.03374

11. Chowdhery, A., et al.: PaLM: scaling language modeling with pathways (2022). arXiv:2204.02311

12. Ernst, M.D., et al.: The Daikon system for dynamic detection of likely invariants. Sci. Comput. Program. **69**(1–3), 35–45 (2007)

13. Fedyukovich, G., Rümmer, P.: Competition report: CHC-COMP-21. In: Hojjat, H., Kafle, B. (eds.) Proceedings 8th Workshop on Horn Clauses for Verification and Synthesis, HCVS@ETAPS 2021, Virtual, 28 March 2021. EPTCS, vol. 344, pp. 91–108 (2021)

14. Gleirscher, M., Foster, S., Woodcock, J.: New opportunities for integrated formal methods. ACM Comput. Surv. (CSUR) **52**(6), 1–36 (2019)

15. Gordon, M., Collavizza, H.: Forward with Hoare. In: Roscoe, A.W., Jones, C.B., Wood, K.R. (eds.) Reflections on the Work of C.A.R. Hoare, pp. 101–121. Springer, London (2010). https://doi.org/10.1007/978-1-84882-912-1_5

16. Hughes, J.: Software testing with QuickCheck. In: Horváth, Z., Plasmeijer, R., Zsók, V. (eds.) CEFP 2009. LNCS, vol. 6299, pp. 183–223. Springer, Heidelberg (2010). https://doi.org/10.1007/978-3-642-17685-2_6

17. Ioannides, C., Eder, K.I.: Coverage-directed test generation automated by machine learning - a review. ACM Trans. Des. Autom. Electron. Syst. **17**(1), 1–21 (2012)

18. Jhala, R., Majumdar, R.: Software model checking. ACM Comput. Surv. **41**(4), 1–54 (2009)

19. Kosmatov, N., Prevosto, V., Signoles, J.: A lesson on proof of programs with Frama-C. Invited tutorial paper. In: Veanes, M., Viganò, L. (eds.) TAP 2013. LNCS, vol. 7942, pp. 168–177. Springer, Heidelberg (2013). https://doi.org/10.1007/978-3-642-38916-0_10

20. Martin, R.C.: Agile Software Development: Principles, Patterns, and Practices. Prentice Hall PTR, Hoboken (2003)

21. Parthasarathy, M., Garg, P.: Machine-learning based methods for synthesizing invariants. Tutorial at CAV 2015 (2015)
22. Richter, C., Hüllermeier, E., Jakobs, M., Wehrheim, H.: Algorithm selection for software validation based on graph kernels. Autom. Softw. Eng. **27**(1), 153–186 (2020)
23. Seghir, M.N., Kroening, D.: Counterexample-guided precondition inference. In: Proceedings of Programming Languages and Systems - 22nd European Symposium on Programming, ESOP 2013, Held as Part of the European Joint Conferences on Theory and Practice of Software, ETAPS 2013, Rome, Italy, 16–24 March 2013, pp. 451–471 (2013)
24. Sen, K., Marinov, D., Agha, G.: Cute: a concolic unit testing engine for C. In: Proceedings of the 10th European Software Engineering Conference Held Jointly with 13th ACM SIGSOFT International Symposium on Foundations of Software Engineering, ESEC/FSE-13, pp. 263–272. Association for Computing Machinery, New York (2005)
25. Si, X., Dai, H., Raghothaman, M., Naik, M., Song, L.: Learning loop invariants for program verification. In: Advances in Neural Information Processing Systems 31, NeurIPS 2018, Montréal, Canada (2018). https://proceedings.neurips.cc/paper/2018
26. Singher, E., Itzhaky, S.: Theory exploration powered by deductive synthesis. In: Silva, A., Leino, K.R.M. (eds.) CAV 2021. LNCS, vol. 12760, pp. 125–148. Springer, Cham (2021). https://doi.org/10.1007/978-3-030-81688-9_6
27. Smallbone, N., Johannson, M., Claessen, K., Algehed, M.: Quick specifications for the busy programmer. J. Funct. Program. **27** (2017)
28. Takeuchi, H., Nonaka, I.: The new new product development game. Harv. Bus. Rev. **64**(1), 137–146 (1986)

Twinning-by-Construction: Ensuring Correctness for Self-adaptive Digital Twins

Eduard Kamburjan[1], Crystal Chang Din[2], Rudolf Schlatte[1],
S. Lizeth Tapia Tarifa[1], and Einar Broch Johnsen[1(✉)]

[1] University of Oslo, Oslo, Norway
{eduard,rudi,sltarifa,einarj}@ifi.uio.no
[2] University of Bergen, Bergen, Norway
crystal.din@uib.no

Abstract. Digital twin applications use digital artefacts to twin physical systems. The purpose is to continuously mirror the structure and behavior of the physical system, such that users can analyse the physical system by means of the digital twin. However, the physical system might change over time. In this case, the digital twin's ensemble of digital artefacts needs to be reconfigured to correctly twin the physical system again. This paper considers a digital twin infrastructure combining MAPE-K feedback loops and semantic reflection to automatically ensure that the digital artefacts correctly twin the physical system; i.e., the resulting system is *twinned-by-construction*. We consider the monitoring of both structural and temporal correctness properties for digital twin, including the time delay required by reconfiguration, and the capture of execution traces to reflect digital threads in the digital twin framework.

1 Introduction

Digital twins are a major innovation driver for the digitisation of key industries. Digital twin applications use digital artefacts to continuously mirror a physical system, such that users can analyse the physical system by means of the digital twin. At their core, they describe applications where a physical system, the *physical twin (PT)*, is mirrored structurally and behaviourally by some digital system, the *digital twin (DT)*; this mirroring turns the DT into a live replica of the PT. It is crucial that the PT and the DT interact with each other; i.e., data flows between them in both directions such that the DT can detect changes in the PT and perform actions. The physical system might change over time. In this case, the digital twin's ensemble of digital artefacts needs to be reconfigured to correctly twin the physical system again. Over its liftetime, the DT can then be seen as a trace of different configurations of digital artefacts, reflecting the changes to the PT. In this paper, we consider DTs that explicitly mirror changes to the PT in the digital system, enabling the user to access the *digital thread* of a physical asset.

© The Author(s), under exclusive license to Springer Nature Switzerland AG 2022
T. Margaria and B. Steffen (Eds.): ISoLA 2022, LNCS 13701, pp. 188–204, 2022.
https://doi.org/10.1007/978-3-031-19849-6_12

In this paper, we discuss the reconfiguration of digital twins from the perspective of X-by-construction (XbC) approaches and self-adaptive systems, and how these reconfigurations can be monitored. We say that a physical system is *twinned* by a digital system if the digital system has the same structure and behavior as the physical system. Static digital twins, i.e., twins that mirror a structure that does not change over time, are *twinned-by-construction* if the initialisation of the digital system ensures this twinning property. However, when the PT evolves over time, self-adaptation at runtime will play a crucial role in not only keeping the DT running, but also to re-establish its twinning property.

To illustrate these interactions between a self-adaptive DT and the PT, we consider an *architecture* for digital twins based on MAPE-K feedback loops [1–3] (Monitor, Analyse, Plan, and Execute based on Knowledge), a well-known method to organize autonomous systems. We distinguish between two different MAPE-K feedback loops for the *digital twin units* and the *digital twin infrastructure* in a digital twin application, where a DT unit is a digital artefact, for example, a simulator that mirrors exactly one part of the physical system, and the DT infrastructure orchestrates an ensemble of DT units.

One of the MAPE-K feedback loops uses the DT infrastructure to make sure that the DT units indeed jointly mirror the PT. Twinning-by-construction (TbC) ensures that the DT infrastructure connects the DT units in such a way that the DT mirrors the structure of the PT. If the physical system changes over time, the DT infrastructure needs to adapt and *re-twin* the digital system and re-establish the structural and behavioural correspondence between PT and DT. The DT infrastructure also realizes other features of the application, e.g., the above-mentioned data flow, the user interfaces, and analysis support over the DT such as the exploration of speculative scenarios, which again can be realised via a second MAPE-K feedback loop that only focuses on the behavioural correspondence between PT and DT.

This paper mainly focuses on the structural correspondence between the PT and the DT, as shown in Fig. 1, and discusses the connection between the concept of twinned-by-construction and self-adaptation at runtime by combining MAPE-K feedback loops with semantically lifted programs [4], and runtime monitoring of properties for self-adaptive systems. Semantically lifted programs combine knowledge graphs and object-oriented programming languages by enabling the program to *semantically reflect* on itself as a knowledge graph. For digital twin applications, we implement the DT units by means of functional mock-up units (FMUs) [5,6] and use ontology-based *asset models* to connect the state of the DT and the PT [7] (see Fig. 1). Knowledge graphs enable a uniform treatment of the DT infrastructure (via semantic reflection) and a physical system (via the asset model). Users can send queries to both the asset model and the DT.

Furthermore, we consider *trace-based TbC* for digital twin applications. Correct twinning captures the property that the current structure of the DT corresponds to the current structure of the PT, as it is expressed in the asset model. Trace-based TbC strengthens this notion of correctness by requiring that the execution *trace* of the DT must also mirror the (execution) *trace* of the PT. Based on this constraint, information concerning physical twin units that are

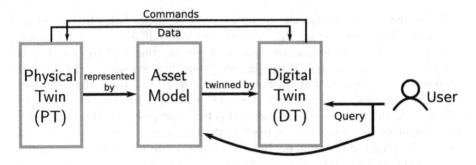

Fig. 1. High-level description of a digital twin architecture: the asset model serves as an interface for structural changes between digital twin (DT) and physical system (PS). Knowledge graphs enable uniform access to both DT and asset model.

no longer present in the *current* configuration of the PT, but were previously present, can be found in the trace of the DT. Consequently, information can be retrieved about DT units corresponding to PT units that no longer exist. Trace-based TbC connects digital twins to the concept of digital threads (see, e.g., [8,9]), which has not been explored so far for DTs using ontologies and asset models.

Contributions and Structure. Our main contributions are (1) a detailed discussion that establishes a conceptual link between digital twins, X-by-construction and self-adaptation at runtime, and (2) an extension of semantical lifting that connects the digital thread with asset models. We introduce the notion of *twinned-by-construction* in Sect. 2 and the role of self-adaptation at runtime in Sect. 3. Section 4 broadens the discussion to digital threads for semantically lifted programs. We discuss related work and conclude the paper in Sect. 5 and Sect. 6

2   Twinned-by-Construction Systems

In this section we discuss twinned-by-construction (TbC) for static digital twins, and the role played by knowledge graphs. We introduce the basics by example and refrain from giving a formal introduction of the technology stack. For a summary of the use of knowledge graphs in digital twins and asset models, we refer to [7]; for a general introduction, we refer to [10].

Asset Model. An asset model serves as an interface between a physical and a digital system. It is a database (or a file) containing an organized description of the composition and properties of assets. An asset model is useful in a digital twin context because it can provide the twin with static configuration data for the digital twin units. The DT infrastructure is responsible for the updates and synchronization between the asset model and the DT. We assume here that the asset model is expressed as, or can be converted into, a knowledge graph.

Example 1. Consider a digital twin that, for some building construction, is twinning the structure of the walls. The building has two walls at the moment: one is left of the other one. As a knowledge graph, this is expressed using the following triples in RDF [11]:

```
as:InProd rdfs:subClassOf as:Asset.
as:Wall   rdfs:subClassOf as:Asset.
as:w1 a as:Wall.        as:w2 a as:Wall.
as:w1 a as:InProd.      as:w2 a as:InProd.
as:w1 as:leftOf as:w2.
```

Each RDF triple consists of three nodes, where in the example each node is either a name of the form `prefix:name`, or the symbol `a` expressing that the first node belongs to the third node, which must be a class. In the example, the first two lines define three classes, the class of all assets (`as:Asset`), and its subclasses of all walls (`as:Wall`) and all assets which are actively used in production `as:InProd`. Lines 3–4 define two objects `as:w1` and `as:w2` which are walls used in production. The last line defined that `as:w1` is left of `as:w2`. The order between the triples listed in the asset model does not matter.

Twinned-by-Construction. If the physical system does not change, the DT can be statically checked to ensure that it correctly mirrors the structure of the PT by statically comparing the asset model with the structure described in the DT infrastructure. Since the core principle of the digital twin is the structural mirroring, the asset model can be used as a guideline to construct the digital twin. In this case, we say that the digital twin is *twinned-by-construction* and the task of establishing the structural connection between PT and DT using an asset model is *twinning-by-construction.*

Figure 2 shows the structure of a correctly twinned system with two physical twin units (e.g., two walls `Asset 1` and `Asset 2`), their two descriptions in the asset model (e.g., `w1` and `w2` in the RDF given above) and two digital twin units `DTU 1` and `DTU 2` (e.g., two wall simulators): Any DT unit twins some part of the asset model, which in turn represents a PT unit. The DT unit and the PT unit are directly connected by data flowing between them. The correct twinning is established over *all* DT and PT units, as the interconnections in the physical system must also be mirrored in the digital one. For Example 1, this would be that the wall simulators are connected according to the `asset:leftOf` guideline.

Given a fixed asset model, an existing DT infrastructure, and a mapping from asset classes to DT units, one can easily define the corresponding structure in the digital twin: first, for each class of the asset define a class in the application with the same spatial information and the used simulation unit. Second, for each object in the asset model create an object of the corresponding class, and replicate the spatial information. We elide the details of this construction, which is the current way to write digital twins, but point out that such systems are already TbC.

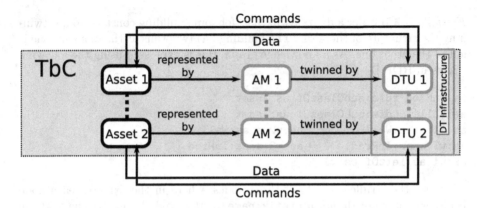

Fig. 2. Structure of a digital twin for two assets (Asset 1 and Asset 2) as PT units.

The Role of Knowledge Graphs. Knowledge graphs (KGs) are the established technique to formalize domain knowledge and add semantics (w.r.t. a domain) to data. In particular, they provide a uniform way to represent, query and reason about data. In the TbC approach, their role is twofold:

Uniform Structure Representation. The asset model can be a knowledge graph,[1] and the information required for twinning can be accessed using standard KG technologies. The DT infrastructure can be translated into a knowledge graph, using semantical lifting [4], that maps program states to KGs, meaning that the information about the structure of the DT has the same format and representation as the structure of the PT.

Uniform Data Access. Starting from the uniform representation of structure, both the user and the DT infrastructure itself can query and reason about the *combined* structure of DT and PT. The user can access the digital twin, e.g., its simulation results, in terms of the asset model. The DT infrastructure can detect structural drift between DT and PT, i.e., if the structural correspondence does not hold when querying over both structures.

3   Twinning-by-Construction and Temporal Properties

In the previous section we discussed how a given asset model, describing the state of a physical system, can be used to construct a digital system that is TbC. Now, we turn our attention to self-adaptation. Self-adaptation is triggered when we observe a deviation of the DT unit with respect to the PT unit and when there are changes in the asset model. When constructing self-adaptive systems in the context of digital twins, it is important to consider a library of reusable DT units, support for a self-adaptation process that takes into consideration requirements for the reconstruction, and support for reasoning, analysis, and tuning during the

---

[1] This approach is taken by several on-going projects, e.g., the READi project [12].

reconstruction process [13]. This can be realised following the MAPE-K feedback loop schema [1–3] with four activities: Monitor, Analyse, Plan, and Execute, over a shared Knowledge.

In addition, we consider properties for both behavioural and structural relations to the assets. The reason for considering these additional properties is that while the physical systems change, the DT infrastructure must preserve the twinning property by reconfiguring the structure between the corresponding DT units within a time bound. This *structural* reconfiguration, which we call *re-twinning*, poses additional temporal constraints on the physical and digital systems in that twinning must be ensured at a certain speed. We now detail these different activities.

MAPE-K Schema for Data Streams. Self-adaptation is needed when we observe model drift, i.e., a deviation between a DT unit and its PT unit. In this context, the *monitor* step collects data streams from the physical and digital system. The *analysis* step can use temporal properties to express expectations on the data stream that are needed for the model in the digital twin to work, e.g., using runtime monitoring (see Fig. 5, top right monitor). In our building example, one may have a restriction that the moisture of the wall is never higher than 1%. If the sensors report a moisture value beyond this threshold, the system triggers an error. During the analysis step, one can also use a *hyperproperty* [14] and compare the data output from the physical system with the data output from the digital system to detect if the difference is above a threshold to trigger an error.

The *planning* step can use *model search techniques* to find the best parameters for the DT unit to adjust the observed output deviation from the PT unit, and the *execute* step will reconfigure the relevant DT units by resetting their parameters. This is a major application scenario for digital shadows,[2] which detect anomalies not only by analysing the data stream, but by the relation of data stream and the digital twin unit.

MAPE-K Schema for Structural Self-adaptation. The connection of digital twin and asset model must also be maintained. As shown in Fig. 3, the self-adaptation process must *detect* structural changes in the asset, and trigger reconfiguration of the digital system such that the temporal TbC properties that were established initially holds again, as initially discussed in [7].

Example 2. Continuing with Example 1, we consider the situation that a third wall as:w3 is added to the building under construction and, consequently, to the asset model. In the knowledge base, the following triples are added:

as:w3 a as:Wall. as:w3 a as:InProd. as:w2 as:leftOf as:w3.

---

[2] A digital shadow is a digital twin with unidirectional data flow: the DT does not send commands back to the PT [15].

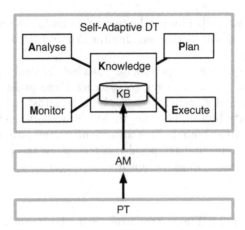

Fig. 3. Structural self-adaptation of a DT following a MAPE-K feedback loop.

Twinning uses the asset model, which is formalized as a knowledge base, to ensure that all assets that are to be twinned are indeed represented by some DT units and that the DT units are correctly connected (i.e., according to the PT). Additionally, TbC ensures that no DT units without a PT equivalent exist in the DT. It is application-specific what assets are modelled and how the DT infrastructure repairs its state – thus, it is not possible to generate a generic DT infrastructure fully automatically from an asset model.

However, in the *monitor* step we can formulate the condition that the DT is twinning the PT correctly by posing the query that returns the mismatches: (1) all assets not represented in the DT and (2) all objects not corresponding to an existing asset in the PT. An example of such a query is shown below. It assumes that the DT infrastructure can be seen as a knowledge base, where all its DT units are represented as instances of a class `dti:DTUnit`, and that each DT unit is connected to the asset it twins via the `dti:twins` property. The following SPARQL [16] query retrieves all assets that occur in the physical system but are not twinned:

```
SELECT ?x { ?x a as:InProd.
            FILTER NOT EXISTS (?y a dti:DTUnit. ?y dti:twins ?x.)
}
```

The *analysis* step is in charge of understanding that the structure is mirrored correctly, which can be expressed in our example simply by using `as:leftOf`. We can similarly define a query that returns all DT units that are not respecting the structure of the assets (shown in Fig. 4), where we assume that the structure of the DT infrastructure that connects DT units is using an analogous property `dti:leftOf`. We say that a system is *simply twinned* if both queries return an empty set. A *simply twinned* system has one DT unit for each PT unit, and all the DT units are correctly connected. Let SIMPLE be the conjunction of the

```
SELECT ?dtu { ?dtu a dti:DTUnit. ?dtu dti:twins ?asset.
    OPTIONAL(
        ?asset as:leftOf ?right.
        FILTER NOT EXISTS (
            ?dtuRight a dti:DTUnit.
            ?dtu dti:leftOf ?dtuRight.
            ?dtuRight dti:twins ?right.
            )
        )
    }
```

Fig. 4. A query to ensure that all twinned units are connected correctly. It returns the set of DT units that are *not* mirroring the structure correctly.

two given queries. Observe that the SIMPLE query only works because there are several sources of data for the knowledge base: the domain knowledge, the asset model and the current state of the DT infrastructure.

The *planning* step identifies the DT units that must be created; in this case, one DT unit for each member of the returned set in the queries, if non-empty.

The *execution* step creates the identified DT units and link them correctly to the existing DT units according to the asset model. The execution step triggers re-twinning, which is done according to the planning step.

Temporal Properties of the DT Infrastructure. It takes time to re-twin and it may be crucial to ensure that re-twinning happens sufficiently fast. For this reason, we also consider temporal properties of the DT infrastructure, which are here represented using Metric Temporal Logic (MTL) [17,18], an extension of LTL with intervals that is suited for online monitoring [19]. The syntax of a MTL formula φ over state predicates p and intervals I[3] is given by

$$\varphi ::= p \mid \textbf{false} \mid \varphi \wedge \varphi \mid \neg\varphi \mid \varphi \, \textbf{U}_I \, \varphi$$

and the abbreviations $\Box_I \, \varphi = \textbf{false} \, \textbf{U}_I \, \varphi$, $\Diamond_I \, \varphi = \neg \Box_I \, \neg\varphi$, $\Box \, \varphi = \Box_{[0,\infty)} \, \varphi$. The intuition for $\Box_I \, \varphi$ is that φ holds at all points in time in the interval I and the intuition for $\Diamond_I \, \varphi$ is that φ holds at some point in the interval I.

A property expressing that if a system is out of sync, then it will be re-twinned within n time units (as shown in Fig. 5), is expressed as follows:

$$n-\textsf{Resync} \equiv \Box\big(\textsf{SIMPLE} \neq \emptyset \rightarrow \Diamond_{[0,n]}\textsf{SIMPLE} \doteq \emptyset\big) \, .$$

Regulating the Rate of Re-twinning. Twinning takes time. So one must make sure that the asset model is not changing too fast. For example, if every change in the physical system triggers re-twinning, then several connected

---

[3] We use discrete time with intervals of the form $[n, m]$ or $[n, \infty)$, where $n, m \in \mathbb{N}$.

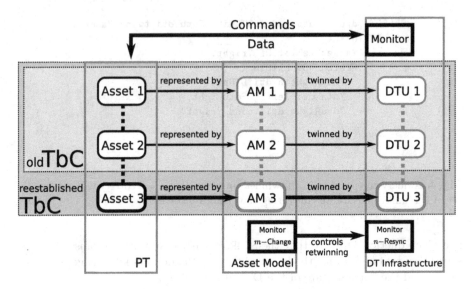

Fig. 5. Refined structure of the digital twin architecture after a change: an new DT unit is added for the new asset and the twinning property must be re-established.

changes (e.g., changing several assets in one maintenance) should be submitted at once to the asset model. Formally, one demands that the distance between any CHANGE is not less than m time units. The following formula expresses this constraint:

$$m-\text{Change} \equiv \Box(\text{CHANGE} \rightarrow \neg\Diamond_{(0,m]}\text{CHANGE}) \ .$$

In our reference architecture, changes in the asset model and the re-twinning process can happen independently: $m-\text{Change}$ monitors the asset model interface and reports if the asset model is updated too often, while $n-\text{Resync}$ monitors the DT infrastructure itself, see Fig. 5.

The rate of change of the asset models, which captures the evolution of the PT, should not be faster than the twinning speed, i.e., the speed of the DT infrastructure that updates according to the changes in the asset model. Thus, the property to be monitored is

$$\text{TEMP}_{m,n} \equiv m > n \wedge m-\text{Change} \wedge n-\text{Resync} \ .$$

4 The Digital Thread as a Temporal Property

So far, we have considered properties that relate the current state of a digital system and the current state of the physical system, as well as temporal properties that ensure that twinning happens at the correct frequency. This, however, does not consider the so-called "digital thread", which must take into account not only the current state of the system, but also its trace of past actions. This requires a specific notion of twinning for traces and has consequences for the structure of the DT infrastructure: not all DT units are relevant for the twinning property of the current state, and the DT units for replaced or removed assets must be handled differently. First, we describe an example of more involved changes in the physical system.

Example 3. Continuing Example 1, the newly built third wall (`as:w3` in the asset model) is used to *replace* the second wall (`as:w2` in the asset model), which is removed in the process. Afterwards `as:w3` is removed as well and `as:w1` remains as the sole wall. The total sequence of actions, the trace, in the physical system is as follows:

1. build walls `as:w1` and `as:w2`,
2. build wall `as:w3`,
3. replace `as:w2` with `as:w3`, and
4. decommission `as:w3`.

The twinning actions in Steps 1 and 2 have been explained in Sect. 2 and 3. Now we continue from Step 3. The following asset model reflects this change by marking that the digital twin unit `as:w2` as decommissioned, `as:w3` as replacing `as:w2`. It updates the information that that `as:w1` is now directly left to `as:w3`:

```
as:w1 a as:Wall. as:w2 a as:Wall. as:w3 a as:Wall.
as:w1 a as:InProd. as:w2 a as:Decom. as:w3 a as:InProd.
as:w1 as:leftOf as:w3. as:w3 as:replaces as:w2.
```

The change on the asset model already realizes the digital thread. We can query about what the PT has performed from the knowledge base. For example, to retrieve the walls that `as:w2` was next to, we can run the following query:

```
SELECT ?x {?x as:leftOf [as:replaces* as:w2]}
```

which gives us `as:w1`. The digital twin however, must keep the information about the DT unit for `as:w2` available as well. As we require that the DT infrastructure represents every physical asset that was part of the asset model at some point in a DT, it is guaranteed that such a DT unit existed, but it *must* still exist now and be ignored for the twinning property of the current state – all assets which are instances of the decommissioned class `as:Decom` must be ignored for it.[4] Thus, we refine the DT infrastructure and introduce the digital twin *graveyard*, see Fig. 6, a data structure where DT units of decommissioned, or otherwise removed, assets are saved, but ignored for the twinning of the *current* state.

The refined structure is shown in Fig. 6: The DT infrastructure contains a DT graveyard structure, where, compared to Fig. 5 one DT unit has been moved and is, consequently *ignored* for the twinning property. Note that the corresponding asset (Asset 1) has been removed from the physical system, but its asset model (AM 1) remains. The moved DT unit is also disconnected from the other DT units, while the asset model contains information about the old structure.

---

[4] This is already modelled in the SIMPLE query above.

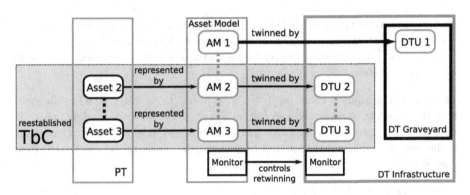

Fig. 6. Structure of the digital twin. The graveyard retains the DT units, which are needed for the digital thread, but must be ignored for the twinned property.

The digital thread is, thus, realised on the asset model (and possible connected to the original designs, requirements, etc.) of the walls, and in the DT infrastructure (using semantic reflection of the graveyard). However, there are further events in the trace of the physical system that are not changing the structure. For example, if a wall is repainted, it is visible in the asset model, but does not require a change in the DT. Similarly, changes in the DT infrastructure that are not structural, such as behavioural reconfigurations, must be made available to the user.

One can easily refine the asset model by recording more information about the events, for example their time and data and additional, explicit information when, how and why `as:w3` was replaced. We refrain from giving a realistic example using a full ontology based asset model like IMF [12], but illustrate the additional information by performing the last step on our building example.

Example 4. Next, we remove wall `as:w3` completely and we add information about the removal. The asset model becomes the following (in terms of Fig. 6, this is the complete asset model including AM1, AM2, and AM3, without general declarations of the classes):

```
as:w1 a as:Wall. as:w2 a as:Wall. as:w3 a as:Wall.
as:w1 a as:InProd. as:w2 a as:Decom. as:w3 a as:Decom.
as:w1 as:leftOf as:w3. as:w3 as:replaces as:w2.
as:w3 as:observed as:ev1. as:w3 as:removedAt as:ev2.
as:ev1 a as:Observation. as:ev1 a as:WaterDamage".
as:ev1 as:at "2022-05-21.12:10:00"^^xsd:date.
as:ev2 a as:Removal. as:ev2 as:byCompany "Parken".
as:ev2 as:at "2022-05-22.12:00:00"^^xsd:date.
```

This marks `as:w3` as decommissioned, but also records two events: `as:ev1` records that there was some water damage at a specific date and `as:ev2` records that a removal was performed at a specific date by the company `Parken`. The fourth line of the asset model connects the `as:w3` with events `as:ev1` and `as:ev2`. The first event `as:ev1`, is not relevant for the structure of the DT infrastructure, yet may trigger a behavioural reconfiguration – our data stream monitor detects the violation of the moisture constraint, but the DT unit is not moved to the graveyard. Yet, the information of the reconfiguration is available in the knowledge graph of the DT infrastructure. For example, consider the following reconfiguration:

```
dti:dtu1 dti:twins as:w3.
dti:dtu1 dti:reconfiguration dti:ev3.
dti:ev3 dti:at "2022-05-21.12:11:00"^^xsd:dateTime.
dti:ev3 dti:newParam "1"^^xsd:int.
dti:dtu1 dti:removal dti:ev4.
dti:ev4 dti:at "2022-05-22.12:01:00"^^xsd:dateTime.
```

Now, the user can run queries to investigate possible causes for a reconfiguration, or the consequences of some event. For example, the following query returns all reconfigurations that happened on the date of a water damage:

```
SELECT ?reconf {
    ?asset as:observed ?ev. ?ev a as:WaterDamage.
    ?dtu dti:twins ?asset. ?dtu dti:reconfiguration ?reconf.
    ?ev as:at ?datetime. ?reconf dti:at ?datetime.}
```

A possible perspective is that we check whether an *event* on asset side has been twinned. However, a reconfiguration can mirror different events (or changes without events, due to model drift), so one cannot in general require a one-to-one correspondence between events in the DT infrastructure and events in the physical system.[5]

The above example shows the intricate interactions of asset models, traces, the re-establishment of twinning properties and self-adaptation at runtime. We now return to the expression of temporal properties and monitoring of twinning process itself.

Monitoring Traces. As discussed, consistency of the updating speed is guaranteed: Formula `TEMP` expresses that every change in the asset model is mirrored in time by the DT infrastructure and the digital twin is simply twinned again. For example, it cannot be the case that the DT updates too slowly and could not perform the addition of `as:w3` in Step 2 in time so that actions in Steps 3 and 4 are not able to be realised.

A part of this is *correctness* w.r.t. simple twinning: Every physical unit (that is correctly handled in the asset model) has a DT unit twinning it. While the

---

[5] Note that while we require a one-to-one correspondence between PT and DT units here, this is only a simplification for *simple* twinning, one can easily extend the system to handle one-to-many twinning relations.

final state of the digital twin has the DT unit for `as:w1`, we know that the DT has also created DT units for the other assets. Next, we discuss how we formalize *temporal simple twinning*, which expresses simple twinning also for decommissioned physical units. And give the following query `TempSimple`:

```
SELECT ?x {
  ?x a dti:DTUnit.
  FILTER NOT EXISTS(
    ?x dti:twins ?asset. ?asset a as:Decom.
    ?asset as:removedAt [a as:Removal; as:at ?datetime1].
    ?x dti:removal [a dti:Remove; dti:at ?datetime2].
    FILTER (
      microsec(?datetime2) - microsec(?datetime1) < 5*60*1000
    )
  )
}
```

If the system is correctly twinned with respect to removal/replacement of PT and DT units, the query should return an empty set. So the query above returns all DT units, excepts those which have a removal event within 5 min of the removal of the corresponding asset they twin, i.e., we define 5 min as the time limit for re-twinning. It is guaranteed that this holds if (1) `TEMP` holds and (2) the DT infrastructure is implemented correctly. Thus, we monitor that the DT infrastructure correctly implements the following temporal property, *trace-based TbC*:

$$\text{TEMP}_{m,n} \wedge \square(\texttt{TempSimple} \neq \emptyset \rightarrow \Diamond_{[0,n]}\texttt{TempSimple} \doteq \emptyset).$$

5   Related Work

The connection of digital twins and asset models so far is mostly used for data integration to handle the numerous heterogeneous data sources of the physical twin. For example, Yan et al. [20] use knowledge bases (KBs) to integrate data in manufacturing equipment, Banerjee et al. [21] use a similar approach to interact with data from IoT sensors in industrial production lines, and Oakes et al. [22] for drivetrains. Going one step further, Wascak et al. [23] aim to use asset models as part of this integration in their abstract digital twin architecture. More abstractly, Kharlamov et al. [24] have investigated the use of KBs for data integration in the context of the energy industry, and used this integrated data to enable machine learning on data streams [25]. Lietaert et al. [26] use KBs similarly to integrate data for machine learning approaches.

To the best of our knowledge, the use of KBs to handle structural drift of the PT and its asset model is hitherto unexplored. Various methods exist to detect parameter or model drift, both statistical, e.g. Woodcock et al. [27] and formal, e.g. [28]. Multiple works have addressed formal modelling and verification of self-adaptive systems to provide assurances [29] using MAPE-K feedback loops. Various approaches, from very methodological such as ENTRUST

[30] to more concrete, using formal techniques, such as ActivFORMS [31] that uses formal models at runtime in the form of timed automata. Recent works explore Petri nets to model self-adaptive systems, along with domain specific language [32–34]. Arcaina et al. have developed Abstract State Machines [3,35] to model interactive MAPE-K loops. Formal verification of MAPE-K loops have been also explored from the perspective of use cases. Feng et al. [36] adapts a case study for DT engineering to verify MAPE-K feedback loops and Päßler et al. [37] develops a formal model of Metacontrol [38] for the heating system of a smart home that considers MAPE-K loops and self-adaptation using a black box approach. Compared to the work presented in this paper, all the previous approaches focuses on the behavioural aspect of self-adaptation, and not on the structural aspect as discussed in this paper. To the best of our knowledge, we are not aware of other approaches that take into account structural self-adaptation and MAPE-K feedback loops.

6   Conclusion

This paper considers a digital twin infrastructure that combines MAPE-K feedback loops and semantic reflection. Whereas feedback loops can be used to realize runtime self-adaptation for the digital twin, semantic reflection enables the structure of the digital twin and of the asset to be uniformly represented in a knowledge base. We show how the resulting knowledge base can be queried by the digital twin application and reasoned over to detect misconfigurations that violate digital twin correctness properties. Consequently, the feedback loops and semantic reflection jointly ensure that the ensemble of digital artefacts is indeed always a correct twin, i.e., the combined digital artefacts are *twinned-by-construction*.

In the paper, we consider the monitoring of both structural and temporal correctness properties for digital twin reconfiguration, including that a structural twin relation is established by the repair function, that the time delay required by reconfiguration is within a given bound, and that the digital thread is reflected in the digital twin framework. To this aim, the knowledge base is extended to capture execution traces, such that the evolution of the physical and digital systems can be compared by querying the knowledge base.

In our current work, the correctness property of *twinning* is specified as an empty query result from a query on the knowledge base that combines the asset model and the semantically reflected digital twin configuration.

In future work, we plan to investigate the feasability of our approach using a bigger case study that will be evaluated the SMOL framework, which supports both semantic reflection and digital artefacts embedded as FMUs. Furthermore, we plan to investigate the static verification of query-based specifications of programs with knowledge bases.

Acknowledgements. This work was partially supported by University of Bergen and the Research Council of Norway via the projects SIRIUS (237898) and PeTWIN (294600).

References

1. Brun, Y., et al.: Engineering self-adaptive systems through feedback loops. In: Cheng, B.H.C., de Lemos, R., Giese, H., Inverardi, P., Magee, J. (eds.) Software Engineering for Self-Adaptive Systems. LNCS, vol. 5525, pp. 48–70. Springer, Heidelberg (2009). https://doi.org/10.1007/978-3-642-02161-9_3

2. Kephart, J.O., Chess, D.M.: The vision of autonomic computing. Computer **36**(1), 41–50 (2003)

3. Arcaini, P., Riccobene, E., Scandurra, P.: Modeling and analyzing MAPE-K feedback loops for self-adaptation. In: Inverardi, P., Schmerl, B.R. (eds.) 10th IEEE/ACM International Symposium on Software Engineering for Adaptive and Self-Managing Systems (SEAMS 2015), pp. 13–23. IEEE Computer Society (2015)

4. Kamburjan, E., Klungre, V.N., Schlatte, R., Johnsen, E.B., Giese, M.: Programming and debugging with semantically lifted states. In: Verborgh, R., et al. (eds.) ESWC 2021. LNCS, vol. 12731, pp. 126–142. Springer, Cham (2021). https://doi.org/10.1007/978-3-030-77385-4_8

5. Blochwitz, T., et al.: Functional mockup interface 2.0: the standard for tool independent exchange of simulation models. In: The Modelica Association Modelica Conference, pp. 173–184 (2012)

6. Kamburjan, E., Johnsen, E.B.: Knowledge structures over simulation units. In: Proceedings of the SCS Annual Modeling and Simulation Conference (ANNSIM) (2022). In press

7. Kamburjan, E., Klungre, V.N., Schlatte, R., Tapia Tarifa, S.L., Cameron, D., Johnsen, E.B.: Digital twin reconfiguration using asset models. In: Proceedings of the 11th International Symposium on Leveraging Applications of Formal Methods (ISoLA 2022) (2022). This volume

8. Gould, L.S.: What are digital twins and digital threads? Automot. Des. Prod. **23** (2018)

9. Margaria, T., Schieweck, A.: The digital thread in industry 4.0. In: Ahrendt, W., Tapia Tarifa, S.L. (eds.) IFM 2019. LNCS, vol. 11918, pp. 3–24. Springer, Cham (2019). https://doi.org/10.1007/978-3-030-34968-4_1

10. Hitzler, P., Krötzsch, M., Rudolph, S.: Foundations of Semantic Web Technologies. CRC Press, Chapman and Hall (2010)

11. W3C, RDF Working Group: Resource description framework https://www.w3.org/RDF

12. Fjosna, E., Waaler, A.: READI information modelling framework (IMF). Asset Information Modelling Framework. Technical report, READI Joint Industry Project (2021). https://readi-jip.org/wp-content/uploads/2021/03/Information-modelling-framework-V1.pdf

13. de Lemos, R., et al.: Software engineering for self-adaptive systems: a second research roadmap. In: de Lemos, R., Giese, H., Müller, H.A., Shaw, M. (eds.) Software Engineering for Self-Adaptive Systems II. LNCS, vol. 7475, pp. 1–32. Springer, Heidelberg (2013). https://doi.org/10.1007/978-3-642-35813-5_1

14. Clarkson, M.R., Schneider, F.B.: Hyperproperties. J. Comput. Secur. **18**(6), 1157–1210 (2010)

15. Kritzinger, W., Karner, M., Traar, G., Henjes, J., Sihn, W.: Digital twin in manufacturing: a categorical literature review and classification. IFAC-PapersOnLine **51**(11), 1016–1022 (2018)

16. W3C, SPARQL Working Group: Sparql 1.1 query language https://www.w3.org/TR/sparq

17. Brandt, S., Kalayci, E.G., Kontchakov, R., Ryzhikov, V., Xiao, G., Zakharyaschev, M.: Ontology-based data access with a horn fragment of metric temporal logic. In: AAAI, pp. 1070–1076, AAAI Press (2017)
18. Koymans, R.: Specifying real-time properties with metric temporal logic. Real Time Syst. **2**(4), 255–299 (1990)
19. Ho, H.-M., Ouaknine, J., Worrell, J.: Online monitoring of metric temporal logic. In: Bonakdarpour, B., Smolka, S.A. (eds.) RV 2014. LNCS, vol. 8734, pp. 178–192. Springer, Cham (2014). https://doi.org/10.1007/978-3-319-11164-3_15
20. Yan, H., Yang, J., Wan, J.: KnowIME: a system to construct a knowledge graph for intelligent manufacturing equipment. IEEE Access **8**, 41805–41813 (2020)
21. Banerjee, A., Dalal, R., Mittal, S., Joshi, K.P.: Generating digital twin models using knowledge graphs for industrial production lines. In: Proceedings of the Web Science Conference (WebSci 2017), pp. 425–430, ACM (2017)
22. Oakes, B.J., Meyers, B., Janssens, D., Vangheluwe, H.: Structuring and accessing knowledge for historical and streaming digital twins. In: Tiddi, I., Maleshkova, M., Pellegrini, T., de Boer, V., (eds.) Joint Proceedings of the Semantics Co-located Events: Poster& Demo Track and Workshop on Ontology-Driven Conceptual Modelling of Digital Twins Co-located with Semantics 2021, vol. 2941 of CEUR Workshop Proceedings. CEUR-WS.org (2021)
23. Waszak, M., Lam, A.N., Hoffmann, V., Elvesæter, B., Mogos, M.F., Roman, D.: Let the asset decide: digital twins with knowledge graphs. In: 19th IEEE International Conference on Software Architecture (ICSA) (2022)
24. Kharlamov, E., Martín-Recuerda, F., Perry, B., Cameron, D., Fjellheim, R., Waaler, A.: Towards semantically enhanced digital twins. In: IEEE BigData, pp. 4189–4193, IEEE (2018)
25. Zhou, B., et al.: SemML: facilitating development of ML models for condition monitoring with semantics. J. Web Semant. **71**, 100664 (2021)
26. Lietaert, P., Meyers, B., Van Noten, J., Sips, J., Gadeyne, K.: Knowledge graphs in digital twins for AI in production. In: Dolgui, A., Bernard, A., Lemoine, D., von Cieminski, G., Romero, D. (eds.) APMS 2021. IAICT, vol. 630, pp. 249–257. Springer, Cham (2021). https://doi.org/10.1007/978-3-030-85874-2_26
27. Woodcock, J., Gomes, C., Macedo, H.D., Larsen, P.G.: Uncertainty quantification and runtime monitoring using environment-aware digital twins. In: Margaria, T., Steffen, B. (eds.) ISoLA 2020. LNCS, vol. 12479, pp. 72–87. Springer, Cham (2021). https://doi.org/10.1007/978-3-030-83723-5_6
28. Deshmukh, J.V., Donzé, A., Ghosh, S., Jin, X., Juniwal, G., Seshia, S.A.: Robust online monitoring of signal temporal logic. Form. Methods Syst. Des. **51**(1), 5–30 (2017). https://doi.org/10.1007/s10703-017-0286-7
29. Weyns, D., et al.: Perpetual assurances for self-adaptive systems. In: de Lemos, R., Garlan, D., Ghezzi, C., Giese, H. (eds.) Software Engineering for Self-Adaptive Systems III. Assurances. LNCS, vol. 9640, pp. 31–63. Springer, Cham (2017). https://doi.org/10.1007/978-3-319-74183-3_2
30. Calinescu, R., Weyns, D., Gerasimou, S., Iftikhar, M.U., Habli, I., Kelly, T.: Engineering trustworthy self-adaptive software with dynamic assurance cases. IEEE Trans. Softw. Eng. **44**(11), 1039–1069 (2017)
31. Iftikhar, M.U., Weyns, D.: ActivFORMS: active formal models for self-adaptation. In: Proceedings of the 9th International Symposium on Software Engineering for Adaptive and Self-Managing Systems (SEAMS 2014), pp. 125–134, ACM (2014)
32. Fakhir, M.I., Kazmi, S.A.R.: Formal specification and verification of self-adaptive concurrent systems. IEEE Access **6**, 34790–34803 (2018)

33. Mian, N.A., Ahmad, F.: Modeling and analysis of MAPE-K loop in self adaptive systems using Petri nets. Int. J. Comput. Sci. Netw. Secur. **17**, 6 (2017)
34. Camilli, M., Capra, L.: Formal specification and verification of decentralized self-adaptive systems using symmetric nets. Discrete Event Dyn. Syst. **31**(4), 609–657 (2021)
35. Arcaini, P., Riccobene, E., Scandurra, P.: Formal design and verification of self-adaptive systems with decentralized control. In: ACM Transactions on Autonomous and Adaptive Systems (2016)
36. Feng, H., et al.: Integration of the MAPE-K loop into digital twins ANNSIM (2022). To appear
37. Päßler, J., Aguado, E., Silva, G.R., Corbato, C.H., Johnsen, E.B., Tapia Tarifa, S.L.: A formal model of Metacontrol in Maude (2022). Under review
38. Corbato, C.H.: Model-based self-awareness patterns for autonomy. PhD thesis, Universidad Politécnica de Madrid (2013)

On Formal Choreographic Modelling: A Case Study in EU Business Processes

Alex Coto[1], Franco Barbanera[2], Ivan Lanese[3], Davide Rossi[4], and Emilio Tuosto[1(✉)]

[1] Gran Sasso Science Institute, L'aquila, Italy
emilio.tuosto@gssi.it
[2] Department of Mathematics and Computer Science, University of Catania, Catania, Italy
[3] Focus Team, University of Bologna/INRIA, Bologna, Italy
[4] University of Bologna, Bologna, Italy

Abstract. Formal choreographic modelling advocates a *correctness-by-construction* principle for the development of sound communication protocols. This principle usually hinges on syntactic or semantic restrictions to rule out models that could lead to communication glitches like message losses or deadlocks.

This paper explores how these restrictions impact on the usability of formal modelling. More precisely, we benchmark the use of a formal choreographic modelling language designed to support the correctness-by-construction principle of message-passing systems. To this purpose, we consider the formal choreographic modelling of real business processes taken from the official documentation of European customs business process models. In fact, following a steadily increasing trend, the European Union started to use BPMN to support the legal provisions of the customs business process models.

1 Introduction

Choreographic models [30] are becoming popular in many application domains. For instance, the *business process modelling notation* (BPMN) [29] is used to design and document both software [31] and other kinds of workflows such as those in the health domain (e.g., [26]) or, as for the case study of this paper, in public administrations (e.g., [34]). Such models are described by means of notations presenting a wide range of levels of formalisation. Semi-formal notations like BPMN are rather expressive and flexible since they tend to feature several mechanisms to ease the representation of complex processes. As a matter

Research partly supported by the EU H2020 RISE programme under the Marie Skłodowska-Curie grant agreement No 778233, by the MIUR project PRIN 2017FTXR7S "IT-MaTTerS" (Methods and Tools for Trustworthy Smart Systems) and by the Progetto di ateneo Unict PIA.CE.RI. 2020–2022 Linea 2. Barbanera, Lanese and Tuosto have also been partially supported by INdAM as members of GNCS (Gruppo Nazionale per il Calcolo Scientifico).

T. Margaria and B. Steffen (Eds.): ISoLA 2022, LNCS 13701, pp. 205–219, 2022.
https://doi.org/10.1007/978-3-031-19849-6_13

of fact, semi-formal approaches are customary among practitioners and usually, once requirements are collected, they are the first step taken in the development phase. Formal approaches, instead, have been developed - mostly in academia - with the aim of supporting the so-called *correctness-by-construction* principle. Accordingly, a choreography holistically describes the interactions of a system and enables the "automatic" extraction of a skeleton description of its single components. Key to this approach is the guarantee that systems obtained that way do enjoy relevant communication properties such as lock-freedom. Researchers strive for the development of solid theories to support the correctness-by-construction principle. Ideally, it would be desirable to attain theories and tools that are flexible and expressive enough to be largely applicable in practice. The present paper analyses through a practical example the distance between a semi-formal and a formal model. We hope that our small *hands-on* analysis sheds some light on the usefulness of formal models.

The correctness-by-construction principle mentioned above hinges on the interplay between the so-called *global* and a *local* view of a formal choreography. The former view specifies the observable behaviour of the process at hand *as a whole* while the latter view specifies the behaviour of each component *in isolation*. The usual design approach rests on two steps:

– First, the designer defines a global view of the process that enjoys suitable properties, often dubbed *well-formedness* conditions.
– Then, local views (and possibly executable artefacts) are algorithmically derived from the global view by means of a *projection* operation guaranteeing relevant communication properties when applied to well-formed global views.

Often, well-formedness conditions are defined in terms of syntactic or semantic restrictions. Several formal modelling languages have been proposed in the literature to realise this correcteness-by-construction principle (see [2,3,6,13,18,23, 28,32,33] to mention but a few, others can be found in the survey in [25]).

In this paper we address the following question:

to what extent well-formedness conditions hinder modelling?

We consider the formal modelling of real business processes taken from the official documentation of European customs business process models available at https://aris9.itsmtaxud.eu/businesspublisher. The documentation of these processes is heavily based on BPMN [29] specifying the interactions among participants involved in the bureaucracy of legal provisions. The type of BPMN diagram adopted for this specification is a collaboration diagram, that is a diagram that can represent both the inner structure of the business process of each involved party (in terms of tasks, choices and so forth) and the structure of the interactions among these parties (in terms of message exchanges). As we shall see, this greatly helps in connecting our formalisation to the case study.

An exhaustive analysis on the family of formal choreographic formalisms would be beyond our possibilities. We therefore choose *global choreographies* [33] (g-choreographies for short) because they have a straightforward semantics and feature an intuitive visual presentation akin to BPMN diagrams, so easing the comparison between the two. We refer the reader to [33] for a formal presentation of g-choreographies; here we will overview them in Sect. 2 and exploit their visual notation to informally describe them by examples in Sect. 4.

The correctness-by-construction principle is rendered in g-choreographies by requiring the so called *well-branchedness* condition [33]. Intuitively, this condition requires that each distributed choice

- has a unique *active* participant, that is only one of the participants of the choice decides which branch has to be followed
- any participant other than the active one is *passive*, namely it either (i) has exactly the same observable behaviour in each branch, or (ii) it is (unambiguously) notified of the choice by a participant already aware of the decision.

Our comparative analysis highlights that well-formedness conditions of formal choreographic models have an heavy impact on the modelling of the processes. As we argue in Sect. 5, this is not only due to the choice of g-choreographies as choreographic formalism but, more generally, to the constraints required to ensure the correctness-by-construction principle.

Besides the typical fact that assumptions have to be made when semi-formal documentation of processes is ambiguous or incomplete, we have observed that the similarity between BPMN and g-choreographies cannot always be exploited. In particular, we have observed that optional sub-processes do clash with the restrictions imposed by g-choreographies and, as argued in Sect. 5, with most of the formal approaches in the literature. More crucially, exploiting similarities may actually be misleading and leads to models that do not faithfully reflect the intended behaviour of the process. This problem can be resolved using design languages that are not well-structured (yet formal), at the cost of renouncing to exploit the affinity.

Structure of the Paper. Section 2 presents a brief background on BPMN and g-choreographies. Section 3 introduces our case study. Section 4 shows the g-choreographies of the case study. Section 5 reports the analysis of our modelling exercise. Finally, Sect. 6 draws some conclusions and sketches future work.

2 Background

In order to support the modelling of business processes, the Object Management Group (https://www.omg.org) introduced the Business Process Model and Notation (BPMN) specification [29]. The main aim of this specification is to provide a notation comprehensible to business users while capturing complex process semantics for technical users. In fact, BPMN is the de facto standard used to describe business processes. In this context a business process is a generic process, in the sense of a coordinated set of activities aiming at achieving a goal, where the goal is the production of goods or the supply of services. BPMN has been designed for a wide array of business users interested in different viewpoints; this translates into the definition of four different diagrams (and their respective underlying metamodels): process, collaboration, conversation and choreography.

Process diagrams focus on detailing the internal structure of a business process. The process is modeled as a network of flow objects (events, activities and gateways) connected by connecting objects (sequence flows). The execution of a process can be thought of as a flow of activities described by the traversing of the process' network by one or more tokens moving through flow objects, carried by connecting objects.

Collaboration diagrams depict the cooperation of different partners' business processes in terms of message exchanges (where message flows are an additional kind of connecting objects). Each partner's internal process can be fully described by a process diagram contained in the partner's pool, or the internal process can be kept opaque by representing the partner as a collapsed pool. Figure 1, detailed later in the paper, depicts a collaboration diagram. Three parties (at the top) are represented by collapsed pools. A fourth participant (at the bottom) is represented by a pool containing the process diagram that details its internal behavior. The interactions between the parties take place in the form of message exchanges represented by message flow (the dashed arrows connecting the various pools).

Choreography diagrams focus on how interactions between participants take place and abstract completely from the internal behavior of each participant. Their network is composed of basic message exchanges (choreography task), a reduced set of events and gateways connected by sequence flows.

Conversation diagrams focus on other interaction-related aspects and are outside the scope of this paper.

In the context of the present work, BPMN choreography diagrams are most definitely relevant, however these diagrams are rarely used, possibly because of their rather convoluted semantics. For example, out of about ~114000 BPMN models present in various projects in GitHub[1] only 333 of them are choreographies (less than 0.3%).

The case study we present mostly adopts BPMN collaboration diagrams. While our focus stays on the interaction between participants, the modeling of the behavior of some of them represented in the diagrams allows us to better understand their internal logic.

To model the processes described in Sect. 3 we adopt the language of *global choreographies* [33] (g-choreographies for short). The reason to choose g-choreographies is that the definition of their formal syntax and semantics is equipped with an intuitive visual presentation akin to BPMN diagrams. In fact, we will appeal to this intuitive presentation and refer to [33] for the technical definitions.

The basic elements of g-choreographies are interactions of the form $A \rightarrow B$: m where A and B are distinct *role names* and m is a *message type* drawn from a given set $\mathcal{M}$ (disjoint from the set $\mathcal{P}$ of role names). Intuitively, $A \rightarrow B$: m represents the fact that participant A sends to B the message m (and B receives it).

---

[1] These models have been identified by (i) searching through the GitHub API the files with the extension .bpmn and then (ii) using pattern matching to identify the ones describing choreographies.

A g-choreography is basically interpreted as a regular language over an alphabet of interactions. For simplicity, we do not consider here another key feature of g-choreographies, namely parallel composition. In fact, the scenarios we consider in Sect. 3 do not require parallel composition. However, in practice parallel composition is sometimes needed. For instance, the documentation for the amendment process discussed in Sect. 3 specifies a procedure which is independent of the ones we consider here and can be formalised using parallel composition of g-choreographies[2]. Instead of giving a formal definition of g-choreographies, we will describe them using examples drawn from our scenarios. The following remarks are worthwhile. In selecting our scenarios we strove to identify parts of the BPMN models that have a straightforward counterpart in g-choreographies as well as parts where the connection is not that clear cut. This, and our consequent modelling choices, are instrumental to make the points of Sect. 5.

3   Legal Provisions

In 2010 the European Union introduced the *customs business process models* [17] on request of member states' customs authorities. These processes are expressed for the most part as a mix of text and BPMN diagrams [29] collected in the repository at https://aris9.itsmtaxud.eu/businesspublisher (and publicly available by following the 'Anonymous access' link there). The purpose of these models is to document and facilitate the reading of the legal provisions.

We will focus on the workflow of the procedures for the entry of goods. A key element within these procedures is the *entry summary declaration* (ENS), a document submitted by *declarants* stating relevant information for the import (nature of the goods, carrier, etc.). These procedures activate several tasks which depend on multiple factors such as where ENS documents were lodged and the transport infrastructures through which the goods enter (i.e. sea, air, or road&rail). Also, after its submission, an ENS goes through a validation process. The validation culminates either in the registration of the ENS or in the request of amendments or additional information. In the latter case, the EU regulations require to notify these requests to the involved parties.

Amendment. We illustrate part of this procedures starting by briefly describing how an amendment[3] gets processed on the *customs office of first entry* (COFE). The process is documented by the L3-ENT-01-05-Process ENS At Office Of First Entry - Amendment diagram in the repository, reported in Fig. 1.

Upon being received by the COFE, the amendment goes through an initial verification process to check, for example, whether the amendment concerns previously submitted information. If the amendment of the ENS is deemed valid, it is registered and multiple participants are notified; according to the documentation,

---

[2] A precise formalisation would involve also other considerations that do not emerge very clearly from the current documentation.

[3] Amendments may be necessary due to changes of e.g., carriers, or dates of travel of the goods, etc.

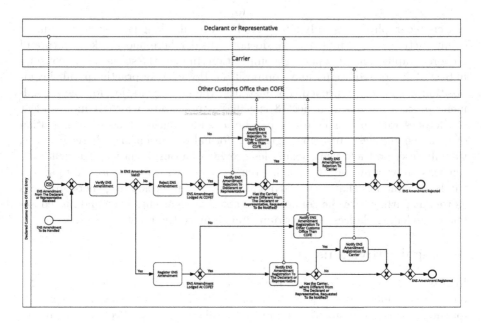

Fig. 1. BPMN specification of the amendment process

- if the amendment was lodged at the COFE, a registration notification is sent to the *declarant*;
- a *carrier* is notified when different from the declarant and asks to be notified;
- if, instead than at COFE, the amendment was lodged in another customs office (OCOFE) then the OCOFE has to be notified;

If the amendment is invalid instead, the participants are notified of the rejection following a communication pattern for notifications similar to the one above.

Arrival of Goods. A more elaborate process describes the arrival of goods. For the purpose of illustration, let us focus on the case where the goods arrive through road and rail as depicted in the set of diagrams collected in the repository (cf. L3-ENT-01-04-Process ENS At Office Of First Entry-Road and Rail), one of which is reproduced[4] in Fig. 2. The diagram in Fig. 2 is more complex than the one in Fig. 1; in fact, it contains nested choices with a loop involving several participants. We now comment on the procedure designed for the arrival of goods as depicted in Fig. 2.

When a full or partial ENS is received at the declared COFE, a first check occurs for the validity and consistency of the information provided. If the ENS is deemed invalid, it is rejected, and this is notified to the declarant so that they can optionally send amendments and iterate the above procedure. Otherwise, the

---

[4] The diagram is hardly readable; it is reported only to give readers a hint on the complexity of these models. Some details of the model can be inferred from the g-choreography Fig. 4 (cf. Sect. 4) corresponding to the diagram in Fig. 2.

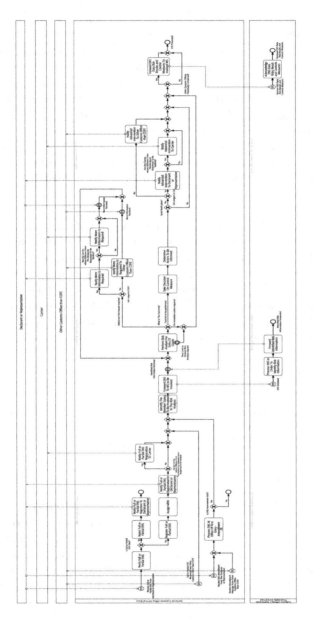

Fig. 2. BPMN specification of the process for the arrival of goods

ENS is registered and automatically assigned a *master reference number* (MRN), which is stored in the system. This registration is notified to the declarant and optionally to the carrier (under the same conditions as for the amendment procedure).

At this point, a risk analysis involving some member states needs to occur. Therefore, the ENS is forwarded to the states and the custom offices deemed to be involved in the risk analysis. These offices should send back information about any identified risks. If any additional information is required by the COFE or the OCOFE (depending on where the ENS was lodged to), the declarant and (optionally) the carrier are requested to send such information to the relevant office. Also, there might be the need for additional controls to be performed, in which case some of the involved participants (i.e., Declarant, Carrier, and OCOFE) might need to be notified, in a similar fashion as when additional information is required. Once the additional controls (if any) are performed, the ENS Data Risk results and control measures should be forwarded to the involved member states customs offices.

Simplifying Assumption. The processes described above are part of a larger workflow, the formalisation of which falls out of the scope of this paper. In fact, in the next sections we will assume that the declarant decided to lodge the ENS to the COFE. The other option would yield basically the same g-choreographies; hence we do not consider it, so reducing the amount of branching and avoiding repetitions. Another assumption is that carrier and declarant do not coincide; the other case can simply be obtained by removing from our formalisation all the branches involving the carrier.

4   Formal Models

We now describe the g-choreographies corresponding to the BPMN diagrams of our case studies. These models have been manually produced from the documentation available at https://aris9.itsmtaxud.eu/businesspublisher. We believe that this process could be partly automated by "compiling" the BPMN models into g-choreographies; however, this is not in the scope of this paper.

Amendment. A g-choreography capturing the amendment process is given by the diagram in Fig. 3. The intuitive graphical notation uses *gates* to represent the combinators of the language; in particular branching and merging points of a non-deterministic choice (and loops) are represented by ◆-gates. Noteworthy, the branching structure of the process in Fig. 3 reflects the one of the BPMN diagram in Fig. 1. Actually, any g-choreography is *well-structured* in the sense that gates behave as well-balanced parenthesis: for each *opening* gate there is a corresponding *closing* one. (In passing we note that well-structuredness is also considered in BPMN modelling and it is studied in e.g., [10] and references

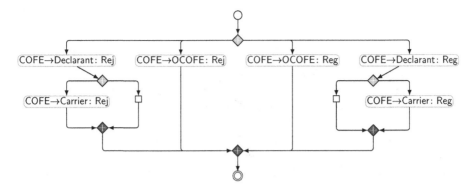

Fig. 3. The amendment process as g-choreography

therein.) Well-structuredness is pictorially represented in Fig. 3 by making closing gates darker than opening ones. For instance, the topmost (opening) ◆-gate
is matched by the bottommost (closing) one; note[5] that this is not the case for
the BPMN diagram of Fig. 1 where the second diamond from the left is not
matched by any closing gateway. The o- and the ⊚-gates mark the start and the
end of the g-choreography, respectively.

The semantics of a g-choreography can be described in intuitive terms as the
sequences of interactions[6] from the o-gate to the ⊚-gate. For instance, in the
diagram of Fig. 3 the topmost ◆-gate allows four possible branches that capture
the options that COFE has to consider when validating an ENS. The following
remarks are worthwhile for our considerations in Sect. 5. Firstly, the diagram in
Fig. 3 should be considered embedded in a larger process where Declarant had
previously sent the ENS either to COFE or OCOFE. Secondly, as per the informal description of the scenario in Sect. 3, the diagram abstracts away from the
details about how COFE decides the next course of action. Finally, the innermost
choices do not respect the conditions that g-choreographies require to guarantee
correctness (which will be described in Sect. 5).

Arrival of Goods. The g-choreography for the arrival of goods process, shown
in Fig. 4, is rather more complicated than the one for the amendment. Since
the former process has more optional interactions than the latter one, Fig. 4 has
several ◆-gates with a branch with an empty box directly connected to the corresponding closing gate; this visually represents the fact that the choice is possibly
resolved without explicit interactions. As said, the diagram is obtained from the
L3-ENT-01-04-Process ENS At Office Of First Entry - Road and Rail
BPMN present in the repository as depicted in Fig. 2.

---

[5] This remark will be reconsidered in Sect. 5.
[6] Formally, these are the words generated by the g-choreography interpreted as a
regular expression on an alphabet of interactions.

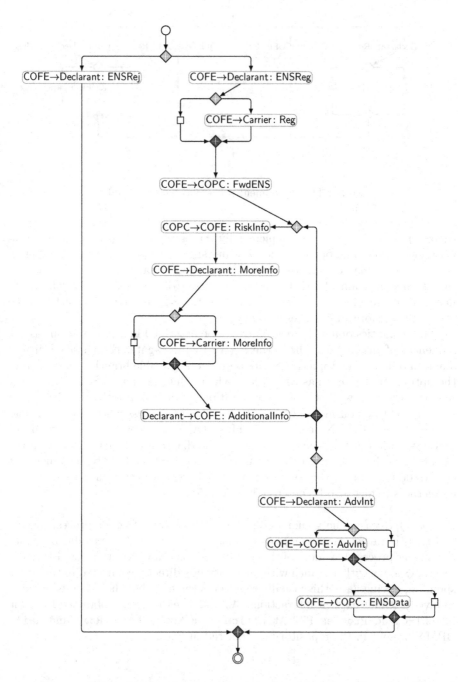

Fig. 4. The arrival of goods process as g-choreography

A source of complexity in this diagram is the presence of the loop for the request of additional information whose entry point is the rightmost ◆-gate. This loop is structurally isomorphic to the corresponding one in the BPMN diagram. We will see in Sect. 5 that this is not however a correct formalisation of the process due to the different semantics.

5   From BPMN to Global Choreographies

This section discusses the nuances of the formalisation of the scenarios with g-choreographies. A definite advantage has been the use of the BPMN diagrams specifying procedures as starting point; indeed these diagrams greatly help in understanding the processes, without having to dive in the actual legislation. In fact, this allowed us to exploit the similarities between g-choreographies and BPMN. Nonetheless, several assumptions and modelling decisions had to be taken due to factors which are worth discussing here. In fact, we believe that they would occur regardless of the formal choreographic language used.

The BPMN diagrams of our scenarios heavily rely on value passing. In fact, several decisions cannot be taken without assuming that some information is properly propagated to participants. For instance, the decision of notifying the carrier is taken according to some information somehow available at COFE through an interaction between carrier and COFE, presumably after carrier and declarant agreed on the ENS. In a modelling language which abstract away from data, such choices either become non deterministic choices (like in our g-choreographies) or explicit interactions. We opted for the first alternative to maintain an higher degree of similarity between BPMN diagrams and g-choreographies as well as because it is not always straightforward to extract the conditions determining such choices from the documentation. For instance, it is not clear from the documentation if an ENS where declarant and carrier coincide can be amended to one where they are different; also, the interpretation of the BPMN diagram would be drastically different if this amendment were possible. This decision has however drawbacks which we now spell out.

A first problem is the one announced at the end of Sect. 4. The loop in Fig. 4 seemingly corresponds to the one in the BPMN diagram but, actually, it has a semantics different than the intend one. In the BPMN diagram, the notification to the carrier is either sent in all iterations or in none of them; this is possible because the decision of COFE is taken according to previously received information which does not change during the iteration. Instead, this is not the case in the g-choreography of Fig. 4: at each iteration COFE can non-deterministically decide to perform the notification or not. To faithfully model the intended behaviour the loop should be preceded by a choice where COFE decides either to iterate and always send the notification or to iterate just the interactions with the declarant.

More in general, choreographic formalisms ensuring correctness-by-construction require that choices are taken by a single participant and communicated to other involved participants via message passing, that is by sending them different messages. This rules out the possibility, quite common in practice and explicitly covered by BPMN's data-based exclusive gateway, that decisions are taken based on data. For instance, in the example above the choice of notifying the carrier or not depends on shared data.

The other issue is also related to the fact that formal choreographic languages are often conceived to support the correctness-by-construction principle. Correctness typically refers to communication properties such as deadlock freedom or guarantees about messages (e.g., no message loss). This requires to limit language expressivity. For instance, many variants of global types (see [25] and references therein) do not allow choices with empty branches. As seen, the BPMN models of the scenarios heavily rely on *optional* communications to some participants (e.g., the notification of rejection to the carrier). Unlike global types, g-choreographies can faithfully reflect this; in fact, optional communications have been rendered as g-choreographies with ◆-gates representing a non-deterministic choice where a branch is empty. However, this bluntly violates the *well-branchedness* condition required for the correctness of g-choreographies [33]. In fact, according to the semantics of g-choreographies, Carrier cannot be certain whether the ENS is rejected or there is a delay in the communication from COFE. An analysis of the g-choreography in Fig. 3 would flag this as a problem whose solution would force us to introduce some interaction on the empty branch. On the other hand, optional processes (like the notification to the carrier) occur rather often in practice. Optional behaviour is supported in *choreography automata* [2], according to the refined theory recently proposed in [19,20]. Optional behaviour can also be specified in [22,24], but there if a participant joins only a part of a choreography, explicit connection and disconnection actions are required. Indeed, choreography automata allow *selective participation*, that is there can be participants occurring only on some of the branches of a non-deterministic choice.

As discussed in Sect. 4, g-choreographies are well-structured. This is often a desirable property of design languages and basically all syntax-based choreographic modelling languages are well-structured. In practice however, well-structured languages may be forced —by their own nature— to handle some typical situations in a cumbersome way. For instance, the BPMN diagram L3-ENT-01 -04-Process ENS At Office Of First Entry - Road and Rail allows amendments to an ENS to arrive while the ENS itself is being processed. This would basically correspond to "jumping" from one branch to another of a choice, which is not allowed by well-structuredness. To circumvent this problem one has to replicate the common behaviour on each branch. Notice that this might not be always straightforward (e.g., when the replication is inside an iteration). In modelling languages such as choreography automata, which are not well-structured, this problem is less acute.

6 Conclusions and Future Work

This work just scratched the surface of the comparison between BPMN modelling, widely used in practice, and formal choreographic approaches, which have been deeply investigated theoretically (see the survey in [25], and in particular all the thread on multiparty session types [23]). We are not aware of other similar attempts while many works study formal semantics and analysis techniques for BPMN (see e.g., [9,10,16] and references therein) and BPMN choreographies (see e.g., [11,12] and references therein). Formal choreographic models are abstractions built to support the correctness-by-construction principle. Typically, these formalisms abstract away from many aspects and focus on specific aspects "in vitro". For instance, some formal models of choreographies feature value passing [4,5,19,27], some others have considered adaptive choreographies [7,8,13,22]. Nonetheless, a formalism comprehensively combining these features is missing and, perhaps, not even worthwhile since it would probably be so complex to be not applicable in practice.

As we have discussed, easy modelling calls for generalised conditions on choreographic models, e.g., participants may be involved only in some branches of a choice. This is in particular the case for optional actions. Such a generalization have been recently considered in [19,22], but they are still missing from many approaches. On the other side, we believe that it is best practice to avoid diagrams which are obscure to the reader, and even less suitable for automatic analysis. An example here is the case of choices which depend on data. We believe that what triggers such choices should instead be made apparent by the messages used in the communications.

Another note is that we found out that most of the available diagrams, including the ones we selected as case studies, represent the view of a system from a single participant (e.g., COFE in our case study). It would be good to develop techniques for composing such local views into a global view along the lines in [1] and in [15].

References

1. Barbanera, F., Dezani-Ciancaglini, M., Lanese, I., Tuosto, E.: Composition and decomposition of multiparty sessions. J. Log. Algebraic Meth. Program. **119**, 100620 (2021)
2. Barbanera, F., Lanese, I., Tuosto, E.: Choreography automata. In: Bliudze, S., Bocchi, L. (eds.) COORDINATION 2020. LNCS, vol. 12134, pp. 86–106. Springer, Cham (2020). https://doi.org/10.1007/978-3-030-50029-0_6
3. Basile, D., ter Beek, M.H., Pugliese, R.: Synthesis of orchestrations and choreographies: bridging the gap between supervisory control and coordination of services. Log. Meth. Comput. Sci. **16**(2), 2–3 (2020)
4. Bocchi, L., Honda, K., Tuosto, E., Yoshida, N.: A theory of design-by-contract for distributed multiparty interactions. In: Gastin, P., Laroussinie, F. (eds.) CONCUR 2010. LNCS, vol. 6269, pp. 162–176. Springer, Heidelberg (2010). https://doi.org/10.1007/978-3-642-15375-4_12
5. Bocchi, L., Melgratti, H.C., Tuosto, E.: On resolving non-determinism in choreographies. Log. Methods Comput. Sci. **16**(3) (2020)
6. Busi, N., Gorrieri, R., Guidi, C., Lucchi, R., Zavattaro, G.: Choreography and orchestration conformance for system design. In: Ciancarini, P., Wiklicky, H. (eds.) COORDINATION 2006. LNCS, vol. 4038, pp. 63–81. Springer, Heidelberg (2006). https://doi.org/10.1007/11767954_5

7. Castellani, I., Dezani-Ciancaglini, M., Pérez, J.A.: Self-adaptation and secure information flow in multiparty communications. Formal Aspects Comput. **28**(4), 669–696 (2016). https://doi.org/10.1007/s00165-016-0381-3
8. Coppo, M., Dezani-Ciancaglini, M., Venneri, B.: Self-adaptive multiparty sessions. Serv. Oriented Comput. Appl. **9**(3), 249–268 (2014). https://doi.org/10.1007/s11761-014-0171-9
9. Corradini, F., Fornari, F., Polini, A., Re, B., Tiezzi, F.: A formal approach to modeling and verification of business process collaborations. Sci. Comput. Program. **166**, 35–70 (2018)
10. Corradini, F., Morichetta, A., Muzi, C., Re, B., Tiezzi, F.: Well-structuredness, safeness and soundness: a formal classification of BPMN collaborations. J. Log. Algebraic Meth. Program. **119**, 100630 (2021)
11. Corradini, F., Morichetta, A., Polini, A., Re, B., Tiezzi, F.: Collaboration vs. choreography conformance in BPMN. Log. Methods Comput. Sci. **16**(4) (2020)
12. Corradini, F., Morichetta, A., Re, B., Tiezzi, F.: Walking through the semantics of exclusive and event-based gateways in BPMN choreographies. In: Alvim, M.S., Chatzikokolakis, K., Olarte, C., Valencia, F. (eds.) The Art of Modelling Computational Systems: A Journey from Logic and Concurrency to Security and Privacy. LNCS, vol. 11760, pp. 163–181. Springer, Cham (2019). https://doi.org/10.1007/978-3-030-31175-9_10
13. Dalla Preda, M., Gabbrielli, M., Giallorenzo, S., Lanese, I., Mauro, J.: Dynamic choreographies: theory and implementation. Log. Meth. Comput. Sci. **13**(2) (2017)
14. de'Liguoro, U., Melgratti, H.C., Tuosto, E.: Towards refinable choreographies. In: Lange, J., Mavridou, A., Safina, L., Scalas, A. (eds.) Proceedings 13th Interaction and Concurrency Experience, ICE 2020, 19 June 2020, Volume 324 of EPTCS, pp. 61–77 (2020)
15. de'Liguoro, U., Melgratti, H.C., Tuosto, E.: Towards refinable choreographies. J. Log. Algebraic Meth. Programm. **127**, 100776 (2022). Extended and revised version of [14]
16. Dijkman, R.M., Dumas, M., Ouyang, C.: Semantics and analysis of business process models in BPMN. Inf. Softw. Technol. **50**(12), 1281–1294 (2008)
17. EU customs BPMN. https://ec.europa.eu/taxation_customs/customs-4/union-customs-code/ucc-bpm_en
18. Fu, X., Bultan, T., Su, J.: Conversation protocols: a formalism for specification and verification of reactive electronic services. TCS **328**(1–2), 19–37 (2004)
19. Gheri, L., Lanese, I., Sayers, N., Tuosto, E., Yoshida, N.: Design-by-contract for flexible multiparty session protocols. In: Ali, K., Vitek, J. (eds.) 36th European Conference on Object-Oriented Programming, ECOOP 2022, 6–10 June 2022, Berlin, Germany, Volume 222 of LIPIcs, pp. 8:1–8:28. Schloss Dagstuhl - Leibniz-Zentrum für Informatik (2022)
20. Gheri, L., Lanese, I., Sayers, N., Tuosto, E., Yoshida, N.: Design-by-contract for flexible multiparty session protocols (artifact). Dagstuhl Artifacts Ser. **8**(2), 21:1–21:5 (2022)
21. Guanciale, R., Tuosto, E.: An abstract semantics of the global view of choreographies. In: Proceedings 9th Interaction and Concurrency Experience, ICE 2016, Heraklion, Greece, 8–9 June 2016, pp. 67–82 (2016)
22. Harvey, P., Fowler, S., Dardha, O., Gay, S.J.: Multiparty session types for safe runtime adaptation in an actor language. In: Møller, A., Sridharan, M. (eds.) 35th European Conference on Object-Oriented Programming, ECOOP 2021, 11–17 July 2021, Aarhus, Denmark (Virtual Conference), Volume 194 of LIPIcs, pp. 10:1–10:30. Schloss Dagstuhl - Leibniz-Zentrum für Informatik (2021)

23. Honda, K., Yoshida, N., Carbone, M.: Multiparty asynchronous session types. J. ACM, **63**(1), 9:1–9:67 (2016). Extended version of a paper presented at POPL08

24. Hu, R., Yoshida, N.: Explicit connection actions in multiparty session types. In: Huisman, M., Rubin, J. (eds.) Fundamental Approaches to Software Engineering - 20th International Conference, FASE 2017, Held as Part of the European Joint Conferences on Theory and Practice of Software, ETAPS 2017, Uppsala, Sweden, 22–29 April 2017, Proceedings, Volume 10202 of Lecture Notes in Computer Science, pp. 116–133. Springer (2017). https://doi.org/10.1007/978-3-662-54494-5_7

25. Hüttel, H., et al.: Foundations of session types and behavioural contracts. ACM Comput. Surv. **49**(1), 3:1–3:36 (2016)

26. Percorsi diagnostici terapeutici e assistenziali adenocarcinoma della prostata. https://www.ispro.toscana.it/sites/default/files/ReteOncologica/PROSTATA. ALLEGATO.D.pdf

27. Jongmans, S.-S., van den Bos, P.: A predicate transformer for choreographies. In: Sergey, I. (ed.) Programming Languages and Systems. PP, pp. 520–547. Springer International Publishing, Cham (2022). https://doi.org/10.1007/978-3-030-99336-8_19

28. Lanese, I., Guidi, C., Montesi, F., Zavattaro, G.: Bridging the gap between interaction- and process-oriented choreographies. In: Cerone, A., Gruner, S., (eds.) Sixth IEEE International Conference on Software Engineering and Formal Methods, SEFM 2008, Cape Town, South Africa, 10–14 November 2008, pp. 323–332. IEEE Computer Society (2008)

29. Object Management Group. Business Process Model and Notation (BPMN). https://www.omg.org/spec/BPMN/2.0.2/PDF

30. Peltz, C.: Web services orchestration and choreography. IEEE Comput. **36**(10), 46–52 (2003)

31. Pillat, R., Oliveira, T., Alencar, P., Cowan, D.: BPMNt: a BPMN extension for specifying software process tailoring. Inf. Softw. Technol. **57**, 95–115 (2015)

32. Qiu, Z., Zhao, X., Cai, C., Yang, H.: Towards the theoretical foundation of choreography. In: Proceedings of the 16th International Conference on World Wide Web, WWW 2007, pp. 973–982 (2007)

33. Tuosto, E., Guanciale, R.: Semantics of global view of choreographies. JLAMP, **95**, 17–40 (2018). Revised and extended version of [21]

34. The r/ukpersonalfinance flowchart v3.0.7. https://flowchart.ukpersonal.finance

Configurable-by-Construction Runtime Monitoring

Clemens Dubslaff[1]([✉])[iD] and Maximilian A. Köhl[2]([✉])[iD]

[1] Technische Universität Dresden, Dresden, Germany
clemens.dubslaff@tu-dresden.de
[2] Saarland University, Saarland Informatics Campus, Saarbrücken, Germany
koehl@cs.uni-saarland.de

Abstract. Most modern systems, be it cyber-physical or mere software systems, are highly configurable. The main challenge when dealing with such *configurable systems* stems from the usually huge number of system variants that can be exponential in the number of configuration options or features. Monitoring systems that react on observations, e.g., sensor data, varying across system configurations or being themselves configurable also face this challenge but have barely been considered in the literature. In this paper, we discuss new aspects for runtime monitoring with variability in the system being monitored as well as the monitor itself. As a first step towards a *configurable-by-construction* runtime monitoring approach, we introduce configurable monitors from an automata-theoretic and stream-based perspective. For this, we harvest existing work on featured transition systems and present a variability-aware variant of the stream-based specification language Lola.

1 Introduction

Modern cyber-physical systems such as cars, airplanes, or robots are highly configurable based on customer needs or through their inherent adaptivity to the environments in which they are operating. For example, cars may come with different driver assistance systems the customer payed for or robots adapt their behaviors depending on whether they operate in a machine-only or human-machine co-adaptive setting. Within software systems we also encounter configurability, e.g., in *software product lines* that can be configured through *features* as incremental or optional functionalities [2,32]. Often the configuration spaces are exponential in the number of configuration options or features, which renders the development, analysis, and explanation of such systems challenging tasks.

The manifold possibilities to configure these systems raise further challenges also in the runtime monitoring setting that have been barely addressed in the existing literature. In this paper, we propose first steps towards a

This work was partially supported by the DFG under the projects TRR 248 (see https://perspicuous-computing.science, project ID 389792660) and EXC 2050/1 (CeTI, project ID 390696704, as part of Germany's Excellence Strategy).

T. Margaria and B. Steffen (Eds.): ISoLA 2022, LNCS 13701, pp. 220–241, 2022.
https://doi.org/10.1007/978-3-031-19849-6_14

configurable-by-construction runtime monitoring approach that is inspired by automata-theoretic runtime verification [6,24], featured transition systems [11], and stream-based runtime monitoring [12,27]. Specifically, we (a) discuss challenges towards *configurable monitors* and variability-aware runtime verification in general, (b) present methods to synthesize concise *featured monitors* from specifications in a featured variant of linear temporal logic (LTL) [11], and (c) introduce a configurable variant of the stream-based specification language Lola [12] together with a family-based analysis for well-formedness and efficient monitorability that exploits commonalities across system variants. While there exist many different approaches to runtime monitoring and verification, automata-based and stream-based approaches are among the most prominent [24]. Hence, we concretize the idea of configurable-by-construction runtime monitoring for both of them.

Outline and Contribution. This paper is structured as follows. We first discuss benefits and open challenges in a configurable runtime monitoring setting (Sect. 2). Then, we introduce an automata-based framework for configurable monitors and their synthesis from featured LTL specifications (Sect. 3) and extend the stream-based specification language Lola to the configurable setting (Sect. 4). These two orthogonal approaches are intentionally presented in self-contained sections to separate concerns and allow interested readers to choose the approach according to their needs. We close the paper by summarizing our findings and related work and provide an outlook on future work (Sect. 5).

2   The Quest of Configurable Runtime Monitoring

Considering monitors to be themselves configurable opens many new challenges. In this section, we first introduce a running example of a configurable system from the automotive systems domain before we discuss selected challenges and how they are addressed in this paper.

2.1   Feature-Oriented Example

While conducting research on real-world runtime monitoring of vehicles [9,22], we encountered the need for monitor configurability. Inspired by this example, we here establish a running example on feature-oriented systems modeling.

Real Driving Emissions Tests. It is well known that the real driving emissions (RDE) regulation, put in force by the European Union [29], can be cast into a runtime monitoring problem using existing stream-based runtime monitoring techniques [22]. An RDE test is supposed to evaluate the emissions of a vehicle under realistic conditions.[1] In recent work, we presented an Android application [9] that enables laypersons to conduct lightweight RDE tests via the

---

[1] Similar test procedures exist for characteristics of electric vehicles, for instance, those issued by the United States Environmental Protection Agency [31].

standard on-board diagnostic (OBD) interface – a component any modern car is required to be equipped with [28]. At its core, our application relies on the runtime monitoring framework RTLola [18]. As different cars usually have different fuel-consumption characteristics, are fully electric, or have different sensors, they provide different information via OBD. To this end, the RTLola specification needs to be adapted to each car based on the car's configuration. Currently, the required RTLola specifications for the different configurations are pieced together in an ad-hoc fashion [9].

For example, to compute the amount of emitted pollutants, such as nitrous oxide (NOx), the *exhaust mass flow* (EMF), i.e., the mass of exhaust emitted per time unit, must be known in addition to the relative concentration (in ppm) of the pollutant in the exhaust gas. While many modern diesel cars come equipped with sensors providing the relative concentration of nitrous oxide, the EMF is rarely provided directly via OBD due to the car not having of an EMF sensor. Fortunately, the EMF can be computed based on various other values such as the mass air flow (MAF) in combination with the fuel rate (FR) or the fuel-air equivalence (FAE) ratio.

Hence, the car is configurable by providing different sensors that can be used for the RDE test. For determining whether the RDE test itself passes, monitoring techniques might be used to establish a monitor observing the sensor data. However, in this case, both the system being monitored as well as the monitor itself should configurable as they depend on the cars sensor configuration.

Feature-Oriented Modeling. Variability in configurable systems can be abstractly described, e.g., using well-known concepts from feature-oriented system development [2]. Here, configuration options are encapsulated in *features* as optional or incremental units of functionality [32] where each set of features stands for a system *configuration*. Not all configurations are feasible in practice: For instance, any car without an EMF sensor or MAF sensor cannot be used for RDE tests since then, the EMF cannot be obtained by neither sensing nor computation. Such constraints on feasible system configurations are usually specified by *feature diagrams* [20] to describe the set of *valid configurations*. Feature diagrams are hierarchical diagrams over features where the parents of features have to be also included in the configuration containing the respective feature. A feature diagram for our RDE example is shown in Fig. 1. Here, if the FR feature is included in the system variant, this requires feature EMFc to be included as well.[2] Branching connectives in feature diagrams might also impose constraints on children, e.g., any configuration that has the RDE feature is also required to include at least one of the features EMF, NOxs, or COs. Differently, the EMFc feature requires both, the MAFs feature and the FR feature to be included towards a valid configuration. In total, there are $3+4\cdot(1+2\cdot3) = 31$ different system variants, e.g., $\{RDE, NOxs\}$ and $\{RDE, EMF, EMFc, MAFs, FAEs\}$, but not $\{RDE, NOxs, EMFc\}$.

---

[2] For brevity, we shorten the feature names for computation and sensor features with tailing c and s, respectively.

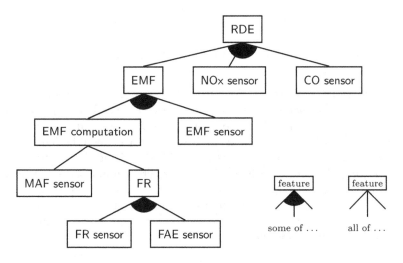

Fig. 1. Feature diagram of the configurable RDE system.

2.2 Challenges

While configurable system design and analysis is a well-established area, e.g., in feature-oriented software development, the link to runtime monitoring techniques is still missing. Indeed, the example of Sect. 2.1 demonstrates that there is a need for specification mechanisms that treat configurations as first-class citizens. It should be clear that similar considerations apply to other scenarios where variability plays a key role, e.g., monitoring of computer networks or microservice-based cloud applications where reconfiguration and scaling happens on a rather frequent basis.

Towards our configurable-by-construction approach to runtime monitoring that establishes the aforementioned link, we now identify five challenges that are to be addressed:

(1) Featured specification languages: As a first step, variability-aware specification languages for runtime monitoring and verification have to be developed or existing languages have to be adapted to account for variability. Such languages should yield *monitor families*, i.e., sets of monitors for different configurations, and may in addition offer support for more advanced scenarios such as online reconfiguration without disrupting any ongoing monitoring.

(2) Family-based monitoring: Given a featured specification, it has to be possible to decide properties of this specification over all possible configurations without suffering from the exponential blowup in the number of features. In particular, in case a monitor has to be configured at runtime, as in Sect. 2.1, separate monitors for each valid configuration are often infeasible. Similar as for family-based analysis approaches, where an *all-in-one* analysis on a family model avoids the combinatorial blowup that arises within a *one-by-one* analysis of each configuration [30], a solution to this challenge could be to aim towards family monitors that are configurable and establish all-in-one family-based monitoring.

(3) Synthesis of monitors: For arriving at a monitor we have to be able to effectively synthesize such from featured specifications. This applies to monitors for single configurations but also to family monitors to enable a family-based monitoring approach as described in (2). It might be also possible that for certain configurations no monitor can be synthesized. The challenge is here to efficiently check *well-formedness* of a configuration, i.e., whether a monitor can be synthesized for the configuration, and to determine all well-formed configurations for which a family monitor can be synthesized. Another interesting question would be: Can we give an upper bound on the required memory and computation time of each single configuration monitor or family monitor?

(4) Matching monitor and system configurations: Configurable monitors can provide monitors with different functionalities depending on the contexts of the monitor or to enable reconfigurations in the case of family monitors. However, their primary use case might be monitoring systems that are themselves configurable. In Sect. 2.1 configurable monitors are required to adapt to the cars configuration of sensors on which the monitor bases its verdict of passing the RDE test. For such cases, mechanisms that match system and monitor configurations have to be developed.

(5) Suitable monitor configurations: Monitor configurations may also be more *suitable* than others [5]. Returning to Sect. 2.1, the EMF sensor might be preferred to EMF computation, as it is presumably more precise than a value computed based on other sensor data. Then, the configuration of monitors turns to an optimization problem: What is the most suitable monitor configuration given a requirement, e.g., the matching to system configurations as of (4)?

2.3   This Paper

Exhaustively addressing all of the challenges raised above goes beyond the scope of this paper. In the following, we tackle some aspects towards configurable monitors by presenting an automata-based and a stream-based approach.

The automata-based approach is used to enhance standard LTL monitorability techniques [24] to the feature-oriented setting, presenting *featured monitors* as formalism to specify family monitors (addressing challenge (2)) and a synthesis algorithm towards monitors for properties in featured LTL [11] (3).

Our stream-based approach relies on the specification language Lola[3], for which we introduce a configurable variant (1). We present family-based anal-

---

[3] This applies to all variants of Lola, including the original variant [12], Lola 2.0 [17], and RTLola [18]. For simplicity, we use "Lola" as an umbrella term here.

ysis algorithms for well-formedness (3) [12] and efficient-monitorability of configurable Lola specifications that exploits commonalities between configurations
and thus mitigates the exponential blowup in the number of features (2).

3   Configurable Automata-Based Monitoring

In this section, we tackle the problem of constructing *featured monitors* by means
of an automata-theoretic approach to runtime monitors [7,24] that are configurable through features.

3.1   Preliminaries

For a finite set X we denote by X^* and X^ω the sets of finite and infinite sequences
of elements in X, respectively, and by $\varepsilon \in X^*$ the empty sequence.

Propositional Logic. By $\mathbb{B}(X)$ we denote the set of *Boolean expressions* over
X, given by the grammar $\phi ::= \texttt{true} \mid x \mid \neg\phi \mid \phi \wedge \phi$ where variables x range
over X. We use well-known Boolean connectives such as $\vee$, $\rightarrow$, etc. from which
a Boolean expression can be easily obtained using standard syntactic transformations such as De Morgan's rule. Further, we define $\texttt{false} = \neg\texttt{true}$. The
satisfaction relation $\vDash \subseteq \wp(X) \times \mathbb{B}(X)$ is defined in the usual way, where for
$Y \subseteq X$ and $\phi \in \mathbb{B}(X)$ we have $Y \vDash \phi$ if ϕ evaluates to $\texttt{true}$ when all variables
in Y are assumed to be $\texttt{true}$ and all variables in $X \setminus Y$ are $\texttt{false}$, respectively.
We denote by $[\![\phi]\!] = \{Y \subseteq X \mid Y \vDash \phi\}$ the set of all ϕ-satisfying sets. With
$\chi(\phi) \in \mathbb{B}(X)$ for a formula $\phi \in \mathbb{B}(X)$ we identify a *characteristic formula* that is
unique modulo ϕ-satisfaction, i.e., for all $\phi, \phi' \in \mathbb{B}(X)$ with $[\![\phi]\!] = [\![\phi']\!]$ we have
$\chi(\phi) = \chi(\phi')$.[4]

Linear Temporal Logic. To specify temporal properties, we rely on *linear
temporal logic (LTL)* [26]. An *LTL formula* over X is given by the grammar

$$\varphi ::= \texttt{true} \mid x \mid \neg\varphi \mid \varphi \wedge \varphi \mid \mathsf{X}\varphi \mid \varphi\mathsf{U}\varphi$$

where x ranges over X. Basically, an LTL formula is a Boolean expression and we
essentially use the same derived notations but with including the next operator
X and the until operator U. The *size* $|\varphi|$ of an LTL formula φ is defined as the
number of contained operators. An infinite sequence $\pi \in X^\omega$ with $\pi = \pi_0\pi_1 \ldots$
satisfies an LTL formula φ, written $\pi \vDash \varphi$, if either $\varphi = \texttt{true}$, $\varphi = x$ and
$\pi_0 = x$, $\varphi = \neg\psi$ and $\pi \nvDash \psi$, $\varphi = \psi \wedge \psi'$ and $\pi \vDash \psi$ as well as $\pi \vDash \psi'$, $\varphi = \mathsf{X}\psi$ and
$\pi_1\pi_2 \ldots \vDash \psi$, and $\varphi = \psi\mathsf{U}\psi'$ and there is a $k \in \mathbb{N}$ such that $\pi_k\pi_{k+1} \ldots \vDash \psi'$ and
$\pi_i\pi_{i+1} \ldots \vDash \psi$ for all $i < k$.

---

[4] A canonical candidate for $\chi(\phi)$ would be the disjunctive normal form $\chi(\phi) = \bigvee_{Y \in [\![\phi]\!]} \left(\bigwedge_{x \in Y} x \wedge \bigwedge_{x \in X \setminus Y} \neg x \right)$, but also any other uniquely chosen formula, e.g.,
focusing on small lengths, would be suitable.

Monitors. We loosely follow definitions for automata-theoretic runtime monitoring according to Bauer et al. [7].

Definition 1. *(Monitor)* *A monitor is a tuple* $\mathcal{A} = (Q, \Sigma, \delta, \iota)$ *where* Q *is a finite set of control states containing* verdict states $\top, \bot \in Q$, Σ *is a finite input alphabet,* $\delta \colon Q \times \Sigma \to Q$ *is a transition function where* $\delta(p, \alpha) = p$ *for all* $p \in \{\top, \bot\}$ *and* $\alpha \in \Sigma$, *and* $\iota \in Q$ *is an initial state.*

Intuitively, a monitor is a deterministic finite state automaton that contains two accepting states $V = \{\top, \bot\}$ that are traps and formalize verdicts $\top$ and $\bot$. For $\pi \in \Sigma^*$ with $\pi = \pi_0 \pi_1 \ldots \pi_n$ we write $\delta(q, \pi)$ for $\delta(\delta(q, \pi_0), \pi_1 \ldots \pi_n)$, i.e., the state reached after consuming π, where $\delta(q, \varepsilon) = q$.

Definition 2. *(Monitor for LTL)* *Let* φ *be an LTL formula over* Σ. *A monitor* $\mathcal{A} = (Q, \Sigma, \delta, \iota)$ *is a monitor for* φ *if for all* $\pi \in \Sigma^*$

$$\delta(\iota, \pi) = \top \ \text{ iff } \ \pi\rho \models \varphi \text{ for all } \rho \in \Sigma^\omega \text{ and}$$
$$\delta(\iota, \pi) = \bot \ \text{ iff } \ \pi\rho \not\models \varphi \text{ for all } \rho \in \Sigma^\omega.$$

Intuitively, a monitor for an LTL formula φ observes a sequence π and yields a verdict $\top$ or $\bot$ if φ is surely satisfied or not satisfied, respectively, w.r.t. to all extensions of π. Conversely, if no verdict state is reached via π, a final decision about satisfaction of φ cannot be drawn.

Theorem 1. *([7]) For any LTL formula* φ *over* Σ *there is a monitor* $\mathcal{A}^\varphi$ *for* φ *with a state space of size* $\mathcal{O}(2^{2^{|\varphi|}})$.

Feature-Oriented Systems. We denote the set of abstract features by F and say that any set $C \subseteq F$ is a *configuration*. To formally describe behaviors of a configurable system family, *featured transition systems (FTSs)* [11] enhance transition systems by *feature guards*, i.e., Boolean expressions over F that are annotated to transitions. Formally, an *FTS* is a tuple $\mathcal{T} = (S, F, \Sigma, \Delta, I)$ where S, F, and Σ are finite sets of states, features, and actions, respectively, $\Delta \subseteq S \times \mathbb{B}(F) \times \Sigma \times S$ is a featured transition relation, and $I \subseteq \mathbb{B}(F) \times S$ is a set of featured initial states. The *projection* of $\mathcal{T}$ onto a configuration $C \subseteq F$ is the transition system $\mathcal{T}|_C = (S, \Sigma, \Delta|_C, I|_C)$ where $I|_C$ is the set of initial states ι for which there is $(\phi, \iota) \in I$ with $C \models \phi$ and $\Delta|_C \subseteq S \times \Sigma \times S$ is the smallest transition relation that satisfies

$$\frac{(s, \phi, \alpha, t) \in \Delta \quad C \models \phi}{\delta(s, \alpha) = t}$$

The semantics of an FTS $\mathcal{T}$ is thus a family of transition systems $\{\mathcal{T}|_C \mid C \subseteq F\}$.[5] To specify variability-aware properties, e.g., for FTSs, *featured linear temporal logic (fLTL)* has been defined as featured extension of LTL [11]. Formulas

---

[5] Note that behaviors for invalid feature configurations can be specified through non-satisfying feature guards on initial states, leading to empty initial state projections.

in fLTL over a feature domain F and an alphabet Σ are of the form $[\phi]\varphi$ where $\phi \in \mathbb{B}(F)$ is a feature guard over F and φ is an LTL formula over Σ. For a set Φ of fLTL formulas, we define $\Phi|_C = \bigwedge_{[\phi]\varphi \in \Phi, C \vDash \phi} \varphi$ as the LTL formula that is effective in a feature configuration $C \subseteq F$.

Example 1. Let us specify properties for the configurable RDE system example (see Sect. 2.1). In case the EMF sensor is present, a desirable property is that no computation of the EMF is triggered, as the EMF should be directly obtained from the EMF sensor. This could be expressed, e.g., by an fLTL formula

$$\psi_0 \;=\; [\mathsf{EMFs}]\neg\Diamond\,comp\text{-}EMF.$$

Another example would be the property that if the EMF computation feature is included and no EMF sensor is present, then after the MAF sensor has been read, in the next step the EMF must be computed. This is expressed by

$$\psi_1 \;=\; [\mathsf{EMFc} \wedge \neg\mathsf{EMFs}]\Box(use\text{-}MAF\text{-}sensor \to \mathsf{X}\,comp\text{-}EMF).$$

$\Diamond$

3.2   Featured Monitors

Combining the concepts of monitors and FTSs, we define *featured monitors*:

Definition 3. (Featured Monitor) *A* featured monitor *is an FTS* $\mathcal{M} = (Q, F, \Sigma, \Delta, I)$ *where Q contains verdict states V and where for all $C \subseteq F$:*

(i) $(q, \mathtt{true}, \alpha, q) \in \Delta$ *for all $q \in V$ and $\alpha \in \Sigma$*
(ii) for all $p \in Q$ and $\alpha \in \Sigma$ there is exactly one $(p, \phi, \alpha, q) \in \Delta$ with $C \vDash \phi$
(iii) there is exactly one $(\phi, \iota) \in I$ with $C \vDash \phi$

Note that any projection $\mathcal{M}|_C$ of a featured monitor $\mathcal{M}$ onto a configuration $C \subseteq F$ is a monitor according to Definition 1 when interpreting $\Delta|_C$ as transition function and $I|_C$ as single state. This monitor is well-defined due to the uniqueness of C-satisfying transitions and initial states. Intuitively, a featured monitor $\mathcal{M}$ ensembles multiple monitors $\mathcal{M}|_C$ for feature configurations $C \subseteq F$.

To combine monitoring functionalities of featured monitors, we define a *featured monitor composition* by a product construction that adjusts feature guards and verdicts. For this, the *verdict composition* on some p and q is defined by

$$p \sqcap q \;=\; \begin{cases} \top & \text{if } p = \top \text{ and } q = \top \\ \bot & \text{if } p = \bot \text{ or } q = \bot \\ \langle p, q \rangle & \text{otherwise.} \end{cases}$$

Definition 4. (Featured Monitor Composition) *Let $\mathcal{M}_i = (Q_i, F, \Sigma, \Delta_i, I_i)$ for $i \in \{0, 1\}$ be two featured monitors over a common feature domain F and alphabet Σ. The composition of $\mathcal{M}_0$ and $\mathcal{M}_1$ is defined by $\mathcal{M}_0 \sqcap \mathcal{M}_1 = (Q, F, \Sigma, \Delta, I)$ where*

- $Q = V \cup (Q_0 \times Q_1)$
- $\Delta \subseteq Q \times \mathbb{B}(F) \times \Sigma \times Q$ is the smallest featured transition relation such that

$$\frac{(p_0, \phi_0, \alpha, q_0) \in \Delta_0 \quad (p_1, \phi_1, \alpha, q_1) \in \Delta_1 \quad p_0 \sqcap p_1 \notin V}{(p_0 \sqcap p_1, \chi(\phi_0 \wedge \phi_1), \alpha, q_0 \sqcap q_1) \in \Delta} \qquad \frac{p \in V \quad \alpha \in \Sigma}{(p, \mathbf{true}, \alpha, p) \in \Delta}$$

- $I = \{(\chi(\phi_0 \wedge \phi_1), \iota_0 \sqcap \iota_1) \mid (\phi_0, \iota_0) \in I_0, (\phi_1, \iota_1) \in I_1\}$.

Recall that $\chi(\phi)$ denotes a uniquely defined ϕ-equivalent Boolean expression and that $V = \{\top, \bot\}$ is the set of verdict states.

Lemma 1. $\mathcal{M}_0 \sqcap \mathcal{M}_1$ *is a featured monitor for any two featured monitors* $\mathcal{M}_0$ *and* $\mathcal{M}_1$ *over a common feature domain and alphabet.*

3.3 Synthesizing Featured Monitors

We use formulas in fLTL to specify variability-aware monitoring properties and describe how to synthesize featured monitors. Recall that for a set Φ of fLTL formulas, we define $\Phi|_C = \bigwedge_{[\phi]\varphi \in \Phi, C \models \phi} \varphi$ as the LTL formula that is effective in a feature configuration $C \subseteq F$.

Definition 5. *(Featured Monitor for fLTL) Let* Φ *be a finite set of fLTL properties over* F *and* Σ*. A featured monitor for* Φ *is a featured monitor* $\mathcal{M}$ *over* F *and* Σ *such that* $\mathcal{M}|_C$ *is a monitor for* $\Phi|_C$ *for all configurations* $C \subseteq F$.

Thus, a featured monitor for a set of fLTL formulas Φ provides a concise representation of a family of monitors that verdicts LTL properties for configurations to be jointly satisfied.

Let now $[\phi]\varphi$ be an fLTL formula over the feature domain F and an alphabet Σ. Further, let $\mathcal{A}^\varphi = (Q, \Sigma, \delta, \iota)$ be the monitor for φ according to Theorem 1. We then define the featured monitor $\mathcal{M}_\phi^\varphi = (Q, F, \Sigma, \Delta, I)$ by

$$\Delta = \{ (q, \chi(\phi), \alpha, \delta(q, \alpha)), (q, \chi(\neg\phi), \alpha, q) \mid q \in Q, \alpha \in \Sigma \}$$

and $I = \{(\chi(\phi), \iota), (\chi(\neg\phi), \top)\}$. Note that $\mathcal{M}_\phi^\varphi$ is indeed a featured monitor for $[\phi]\varphi$ since for all configurations $C \subseteq F$ with $C \models \phi$ we have that $\mathcal{M}_\phi^\varphi|_C = \mathcal{A}^\varphi$ and $\mathcal{A}^\varphi$ is a monitor for φ.

Theorem 2. *For any set of fLTL formulas* Φ*, we have that* $\mathcal{M}^\Phi = \bigsqcap_{[\phi]\varphi \in \Phi} \mathcal{M}_\phi^\varphi$ *is a featured monitor for* Φ.[6]

Example 1. Let us describe how to synthesize a featured monitor from the set of fLTL formulas $\Phi = \{\psi_0, \psi_1\}$ from Example 1. First, we construct monitors for ψ_0 and ψ_1 according to Theorem 1 and, following the construction for $\mathcal{M}_\phi^\varphi$

---

[6] The corner case where $|\Phi| = 0$ is covered by the $\top$-verdicting featured monitor $\mathcal{M}_{\mathbf{true}}^{\mathbf{true}}$ that arises from $\mathcal{A}^{\mathbf{true}} = (V, \Sigma, \delta, \top)$ where $\delta(p, \alpha) = p$ for all $p \in V$ and $\alpha \in \Sigma$.

$\mathcal{M}_0$: $\mathcal{M}_1$:

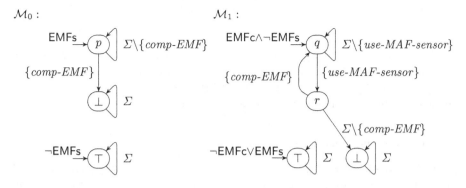

Fig. 2. Synthesized featured monitors $\mathcal{M}_0$ and $\mathcal{M}_1$ for ψ_0 and ψ_1, respectively

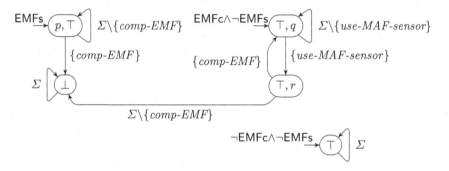

Fig. 3. Featured monitor composition $\mathcal{M}^\Phi = \mathcal{M}_0 \sqcap \mathcal{M}_1$ for $\Phi = \{\psi_0, \psi_1\}$

above, include feature guards towards $\mathcal{M}_0$ and $\mathcal{M}_1$. In Fig. 2 we depict both $\mathcal{M}_0$ and $\mathcal{M}_1$. For brevity, we only show the reachable parts where feature guards are satisfiable, annotated the transitions with the set of possible actions for the transition, and only indicated the feature guard once in initial states.

In Fig. 3 we show the featured monitor $\mathcal{M}^\Phi = \mathcal{M}_0 \sqcap \mathcal{M}_1$ obtained by the construction of Theorem 2. Note that there is also an initial state (`false`, $\langle p, q \rangle$) not depicted in Fig. 3 due to the unsatisfiable feature guard. The featured monitor $\mathcal{M}^\Phi$ as of Fig. 3 provides a non-trivial $\perp$-verdict and only a trivial $\top$-verdict for configurations that do not have EMF computation nor sensor. This configuration can be considered as non-valid, since then, no RDE test is possible (see Sect. 2.1). However, there are also properties that have both, non-trivial $\perp$- and $\top$-verdicts: Consider the property of passing the NOx emission test in an RDE setup, i.e., that within 60 and 120 min, a valid RDE situation arises and the NOx emissions are below a threshold of 80 mg/km. To specify this property in fLTL, observe that time intervals can be expressed in LTL by chains of X-operators, e.g., $\Diamond^{[2,4]}\varphi$ stands for the formula $XX(\varphi \vee X(\varphi \vee X\varphi))$ specifying φ to hold within 2 and 4 time units. With this at hand, the fLTL property for the NOx passing RDE test could be specified by

$$\psi_{\text{passed}}^{\text{NOx}} \;=\; [\text{NOxs}]\lozenge^{[60,120]}(\textit{valid-RDE} \wedge \textit{NOx-emission} < 80).$$

If the test is valid within the time interval and the emissions are below the threshold, then the featured monitor verdicts $\top$, while when passing the upper time bound of 120 without reaching a valid RDE state where the emissions are below the threshold, the featured monitor verdicts $\bot$. $\diamond$

3.4 Concise Featured Monitors

In the last sections, we introduced featured monitors and provided a method to synthesize such from fLTL specifications. To keep the presentation clean, we disregarded several technicalities that, however, would increase feasibility of the approach. First, our definitions always range over all possible configurations $C \subseteq F$ but could well be defined to range over valid configurations only. Second, our synthesis construction could be enhanced by reduction steps to obtain more concise featured monitors. For instance, we could join featured transitions (p, ϕ, α, q) and (p, ϕ', α, q) towards $(p, \chi(\phi \vee \phi'), \alpha, q)$ as well as featured initial states (ϕ, ι) and (ϕ', ι) towards $(\chi(\phi \vee \phi'), \iota)$. Transforming featured monitors into the related formalism of FTSs, we can directly apply dedicated bisimulation techniques [8] towards a compact featured monitor. For this, we label the verdict states $\top$ and $\bot$ by corresponding atomic propositions $\top$ and $\bot$, respectively, and keep all other states not labeled at all. Featured bisimulation is then achieved w.r.t. verdicts, preserving the featured monitor properties.

4 Configurable Stream-Based Monitoring

As discussed in Sect. 2, there is a need for featured specification languages for runtime monitoring. We now address this challenge by presenting an extension of the stream-based specification language Lola [12]. For simplicity, we will do so for the original variant of Lola [12]. Our extension is orthogonal to the extensions introduced by Lola 2.0 [17] and RTLola [18]. It should be straightforward to use the same techniques to introduce variability to those extensions.

We first restate the syntax and semantics of Lola as well as the central theorem necessary for constructing monitors out of Lola specifications. As our contribution, we then (a) introduce a notion of composability of Lola specifications, (b) use this notion to define *configurable Lola specifications*, and (c) present a family-based analysis for configurable Lola specifications ensuring that a monitor can be constructed for each configuration of interest and that the amount of memory it requires is independent of the length of its input.

4.1 Preliminaries

Let's start by introducing the stream-based specification language Lola.

Definition 6. *(Lola Specification* [12][7] *) Let T be a set of* data types *and $\mathbb{S}$ be a set of* typed stream variables, *i.e., each $s \in \mathbb{S}$ has an associated type $T_s \in T$. A* Lola specification *over T and $\mathbb{S}$ is a partial function $f : \mathbb{S} \rightharpoonup \mathbb{E}$ assigning* stream variables *to typed stream expressions. The set of typed stream expressions $\mathbb{E}$ is defined inductively by:*

(i) Constants and stream variables of type T are expressions of type T.

(ii) Let $g : T_1 \times \cdots \times T_k \to T$ be a k-ary operator and $\eta_1, \ldots, \eta_k$ be expressions of type $T_1, \ldots, T_k$, then $g(\eta_1, \ldots, \eta_k)$ is an expression of type T.

(iii) Let η be a Boolean expression and η_1 and η_2 be expressions of some type T, then $\mathrm{ite}(\eta, \eta_1, \eta_2)$ is an expression of type T.

(iv) Let s be a stream variable of type T, c be a constant of type T, and $z \in \mathbb{Z}$, then $s[z, c]$ is a stream expression of type T.

A Lola specification f defines stream expressions for the set $\mathrm{dom}(f) \subseteq \mathbb{S}$ of stream variables. Those variables are coined *dependent* while the remaining variables are coined *independent*. The idea is that the stream expressions constrain the values the dependent variables can have at certain points in time.

The semantics of Lola is defined in terms of *evaluation models*. An evaluation model σ of length N assigns a sequence $\sigma(s) = \sigma_1(s) \cdots \sigma_N(s)$ of values of type T_s, coined a *stream*, to each stream variable $s \in \mathbb{S}$. Note that the individual streams all have the same length N. Given an evaluation model σ we inductively define an evaluation function $\llbracket \cdot \rrbracket_t$ for stream expressions at time t:

$$\llbracket c \rrbracket_t = c \qquad \llbracket s \rrbracket_t = \sigma_t(s) \qquad \llbracket g(\eta_1, \ldots, \eta_k) \rrbracket_t = g(\llbracket \eta_1 \rrbracket_t, \ldots, \llbracket \eta_k \rrbracket_t)$$

$$\llbracket \mathrm{ite}(\eta, \eta_1, \eta_2) \rrbracket_t = \begin{cases} \llbracket \eta_1 \rrbracket_t & \text{if } \llbracket \eta \rrbracket_t = \text{true} \\ \llbracket \eta_2 \rrbracket_t & \text{otherwise} \end{cases}$$

$$\llbracket s[z, c] \rrbracket_t = \begin{cases} \sigma_{t+z}(s) & \text{if } 1 \le t + z \le N \\ c & \text{otherwise} \end{cases}$$

An evaluation model σ *is consistent with* a Lola specification f, denoted by $\sigma \vDash f$, if and only if $\llbracket f(s) \rrbracket_t = \sigma_t(s)$ for all $s \in \mathrm{dom}(f)$ and $1 \le t \le N$. That is, the values of each dependent stream variable $s \in \mathrm{dom}(f)$ over time are consistent with the expressions specified by f.

Let us now have a look at a concrete example taken from Sect. 2.1. The RDE regulation stipulates that the acceleration a_t at time t shall be computed as follows [29, ANNEX IIIA, Appendix 7a, 3.1.2]:

$$a_t = (v_{t-1} + v_{t+1})/(2 \cdot 3.6)$$

---

[7] We slightly deviate from the original definition for notational convenience. In particular, we do not allow expressions of the form $\eta[z, c]$ where η is an arbitrary stream expression. It has been shown that those can be rewritten to $s'[z, c]$ by introducing an additional stream variable s' such that $f(s') = \eta$.

Hence, the acceleration at time t shall be computed using the velocity v at time $t-1$ and $t+1$. The translation into Lola is straightforward:

$$f(a) = \frac{v[-1,0] + v[+1,0]}{2 \cdot 3.6}$$

By using an offset expression of the form $s[z,c]$ we can access the value of the stream variable v in the past as well as the future. The default value c in an offset expression is used at time t if and only if the time $t+z$ lies outside of the streams provided by the evaluation model. Offset expressions are arguably the most innovative feature of Lola and responsible for its great expressive power. We refer to the original Lola paper for a detailed discussion [12].

Online Monitoring and Well-Formedness. An online monitor for a Lola specification incrementally computes values for the dependent stream variables based on incrementally observed independent stream variables. In the following, we refer to the streams for the independent variables as *input streams* and to the streams for the dependent variables as *output streams*.

Using this terminology, an online monitor for a specification f computes output streams from input streams such that those streams together form an evaluation model consistent with the given specification. Being able to construct such a monitor is the primary purpose of a Lola specification.

In case of our example, assume that v is an independent variable, i.e., the velocity is provided as an input to the monitor, the monitor will then compute the stream for the acceleration a as defined by the RDE regulation.

Unfortunately, with the provided definitions, it might be impossible to compute output streams from input streams as no evaluation model may exist or there might be multiple such models for a given set of input streams leading to ambiguity [12]. To address this issue, a notion of well-definedness is introduced: A Lola specification is *well-defined* if and only if for any set of appropriately typed input streams, all of the same length, it has exactly one consistent evaluation model [12]. This restriction ensures that the monitor is well-defined.

From a practical perspective, however, well-definedness is difficult to deal with. Instead, the original paper [12] introduces a purely syntactic criterion called *well-formedness* such that the following central theorem holds:

Theorem 3. *([12]) If a specification is well-formed, then it is well-defined.*

Now, well-formedness is defined by means of a *dependency graph*:

Definition 7. *(Dependency Graph) Let f be a Lola specification over the stream variables $\mathbb{S}$. The dependency graph for f is a directed and weighted multi-graph $G = \langle \mathbb{S}, E \rangle$ where E is the set of edges. An edge is a triple $\langle s_x, s_y, z \rangle$ where $s_x, s_y \in \mathbb{S}$ and $z \in \mathbb{Z}$. The set E of edges contains an edge $\langle s_x, s_y, z \rangle$ if and only if $s_x \in \mathrm{dom}(f)$ and the expression $f(s_x)$ contains an offset expression $s_y[z,c]$ for some constant c.*

Intuitively, the existence of an edge $\langle s_x, s_y, z \rangle$ in E records the fact that the stream for s_x depends on the stream for s_y with an offset of z. If there exists a cycle whose weights z sum up to zero, i.e., a *zero-weight cycle*, then the value at a given time circularly depends on the very same value leading to ambiguity issues. Well-formedness forbids precisely such viscous cycles.

Definition 8. *(**Well-Formedness**) A specification is* well-formed *if and only if its dependency graph does not contain any zero-weight cycle.*

By checking well-formedness of a specification, we make sure that a monitor for it is uniquely defined. It is this property of well-formedness that has to be checked in order to ensure that a monitor can be constructed using the techniques presented in the original Lola paper [12]. We refer to this paper for further details regarding the monitor construction and Theorem 3. Note that the *zero-weight cycle problem*, i.e., the problem of deciding whether a zero-weight cycle exists, is known to be NP-complete, which can be shown by a simple reduction from the NP-complete subset-sum problem [3, Theorem 3.12].

4.2 Configurable Lola

We now introduce an extension of Lola that yields monitor families and accounts for variability. To this end, we first define a notion of composition enabling the combination of multiple Lola specifications into one.

Definition 9. *(Composition) Two Lola specifications f_1 and f_2 are composable if and only if their dependent variables are disjoint. Formally that is $\mathrm{dom}(f_1) \cap \mathrm{dom}(f_2) = \emptyset$. For two composable specifications f_1 and f_2, we define their composition $f_1 \parallel f_2 : \mathrm{dom}(f_1) \cup \mathrm{dom}(f_2) \to \mathbb{E}$ as follows:*

$$(f_1 \parallel f_2)(s) := \begin{cases} f_1(s) & \text{if } s \in \mathrm{dom}(f_1) \\ f_2(s) & \text{if } s \in \mathrm{dom}(f_2) \end{cases}$$

Note that the composition $f_1 \parallel f_2$ is itself a Lola specification. The set of dependent variables of $f_1 \parallel f_2$ is $\mathrm{dom}(f_1) \cup \mathrm{dom}(f_2)$.

Without the restriction to composable specifications, the composition of two specifications would be problematic since the sets of dependent variables may overlap, thus, containing multiple potentially different equations for the same variable thereby leading to ambiguity.

Note that the composition operator $\parallel$ is associative and commutative. For that reason, the order of composition does not matter and any set of pairwise composable Lola specifications has a unique composition.

Leveraging this notion of composability, we now have all the tools to formally introduce *configurable Lola specifications*:

Definition 10. *(Configurable Lola Specification) A configurable Lola specification is a set $F = \{f_1, \ldots, f_m\}$ of Lola specifications, i.e., f_i is a Lola*

EMF sensor feature (EMFs):

```
input emf_sensor: Float64; // g/s
output emf = emf_sensor;
```

EMF computation feature (EMFc):

```
input maf_sensor: Float64; // g/s
input fuel_rate: Float64; // g/s
output emf = maf_sensor + fuel_rate;
```

FR sensor feature (FRs):

```
input fuel_rate_sensor: Float64; // g/s
output fuel_rate = fuel_rate_sensor;
```

FR computation feature (FRc):

```
input maf_sensor: Float64; // g/s
input fuel_air_equivalence_sensor: Float64; // ratio
output fuel_rate = maf_sensor / (14.5 * fuel_air_equivalence_sensor)
```

Fig. 4. Features extracted from the different RDE Lola specifications [9, 22].

specification for each $1 \leq i \leq m$. *We call the individual specifications* f_i *features of* F. *A configuration* C *of* F *is a subset of* F *such that all features included in the subset are pairwise composable.*

By composition as defined in Definition 9, every configuration gives rise to a uniquely defined composite specification. In the following, we make use of this fact and simply treat configurations as if they are Lola specifications. In particular, we apply the concepts of well-formedness and efficient monitorability directly to configurations.

Featured Lola specifications make variability a first-class concept enabling the specification of configurable-by-construction runtime monitors. Returning to Sect. 2.1, we can now use different features for the different ways the EMF and fuel rate can be determined (see also Fig. 1). Figure 4 shows four features, two for obtaining the EMF and two for computing the fuel rate. It is also a natural consequence of Definition 10 that the different ways to compute the EMF or fuel rate are mutually exclusive because those features overlap in their dependent stream variables (defined using the `output` keyword), i.e., they are not composable. Using a configurable Lola specification, those features can now systematically be combined as required.

Well-formedness of Configurations. As with ordinary Lola specifications, we have to ensure that any configuration is well-formed or at least determine the configurations which are not. In particular, when reconfiguration at runtime is required, we have to ensure that any configuration of interest gives rise to a well-formed composite specification. Otherwise, at runtime, it might turn out impossible to construct a monitor for a certain configuration.

In case a feature is already not well-formed itself, we can conclude that any configuration containing this feature will also be not well-formed:

Lemma 2. *If any of the individual features is not well-formed, then any configuration containing the respective feature is not well-formed.*

This is easy to see as the dependency graph of the feature is a subgraph of the dependency graph of the configuration. Hence, any zero-weight cycle will also exist in the dependency graph of the configuration thereby rendering the configuration itself not well-formed.

Unfortunately, the reverse is not true, i.e., even if the individual features are all well-formed, this does not imply that any configuration is also well-formed. The dependency graph of a configuration combines those of the features and may thereby introduce new zero-weight cycles that are not present in the dependency graphs of any of the features when considered in isolation.

An obvious way to decide whether all configurations are well-formed would be to construct the specification for each configuration and then determine whether it is well-formed. Considering each configuration of a configurable Lola specification in isolation and checking its well-formedness is, in general, exponential in the number of features of that specification, thus rendering it infeasible as soon as the amount of features grows large. As we will see, using a family-based analysis for checking well-formedness prevents this blowup by exploiting commonalities between different configurations.

4.3   Family-Based Specification Analysis

For checking well-formedness and efficient monitorability for all configurations without an exponential blowup, we present a family-based analysis that exploits commonalities between configurations. Instead of using a dependency graph for each configuration in isolation, we construct a *family dependency graph*:

Definition 11. *(Family Dependency Graph)* Let $F = \{f_1, \ldots, f_m\}$ be a *configurable Lola specification with m features over the stream variables $\mathbb{S}$. The family dependency graph for F is a directed, weighted, and feature-labeled multigraph $G = \langle \mathbb{S}, E \rangle$ where E is the set of* edges. *An edge is a quadruple $\langle s_x, s_y, z, i \rangle$ where $s_x, s_y \in \mathbb{S}$, $z \in \mathbb{Z}$, and $1 \leq i \leq m$. The set E of edges contains an edge $\langle s_x, s_y, z, i \rangle$ if and only if $s_x \in \mathrm{dom}(f_i)$ and the expression $f_i(s_x)$ contains an expression $s_y[z, c]$ for some constant c.*

Intuitively, the existence of an edge $\langle s_x, s_y, z, i \rangle$ in E records the fact that the stream for s_x depends on the stream for s_y with an offset of z when activating the feature f_i. The family dependency graph is a superimposition of the dependency graphs of each individual feature with additional edge labels for the features they belong to. Hence, the following criterion is easily established:

Lemma 3. *If the family dependency graph of a configurable Lola specification does not contain a zero-weight cycle, then every configuration is well-formed.*

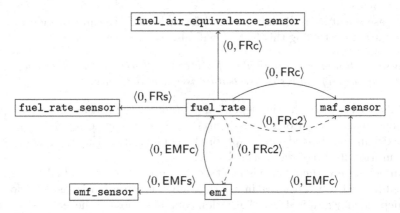

Fig. 5. Family dependency graph (without the dashed lines) for the configurable Lola specification in Fig. 4. The arrows are to be read as "depends on" with the given offset and feature. The dashed lines are with the additional FRc2 feature.

Clearly, the dependency graph of every configuration is a subgraph of the family dependency graph. Therefore, if the family dependency graph does not contain a zero-weight cycle then the dependency graphs of any individual configuration cannot contain such a cycle either.

Figure 5 shows the family dependency graph (without the dashed lines) for the configurable Lola specification in Fig. 4. It does not contain any zero-weight cycles, in fact, it does not contain any cycles at all. Hence, all configurations for the configurable Lola specification are well-formed.

Lemma 3 gives us a sufficient criterion for well-formedness of every configuration. This criterion can be checked with the same algorithms and techniques as checking well-formedness of an individual specification. In contrast to the naive approach, which would consider each configuration individually, these algorithms can now exploit commonalities between the dependency graphs of the different configurations thereby mitigating the exponential blowup due to the often exponential number of configurations.

A Necessary Criterion. While Lemma 3 gives us a sufficient criterion for well-formedness of all configurations, this is actually not a necessary criterion. Intuitively, only those zero-weight cycles pose a problem that can actually arise from a configuration, i.e., a set of pairwise composable features. By adding this additional condition for cycles, we obtain the following theorem:

Theorem 4. *Every configuration is well-formed if and only if every zero-weight cycle in the family dependency graph contains at least two edges labeled with features which are not composable.*

The dependency graph of an individual configuration can be obtained from the family dependency graph by removing all edges corresponding to features which are not enabled. Now, if a zero-weight cycle in the family dependency graph contains at least two edges labeled with features which are not composable, this cycle will not be included in a dependency graph of any of the configurations as a configuration can only contain features which are pairwise composable. If this is the case for all zero-weight cycles of the family dependency graph, then none of these cycles will be included in the dependency graph of any of the configurations. As a result, all configurations are well-formed. Conversely, if a zero-weight cycle exists which does not contain two edges that are labeled with non-composable features, then the respective features on this cycle can be composed to form a specification which is not well-formed.

Consider an extension of the configurable Lola specification in Fig. 4 with the following additional feature (FRc2) for computing the fuel rate:

```
input maf_sensor: Float64; // g/s
input emf: Float64; // g/s
output fuel_rate = emf - maf_sensor;
```

This introduces additional edges in the dependency graph (dashed edges in Fig. 5). With this feature, the family dependency graph now contains one elementary zero-weight cycle between fuel_rate and emf. Indeed, a configuration with both the FRc2 and EMFc feature is not well-formed. Enabling both features would mean that the fuel_rate should be computed based on the emf but at the same time the emf should be computed based on the fuel_rate. This cycle yields that a monitor is no longer well-defined. Note that FRc2 and EMFc are composable because they contain no overlapping definitions. With the family-based analysis this can be detected solely relying on the family dependency graph and without considering all $2^5 = 32$ configurations one-by-one.

Complexity. As the zero-weight cycle problem, the problem of finding a zero-weight cycle not containing two edges that are labeled with non-composable features is also NP-complete. It is more general than the zero-weight cycle problem because it contains an additional condition on cycles. It also lies in NP because it is easy to verify in polynomial time that a cycle is zero-weight and does not contain two edges that are labeled with non-composable features.

For practical purposes, it makes sense to collapse all edges $\langle s_x, s_y, z, i \rangle$ between the same vertices s_x and s_y that have the same weight z into a single edge $\langle s_x, s_y, z, I \rangle$ where I is the set of all feature labels found on any of these edges. This can drastically reduce the number of edges and thereby the number of potential zero-weight cycles to be considered.

Efficient monitorability. Recall that an additional property of Lola specifications that is of practical interest is *efficient monitorability*. Efficiently monitorable specifications are guaranteed to be monitorable with a bounded amount of memory independent of the length of the involved streams. A Lola specification is efficiently monitorable if and only if its dependency graph does not have positive cycles [12]. Our family-based analysis and Theorem 4 is easily extended to the question whether all configurations are efficiently monitorable:

Theorem 5. *Every configuration is efficiently monitorable if and only if every positive-weight cycle in the feature dependency graph contains at least two edges labeled with features which are not composable.*

Practical impact. Checking the family dependency graph instead of the dependency graph of each configuration in isolation can mitigate the exponential blowup in the number of features. At the same time, it enables analyzing a configurable Lola specification and makes sure that any configurations that appear in practice will indeed give rise to a well-formed and efficiently monitorable specification. This, in turn, means that a monitor can be synthesized and that its memory consumption will be bounded. Based on found zero-weight cycles, configurations that would not lead a well-formed specification can be identified ahead-of-time, providing a static guarantee for configurations at runtime.

We want to point out that Lola specifications can be parametrized and that parametrization can also be used for configurable monitors. However, while emulating features as we considered them with parameters and ite expressions is possible to some extent, the traditional well-formedness analysis will not understand that the different cases of "ite" are mutually exclusive. Thus, it would essentially correspond to a coarse-grained analysis according to Theorem 3. Instead, the analysis we propose here is more fine-grained. In addition, when emulating features using parameters, the independent variables of all features would be merged with no explicit distinction about which actually have to be provided and which are merely an encoding artifact. Thus, our work complements parameters offering a more fine-grained analysis and explicit treatment of features and independent variables. Together, parameters and features as we considered them make Lola a perfect fit for configurable-by-construction runtime verification.

5   Concluding Remarks

We presented initial concepts towards a *configurable-by-construction* approach for runtime monitoring, introducing *featured monitors* to serve the automata-theoretic view on runtime monitoring, and *configurable Lola specifications* that take on a stream-oriented view.

Related Work. While we addressed some of the challenges for configurable-by-construction runtime verification, this is still a largely uncharted field. In the feature-oriented systems domain, Kim et al. [21] lift static analysis techniques to determine those feature configurations where safety properties could be violated and hence should be monitored during runtime. They address different problems than we consider in this paper, not considering variability in the monitor itself.

In addition to the Lola family [12,17,18] there are also other stream-based specification languages, in particular, TeSSLa [23] and Striver [19]. We expect our insights on configurability to at least partially carry over to them. In addition, there are also stream-based specification mechanisms based on automata theory [1] that provide the opportunity to consider the interplay between our notion of featured monitors and configurable Lola specifications.

Future Work. Two notable dimensions that we did not consider yet in this paper concerns the question of uninterrupted online reconfiguration and the systematic matching of monitor and system configurations. For this future work, we could harvest results on reconfigurable systems analysis [13,14]. Monitors that take causality information on the system into account [4] could be also considered in the feature-oriented setting [16] and could trigger preemptive reconfigurations of features. Feature-oriented concepts can well be used to describe context-dependent systems [15,25] or role-based systems [10]. Thus, our runtime monitoring approach also enables monitoring systems to verdict contexts and roles entities play, e.g., whether a network device has the role of a server, client, or relay in different contexts.

To enhance the expressiveness of featured monitor specifications, our synthesis algorithm to obtain featured monitors from sets of fLTL formulas could surely be extended to arbitrary Boolean expressions over fLTL formulas. This requires the definition of further composition operators on verdicts and featured monitors, for which we solely defined the conjunctive counterpart ⊓ in this paper.

References

1. Alur, R., Mamouras, K., Stanford, C.: Automata-based stream processing. In: Proceedings of the 44th International Colloquium on Automata, Languages, and Programming (ICALP 2017). Schloss Dagstuhl, Leibniz-Zentrum für Informatik (2017)
2. Apel, S., Batory, D., Kästner, C., Saake, G.: Feature-oriented software product lines. In: Concepts and Implementation. Springer, Heidelberg (2013). https://doi.org/10.1007/978-3-642-37521-7
3. Baier, C., Bertrand, N., Dubslaff, C., Gburek, D., Sankur, O.: Stochastic shortest paths and weight-bounded properties in Markov decision processes. In: Proceedings of the 33rd Annual ACM/IEEE Symposium on Logic in Computer Science (LICS 2018), pp. 86–94. ACM, NY (2018)
4. Baier, C., et al.: From verification to causality-based explications. In: Proceedings of the 48th International Colloquium on Automata, Languages, and Programming (ICALP 2021). LIPIcs, vol. 198, pp. 1:1–1:20. Leibniz-Zentrum für Informatik (2021)
5. Baier, C., Dubslaff, C., Hermanns, H., Klauck, M., Klüppelholz, S., Köhl, M.A.: Components in probabilistic systems: suitable by construction. In: Margaria, T., Steffen, B. (eds.) ISoLA 2020. LNCS, vol. 12476, pp. 240–261. Springer, Cham (2020). https://doi.org/10.1007/978-3-030-61362-4_13
6. Bartocci, E., Falcone, Y., Francalanza, A., Reger, G.: Introduction to runtime verification. In: Bartocci, E., Falcone, Y. (eds.) Lectures on Runtime Verification. LNCS, vol. 10457, pp. 1–33. Springer, Cham (2018). https://doi.org/10.1007/978-3-319-75632-5_1
7. Bauer, A., Leucker, M., Schallhart, C.: Monitoring of real-time properties. In: Arun-Kumar, S., Garg, N. (eds.) FSTTCS 2006. LNCS, vol. 4337, pp. 260–272. Springer, Heidelberg (2006). https://doi.org/10.1007/11944836_25
8. Belder, T., ter Beek, M.H., de Vink, E.P.: Coherent branching feature bisimulation. In: Proceedings 6th Workshop on Formal Methods and Analysis in SPL Engineering (FMSPLE@ETAPS 2015). EPTCS, vol. 182, pp. 14–30 (2015)

9. Biewer, S., Finkbeiner, B., Hermanns, H., Köhl, M.A., Schnitzer, Y., Schwenger, M.: RTLola on board: testing real driving emissions on your phone. In: TACAS 2021. LNCS, vol. 12652, pp. 365–372. Springer, Cham (2021). https://doi.org/10. 1007/978-3-030-72013-1_20

10. Chrszon, P., Baier, C., Dubslaff, C., Klüppelholz, S.: From features to roles. In: Proceedings of the 24th ACM International Systems and Software Product Line Conference (SPLC 2020), pp. 19:1–19:11. ACM (2020)

11. Classen, A., Cordy, M., Schobbens, P.Y., Heymans, P., Legay, A., Raskin, J.F.: Featured transition systems: foundations for verifying variability-intensive systems and their application to LTL model checking. IEEE Trans. Softw. Eng. **39**(8), 1069–1089 (2013)

12. d'Angelo, B., et al.: LOLA: runtime monitoring of synchronous systems. In: Proceedings of the 12th International Symposium on Temporal Representation and Reasoning (TIME 2005), pp. 166–174. IEEE Computer Society Press (2005)

13. Dubslaff, C.: Quantitative analysis of configurable and reconfigurable systems. Ph.D. thesis, TU Dresden, Institute for Theoretical Computer Science (2021)

14. Dubslaff, C., Baier, C., Klüppelholz, S.: Probabilistic model checking for feature-oriented systems. In: Chiba, S., Tanter, É., Ernst, E., Hirschfeld, R. (eds.) Transactions on Aspect-Oriented Software Development XII. LNCS, vol. 8989, pp. 180–220. Springer, Heidelberg (2015). https://doi.org/10.1007/978-3-662-46734-3_5

15. Dubslaff, C., Koopmann, P., Turhan, A.-Y.: Ontology-mediated probabilistic model checking. In: Ahrendt, W., Tapia Tarifa, S.L. (eds.) IFM 2019. LNCS, vol. 11918, pp. 194–211. Springer, Cham (2019). https://doi.org/10.1007/978-3-030-34968-4_11

16. Dubslaff, C., Weis, K., Baier, C., Apel, S.: Causality in configurable software systems. In: Proceedings of the 44th International Conference on Software Engineering (ICSE) (2022)

17. Faymonville, P., Finkbeiner, B., Schirmer, S., Torfah, H.: A stream-based specification language for network monitoring. In: Falcone, Y., Sánchez, C. (eds.) RV 2016. LNCS, vol. 10012, pp. 152–168. Springer, Cham (2016). https://doi.org/10. 1007/978-3-319-46982-9_10

18. Faymonville, P., et al.: StreamLAB: stream-based monitoring of cyber-physical systems. In: Dillig, I., Tasiran, S. (eds.) CAV 2019. LNCS, vol. 11561, pp. 421–431. Springer, Cham (2019). https://doi.org/10.1007/978-3-030-25540-4_24

19. Gorostiaga, F., Sánchez, C.: Striver: stream runtime verification for real-time event-streams. In: Colombo, C., Leucker, M. (eds.) RV 2018. LNCS, vol. 11237, pp. 282–298. Springer, Cham (2018). https://doi.org/10.1007/978-3-030-03769-7_16

20. Kang, K.C., Cohen, S.G., Hess, J.A., Novak, W.E., Peterson, A.S.: Feature-oriented domain analysis (FODA) feasibility study. Carnegie-Mellon University Software Engineering Institute, Tech. rep. (1990)

21. Kim, C.H.P., Bodden, E., Batory, D., Khurshid, S.: Reducing configurations to monitor in a software product line. In: Barringer, H., et al. (eds.) RV 2010. LNCS, vol. 6418, pp. 285–299. Springer, Heidelberg (2010). https://doi.org/10.1007/978-3-642-16612-9_22

22. Köhl, M.A., Hermanns, H., Biewer, S.: Efficient monitoring of real driving emissions. In: Colombo, C., Leucker, M. (eds.) RV 2018. LNCS, vol. 11237, pp. 299–315. Springer, Cham (2018). https://doi.org/10.1007/978-3-030-03769-7_17

23. Leucker, M., Sánchez, C., Scheffel, T., Schmitz, M., Schramm, A.: TeSSLa: runtime verification of non-synchronized real-time streams. In: Proceedings of the 33rd ACM Symposium on Applied Computing (SAC 2018). ACM, France (2018)

24. Leucker, M., Schallhart, C.: A brief account of runtime verification. J. Log. Algebr. Program. **78**(5), 293–303 (2009)
25. Mauro, J., Nieke, M., Seidl, C., Yu, I.C.: Context aware reconfiguration in software product lines. In: Proceedings of the 10th Workshop on Variability Modelling of Software-Intensive Systems (VaMoS 2016), pp. 41–48. ACM (2016)
26. Pnueli, A.: The temporal logic of programs. In: Proceedings of the 18th Symposium on Foundations of Computer Science (SFCS 1977), pp. 46–57. IEEE (1977)
27. Sánchez, C.: Online and offline stream runtime verification of synchronous systems. In: Colombo, C., Leucker, M. (eds.) RV 2018. LNCS, vol. 11237, pp. 138–163. Springer, Cham (2018). https://doi.org/10.1007/978-3-030-03769-7_9
28. The European Parliament and the Council of the European Union: Directive 98/69/ec of the European parliament and of the council. Official Journal of the European Communities (1998). https://eur-lex.europa.eu/LexUriServ/LexUriServ.do?uri=CELEX:31998L0069:EN:HTML
29. The European Parliament and the Council of the European Union: Commission Regulation (EU) 2017/1151 (2017). https://data.europa.eu/eli/reg/2017/1151/oj
30. Thüm, T., Apel, S., Kästner, C., Schaefer, I., Saake, G.: A classification and survey of analysis strategies for software product lines. ACM Comput. Surv. **47**(1s), 6:1–6:45 (2014)
31. United States Environmental Protection Agency. https://www.epa.gov/greenvehicles/explaining-electric-plug-hybrid-electric-vehicles
32. Zave, P.: Feature-oriented description, formal methods, and DFC. In: Gilmore, S., Ryan, M. (eds.) Language Constructs for Describing Features. Springer, London (2001). https://doi.org/10.1007/978-1-4471-0287-8_2

Runtime Verification of Correct-by-Construction Driving Maneuvers

Alexander Kittelmann[1,2]($\boxtimes$), Tobias Runge[1,2], Tabea Bordis[1,2], and Ina Schaefer[1,2]

[1] TU Braunschweig, Brunswick, Germany
[2] Karlsruhe Institute of Technology, Karlsruhe, Germany
{alexander.kittelmann,tobias.runge,tabea.bordis,
ina.schaefer}@kit.edu

Abstract. Cyber-physical systems play an increasingly vital role in our everyday lives by leveraging technology to mitigate human error. These systems are inherently safety-critical, which requires the highest standards in quality assurance. Therefore, designing safe behaviors for these systems in a manageable fashion and maximizing trust early on by formally verifying them against a formal specification mandates a software engineering process that prioritizes appropriate abstractions in the early design phase. However, even if models are formally verified at design time, their appropriateness in the real world stills needs to be validated at runtime, as specifications are usually incomplete. In this work, we introduce a methodology for refining verified cyber-physical systems modeled by hybrid mode automata to executable source code amenable for runtime verification. In particular, we employ ARCHICORC, which lifts the *correctness-by-construction* paradigm for programs to component-based architectures, and comes with facilities for code generation. Subsequent simulations of the executable and verified maneuvers allow to validate their initial requirements in a diverse set of scenarios.

Keywords: Correctness-by-construction · Cyber-physical systems · Runtime verification

1 Introduction

Cyber-physical systems are ubiquitous in many products that we use in our daily lives, including avionic systems [45], automobiles [15], robotics [30], and even medical equipment [25]. To reduce development complexity, their safety-critical nature mandates sophisticated elicitation of requirements and formal reasoning techniques (e.g., formal verification) during the design stage. Model-based development is such an approach in modern software engineering, which allows to express cyber-physical systems in a way that makes their analysis, visualization, and simulation tractable. The goal is to start with an abstract behavioral model of a system that is already amenable to various analyses (e.g., scalable formal

T. Margaria and B. Steffen (Eds.): ISoLA 2022, LNCS 13701, pp. 242–263, 2022.
https://doi.org/10.1007/978-3-031-19849-6_15

verification) to identify conceptual design flaws as early as possible. Moreover, the typical model-based design process spans multiple layers. That is, a *refining process* is applied to add more details to the current model and to perform more complex analyses. Eventually, the model is refined to executable source code.

A challenge is that the initial set of requirements used for successfully verifying an abstract model's behavior can often not guarantee that the system behaves *completely safe* after deployment. That is, elicitated requirements are typically incomplete for real-world execution of cyber-physical systems. Therefore, it is of paramount importance to *validate* the executable model under real-world conditions. To be cost-effective, the validation process aims at inspecting completeness of requirements by *simulating* the modeled behavior using one of many data-driven validation techniques (i.e., run-time verification) [33]. Model parts that violate any safety concerns can then be localized and improved, resulting in an iterative development process. Examples of such simulation and analysis tools include MATLAB/SIMULINK [3], PTOLEMY II [41], and AADLSIM [8]. Most of these simulation frameworks focus on rich specification languages, problems orthogonal to functional safety (e.g., uncertainty or performance), and are tied to specific modeling languages.

An important challenge is the gap between design model and the actual implementation that is simulated. Most of the aforementioned approaches already work with detailed enough design models amenable to simulation (e.g., MATLAB/SIMULINK [3]). However, this puts a lot of burden onto the early development of such systems due to high complexity in the modeling phase. Moreover, formal verification (e.g., establishment of correctness proofs) becomes intractable for these models. In contrast, maximizing abstraction of the initial design model is necessary to make formal verification scalable. However, this requires to *add* details to the implementation model before simulation, which increases the chances to introduce new defects and invalidates verification and simulation results.

In this work, we address this challenge by presenting an abstract formalism to specify and verify behavior of cyber-physical systems, and then derive *correct-by-construction* implementations including facilities for monitoring for virtual simulation and run-time verification. In Fig. 1, we give a high-level overview of the key ingredients of our proposed verification and validation pipeline, which depicts an iterative and incremental development process consisting of four consecutive steps.

First, we propose to model and specify the intended behavior of cyber-physical systems with so-called *hybrid mode automata*. To verify these models and to generate correctness proofs, we translate them to differential dynamic logic ($d\mathcal{L}$) [40] and employ the interactive theorem prover KEYMAERA X [34]. Second, the modeled hybrid mode automata are then translated to a component-based architecture. In particular, we exploit ARCHICORC [22], which builds on top of CORC [44] (a tool suite for correct-by-construction programs) and enables a developer to establish a component-based *correct-by-construction architecture*. Third, the architecture is automatically translated to source code in a general-purpose programming language (e.g., JAVA or C++). Although the code genera-

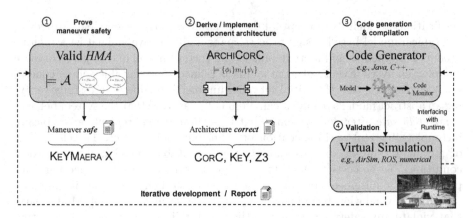

Fig. 1. Schematic overview of steps in the proposed verification and validation pipeline.

tion itself is unverified per se, each part of this process is verifiable when following best practices. That is, behaviors of components ideally follow the correctness-by-construction approach and checking validity of connections between components (horizontally and vertically) reduces to satisfiability checks based on their interface specifications. Moreover, the implementation also comes with facilities for monitoring, which are automatically generated from the formal specification.

Finally, the derived executable is verified on a set of scenarios (i.e., run-time verification by simulation). For the visual simulation environments, we integrate AirSim [47] by Microsoft, which is used for ground and air vehicles, and the robot operating system (ROS) together with Gazebo, which is a mature framework and visualization environment for robotic systems. Validation is supported by the automated monitoring of safety conditions. Monitoring functions are automatically generated from the hybrid mode automata as part of the third step. This allows to classify monitor violations as *passable* (i.e., violation does not have an impact on safety), *severe* (i.e., violation does have a high chance of impacting safety), or even *fatal* (e.g., vehicle collided with an object).

In summary, we make the following contributions.

- **Technique:** We propose a verification and validation pipeline for behaviors of cyber-physical systems that starts with an abstract model amenable to formal verification, and allows to derive a correct-by-construction and fully-functional implementation amenable to run-time verification.
- **Tool support:** We implemented our technique as part of the tool chain SKEDITOR by leveraging ARCHICORC, a model-based framework for developing correct-by-construction component-based architectures. As simulation environment, we integrated AirSim [47] by Microsoft.
- **Evaluation:** We performed an empirical study on five case studies in the context of automated driving, which differ in complexity and safety requirements. In our study, we verified at run-time that none of the case studies violated their safety requirements, which affirms that deriving fully-functional behaviors from highly-abstract verified models is feasible.

2   Workflow by Example

In this section, we aim at exemplifying our proposed workflow on an automatic distance control for road vehicles.

To formally reason about cyber-physical systems, they are often mathematically modeled by *hybrid systems* [1,7,16], which mix discrete and continuous behavior in a single formalism and abstract away from unnecessary details. Modeling approaches include *hybrid automata* [2] and *hybrid programs* [40].

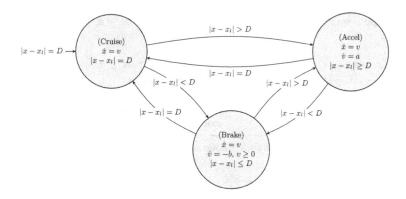

Fig. 2. Simplified hybrid system of a vehicle with automatic distance control.

In Fig. 2, we give an example of a simplified hybrid automaton representing the aforementioned automatic distance control with three possible states, namely Cruise, Accel, and Brake. Variables x and x_l define the current position on a straight line of both the host vehicle and the leading vehicle, and constant D represents the ideal distance between them. Moreover, variables v, a, and b define the current velocity, acceleration, and braking force, respectively. The goal of the distance control is to ensure that the distance between both vehicles remains approximately equal to D. The vehicle is in cruise mode when the distance to the leading vehicle is equal to distance D, which also means that acceleration a is set to zero (i.e., resulting in constant speed). In each control cycle, the current state evolves by applying the respective differential equations and is then evaluated, such that the automaton may transition into a different state. That is, if the leading vehicle increases or decreases the distance, the automaton switches to either state Accel or state Brake. The condition $v \geq 0$ in state Brake ensures that velocity v will not be allowed to become negative.

Step 1: Hybrid Mode Automaton. For modeling the behavior of cyber-physical systems, we propose *hybrid mode automata*, which is a customized combination of *hybrid automata* [16] and *mode automata* [28,29]. Hybrid mode automata consist of a number of discrete modes with guarded transitions between them. Although their expressiveness is equal to the expressiveness of hybrid automata, a key difference is that a *discrete* and simple program is projected onto each mode, which is executed each time a mode is entered. This reduces the number of transitions by allowing more than a single computation step per mode. Furthermore, each mode is allowed to have exactly one system of ordinary differential equations that represents how variables change over time. In Listing 1, we present an excerpt of a possible variation of the distance control as a hybrid mode automaton in our own domain-specific language [20].

```
1   automaton Distance              init Cruise
2     input variables:             mode Accel:
3       x, xₗ, D : ℝ                 controller:
4     output variables:               if(D<100.0) {a := C} else
5       a : ℝ                         {a := *; assume a ≤ A};
6                                   dynamics:
7     assumption:                     {x'=v, v'=a & v >= 0}
8       |x − xₗ| ≥ D                 transitions:
9     guarantee:                      to Cruise when |x − xₗ| = D;
10      |x − xₗ| ≥ D                  to Brake when |x − xₗ| < D;
11                                  mode Cruise: ...
```

Listing 1. Excerpt of a hybrid mode automaton for the distance control.

Besides transitions, each mode is comprised of a controller and dynamics part. The controller part lets a user define how variables may change (without elapsed time after entering the mode), while the dynamics part specifies the physical evolution of variables over time. Here, mode Accel assigns acceleration variable a the constant C if the distance to the leading vehicle is less than 100 m, and otherwise may assume any value for a that is less then the (constant) maximum acceleration A. Additionally, we allow to specify *assumptions* and *guarantees* of the complete automaton using first-order logical formulas (with real-valued arithmetic). Assumptions state the initial condition before executing the automaton, while guarantees state safety *invariants* that are not allowed to be violated during *any time* of the execution. Execution of such automata can be formally verified against the pair of assumptions and guarantees using a deductive calculus.

Step 2 and 3: Correct-by-Construction Architecture and Code Generation. After a maneuver represented by the hybrid mode automaton is modeled and verified, we use it to generate a component-based architecture amenable to runtime execution (e.g., for the purpose of simulation). As mentioned before, nondeterminstic assignments must be concretized manually during the implementation phase, which could potentially violate the safety guarantees. To propose a guideline for developers to implement nondeterminstic assignments in a correct-by-construction fashion, we employ the tool suite ARCHICORC [22]. At its core ARCHICORC [22] is a architecture modeling framework build on top of CORC [44]. CORC enables users to start with a specification (i.e., precondition and postcondition) and to develop correct-by-construction algorithms in an imperative language applying only sound refinement rules.

A hybrid mode automaton is translated to ArchiCorC's own domain-specific language consisting of required and provided interface definitions, as well as a textual representation for the atomic component that links provided methods to real implementations. In particular, a component resulting from a hybrid mode automaton provides an interface that includes (1) a *control method* representing a single execution of the automaton (i.e., mode switch and execution of the discrete program), (2) methods for nondeterminstic assignments that must be implemented by hand (ideally using CorC), and (3) a method for monitoring the current state. The following interfaces in ArchiCorC's interface language exemplify this translation for the automatic headway control.

```
archicorc_interface IHeadwayReq {          archicorc_interface IHeadwayProv {
  // Parameters                              // Output variables
  double D;                                  double a;
  // Input variables                         // State ID
  double x, xₗ;                              int state_id;
}
                                            //@ requires |x − xₗ| ≥ D;
                                            //@ ensures |x − xₗ| ≥ D;
                                            void ctrlStep(void);

                                            // Resolve nondet. assignment
                                            //@ requires |x − xₗ| > D ∧ D ≥ 100;
                                            //@ ensures |x − xₗ| > D ∧ D ≥ 100 ∧ a ≤ A;
                                            double a₁();

                                            // Monitoring
                                            bool monitorSatisfied(State prior);
                                          }
```

As illustrated above, key element of the provided interface is the `ctrlStep` method that advances the state each cycle. Automated code generated for the `ctrlStep` methods resembles the structure of the corresponding hybrid mode automaton. We translate the corresponding hybrid mode automaton to a *logical formula*, which is then used as postcondition, while using the hybrid mode automaton's assumption and environmental conditions as precondition. Finally, we add a method to the component for *monitoring* whether any control actions violate the original (and verified) controller model. Input argument `State` is a simple structure used as shorthand for the collection of input and output variables. We discuss the generation of monitor code in the next section in more detail.

Step 4: Simulation and Monitoring. Finally, the generated implementation is executed in a simulation environment to validate whether the verified maneuver is appropriate in practice. To rule our any defects besides an insufficient specification, it is important to ensure that the executable implementation adheres to the same correctness guarantees as the modeled and verified controller. For this, we apply runtime monitoring that reports on violations during runtime with respect to the modeled controller. On a higher level, execution of the hybrid mode automaton is split into executing the modes and transitioning between them. In general, this results in disjunctions of modes including information about when a mode can be executed (i.e., using the guards of incoming transitions per mode). Our automatic headway controller results in the disjunction

$$\Big((|x - xl| > D \wedge \mathsf{Accel}) \vee (|x - xl| = D \wedge \mathsf{Cruise}) \vee (|x - xl| < D \wedge \mathsf{Brake}) \Big).$$

3   Modeling and Verifying Maneuvers with Hybrid Mode Automata

In this section, we formalize *hybrid mode automata*, which are used for modeling, specifying, and verifying behaviors of cyber-physical systems. In Sect. 3.1, we present syntax and semantics of hybrid mode automata. In Sect. 3.2, we present how to translate hybrid mode automata to *differential dynamic logic* for proving their correctness against a specification.

3.1   Formalization of Hybrid Mode Automata

As presented in the previous section, we propose to model the behavior of cyber-physical systems by means of *hybrid mode automata*. We first give a definition of the syntax of hybrid mode automata and explain specific parts of it afterwards.

Definition 1 (Syntax of Hybrid Mode Automata ($\mathcal{HMA}$)). *A hybrid mode automaton $\mathcal{A}$ is a tuple $\langle Q, q^0, V^{\mathsf{in}}, V^{\mathsf{out}}, \mathsf{Trans}, \mathsf{Dyn}, \mathsf{Ctrl} \rangle$ where:*

- *Q is a finite set of modes,*
- *$q^0 \in Q$ is the initial mode,*
- *V^{in} and V^{out} are sets of input and output variables in $\mathbb{R}$, respectively. We require that $V^{\mathsf{in}} \cap V^{\mathsf{out}} = \emptyset$,*
- *$\mathsf{Trans} \subseteq Q \times G(V) \times Q$ is the set of transitions, which are labeled by a first-order logical formula G over the input and output variables. We use the notation $q \xrightarrow{g} q'$ for $(q, g, q') \in \mathsf{Trans}$,*
- *$\mathsf{Dyn} : Q \to \mathsf{ODE}$ maps a mode to a (possibly empty) system of ordinary differential equations,*
- *$\mathsf{Ctrl} : Q \to \mathsf{HMAL}_{\mathsf{disc}}$ maps a mode to the discrete control part.*

The two elements of hybrid mode automata that need further explanation are the maps Dyn and Ctrl. As described in Sect. 2, each mode is associated with a set of ordinary differential equations and a sequence of *discrete computation steps* (e.g., assigning a value to a specific variable). Semantically, the discrete computations are executed sequentially and instantaneously (i.e., without elapsed time) after a mode is entered. Afterwards, the differential system runs for indefinite amount of time and lets specific variables evolve accordingly. In particular, to model discrete computations and ODEs, we adopt a simplified version of the syntax and semantics of *hybrid programs* provided by Platzer [40].[1]

---

[1] Further information on the syntax and semantics of hybrid programs beyond our application in this work can be found in A. Platzer's textbook *Logical Foundations of Cyber-Physical Systems* [40].

We denote by ODE the set of differential systems, where an element $ode \in$ ODE has the following syntax:

$$ode \equiv x_1' = f_1(x_1), \ldots, x_n' = f_n(x_n) \& H. \qquad (1)$$

Here, $x_1, \ldots, x_n$ are variables that change over time by equations $f_1, \ldots, f_n$, and H is an *evolution constraint* in first-order logic that restricts the maximum evolution of these variables. For example, the ODE $\left[v' = -2 \& v \geq 0\right]$ decrements variable v by 2 over an arbitrary amount of time but only as long as v remains non-negative.

The language we use for implementing discrete computations in modes will be denoted HMAL (for *Hybrid Mode Automata Language*) and is a subset of hybrid programs (excluding nondeterministic repetitions and nondeterministic choice). We provide the following syntax for HMAL.

Definition 2 (Syntax of HMAL). *The syntax of language HMAL is defined by the following grammar, where S_1 and S_2 are programs of HMAL, $x, x_1, \ldots, x_n$ are real-valued variables, θ is a term, $P, Q,$ and H are first-order logical formulas in real arithmetic, and $x' = f(x)$ is a system of ODEs:*

$$S_1, S_2 ::= S_1; S_2 \mid x := \theta \mid \textsf{havoc } x_1, \ldots, x_n \mid \textsf{assume } H \mid \textsf{skip}$$
$$\mid \textsf{if}(H)\{S_1\}\textsf{else}\{S_2\} \mid \textsf{assert } H$$

Language HMAL consists of seven constructs. *Sequential composition* first runs the program defined by S_1 and then the program defined by S_2. *Discrete assignment* assigns a value of term Θ to variable x. *Nondeterministic assignment* represented by the keyword **havoc** $(\cdot)$ assigns arbitrary real numbers to variables $x_1, \ldots, x_n$. These assignments must be concretized when deriving an executable implementation. **assume** H is used to check that a particular formula holds at the respective position. **skip** is shorthand for **assume** true. The selection statement **if**(H) $\{S_1\}$ **else** $\{S_2\}$ runs program S_1 if condition H holds, and runs program S_2 otherwise. Finally, an *assertion* is similar to an assumption, where the checkable condition H valuates to either true or false depending on the current state. A violation of H will not just abort the current run, but the program will transition to a designated *error state*, which itself does not have outgoing transitions. This way, we mark violations of H explicitly as erroneous behavior.

After presenting the syntax of both HMAL and ODEs, we present their semantics next. Execution semantics of HMAL and ODEs are each based on the transitioning between *states*. In particular, Let $\mathbb{R}$ represent the set of real numbers and let V denote the set of real-valued variables. A state is a function σ from V to $\mathbb{R}$, i.e., $\sigma : V \to \mathbb{R}$.

Definition 3 (Semantics of HMAL and ODEs). *Let V be a finite set of real-valued variables and let Σ be the set of all possible states. The semantics of a program $S \in$ HMAL leads to the following denotational definition of the transition relation $[\![S]\!]_{\mathsf{HMAL}}, [\![S]\!]_{\mathsf{ODE}} \subseteq \Sigma \times \Sigma$, where $\sigma, \sigma' \in \Sigma$ represent the initial and final state, respectively, and σ^{error} is the error state:*

- $[S\,;\,S']_{\mathsf{HMAL}} = \{(\sigma,\sigma')\,|\,(\sigma,\sigma_{im}) \in [S]_{\mathsf{HMAL}}, (\sigma_{im},\sigma') \in [S']_{\mathsf{HMAL}}\}$ *with intermediate state* σ_{im},
- $(\sigma,\sigma') \in [x := \Theta]_{\mathsf{HMAL}}$ *iff* $\sigma'(x) = \mathtt{eval}(\Theta,\sigma)$ *and* $\forall y \in V$ *with* $x \neq y$ *it follows that* $\sigma(x) = \sigma'(y)$,
- $(\sigma,\sigma') \in [\mathbf{havoc}\ x_1,\ldots,x_n]_{\mathsf{HMAL}}$ *iff* $\forall x \in \{x_1,\ldots,x_n\}$, $\forall y \in V$ *with* $x \neq y$ *it follows that* $\sigma(y) = \sigma'(y)$,
- $(\sigma,\sigma') \in [\mathbf{assume}\ H]_{\mathsf{HMAL}}$ *iff* $\sigma = \sigma'$ *and the assignment of variables in state* σ *satisfies formula* H *(i.e.,* $\sigma \models H$*)*,
- $(\sigma,\sigma') \in [\mathbf{if}(H)\{S_1\}\mathbf{else}\{S_2\}]_{\mathsf{HMAL}}$ *iff* $(\sigma,\sigma') \in [\mathbf{assume}\ H;S_1]_{\mathsf{HMAL}} \cup [\mathbf{assume}\ \neg H;S_2]_{\mathsf{HMAL}}$,
- $\Big[(\sigma,\sigma^{\mathsf{error}}) \in [\mathbf{assert}\ H]_{\mathsf{HMAL}}$ *iff* $(\sigma,\sigma) \in [\mathbf{assume}\ \neg H]_{\mathsf{HMAL}}\Big]$ *and* $\Big[(\sigma,\sigma') \in [\mathbf{assert}\ H]_{\mathsf{HMAL}}$ *iff* $(\sigma,\sigma') \in [\mathbf{assume}\ H]_{\mathsf{HMAL}}\Big]$,
- *For ODEs:* $(\sigma,\sigma') \in [x' = f(x)\ \&\ H]_{\mathsf{ODE}}$ *iff* $\gamma : [0,r] \to \Sigma$ *is a solution of the ODE* $x' = f(x)$ *with* $\gamma(0) = \sigma$, $\gamma(r) = \sigma'$, *and each state in between* $\gamma(0)$ *and* $\gamma(r)$ *satisfies formula* H *with respect to differential equation* $x' = f(x)$ *(i.e.,* $\gamma \models x' = f(x)\ \&\ H$*)*.

Both constructs, language HMAL and the definition of ODEs, are inspired by the syntax and semantics of hybrid programs [37–40]. The language of hybrid programs itself is only a simple nondeterministic programming language with support for differential equations. The reason to closely follow hybrid programs is twofold. First, hybrid programs provide a very simple programming model, which is expressively sufficient for us to describe the intended controller logic at this design stage. However, hybrid programs additionally provide means for nondeterministic repetition and nondeterministic choice, which we eliminated. The reason for the former is that a mode only performs one execution per time step before it transitions, which makes repetition unnecessary. The reason for the latter is that nondeterministic choice needs to be resolved when deriving a concrete implementation. We restrict language HMAL to nondeterministic assignment only, which is simpler to resolve. The second reason is that we aim at leveraging $d\mathcal{L}$ [37–40] for verifying hybrid mode automata. As $d\mathcal{L}$ is defined over hybrid programs, it is natural to only make some necessary modifications. Finally, we can give a definition of the execution semantics of hybrid mode automata.

Definition 4 (Execution Semantics of Hybrid Mode Automata). *Let* σ_i^{in} *and* σ_i^{out} *denote valuations of variables in* V. *A valid run of a hybrid mode automaton* $\mathcal{A} = \langle Q, q^0, V^{\mathsf{in}}, V^{\mathsf{out}}, \mathsf{Trans}, \mathsf{Dyn}, \mathsf{Ctrl}\rangle$ *is a sequence of mode switches* $l_0,\ldots,l_k \in Q$ *of the form* $\mathrm{run}_{\mathcal{A}} = \langle \sigma_0^{\mathsf{in}}, l_0, \sigma_0^{\mathsf{out}}\rangle,\ldots,\langle \sigma_n^{\mathsf{in}}, l_n, \sigma_n^{\mathsf{out}}\rangle$ *such that*

- σ_i^{in} *and* σ_i^{out} *are input and output valuations of variables in* V *in mode* l_i,
- *for all* $k = 0,\ldots n$,

$$(\sigma_k^{\mathsf{in}}, \sigma_k^{\mathsf{out}}) \in \{(\sigma^{\mathsf{in}}, \sigma^{\mathsf{out}})\,|\,(\sigma^{\mathsf{in}}, \sigma^{\mathsf{im}}) \in [\mathsf{Ctrl}(l_k)]_{\mathsf{HMAL}}, (\sigma^{\mathsf{im}}, \sigma^{\mathsf{out}}) \in [\mathsf{Dyn}(l_k)]_{\mathsf{ODE}}\},$$

- the initial execution is performed after taking the first transition from initial mode q^0, such that $\langle q^0, G, l_0 \rangle \in$ Trans and $\sigma_0^{in} \models G$,
- for each $i = 0, \ldots, n - 1$, $\langle \sigma_i^{in}, l_i, \sigma_i^{out} \rangle$ is followed by $\langle \sigma_{i+1}^{in}, l_{i+1}, \sigma_{i+1}^{out} \rangle$ if and only if there exists a transition $(l_i, G, l_{i+1}) \in$ Trans and $\sigma_{i+1}^{in} \models G$.

Execution of a hybrid mode automaton begins with taking a transition from the initial mode, and afterwards sequentially running the currently active mode's discrete program and ODEs. We assume that guards of outgoing transitions of a mode do not overlap. If no applicable outgoing transition exists, we assume a self-transition. Assuming a logical clock, this ensures that each cycle the discrete program of the currently active mode is executed, and that the dynamical systems evolves over time. That is, the execution semantics of a hybrid mode automaton resembles a trace semantics.

3.2   Verification Based on Differential Dynamic Logic

Differential dynamic logic $(d\mathcal{L})$ [37–40] is a *first-order modal logic* for specifying and proving safety properties of hybrid programs. That is, formulas in $d\mathcal{L}$ that do not contain modalities are classical first-order logical formulas with real arithmetic. Additionally, the modal operators $[\alpha]$ and $\langle\alpha\rangle$ for a hybrid program α express special reachability properties. Essentially, $d\mathcal{L}$ formula $[\alpha]\phi$ is *true* iff ϕ is true for all reachable states of α (i.e., upon complete execution of α), and $d\mathcal{L}$ formula $\langle\alpha\rangle\phi$ is *true* iff ϕ is true in some reachable state of α.

As language HMAL is defined with the semantics of hybrid programs in mind, we prove the correctness of hybrid mode automata for a given specification by translating them to $d\mathcal{L}$. For this, we define the translation function $\text{trans}_{\mathcal{HMA}}$ that relates hybrid mode automata and hybrid programs. As depicted in Listing 1, a user defines valid assumptions Φ (i.e., precondition) and guarantees Ψ (i.e., postcondition) of the respective behavior in first-order logic with real-valued arithmetic. Assumptions must hold prior to executing the hybrid mode automaton, whereas guarantees are invariants that must hold at every real point in time during the continuous dynamics. The safety requirement in $d\mathcal{L}$ is then expressed as

$$\Phi \;\rightarrow\; [\text{trans}_{\mathcal{HMA}}]\Psi \tag{2}$$

For example, the automatic distance control assumes initially that the difference in positions of host and leading vehicle is greater than the minimal allowed distance. Only then can it guarantee that the difference in positions will remain greater throughout the execution.

To prove the validity of $d\mathcal{L}$ formulas deductively, a sound set of axioms and proof rules (i.e., a deductive calculus) is required. The KEYMAERA X theorem prover [13] implements such a calculus for $d\mathcal{L}$ and is built on top of a *small trusted kernel* written in SCALA to also increase trust in the tool support itself. In Fig. 3, we give a schematic overview of the modeling and verification procedure. For brevity, we omit the definition of $\text{trans}_{\mathcal{HMA}}$ that translates hybrid mode

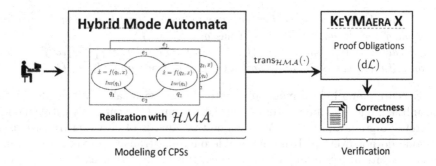

Fig. 3. Schematic overview of the verification process.

automata to $d\mathcal{L}$, as it is only of technical nature and can be found in previous work [20]. After we proved validity of a hybrid mode automaton with respect to the pair of assumptions and guarantees, the next goal is to derive a correct-by-construction implementation amenable to runtime verification. This way, we may rule out the introduction of new implementation defects and can focus on validating completeness of the specified safety guarantees.

4   Runtime Verification of $\mathcal{HMA}$ Models

In this section, how monitor conditions of the controller model are generated to validate whether the implementation behaves as intended.

4.1   Generating Monitor Conditions for Runtime Verification

In the previous sections, we described how to derive an implementation from an $\mathcal{HMA}$ model. Although models and abstraction are necessary to reduce complexity (e.g., for asserting correctness), any model has the tendency to deviate from the real world. It is therefore important to monitor at runtime that the properties proven with respect to the model are also ensured during execution. For instance, if at some point compliance of model and implementation cannot be guaranteed anymore, it is important to initiate fallback options that may still hinder catastrophic behavior (e.g., emergency braking).

To be able to assess whether our controller behaves as intended, we additionally generate executable monitor code for the controller in a dedicated method with signature **bool** `monitorSatisfied(State prior)`. Eventually, the monitor code can be used throughout runtime to report condition violations of the controller (i.e., deviations of controller model and implementation) that would otherwise be unnoticed. In particular, the generated code compares the current state of the controller with the previous state, which we explicitly provide as argument (the current state is obtained from the atomic component itself). If

$$\mathsf{trans_{mon}}(\mathsf{Ctrl}(q)) \doteq \mathsf{trans_{mon}}(S) \wedge V = V^{\mathsf{post}} \qquad with\,\mathsf{Ctrl}(q) \equiv S$$

$$\mathsf{trans_{mon}}(S_1; S_1) \doteq \mathsf{trans_{mon}}(S_1) \wedge \mathsf{trans_{mon}}(S_1)$$

$$\mathsf{trans_{mon}}(x := \theta) \doteq x^{\mathsf{post}} = \theta$$

$$\mathsf{trans_{mon}}(\mathbf{havoc}\ x_1, \ldots, x_n) \doteq \mathsf{true}$$

$$\mathsf{trans_{mon}}(\mathbf{assume}\ H) \doteq H[x \mapsto x^{\mathsf{post}}]$$

$$\mathsf{trans_{mon}}(\mathbf{assert}\ H) \doteq H[x \mapsto x^{\mathsf{post}}]$$

$$\mathsf{trans_{mon}}(\mathbf{skip}H) \doteq \mathsf{true}$$

$$\mathsf{trans_{mon}}(\mathbf{if}(H)\{S_1\}\mathbf{else}\{S_2\}) \doteq \Big(H[x \mapsto x^{\mathsf{post}}] \wedge \mathsf{trans_{mon}}(S_1)\Big)$$
$$\vee \Big(\neg H[x \mapsto x^{\mathsf{post}}] \wedge \mathsf{trans_{mon}}(S_2)\Big)$$

Fig. 4. Translation of a mode to a logical formula for the monitoring condition.

the current state is not a valid poststate of the given prestate according to our modeled controller, the monitor is not satisfied. This is guaranteed by using MODELPLEX [32] in our process that, given a $d\mathcal{L}$ model, generates monitor code for the controller model automatically.

In particular, the monitor conditions we generate are formulas that relate the current and next state with respect to the $\mathcal{HMA}$ model. That is, a monitor condition $\mathsf{mon}(v^{\mathsf{curr}}, v^{\mathsf{post}})$ compares the previous state comprised of variables v^{curr} with the next state comprised of variables v^{post}, and valuates to false whenever the program statements of the $\mathcal{HMA}$ model lead to a different model state than observed in the current state at runtime. In Fig. 4, we depict the rules for translating the program statements of a mode of a hybrid mode automaton to the logical counterpart for the monitoring condition. That is, if a particular mode is executed on the implementation level, the monitor condition for the respective controller program of the $\mathcal{HMA}$ model is based on this translation scheme. Importantly, variables that do not change by the modeled controller must evaluate to the same value in the current and next state. We represent this by the set of unmodified variables V in the beginning of the translation, which we explicitly add to the monitor condition.

4.2 Simulation

Simulation is an integral part of our verification and validation pipeline. There exist numerous simulation environments to choose from, which all come with advantages and drawbacks. Most popular in the research community, GAZEBO [23] is a simulation platform that offers a modular design that allows developers to integrate different physics engines and to create complex robotic systems with arbitrary sensor models and simple 3D worlds. Furthermore, GAZEBO maintains a close relationship with the robot operating system

(ROS) [24,42], one of the most prominent open-source frameworks for personal and industrial robotic systems. Therefore, GAZEBO is typically used for simulating systems based on ROS modules. Although GAZEBO comes with numerous features to increase realism in simulations, its rendering engine cannot compete with engines such as the Unreal engine or Unity, which makes it difficult to create visually-rich environments close to real-world scenarios.

To focus on visually-rich environments, AIRSIM [47] is a recent platform based on the Unreal engine that focuses primarily on automotive vehicles and flying drones. Most appealing, AirSim comes with pre-existing physical models of automotive vehicles and numerous 3D worlds (e.g., urban neighborhood or city), which saves development time and reduces the risk of introducing insufficient physical behavior. Especially, using independently-developed models and simulation environments is necessary in our evaluation to not invalidate empirical results.

In our validation and verification pipeline, we currently integrate both simulation platforms mentioned before. We primarily use GAZEBO/ROS for robotic systems, and AirSim for automotive vehicles, such as applied in our evaluation for various driving maneuvers. Moreover, the modularity of our tool suite allows to extend the current set of simulation environments and to add new ones in a plug-and-play fashion.

5   Evaluation

The above sections raised two important research questions that we try to investigate by an empirical experiment and a qualitative assessment:

RQ-1: *To what degree do safety guarantees that are verified at design time hold at execution level?*

RQ-2: *What are lessons learned drawn from our experiences following the proposed verification and validation pipeline?*

With **RQ-1**, we investigate the *feasibility* of our verification and validation pipeline. In particular, we evaluate whether safety guarantees can be transferred from the verification model to the execution model following the guidelines of ARCHICORC and inspecting the generated monitor objects. Finally, with **RQ-2**, we discuss our experiences with the proposed verification and validation process.

We characterize our non-trivial case study of a road vehicle and the evaluated subject maneuvers in Sect. 5.1. In Sect. 5.2, we present results and discuss the research questions.

5.1   Case Studies and Setup

We aim at evaluating our pipeline in the context of automated driving maneuvers. In particular, we employ AirSim [47] as simulation environment to validate to what extent correctness guarantees of verified $\mathcal{HMA}$ models can be transferred to implementation level. For automatic driving, the final goal is indeed to develop such $\mathcal{HMA}$ models for each maneuver from a catalog of basic driving maneuvers that can be safely applied in road traffic. The purpose of this evaluation, however, is a *proof of concept* of our verification and validation pipeline.

In total, we created five maneuvers including validation scenarios in AirSim to demonstrate the applicability of our verification and validation pipeline. All studied maneuvers are modeled as hybrid mode automata, verified, and eventually implemented in C++ supported by ARCHICORC. As ARCHICORC is limited with respect to floating-point reasoning, parts of the implementation remain unverified. However, such parts are already in a form that allows to verify them when reasoning with floating-point arithmetic becomes available. A short description of the maneuvers and their safety requirements is given in the following.

Explore World (Vehicle version). The goal of this maneuver is to randomly explore an area without colliding with any object. Due to the vehicle's kinematics, the turning circle must be considered explicitly. Safety goals are (1) respecting a maximum velocity ($v \leq v_{max}$), and (2) avoiding collision.

Safe Halt. The goal of this maneuver is to drive forward in a straight line and come to a halt if needed (i.e., either in front of an obstacle or a particular point) without collision or overstepping. Safety goals are again (1) respecting a maximum velocity ($v \leq v_{max}$), and (2) avoid collision.

Lane Keeping Assistance. This maneuver captures the lateral aspects of following a lane without deviating too far from the lane's center point. For this, the vehicle must drive on a lane with perceivable solid lane markings. Safety goal is to respect a maximum lane deviation ($y \leq y_{max}$).

Adaptive Cruise Control (Unoptimized and Optimized). This maneuver captures the longitudinal aspects of following a car while keeping a safe distance. We further split the *adaptive cruise control* maneuver into two versions, an optimized version and an unoptimized version. The optimized version resembles a more sophisticated controller on the modeled level without nondeterministic assignments, whereas the unoptimized version is simpler and delegates concretization of the acceleration part to the implementation level. Safety goal is to avoid collision with the leading vehicle.

As our evaluation aims at investigating whether our concept is feasible, we only built simple scenarios to test each driving maneuver in isolation. For the *Explore World* maneuver, we created a closed world with numerous static obstacles. For the *Safe Halt* maneuver, we used the same world, but placed the vehicle in front of an obstacle in a straight line. For the lane keeping assistance, we modeled a street and encoded the ground truth of the lane markings to eliminate sensor uncertainty. For the adaptive cruise control, we added a second leading vehicle in front of our vehicle that drives in a straight line.

Table 1. Simulation results.

Maneuver	Safety goal	Fail statistics				
		Non.-Det.	Passable	Severe	Failure rate (∅)	Sim. time
Explore world	$v \leq v_{max}$; no collision	Yes	100%	0%	1.07%	5 m
Safe halt	$v \leq v_{max}$; no collision	no	100%	0%	3.03%	ca. 6–12 s.
LKA	Lane deviation ($y \leq y_{max}$)	Yes	100%	0%	1.63%	30 s
ACC (Unoptimized)	No collision	Yes	100%	0%	2.72%	30 s
ACC (Optimized)	No collision	No	100%	0%	2.36%	30 s

5.2   Results and Insights

In the following, we share results obtained with our case studies. In particular, we are interested in usefulness and feasibility of our proposed approach. First, we investigate whether safety guarantees from verified $\mathcal{HMA}$ models can be transferred to the implementation level. Second, we discuss our experiences. The concrete models are contained as examples in the tool suite SKEDITOR [21], which integrates this work as part of its maneuver-centric development approach for cyber-physical systems.[2]

RQ-1: Validation and Safety Violations

In the following, we investigate the feasibility of our approach by simulating simulating each case study in AirSim and validating their correctness by employing the generated monitors. As mentioned before, each maneuver (i.e., $\mathcal{HMA}$ model) was successfully verified, which leads to the question whether correctness guarantees transfer to the implementation level. In Table 1, we summarize results from the performed experiments. In particular, for the fail statistics, we report three values. First, column *passable* reports on the percentage of monitor violations that we consider as acceptable. These stem from violations of nondeterministic assignments or other issues in the initial state, but do not violate the safety invariants. Second, column *severe* reports on the percentage of violations of the safety invariants. Finally, *failure rate* is the time spent in monitor-violating states with respect to the simulation time.

We observe that none of the five maneuvers violated any of the safety invariants during their simulation, which is why all reported violations are considered as *passable*. Furthermore, the failure rates are all low. However, we identified that oftentimes the initial state (i.e., a halted state with zero velocity for all five case studies) violates the monitor condition for the control part, while during movement the failure rate converges towards zero. Other times, the failure rate increases for a short amount of time. We assume that the conversion of arithmetic reals to floating-point precision results in sporadic problems.

---

[2] https://github.com/AlexanderKnueppel/Skeditor.

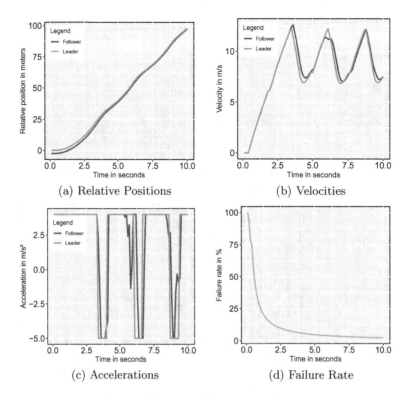

(a) Relative Positions

(b) Velocities

(c) Accelerations

(d) Failure Rate

Fig. 5. Measurements for the *Adaptive Cruise Control* case study with the leading vehicle keeping a velocity between 8 and 12 m/s.

RQ-2: Experiences

In the following, we discuss experiences following the proposed development and simulation process using the *Optimized Adaptive Cruise Control* and *Safe Halt* case studies as two representative examples. In Fig. 5, we depict the position, velocity, acceleration, and failure rate over time of the *Optimized Adaptive Cruise Control* case study. The leading vehicle alternates between accelerating and braking as shown by the acceleration (lower left), and aims at keeping the velocity between 8 m/s and 12 m/s (upper right). The position (upper left) of the ego car shows that it tightly follows the leading car, but always keeps a minimal distance that is considered safe. The failure rate (lower right) shows the aforementioned issue, where the initial state violates the monitor condition due to imprecision, but afterwards the monitor condition is not violated anymore.

In contrast to the optimized version, the unoptimized version is simpler and provides nondeterminstic assignments for braking and acceleration. Moreover, the implementation switches accelerations only between the maximum braking force B and maximum acceleration force A. Although safety invariants still held at execution, we considered this behavior to be less convenient for human drivers.

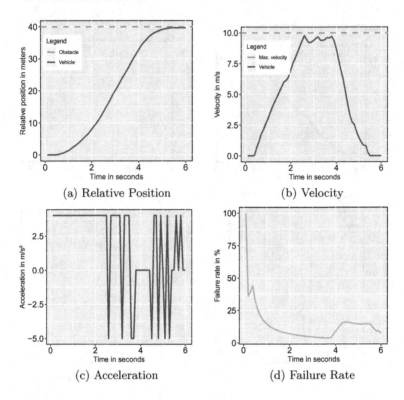

(a) Relative Position   (b) Velocity

(c) Acceleration   (d) Failure Rate

Fig. 6. Measurements for the *Safe Halt* case study with a maximum velocity of 10 m/s.

We realized that optimizing this behavior is best addressed in the modeling phase, as we decided to add additional modes for more fine-grained control.

In this specific case, we considered that resolving nondeterministic choice at implementation level to realize the same optimization would be significantly more difficult for two reasons. First, modes and their implementation in HMAL provide a *local* view on the parameters involved (e.g., velocity), whereas the implementation is much more detailed and scattered. The unoptimized version sets the acceleration to a fixed constant. The optimized version, however, views the acceleration as a function depending on variables and parameters, such as velocity, distance to leading vehicle, and worst-case execution time. Considering optimality of such functions increases effort during the implementation phase. Second, verifying correctness of such optimization is also more promising in the modeling, as numerical optimization is best addressed with differential dynamic logic.

The second example illustrating the *safe halt* case study is shown in Fig. 6. The vehicle must keep a maximum velocity of 10 m/s and starts 40 m in front of an obstacle. Similar to the unoptimized adaptive cruise control case study, the vehicle only switches accelerations between the maximum braking force B and maximum acceleration force A (upper left). The failure rate (lower right) shows an increase in monitor violations after four seconds. Although we did not exactly locate the cause for this issue, as both safety guarantees were not violated, we assume that sensor uncertainties may play a role.

While failure rates should not be dismissed, the above experiments increase our confidence in the proposed link from verified $\mathcal{HMA}$ models to actual implementations. All evaluated maneuvers transferred their safety guarantees to the simulation. Although the first two case studies required more implementation effort (e.g., due to interfacing with AirSim and processing sensor data), the automatic code generation and reuse of existing implementations allowed us to implement the final three case studies considerably faster. Moreover, three of the five maneuvers used non-deterministic assignments in their hybrid mode automata, which had to be resolved manually by us following the correctness-by-construction approach. This ensured that no new defects were introduced and that violations of monitor conditions can, in principle, always be traced back to an incomplete specification. We therefore believe that our verification and validation pipeline is particularly valuable for virtual prototyping of maneuvers and experimenting with their set of requirements.

6 Related Work

To enable the correctness-by-construction approach in our tool chain, we integrated CORC [44] into ARCHICORC. The reason for this decision are manifold. First, the feature set and future plans of CORC are sufficient for the purpose of ARCHICORC. In particular, both tools target object-oriented languages and the small kernel of CORC's theoretical foundation increases trust in its correctness. Second, CORC and ARCHICORC are based on the same technology stack, namely the *Eclipse Modeling Framework*. This leads to easier maintenance of the bridge between both tool suits and provides better user experience, as ARCHICORC artifacts and CORC programs can all be part of the same module. Third, CORC is well-maintained and actively developed, whereas most other frameworks in the field of stepwise program construction are not maintained anymore and also never reached a level of maturity, which we would consider sufficient enough for proper integration into ARCHICORC.

In spite of its young age, CORC was already extended in several directions. First, Runge et al. [43] extended CORC with a notion of information flow control-by-construction. Instead of checking confidentiality of data post-hoc by static information-flow analyses, information flow control-by-construction defines refinement rules for constructing secure programs. Second, Bordis et al. [6] introduced VARCORC, which is an offspring of CORC that focuses on correctness-by-construction for software product lines, instead of only considering monolithic programs. Finally, ARCHICORC, as presented in this chapter, lifts CORC to an architectural level by bundling correct-by-construction implementations in software components and providing means for code generation.

In the literature, many languages, techniques, frameworks, and tools exist to formally and semi-formally address the diverse set of challenges of industrial cyber-physical systems development. These challenges include large system sizes, heterogeneity of connected modules, stakeholders from a multitude of disciplines, requirements elicitation, and also software evolution and maintenance themselves. Popular modeling languages include AADL [10,26,31,48,49], MODELICA [9,14], ALLOY [17,19], UML [4,11,18,27], and its variants SysML [12,35,36] and MARTE [5,46]. While all these languages greatly contributed to the research of system's design and analysis, their purpose is (1) to provide rich modeling facilities for almost all parts of a cyber-physical system, and (2) to eventually use these models as basis for real production code. Both goals make these languages inherently complex. For instance, AADL is used to model both hardware and software architectures of real-time embedded systems in great detail. In contrast, we aim to thrive for simplicity and focus on the functional modeling of maneuvers only to scale and leverage formal verification.

7 Conclusion

We presented a verification and validation pipeline for cyber-physical systems, where we explained how verified abstract maneuvers represented by hybrid mode automata can be refined in a correct-by-construction fashion to a component-based architecture amenable to simulation and runtime verification. In particular, we employed ARCHICORC, which (1) allows to manually resolve nondeterministic assignments relying on the correctness-by-construction approach for programs and (2) automatically generates code in a general-purpose programming language that can be considered correct-by-construction as well. To validate the executable maneuver at run-time, we added functionality for automatically generating monitor conditions based on the corresponding hybrid mode automaton. As the verified model is highly abstract, monitoring ensures that the safety obligations can be checked during runtime in case of hardware issues or environmental uncertainties.

We simulated the derived controller implementations in AirSim to inspect the appropriateness of the abstract model of a maneuver. The pursued and accomplished goal is that the link from a formal $\mathcal{HMA}$ model to execution is achievable in practice for non-trivial maneuvers. We have evaluated that all five case studies indeed transferred their correctness guarantees to the execution stage.

References

1. Alur, R.: Formal verification of hybrid systems. In: Proceedings of the International Conference on Embedded Software and Systems, pp. 273–278 (2011)
2. Alur, R., et al.: The algorithmic analysis of hybrid systems. Theoret. Comput. Sci. **138**(1), 3–34 (1995)
3. Angermann, A., Beuschel, M., Rau, M., Wohlfarth, U.: Matlab-simulink-stateflow. De Gruyter Oldenbourg (2020)

4. Bernardi, S., Gentile, U., Marrone, S., Merseguer, J., Nardone, R.: Security modelling and formal verification of survivability properties: application to cyber-physical systems. J. Syst. Softw. **171**, 110746 (2021)
5. Bernardi, S., Merseguer, J.: A UML profile for dependability analysis of real-time embedded systems. In: Proceedings of the International Workshop on Software and Performance (WOSP), pp. 115–124 (2007)
6. Bordis, T., Runge, T., Knüppel, A., Thüm, T., Schaefer, I.: Variational correctness-by-construction. In: Cordy, M., Acher, M., Beuche, D., Saake, G. (eds.) Proceedings of the International Working Conference on Variability Modelling of Software-Intensive Systems (VAMOS), pp. 7:1–7:9. ACM (2020). https://doi.org/10.1145/3377024.3377038
7. Branicky, M.S.: Introduction to hybrid systems. In: Hristu-Varsakelis, D., Levine, W.S. (eds.) Handbook of Networked and Embedded Control Systems. Control Engineering, pp. 91–116. Birkhäuser, Boston (2005). https://doi.org/10.1007/0-8176-4404-0_5
8. Buzdalov, D., Khoroshilov, A.: A discrete-event simulator for early validation of avionics systems. In: Proceedings of the Workshop on Architecture Centric Virtual Integration (ACVIP), p. 28 (2014)
9. Elmqvist, H., Mattsson, S.E., Otter, M.: Object-oriented and hybrid modeling in modelica. J. Eur. des systèmes automatisés **35**(4), 395–404 (2001)
10. Feiler, P.H., Gluch, D.P.: Model-Based Engineering with AADL: An Introduction to the SAE Architecture Analysis & Design Language. Addison-Wesley, Boston (2012)
11. France, R., Evans, A., Lano, K., Rumpe, B.: The UML as a formal modeling notation. Comput. Stand. Interfaces **19**(7), 325–334 (1998)
12. Friedenthal, S., Moore, A., Steiner, R.: A Practical Guide to SysML: the Systems Modeling Language. Morgan Kaufmann, San Francisco (2014)
13. Fulton, N., Mitsch, S., Quesel, J.-D., Völp, M., Platzer, A.: KeYmaera X: an axiomatic tactical theorem prover for hybrid systems. In: Felty, A.P., Middeldorp, A. (eds.) CADE 2015. LNCS (LNAI), vol. 9195, pp. 527–538. Springer, Cham (2015). https://doi.org/10.1007/978-3-319-21401-6_36
14. Gómez, F.J., Aguilera, M.A., Olsen, S.H., Vanfretti, L.: Software requirements for interoperable and standard-based power system modeling tools. Simul. Model. Pract. Theory **103**, 102095 (2020)
15. Goswami, D., et al.: Challenges in automotive cyber-physical systems design, pp. 346–354 (2012). https://doi.org/10.1109/SAMOS.2012.6404199
16. Henzinger, T.A.: The theory of hybrid automata. In: Inan, M.K., Kurshan, R.P. (eds) Verification of Digital and Hybrid Systems. NATO ASI Series, vol. 170, pp. 265–292. Springer, Berlin, Heidelberg (2000). https://doi.org/10.1007/978-3-642-59615-5_13
17. Jackson, D.: Alloy: a lightweight object modelling notation. ACM Trans. Softw. Eng. Methodol. (TOSEM) **11**(2), 256–290 (2002)
18. Jue, W., Song, Y., Wu, X., Dai, W.: A semi-formal requirement modeling pattern for designing industrial cyber-physical systems. In: Proceedings of the Annual Conference of the IEEE Industrial Electronics Society (IES), vol. 1, pp. 2883–2888. IEEE (2019)
19. Kang, E., Adepu, S., Jackson, D., Mathur, A.P.: Model-based security analysis of a water treatment system. In: Proceedings of the International Workshop on Software Engineering for Smart Cyber-Physical Systems (SEsCPS), pp. 22–28. IEEE (2016)

20. Kittelmann, A.: Maneuver-centric formal engineering approach for cyber-physical systemsA. Ph.D. thesis, Braunschweig, Technische Universität Carolo-Wilhelmina zu Braunschweig (2022). https://doi.org/10.24355/dbbs.084-202204121019-0
21. Knüppel, A., Jatzkowski, I., Nolte, M., Thüm, T., Runge, T., Schaefer, I.: Skill-based verification of cyber-physical systems. In: FASE 2020. LNCS, vol. 12076, pp. 203–223. Springer, Cham (2020). https://doi.org/10.1007/978-3-030-45234-6_10
22. Knüppel, A., Runge, T., Schaefer, I.: Scaling correctness-by-construction. In: Margaria, T., Steffen, B. (eds.) ISoLA 2020. LNCS, vol. 12476, pp. 187–207. Springer, Cham (2020). https://doi.org/10.1007/978-3-030-61362-4_10
23. Koenig, N., Howard, A.: Design and use paradigms for gazebo, an open-source multi-robot simulator. In: Proceedings of the International Conference on Intelligent Robots and Systems (IROS), vol. 3, pp. 2149–2154. IEEE (2004)
24. Koubaa, A.: Robot Operating System (ROS). The Complete Reference (Volume 1) SCI, vol. 625. Springer, Cham (2016). https://doi.org/10.1007/978-3-319-26054-9
25. Lee, I., et al.: Challenges and research directions in medical cyber-physical systems. Proc. IEEE **100**(1), 75–90 (2012). https://doi.org/10.1109/JPROC.2011.2165270
26. Lin, Q., Adepu, S., Verwer, S., Mathur, A.: Tabor: a graphical model-based approach for anomaly detection in industrial control systems. In: Proceedings of the Asia Conference on Computer and Communications Security (ASIACCS), pp. 525–536 (2018)
27. Mancini, T., et al.: Parallel statistical model checking for safety verification in smart grids. In: Proceedings of the International Conference on Communications, Control, and Computing Technologies for Smart Grids (SmartGridComm), pp. 1–6. IEEE (2018)
28. Maraninchi, F., Rémond, Y.: Mode-automata: about modes and states for reactive systems. In: Hankin, C. (ed.) ESOP 1998. LNCS, vol. 1381, pp. 185–199. Springer, Heidelberg (1998). https://doi.org/10.1007/BFb0053571
29. Maraninchi, F., Rémond,.Y.: Mode-automata: a new domain-specific construct for the development of safe critical systems. Sci. Comput. Program. **46**(3), 219–254 (2003)
30. Michniewicz, J., Reinhart, G.: Cyber-physical robotics - automated analysis, programming and configuration of robot cells based on cyber-physical-systems. Proc. Technol. **15**, 566–575 (2014). https://doi.org/10.1016/j.protcy.2014.09.017
31. Misson, H.A., Gonçalves, F.S., Becker, L.B.: Applying integrated formal methods on cps design. In: Proceedings of the Brazilian Symposium on Computing Systems Engineering (SBESC), pp. 1–8. IEEE (2019)
32. Mitsch, S., Platzer, A.: Modelplex: verified runtime validation of verified cyber-physical system models. Formal Methods Syst. Des. **49**(1), 33–74 (2016)
33. Müller, A., Mitsch, S., Retschitzegger, W., Schwinger, W.: Towards cps verification engineering. In: Proceedings of the International Conference on Information Integration and Web-Based Applications & Services, pp. 367–371. iiWAS 2020, Association for Computing Machinery, New York, NY, USA (2020). https://doi.org/10.1145/3428757.3429146
34. Müller, A., Mitsch, S., Schwinger, W., Platzer, A.: A component-based hybrid systems verification and implementation tool in Keymaera x (tool demonstration). In: Chamberlain, R., Taha, W., Törngren, M. (eds.) CyPhy/WESE -2018. LNCS, vol. 11615, pp. 91–110. Springer, Cham (2019). https://doi.org/10.1007/978-3-030-23703-5_5
35. Neghina, M., Zamfirescu, C.-B., Pierce, K.: Early-stage analysis of cyber-physical production systems through collaborative modelling. Softw. Syst. Model. **19**(3), 581–600 (2019). https://doi.org/10.1007/s10270-019-00753-w

36. Pagliari, L., Mirandola, R., Trubiani, C.: Engineering cyber-physical systems through performance-based modelling and analysis: a case study experience report. J. Softw. Evol. Process **32**(1), e2179 (2020)
37. Platzer, A.: Differential dynamic logic for hybrid systems. J. Autom. Reason. **41**(2), 143–189 (2008). https://doi.org/10.1007/s10817-008-9103-8
38. Platzer, A.: Logical Analysis of Hybrid Systems - Proving Theorems for Complex Dynamics. Springer, Cham (2010). https://doi.org/10.1007/978-3-642-14509-4
39. Platzer, A.: Logics of dynamical systems. In: Proceedings of the International Symposium on Logic in Computer Science (LICS), pp. 13–24. IEEE Computer Society (2012). https://doi.org/10.1109/LICS.2012.13
40. Platzer, A.: Logical Foundations of Cyber-physical Systems. Springer, Cham (2018). https://doi.org/10.1007/978-3-319-63588-0
41. Ptolemaeus, C.: System Design, Modeling, and Simulation: Using Ptolemy II, vol. 1. Ptolemy.org Berkeley (2014)
42. Quigley, M., et al.: Ros: an open-source robot operating system. In: Procedings of the Workshop on Open Source Software, vol. 3, p. 5. Kobe, Japan (2009)
43. Runge, T., Knüppel, A., Thüm, T., Schaefer, I.: Lattice-based information flow control-by-construction for security-by-design, pp. 44–54. ACM (2020). https://doi.org/10.1145/3372020.3391565
44. Runge, T., Schaefer, I., Cleophas, L., Thüm, T., Kourie, D., Watson, B.W.: Tool support for correctness-by-construction. In: Hähnle, R., van der Aalst, W. (eds.) FASE 2019. LNCS, vol. 11424, pp. 25–42. Springer, Cham (2019). https://doi.org/10.1007/978-3-030-16722-6_2
45. Sampigethaya, K., Poovendran, R.: Aviation cyber-physical systems: Foundations for future aircraft and air transport. Proc. IEEE **101**(8), 1834–1855 (2013). https://doi.org/10.1109/JPROC.2012.2235131
46. Seceleanu, C., et al.: Analyzing a wind turbine system: From simulation to formal verification. Sci. Comput. Program. **133**, 216–242 (2017)
47. Shah, S., Dey, D., Lovett, C., Kapoor, A.: AirSim: high-fidelity visual and physical simulation for autonomous vehicles. In: Hutter, M., Siegwart, R. (eds.) Field and Service Robotics. SPAR, vol. 5, pp. 621–635. Springer, Cham (2018). https://doi.org/10.1007/978-3-319-67361-5_40
48. Zhang, L.: Specifying and modeling automotive cyber physical systems. In: Proceedings of the International Conference on Computational Science and Engineering (CSE), pp. 603–610. IEEE (2013)
49. Zhang, L.: Modeling large scale complex cyber physical control systems based on system of systems engineering approach. In: Proceedings of the International Conference on Automation and Computing (ICAC), pp. 55–60. IEEE (2014)

Leveraging System Dynamics in Runtime Verification of Cyber-Physical Systems

Houssam Abbas[1] and Borzoo Bonakdarpour[2]([⊠])

[1] Oregon State University, Corvalis, OR, USA
houssam.abbas@oregonstate.edu
[2] Michigan State University, East Lansing, USA
borzoo@msu.edu

Abstract. Cyber-physical systems consist of control software systems that interact with physical components that obey the fundamental laws of physics. It has been long known that exhaustive verification of these systems is a computationally challenging problem and distribution makes the problem significantly harder. In this paper, we advocate for runtime verification of cyber-physical systems and layout a road map for enhancing its effectiveness and efficiency by exploiting the knowledge of dynamics of physical processes.

1 Introduction

Cyber-physical systems (CPS), the Internet of Things (IoT), and edge applications appear in many different applications in our daily lives. CPS generally have safety-critical nature and as in other such systems, *runtime verification* (RV) is a complementary approach to static verification and testing in order to gain assurance about the health of the system. CPS is particularly becoming *distributed* over networks of *agents*, e.g., in sensors in infrastructures, health-monitoring wearables, networks of medical devices, and autonomous vehicles. Moreover, CPS and IoT often have to deal with resource constraints and any improvement in minimizing resource utilization and consumption is in pressing need.

While there have been proposals for monitoring CPS [2,4,5], predictive monitoring [3], monitoring using worst-case bounds [6], mitigating the effects of timing inaccuracies [1,12], and for minimally intrusive CPS monitoring [9], to our knowledge, the work on distributed RV and exploiting system dynamics to reduce the overhead of RV is limited to [11]. System dynamics is especially an interesting feature of CPS, as physical processes are assumed to obey the laws of physics. For example, a car cannot accelerate from 1–150 km/h in only one second. Knowing this could significantly assist in designing runtime monitors that monitor the state of the system while ignoring scenarios that cannot be reached.

Our goal in this paper is to explore the idea of combining RV with a precomputed knowledge of system dynamics to enhance the effectiveness of RV and

This work is sponsored by the NSF CCF Award 2118356.

reduce its runtime overhead. To this end, we introduce a set of ideas on the types of dynamics knowledge that can be available and how it might be leveraged by a runtime monitor, in the centralized and distributed setups. Specifically, we look at:

- Types of dynamics knowledge: from simple bounds on the state changes to full knowledge of the dynamics but only over a short amount of time.
- Different system models: we consider continuous-time and discrete-time models in a unified manner, to maintain maximum applicability of the monitors.
- Different ways to leverage the dynamics: from skipping parts of the signal where nothing interesting can happen, to early termination of the monitoring process.

We also discuss that the impact of the knowledge of the dynamics when the monitor is distributed over the agents, with each agent knowing only its own dynamics, and show how access to information about offline model-checking runs on the model can be leveraged.

The Model-Based Design Cycle and Runtime Verification. Knowledge of the dynamics, and offline formal verification, are possible in the model-based design cycle, in which a model of the system-under-development is created, refined and ultimately synthesized. Thus, by construction, the system can predict its own future, up to a certain horizon, and up to a certain accuracy. This knowledge, available by construction, can accelerate or improve the accuracy of online RV.

Organization. The rest of the paper is organized as follows. In Sect. 2, we present the preliminary concepts. Section 3 discusses the role of system dynamics in improving the runtime overhead. We discuss the distributed setting and its challenges in Sect. 4 and the impact having access to verified dynamics in Sect. 5. Finally, we conclude in Sect. 6.

2   Preliminary Concepts

First, we set some notations. The set of reals is $\mathbb{R}$, the set of non-negative reals is $\mathbb{R}_+$, and the set of positive reals is $\mathbb{R}_+^*$. The set of integers $\{1, \ldots, N\}$ is abbreviated as $[N]$.

2.1   Signal Model

In this section, we review our signal model, i.e., our model of the output signal of an agent from [11].

Definition 1. *An* output signal *is a function* $x : I \to \mathbb{R}^d$, *which is right-continuous, left-limited, and is not Zeno. Here, I is an interval in $\mathbb{R}_+$ (which could be all of $\mathbb{R}_+$), and will be referred to as the* timeline *of the signal.* ∎

Right-continuity means that at all t in its support, $\lim_{s \to t_+} x(s) = x(t)$. *Left-limitedness* means the function has a finite left-limit at every t in its support: $\lim_{s \to t_-} x(s) < \infty$. *Not being Zeno* means that x has a finite number of discontinuities in any bounded interval in its support. This ensures that the signal cannot jump infinitely often in a finite amount of time. A *discontinuity* in a signal $x(\cdot)$ can be due to a discrete event internal to agent A (like a variable updated by software), or to a message sent to or received from another agent A'.

2.2   Signal Temporal Logic (STL) [8]

Let AP be a set of *atomic propositions*. The syntax for *signal temporal logic* (STL) is defined for infinite traces using the following grammar:

$$\varphi := \top \mid p \mid \neg\varphi \mid \varphi \wedge \varphi \mid \varphi \mathcal{U}_{[a,b]} \varphi$$

where $\top$ is the logical constant standing for `true`, $p \in$ AP and $\mathcal{U}$ is the 'until' temporal operator. We view other propositional and temporal operators as abbreviations, that is, $\bot = \neg\top$ (`false`), $\Diamond_{[a,b]} \varphi = \top \mathcal{U}_{[a,b]}\varphi$ (*eventually*), $\Box_{[a,b]} \varphi = \neg(\Diamond_{[a,b]} \neg\varphi)$ (*always*). We denote the set of all STL formulas by Φ_{STL}.

Let a *trace* $\sigma = (x_1, \ldots, x_N)$ be a set of N signals with common support $\mathbb{R}_+$. Thus, a trace is, by definition, of infinite duration. This models that all agents are executing concurrently, and that time does not stop. Even if the agent does nothing over some interval $[a, b]$, its physical output signal still has a value. This models the output of a set of N agents operating concurrently. Each signal might be d-dimensional. For simplicity of presentation and without loss of generality in this paper, we assume $d = 1$.

To every atom p in AP is associated an N-ary function $f_p : \mathbb{R}^N \to \mathbb{R}$.

Let $\models$ denote the *satisfaction* relation. We write $\sigma, t \models \varphi$ to signify 'the infinite trace σ satisfies formula φ starting at time t'. Since the signals share a support, time t is in that shared support. Satisfaction is formally defined as follows.

$$
\begin{array}{lll}
(\sigma, t) \models \top & & \text{(no condition, } \top \text{ is satisfied by all traces at all times)} \\
(\sigma, t) \models p & \text{iff} & f_p(x_1(t), \ldots, x_n(t)) > 0 \\
(\sigma, t) \models \varphi \wedge \psi & \text{iff} & (\sigma, t) \models \varphi \wedge (\sigma, t) \models \psi \\
(\sigma, t) \models \neg\varphi & \text{iff} & \neg((\sigma, t) \models \varphi) \\
(\sigma, t) \models \varphi \mathcal{U}_{[a,b]}\psi & \text{iff} & \exists t' \in [t+a, t+b] : (\sigma, t') \models \psi \wedge \\
& & \forall t'' \in [t, t') : (\sigma, t'') \models \varphi
\end{array}
$$

Note that for the Until operator, formula φ is required to hold starting at the evaluation moment t up to and excluding the 'hand-over' moment t'. When $t = 0$ we write $\sigma \models \varphi$ instead of $(\sigma, 0) \models \varphi$. For example, given the trace σ shown in Fig. 1, the STL formula $\varphi = p \mathcal{U}_{[4,6.5]} q$ holds at time 0, that is, $\sigma \models \varphi$. However, φ does not hold after time 2, as in that case, q must be observed after time $2 + 4$ and before $2 + 6.5$, which does not happen.

A subtlety of the online monitoring setup is that only a finite-duration segment of a trace is available at any given time, not an infinite trace. This is handled in the classical manner: given a finite duration signal x, we say it satisfies/violates φ iff every extension $(x.y)$, where y is an infinite signal, satisfies/violates φ. Otherwise, the monitor returns Unknown. Here, the dot '.' denotes concatenation in time.

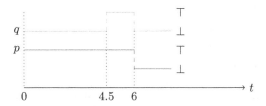

Fig. 1. A trace σ generated by a system.

3   Exploiting Knowledge of System Dynamics

RV first emerged as a set of techniques for monitoring a signal against a specification, without paying any attention to the dynamics that generates the signal. This was deliberate: the setup imagined by RV pioneers was one in which a model of the systems was not available, or was available but too complicated for exhaustive verification (i.e., model checking). The advantage of ignoring the signal-generating dynamics is that the resulting monitor is maximally applicable: all it needs is the signal to monitor. It might also be thought that this creates a faster monitor, since taking signal dynamics into account might add a computational burden.

In this section, we argue that this is not always the case – indeed, we argue that exploiting available knowledge of signal dynamics can reduce the monitor's run time. In a sense, this parallels earlier developments in cyber-physical systems which brought together computer scientists and control theorists to develop model-checking and verification algorithms for hybrid dynamical systems. The new model checking algorithms had to account for the dynamics to verify properties expressed in terms of the state variables.

3.1   Motivating Example

To motivate the benefit of using systems dynamics, we repeat one of our examples from [11] (see Fig. 2). From knowing the rate bound $|\dot{x}| \leq 1$ (shown by a dashed line), the monitor concludes that the earliest x can satisfy the atom $x \geq 3$ is τ_1. Similarly for y. Given that $\tau_1 > \tau_2$, the monitor discards, roughly speaking, the fragment $[0, \tau_2]$ from each signal and monitors the remaining pieces.

In [11] we demonstrated that such dynamics knowledge can significantly reduce the runtime of the monitor. This paper explores other possibilities for exploiting other forms of knowledge.

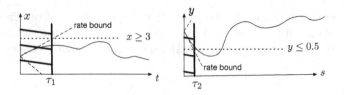

Fig. 2. Leveraging dynamics.

3.2   System Model

We consider signals x generated by a system under observation. A system is modeled as a tuple $\Sigma = (X, I, U, f, H)$, where $X \subseteq \mathbb{R}^d$ is the state space, $I \subset X$ is the set of initial states, $U \subset \mathbb{R}^m$ is the input space, $f : X \times U \to X$ is the transition function, and $H : X \to \mathbb{R}^o$ is the output or observation function.

The model is either an Ordinary Differential Equation (ODE) in continuous time

$$\dot{x}(t) = f(x(t), u(t)), \quad x(0) \in I, u(t) \in U, t \in [0, \infty)$$

or a Difference Equation (DEs) in discrete time

$$x(t+1) = f(x(t), u(t)), \quad x(0) \in I, u(t) \in U, t \in \mathbb{N}$$

The DE can model, as a special case, finite state automata: in this case f models the transition relation of the automaton. In both cases, u is the input signal, provided by the system's controller; in the discrete-time case, u is of course a (discrete-time) sequence. We write $x \xrightarrow{\bar{u}} x'$ to indicate a transition from x to x' under input signal or sequence $\bar{u}$ of unspecified length.

3.3   Knowledge of Signal Dynamics

In this section, by 'signal dynamics', we mean the dynamics of the model that is generating the monitored signal. E.g., the signal x might be the position of a car which obeys an ODE

$$\dot{x}(t) = v(t)cos(\theta(t)),$$

where $\dot{v}(t) = a(t)$, a is the acceleration input, and $\theta(t)$ is the steering input. Thus the input signal is 2-dimensional: $u = [a, \theta]$.

The monitor, which runs on-board the system, may have different kinds of knowledge about the dynamics:

1. **Bounds on the signal's derivative/difference**: $|\dot{x}(t)| \leq L$ or $|x(t+1) - x(t)| \leq L$. This is the simplest form of knowledge that we consider.
2. **Local model**: To each value of the state, the monitor associates a local approximation of the dynamics. That is, if the measured state at time t is x, the monitor considers that the signal obeys $\dot{x}(t) = f_x(x(t), u(t))$, where f_x is the local model. We do not commit to how f_x and f are related: the

former may be a linearization of the latter, or something else entirely. For f_x to be useful, we must assume that its error to f is bounded, namely $\|f_x(y, u) - f(y, u)\| \leq e(x)$ for all x, y and u. (Note that sometimes f_x does not take the same input as f, in which case we must also assume some mapping from f-inputs to f_x-inputs). Presumably f_x is also faster to simulate than f. Similar equations apply to the DE case.

3. **Simulating model**: In this case, the monitor has access to a dynamical model $\Sigma' = (X_g, I_g, U_g, g, H)$, with state space X_g and control space U_g, which *simulates* f. This means that there is relation R between X_f and X_g, called the *simulation relation*, such that:

   (a) Any two related states have the same output: $H(x_f) = H(x_g)$ for all $(x_f, x_g) \in R$. Thus, an observer cannot tell whether they are observing a state of f or g.

   (b) For every x in I_f there exists a point y in I_g s.t. $(x, y) \in R$ (initial conditions are related).

   (c) For every $(x, y) \in R$ it holds that: $x \xrightarrow{\overline{u}} x'$ in the f-system implies the existence of a transition $y \xrightarrow{\overline{u}'} y'$ in the g-system s.t. $(x', y') \in R$. That is, related states evolve into related states.

   We say g *simulates* f. Note that every f-behavior has a corresponding g-behavior, but not necessarily the other way around.

   The notion of ϵ-simulation generalizes the above definition by requiring bounded error between related states rather than equality. That is, $\|H(x_f) - H(x_g)\| \leq \epsilon$ for all $(x_f, x_g) \in R$

4. **Short model**: the monitor has access to the 'true' model f but can only execute it for a short amount of time. E.g., it can only solve the ODE up to time 5, or it can only see 5 hops ahead in the automaton.

We do not consider the case where the monitor has access to the true model f and can execute it to any length since then, the monitor can predict exactly the future trajectory and monitor it in a dynamics-agnostic manner.

Of course, there may be combinations of the above types of knowledge, e.g., a short local model.

3.4   Using Partial Knowledge

How might the monitor use these kinds of partial knowledge? And why would that reduce the monitoring overhead? By default, we present all examples for continuous-time signals. Obvious modifications can be made for the DE case, unless otherwise indicated. Our approach in this section will be to start from simple concrete examples which clarify the basic idea and technique to leverage dynamics in runtime monitoring. We then raise some of the challenges that will arise when we try to generalize, and suggest ways forward.

Early Termination: the most concrete idea, and one which can be readily implemented on top of existing software, is to use the dynamics knowledge to potentially terminate monitoring early. For instance, consider the atom $p :=$ $(x \geq 0)$ and suppose the formula is $\Diamond p$. So far no p has been observed, and at the present moment t, $x(t) = -5$. If the monitor knows that $\dot{x}(s) \leq -1$ from here on out $(s \geq t)$ then it can immediately declare a violation since x will never go positive.

The same principle applies if the monitor has a local model with a known deviation e to the true dynamics. The local bound provides a more refined bound, one that is not uniform, thus reducing the conservatism of the answer, but at the cost of solving the local model's time-varying ODE.

A simulating model is also useful for achieving the same task if the simulation relation meets a certain property. Namely, the state space of g, X_g, is obtained by partitioning X, where the states in each part all satisfy a particular combination of atoms. Formally, X_g is the quotient set of X by the equivalence relation

$$x \equiv y \text{ iff for all atomic propositions } p, \ x \models p \text{ iff } y \models p.$$

We say that the simulation *respects* AP. If the simulation relation respects AP, then it is enough to execute g to get a peek at the future. This is because g contains all the information necessary to monitor the formula: In such a case, the monitor executes g however long is feasible and tries to predict a violation or satisfaction, if they occur within the prediction horizon.

The above reasoning might be generalized somewhat if we find a notion of approximate satisfaction of an atom, which we then lift to the notion of a simulation relation that approximately respects AP. This might coincide with the notion of *approximate simulation* introduced in 2. Approximate simulations are well-known in the hybrid systems literature and have been successfully used to verify the *safety* of complex dynamics by reasoning over the simulating system. For general properties expressed in a temporal logic, this is more complicated as it compounds the errors in complex ways. One possible approach is to study the formula's language directly, and lift the approximate simulation to the languages. It is less clear whether a general simulating model, which does not (approximately) respect AP, can enable early termination.

It is fairly obvious that a short model can help in early termination: just execute the model as long as feasible, say for H time units, and see if the predicted trajectory already satisfies or violates the spec. However, since we assume the execution horizon H to be very short, this will probably waste more energy in trajectory prediction than it saves in early termination, since most predictions won't yield a decisive verdict. An interesting research direction arises if we assume that the monitor can *query* the model f at particular states: meaning that it can simulate f for H units *from a state q of its choosing*, not necessarily the current state $x(t)$. If this is possible, then the monitor can pre-emptively explore the model's behavior around potentially troublesome states from which violations of the formula can arise. Research is needed to define "troublesome states", and to do so in a way that takes into account the current on-going execution and the ways in which the formula can still be violated.

If f is an ODE or DE, the model can be queried in a straightforward fashion by setting the initial condition to q – but the difficulty immediately arises of what input signal to apply to solve the ODE $\dot{x} = f(x, u)$. If the controller is a state-feedback controller, the answer is trivial, but in general, this is an open question. If f is an automaton, querying it requires communication between the monitor and the system itself (or perhaps the controller), in which the monitor asks to obtain that piece of the automaton which is centered on q; i.e., q and its out-neighbors up to H hops away. Whether this is realistic or not depends on the system architecture: for instance, many systems do not carry a model of their own dynamics at all, or that model is not all available in memory at any given point in time due to memory constraints.

Skipping Parts of the Signal: The same types of knowledge might allow skipping parts of the signal: they are not monitored, thus saving in monitoring energy consumption, or freeing the monitor for other tasks, like monitoring multiple signals in alternating fashion. This is true for instance if the monitor knows bounds $|x(t)| \leq L$. Let's reprise the above example: consider the atom $p := (x \geq 0)$ and suppose the formula is $\Diamond p$. So far no p has been observed, and at the present moment t, $x(t) = -5$. If the monitor knows that $|\dot{x}| \leq 1$ from here on out, then it knows x will remain negative at least for the next $5\,\mathrm{s}$. So it can ignore the next $5\,\mathrm{s}$ of the signal, saving processing power, and start observing again at $t + 5$. The same reasoning applies if the monitor has a local model, the only difference being that we now have possibly less conservative bounds on the derivative and trajectory.

The use of a simulating model to skip signal segments is much less obvious. One of the difficulties is that the simulating model g does not have the same notion of time as the original model f. While every f-transition $x \xrightarrow{u} x'$ has a corresponding transition $y \xrightarrow{u'} y'$ in the g-system, the two transitions do not necessarily take the same amount of time, and in general, there is no known relation between the timelines. In fact, one of the reasons we develop a simulating model is that it can abstract away or accelerate time, allowing us to run faster simulations with it.

The use of a short model is also not obvious, because of the short horizon. It is not clear to us whether adding the ability to query the short model at will helps: questions of where and when to query it must be driven by the formula being monitored and the history of the system trajectory so far, and all of these are challenging research questions.

An additional challenge to all the above methods in the case of a general temporal logic formula is that the monitor must track all the ways the formula might be satisfied or violated, to avoid skipping signal segments that affect the truth value of the formula. While in principle possible (for a finite duration trajectory), it poses a heavy memory burden on the RV module, which needs to be lightweight. A partial workaround is to simply track each atom individually and avoid any truth value changes of the atoms. This is only a partial workaround:

as shown in the example, the truth value can change simply due to time passing, without change in the values of any atoms.

4   Monitoring Distributed CPS

If the system under monitoring consists of multiple nodes or agents, each of which has a local clock, then new challenges arise for runtime monitoring. These challenges further complicate our attempts at leveraging system dynamics.

At the highest level, the biggest challenge is that local clocks can and do drift: thus when one agent reports $x_1(5) = 3$ and the other agent reports $x_2(5) = 2$, these are not necessarily truly synchronous readings. I.e., the first clock reads 5 at a different (physical) time than the second clock. Such drift can obviously affect the validity of the monitor's calculations.

The second high-level challenge, which is independent of clock drift, is that each agent only has access, a priori, to its own state. So formulas that couple agents' states, like $(x_1 > 0)\,\mathcal{U}\,(x_2 > 3)$, require communication between agents and exchange of information. Thus we must design a low-overhead communication protocol between the agents.

In this section, we first describe the formal setup of a distributed CPS. Then we describe the challenges that arise when trying to leverage system dynamics' knowledge in RV.

4.1   Distributed CPS Architecture

We assume a loosely coupled system. Specifically, the system consists of N reliable *agents* that do not fail, denoted by $\{A_1, A_2, \ldots, A_N\}$, without any shared memory or global clock. The output signal of agent A_n is denoted by x_n, for $1 \leq n \leq N$. We will need to refer to some global clock which acts as a 'real' time-keeper. However, this global clock is a theoretical object used in definitions and theorems, and is *not* available to the agents. Messages that are passed between agents as part of their normal functioning (i.e., independently of the monitoring task) can be modeled as instantaneous changes in signal value, and will not be modeled separately here. We make two assumptions:

– *(A1) Partial synchrony.* The *local clock* (or time) of an agent A_n can be represented as an increasing function $c_n : \mathbb{R}_+ \to \mathbb{R}_+$, where $c_n(\chi)$ is the value of the local clock at global time χ. Then, for any two agents A_n and A_m, where $m, n \in [N]$, we have:

$$\forall \chi \in \mathbb{R}_+ . |c_n(\chi) - c_m(\chi)| < \varepsilon$$

with $\varepsilon > 0$ being the maximum *clock skew*. The value ε is assumed fixed and known by the monitor in the rest of this paper. In the sequel, we make it explicit when we refer to 'local' or 'global' time.
– *(A2) Deadlock-freedom.* The agents being analyzed do not deadlock.

Assumption (A1) is met by using a clock synchronization algorithm, like NTP [10], to ensure bounded clock skew among all agents. Assumption (A2) is stronger, meaning that some systems do indeed deadlock, while others are explicitly guaranteed not to deadlock.

In the discrete-time setting, a distributed signal is defined as a set of events (where an event is a value change in an agent's variables, due to a software update for example). We now update this definition for the continuous-time setting of this paper. Namely, we define a distributed signal to be a set of signals (one per agent), where each timeline is measured using the *local* clock c_n defined above, an event on the nth agent is a pair $(t, x_n(t))$, and inter-agent events are partially ordered by a variation of the *happened-before* ($\rightsquigarrow$) relation [7], extended by our assumption (A1) on bounded clock skew among all agents. The formal definition follows.

Definition 2. *A distributed signal on N agents is a pair $(E, \rightsquigarrow)$, where $E = (x_1, x_2, \ldots, x_N)$ is a vector of signals, one for each agent. All signals x_k share a support, modeling that all agents execute in parallel and that time (measured locally) does not stop. The relation $\rightsquigarrow$ is a relation between events in signals such that:*

(1) In every signal x_n, all events are totally ordered, that is,

$$\forall n \in [N].\ \forall t, t' \in I_n.\Big(t < t'\Big) \Rightarrow$$
$$\Big((t, x_n(t)) \rightsquigarrow (t', x_n(t'))\Big),$$

where the set I_n is a bounded nonempty interval.

(2) If the time between any two events is more than the maximum clock skew ε, then the events are totally ordered, that is,

$$\forall m, n \in [N].\ \forall t, t' \in I_n.\Big(t + \varepsilon < t'\Big) \Rightarrow$$
$$\Big((t, x_m(t)) \rightsquigarrow (t', x_n(t'))\Big). \qquad \blacksquare$$

We use a new symbol E for the trace in a distributed signal, rather than σ, to emphasize that signals in E are partially synchronous, and that their supports are bounded (which is a technical requirement - see [11]).

Example. Figure 3 shows two timelines, generated by two agents executing concurrently. Every moment in each timeline corresponds to an event $(t, x_n(t))$, $n \in [2]$. Thus, we see that the following hold: $(1, x_1(1)) \rightsquigarrow (2.3, x_1(2.3))$, $(2.3, x_1(2.3)) \rightsquigarrow (2.94, x_2(2.94))$, $(1, x_2(1)) \rightsquigarrow (2.94, x_2(2.94))$, and $(2.94, x_2(2.94)) \not\rightsquigarrow (3, x_1(3))$.

The classic case of complete asynchrony is recovered by setting $\varepsilon = \infty$. Because the agents are only synchronized within an ε, it is not possible to actually evaluate all signals at the same moment in global time. The notion of *consistent cut* and its frontier, defined next, capture *possible* global states: that is, states that could be valid global states (see Fig. 3).

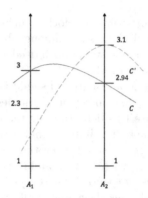

Fig. 3. Two partially synchronous continuous concurrent timelines with $\varepsilon = 0.1$. C is a consistent cut. C' is not a consistent cut: indeed $(1, x_1(1)) \rightsquigarrow (3.1, x_2(3.1))$ by definition of happened-before. Moreover, $(3.1, x_2(3.1)) \in C'$ but $(1, x_1(1))$ is not in C', which violates the definition of consistent cut.

Definition 3. *Let $(E, \rightsquigarrow)$ be a distributed signal over N agents and S be the set of all events defined as follows:*

$$S = \left\{ (t, x_n(t)) \mid x_n \in E \wedge t \in I_n \wedge I_n \subseteq \mathbb{R}_+ \right\}.$$

A consistent cut C is a subset of S if and only if when C contains an event e, then it contains all events that happened before e. Formally,

$$\forall e, f \in S \ . \ (e \in C) \wedge (f \rightsquigarrow e) \Rightarrow (f \in C).$$

■

From this definition and Definition 2 it follows that if $(t', x_n(t'))$ is in C, then C also contains every event $(t, x_m(t))$ s.t. $t + \varepsilon < t'$. Observe that due to time asynchrony, at any global time $\chi \in \mathbb{R}_+$, there exists infinite number of consistent cuts denoted by $\mathcal{C}(\chi)$. This is attributed to the fact that between any two local time instances t_1 and t_2 on some signal x, there exists infinite number of time instances. Therefore, infinite number of consistent cuts can be constructed.

A consistent cut C can be represented by its *frontier*

$$\mathrm{front}(C) = \left\{ (t_1, x_1(t_1)), \ldots, (t_N, x_n(t_N)) \right\},$$

in which each $(t_n, x_n(t_n))$, where $1 \le n \le N$, is the last event of agent A_n appearing in C. Formally:

$$\forall n \in [N] \ . \ (t_n, x_n(t_n)) \in C \text{ and}$$

$$t_n = \max \left\{ t \in I_n \mid (t, x_n(t)) \in C \right\}.$$

Example. Assuming $\varepsilon = 0.1$ in Fig. 3, it comes that all events below (thus, before) the solid arc form a consistent cut C with frontier $\mathsf{front}(C) = \{(3, x_1(3)), (2.94, x_2(2.94))\}$. On the other hand, all events below the dashed arc do *not* form a consistent cut since $(2.3, x_1(2.3)) \rightsquigarrow (3.1, x_2(3.1))$ and $(3.1, x_2(3.1))$ is in the set C', but $(2.3, x_1(2.3))$ is not in C'.

4.2 Additional Challenges in the Distributed Setup

We can conceive of numerous additional challenges arising in the distributed setup.

The first class of challenges of distributed monitoring is that the knowledge of the dynamics is distributed over the agents, with each agent knowing only its own dynamics a priori. Already, even if we assume total synchrony between the agents, there is a need to design a protocol by which this information is shared, or some summary of it is exchanged. We will give an example of the complexity of the task: assume that each agent has bounds on its own dynamics. In the centralized setting, this can be used to skip parts of the signal, as described earlier. In the distributed setup, this cannot be done directly: indeed whether a formula will change truth value in the next second, say, depends on the bounds of two or more agents. The relevant segment of x_1 (signal of agent 1 that should be monitored) depends on the relevant segment of x_2 and vice versa. E.g., if the atom is $(x_1 + x_2 > 0)$ then, without knowing the bounds of x_2, the entire x_1 can be relevant for monitoring.

On the other hand, if agent 1 know that $-1 \leq x_2 \leq 1$ then it can conclude the only relevant portion of x_1 is $1 \leq x_1$. Agent 1 can then send only those segments where its signal is larger than 1. Thus there are at least two kinds of tokens (packets of information) that must be exchanged: tokens with bounds (from Agent 2 to Agent 1) and tokens with pieces of the signal (from Agent 1 to Agent 3, etc.).

Secondly, the partial synchrony creates difficulties in trying to leverage the model knowledge. Indeed, even on a single agent whose clock is drifting relative to global physical time ($c_n(\chi) \neq \chi$), there is an error between the model predictions, which embody an error-free timeline, and the measurements, which integrate a drifting timeline. For example, assume the monitor has a short model, which it uses to predict the trajectory $x_1[0, 1] \to \mathbb{R}$. Based on this it concludes it can ignore the segment $x_1[0 : 0.3]$, i.e., the first 0.3 s of the signal, *measured on a perfect clock*. But its local clock has an unknown, ε-bounded drift from physical time. So, measured on its local clock, the conservative thing is to skip $x_1[0 : 0.3 - \varepsilon]$.

It might be that the general case is a tedious, but ultimately straightforward, generalization of this calculation: conservatively ignore shorter pieces. The technical problem is then to build an inductive argument for the general case, taking into account the nature of the dynamics knowledge that is available.

The case of a simulating model is particularly interesting: recall that Σ_g simulates Σ_f if for every $(x, y) \in R$ it holds that: $x \xrightarrow{\overline{u}} x'$ in the f-system implies the existence of a transition $y \xrightarrow{\overline{u}'} y'$ in the g-system s.t. $(x', y') \in R$. The key characteristic is that $\overline{u}$ and $\overline{u}'$ are not necessarily of the same duration - indeed, in general, it is difficult to get some kind of relation between the two durations. So far in the literature, the properties verified on the simulating g-system have not depended on time. It is not at all clear how we might apply a conservative ε-shortening to the time bounds when the relation between the g and f timelines is unknown.

5 Using Verified Dynamics

In this section, we explore a different kind of information: the monitor does not have access to any kind of model. Rather, it has access to information about offline model-checking runs on the model. That is, offline, the designer ran a series of model-checking runs on the model, and the verdicts of these runs are available to the monitor. Every piece of information is thus structured as a tuple (x, h, V, ϕ), where:

1. x is the state from which the verification ran
2. h is the verification horizon, if applicable. E.g., in bounded model checking, this would be the bound.
3. ϕ is the formula against which the model was checked. That is, the designer checked whether the model satisfies $M, x \models \phi$. (Here, M is the model).
4. $V \in \{\top, \bot\}$ is the verdict, or result, of the verification.

Such information is naturally available in a model-based design cycle where formal methods play a role. Note we allow the possibility that the model-checking runs were limited, both in terms of their bounds, and in terms of the states they are run from.

The runtime monitor is monitoring for some property(ies) ψ that, in general, is different from ϕ. The question then: can the monitor leverage the knowledge that $M, x \models \phi$ to monitor ψ more efficiently? Intuitively, that should be possible some of the time: when the current state is 'near' x, and the formula ψ is somehow related to ϕ.

The following trivial cases illustrates that intuition: if the current state is exactly x, and $\psi = \phi$, the obviously there is no need to monitor. Or, assume the model is a finite automaton. The current state is within $s \leq h$ hops of x, and $\psi \Rightarrow \Diamond_s \phi$. Here too, it is not necessary to monitor since the satisfaction of ϕ now is implied by that of ψ earlier.

A more involved example is provided by offline reachability: suppose the model has been verified to not enter a set of states S within h time units if it starts from some set J. (Reachability tools like SpaceEx and Flow* could be used for this). Such a guarantee holds under some assumptions on the system's environment, say the assumption that any disturbance w is bounded: $|w(t)| \leq 1$ for all time t. Now the atomic proposition p that '$x \in S$' might appear in formulas that are monitored online. The offline reachability result can be leveraged in the monitor in a predictive manner: whenever the state x is about to enter (or enters) set J, every appearance of p in the monitored formula can be replaced by `false`, as long as it appears within the scope of a temporal operators whose combined intervals add up to less than h time units.

The challenge is to formalize then generalize this intuition to more cases. We will also need to account for the fact that the monitor does not actually know the current state: in general, it only has access to observables, i.e., to $H(x(t))$ rather than $x(t)$.

6 Conclusion

In this paper, we explored the idea of combining runtime verification (RV) with a pre-computed knowledge of system dynamics to enhance the effectiveness of RV and improve its runtime overhead. To this end, we introduced a set of ideas on how different aspects of system dynamics can be potentially leveraged to equip the monitor with tools to decrease it involvement by ruling out certain scenarios.

Our next natural step is to materialize these ideas by developing the theory as well as conducting rigorous experiments to validate our results. *Stream-based* runtime verification techniques such as RTLola[1] allows real-time monitoring for cyber-physical systems and networks but they currently cannot handle data streams coming from components that do not share a common clock and do not take system dynamics into account. Thus, longer-term interesting problem is to integrate our ideas in this on using system dynamics as well as our results in [11] with RTLola.

References

1. Abbas, H., Mittelmann, H., Fainekos, G.: Formal property verification in a conformance testing framework. In: ACM-IEEE International Conference on Formal Methods and Models for System Design (MEMOCODE), October 2014
2. Annpureddy, Y., Liu, C., Fainekos, G., Sankaranarayanan, S.: S-TaLiRo: a tool for temporal logic falsification for hybrid systems. In: Abdulla, P.A., Leino, K.R.M. (eds.) TACAS 2011. LNCS, vol. 6605, pp. 254–257. Springer, Heidelberg (2011). https://doi.org/10.1007/978-3-642-19835-9_21
3. Dokhanchi, A., Hoxha, B., Fainekos, G.: Online monitoring for temporal logic robustness. In: Proceedings of Runtime Verification (2014)
4. Donzé, A., Ferrère, T., Maler, O.: Efficient robust monitoring for STL. In: Proceedings of the 25th International Conference on Computer Aided Verification (CAV), pp. 264–279 (2013)
5. Donzé, A., Maler, O.: Robust satisfaction of temporal logic over real-valued signals. In: Proceedings of the 8th International Conference on Formal Modeling and Analysis of Timed Systems (FORMATS), pp. 92–106 (2010)
6. Deshmukh, J.V., Donzé, A., Ghosh, S., Jin, X., Juniwal, G., Seshia, S.A.: Robust online monitoring of signal temporal logic. Formal Methods Syst. Des. **51**(1), 5–30 (2017). https://doi.org/10.1007/s10703-017-0286-7

---

[1] https://www.react.uni-saarland.de/tools/rtlola/.

7. Lamport, L.: Time, clocks, and the ordering of events in a distributed system. Commun. ACM **21**(7), 558–565 (1978)
8. Maler, O., Nickovic, D.: Monitoring temporal properties of continuous signals. In: Proceedings of the Formal Techniques, Modelling and Analysis of Timed and Fault-Tolerant Systems (FORMATS/FTRTFT), pp. 152–166 (2004)
9. Medhat, R., Bonakdarpour, B., Kumar, D., Fischmeister, S.: Runtime monitoring of cyber-physical systems under timing and memory constraints. ACM Trans. Embed. Comput. Syst. **14**(4), 79:1–79:29 (2015)
10. Mills, D.: Network time protocol version 4: Protocol and algorithms specification. RFC 5905, RFC Editor, June 2010
11. Momtaz, A., Basnet, N., Abbas, H., Bonakdarpour, B.: Predicate monitoring in distributed cyber-physical systems. In: Proceedings of the 21st International Conference on Runtime Verification (RV) 2021, pp. 3–22 (2021)
12. Jan-David, Q.: Similarity, Logic, and Games: Bridging Modeling Layers of Hybrid Systems. Ph.D. thesis, Carl Von Ossietzky Universitat Oldenburg, July 2013

Automated Repair of Security Errors in C Programs via Statistical Model Checking: A Proof of Concept

Khanh Huu The Dam[1], Fabien Duchene[1(✉)], Thomas Given-Wilson[1],
Maxime Cordy[2], and Axel Legay[1]

[1] UCLouvain, Louvain-La-Neuve, Belgium
{khan.dam,fabien.duchene,thomas.given-wilson,axel.legay}@uclouvain.be
[2] University of Luxembourg, Esch-sur-Alzette, Luxembourg
maxime.cordy@uni.lu

Abstract. One major challenge in software development is finding and repairing programming errors. Recently, formal methods such as model checking have become a popular approach to finding errors due to their formal guarantees about error status and evidence of the error in the form of a trace. Another recently growing area, automated program repair, aims to fix errors using automated approaches that do not require programmer intervention. This paper gives a proof of concept that one can combine these two areas using state-of-the-art approaches in both: the discovery of program errors and traces exhibiting these errors; and automated program repair building on test cases generated from traces. This naturally links together the discovery, learning, repairing, and validation of repair in a single package.

1 Introduction

The discovery and repair of errors are major challenges in software engineering that take developers considerable effort. This is why software engineering research has intensively worked on improving techniques to assess program correctness and to repair program errors.

Formal methods have become a popular approach to finding errors in hardware and software systems. Formal methods offer great promise in that they can provide guarantees regarding the presence or absence of errors in the system. *Model Checking* (MC) [7], for instance, exhaustively explores the possible executions of the system (or a model of the system) in search of errors – typically expressed as violations of a given temporal property. Formal methods contrasts with other approaches more prominently used in software development, such as testing techniques whose offered guarantees are limited to the behavior that (manually or generated) test cases cover.

Formal methods were initially restricted to the verification of system models (e.g. transition systems) that would directly be provided by the user. More recent tools enable the verification of source code directly. These tools implement a variety of analysis approaches, including: heuristics [29]; model

T. Margaria and B. Steffen (Eds.): ISoLA 2022, LNCS 13701, pp. 279–298, 2022.
https://doi.org/10.1007/978-3-031-19849-6_17

checking [7] and variations [17]; symbolic verification [10], and runtime analysis [12]. Unfortunately, all those approaches either suffer from the state-space explosion problem (i.e. the program state space is too large to be explored exhaustively) or from difficulties in handling the memory model of the system under verification. These two limitations hinders the practical applicability of formal methods to real-world programs.

Statistical Model Checking (SMC) [14,20,33] resolves these complexity limitations, albeit at the cost of some statistical uncertainty in the results. Instead of exhaustive exploration, SMC simulates multiple executions of a system and monitors these executions in regards to expected properties. Then, SMC uses statistical algorithms to extrapolate its conclusions to the system globally. While SMC can efficiently find errors and avoid the aforementioned complexity issues, SMC provides only a statistical likelihood of the absence of errors. So far, SMC has been mostly applied to verify safety and liveness properties on (stochastic) models of systems. This includes for example, properties of biological systems [9,16], robotics [26], security [30], or of railway systems [3]. On the other hand, with the exception of [18,24], SMC has not been used to verify properties on program code. Program code analysis applications are generally limited to specific reachability properties and restricted fragments of programming languages. In particular, the verification of security properties that depend on space and time memory failures (e.g. out of bounds, overflows, read-only memory access, etc.) has not yet been explored, whereas such failures are prominent in popular languages such as C. The verification of such properties is critical because their violation leads to serious errors that conventional testing techniques (that lean on a test suite) cannot unveil [23].

The main challenge in applying SMC and other formal methods to program code is to accurately and efficiently model the possible values within the program and its complex internal information. The true possible values of a program execution can be difficult to determine because of the large domains of values to consider (e.g. all 64-bit Integers) and the difficulty of tracking complex runtime relationships between successive values. Similarly, building an accurate but abstract model of memory organization is challenging, since the compiler and operating system have specific features that are opaque to the verification engine. All these challenges ultimately lead to inaccuracies in the verification results and, in turn, to an increasing risk of overlooking pernicious security vulnerabilities.

In [5], we have proposed the *C Statistical Model Checker* (C-SMC) approach and tool in order to address these challenges and enable the discovery a wide range of security errors. C-SMC combines the inherent strengths of SMC with a runtime engine to connect the program under verification with a real executions. This allows us to reason on contextual information such as memory, stack, registers, warning flags, etc. The runtime engine feeds the SMC engine with information over the program executions without having to derive a formal model of the entire hardware and operating system's behavior. We, more specifically, use a debugging engine – viz. GDB [1] – to inform the analysis on the true instantiations of memory and internal system hardware to determine concrete values. As C-SMC builds on SMC, this approach can handle many independent executions of the program and effectively combine the analysis results of these executions in order to determine the likelihood to satisfy given properties.

Automated Program Repair (APR) [11] is a popular area of research that aims to automate code modifications in order to fix existing errors without programmer intervention. APR is typically used once the presence of an error has been detected in the program, e.g. via formal methods or a tool such as C-SMC.

The process of most APR approaches fall in the subarea of "generate and validate". During the *generation* part the APR uses test case results in order to locate suspicious code statements possibly responsible for the error and, then, alter these statements in order to produce candidate patches. During the *validation* part the APR methods execute the program test suite on the patched code and discard all patches that make some tests fail.

Contribution. The present paper is a proof of concept of how to enrich C-SMC with a program repair module. The tool is used both to generate error trace as well as to evaluate potential patches. Concretely, C-SMC can discover errors and produce test cases that can then be the input to APR, and further C-SMC can validate the patches generated as part of the APR itself. We show how an APR approach can benefit from the statistical nature of SMC and the information that C-SMC produces regarding the errors discovered.

Conceptually, we propose to use the set of traces that C-SMC produce as inputs for APR. The traces are divided into positive traces (that raise no error) and negative traces (that exhibit the error). Hence, we lean on the capability of SMC to provide multiple traces that reveal the error – and to do so without guidance from developer-written or automatically generated tests. Based on the traces, we determine the set of suspicious statements through reverse data-flow analysis from the statement where the error was revealed.

We, then, propose a neural agent-based method that, given a set of suspicious statements, looks for the sequence of actions (statement alterations) that maximizes the likelihood to repair the error. Candidate sequences of actions produce in turn potential patches whose correctness is validated via C-SMC to speed up the process.

We evaluate our repair approach on the benchmark from [5]. Our repair approach fixes 8 out of the 9 errors and – compared to a random baseline – does so while producing 23% to 91% fewer candidates patches in all cases but one. Put together, SMC and APR effectively automate the detection and repair of memory usage-related errors to an extent that previous approaches could not achieve. Our approach complements the state of the art on software testing and repair, which has mostly focused on test-based approaches. Here we find a productive union of formal methods – viz. SMC – and APR that yield a complete package for error detection and repair.

To summarize, our main contributions are as follows. (1) Propose the first approach for automated error detection and program repair that builds on statistical model checking. Our approach can detect and repair pernicious security errors that conventional test cases are not likely to trigger. (2) Propose a novel genetic algorithmic searching approach to find an effective program repair efficiently. (3) Demonstrate an implementation of our approach on top of established tools and technologies. (4) Evaluate our approach using a benchmark of eight memory usage-related errors and one arithmetic error. Our evaluation results suggest that (a) our detection method could find all of the nine errors, and (b) our repair method could fix eight of these errors and do so with fewer generated patches for seven of these eight errors.

Structure. The structure of the paper is as follows. Section 2 provides background and related work that are necessary to understand the paper. Section 3 presents an illustrative example used in this work. Section 4 describes the novel genetic algorithmic repair agent. Section 5 presents our implementation and experimental results. Section 6 concludes.

Note on Content. As said above, this paper is a proof of concept paper that is written to generate discussions with the community. Consequently, many formal details are left out of this presentation.

2   Background and Related Work

We consider systems/programs where executions are represented by traces, i.e., sequences of states. Each state represents the status of the system under verification at a given moment of time. States and traces can be abstracted as mathematical objects such as (sequences of) Boolean variables [7]. When considering languages such as C, a state represents the current location in the program (line of code), its memory, and the set of instructions/statements that are available from this state. A state can also contain information about the execution environment. A trace moves from on state to another state by following a transition. When considering languages such as C, such transition represents the execution of an instruction.

2.1   Essentials of Statistical Model Checking

Statistical Model Checking (SMC) [14,20,33] is a variety of probabilistic model checking (see e.g. [2]) that exploits execution traces to avoid an explicit representation of the state space. The evaluation of properties is instead calculated from an empirical distribution of the executions of the system. Given a number of statistically independent traces of a stochastic model, and the capabilities to decide whether a trace satisfies a property, it is possible to estimate the probability that the model will satisfy the property.

Note that unlike model checking [7], SMC provides results that are not complete and may only provide an approximation of the true properties of the system. Thus, an estimate of the behavior may be obtained with a specified confidence provided by, e.g. the Okamoto bound [14,25]. Further, it is possible to efficiently evaluate the truth of a hypothesis without needing to calculate the actual probability using, e.g. the sequential probability ratio test [31,33]. SMC can also be used to compute the probability of rare errors [21].

To apply SMC requires building a model of the system and expressing the properties to be checked. Typically the model can be defined as a *labeled transition system* (LTS) and the properties expressed in a logic such as *bounded linear temporal logic* (BLTL) that can express complex behavioral properties with nested temporal causality.

2.2   Trace Execution Properties

Expressing properties formally is key in software verification. Based on definitions above, properties about a program can be defined in terms of properties over states, over individual traces, and over sets of traces. We first focus on the first two types of properties. The last one, which corresponds to the verification of the whole program, will be handled in the next (sub-)section.

A propositional logic can define properties about each state individually. To be able to consider all the states of an execution trace, this propositional logic needs to be extended. One popular extension is *Linear Temporal Logic* LTL [27]. LTL allows us to make hypotheses of unbounded traces via temporal operators. As SMC restricts to finite trace executions, we consider a bounded LTL, where each temporal operator is bounded for the number of states to which it applies.

Bounded Linear Temporal Logic (BLTL) is an enhancement of LTL that adds bounds expressed in step or time units. The syntax of BLTL is as follows:

$$\phi, \psi \quad ::= \quad p \mid \phi \vee \psi \mid \neg \phi \mid \phi\, U_{\leq t}\, \psi \mid X_{\leq t}\, \phi\,. \tag{1}$$

The p is propositional variables, disjunction $\phi \vee \psi$ and negation $\neg\phi$ are all as in LTL. The formula $X\phi$ is true if ϕ is true in the next state from the current state. The formula $\phi\, U_{\leq t}\, \psi$ is true if both: ψ becomes true before t in the sequence from the current state; and ϕ remains true in every state before the state where ψ becomes true. For a formal definition of BLTL semantics, see [35]. A BLTL formula is expressed with respect to a trace. It is also helpful to have conjunction $(\phi \wedge \psi)$ and implication $(\phi \Rightarrow \psi)$ that are defined in the usual manner. Similarly the *always* (G) and *eventually* (F) operators can be defined using the BLTL syntax above as follows. Eventually is defined as $F_{\leq t}\phi = \mathbf{true}\, U_{\leq t}\, \phi$ and means that the formula ϕ should become true before t. Always is defined as $G_{\leq t}\phi = \neg F_{\leq t}\neg\phi$ and means that ϕ must always hold for the next t.

Let $w = s_0, s_1, ..., s_L, ...$ be an execution trace, and denote by $w^j = s_j, ..., s_L, ...$ the portion of the trace starting from j (included). The truthfulness of the formulas can be decided using the rules described in Table 1.

BLTL allows us to express reachability properties such as "the software should eventually reach a state where variable x is equal to 1". The logic can also be used to express more elaborated causalities such as "always, if the software reaches a state where x is equal to 1, it will eventually reach a state where y is equal to 1". This expressive power allows us to express a wide range of safety and security properties. BLTL properties can be verified with monitoring procedures [13]. Such procedures, inspect successive states of an execution trace until it can decide whether the property is satisfied. BLTL properties, which are a fragment of safety properties, can be monitored over finite traces using well-established techniques such as those presented in [13].

Table 1. BLTL rules.

$w \models F_{\leq t}\phi$	iff $w \models$ true $U_{\leq t}\phi$
$w \models G_{\leq t}\phi$	iff $w \models \neg(F_{\leq t}\neg\phi)$
$w \models \phi U_{\leq t}\psi$	iff $\exists i, t_0 \leq t_i \leq t_0 + t$ and $w^i \models \psi$ and $\forall j, 0 \leq j < i, w^j \models \phi$
$w \models X_{\leq t}\phi$	iff $\exists i, i = max(j \vert t_0 \leq t_j \leq t_0 + t)$ and $w^i \models \phi$
$w \models X_{\leq}\phi$	iff $w^1 \models \phi$
$w \models \phi \vee \psi$	iff $w \models \phi$ or $w \models \psi$
$w \models \phi \wedge \psi$	iff $w \models \neg\phi \vee w \models \neg\psi$
$w \models \phi \Rightarrow \psi$	iff $w \models \neg\phi \vee \psi$
$w \models \neg\phi$	iff $w \not\models \varphi$
$w \models$ true	always
$w \models$ false	never

2.3 Probabilistic Verification

We now turn to properties defined over sets of trace executions, that is properties defined on the whole system. We are interested in solving the probabilistic BLTL problem, that is to compute the probability for the system to satisfy a BLTL property ϕ. Such probability being defined as the probability that a random trace of the system satisfies ϕ.

Statistical model checking [19] has been proposed as an efficient approach to solve such problem. SMC statistically measures the truthfulness of properties over a smaller number of traces. This is done by performing a fixed number of simulations of the system and using an algorithm to estimate the probability that the system satisfies the property. As the number of observed executions is finite, this answer comes together with a confidence interval [19].

There is a wide range of statistics algorithms that can be used to estimate the probability to satisfy a given property. This includes, e.g., importance splitting and sampling [19] that can also be used to efficiently exhibit traces that do not satisfy the property. As the study of those algorithms is not the topic of this paper, we propose to work with the most simple one that is based on the Monte Carlo estimator. The estimator relies on the following proportion:

$$\bar{\gamma} = \frac{\sum_{i=1}^{N} \mathbf{1}(w_i \models \phi)}{N} \text{ where } \mathbf{1}(x) = \begin{cases} 1 & \text{if } x \text{ is true} \\ 0 & \text{otherwise.} \end{cases} \quad (2)$$

where N is the number of simulation being performed. Let γ be the true probability to satisfy ϕ and P be a probability evaluation. Let ϵ (precision) and δ (confidence)be small values. The Chernoff-Hoeffding bound [15] guarantees that $P(\vert\bar{\gamma} - \gamma\vert \geq \epsilon) \leq \delta$ is given by $N = \lceil \frac{ln2 - ln\delta}{2\epsilon^2} \rceil$. Thus, by controlling the number of trace executions verified, the user entirely controls the preciseness of the $\bar{\gamma}$ estimator.

2.4   SMC Tools

As seen in the previous section, SMC mainly depends on sub-parts that include the type of execution trace property that has to be monitored and the statistical algorithm used to compute the stochastic guarantee. Implicitly, SMC also depends on the type of system under verification and on the capacity to generate an arbitrary number of execution traces from this system.

In [34], the authors proposed YMER, a tool that can be used to verify BLTL properties of Markov Chains with an hypothesis testing procedure. That is, the tool decides between two hypothesis rather than computing an exact probability. In [8] Monte Carlo is applied to verify properties of Metric Temporal Logic over stochastic timed automata. Those tools have been shown to be very efficient on various problems. However, they are rather static in the sense that they do not exploit the intrinsic modularity of SMC. As an example, YMER does not permit replacing the hypothesis testing algorithm by a Monte Carlo one. None of those tools allows replacing classical BLTL with an algorithm that would consider debugger expression. On the top of this, none of those tools consider C code.

In [4,22], Boyer et al. introduced Plasma a Statistical Model Checking (SMC) [19] tool that can provide the ability to create custom statistical model checkers. Especially, Plasma works with open source plugins that can (1) specify the property under verification (this includes BLTL as well as many other logics such as those introduced in [6]), (2) monitor traces, (3) generate traces in an efficient manner, i.e., to minimize the number of traces needed to compute the probability to satisfy a given property. Those plugins can be customized to adapt to a wide range of properties and systems.

In a recent work [5], we have introduced C-SMC, a new open source plugin that allows us to monitor security properties of C program. C-SMC monitors BLTL properties via and extension that exploits states of the GDB debugger as input instead of Boolean abstraction. Using this, BLTL properties can refer to variables, registers, memory, locations and next instructions of a given state of the C program. In addition properties can also refer to special flags of the GDB debugger. C-SMC has been able to detect security and safety flaws such as buffer and integer overflows. It can also be used to detect overflow that depends on contextual information coming e.g. from global variables. The later one shall be showed in our motivating example.

3   Illustrative Example

Consider the illustrative binary search example given in Listing 1.1. Variable r should be initialized to size-1 but is initialized to size. This error will lead the search to occasionally go out of the bounds of the array being inspected. Consider an array of size 10 (indexed from 0 to 9) containing numbers 1 to 10. If the search function is called with a value that is greater than the greatest value of the array (10 in this example) then it will go out of bounds looking for the value located at arr[size] (10 in this case).

This behavior will often lead to no consequences (because even if the access is out of bounds it is still checking a valid address on the stack) and thus be undetected. However, when looking for a value not contained in the array, 11 for instance, it is *possible* that the memory address located just after the end of the array contains the searched for value. In this case, the output of the search function will be invalid. This error is very hard to reproduce and to express. Indeed, the `search` function itself does not contain the information about the input values (i.e. `arr` and `size` and

```
1  int search(int arr[],int size
       ,int elem) {
2    int l = 0;
3    int r = size; //not size-1
4    int m = 0;
5    while (r >= 1) {
6      m = (l+r) / 2;
7      if (arr[m] == elem) {
8        return m;
9      } else if (arr[m] > elem)
         {
10        r = m - 1;
11     } else {
12        l = m + 1;
13     }
14   }
15   return -1;
16  }
```

Listing 1.1. Binary Search Example.

whether or not `size` is correct) and so most analysis engines can only warn about a *potential* out of bounds access for all instances of `arr[m]` or report no errors.

Pernicious security errors like the above are difficult to reveal through conventional testing. This is due to the fact that testing focuses on comparing outputs for a given set of inputs. As an example, we show in Listing 1.2 a set of 14 test cases that thoroughly check whether the search function works correctly when invoked on (1) all elements that the array contains and (2) close elements that the array does not contain. For conciseness, we have concatenated all these cases into a single piece of code. In this code, the `report_fail` function is used to report when some test yields an incorrect result.

```
1  int tab[8] = {-3,-1,0,4,5,6,7,8};
2  int input[14] = {-3,-1,0,4,5,6,7,8,-2,1,2,3, -(rand() % (
      MAXINT - 3)) - 4,(rand() % (MAXINT - 8)) + 9};
3  int i = 0;
4  while (i < 8) { // Test good values
5    int y = search(tab,sizeof(tab)/sizeof(tab[0]),input[i]);
6    if (y != i) { report_fail(input[i]); }
7    i++;
8  }
9  while (i < 14) { // Test random values outside the good
      values
10   int y = search(tab,sizeof(tab)/sizeof(tab[0]),input[i]);
11   if (y != -1) { report_fail(input[i]); }
12   i++;
13  }
```

Listing 1.2. Test Cases for the `search` function

Observe that all these test cases will usually pass. Thus, although developers can strenuously test the `search` function and find other potential errors, it is likely that the out of bounds access error will never occur during the test execution. This error would actually occur in the unlikely event where the searched value is not in the array but resides in memory exactly at the memory address located right after the end of the array. In such a case, the search function would return an index value equal to the size of the array, while the special value -1 is expected. This example already demonstrates that test cases are inappropriate to detect errors related to memory usage because the error is independent of the particular inputs on which the function is tested. Even if every possible `int` value was covered in the test suite, the error would likely remain undetected. To detect this error with C-SMC instead of checking the value of the output for a given input, we monitor the value of the variable `m` using the formula $m = 0|(0 <= m \& m < size$. With this formula we can check that at any moment, `m` does not go out of bounds. This allows us to detect an error that is very hard to reproduce or detect with unit tests or analysis engines.

3.1 SMC-Based Validation

Consider again the binary search example shown in Listing 1.1, where the upper bound of the binary search `r` is initialized beyond the end of the array `arr`. A natural check for array data structure is to ensure there is no access (read or write) beyond the limit of the array. This can be formulated as a BLTL property:

$$\neg(\texttt{arr[x]} \wedge \texttt{x} \geq |\texttt{arr}|), \tag{3}$$

where `arr[x]` indicates an access to the array `arr` at offset `x` and $\texttt{x} \geq |\texttt{arr}|$ indicates that `x` is greater than or equal to the size of `arr`.

In the example code, there are two accesses to an array, one at lines 7 and one at line 9. However, the value `m` that records the accessed index is modified at each loop iteration, based on the values of `size`, `elem`, and the values contained in `arr`. Hence, the above property can be reformulated as:

$$G_{\leq 1000}(line = 7 \vee line = 9) => m \geq 0 \wedge m < size, \tag{4}$$

where *line* indicates the line number in C code, *m* and *size* are variables *m* and *size* in C code of Listing 1.1.

Assume that C-SMC tested with the following input values for `search` to generate tests (and in particular this limits the scope of our search).

```
1  int tab[8] = {1,2,3,4,5,6,7,8};
2  int v = (rand() % 10);
3  int i = search(tab, 8, v);
```

Listing 1.3. Simple Example of Search C Code Input

After running 4 tests with C-SMC we may discover that the program works properly for $v \in \{6, 2, 3\}$ while 9 causes a problem. Observe that applying SMC to search could yield an infinite number of traces that exhibit both good and bad behavior depending on the input arguments given to the search function. As an example, consider the inputs given in Listing 1.2. They will generate traces that satisfy Property 4 when v is assigned to a value located between index 0 and 12 of the input array (input[0:12]) given in line 2 of Listing 1.2. They will generate traces that do not satisfy Property 4 when v is assigned to input[13]. In fact, all searches for a value $v \leq 8$ will provide a GOOD trace, and all searches for values $v > 8$ will provide a BAD trace. Note that the capabilities to identify GOOD and BAD traces depends on the randomized algorithm used to generate inputs. There exists various strategies to reach this objective. Including, e.g., importance splitting and sampling.

BLTL can also be used to describe other classes of properties that are beyond the scope of classical testing. As an example, it is worth checking that the program terminates after a bounded number of steps. The latter can be expressed by:

$$F_{\leq 1000}(line = 15 \vee line = 16) \tag{5}$$

In addition, we can also use BLTL to specify expected (input, output) pairs just like in typical test cases. Such BLTL formulae would take the form:

$$G_{\leq 1000}(line = 16 => eax = gt) \tag{6}$$

where eax is a reserved symbol to indicate the return value of the function and gt is a specific, user-defined target output.

3.2   Using Traces for Automated Program Repair

We now turn to illustrate how to repair the program. Observe that the trace monitoring process of SMC has the potential to locate error statements/lines. Those can be exploited to produce a set of possible changes, i.e., actions, for fixing the program according to the execution traces. The key principle is to start from the statement where SMC detected the violation of a property, and apply a reverse data-flow analysis to determine all previously executed statements that share a (direct or indirect) data dependency with the statement where the violation was located. It then examines the abstract syntax tree of the program in order to determine the constituents of these statements and, in turn, determines the set of actions (statement alterations) that the repair agent will consider. For example, a BAD trace given by C-SMC contains lines 2, 3, 5, 6, 7, 9, 10 and 12, and this trace is ended at line 7. Applying the reverse data-flow analysis from line 7, we locates error statements at lines 6, 10, 12, 3 and 2. We can then generate possible changes to each of these lines. This approach is similar to fault-spectrum localisation as presented in [32].

We want to use a repair agent that takes as input the set of possible actions that the trace analysis component identified based on the error trace. It then produces different sequences of actions (based on the taken set) and applies these sequences to generate a set of independent patches that are themselves verified with C-SMC. This process continues until the faulty program is fixed or until the computational budget (expressed in number of produced patches) is reached.

For instance, the agent has fixed our binary search error example by modifying the line where variable r is initialized, as shown in Listing 1.4.

In the rest of this paper, we describe a trace analysis framework that can be used in combination with a genetic algorithm based repair agent. We then report on case studies that implement this proof of concept.

4   Designing a Repair Agent

```
1  int search(int arr[],int
       size,int elem) {
2    int l = 0;
3    int r = size - 1;//
         patched
4    int m = 0;
5    while (r >= 1) {
6      m = (l+r) / 2;
7      if (arr[m] == elem) {
8        return m;
9      } else if (arr[m] >
           elem) {
10         r = m - 1;
11     } else {
12         l = m + 1;
13     }
14   }
15   return -1;
16 }
```

Listing 1.4. Binary Search Function C Code

Our objective is to develop a repair agent that exploits the information contained in execution traces generated by the SMC engine. We first show how to reason on a trace. Especially, we give intuition on how a trace can be corrected. Recall that each trace contains lines (i.e. location in program's code) which are reached by the execution and a property field which specifies the property violated by the program. Intuitively, the error statements/lines appear to BAD traces. The last line in a BAD trace indicates where the property has been violated and the error occurs. Let $\mathcal{L}$ be a set of lines which may cause the error. Let $\mathcal{T}$ be a set of BAD traces from C-SMC. $\mathcal{L}$ is computed as follows. Initially, $\mathcal{L} = \{\ell_i | \ell_i$ is the last line in the trace $t_i \in \mathcal{T}\}$. Then, $\ell \in t$ is iteratively added to $\mathcal{L}$ if there exist a $\ell' \in \mathcal{L}$, and (ℓ', ℓ) are data dependent (this can be done via classical taint analysis techniques).

Table 2 shows lines appearing in execution traces of the illustrative example (Listing 1.1) computed by C-SMC on the three properties given in Eqs. 4, 5 and 6. The error lines, which are marked with a X, are given by $\mathcal{L} = \{2, 3, 6, 7, 10, 12\}$. In order to fix the faulty program, we propose to apply an action to the error lines. An action is implemented by either replacing or inserting a new statement at a given error line. An action $a = (\ell, c)$ means that a change c is implemented at line ℓ. The change c is generated by three ways as follows. First, one can change operators of an expression. For example, if <name> <operator> <name> is an expression, then <operator> can be changed by taking an operator in either the arithmetic operators or the comparison operators. Second, one can replace the current patterns of an expression by existing patterns in the program. The replacement is applied to an expression which matches to an expression pattern in the library. The existing expression matches to a pattern if

Table 2. Error lines for the example in Listing 1.1.

Line	1	2	3	4	5	6	7	8	9	10	11	12	13	14	15	16
Property 1 (Eq. 4)	-	X	X	-	-	X	X	-	-	X	-	X	-	-	-	-
Property 2 (Eq. 5)	-	-	-	-	-	-	-	-	-	-	-	-	-	-	-	-
Property 3 (Eq. 6)	-	-	-	-	-	-	-	-	-	-	-	-	-	-	-	-

its abstract syntax tree can be transformed to the pattern's abstract syntax tree, or if they contain the same numbers of `<name` and `<operator>`. For example, if (`<name>` `<operator>` `<name>`)`<operator>` `<name>` is an expression and it matches to the pattern `<name>` `<operator>`(`<name>` `<operator>` `<name>`), a change is made by the `<name>` in the pattern by the `<name>` in the expression. Third, a change can be created by inserting a new statement. Consider, e.g., the insertion of the control statements if else, or the addition of special statements such as break, continue, exit, return.

4.1   A SMC-Based Program Repair Algorithm

Our objective is to fix the faulty program by finding a subset of actions (called patch) from actions given by the trace analysis. By fixing the program, we mean that all properties under verification are satisfied with probability one. We here propose the use of a genetic algorithm and heuristics to generate the patch in an efficient manner.

Let $\overline{gp}$ denote a faulty program. Let $\mathcal{A}_{\overline{gp}}$ denotes a finite set of actions given by the trace analysis part to fix the faulty program $\overline{gp}$. Let $\Pi_{\overline{gp}}$ be a power set of $\mathcal{A}_{\overline{gp}}$ (the set of patches). A patch $\rho = \{a \in \mathcal{A}_{\overline{gp}}\} \in \Pi_{\overline{gp}}$ is applied to $\overline{gp}$ to transform $\overline{gp}$ to gp, i.e., $\overline{gp} \xrightarrow{\rho} gp$. Let $\mathcal{G}$ be a finite set of programs, i.e., $\mathcal{G} = \{gp | \exists \rho \in \Pi_{\overline{gp}} : \overline{gp} \xrightarrow{\rho} gp\}$. Our task is to find a patch $\rho* \in \Pi_{\overline{gp}}$ such that $\overline{gp} \xrightarrow{\rho*} gp*$ and $gp*$ is a fixed program. Note that the faulty program $\overline{gp}$ is fixed by a patch $\rho*$, i.e., $\overline{gp} \xrightarrow{\rho*} gp*$, if all the properties given in the environment are satisfied by $gp*$.

Let f be an objective function $f : \mathcal{G} \to [0.0, 1.0]^m$ where $[0, 1]^m$ denotes the output of m properties of a program $gp \in \mathcal{G}$, e.g., $f(gp) = [0.0, 1.0, 0.2]$ indicates that the program gp has 0% chance for holding the property 1, 100% chance for holding the property 2 and 20% chance for holding the property 3. The program $gp*$, i.e., $\overline{gp} \xrightarrow{\rho*} gp*$, satisfies all properties such as $f(gp*) = [1.0]^m$. Let $\mathbf{s} = f(gp)$ be a validation-state of the program gp, i.e., a vector whose components represent the probability to satisfy the properties under verification. Consider $\mathbf{s}_0 = f(\overline{gp})$ to be the initial validation-state, i.e. the initial probability value for each property that the program must eventually satisfy.

Our genetic algorithm works by evaluating a population of patches. In case, those patches do not lead to s_*, mutation and recombination operators shall be called. Given a validation-state, our objective is to derive actions that will lead to better patches and eventually to a better validation-state. For doing so, we propose to use a Q-function [28] to specify the relation of states and actions, as follows. For every observed patch $\rho \in \Pi_{\overline{gp}}$:

$$Q(\mathbf{s}, a) = r + \gamma \max_{a'} Q(\mathbf{s'}, a'), \forall a \in \rho., \tag{7}$$

where γ is a coefficient in $[0, 1]$, r and $\mathbf{s'}$ are reward and validation-state respectively. We assume the reward to be 0 when the system is not repaired and 1 if it is repaired. In practice, we will stick to those two values. In theory, a reward of $0, 5$ would mean that the program is half fixed. Initially, we have $Q(\mathbf{s}, a) = 0$ for every state $\mathbf{s}$ and every action $a \in \mathcal{A}_{\overline{gp}}$. The reward r gets 1.0 if the faulty program is fixed. Otherwise, it gets -1.0.

Intuitively, $Q(\mathbf{s}, a)$ indicates the probability to choose action a at validation-state $\mathbf{s}$. The Q-function is updated for every patch and its values later are used to generate a new patch. For instance, if there is a patch $\rho = \{a_1, a_2\}$ and the state transitions $\mathbf{s_0} \xrightarrow{a_1} (\mathbf{s_1}, r_1) \xrightarrow{a_2} (\mathbf{s_2}, r_2)$, then the Q-function is updated as follows: $Q(\mathbf{s_0}, a_1) = r_1 + max_{a'}Q(\mathbf{s_1}, a')$ and $Q(\mathbf{s_1}, a_2) = r_2 + max_{a'}Q(\mathbf{s_2}, a')$. In this work, we implement a ϵ greedy selection algorithm to choose an action for the patch generation, such that, at a state $\mathbf{s}$ an action is either chosen by $\arg\max_{a \in \mathcal{A}_{\overline{gp}}}(Q(\mathbf{s}, a))$ with a given probability ϵ or chosen any action $a \in \mathcal{A}_{\overline{gp}}$ with probability $1 - \epsilon$.

Input : $\epsilon, Q(\mathbf{s}), \mathcal{A}$
Output: an action a
1 **if** $random() < \epsilon$ **then**
2 | $a \leftarrow \arg\max_{a \in \mathcal{A}}(Q(\mathbf{s}, a))$
3 **else**
4 | $a \leftarrow random(\mathcal{A})$
5 **end**

Algorithm 1: ϵ greedy selection algorithm (GreedySelection())

To estimate the values of Q-function, we implement an estimator neural network $NN(\mathbf{s}, \mathbf{s'})$. The network takes the source validation-state $\mathbf{s}$ and the destination validation-state $\mathbf{s'}$ as inputs. It outputs the value of the Q-function at validation-state $\mathbf{s}$. Output values are used to compute a patch for the transition $\mathbf{s} \rightarrow \mathbf{s'}$. Hence, if there is a transition $\mathbf{s} \rightarrow \mathbf{s'}$, the values of Q-function at the state $\mathbf{s}$, i.e., $Q'(\mathbf{s}) \approx Q(\mathbf{s}, a)_{a \in \mathcal{A}_{\overline{gp}}}$, which are used to compute a patch $\rho: \mathbf{s} \xrightarrow{\rho} \mathbf{s'}$, are computed as follows.

$$Q'(\mathbf{s}) = NN(\mathbf{s}, \mathbf{s'}) \tag{8}$$

For every patch, the neural network is updated by the actual values of actions in this patch with the following Mean Squared Error loss function.

$$MSE = \frac{1}{n} \sum_{i=1}^{n} (Y_i - \bar{Y}_i)^2, \tag{9}$$

where $Y_i = Q'(\mathbf{s}, a_i)$ and $\bar{Y}_i = Q(\mathbf{s}, a_i)$ are predicted/actual values of the action a_i at the state $\mathbf{s}$, respectively. n is the number of actions, i.e., $n = |\rho|$. Note that

---

Input : a set of actions $\mathcal{A}_{\overline{gp}}$, MaxPopulation, the estimator neural network
            NN, τ is the threshold to create an optimal patch, and the initial/final
            states of C program $s_0, s*$

Output: $\rho*$ is an optimal patch to fix the faulty program

1 $P \leftarrow \{\{a\}_{\mathcal{A}_{\overline{gp}}}\}$
2 $N \leftarrow 0$
3 isdone $\leftarrow$ False
4 **while** *not isdone and $N \leq$ MaxPopulation* **do**
5 $\quad$ $N \leftarrow N + |P|$
6 $\quad$ $S \leftarrow \emptyset$
7 $\quad$ **foreach** $\rho \in P$ **do**
8 $\quad\quad$ $s \leftarrow$ Evaluate(ρ)
9 $\quad\quad$ UpdateQ(s, ρ, NN)
10 $\quad\quad$ $S \leftarrow S \cup \{s\}$
11 $\quad\quad$ **if** $s = s*$ **then**
12 $\quad\quad\quad$ isdone $\leftarrow$ True
13 $\quad\quad\quad$ $\rho* \leftarrow \rho$
14 $\quad\quad\quad$ **break**
15 $\quad\quad$ **end**
16 $\quad$ **end**
17 $\quad$ parents $\leftarrow$ SelectParent($P, S, nparent$)
18 $\quad$ $P \leftarrow$ CreatePopulation(parents, S, NN, $s_0, s*$)
19 **end**
20 **if** *not isdone* **then**
21 $\quad$ $Q(s_0) \leftarrow$ NN($s_0, s*$)
22 $\quad$ $\rho* \leftarrow \{a \in \mathcal{A}_{\overline{gp}} | Q(s_0, a) \geq \tau\}$
23 **end**

Algorithm 2: The patch generation algorithm

---

if $s \xrightarrow{\rho} s'$, $Q(s, a_i)_{a_i \in \rho}$ is computed by Eq. 7 and $Q'(s, a_i)_{a_i \in \rho}$ is a value of $Q'(s)$, which is predicted by NN, i.e., $Q'(s) = NN(s, s')$.

We are now ready to present the genetic algorithm for patch generation as shown in Algorithm 2. Intuitively, patches are created from one action in the set of actions given by the trace analysis part (line 1). Then, each patch is evaluated by SMC (line 8). The validation-states obtained from this evaluation are used to update the neural network NN (line 9). If there exists a patch which can fix the faulty program, i.e., the state of the current patch is the final state $s*$, the algorithm terminates (line 11–14). Otherwise, it creates a parent set from the current population, i.e., P, and generates a new population from this set (lines 17–18). If the optimal patch is not found after exceeding the limit number, i.e., MaxPopulation, the threshold τ is used to choose actions for creating an "optimal" patch (line 21–22). The threshold τ is used to select actions in a patch. We use τ to vary the number of actions in a patch. Although the patch chosen by τ may not be a good one for fixing the faulty program, it can be a recommendation for the developers to fix their code. Algorithm 3 presents the parent selection algorithm. This algorithm conserves n selected parents by exploiting an Euclidean distance between the

Input : a population P, a set S of states of population P, n is the number of selected parents

Output: a parent set is the subset of P

1 Compute the Euclidean distance between the state of each patch and the final state $[1.0]^m$.

2 Select n patches from P which have the shortest distance from the final state.

Algorithm 3: The Parent Selection algorithm (SelectParent())

Input : The parent population P,S, NN and the initial/final states of C program $s_0, s*$

Output: a population P'

1 $Q(s_0) \leftarrow NN(s_0; s*)$

2 $a \leftarrow GreedySelection(\epsilon, Q(s_0), A_{\overline{gp}})$

3 $P' \leftarrow \{a\}$

4 **foreach** $\rho \in P$ **do**

5 $\quad$ $s \leftarrow S[\rho]$ $\quad$ // the state of the C-program after applying patch ρ

6 $\quad$ $Q(s) \leftarrow NN(s, s*)$

7 $\quad$ $a_{max} = \arg\max_{a \in A_{\overline{gp}}} Q(s, a)$

8 $\quad$ $a_{min} = \arg\min_{a \in \rho} Q(s, a)$

9 $\quad$ $P' \leftarrow P' \cup \{\rho \cup \{a_{max}\}\}$

10 $\quad$ $P' \leftarrow P' \cup \{\rho \setminus \{a_{min}\}\}$

11 **end**

12 **foreach** $\rho_1 \in P$ **do**

13 $\quad$ $s_1 \leftarrow S[\rho_1]$

14 $\quad$ $Q(s_1) \leftarrow NN(s_1, s*)$

15 $\quad$ $\rho_1' \leftarrow$ Sort ρ_1 by $Q(s_1)$

16 $\quad$ **foreach** $\rho_2 \in P$ **do**

17 $\quad\quad$ $s_2 \leftarrow S[\rho_2]$

18 $\quad\quad$ $Q(s_2) \leftarrow NN(s_2, s*)$

19 $\quad\quad$ $\rho_2' \leftarrow$ Sort ρ_2 by $Q(s_2)$

20 $\quad\quad$ $P' \leftarrow P' \cup$ switch a part of ρ_1' and $\rho'2$

21 $\quad$ **end**

22 **end**

Algorithm 4: The Population Generation algorithm (CreatePopulation())

validation state obtained for each patch and the expected final validation-state. Algorithm 4 presents the recombination and mutation operations. Initially, the new population P' is created from the parent population starting with a patch of one action that is selected by Function GreedySelection. Then, P' is grown up by two operators (lines 1–3). The first operator is the mutation operator. It implements two operations: (1) to add an action with the highest Q-value into ρ, (2) to remove an action $a \in \rho$ with the lowest Q-value (lines 4–11). The second operator called recombination replace a pair (ρ_1, ρ_2) by a pair (ρ_1', ρ_2') that is created by exchanging actions which are associated with the highest Q-values in ρ_1 and ρ_2 (lines 12–21).

5   Implementation and Experimental Results

We implemented the APR process described in Sect. 4 with three modules: the environment module, trace analysis module, and agent module.

The *environment module* has two roles: C program evaluation and program repair evaluation. The C program evaluation is done by interfacing with C-SMC and inputting the C program and BLTL properties. If any property of the C program is not satisfied then repair must be triggered (otherwise the program is error free and no further action taken). The traces from C-SMC are gathered along with their result (GOOD or BAD) and these are sent to the trace analysis module. The program repair role takes a patch from the agent module and produces the state of the C program after applying the patch.

The *trace analysis module* takes a set of traces from the environment module and the C program as inputs, and produces a set of actions to fix the C program. For the motivating example, it analyses the BAD traces of Eq. 4 and generates actions to fix the C program at lines 2, 3, 5, 6, 7, 8, 9, 10, 12. Then, these actions are sent to the agent module for patch generation.

The *agent module* takes the lines from the trace analysis module and implements the algorithms detailed in Sect. 4 to generate a patch to apply to the C program. The agent module then sends this to the environment module to evaluate the efficacy of the patch and provide this as data for further patch generation using the genetic techniques described in Sect. 4.

5.1   Experimental Results

In this section, we evaluate the performance of the C-SMC based APR tool with Q-function on the motivating example in Listing 1.1 and in three variants. Our objective is to evaluate the performance of a Q-function with respect to a random strategy to select actions to mutate and recombine in the genetic algorithm.

In this experiment, we choose the maximum population to be 3000 patches, i.e., $MaxPopulation = 3000$ and we applied the randomized strategy for action selection. The results are reported in Table 3. The motivating example in Listing 1.1 starts in validation-state $s_0 = [0.9, 1.0, 1.0]$. It is fixed by the APR tool after 50 patches out of a population of 112 patches by the random strategy. Variant 1 is obtained by replacing $l = m + 1$ with $l = m - 1$ at line 12. The initial validation-state is given by $s_0 = [1.0, 1.0, 0.6]$. It is fixed by our tool after 72 patches while it takes a population of 210 patches to fix it with a random strategy. Variant 2 is obtained by replacing $r = size$ with $r = size - 1$ at line 3, $m = (l + r)/2$ with $m = (r - l)/2$ at line 6 and $l = m + 1$ with $l = m - 1$ at line 12. Its initial validation state is given by $s_0 = [1.0, 1.0, 0.4]$. It is fixed after 290 patches by our tool while the random strategy takes 2259 patches. Variant 3 is obtained by replacing $r = m - 1$ with $r = m + 1$ at line 10 and $l = m + 1$ with $l = m - 1$ at line 12. Its initial validation-state is given by $s_0 = [1.0, 1.0, 0.6]$. It is fixed after 290 patches by our tool. A random strategy could not fix it after a population of 3000 patches. The results show that the use of an optimized Q-function drastically improve the selection of patches.

Table 3. Comparison of the APR tool with Q-function and the random strategy.

| | Size of population to fix the fault | | | |
	Motivating example	Variant 1	Variant 2	Variant 3
APR tool with random strategy	112	210	2259	>3000
APR tool with Q function	50	72	290	2012

Table 4. Evaluation of the APR tool on other C code.

| | Size of population to fix the fault | |
	APR tool with random strategy	APR tool with Q-function
Binary search	112	50
Binary search (variant 1)	210	72
Binary search (variant 2)	2259	290
Binary search (variant 3)	>3000	2012
Static out-of-bounds	4	2
Random out-of-bounds	4	2
Divide by zero	1	3
Buffer overflow	25	3
Local binary search	13	10
Pointer to pointer	2	1
Read-only memory	Failed	Failed
Integer overflow	10	3

The C-SMC based APR tool with Q-function was also applied to the nine benchmark error programs from [5] that are available on GitHub[1]. The results are shown in Table 4. Observe that in all cases (except for "read-only memory") the combination of C-SMC with APR was able to not only find the error, but also successfully repair the error. The failure to repair the "read-only memory" example is due to there being no reasonable way for the patch generation algorithm to create a suitable repair. While this example was relevant to demonstrate the capabilities to detect such errors, it would be difficult to fix given the patch algorithms possible changes, and also to preserve the program's behavior. Further, in all cases (except for "divide by zero") the APR tool with Q-function proved to be more effective than the random strategy.

Due to space limitation, a detailed analysis of the benchmarks is given in the aforementioned GitHub. These results demonstrate that the approach is effective both in concept and in practice, and further that the APR Q-function strategy is an improvement over the default (random) genetic algorithm.

---

[1] https://github.com/csvl/bugs.

6   Conclusions and Future Work

The challenge of finding and repairing errors in software development is complex and ongoing. Formal methods such as SMC provide a strong basis for finding and proving the existence of errors, including a trace to demonstrate the error. The statistical nature of SMC allows the generation of multiple correct and erroneous traces of the program. These traces form a natural set of test cases that can be the input for APR approaches. Combining SMC with APR is an effective solution to find errors and provide the necessary information to repair them.

This paper presents a proof of concept showing that this approach is effective in discovering, learning, repairing, and validating the repair in a single tool. Further, the proposed Q-function for improving the genetic algorithmic search for a patch improves the efficacy of the patch generation. This is demonstrated by the implementation here exploiting C-SMC and demonstrating effective discovery and repair of errors.

Future Work. We would like to extend our approach to guided simulations approaches such as importance sampling and splitting. This shall help us to find error traces in a more efficient manner and hence improve the efficiency of the repair agent. We also would like to apply the work to a wider class of systems. Especially, we would be interested in applying the approach to real-time version of C. This could be done by exploiting recent work on stochastic timed automata implemented in UPPAAL-SMC [18]. The limitations of the "read-only memory" benchmark also motive the use of more complex repair tools in the agent and other methods of patch generation. Finally, observe that this paper is a proof of concept. Comparison with other tools shall be investiguated in near future.

References

1. GDB: The GNU Project Debugger. https://www.gnu.org/software/gdb/. Accessed 14 Oct 2020
2. Baier, C., Katoen, J.-P.: Principles of Model Checking. MIT Press, Cambridge (2008)
3. Basile, D., ter Beek, M.H., Legay, A.: Strategy synthesis for autonomous driving in a moving block railway system with UPPAAL STRATEGO. In: Gotsman, A., Sokolova, A. (eds.) FORTE 2020. LNCS, vol. 12136, pp. 3–21. Springer, Cham (2020). https://doi.org/10.1007/978-3-030-50086-3_1
4. Boyer, B., Corre, K., Legay, A., Sedwards, S.: PLASMA-lab: a flexible, distributable statistical model checking library. In: Joshi, K., Siegle, M., Stoelinga, M., D'Argenio, P.R. (eds.) QEST 2013. LNCS, vol. 8054, pp. 160–164. Springer, Heidelberg (2013). https://doi.org/10.1007/978-3-642-40196-1_12
5. Chenoy, A., Duchene, F., Given-Wilson, T., Legay, A.: C-SMC: a hybrid statistical model checking and concrete runtime engine for analyzing C programs. In: Laarman, A., Sokolova, A. (eds.) SPIN 2021. LNCS, vol. 12864, pp. 101–119. Springer, Cham (2021). https://doi.org/10.1007/978-3-030-84629-9_6
6. Clarke, E.M., Donzé, A., Legay, A.: On simulation-based probabilistic model checking of mixed-analog circuits. Formal Methods Syst. Des. **36**(2), 97–113 (2010)

7. Clarke, E.M., Henzinger, T.A., Veith, H.: Introduction to model checking. In: Clarke, E., Henzinger, T., Veith, H., Bloem, R. (eds.) Handbook of Model Checking, pp. 1–26. Springer, Cham (2018). https://doi.org/10.1007/978-3-319-10575-8_1

8. David, A., Larsen, K.G., Legay, A., Mikucionis, M., Poulsen, D.B.: Uppaal SMC tutorial. Int. J. Softw. Tools Technol. Transf. **17**(4), 397–415 (2015)

9. David, A., Larsen, K.G., Legay, A., Mikucionis, M., Poulsen, D.B., Sedwards, S.: Statistical model checking for biological systems. Int. J. Softw. Tools Technol. Transf. **17**(3), 351–367 (2015)

10. Godefroid, P., Klarlund, N., Sen, K.: DART: directed automated random testing. In: Sarkar, V., Hall, M.W. (eds.) Proceedings of the ACM SIGPLAN 2005 Conference on Programming Language Design and Implementation, Chicago, IL, USA, 12–15 June 2005, pp. 213–223. ACM (2005)

11. Goues, C.L., Pradel, M., Roychoudhury, A., Chandra, S.: Automatic program repair. IEEE Softw. **38**(4), 22–27 (2021)

12. Havelund, K.: A scala DSL for rete-based runtime verification. In: Legay, A., Bensalem, S. (eds.) RV 2013. LNCS, vol. 8174, pp. 322–327. Springer, Heidelberg (2013). https://doi.org/10.1007/978-3-642-40787-1_19

13. Havelund, K., Roşu, G.: Synthesizing monitors for safety properties. In: Katoen, J.-P., Stevens, P. (eds.) TACAS 2002. LNCS, vol. 2280, pp. 342–356. Springer, Heidelberg (2002). https://doi.org/10.1007/3-540-46002-0_24

14. Hérault, T., Lassaigne, R., Magniette, F., Peyronnet, S.: Approximate probabilistic model checking. In: Steffen, B., Levi, G. (eds.) VMCAI 2004. LNCS, vol. 2937, pp. 73–84. Springer, Heidelberg (2004). https://doi.org/10.1007/978-3-540-24622-0_8

15. Hoeffding, W.: Probability Inequalities for sums of Bounded Random Variables. In: Fisher, N.I., Sen, P.K. (eds.) The Collected Works of Wassily Hoeffding, pp. 409–426. Springer, New York (1994). https://doi.org/10.1007/978-1-4612-0865-5_26

16. Jha, S.K., Clarke, E.M., Langmead, C.J., Legay, A., Platzer, A., Zuliani, P.: A Bayesian approach to model checking biological systems. In: Degano, P., Gorrieri, R. (eds.) CMSB 2009. LNCS, vol. 5688, pp. 218–234. Springer, Heidelberg (2009). https://doi.org/10.1007/978-3-642-03845-7_15

17. Karakaya, K., Bodden, E.: Sootfx: a static code feature extraction tool for java and android. In: 21st IEEE International Working Conference on Source Code Analysis and Manipulation, SCAM 2021, Luxembourg, 27–28 September 2021, pp. 181–186. IEEE (2021)

18. Kulczynski, M., Legay, A., Nowotka, D., Poulsen, D.B.: Analysis of source code using UPPAAL. In: Proença, J., Paskevich, A. (eds.) Proceedings of the 6th Workshop on Formal Integrated Development Environment, F-IDE@NFM 2021, Held online, 24–25th May 2021. EPTCS, vol. 338, pp. 31–38 (2021)

19. Legay, A., Delahaye, B., Bensalem, S.: Statistical model checking: an overview. In: Barringer, H., et al. (eds.) RV 2010. LNCS, vol. 6418, pp. 122–135. Springer, Heidelberg (2010). https://doi.org/10.1007/978-3-642-16612-9_11

20. Legay, A., Lukina, A., Traonouez, L.M., Yang, J., Smolka, S.A., Grosu, R.: Statistical model checking. In: Steffen, B., Woeginger, G. (eds.) Computing and Software Science. LNCS, vol. 10000, pp. 478–504. Springer, Cham (2019). https://doi.org/10.1007/978-3-319-91908-9_23

21. Legay, A., Sedwards, S., Traonouez, L.-M.: Rare events for statistical model checking an overview. In: Larsen, K.G., Potapov, I., Srba, J. (eds.) RP 2016. LNCS, vol. 9899, pp. 23–35. Springer, Cham (2016). https://doi.org/10.1007/978-3-319-45994-3_2

22. Legay, A., Sedwards, S., Traonouez, L.-M.: Plasma lab: a modular statistical model checking platform. In: Margaria, T., Steffen, B. (eds.) ISoLA 2016. LNCS, vol. 9952, pp. 77–93. Springer, Cham (2016). https://doi.org/10.1007/978-3-319-47166-2_6

23. Liu, K., Koyuncu, A., Bissyandé, T.F., Kim, D., Klein, J., Traon, Y.L.: You cannot fix what you cannot find! an investigation of fault localization bias in benchmarking automated program repair systems. In: 12th IEEE Conference on Software Testing, Validation and Verification, ICST 2019, Xi'an, China, 22–27 April 2019, pp. 102–113. IEEE (2019)

24. Ngo, V.C., Legay, A.: Formal verification of probabilistic SystemC models with statistical model checking. J. Softw. Evol. Process. **30**(3), e1890 (2018)

25. Okamoto, M.: Some inequalities relating to the partial sum of binomial probabilities. Ann. Inst. Stat. Math. **10**, 29–35 (1959)

26. Palopoli, L., et al.: Navigation assistance and guidance of older adults across complex public spaces: the DALi approach. Intell. Serv. Robot. **8**(2), 77–92 (2015)

27. Pnueli, A.: The temporal logic of programs. In: 18th Annual Symposium on Foundations of Computer Science (SFCS 1977), Providence, RI, USA, pp. 46–57. IEEE, September 1977

28. Sutton, R.S., Barto, A.G.: Reinforcement Learning - An Introduction. Adaptive Computation and Machine Learning, MIT Press, Cambridge (1998)

29. Tasharofi, S., Karmani, R.K., Lauterburg, S., Legay, A., Marinov, D., Agha, G.: TransDPOR: a novel dynamic partial-order reduction technique for testing actor programs. In: Giese, H., Rosu, G. (eds.) FMOODS/FORTE -2012. LNCS, vol. 7273, pp. 219–234. Springer, Heidelberg (2012). https://doi.org/10.1007/978-3-642-30793-5_14

30. ter Beek, M.H., Legay, A., Lluch-Lafuente, A., Vandin, A.: Quantitative security risk modeling and analysis with RisQFLan. Comput. Secur. **109**, 102381 (2021)

31. Wald, A.: Sequential tests of statistical hypotheses. Ann. Math. Stat. **16**(2), 117–186 (1945)

32. Wen, W.: Software fault localization based on program slicing spectrum. In: Glinz, M., Murphy, G.C., Pezzè, M. (eds.) 34th International Conference on Software Engineering, ICSE 2012, 2–9 June 2012, Zurich, Switzerland, pp. 1511–1514. IEEE Computer Society (2012)

33. Younes, H.L.S., Simmons, R.G.: Probabilistic verification of discrete event systems using acceptance sampling. In: Brinksma, E., Larsen, K.G. (eds.) CAV 2002. LNCS, vol. 2404, pp. 223–235. Springer, Heidelberg (2002). https://doi.org/10.1007/3-540-45657-0_17

34. Younes, H.L.S.: Ymer: a statistical model checker. In: Etessami, K., Rajamani, S.K. (eds.) CAV 2005. LNCS, vol. 3576, pp. 429–433. Springer, Heidelberg (2005). https://doi.org/10.1007/11513988_43

35. Zuliani, P., Platzer, A., Clarke, E.M.: Bayesian statistical model checking with application to stateflow/simulink verification. Formal Methods Syst. Des. **43**(2), 338–367 (2013)

Towards Safe and Resilient Hybrid Systems in the Presence of Learning and Uncertainty

Julius Adelt, Paula Herber$^{(\boxtimes)}$, Mathis Niehage, and Anne Remke

University of Münster, Einsteinstr. 62, 48149 Münster, Germany
{julius.adelt,paula.herber,mathis.niehage,anne.remke}@uni-muenster.de

Abstract. Intelligent hybrid systems pose a major challenge for the analysis of safety and resilience. Deductive formal verification methods for such systems typically use strong abstractions and focus only on the worst-case behavior. This often seriously impedes performance. Quantitative analyses based on simulations and statistical model checking, on the other hand, are much better suited to take performance properties into account, but generally do not provide guarantees for all possible behaviors. In this paper, we present a novel approach to combine deductive formal verification and quantitative analysis. Our approach enables us to construct provably safe and resilient systems, which still achieve certain performance levels with a statistical guarantee. We demonstrate the applicability of our approach with a case study of an intelligent water distribution system, which is resilient towards pump failures.

Keywords: Hybrid systems · Resilience · Reinforcement learning · Formal verification · Statistical model checking

1 Introduction

With the advent of Industry 4.0, self-driving cars, and autonomous systems controlling supply systems and critical infrastructure, the complexity of safety-critical hybrid systems is steadily increasing. The complexity is driven by several factors: they combine discrete and continuous behavior, they are real-time dependent, and highly concurrent. In addition, while we are moving towards autonomous systems with learning components, we have to cope with the trial-and-error learning process and uncertainties in the dynamic environment, e.g. failures of components, stochastic repair processes, or varying supplies and demands. To ensure that hybrid systems are functioning correctly even in unexpected situations and under external disruptions, it is crucial to ensure their safety, but also their resilience, i.e. they have to remain operational in the presence of stressors and to adapt their functioning in case stressors persist [24]. Existing approaches for the verification of hybrid systems either focus on the rigorous verification of safety guarantees [4,12], or employ probabilistic techniques to optimize the probability that a stochastic hybrid system satisfies a temporal logic formula [28,29]. While the former often involves worst-case

T. Margaria and B. Steffen (Eds.): ISoLA 2022, LNCS 13701, pp. 299–319, 2022.
https://doi.org/10.1007/978-3-031-19849-6_18

considerations that impede the performance, the latter does not yield guarantees for all possible behaviors.

In this paper, we propose an approach to combine deductive formal verification with probabilistic techniques to ensure safety and resilience of hybrid systems in the presence of learning and uncertainty. Our key idea is twofold: First, we verify safety and resilience using deductive verification while we abstract from uncertainties using non-deterministic over-approximations. Second, we use a probabilistic approach to find a near-optimal scheduler, which maximizes resilience and the probability that a given performance property is satisfied. The former gives us potentially pessimistic *guarantees*. The latter allows a fine-grained control over control decisions, maximizes resilience and takes performance properties under stochastic assumptions about the environment into account. For deductive verification, we automatically transform system descriptions that are modeled in the industrial design language Simulink into a formal model in differential dynamic logic (d$\mathcal{L}$) [25] and verify safety and resilience with the interactive theorem prover KeYmaera X [12]. This provides us with a correct-by-construction approach, where only models with potentially pessimistic guarantees may be used for later execution and code generation. We capture the safe behavior of learning components with hybrid contracts [2]. To verify resilience, we define hybrid contracts that explicitly capture the dynamical adaptation of the system to potential stressors. The hybrid contracts define safe behavior of learning components and thus provide potentially pessimistic guarantees for their runtime behavior. To find a near-optimal scheduler, we use (discretized) Q-learning together with a simulation of the continuous system [31]. The learning process exploits hybrid contracts that are defined during the deductive verification process to ensure safety, and thus follows a correct-by-construction approach. The system then learns to adapt to reoccurring stressors. We meet predefined performance goals, and compute the probability that a given formula is satisfied using statistical model checking.

We demonstrate the applicability of our approach with a case study of an intelligent water distribution system with reinforcement learning and three pumps with stochastic failure probabilities and repair times, which is inspired by a Simulink model by The MathWorks [43]. We formally verify that the tank never runs empty and that it provides full service with three pumps and degraded service with fewer pumps. With our combined approach, we provide a near-optimal scheduler that is guaranteed to be safe and resilient by construction. It maximizes resilience and the probability that the energy consumption is kept below a given limit.

The paper is structured as follows: Sect. 2 introduces preliminaries and Sect. 3 discusses related work. Section 4 combines deductive formal verification and quantitative analysis for the design of safe and resilient hybrid systems. We summarize experimental results in Sect. 5 and conclude in Sect. 6.

2   Background

In this section, we introduce reinforcement learning and the necessary background of our deductive verification approach and our quantitative analysis.

2.1   Reinforcement Learning (RL)

Reinforcement learning is a class of machine learning methods for learning in a trial and error approach by interacting with an environment through actions [39]. The goal of an RL algorithm is to optimize a reward by learning a policy $\pi(a|s)$ that determines which actions to take in which states. The mathematical basis are Markov decision processes (MDPs) [39]. An MDP is a tuple (S, A, R, p), where S is a set of states, A a set of actions, $R \subset \mathbb{R}$ a set of rewards, and p a probability distribution, which describes the MDPs dynamics. In an MDP, an agent and an environment interact in discrete time steps. At each step t, the agent chooses an action $a_t \in A$ to apply in the current state $s_t \in S$. Then the RL agent receives a new state $s_{t+1} \in S$ resulting from the applied action and a reward $r_{t+1} \in R$. The probabilities of states s, actions a and rewards r at times t are given by random variables S_t, A_t and R_t. The expected reward r and next state s' resulting from the application of a in s can be expressed as the probability distribution $p(s', r|s, a) \doteq Pr\{S_t = s', R_t = r|S_{t-1} = s, A_{t-1} = a\}$.

2.2   Simulink and the RL Toolbox

Simulink [40] is an industrially well established graphical modeling language for hybrid systems. It comes with a tool suite for simulation and automated code generation. Simulink models consist of blocks that are connected by discrete or continuous signals. The Simulink block library provides a large set of predefined blocks, from arithmetics over control flow blocks to integrators and complex transformations. Together with the MATLAB library, linear and non-linear differential equations can be modeled and simulated.

Figure 1a shows a Simulink model of a simple water tank. The model has two input ports, one for an input water supply i and one for the current water demand d. The water level h is computed by integrating the difference of inflow and demand d over time in an integrator block. The inflow is controlled by a switch block. If the water level exceeds h_{OK}, the inflow is stopped, and the constant 0 is used instead. Otherwise, the value supplied at input port i is used. To model discrete sampling of the water level, the model features a zero order hold h_{Hold}, which updates its output in fixed sampling steps before the switch.

The RL toolbox [41] provides an RL agent block, which enables the simulation of reinforcement learning algorithms directly within Simulink. The RL agent acts in fixed sampling steps. In each time step, it samples observations s_t and rewards r_t, and outputs an action a_t chosen by its RL algorithm.

2.3   Differential Dynamic Logic

Differential dynamic logic (d$\mathcal{L}$) [35] is a logic for formally specifying and reasoning about properties of hybrid systems, which are described as hybrid programs.

The syntax is as follows: $\alpha; \beta$ models a sequential composition of two hybrid programs α and β. $\alpha \cup \beta$ (or $\alpha + + \beta$) models a non-deterministic choice. A non-deterministic loop α^* executes α zero or more times. The hybrid program

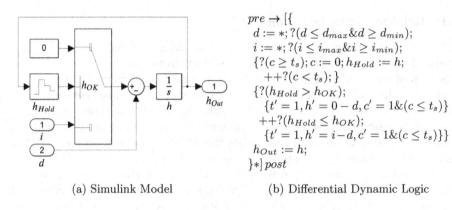

(a) Simulink Model   (b) Differential Dynamic Logic

Fig. 1. Reinforcement Learning, Simulink, and d$\mathcal{L}$

$x := e$ evaluates the term e and assigns it to the variable x. $x := *$ denotes a non-deterministic assignment. $?\mathcal{Q}$ is a test, which checks whether the formula $\mathcal{Q}$ is fulfilled. Finally, $\{x'_1 = \theta_1, x'_2 = \theta_2, x'_n = \theta_n \ \& \ \mathcal{Q}\}$ is a continuous evolution, which evolves a set of variables x with a set of differential equations θ. A continuous evolution may progress as long as the evolution domain $\mathcal{Q}$ is satisfied. d$\mathcal{L}$ provides two modalities for reasoning about reachable states of hybrid programs. $[\alpha]\phi$ states that a formula ϕ holds in every state reachable by α. $\langle\alpha\rangle\phi$ states that there exists a state reachable by α in which ϕ holds. Specifications for hybrid programs are defined as $pre \rightarrow [\alpha]post$.

A d$\mathcal{L}$ specification can be deductively verified with the interactive theorem prover KeYmaera X [12]. Deductive reasoning avoids the state space explosion problem and can also be used for parameterized and infinite-state systems, but requires high expertise, e.g., for the manual definition of invariants.

2.4   Transformation from Simulink to d$\mathcal{L}$

In [25], we have presented a fully-automatic transformation of hybrid Simulink models into d$\mathcal{L}$. We have defined d$\mathcal{L}$ expressions that precisely capture the semantics of all Simulink blocks in a given model, connect them according to the signal lines, and expand control conditions such that assignments and evaluations are only performed if the control conditions are satisfied. A simplified illustrating example is shown in Fig. 1b. The d$\mathcal{L}$ model corresponds to the simple Simulink water tank in Fig. 1a. The inputs i and d are modeled by constrained non-deterministic assignments, i.e., an arbitrary value from the given input range can be assigned at any time. The integrator block is captured by a continuous evolution. Depending on the control flow condition of the switch ($h_{Hold} > h_{OK}$), the water level h evolves with $0 - d$ or $i - d$. The discrete zero order hold block is captured using discrete assignment together with a test formula, which ensures that the assignment is only made whenever a clock variable c is equal to the discrete sample time. The clock variable c is evolved in the continuous evolution and $c \leq t_s$ is added to the evolution domain to ensure that no discrete sampling step is missed. A nondeterministic repetition models the global simulation loop.

To enable compositional verification, we have introduced the concept of Simulink services [26]. A service is a group of blocks whose joint functionality can be described by a hybrid contract, i.e., by a tuple $hc = (\phi_{in}, \phi_{out})$ specifying assumptions on the inputs and guarantees on the outputs. By specifying a hybrid contract, a service can be individually verified, and then be replaced by its contract, which enables us to abstract from the inner workings of the service.

2.5   Stochastic Hybrid Model

In dynamic environments, we often have to cope with uncertainties such as varying demands, failures, unknown repair times, or external disruptions. A flexible approach to cope with uncertainties and to express expectations about a dynamic environment in terms of, e.g. a demand distribution, failure probabilities and stochastically distributed repair times, are stochastic hybrid models. A variety of model formalisms for stochastic hybrid systems exists, e.g. [1,6,16,28], with highly different semantics. An interface for different stochastic hybrid systems has been defined as Stochastic Hybrid Model (SHM) in [31]. It currently supports modeling formalisms which combine discrete, continuous variables and random delays with discrete nondeterminism. This results in a model with $n_d \in \mathbb{N}$ discrete modes $m_j \in \mathbb{N}$, $j \in \{1, \ldots, n_d\}$, and $n_c \in \mathbb{N}$ continuous variables $x_i \in \mathbb{R}$, $i \in \{1, \ldots, n_c\}$, which span a hybrid and uncountable state space S. A system of first-order ordinary differential equations $\dot{x} = f_j(t, x(t))$, where f_j is a Lipschitz continuous function describing the evolution of a continuous variable.

The specific semantics of an SHM is adopted from an existing modeling formalism, e.g. stochastic hybrid automata (SHA) [16] or hybrid Petri nets with general transitions (HPnG) [14,33]. We use the latter in the case study of this paper. The chosen semantics excludes Zeno behaviour and induces a finite number of deterministic events and random delays up to a finite time bound. Events are caused by enabled actions, which are collected in a finite set A_Γ per state $\Gamma \in S$. If $|A_\Gamma| = 0$, only time can pass and if $|A_\Gamma| \geq 2$, a nondeterministic conflict occurs between different actions. The state Γ is updated according to the specific semantics after choosing and executing one action.

As proposed in [31], we use a *discrete event system (DES)* to simulate specific instances of an SHM formalism according to its semantics. The simulation runs until a predefined time-bound or until a nondeterministic conflict occurs. After choosing an action, the DES continues with the execution of the action. Resolving a nondeterministic conflict can be done by a scheduler which assigns at each state all available actions a probability by a discrete probability distribution.

Memoryless prophetic and nonprophetic schedulers are supported in [31]. In this paper, we focus on memoryless nonprophetic schedulers, as prophetic schedulers require an amount of information that appears unrealistic in many practical settings. A *memoryless nonprophetic scheduler* for a SHM is a measurable function $\mathfrak{s} \colon S \to \mathrm{Dist}(\mathcal{A})$ that maps every state $\Gamma \in S$ to a discrete probability distribution over the set of all actions $\mathcal{A}$ with $support(\mathfrak{s}(\Gamma)) \subseteq A_\Gamma$.

2.6 Signal Temporal Logic

A property in signal temporal logic (STL) [29] expresses linear-time properties over the state of a hybrid model. Whether a property specified in STL at time t is satisfied in a simulation of the DES can be decided by a model checker which monitors the state evolution. The context-free grammar

$$\Psi ::= tt \mid AP \mid \neg\Psi \mid \Psi \wedge \Psi \mid \Psi\, U^{[t_1,t_2]}\, \Psi$$

constructs a signal temporal logic property Ψ. It consists of true (tt) and continuous atomic properties (AP) comparing a function $f : S \to \mathbb{R}$ with the value zero: $f(\Gamma) > 0$. They can be combined with a logical *and* or with a time-bounded *until*-operator and negated. STL as in [29] only supports continuous signals, i.e. continuous variables in our context. By mapping discrete modes to continuous signals, they can be included as well. We refer to our own previous work [34] for the semantics of STL in the context of HPnGs.

Statistical model checking can be used to estimate the probability of a STL property Ψ at a time t via multiple simulation runs for a given scheduler. The model checker returns for each run whether the run fulfils Ψ or not. Hence, given n simulation runs, a sequence of independent values $p_1, \ldots, p_n \in \{0,1\}$ can be computed where each $p_i, i \in \{1, \ldots, n\}$, is a sample of a Bernoulli distribution indicating whether run i fulfils Ψ at time t. The actual probability p can be estimated by the arithmetic mean $\hat{p} = \frac{1}{n}\sum_{i=1}^{n} p_i$ and a confidence interval $\hat{p} \in [a, b]$. The number of simulation runs depends on the chosen interval width and the confidence level.

Resolving nondeterminism with a scheduler determines the following evolution of the system. Thus, the scheduler influences the probability that indicates whether the STL property is fulfilled at time t. Hence, a interval of possible probabilities can be obtained by choosing schedulers from the set of all memoryless nonprophetic schedulers $\mathfrak{S}^n$ (cf. [31]). In the following, the boundaries of the interval are referred to as minimum and maximum probabilities.

2.7 Learning Optimal Decisions for Stochastic Hybrid Systems

Using reinforcement learning as summarized in Sect. 2.1 requires a finite state space and a discrete notion of time. Neither the DES, nor its embedded SHM compy with these requirements. The requirement of discrete time is not problematic in our setting since decisions occur only at discrete time points over a finite set of actions. To handle the uncountable state space, [31] suggests a discretization of the continuous variables and proves the optimality of the approach for a decreasing discretization distance.

The main idea is that the DES is simulated until a nondeterministic conflict occurs. Then the conflict set and the discretized state are given to the scheduler which resolves the conflict. The STL property is checked after the simulation run reached its time-bound and a reward is given to the learner based on whether the STL property is fulfilled. If the goal is to maximize the probability of the

STL formula, a positive reward is given if the property is satisfied. Otherwise when minimizing, a reward is given if the STL property is not fulfilled.

The scheduler is trained for a predefined number of runs. Then, statistical model checking estimates the probability of the STL property for that scheduler.

3   Related Work

In the last decade, a variety of approaches have been proposed for the formal verification of systems that are modeled in Simulink. However, many of them, e.g. [5,20,36], including the Simulink Design Verifier [42], are limited to discrete subsets of Simulink. Formal verification methods that support hybrid systems modeled in Simulink are, e.g., proposed in [8,9,30,44]. In [9] and [30], Simulink is translated into hybrid automata. However, the models are verified by exploring the state space via reachability analysis, which does not scale for larger systems. In [8,44], the authors present and approach to automatically transforms a given Simulink model into Hybrid CSP and to enable the verification with Hybrid Hoare Logic in the HHL Prover. By using Hybrid CSP as underlying formalism, the authors inherit compositionality from a highly expressive process algebra. However, both the property specification and the verification process with Hybrid CSP require a very high level of expertise. Furthermore, none of these methods enables verification of intelligent Simulink models.

Formal methods are used to ensure the safety of reinforcement learning. In [3], the use of a shield is proposed, which substitutes unsafe for safe actions and is synthesized from a safety automaton and an abstraction of the environment. This idea has attracted quite some interest. A survey on shield synthesis for reinforcement learning is given in [23]. In [13], the safety of an RL controller is ensured via verified runtime monitors based on a differential dynamic logic model. However, the resulting knowledge about safe actions is not used in quantitative analyses, i.e., they do not get an optimized probability for meeting a performance property while only choosing guaranteedly safe actions.

Reinforcement learning has also been used on MDPs to improve performance and safety (e.g. [19]), as well as to deal with *unknown* stochastic behavior [7,18], and with linear-time logic specifications (e.g. [7,17,37]).

Applying machine learning on (infinite-state) stochastic hybrid systems in continuous time requires discretization. A formal approach to discretization has been taken in [21], which includes discretization of a continuous environment as well as reinforcement learning. Learning for SHS is considered, e.g. in a variant of ProbReach, which applies a the cross-entropy method for resolving nondeterminism [38]. Also [10] enriches an SMT-based approach with decision trees and AI planning algorithms to handle nondeterminism. More generally, Fulton et al. [11] provide an overview on challenges related to learning.

Finally, there has been some work on combining rigorous formal and statistical methods. In [22], the authors incorporate statistical hypothesis testing to compute promising configurations of program verifiers automatically. However, they do not support hybrid systems, and they do not consider both safety and

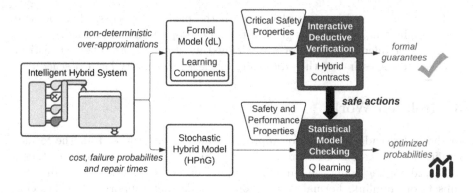

Fig. 2. Combining deductive verification and quantitative analysis

performance properties. In [15], the authors present a formal framework for an integrated qualitative and quantitative model-based safety analysis. This approach is more closely related to our work and also exploits the idea to combine the best out of both worlds from formal verification and quantitative analysis. However, they again do not support hybrid systems, do not consider deductive verification methods and also not the integration of learning components.

4   Combining Deductive and Quantitative Analyses

In this paper, we propose an approach to combine deductive formal verification with quantitative analysis to ensure safety and resilience of hybrid systems in the presence of learning and uncertainty. Our key idea is to use interactive deductive verification to provide safety and a statistical model checking approach combined with Q-learning to take performance properties into account.

Our overall approach is shown in Fig. 2. Our goal is to ensure safety and resilience of intelligent hybrid systems. To provide formal guarantees for the safe and resilient behavior of intelligent hybrid systems, we first translate given system descriptions (e.g. a Simulink model) into a formal model in d$\mathcal{L}$ [25,27], as shown in the upper part of Fig. 2. In the transformation process, we abstract from uncertainties and the learning process using non-deterministic over-approximations, as proposed in [2]. Then, we use the formal d$\mathcal{L}$ representation as an input to an interactive deductive verification tool for hybrid systems, namely KeYmaera X. We capture critical properties that establish safety and resilience in d$\mathcal{L}$ (e.g., a water tank never runs empty). Additionally, we capture the requirements imposed on the learning components by these properties with hybrid contracts, as proposed in [2,26]. Finally, we deductively verify that the overall system satisfies the given properties for an unbounded time and potentially even for a system model with unbounded parameters under the assumption that the learning components adhere to the hybrid contract at runtime. This provides us with a correct-by-construction approach: the resulting verified model is guaranteed to be correct (with respect to the verified safety properties), and can be optimized and refined using simulation-based approaches and automated code generation in later stages of the development process.

To take performance properties into account, we use a simulation-based approach to find a near-optimal scheduler, which maximizes or minimizes the probability that a given performance property is satisfied. To this end, we first (manually) translate the given system description into a stochastic hybrid model (SHM), for example a HPnG, as shown in the lower part of Fig. 2. We define safety and performance properties in STL. Then, we combine simulation with Q-learning, as proposed in [31], to compute a non-prophetic scheduler that optimizes the probability that the given STL formula is satisfied. Thereby, we restrict ourselves to exploiting only safe actions defined by the hybrid contracts that we have used for deductive formal verification to ensure that the resulting scheduler is correct by construction with respect to the (deductively) verified safety properties. With that, we compute an optimized probability that general safety properties (e.g. there is always a reasonable amount of water available) or performance properties (e.g., the energy consumption of the pump is never above a certain limit) are satisfied, while we still ensure that the critical safety properties are never violated.

In the following subsections, we first introduce an intelligent water distribution system [43] with some adaptations as a motivational example, and (informally) discuss its major requirements with respect to safety, resilience, and performance. Secondly, we present our approach for the deductive verification, which enables correct-by-construction design, but may impede performance. Third and finally, we present our simulation-based probabilistic approach that exploits the safe actions defined by the hybrid contracts used for deductive verification while optimizing for more general safety and performance properties.

4.1 An Intelligent Water Distribution System

Our motivational example is a water distribution system (WDS) that uses a reinforcement learning agent to learn how to satisfy a water demand by consumers as best as possible, while being energy efficient. Our model is inspired by [43]. Figure 3 depicts our system intuitively. The system consists of three pumps (p_1, p_2, p_3), which are used to constantly pump fluid from a reservoir into a water tank. Using pumps is associated with a cost. The usage of pumps is controlled by the systems' RL agent. The RL agent can activate the pumps (actions $a_1 - a_3$), and it can limit the outflow to a maximum supply s_{max}. The RL agent makes these control decisions in discrete sampling steps, while the overall behavior of the system is hybrid. If a pump is turned on by the RL agent, it pumps fluid with a constant rate r into the tank. The overall inflow i is determined by the activated pumps. The fluid in the tank is used to satisfy a consumer demand d. This demand ranges from 0 to s_{max}. The continuous change of the tanks water level h is described by the differential equation $h' = i - d$.

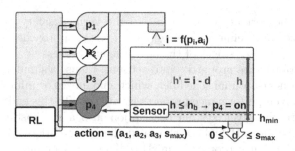

Fig. 3. Intelligent WDS inspired by [43]

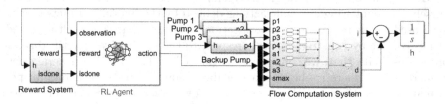

Fig. 4. Simulink model of the intelligent WDS inspired by [43]

Safety. A critical safety property is that the water tank should never run empty. We capture this with the safety property $h > h_{min}$, which should hold in any reachable state. To ensure that a minimum supply of water is always available, the system features a backup pump (p_4), which is not controlled by the RL agent and turns on as soon as the water level falls below a backup level h_b. The backup pump has the highest cost of all pumps. To ensure that the safety requirement $h > h_{min}$ is fulfilled, the agent has to limit the supply accordingly.

Resilience. A resilient system should be able to keep working under the influence of external stressors [24]. To achieve this, the system needs the capability to dynamically adapt to unexpected disruptions. In our model, pumps can break during usage. We model a possible adaptation to this by defining a degraded service level, where the RL agent limits the maximum water supply s_{max} to s_{deg}. As a result, the supply limit s_{max} is chosen from the interval $[s_{deg}, s_{full}]$, where s_{full} is the highest service level, which ensures that the maximum possible consumer demand can be satisfied, and s_{deg} is the degraded service level, which ensures that only critical consumers can be supplied but that the system is still functional even with a limited number of working pumps.

Performance. The pumps in our intelligent WDS are associated with varying cost in terms of their energy usage. A crucial performance property of our system is that the energy consumption stays below a certain limit.

```
1    pre → [{
2      smallStep := 0;
3      /* pumps 1-3 */
4      p₁ := *; ?(p₁ = 1.0|p₁ = 0.0); p₂ := *;  ?(p₂ = 1.0|p₂ = 0.0); p₃ := *;  ?(p₃ = 1.0|p₃ = 0.0);
5      /* backup pump triggered by sensor */
6      p₄ := *;  ?(p₄ = 1.0|p₄ = 0.0); ?(h ≤ h_b → p₄ = 1.0);
7      /* RL agent embedding */
8      { ?(c_RL ≥ t_S);
9        c_RL := 0; a₁ := *; a₂ := *; a₃ := *; s_max := *; ?(hc_RL);
10     ++
11       ?(c_RL < t_S); }
12     /* in- and outflow calculation */
13     i := *;  ?(i = (min(p₁, a₁) + min(p₂, a₂) + min(p₃, a₃) + p₄) · r);
14     d := *;  ?(d ≥ 0) & (d ≤ s_max));
15     /* continuous behavior */
16     { ?(h ≤ h_b);
17       { t' = 1, c'_RL = 1, h' = (i − d), smallStep' = 1 &(h ≤ h_b | smallStep ≤ ϵ) & c_RL ≤ t_S}}
18     ++
19     {{ ?(!(h ≤ h_b));
20       { t' = 1, c'_RL = 1, h' = (i − d), smallStep' = 1 &( !(h ≤ h_b) | smallStep ≤ ϵ) & c_RL ≤ t_S}}}
21   }*] h > h_min
```

Fig. 5. Intelligent WDS in d$\mathcal{L}$

4.2 Formal Verification of Safety and Resilience

Our intelligent WDS is originally modeled in the industrial modelling language
Simulink. The model is depicted in Fig. 4. The system features an RL agent from
the RL toolbox [41], which chooses pump activations (a_1, a_2, a_3) and maximum
supply s_{max}. It further consists of services for each pump, which forward a binary
status $(working = 1, broken = 0)$, a flow computation service for computing in-
and out-flow (i and d) from the pump's status (p_i), activations (a_i) and maximum
supply (s_{max}), and an integrator block, which computes the current water level
h. To formally verify safety and resilience, we first transform the Simulink model
into d$\mathcal{L}$ [25]. Then, we capture the safe behavior of the RL agent with hybrid
contracts in d$\mathcal{L}$, and verify the model under the assumption that the RL agent
complies with its contract [2] deductively in KeYmaera X.

The formal d$\mathcal{L}$ model resulting from our approach is shown in Fig. 5. It uses
symbolic constants for system parameters like sampling time t_S, service levels
s_{full}, s_{degr} and minimum water height h_{min}. This enables verifying properties for
a range of safe system parameters and every possible input scenario. The services
for individual pumps are captured by hybrid contracts (Line 4) that only capture
the possible value range of pump failures ($on = 1, off = 0$), while abstracting
from details like failure probabilities. The contract in Line 6 captures the backup
pump, which turns on whenever the water height falls below the backup level h_b.
Line 8 to 11 contain our embedding of the RL agent. Whenever the clock c_{RL}
reaches the sampling time of the agent t_S, new values for the RL agent's actions
are chosen. These values are subject to the contract of the RL agent (hc_{RL}).
Lines 13 and 20 capture the computed values for in- and outflow (i and d). In
Line 16 to 20, the continuous variables of the system, including the water level,
evolve according to their differential equations. The evolutions are bounded by
the evolution domain $c_{RL} ≤ t_S$ to ensure that no sampling times of the RL agent
are missed. To ensure that the backup pumps contract is evaluated in time, its

Table 1. Safety contract

Assumption	Guarantee
True	$h - s_{max} * t_S > h_{min}$

Table 2. Resilience contract

Assumption	Guarantee
$h > h_{full}$	$s_{max} = s_{full}$
$h \leq h_{deg}$	$s_{max} = s_{deg}$
$h > h_{deg}$ & $h \leq h_{full}$	$h - s_{max} * t_S > h_{min}$

condition ($h \leq h_b$) and the negation ($!(h \leq h_b)$) are added to the control flow conditions of the system's continuous evolutions. To enable switching between the conditions, a small delay (*smallStep*) is added to the evolution domains [25]). The safety property $h > h_{min}$, which must hold in every reachable state, was manually added after the [ ] modal operator (Line 21).

Hybrid Contract for Ensuring Safety. To ensure that the tank never runs empty ($h > h_{min}$), the agent must manage maximum water supply and pump usage safely. The transformed model contains nondeterministic over-approximations to abstract from uncertainties, like pump failure times and water demand behavior. This ensures that proofs hold for every possible behavior of the environment. However, it also means that, to ensure safety, a hybrid contract for the RL agent has to always consider the worst case environmental behavior. The worst case possible behavior (regarding the safety property $h > h_{min}$) in our model is the failure of all three pumps. We define the safe behavior of the RL agent with the hybrid contract shown in Table 1. The contract ensures that the maximum water supply is always limited to a value (s_{max}) that can be satisfied by the current water level (h) without falling below h_{min} until the next decision is made in one sampling step (t_S). To account for the possible failure of all pumps, the contract does not make use of pump activation and always assumes the inflow to be zero.

Hybrid Contracts for Ensuring Resilience. To ensure resilience, we define the contract shown in Table 2. The first guarantee ensures that the agent always supplies the full service level $s_{max} = s_{full}$ whenever the water level is above $h_{full} = s_{full} \cdot t_S + h_{min}$. The second guarantee specifies that the agent supplies the degraded service level if the water level is too low, i.e., it chooses $s_{max} = s_{deg}$ if $h \leq h_{deg} = s_{deg} \cdot t_S + h_{min}$. This degraded service is guaranteed by the backup pump, which turns on before the tank runs empty. The third guarantee specifies that the agent supplies intermediate but safe levels between the two boundaries.

4.3 Resilient Scheduling Under Uncertainty

As sketched in Sect. 2.7, in the quantitative approach [31], a DES simulates a specific instance of an SHM. Then Q-learning is used to find optimal actions for nondeterministic conflicts, which optimize the probability that a predefined STL formula holds. Hence, the model of the WDS, as depicted in Fig. 3 must be expressed in a model formalism suitable for the SHM interface, as shown in Sect. 2.5. Here, we chose Hybrid Petri Nets with general transitions [14].

Table 3. Fail and repair distributions for the three pumps.

Pump	Fail: folded normal		Repair: uniform	
	μ	σ	a	b
p_1	30	6	7	10
p_2	20	4	3	5
p_3	5	1	1	2

Model as SHM. To obtain quantitative results, we parameterize the variables of the model, as follows. The water tank has an initial value of 5.5m and the minimum level is set to $h_{min} = 2$ m. Each pumps fills, if active, the tank with 0.15 m per hour. When active, pumps consume energy, which leads to cost 0.1 for p_1, p_2 and p_3, and to cost 0.15 for p_4. While the backup pump can not fail, the three ordinary pumps can fail and can be repaired. The parameters for the corresponding probability distributions are provided in Table 3.

The nondeterministic conflict set is formed by all possible actions, i.e., the different combinations $\mathcal{A} = \{(a_1, a_2, a_3) \mid a_i \in \{0, 1\}\}$, which indicates the choice of pumps. Note that $a_i = 1$ indicates that pump p_i is chosen, but not necessarily corresponds to an active pump. An action must then be taken at the initial time and after every sampling time $t_S = 10$. At the same time instances, a choice between three different service levels, $\mathcal{S} = \{s_{full}, s_{mid}, s_{deg}\}$ with $s_{full} = 0.3, s_{mid} = 0.2$, and $s_{deg} = 0.15$ is required. This results in action set $\mathcal{A} \times \mathcal{S}$.

Applying contracts from Sect. 4.2, we compute resilient schedules to ensure a combination of safety and resilience. This restricts the nondeterministic set $\mathcal{S}$, as the service level follows directly from the chosen contract, as indicated in Table 2. Hence, the contract serves as scheduler for the service level.

Resilience with respect to a desired property Ψ is then encoded as STL *until* formula $tt\ U^{[0,t]} \neg \Psi$, with $\Psi = (h > h_{full})$. Minimizing the probability that this formula holds then increases resilience, as the probability to reach a state where Ψ does not hold before time t decreases. *Performance* with respect to energy consumption can be incorporated into the desired property $\Psi = (h > h_{full} \wedge \text{cost} < c)$, where h is a constant restricting the height of the water level and c forms an upper bound for the incurred energy cost.

5 Evaluation

In this section, we summarize and discuss our experimental results obtained by the two different approaches.

Table 4. Verified d$\mathcal{L}$ properties and manual verification effort

d$\mathcal{L}$ Property	Number of invariants	Estimated time in hh:mm	Manual proof steps
(1) $h > h_{min}$	8	6:00	212
(2) $s_{max} \geq s_{deg}$	1	0:15	9
(3) $obs_h > h_{full} \rightarrow s_{max} = s_{full}$	1	0:10	5
(4) $i = i_{max} \wedge i \cdot clk_{lc} \geq h_{full} + h_{\delta,RL} \rightarrow s_{max} = s_{full}$	11	8:00	332

5.1   Deductive Verification

For the evaluation of our deductive verification approach, we have verified the d$\mathcal{L}$ properties (1)–(4) of Table 4 for our intelligent WDS for all reachable states ([.] modality). The table only shows postconditions. Preconditions like assumptions on safe ranges of system parameters are omitted for brevity. Our Simulink2dL transformation tool and all proofs can be found online[1]. d$\mathcal{L}$ property (1) is a typical safety property, which specifies that the tank never runs empty. d$\mathcal{L}$ properties (2)–(4) capture the resilience of the system by guaranteeing service levels under different circumstances. d$\mathcal{L}$ property (2) states that the system always at least offers the degraded service level. d$\mathcal{L}$ property (3) states that the full service level s_{full} is offered whenever the water level sampled by the RL agent obs_h is above h_{full}. d$\mathcal{L}$ property (4) captures that the full service level is enabled, if no pumps fail and the RL agent uses all three pumps for a sufficiently long time. Here $i_{max} = 3 \cdot r$ marks the maximum possible inflow by using all pumps except for the backup pump (p_4). clk_{lc} is a fresh clock that is reset on any pump activation changes (changes of a_i or p_i) and $h_{\delta,RL} = (i + r) \cdot t_S$ is the maximum water level change in one sampling time of the RL agent. Table 4 summarizes the time and effort spent for the verification.

5.2   Quantitative Analysis

While deductive verification guarantees properties (1)–(4) in Table 4, HYPEG [32] provides statistical guarantees w.r.t. a finite time bound. Hence, safety and resilience are considered quantitatively. We use a confidence level of 99% and a half interval width of 0.01. Additionally, we train schedulers which solve nondeterministic conflicts. All considered STL properties are summarized in Table 5.

Safety. Table 6 presents the probability that the safety property Φ_s holds before time 24 h to 96 h. As base case, we consider a purely probabilistic scheduler (U, U), which chooses pumps and a service level according to the uniform distribution from the complete action set $\mathcal{A} \times \mathcal{S}$. Scheduler (L, L) minimizes the probability that the Φ_s holds. Training is done over the full action set $\mathcal{A} \times \mathcal{S}$ and for different predefined maximum times. Note that a new scheduler is learned

---

[1] https://www.uni-muenster.de/EmbSys/research/Simulink2dL.html.

Table 5. STL properties describing the three considered optimization goals.

Safety	$\Phi_s = tt\ U^{[0.0,maxTime]} \neg(h > 2.0)$
Resilience	$\Phi_r = tt\ U^{[0.0,maxTime]} \neg(h > 5.0)$
Performance	$\Phi_p = tt\ U^{[0.0,maxTime]} \neg(h > 5.0 \wedge cost \leq 0.2 \cdot maxTime)$

Table 6. Estimated probability for Φ_s for a combination of uniform (U), learned (L) and contract-based (C) schedulers for the action set $\mathcal{A} \times \mathcal{S}$ and different maximum times. Schedulers are indicated as tuples, indicating the considered strategy for $\mathcal{A}$ and $\mathcal{S}$, respectively.

	24 h	48 h	72 h	96 h
(U, U)				
Mean p	0.027	0.124	0.244	0.358
Sim. time	1.7 s	3.5 s	6.5 s	10.6 s
Sim. runs	5000 (min)	7204	12 229	15 250
(L, L)				
Mean p	0.0	4.0×10^{-4}	0.0024	0.057
Train time	1419.7 s	2348.7 s	3917.2 s	5237.1 s
Sim. time	3.7 s	5.8 s	9.0 s	11.9 s
Sim. runs	5000 (min)	5000 (min)	5000 (min)	5000 (min)
(U, C)				
Mean p	0.0	0.0	0.0	0.0
Sim. time	1.9 s	2.1 s	3.1 s	3.8 s
Sim. runs	5000 (min)	5000 (min)	5000 (min)	5000 (min)

for every time bound. Finally, scheduler (U, C) chooses the pump according to a uniform distribution and resolves $\mathcal{S}$, i.e., defines a demand, according to the contract given by the deductive approach.

For each scheduler, the estimated mean probability that Φ_s holds is provided together with the simulation time and the number of simulation runs. Furthermore, the training times for the learned schedulers are listed.

Overall, the uniform scheduler (U, U) yields the highest probability of a safety violation, which is furthermore increasing with a larger time horizon. The learned scheduler (L, L) is better than the base case (U, U), but not as good as the contract-based scheduler (U, C), even though it can choose from the full action set $\mathcal{A} \times \mathcal{S}$. Recent work [31] has shown that the learned scheduler will be optimal for a vanishing discretization and an infinite amount of training runs.

We performed 2 million training runs with a learning rate decreasing from 0.1, a discount factor 1 and epsilon greedy parameter 0.15. As discretization of the continuous variables, the valuations are truncated after the first digit.

The contract always determines the service level based on the current water level and is encoded in the model via guard arcs which only enable one service

Table 7. Estimated probability for Φ_r, for learned or uniform scheduling of $\mathcal{A}$ and a contract-based resolution of $\mathcal{S}$ and different time bounds.

	24 h	48 h	72 h	96 h
(U, C)				
Mean p	0.867	0.982	0.998	1.000
Sim. time	2.4 s	2.2 s	2.7 s	3.6 s
Sim. runs	7679	5000 (min)	5000 (min)	5000 (min)
(L, C)				
Mean p	6.0×10^{-4}	4.0×10^{-4}	0.005	0.0028
Train time	976.3 s	1804.4 s	2863.0 s	3677.6 s
Sim. time	2.5 s	4.7 s	7.4 s	9.4 s
Sim. runs	5000 (min)	5000 (min)	5000 (min)	5000 (min)

level action at a time. Since appropriate service level actions are sufficient to ensure safety, pump actions are irrelevant. The computation times depend on the number of runs performed and the considered time horizon. The simulation times of (U, C) are smaller than those of (U, U), since fewer decisions need to be sampled. The simulation times for (L, L) are the highest, as every action requires a lookup in the Q-table, instead of drawing a uniform sample.

In the current case study the approach suffers from the fact that the reward is collected only after a sequence of consecutive choices has been made. Hence, more training runs are required, especially for 96 h.

Clearly, the contract-based scheduler (U, C) outperforms all other schedulers in Table 6. However, it requires a predefined contract (cf. Section 5.1).

Resilience. In the following, we use the predefined contract to assure safety for all schedulers, hence we only consider schedulers (U, C) and (L, C). This approach allows to optimize the probability to maintain the full service level without the risk of a safety violation. The full service level is chosen if the water level is larger than $h_{full} = 5$. Table 7 shows the results for schedulers (U, C) and (L, C) for Φ_r (cf. Table 5).

The learned scheduler (L, C) is able to keep the estimated probability that a reduced service level is reached very close to zero, even for longer time bounds. In contrast, (U, C) is not able to realize the full service level with probability above 0.86, even for short time horizons, the probability of a reduced service level for time bound 96 even equals one.[2] The estimated probability increases with the time horizon for both scheduler, as a longer sequence of choices increases the probability to take a bad action.

Training used the same parameters as in Table 6. Note that the training and simulation times for (L, C) are smaller than the respective times of the of

---

[2] Scheduler (U, C) obtains different probabilities in Tables 6 and 7, since those probabilities relate to different STL properties.

Table 8. Estimated probability for Φ_p for either a uniform or a learned resolution of $\mathcal{A}$, and a contract-based resolution of $\mathcal{S}$. Learning is either done to optimize resilience (L_{res}), or to optimize performance (L_{perf}) and for different time bounds.

	24 h	48 h	72 h	96 h
(U, C)				
Mean p	0.966	0.994	1.000	1.000
Sim. time	1.9 s	1.9 s	2.8 s	3.6 s
Sim. runs	5000 (min)	5000 (min)	5000 (min)	5000 (min)
(L_{res}, C)				
Mean p	0.732	0.970	0.883	0.887
Train time	976.3 s	1804.4 s	2863.0 s	3677.6 s
Sim. time	6.6 s	4.7 s	10.5 s	12.7 s
Sim. runs	13021	5000 (min)	6846	6631
(L_{perf}, C)				
Mean p	0.0168	0.111	0.038	0.078
Train time	971.3 s	1779.7 s	2860.0 s	3633.1 s
Sim. time	2.6 s	6.0 s	7.3 s	9.3 s
Sim. runs	5000 (min)	6535	5000 (min)	5000 (min)

(L, L) (cf. Table 6). This speedup results from using the contract to choose actions concerning the service level, which is faster than learning them.

Performance. Energy cost induced by pumps have not been considered so far, but could be optimized as well. The desired cost corresponds to the cost accumulated by two pumps, since without pump failures, two pumps achieve the full service level. However, to account for pump failures, a buffer needs to be accumulated which incurs additional cost.

In the following Φ_p is minimized over the choices in $\mathcal{A}$, which can be done safely for the predefined contract. The corresponding results are shown in Table 8 for three schedulers, namely (U, C), or trained either towards on resilience (L_{res}, C), similar to (L, C) from Table 7, or trained towards minimizing Φ_p, denoted (L_{perf}, C). Clearly (U, C) and (L_{res}, C) are agnostic of cost and not able to achieve a low probability for Φ_p. However note, that (L_{res}, C) outperforms (U, C), which additionally struggles to maintain the desired height of the water level.

Schedulers trained on performance keep the estimated probability of Φ_p well below 0.1, with the exception of the scheduler learned for 48 h. This is due to the underlying distributions of the pump failures which make it harder at this specific time to consistently stay above $h_{full} = 5$ and have limited accumulated costs. The training times for all instances of (L_{res}, C) and (L_{perf}, C) increase with the considered maximum time and similar for the two different training objectives.

The deductive verification omits parts of the model, e.g. energy costs and failure distributions. The quantitative analysis exploits this information. Hence, we have a trade-off between the strengths of the results and the underlying assumptions. With our combination, we get the best of both worlds: safety and resilience are proven in a reduced model and resilience and performance are optimized for a verified system while still giving statistical guarantees.

6   Conclusion

In this paper, we have presented an approach for the design and verification of safe and resilient hybrid systems in the presence of learning and uncertainty. To achieve this, we explicitly define critical safety properties and safe dynamic adaptations to external disruptions as hybrid contracts. Then, we formally verify that critical properties are ensured under all circumstances using deductive verification with the differential dynamic logic d$\mathcal{L}$ and the interactive theorem prover KeYmaera X. Finally, we perform a quantitative analysis based on statistical model checking and Q learning to maximize resilience and the probability that performance goals are met for the verified system. Our approach is correct-by-construction in the sense that safety and resilience guarantees are maintained by exploiting hybrid contracts that are used for deductive verification in the quantitative analysis, i.e., only provably safe actions are taken in the optimization process. Our main contribution is a novel combination of deductive formal verification and quantitative analyses, which enables us to verify complex properties of intelligent hybrid systems in dynamic environments without impeding performance. With that, we get a more fine-grained control over potentially conflicting safety, resilience, and performance requirements than existing approaches. We have shown the applicability of our approach with an intelligent water distribution system modeled in the widely used industrial design language Simulink. In particular, we have shown that we can verify safe and resilient behavior while still maintaining efficient energy consumption with a maximal probability.

In future work, we plan to extend our approach to more sophisticated properties that reflect resilience. In addition, we plan to investigate the potential reuse of hybrid contracts and invariants for recurring properties and systems.

References

1. Abate, A., Katoen, J.P., Lygeros, J., Prandini, M.: Approximate model checking of stochastic hybrid systems. Eur. J. Control. **16**(6), 624–641 (2010)
2. Adelt, J., Liebrenz, T., Herber, P.: Formal verification of intelligent hybrid systems that are modeled with simulink and the reinforcement learning toolbox. In: Huisman, M., Păsăreanu, C., Zhan, N. (eds.) FM 2021. LNCS, vol. 13047, pp. 349–366. Springer, Cham (2021). https://doi.org/10.1007/978-3-030-90870-6_19
3. Alshiekh, M., Bloem, R., Ehlers, R., Könighofer, B., Niekum, S., Topcu, U.: Safe reinforcement learning via shielding. In: Proceedings of the AAAI Conference on Artificial Intelligence, vol. 32 (2018)

4. Alur, R.: Formal verification of hybrid systems. In: ACM International Conference on Embedded Software (EMSOFT), pp. 273–278 (2011)
5. Araiza-Illan, D., Eder, K., Richards, A.: Formal verification of control systems' properties with theorem proving. In: UKACC International Conference on Control (CONTROL), pp. 244–249. IEEE (2014)
6. Bertrand, N., et al.: Stochastic timed automata. Log. Methods Comput. Sci. **10**(4) (2014)
7. Cai, M., Peng, H., Li, Z., Kan, Z.: Learning-based probabilistic LTL motion planning with environment and motion uncertainties. IEEE Trans. Autom. Control **66**(5), 2386–2392 (2021)
8. Chen, M., et al.: MARS: a toolchain for modelling, analysis and verification of hybrid systems. In: Hinchey, M.G., Bowen, J.P., Olderog, E.-R. (eds.) Provably Correct Systems. NMSSE, pp. 39–58. Springer, Cham (2017). https://doi.org/10.1007/978-3-319-48628-4_3
9. Chutinan, A., Krogh, B.H.: Computational techniques for hybrid system verification. IEEE Trans. Autom. Control **48**(1), 64–75 (2003)
10. Ellen, C., Gerwinn, S., Fränzle, M.: Statistical model checking for stochastic hybrid systems involving nondeterminism over continuous domains. Int. J. Softw. Tools Technol. Transf. **17**(4), 485–504 (2015)
11. Fulton, N., Hunt, N., Hoang, N., Das, S.: Formal Verification of End-to-End Learning in Cyber-Physical Systems: Progress and Challenges. arXiv:2006.09181 (2020)
12. Fulton, N., Mitsch, S., Quesel, J.-D., Völp, M., Platzer, A.: KeYmaera X: an axiomatic tactical theorem prover for hybrid systems. In: Felty, A.P., Middeldorp, A. (eds.) CADE 2015. LNCS (LNAI), vol. 9195, pp. 527–538. Springer, Cham (2015). https://doi.org/10.1007/978-3-319-21401-6_36
13. Fulton, N., Platzer, A.: Safe reinforcement learning via formal methods: toward safe control through proof and learning. In: Proceedings of the AAAI Conference on Artificial Intelligence, vol. 32 (2018)
14. Gribaudo, M., Remke, A.: Hybrid Petri nets with general one-shot transitions. Perform. Eval. **105**, 22–50 (2016)
15. Gudemann, M., Ortmeier, F.: A framework for qualitative and quantitative formal model-based safety analysis. In: IEEE International Symposium on High Assurance Systems Engineering, pp. 132–141. IEEE (2010)
16. Hahn, E.M., Hartmanns, A., Hermanns, H., Katoen, J.P.: A compositional modelling and analysis framework for stochastic hybrid systems. Form. Methods Syst. Des. **43**(2), 191–232 (2013)
17. Hahn, E.M., Perez, M., Schewe, S., Somenzi, F., Trivedi, A., Wojtczak, D.: Faithful and effective reward schemes for model-free reinforcement learning of omega-regular objectives. In: Hung, D.V., Sokolsky, O. (eds.) ATVA 2020. LNCS, vol. 12302, pp. 108–124. Springer, Cham (2020). https://doi.org/10.1007/978-3-030-59152-6_6
18. Hasanbeig, M., Kantaros, Y., Abate, A., Kroening, D., Pappas, G.J., Lee, I.: Reinforcement learning for temporal logic control synthesis with probabilistic satisfaction guarantees. In: IEEE Conference on Decision and Control (CDC), Nice, France, pp. 5338–5343. IEEE (2019)
19. Hasanbeig, M., Abate, A., Kroening, D.: Cautious reinforcement learning with logical constraints. In: International Foundation for Autonomous Agents and Multiagent Systems, AAMAS 2020, pp. 483–491 (2020)
20. Herber, P., Reicherdt, R., Bittner, P.: Bit-precise formal verification of discrete-time MATLAB/Simulink models using SMT solving. In: International Conference on Embedded Software (EMSOFT), pp. 1–10. IEEE (2013)

21. Junges, S., Jansen, N., Katoen, J.-P., Topcu, U., Zhang, R., Hayhoe, M.: Model checking for safe navigation among humans. In: McIver, A., Horvath, A. (eds.) QEST 2018. LNCS, vol. 11024, pp. 207–222. Springer, Cham (2018). https://doi.org/10.1007/978-3-319-99154-2_13

22. Knüppel, A., Thüm, T., Schaefer, I.: GUIDO: automated guidance for the configuration of deductive program verifiers. In: IEEE/ACM International Conference on Formal Methods in Software Engineering (FormaliSE), pp. 124–129. IEEE (2021)

23. Könighofer, B., Lorber, F., Jansen, N., Bloem, R.: Shield synthesis for reinforcement learning. In: Margaria, T., Steffen, B. (eds.) ISoLA 2020. LNCS, vol. 12476, pp. 290–306. Springer, Cham (2020). https://doi.org/10.1007/978-3-030-61362-4_16

24. Laprie, J.C.: From dependability to resilience. In: IEEE/IFIP International Conference on Dependable Systems and Networks (DSN), pp. G8–G9 (2008)

25. Liebrenz, T., Herber, P., Glesner, S.: Deductive verification of hybrid control systems modeled in simulink with KeYmaera X. In: Sun, J., Sun, M. (eds.) ICFEM 2018. LNCS, vol. 11232, pp. 89–105. Springer, Cham (2018). https://doi.org/10.1007/978-3-030-02450-5_6

26. Liebrenz, T., Herber, P., Glesner, S.: A service-oriented approach for decomposing and verifying hybrid system models. In: Arbab, F., Jongmans, S.-S. (eds.) FACS 2019. LNCS, vol. 12018, pp. 127–146. Springer, Cham (2020). https://doi.org/10.1007/978-3-030-40914-2_7

27. Liebrenz, T., Herber, P., Glesner, S.: Service-oriented decomposition and verification of hybrid system models using feature models and contracts. Sci. Comput. Program. 211, 102694 (2021)

28. Lygeros, J., Prandini, M.: Stochastic hybrid systems: a powerful framework for complex, large scale applications. Eur. J. Control. 16(6), 583–594 (2010)

29. Maler, O., Nickovic, D.: Monitoring temporal properties of continuous signals. In: Lakhnech, Y., Yovine, S. (eds.) FORMATS/FTRTFT -2004. LNCS, vol. 3253, pp. 152–166. Springer, Heidelberg (2004). https://doi.org/10.1007/978-3-540-30206-3_12

30. Minopoli, S., Frehse, G.: SL2SX translator: from Simulink to SpaceEx models. In: International Conference on Hybrid Systems: Computation and Control, pp. 93–98. ACM (2016)

31. Niehage, M., Hartmanns, A., Remke, A.: Learning optimal decisions for stochastic hybrid systems. In: ACM-IEEE International Conference on Formal Methods and Models for System Design (MEMOCODE), pp. 44–55. ACM (2021)

32. Pilch, C., Edenfeld, F., Remke, A.: HYPEG: statistical model checking for hybrid petri nets: tool paper. In: EAI International Conference on Performance Evaluation Methodologies and Tools (VALUETOOLS), pp. 186–191. ACM Press (2017)

33. Pilch, C., Niehage, M., Remke, A.: HPnGs go non-linear: statistical dependability evaluation of battery-powered systems. In: IEEE International Symposium on Modeling, Analysis, and Simulation of Computer and Telecommunication Systems (MASCOTS), pp. 157–169. IEEE (2018)

34. Pilch, C., Remke, A.: Statistical model checking for hybrid petri nets with multiple general transitions. In: Annual IEEE/IFIP International Conference on Dependable Systems and Networks (DSN), pp. 475–486. IEEE (2017)

35. Platzer, A.: Differential dynamic logic for hybrid systems. J. Autom. Reason. 41(2), 143–189 (2008)

36. Reicherdt, R., Glesner, S.: Formal verification of discrete-time MATLAB/Simulink models using boogie. In: Giannakopoulou, D., Salaün, G. (eds.) SEFM 2014. LNCS, vol. 8702, pp. 190–204. Springer, Cham (2014). https://doi.org/10.1007/978-3-319-10431-7_14

37. Sadigh, D., Kim, E.S., Coogan, S., Sastry, S.S., Seshia, S.A.: A learning based approach to control synthesis of Markov decision processes for linear temporal logic specifications. In: IEEE Conference on Decision and Control, pp. 1091–1096. IEEE (2014)

38. Shmarov, F., Zuliani, P.: Probabilistic hybrid systems verification via SMT and Monte Carlo techniques. In: Bloem, R., Arbel, E. (eds.) HVC 2016. LNCS, vol. 10028, pp. 152–168. Springer, Cham (2016). https://doi.org/10.1007/978-3-319-49052-6_10

39. Sutton, R.S., Barto, A.G.: Reinforcement Learning: An Introduction, 2nd edn. The MIT Press, Cambridge; London (2018)

40. The MathWorks: Simulink. https://de.mathworks.com/products/simulink.html

41. The MathWorks: Reinforcement Learning Toolbox. https://www.mathworks.com/products/reinforcement-learning.html

42. The MathWorks: Simulink Design Verifier. https://de.mathworks.com/products/simulink-design-verifier.html

43. The MathWorks: Simulink Example: Water Distribution System Scheduling Using Reinforcement Learning. https://de.mathworks.com/help/reinforcement-learning/ug/water-distribution-scheduling-system.html

44. Zou, L., Zhan, N., Wang, S., Fränzle, M.: Formal verification of simulink/stateflow diagrams. In: Finkbeiner, B., Pu, G., Zhang, L. (eds.) ATVA 2015. LNCS, vol. 9364, pp. 464–481. Springer, Cham (2015). https://doi.org/10.1007/978-3-319-24953-7_33

Non-functional Testing of Runtime Enforcers in Android

Oliviero Riganelli[✉][ID], Daniela Micucci[ID], and Leonardo Mariani[ID]

University of Milano-Bicocca, Milan 20126, Italy
{oliviero.riganelli,daniela.micucci,leonardo.mariani}@unimib.it

Abstract. Runtime enforcers can be used to ensure that running applications satisfy desired correctness properties. Although runtime enforcers that are correct-by-construction with respect to abstract behavioral models are relatively easy to specify, the concrete software enforcers generated from these specifications may easily introduce issues in the target application. Indeed developers can generate test suites to verify the *functional* behavior of the enforcers, for instance exploiting the same models used to specify them. However, it remains challenging and tedious to verify the behavior of enforcers in terms of *non-functional* performance characteristics. This paper describes a practical approach to reveal runtime enforcers that may introduce *inefficiencies* in the target application. The approach relies on a combination of automatic test generation and runtime monitoring of multiple key performance indicators. We designed our approach to reveal issues in four indicators for mobile systems: responsiveness, launch time, memory, and energy consumption. Experimental results show that our approach can detect performance issues that might be introduced by automatically generated enforcers.

Keywords: Runtime enforcement · Testing enforcers · Non-functional testing · Android apps

1 Introduction

Mobile applications are extremely popular. Indeed, there are applications to support virtually any task, as witnessed by the more than 3 million applications available for download in Google Play in the first quarter of 2022 [36].

Mobile applications interact with the hosting device, exploiting the available resources, such as the camera, memory, battery, and Wi-Fi antenna. Unfortunately, mobile applications may easily misuse resources, causing issues to the underlying system and the rest of the applications running in the device. For instance, an application may acquire the camera without releasing it, preventing the access to the camera to the other applications.

To prevent these problems, users of mobile applications can install and activate software enforcers [10–12,15,32] that guarantee that specific correctness policies are satisfied (e.g., the camera is always released after it has been

T. Margaria and B. Steffen (Eds.): ISoLA 2022, LNCS 13701, pp. 320–334, 2022.
https://doi.org/10.1007/978-3-031-19849-6_19

acquired). These enforcers can be typically generated automatically from a model-based representation of the processes involved in the policy that must be enforced. For instance, I/O automata can model the behavior of apps and services running in a mobile device, and edit automata [20] can be used to specify enforcers that can correct executions to avoid policy violations. Software enforcers derived from these models are guaranteed to fix the execution since they are correct-by-construction, as long as both the specified models and the code generation process are correct.

However, models are abstractions of the behavior of the software and its environment, and often miss many relevant details that might affect the correctness of the enforcers. For this reason, software enforcers, even when generated automatically, have to be tested. In previous work [13], we addressed the challenge of automatically generating test cases that cover the functional specification used to generated the enforcers, and to ensure correctness-by-construction before the enforcers are deployed. However, correctness-by-construction is limited to the functional aspect of the enforcers. In this paper, we address the challenge of enriching the testing strategy with the capability to collect and analyze non-functional indicators to ensure non-functional properties, specifically through the detection of performance problems that might be introduced into the target system in an attempt to apply (functional) policy. We experimented our approach with several enforcers, indicators, and faults, demonstrating the usefulness of addressing both the functional and non-functional aspects when verifying software enforcers.

The paper is organized as follows. Section 2 provides background information about software enforcement. Section 3 describes the test case generation strategy for software enforcers, augmented to deal with performance problems. Section 4 reports the results that we obtained with the evaluation of the approach. Section 5 discusses related work. Finally, Sect. 6 provides final remarks.

2   Background

In this section we introduce the notion of runtime policy and policy enforcement.

2.1   Runtime Policy

A runtime policy is a predicate over a set of executions. More formally, let Σ be a finite set of observable program actions a. An *execution* σ is a finite or infinite non-empty sequence of actions $a_1; a_2; \ldots; a_n$. Σ^* is the set of all finite sequences, Σ^ω is the set of infinite sequences, and $\Sigma^\infty = \Sigma^* \cup \Sigma^\omega$ is the set of all sequences. Given a set of executions $\chi \subseteq \Sigma^\infty$, a *policy* is a predicate P on χ. A policy P is satisfied by a set of executions χ if and only if $P(\chi)$ evaluates to *true*.

A policy may concern any behavior of an application, including resource usage and security. For example, an Android policy [1] requires that anytime an Android app stops using the camera, it explicitly releases the camera to make it available to the other apps. More in details, *"if an activity*[1] *is using the camera and the activity receives an invocation to the callback method onPause()*[2]*, the activity must release the camera."* We refer to this policy throughout the paper to describe our approach.

2.2   Policy Enforcement Models

A policy enforcement model specifies how executions must be changed to make them satisfy a given policy. Policy enforcers can be represented with finite-state models, such as edit and input/output automata. For instance, Fig. 1 shows an input/output automaton that specifies an enforcement model that can enforce a faulty activity that does not release the camera to release it.

The inputs are the events intercepted by the enforcer (represented with the *req* subscript in the model) while the outputs (represented with the *api* subscript) are the events emitted by the enforcer in response to the intercepted events. When the input and the output in a same transition match (regardless of the subscript), the enforcer is not changing the execution. If the output differs from the input, the enforcer is changing the execution suppressing and/or adding events.

Referring to the example model in Fig. 1, state s_0 represents the case the camera has not been acquired yet, and the enforcer is ready to intercept events without altering the execution. In fact, both pausing the current activity (event `activity.onPause()`) and acquiring the camera (event `camera.open()`) are events compatible with the policy related to the access to the camera. Once the camera is acquired (event `camera.open()` from state s_0), the camera must be released before the activity can be paused. In state s_1, the enforcer is thus ready to accept the `camera.release()` event. On the contrary, if the activity is paused, the `activity.onPause()` event would violate the policy (i.e., the activity would be paused without releasing the camera), and thus the enforcer modifies the execution emitting the sequence of events `camera.release()` `activity.onPause()`, which guarantees the satisfaction of the policy.

Enforcement strategies must be translated into software components (i.e., software enforcers) that enforce the specified strategies at runtime. This translation could be done manually, semi-automatically, or automatically. In all the cases, the resulting components may include bugs, due to issues in the translation process and the extra code added by developers to obtain fully functional components, and must be tested extensively before they can be deployed and used.

To detect functional bugs, we developed Test4Enforcers [13], a tool that automatically generates test cases that cover the functional specification used to generate the enforcers. In this paper, we describe how we extended Test4Enforcers

---

[1] Activities are the entry point of interactions between users and apps https://developer.android.com/guide/components/activities.

[2] onPause() is a callback method that is invoked by the Android framework every time an activity is paused.

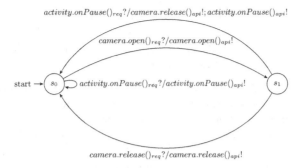

Fig. 1. Enforcer for systematically releasing the camera when the activity is paused.

with the capability to detect performance bugs by collecting and analyzing non-functional indicators.

3 Test4Enforcers

Test4Enforcers detects bugs by implementing a two-step detection strategy. The first step, *test case generation*, generates test cases that cover the behavior of the enforcer, considering both the case the enforcer has to modify the execution to enforce the policy and the enforcer does not need to change the execution since it already satisfies the policy. The second step, *test case execution*, executes the generated test cases in the target environment both with and without the policy enforcer by collecting the Key Performance Indicators (KPIs) that are analyzed to detect any non-functional bug.

3.1 Test Case Generation

Test case generation consists of 3 activities, as shown in Fig. 2.

i) The *Generation of the Test Sequences* activity generates the test sequences that must be covered to thoroughly test the behavior of the enforcer according with the enforcement model.

ii) The *GUI Ripping with Tracing* activity runs a GUI Ripping process that explores the GUI of the app under test while tracing the events that are in the alphabet of the enforcement model. The output of this activity is an augmented GUI model with states representing the GUI states visited during the ripping process and the transitions representing the GUI actions that caused the state change. The model is augmented since each transition is annotated with the events in the alphabet of the enforcement model that have been executed as a consequence of the state change.

iii) The *Concrete Test Case Generation* activity uses the augmented GUI model to identify the sequences of UI interactions that exercise the test sequences identified in the first step as the ones relevant to verify the behavior of the enforcer. These UI interactions, enriched with program oracles, are the test cases that can be executed to validate the activity of the enforcer. In the following, we briefly describe each activity, explaining how we extended the approach to collect and verify the non-functional impact of the enforcer. More information about Test4Enforcers can be found in [13].

Generation of the Test Sequences. In this activity, Test4Enforcers generates the sequences of operations that must be exercised to validate an enforcer whose behavior is captured by an enforcement model (we assume the model is correctly specified and verified [33]). To this end, Test4Enforcers uses the *Harmonized State Identifiers* (HSI) method [7,24], which is a variant of the W-method [8, 18,34] that does not require the model of the system to be completely specified. In fact, not every combination of event is feasible in an enforcement model, for instance due to the constraints of the environment (e.g., it is not possible to pause an app that is already paused).

We use HSI since it works well to reveal implementation errors, such as erroneous next-states, extra/missing states, etc. In a nutshell, HSI supports the generation of tests that cover every transition in the model and that check the identity of the state reached by each transition to ensure that the implementation of the model is correct.

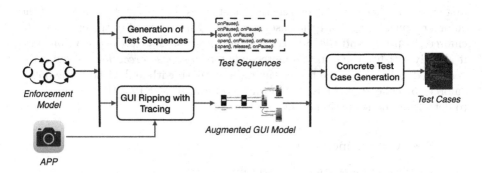

Fig. 2. Test case generation with Test4Enforcers.

HSI exploits the notions of *transition cover*, to cover all the transitions, and *separating families*, to check the identity of the states reached by each transition. Informally, a transition cover P for an automaton A is a set of input sequences, including the empty sequence ϵ, that exercises all the transitions in A (every transition must occur as the last element of at least an input sequence). A separating family H includes an element H_i for each state s_i of the mode. The element H_i is a set input sequences that can be executed to distinguish the state s_i from the other states of the system (that is, the outputs observed by executing the sequences of inputs in H_i from s_i are different from the ones produced by any other state of the system).

The final set of test sequences are obtained by concatenating each element tc_i in the transition coverage set P with every input sequence in the separating family associated with the state reached after executing tc_i. Namely, if tc_i reaches state s_i, the elements in the separating family H_i are concatenated to tc_i to obtain the final set of test sequences (note that the prefix t_i must be executed multiple times, depending on the number of elements in H_i). This process may generate redundant combinations that are filtered out from the final set of input sequences to be exercised.

In our example, this process generates the following sequences to be covered with test cases:

$activity.onPause()_{req}$,
$activity.onPause()_{req}\ activity.onPause()_{req}$,
$camera.open()_{req}\ activity.onPause()_{req}$,
$camera.open()_{req}\ activity.onPause()_{req}\ activity.onPause()_{req}$,
$camera.open()_{req}\ camera.release()_{req}\ activity.onPause()_{req}$

GUI Ripping with Tracing. GUI Ripping is an exploration strategy that can be used to explore the GUI of an app under test with the purpose of building a state-based representation of its behavior [26]. GUI ripping generates the state-based model of the app under test by systematically executing every possible action on every state encountered during the exploration, until a given time or action budget expires. Our implementation of Test4Enforcers targets Android apps and uses DroidBot [19] configured to execute actions in a breadth-first manner to build the state-based model.

A state s of the app under test is represented by its visible views $s = \{v_i | i = 1 \ldots n\}$. Each view v_i is defined by a set of properties $v_i = \{p_{i1}, \ldots, p_{ik}\}$, with each property being a key-value pair. For instance, `EditText` is an Android view for entering text and it has properties such as `clickable`, to specify if the view reacts to click events, and `text` to store the text present in the view.

Operations that change the set of visible views (e.g., because an activity is closed and another one is opened) or the properties of the views (e.g., because some text is entered in an input field) change the state of the app. DroidBot uses the following set of actions A_{app} during GUI ripping: *touch* and *long touch*, which execute a tap and a long tap on a clickable view, respectively; *setText*, which enters a pre-defined text inside an editable view; *keyEvent*, which presses a navigation button; and *scroll*, which scrolls the current window.

The state-based representation of the execution space produced by GUI Ripping includes all the visited states and the executed actions. Test4Enforcers enriches the model generated by GUI ripping with the information reported by a tracer, which associates each transition with a sequence of methods belonging to the enforcer's alphabet, if executed during the transition between state. The state-based model thus shows both the UI interactions that can be executed on the app, their effect on the state of the app, and the internal events that are activated when they are executed.

Figure 3 shows an excerpt of the model obtained by running the ripping activity on the fooCam app[3] while considering the alphabet of the enforcer shown in Fig. 1. For simplicity, we represent the states with the screenshots of the app. The labels above transitions represent UI interactions, while the labels below transitions, when present, represent events in the alphabet of the enforcer collected by the monitor. For instance, when the *KeyEvent(Back)* UI interaction is executed and the app moves from the state *MainActivity* to the state *Launcher*, the sequence of internal events *camera.release() activity.onPause()* is observed.

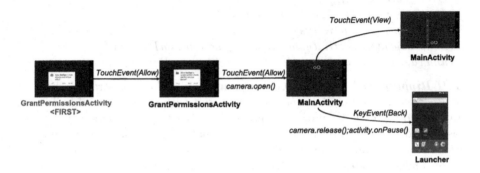

Fig. 3. Excerpt of a model derived with GUI Ripping.

Concrete Test Case Generation. Generating concrete (i.e., executable) test cases consists of finding the sequences of GUI interactions that cause the execution of the desired sequences of events belonging to the alphabet of the enforcer, as identified by the HSI method. To this end, Test4Enforcers exploits both the augmented model derived with GUI ripping and the sequences generated with the HSI method. In particular, Test4Enforcers aims to generate a test suite that contains a test case for each target sequence of events generated with the HSI method. These tests are identified by searching for a path in the GUI model that covers the sequence under consideration according to the annotations on the transitions. For instance, if the sequence to be covered is *camera.open() camera.release() activity.onPause()* and the GUI model is the one in Fig. 3, the sequence *TouchEvent(Allow) TouchEvent(Allow) KeyEvent(Back)* is identified as the concrete test to execute. In fact, the execution of the identified UI events is expected to produce the desired internal computation (based on the labels on the transitions).

If there is at least one path in the GUI model that covers the sequence under consideration, the corresponding test case is generated. Since a path derived from the model is not necessarily feasible, Test4Enforcers identifies the 10 shortest paths that cover the target sequence and executes them sequentially until it is

---

[3] fooCam is a HDR camera app that can take multiple shots with different exposure settings. The app is available on the Google Play Store at the following link: https://play.google.com/store/apps/details?id=net.phunehehe.foocam2&hl=EN.

able to exercise the target sequence. If the right test is found, a *differential oracle* is embedded in the test case. A differential oracle is an oracle that determines the correctness of a test execution by comparing two executions of the same test on two different programs. In our case, the compared programs are the app *with* and *without* the enforcer deployed. Test4Enforcers injects two different differential oracles: the *transparent-enforcement oracle* and the *actual-enforcement oracle*.

A test is assigned with the *transparent-enforcement oracle* when the test must *produce the same result if executed on both the apps with and without the enforcer in place*. In other words, the exercised sequence does not require any change performed by the enforcer. For instance, the sequence *camera.open() camera.release() activity.onPause()* is not altered by the enforcer in Fig. 1 and thus the transparent-enforcement oracle is used to determine the correctness of the test that covers this sequence, that is, no behavioral differences must be observed when this sequence is executed in both the app without and the app with the enforcer.

A test is assigned with the *actual-enforcement oracle* when the test must *produce a different outcome when executed on the app with and without the enforcer in place*. In other words, the tested sequence corresponds to a path that requires the intervention of the enforcer. For instance, the sequence *camera.open() activity.onPause()* causes the intervention of the enforcer shown in Fig. 1, which outputs the extra event *camera.release()*. The test corresponding to that sequence is thus labeled as *producing the same result until the activity.onPause() event, and a potentially different result afterwards*, and the actual-enforcement oracle is embedded in the test.

3.2   Test Execution

The test execution step aims to automatically identify, if present, any problem introduced by the enforcer in the target app. The transparent-enforcement and actual-enforcement oracles can detect functional misbehaviors. Here we describe how Test4Enforcers can detect non-functional problems, performance degradations in particular, introduced by enforcers.

Test execution requires three inputs: 1) The enforcer implementation that must be tested; 2) One or more apps to be used to concretely test the enforcer; and 3) The automatic test suites generated in the previous step to exercise the enforcer's behavior.

The output is a list of KPIs whose values indicate performance degradation when the enforcer is active. As shown in Fig. 4, this step performs two main activities: *i) Test Execution*, which runs the test suite that exercises the enforcer behaviour and collects the KPI values from executions with and without the enforcer, and *ii) Performance Comparison*, which identifies performance degradation by comparing the KPI values obtained with and without the enforcer.

Test Execution. This activity runs the automatic test suite and collects KPI values about the performance of the running app. Specifically, we used profiler tools [3,5] that come with Android Studio [6] and allow us to obtain KPIs on

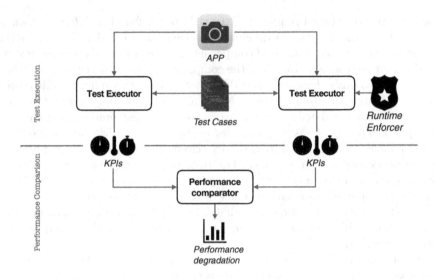

Fig. 4. Detection of non-functional programs with Test4Enforcers.

CPU, memory, network, and energy usage. The test suite is executed ten times to compute stable median values not affected by outliers for each KPI.

The execution of the test suite is performed by two instances of the Test Executor components, which can be executed either sequentially or in parallel (e.g., on a cloud infrastructure). One instance runs the test suite on the unaltered version of the app under test, to collect KPIs about the app's performance when no enforcer is deployed. The collected values represent the baseline for the detection of performance degradation. The other instance of the Test Executor runs the test suite on the app enriched with the software enforcer, to collect data about the potential degradation of the performance.

Performance Comparison. The performance comparison activity interprets the results produced by Test Execution and reports any performance degradation. We currently support four non-functional performance characteristics [14]: responsiveness, launch time, memory consumption, and energy consumption. The reported performance degradations depend on some thresholds and parameters whose default values can be changed by users according to the specific context. We report below the values we used in our evaluation.

Responsiveness refers to the ability of a mobile app to respond to user iterations in a timely manner. A highly responsive app improvers the user satisfaction, since users prefer to not wait for too long when interacting with an app. On the other hand, an app with poor responsiveness can have a negative impact on user experience and its success on the market. Consequently, the enforcer should not negatively impact responsiveness.

In the case of Android apps, response times of less than 200 ms is known to not negatively impact user satisfaction [37], while delays that last almost a second do not significantly affect users but can be recognized by users, while longer delays have a clearly negative impact on the user experience.

By measuring the CPU usage time in event handler methods, we can measure the response time to GUI events. If any UI interaction requires more than 200 ms [37] to be served only when the enforcer is active, a poor responsiveness caused by the enforcer is reported to the user.

Launch time is another KPI analyzed by Test4Enforcers. It represents the amount of time necessary to boot the app. During start-up, the app initializes all its components, including initializing objects, creating and initializing activities, inflating the layout, and drawing the app for the first time. This is the first performance characteristic that a user is exposed to. Since from the first usage, users normally expect a short launch time, otherwise, the experience and satisfaction might be negative. The launch time is considered to be excessive when it exceeds 5 s, as reported in the Android documentation [2].

To detect any degradation of this performance characteristic, Test4Enforcers measures the time the app needs to produce the first frame. If the value of this KPI exceeds 5 s only when the enforcer is active then a degradation of the startup time caused by the enforcer is reported to developers.

Memory consumption is another important performance characteristic for mobile apps as these are running on devices with limited resources. For instance, a memory leakage can lead to performance degradation due to the frequent triggering of the garbage collection process. These slowdowns can then evolve into freezes and even app crashes. In order to be able to detect a degradation in memory consumption, we analyze KPIs that can give information regarding the memory usage and report a degradation when the execution with the enforcer introduces an overhead of more than 5% compared to the baseline without enforcer.

Power consumption is a crucial characteristic of mobile systems. Running an enforcer with abnormal power consumption can drastically reduce battery life, affecting the user experience. Therefore, it is very important to solve problems of energy inefficiencies introduced by enforcers. To detect energy hotspots and bugs introduced by enforcers, Test4Enforcers collects and analyzes KPI values regarding battery usage, and reports a degradation when execution with the enforcer introduces more than 5% overhead compared to baseline without enforcers.

4   Evaluation

We evaluated the capability of Test4Enforcers to capture performance degradations introduced by faulty enforcers. In particular, we addressed the following research question: *Can Test4Enforcers detect actual performance bugs?*

To investigate this research question, we selected fooCam as the app under test. It is a camera app that can automatically take multiple successive shots with different exposure settings. FooCam has been already used in previous works about API misuses [23, 31, 32].

The enforcer used to validate the effectiveness of Test4Enforcers in detecting performance bugs is an implementation of the enforcement model shown in Fig. 1 that has been tested to have no functional bugs [13].

To evaluate the performance of Test4Enforces, we injected bugs that can cause performance degradation into the source code of the enforcer. In particular, we injected 4 bugs that affect the main non-functional performance characteristics of mobile apps [14]:

- A responsiveness bug that introduces a delay in reacting to GUI events.
- An app startup bug that delays the loading of the app's initial screen.
- A CPU hog bug that executes some CPU intensive tasks that significantly increase memory consumption.
- A memory leak bug that executes tasks that allocate memory without releasing it.

Figure 5 shows the boxplots that compare the collected values of the KPIs, one for each performance characteristic validated by Test4Enforcers. The three boxes in each plot shows the distribution of values obtained when the app is executed without the enforcer (label *w/o enforcer*), with the correct enforcer (label *with enforcer*) and with the faulty enforcer (label *with faulty enforcer*). Each box represents a population of 10 samples obtained by running the same test case 10 times.

Figure 5a shows the values obtained for the *Estimated Power Use* KPI, which calculates the app's power consumption. We can notice that the enforcer has a small impact on energy consumption, which confirms the suitability of the enforcement technology on the power perspective. The faulty enforcer instead introduces the battery usage by more than 14%, which can be detected by Test4Enforcers when comparing the collected KPIs.

Figure 5b shows the values of the KPI "Total Propotional Set Size" (PSS), which represents the RAM used by the app. Test4Enforcers can detect the problem introduced by the faulty enforcer since memory consumption is increased by more than 5%, while it is not the case when the correct enforcer is introduced. In this case, we could notice a difference in memory consumption since the enforcer has to collect and store information about the status of the system. However, the memory overhead is below 5%.

Figures 5c and 5d report the collected values for launch time and responsiveness. The red lines in these plots represent the threshold values (5 s and 200 milliseconds) that should not be passed, as reported in the literature and discussed in the previous section. Results show that the correct enforcers introduce a marginal overhead in launch time and responsiveness, while the faulty enforcers introduce a performance degradation that could be automatically detected.

In conclusion, Test4enforcers was always able to stimulate the behavior of the enforcers and correctly evaluates their performance, helping developers timely identifying performance bugs.

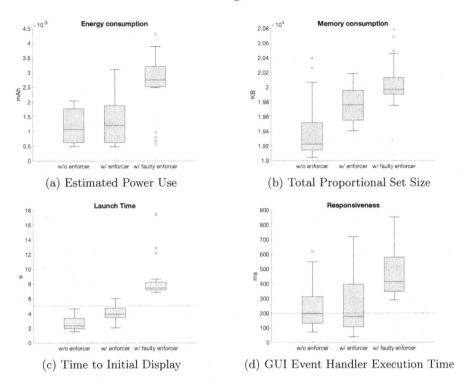

(a) Estimated Power Use

(b) Total Proportional Set Size

(c) Time to Initial Display

(d) GUI Event Handler Execution Time

Fig. 5. Comparison of KPIs in executions without enforcer, with enforcer, and with faulty enforcer. (Color figure online)

5 Related Work

Runtime enforcement is a powerful technique that enforces the behaviour specified by a set of correctness policies on a running system. In particular, runtime enforcement strategies modify executions assuring that policies are satisfied despite the potentially incorrect behavior of the monitored software [12,15]. Runtime enforcement has been applied in multiple domains, including mobile apps [10,11,29,31] operating systems [35], web-based applications [25], control systems [17], and cloud systems [9]. Among these many domains, in this paper we focus on the Android environment, which has been already considered in the work by Falcone et al. [11], who studied how to enforce privacy policies by detecting and disabling suspicious method calls, and more recently by Riganelli et al. [30–32], who studied how to augment classic Android libraries with proactive mechanisms that can automatically suppress and insert API calls to enforce resource usage policies.

While runtime enforcement strategies focus on the definition of models and strategies to specify and implement the enforcers, Test4Enforcers is complemental to this effort, since it derives the test cases that should be executed on apps with and without the enforcers to verify the correctness and performance of the implemented enforcer. In particular, performance is a crucial issue especially in mobile systems that have limited resources.

Performance testing refers to the execution of test cases to evaluate the behavior of an application with respect to performance aspects, such as responsiveness or efficiency [27]. Despite the large number of approches aimed at automating functional testing in mobile apps [16], studies highlight the lack of approaches that include performance testing [22,28]. Developers depend on manual testing and analysis to detect performance bugs [21] by using tools for profiling and debugging their applications [4,14]. Test4Enforcers automates the performance testing of runtime enforcers in mobile devices by automatically generating and executing test cases that interact with an app's GUI in order to verify both the behavior and performance of an enforcer.

Verification and Validation of runtime enforcement concerns with checking that the software enforcer is indeed delivering the intended behavior. In fact, although the enforcer is meant to correct the behavior of a monitored software, the enforcer itself might still be wrong and its activity might compromise the correctness of the system rather than improving it. A recent work in this direction is the one by Riganelli et al. [33] that provides a way to verify if the activity of multiple enforcers may interfere. The proposed analysis is however entirely based on the models and the many problems that might be introduced by the actual software enforcers cannot be revealed with that approach. Test4Enforcers provides a complemental capability, that is, it can test if the implementation of the enforcer behaves as expected once injected in the target system.

6   Conclusion and Future Work

Software enforcers can be effectively used to modify executions to ultimately guarantee that correctness policies are satisfied. Since software enforcers are active in the operational environment (e.g., in the end user environment), it is compulsory to use dependable enforcers that cannot affect negatively the target app. It is thus important to extensively validate enforcers before they can be used.

In this paper we presented Test4Enforcers, which can be used to validate the correctness of software enforcers on both a functional and non-functional perspective. Early results show that the generated test cases can feasibly detect problems, preventing the distribution of faulty enforcers.

Future work mainly concerns with experimenting Test4Enforcers with a larger set of apps and enforcers, and collecting additional evidence about the effectiveness of the approach.

Acknowledgements. We would like to thanks Alice Hoa Galli for her help with the experiments.

References

1. Android Docs: Camera API (2020). https://developer.android.com/guide/topics/media/camera
2. Android Docs: App startup time (2022). https://developer.android.com/topic/performance/vitals/launch-time
3. Android Docs: dumpsys (2022). https://developer.android.com/studio/command-line/dumpsys
4. Android Docs: Profile your app performance (2022). https://developer.android.com/studio/profile
5. Android Docs: The Android Profiler (2022). https://developer.android.com/studio/profile/android-profiler
6. Android Docs: The Android Studio. https://developer.android.com/studio (2022)
7. Belli, F., Beyazıt, M., Endo, A.T., Mathur, A., Simao, A.: Fault domain-based testing in imperfect situations: a heuristic approach and case studies. Software Qual. J. **23**(3), 423–452 (2015)
8. Chow, T.S.: Testing software design modeled by finite-state machines. IEEE Trans. Software Eng. **3**, 178–187 (1978)
9. Dai, Y., Xiang, Y., Zhang, G.: Self-healing and hybrid diagnosis in cloud computing. In: Proceedings of the International Conference on Cloud Computing (CloudCom) (2009)
10. Daian, P., Falcone, Y., Meredith, P.O., Serbanuta, T., Shiriashi, S., Iwai, A., Rosu, G.: Rv-android: Efficient parametric android runtime verification, a brief tutorial. In: Proceedings of the International Conference on Runtime Verification (RV) (2015)
11. Falcone, Y., Currea, S., Jaber, M.: Runtime verification and enforcement for android applications with RV-Droid. In: Proceedings of the International Conference on Runtime Verification (RV) (2012)
12. Falcone, Y.: You should better enforce than verify. In: Proceedings of the International Conference on Runtime Verification (RV) (2010)
13. Guzman, M., Riganelli, O., Micucci, D., Mariani, L.: Test4enforcers: Test case generation for software enforcers. In: Proceedings of the International Conference on Runtime Verification (RV) (2020)
14. Hort, M., Kechagia, M., Sarro, F., Harman, M.: A survey of performance optimization for mobile applications. IEEE Trans. Softw. Eng. (2021)
15. Khoury, R., Tawbi, N.: Which security policies are enforceable by runtime monitors? a survey. Comput. Sci. Rev. **6**(1), 27–45 (2012)
16. Kong, P., Li, L., Gao, J., Liu, K., Bissyandé, T.F., Klein, J.: Automated testing of android apps: a systematic literature review. IEEE Trans. Reliability (2019)
17. Lanotte, R., Merro, M., Munteanu, A.: Runtime enforcement for control system security. In: Proceedings of the Computer Security Foundations Symposium (CSF) (2020)
18. Lee, D., Yannakakis, M.: Principles and methods of testing finite state machines-a survey. Proc. IEEE **84**(8), 1090–1123 (1996)
19. Li, Y., Ziyue, Y., Yao, G., Xiangqun, C.: Droidbot: a lightweight ui-guided test input generator for android. In: Proceedings of the International Conference on Software Engineering Companion (ICSE) (2017)
20. Ligatti, J., Bauer, L., Walker, D.: Edit automata: enforcement mechanisms for run-time security policies. Int. J. Inf. Secur. **4**, 2–16 (2005)

21. Linares-Vasquez, M., Vendome, C., Luo, Q., Poshyvanyk, D.: How developers detect and fix performance bottlenecks in android apps. In: Proceedings of the International Conference on Software Maintenance and Evolution (ICSME) (2015)
22. Linares-Vásquez, M., Moran, K., Poshyvanyk, D.: Continuous, evolutionary and large-scale: a new perspective for automated mobile app testing. In: Proceedings of the International Conference on Software Maintenance and Evolution (ICSME) (2017)
23. Liu, J., Wu, T., Yan, J., Zhang, J.: Fixing resource leaks in android apps with light-weight static analysis and low-overhead instrumentation. In: Proceedings of the International Symposium on Software Reliability Engineering (ISSRE) (2016)
24. Luo, G., Petrenko, A., Bochmann, G.V.: Selecting test sequences for partially-specified nondeterministic finite state machines. In: Proceedings of the IFIP WG 6.1 International Workshop on Protocol Text Systems (1995)
25. Magalhães, J.a.P., Silva, L.M.: Shõwa: A self-healing framework for web-based applications. ACM Trans. Autonomous Adaptive Syst. **10**(1), 4:1–4:28 (2015)
26. Memon, A.M., Banerjee, I., Nguyen, B.N., Robbins, B.: The first decade of gui ripping: Extensions, applications, and broader impacts. In: Proceedings of the Working Conference on Reverse Engineering (WCRE) (2013)
27. Molyneaux, I.: The art of application performance testing: from strategy to tools. "O'Reilly Media, Inc." (2014)
28. Muccini, H., Di Francesco, A., Esposito, P.: Software testing of mobile applications: challenges and future research directions. In: Proceedings of the International Workshop on Automation of Software Test (AST) (2012)
29. Riganelli, O., Micucci, D., Mariani, L.: Healing data loss problems in android apps. In: Proceedings of the International Workshop on Software Faults (IWSF), co-located with the International Symposium on Software Reliability Engineering (ISSRE) (2016)
30. Riganelli, O., Micucci, D., Mariani, L.: Increasing the reusability of enforcers with lifecycle events. In: Proceedings of the International Symposium on Leveraging Applications of Formal Methods, Verification and Validation (ISOLA) (2018)
31. Riganelli, O., Micucci, D., Mariani, L.: Policy enforcement with proactive libraries. In: Proceedings of the IEEE/ACM International Symposium on Software Engineering for Adaptive and Self-Managing Systems (SEAMS) (2017)
32. Riganelli, O., Micucci, D., Mariani, L.: Controlling interactions with libraries in android apps through runtime enforcement. ACM Trans. Autonomous Adaptive Syst. **14**(2), 8:1–8:29 (2019)
33. Riganelli, O., Micucci, D., Mariani, L., Falcone, Y.: Verifying policy enforcers. In: Proceedings of the International Conference on Runtime Verification (RV) (2017)
34. Sidhu, D.P., Leung, T.K.: Formal methods for protocol testing: a detailed study. IEEE Trans. Software Eng. **15**(4), 413–426 (1989)
35. Sidiroglou, S., Laadan, O., Perez, C., Viennot, N., Nieh, J., Keromytis, A.D.: ASSURE: automatic software self-healing using rescue points. In: Proceedings of the International Conference on Architectural Support for Programming Languages and Operating Systems (ASPLOS) (2009)
36. Statista: Number of apps available in leading app stores as of 2022 (2022). https://www.statista.com/statistics/276623/number-of-apps-available-in-leading-app-stores/
37. Yang, S., Yan, D., Rountev, A.: Testing for poor responsiveness in android applications. In: Proceedings of the International Workshop on the Engineering of Mobile-Enabled Systems (MOBS) (2013)

Automata Learning Meets Shielding

Martin Tappler[1,2], Stefan Pranger[1], Bettina Könighofer[1(✉)], Edi Muškardin[2,1], Roderick Bloem[1,2], and Kim Larsen[3]

[1] Graz University of Technology, Graz, Austria
martin.tappler@ist.tugraz.at,
{stefan.pranger,roderick.bloem,bettina.koenighofer}@iaik.tugraz.at
[2] TU Graz-SAL DES Lab, Silicon Austria Labs, Graz, Austria
edi.muskardin@silicon-austria.com
[3] Aalborg University, Aalborg, Denmark
kgl@cs.aau.dk

Abstract. Safety is still one of the major research challenges in reinforcement learning (RL). In this paper, we address the problem of how to avoid safety violations of RL agents during exploration in probabilistic and partially unknown environments. Our approach combines automata learning for Markov Decision Processes (MDPs) and shield synthesis in an iterative approach. Initially, the MDP representing the environment is unknown. The agent starts exploring the environment and collects traces. From the collected traces, we passively learn MDPs that abstractly represent the safety-relevant aspects of the environment. Given a learned MDP and a safety specification, we construct a shield. For each state-action pair within a learned MDP, the shield computes exact probabilities on how likely it is that executing the action results in violating the specification from the current state within the next k steps. After the shield is constructed, the shield is used during runtime and blocks any actions that induce a too large risk from the agent. The shielded agent continues to explore the environment and collects new data on the environment. Iteratively, we use the collected data to learn new MDPs with higher accuracy, resulting in turn in shields able to prevent more safety violations. We implemented our approach and present a detailed case study of a Q-learning agent exploring slippery Gridworlds. In our experiments, we show that as the agent explores more and more of the environment during training, the improved learned models lead to shields that are able to prevent many safety violations.

Keywords: Automata learning · Shielding · Markov Decision Processes

1 Introduction

Nowadays systems are increasingly autonomous and make extensive use of machine learning. The tremendous potential of autonomous, AI-based systems

T. Margaria and B. Steffen (Eds.): ISoLA 2022, LNCS 13701, pp. 335–359, 2022.
https://doi.org/10.1007/978-3-031-19849-6_20

is contrasted by the growing concerns about their safety [11]. Their huge complexity makes it infeasible to formally prove their correctness or to cover the entire input space of a system with test cases. An especially challenging problem is ensuring safety during the learning process [21]. In model-free *reinforcement learning* (RL) [34], an agent aims to learn a task through trial-and-error via interactions with an unknown environment. While the model-free RL approach is very general as well as scalable and has successfully been applied in various challenging application domains [20], the learning agent needs to explore unsafe behavior in order to learn that it is unsafe.

Shielding [4] is a runtime enforcement technique that applies correct-by-construction methods to automatically compute shields from a given safety temporal logic specification [5] and a model that captures all safety-relevant dynamics of the environment. Shields have been categorized into post-shields and pre-shields. Post-shields monitor the actions selected by the agent and overwrite any unsafe action with a safe one. Pre-shields are implemented before the agent and block, at every time step, unsafe actions from the agent (also referred to as action masking). Thus, the agent can only choose from the set of safe actions. In this paper, we use pre-shielding since this setting allows the agent maximal freedom in exploring the environment.

In the *non-probabilistic setting* [6], shields guarantee that the safety specification will never be violated, working under the assumption that a complete and faithful environmental model of the safety-relevant dynamics is available. Shielding in the *probabilistic setting* [19], which is the standard setting in RL, assumes to have an environmental model in form of a Markov decision process (MDP) available. Given such an MDP $\mathcal{M}$ and a safety specification φ, the shield computes how likely it is that executing an action from the current state will result in violating φ within a given finite horizon. At any state s, an actions a is called *unsafe* if executing a incurs a probability of violating φ within the next k steps greater than a relative threshold λ w.r.t. the optimal safety probability possible in s. The resulting shield prohibits safety violations that can be prevented by planning ahead k steps into the future. Shielding requires a complete and accurate environmental model, but it is rarely the case that such a model is available. However some data about the environment often exists, for example, a RL agent collects data by exploring the environment.

Automata learning [1,17,38] is a well-established technique to automatically learn automata models of black-box systems from observed data. The data used for automata learning is usually given in the form of observation traces, which are sequences of observations of the environment's state and actions chosen by the agent. *Passive MDP learning* [23,24] is able to learn MDP models from a multiset of sampled observation traces. Thus, the learned MDP depends on the given sampled traces.

Our Approach. In this paper, we consider the setting of RL in an initially unknown environment. The goal is to reduce safety violations during the exploration phase of the RL-agent by combining *passive MDP learning* with *probabilistic shielding* in an iterative approach. Initially, the MDP representing the environment is unknown. During runtime, the agent collects observation traces while exploring the environment. After having a large enough initial multiset of traces, we first transform the sequences of observed states in the traces into observations, which include only the safety-relevant information, using a suitable abstraction function. The abstract traces are then used to learn a first estimate of the safety-relevant MDP. From this initial MDP and a given safety specification, we construct an initial shield. After the shield is constructed, the agent is augmented with the shield, i.e., the shield blocks unsafe actions from the agent and the agent can pick from the set of safe actions. The newly collected traces are added to the multiset of all traces. After collecting a predefined number of new traces, our approach learns a new safety-relevant MDP from the multiset of all collected traces and creates a new shield.

At every iteration, the shield is built from an MDP that approaches more and more the real MDP underlying the environment modulo the abstraction to safety-relevant observations. Thus, the resulting shields are getting more informed and prevent the agent from entering more safety-critical situations.

Outline. The rest of the paper is structured as follows. We present the related work in Sect. 2 and discuss the relevant foundations in Sect. 3. We present our approach for safe learning via shielding and automata learning in Sect. 4. We present our experimental results in Sect. 5 and conclude in Sect. 6.

2   Related Work

We combine automata learning and probabilistic verification to create safety shields in our approach. Early work on such combinations has been performed by Cobleigh et al. [10], who propose to learn assumptions for compositional reasoning. More closely related to our work is black box checking by Peled et al. [31], where they present a technique for model checking of deterministic black-box systems. Learning-based testing by Meinke and Sindhu [26] follows a similar approach of incremental learning of hypothesis models and model checking of these hypotheses. In previous work [3], we proposed a technique inspired by black box checking for probabilistic reachability checking of stochastic black-box systems. As in this paper, we applied IOALERGIA [23, 24] to learn MDPs. Rather than computing safety shields from learned MDPs, we computed policies to satisfy reachability objectives. We also proposed a technique for L^*-based learning of MDP [35], which may serve as a basis for RL and shielding. In this paper, we combine stochastic learning and abstraction with respect to safety-relevant features to improve RL. Nouri et al. [30] also apply abstraction on traces with respect to properties of the system under consideration in order to learn abstract probabilistic models. In contrast to us, they aim to improve the runtime of statistical model-checking and they learn Markov chains that are not controllable via inputs.

Recently, various authors have proposed combinations of automata learning and reinforcement learning [13,14,18,42]. By learning finite-state models, such as so-called reward machines, they provide additional high-level structure for

RL. This enables RL when rewards are non-Markovian, i.e., the gain depends not only on the current state and action, but on the path taken by the agent. DeepSynth [16] follows a similar approach to improve RL with sparse rewards. Related to these approaches, Muskardin et al. [29] propose a combination of reinforcement learning and automata learning to handle partial observability, i.e., non-Markovian environments.

Fu and Topcu [12] presented an approach for a learning-based synthesis of policies for MDPs w.r.t. temporal logic specifications that are probably approximately correct. In contrast to us, they assume the topology of the MDP to be known, so that only transition probabilities need to be learned.

Alshiekh et al. [4] proposed shielding for RL. Jansen et al. [19] proposed the first method to compute safety shields using a bounded horizon in MDPs. Giacobbe et al. [15] applied the same technique on 31 Atari 2600 games. The approach was further extended by Könighofer et al. [22]. Instead of analyzing the safety of all state-action pairs ahead of time, the approach uses the time between two successive decisions of an agent to analyze the safety of actions on the fly. Pranger et al. [33] proposed an iterative approach to shielding that updates the transition probabilities of the MDP based on observed behavior and computes new shields in regular intervals. To construct our shields, we use the approach proposed by Jansen et al. [19]. Similarly to Pranger et al. [33], we iteratively construct new shields, but do not rely on a known topology of the MDP.

As in our approach, Waga et al. [40] use automata learning to dynamically construct shields during runtime. The main difference to our work is that they assume that the environment behaves deterministically, whereas we allow probabilistic environmental behavior which is the standard assumption in reinforcement learning.

3   Preliminaries

Basics. Given a set E, we denote by $Dist(E)$ the set of probability distributions over E, i.e. for all μ in $Dist(E)$ we have $\mu : E \to [0,1]$ such that $\sum_{e \in E} \mu(e) = 1$. In Sect. 4, we apply two randomized functions *coinFlip* and *randSel*. The function *coinFlip* is defined by $\mathbb{P}(coinFlip(p) = \top) = p$ and $\mathbb{P}(coinFlip(p) = \bot) = 1 - p$ for $p \in [0,1]$. The function *randSel* samples an element e from a given set E according to uniform distribution, i.e., $\forall e \in E : \mathbb{P}(randSel(E) = e) = \frac{1}{|E|}$.

3.1   Markov Decision Processes and Reinforcement Learning

Definition 1. *A **Markov decision process (MDP)** is a tuple $\langle S, s_0, A, P \rangle$ where S is a finite set of states, $s_0 \in S$ is the initial state, A is a finite set of actions, and $P : S \times A \to Dist(S)$ is the probabilistic transition function.*

For all $s \in S$ the available actions are $A(s) = \{a \in A \mid \exists s', P(s, a)(s') \neq 0\}$ and we assume $|A(s)| \geq 1$. We associate an MDP $\mathcal{M}$ with a *reward function* $\mathcal{R} : S \times A \times S \to \mathbb{R}$.

Traces. A finite *path* ρ through an MDP is an alternating sequence of states and actions, i.e. $\rho = s_0 a_1 s_1 \cdots a_{n-1} s_{n-1} a_n s_n \in s_0 \times (\mathcal{A} \times \mathcal{S})^*$. The set of all paths of an MDP $\mathcal{M}$ is denoted by $Path_{\mathcal{M}}$. We refer to a path augmented with the gained reward as a *reward trace* $\tau = s_0 a_1 r_1 s_1 \cdots s_{n-1} a_n r_n s_n$ with $r_i = \mathcal{R}(s_{i-1}, a_i, s_i)$. In the remainder of the paper, we treat reward traces also as sequences of triples (a_i, r_i, s_i) comprising an action, the gained reward, and the reached state.

Policies. A memoryless policy defines for every state in an MDP a probability distribution over actions. Given an MDP $\mathcal{M} = \langle S, A, s_0, \mathcal{P} \rangle$, a *memoryless policy* for $\mathcal{M}$ is a function $\sigma : \mathcal{S} \to Dist(\mathcal{A})$. A *memoryless deterministic policy* $\sigma : \mathcal{S} \to \mathcal{A}$ is a function over action given states.

Reinforcement Learning. An RL agent learns a task through trial-and-error via interactions with an unknown environment. The agent takes *actions* and receives feedback in form from *observations* on the state of the environment and *rewards*. The goal of the agent is to maximize the expected accumulated reward.

Typically, the environment is modeled as an MDP $\mathcal{M} = \langle \mathcal{S}, s_0, \mathcal{A}, \mathcal{P} \rangle$ with associated reward function $\mathcal{R}$. At each step t of a training episode, the agent receives an observation s_t. It then chooses an action $a_{t+1} \in \mathcal{A}$. The environment then moves to a state s_{t+1} with probability $\mathcal{P}(s_t, a_{t+1})(s_{t+1})$. The reward is determined with $r_{t+1} = \mathcal{R}(s_t, a_{t+1}, s_{t+1})$. We refer to negative rewards $r_t < 0$ as *punishments*. The *return* $\mathtt{ret} = \Sigma_{t=1}^{\infty} \gamma^t r_t$ is the cumulative future discounted reward, where r_t is the immediate reward at time step t, and $\gamma \in [0,1]$ is the discount factor that controls the influence of future rewards. The objective of the agent is to learn an *optimal policy* $\sigma^* : \mathcal{S} \to \mathcal{A}$ that maximizes the expectation of the return, i.e. $\max_{\sigma \in \Sigma} \mathbb{E}_{\sigma}(\mathtt{ret})$. A training episode ends after a maximum episode length of t_{max} steps.

Q-learning is one of the most established RL algorithms. The Q-function for policy σ is defined as the expected discounted future reward gained by taking an action a from a state s and following policy σ thereafter. Tabular Q-learning [41] uses the experience (s_t, a_t, r_t, s_{t+1}) to learn the Q-function $Q^*(s, a)$ corresponding to an optimal policy $\sigma^*(s, a)$. The update rule is defined as

$$Q(s_i, a_{i+1}) \leftarrow (1 - \alpha) \cdot Q(s_i, a_{i+1}) + \alpha(r_{i+1} + \gamma \cdot \max_{a \in A}(Q(s_{i+1}, a))),$$

where α is the learning rate and γ is the discount factor.

Definition 2. *A **deterministic labeled MDP** $\mathcal{M}_L = \langle \mathcal{S}, s_0, \mathcal{A}, \mathcal{P}, L \rangle$ is an MDP with a labeling function $L : \mathcal{S} \to O$ mapping states to observations from a finite set O. The transition function $\mathcal{P}$ must satisfy the following determinism property: $\forall s \in \mathcal{S}, \forall a \in \mathcal{A} : \delta(s, a)(s') > 0 \wedge \delta(s, a)(s'') > 0$ implies $s' = s''$ or $L(s') \neq L(s'')$.*

In this paper, we use passive automata learning to compute abstract MDPs of the environment in the form of deterministic labeled MDPs. These MDPs represent safety-related information only and will not be used for RL but for shielding. Therefore, there is no need to use rewards in combination with deterministic labeled MDPs.

Given a path ρ in a deterministic labeled MDP $\mathcal{M}_L$. Applying the labeling function on all states of a path ρ results in a so called *observation trace* $L(\rho) = L(s_0)a_1L(s_1)\cdots a_{n-1}L(s_{n-1})a_nL(s_n)$. Note that due to determinism, an observation trace $L(\rho)$ uniquely identifies the corresponding path ρ.

3.2   Learning of MDPs

We learn deterministic labelled Markov decision processes (MDPs) via IOALERGIA [23,24], which is an adaptation of ALERGIA [8]. IOALERGIA takes a multiset $\mathcal{T}_o$ of observation traces as input and first constructs a tree representing the observation traces, by merging common prefixes. The tree has edges labeled with actions and nodes that are labeled with observations. Each edge corresponds to a trace prefix with the label sequence that is visited by traversing the tree from the root to the edge. Additionally, edges are associated with frequencies that denote how many traces in $\mathcal{T}_o$ have the trace corresponding to an edge as a prefix. Normalizing these frequencies would already yield tree-shaped MDP.

For generalization, the tree is transformed into an MDP with cycles through an iterated merging of nodes. Two nodes are merged if they are compatible, i.e., their future behavior is sufficiently similar. For this purpose, we check whether the observations in the sub-trees originating in the nodes are not statistically different. The parameter $\epsilon_{\text{ALERGIA}}$ controls the significance level of the applied statistical tests. If a node is not compatible with any other potential node, it is promoted to an MDP state. Once all potential pairs of nodes have been checked, the final deterministic labeled MDP is created by normalizing the frequencies on the edges to yield probability distributions for the transition function $\mathcal{P}$. In this paper, we refer to this construction as MDP learning and we denote calls to IOALERGIA by $\mathcal{M}_{\sqcup} = \text{IOALERGIA}(\mathcal{T}_o, \epsilon_{\text{ALERGIA}})$, where $\mathcal{M}_{\sqcup}$ is the deterministic labeled MDP learned from the multiset of observation traces $\mathcal{T}_o$.

3.3   Shielding in MDPs

Specifications and Model Checking. We consider specifications given in the safety fragment of linear temporal logic (LTL) [5]. For an MDP $\mathcal{M}$ and a safety specification φ, probabilistic model checking employs linear programming or value iteration to compute the probabilities of all states and actions of the $\mathcal{M}$ to satisfy an φ. Specifically, the probabilities $\eta_{\varphi,\mathcal{M}}^{\max} : \mathcal{S} \times \mathbb{N} \to [0,1]$ or $\eta_{\varphi,\mathcal{M}}^{\min} : \mathcal{S} \times \mathbb{N} \to [0,1]$ give for all states the maximal (or minimal) probability over all possible policies to satisfy φ, within a given number of steps. For instance, a safety property $\varphi = \mathbf{G}(\neg \mathcal{S}_{unsafe})$ could encode that a set of unsafe states $\mathcal{S}_{unsafe} \in \mathcal{S}$ must not be entered. Then $\eta_{\varphi,\mathcal{M}}^{\max}(s,h)$ is the maximal probability to not visit $\mathcal{S}_{unsafe}$ from state $s \in \mathcal{S}$ in the next h steps.

Shield Construction. Given an MDP $\mathcal{M}$, a safety specification φ, and a finite horizon h, the task of the shield is to limit the probability to violate the safety specification φ within the next h steps.

For any state $s \in \mathcal{S}$ and action $a \in \mathcal{A}(s)$, the *safety-value* $val_{\varphi,\mathcal{M}}(s,a,h)$ is computed which gives the maximal probability to stay safe from s after executing a, i.e.,

$$val_{\varphi,\mathcal{M}}(s,a,h) = \eta^{\max}_{\varphi,\mathcal{M}}(\mathcal{P}(s,a),h-1).$$

The *optimal safety-value* $optval_{\varphi,\mathcal{M}}(s)$ of s is the maximal safety value of any action a in state s within the next $h-1$ steps, i.e.,

$$optval_{\varphi,\mathcal{M}}(s,h) = \max_{a \in \mathcal{A}(s)} val_{\varphi,\mathcal{M}}(s,a,h) = \eta^{\max}_{\varphi,\mathcal{M}}(\mathcal{P}(s,a),h-1).$$

An action a in s is *unsafe* if the safety value of a is lower than the optimal safety-value by some threshold λ_{sh}, i.e., an action a in state s is *unsafe* iff

$$val_{\varphi,\mathcal{M}}(s,a,h) < \lambda_{sh} \cdot optval_{\varphi,\mathcal{M}}(s,h).$$

We refer to actions that are not unsafe as safe actions.

The task of the shield is to block any unsafe action from the agent, thereby restricting the set of available actions $\mathcal{A}(s)$ to the set of safe actions. A shield is a relation $\pi_{\square} : \mathcal{S} \to 2^{\mathcal{A}(s)}$ allowing at least one action for any state.

4   Learned Shields for Safe RL

In this section, we present our iterative approach for safe reinforcement learning via automata learning and shielding. We first discuss the setting in which the RL agents operates and give our problem statement. Then we give an overview of our approach. Finally, we discuss the individual steps of our approach in detail.

4.1   Setting and Problem Statement

Setting. We consider an RL agent acting in an unknown environment that can be modeled as an MDP $\mathcal{M} = \langle \mathcal{S}, s_0, \mathcal{A}, \mathcal{P} \rangle$ with an associated reward function $\mathcal{R} : \mathcal{S} \times \mathcal{A} \times \mathcal{S} \to \mathbb{R}$. However, since the environment is unknown at the beginning of the learning phase, the agent has no knowledge about the structure of $\mathcal{M}$.

We assume that the safety critical properties are given in form of an LTL formula φ. Without knowledge about the safety-relevant dynamics of the environment, it is not possible to prohibit violating φ while the RL agent is exploring the environment.

During the exploration phase of the RL agent, a multiset of reward traces is collected. We assume to have an observation function $Z : \mathcal{S} \to O$ given that maps any state $s \in \mathcal{S}$ states to a safety-relevant observation $o \in O$.

Problem Statement. Consider the setting as discussed above. The goal of our approach is to use the available data from the environment in form of collected traces and the given safety specification to prevent safety violations if possible.

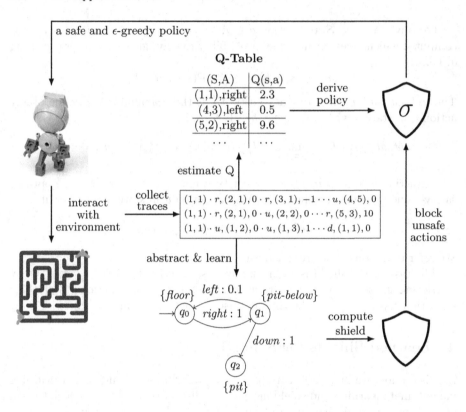

Fig. 1. Iterative safe reinforcement learning via learned shields.

4.2   Overview of Iterative Safe RL via Learned Shields

Our approach combines automata learning, shielding, and reinforcement learning in an iterative manner. Our approach performs n_{iter} iterations. At the first iteration with $i = 1$, we start from an empty multiset of reward traces $\mathcal{T} = \emptyset$, an initial learned $\mathcal{M}_{\square 0}$ with a single state and a self-loop for any action, and an initial shield $\pi_{\square 0}$ that allows at every step any action.

At each iteration i of n iterations, our approach works as follows:

Step 1 - Exploration. The RL agent explores the environment to learn the optimal policy. At each iteration i, the agent trains for a number of $n_{episodes}$. The agent is augmented by a shield $\pi_{\square i-1}$ that restricts its available actions. The learned MDP $\mathcal{M}_{\square i-1}$ is simulated in parallel during the exploration. Each training episode yields a reward trace τ that is added to the multiset of all collected traces $\mathcal{T}$, i.e., $\mathcal{T}' = \{\tau\} \uplus \mathcal{T}$.

Step 2 - MDP Learning. After executing $n_{episodes}$ episodes, we learn a deterministic labeled MDP $\mathcal{M}_{\square i}$ from $\mathcal{T}$.

Step 3 - Shield Construction. Using $\mathcal{M}_{\square i}$, a given specification φ, and a finite horizon h, we compute a shield $\pi_{\square i}$ and continue in **Step 1**.

Figure 1 provides a graphical overview of the proposed approach. Based on this figure, we discuss the individual steps of our approach in detail. For each iteration $1 \leq i \leq n_{iter}$ our approach performs the following steps.

Step 1 - Exploration. The agent interacts with an unknown stochastic environment $\mathcal{M} = \langle S, s_0, \mathcal{A}, \mathcal{P} \rangle$, depicted by a maze. The agent picks actions that are considered to be safe by the current shield and receives observations of the state of the environment and rewards. At iteration i, we have given the set of collected reward traces $\mathcal{T}$, the learned MDP $\mathcal{M}_{\square i-1} = \langle S_\square, s_{\square 0}, \mathcal{A}_\square, \mathcal{P}_\square, L \rangle$, and the current shield $\pi_{\square i-1}$. Each episode resets the environment and starts in a fixed initial state $s_0 \in S$ for $\mathcal{M}$ and $s_{\square 0} \in S_\square$ for $\mathcal{M}_\square$. At every step t, the agent observes $s_t \in S$. Based on the observed label $Z(s_t)$, the learned MDP $\mathcal{M}_{\square i-1}$ moves to state $s_{\square t}$. We give in Sect. 4.3 the details on how to simulate $\mathcal{M}_{\square i}$.

The shield determines the set of safe actions $\mathcal{A}_\square = \pi_{\square i-1}(s_{\square t})$ and sends it to the agent. The agent selects a next action $a_{t+1} \in \mathcal{A}_\square(s)$. The environment executes a_{t+1} and sends the agent a reward r_{t+1} and state observation s_{t+1}. Based on $(s_t, a_{t+1}, r_{t+1}, s_{t+1})$, the agent performs a policy update. Figure 1 represents the learned Q-function of the RL agent as a Q-table, from which we derive an ϵ-greedy policy for training. Please note that our approach is general and applicable to deep Q-learning as well as to tabular Q-learning.

A training episode ends after a maximal number of t_{max} steps. It may end earlier in case of violating safety or performing the task that needs to be learned (e.g., reaching a certain goal state). Each episode yields a reward trace $\tau = s_0 a_1 r_1 s_1 \cdots s_{n-1} a_n r_n s_n$ that is added to the multiset $\mathcal{T}$ of all collected traces, i.e., $\mathcal{T}' = \{\tau\} \uplus \mathcal{T}$.

Step 2 - MDP Learning. After $n_{episodes}$ training episodes, resulting in a new reward trace per episode, we learn a new model of the environment dynamics. Given the multiset of reward traces $\mathcal{T}$ observed while exploring the environment, we abstract away all information in the traces that is not relevant to safety. For each reward trace $\tau = s_0 a_1 r_1 s_1 \cdots s_{n-1} a_n r_n s_n \in \mathcal{T}$, we first discard the rewards to obtain a path $\rho = s_0 a_1 s_1 \cdots s_{n-1} a_n s_n$ and second apply the abstraction function Z to obtain an observation trace $\tau_o = Z(\rho) = Z(s_0) a_1 Z(s_1) \cdots Z(s_{n-1}) a_n Z(s_n)$. For example, the states in the path ρ may represent the exact coordinates of the agent's positions and distance measurements. Relevant for safety might only be the distances. In such a case, the abstraction function Z would abstract away the concrete position and only keep the distances.

To compute the deterministic labeled MDP $\mathcal{M}_{\square i}$, we invoke IOALERGIA by calling IOALERGIA($\mathcal{T}_0, \epsilon_{\text{ALERGIA}}$), where $\epsilon_{\text{ALERGIA}}$ is a parameter specifying the significance level of statistical tests performed by IOALERGIA.

Additionally, we make $\mathcal{M}_{\square i}$ *action-complete*. During the training phase, we propose to make $\mathcal{M}_{\square i}$ with $i < n$ action-complete by adding self-loop transitions to all state-action pairs $(s_\square, a_\square)$ where $\mathcal{P}_\square(s_\square, a_\square)$ is not defined. That is, we set for all such state-action pairs $\mathcal{P}_\square(s_\square, a_\square) = \{s_\square \mapsto 1\}$. The rationale behind this is that whenever an action's effect is unknown, we assume that it leaves the safety of the corresponding state unchanged.

Algorithm 1. A single RL training's episode using a learned shield.

Input: Q-function Q, a learned deterministic labeled MDP $\mathcal{M}_\square = \langle S_\square, \mathcal{A}_\square, s_{\square 0}, \mathcal{P}_\square, L \rangle$, exploration rate ϵ, safety shield $\pi_\square$, environment with **step** and **reset**

Output: Updated Q-function Q

  1: $s_\square \leftarrow s_{\square 0}$
  2: $s \leftarrow$ **reset**
  3: $t \leftarrow 0$ ▷ steps
  4: **while** $t < t_{max}$ **do**
  5:      $\mathcal{A}_\square \leftarrow \pi_\square(s_\square)$ ▷ safe actions for s
  6:      **if** $coinFlip(\epsilon)$ **then**
  7:          $a \leftarrow randSel(\mathcal{A}_\square)$
  8:      **else**
  9:          $a \leftarrow \mathrm{argmax}_{a' \in \mathcal{A}_\square} Q(s, a')$
10:      $r, s' \leftarrow$ **step**(a) ▷ step in environment
11:      $s_\square \leftarrow s'_\square$ where $\mathcal{P}(s_\square, a)(s'_\square) > 0$ and $L(s'_\square) = Z(s')$ ▷ step in learned MDP
12:      UPDATEQ(s, a, r, s')
13:      **if** s' is a terminal state **then**
14:          **break**
15:      $t \leftarrow t + 1$

For the final shield $\pi_\square$ that will be used permanently after training, we propose a more conservative approach and to make $\mathcal{M}_{\square i}$ with $i = n$ action-complete by adding a special sink state $s_{\neg \varphi}$ that violates φ and adding transitions to $s_{\neg \varphi}$. In the training phase, the resulting shield $\pi_\square$ would not be suitable since it would prohibit exploration. For the exploration phase, however, the behavior of $\pi_\square$ may be desirable since it blocks behavior that has not been explored sufficiently.

Step 3 - Shield Construction. The abstract MDP $\mathcal{M}_{\square i}$ encodes the safety-relevant information about the environment. We use $\mathcal{M}_{\square i}$, the safety specification φ, and a finite horizon h, to compute the safety values of all state-action pairs in $\mathcal{M}_{\square i}$. Based on a given relative threshold λ_{sh}, we compute a shield $\pi_{\square i}$ which allows for any state all actions that are safe w.r.t. λ_{sh} and the optimal safety value. After constructing the shield $\pi_{\square i}$, the current shield of the agent is set to $\pi_{\square i}$. The agent continues to explore the environment and learn the optimal strategy using $\pi_{\square i}$ (Step 1).

4.3 Details for Training Using Learned Shields

In this section we discuss a single RL episode of an agent augmented with a learned shield in detail. The pseudocode is given in Algorithm 1. The RL agent interacts with the environment through two operations: **reset** and **step**[1].

reset: This operation resets the environment to a fixed initial state. This state s_0 from the unknown environment MDP is also returned from **reset**.

---

[1] The convention of OpenAI gym [7].

step: The operation **step**(a) takes an action a and executes a causing a probabilistic state transition. It returns a pair r, s', where r is the reward gained by performing a and s' is the reached state when executing a.

The algorithm starts with initializing the learned MDP state as well as the environment state (Line 1 and 2). Then we enter a loop in which the agent performs a maximum of t_{max} steps.

The RL agent applies ϵ-greedy learning, i.e., it explores a random action with probability ϵ and otherwise performs the optimal action according to the RL agent's current knowledge. Note that both, random exploration and exploitation, are shielded, i.e., actions are chosen from the set of safe actions.

For every step, the shield provides a set of safe actions (Line 5). With probability ϵ, the RL agent selects a random safe action in Line 7. Otherwise, it determines the currently optimal action in Line 9. The chosen action is executed in Line 10. In Line 11, the state of $\mathcal{M}_\square$ is updated. To conclude the training step, we update the agent's Q-table.

If the agents visits a terminal state, the loop terminates before performing t_{max} steps (Line 13). A terminal state may, for instance, be reached by completing the task to be solved or by violating safety.

Execution Phase. After training, we use the same approach to execute an agent, but with ϵ set to 0, such that only safe and optimal actions are executed.

5   Experiments

In our experimental evaluation, we evaluated our approach on 24 slippery grid-world environments of varying shapes and sizes. We implemented a tabular Q-learning agent that should learn to reach a given goal state quickly while staying safe. We learn deterministic labeled MDPs using IOALERGIA implemented in AALPY [28]. The shields are created from the learned MDPs using the shield synthesis tool TEMPEST [32]. In our experiments, we discuss the scalability of our approach and its effectiveness by comparing the averaged gained reward during training with and without learned shields.

Experimental Setup. All experiments have been executed on a desktop computer with a 4×2.70 GHz Intel Core i7-7500U CPU, 7.7 GB of RAM running Arch Linux.

Availability. An implementation of our framework for iterative safe RL via learned shields is available online, together with several examples and detailed execution instructions to reproduce our results[2]. The implementation includes a shielded tabular Q-learning agent written in Python.

Usability. Our prototype implementation allows users to easily perform their own experiments. AALPY's IOALERGIA implementation has a simple text-based interface and TEMPEST uses the well-established PRISM MDP format that is

---

[2] https://github.com/DES-Lab/Automata-Learning-meets-Shielding.

also supported by AALPY, as well as a property language similar to PRISM and Storm. Furthermore, our prototype implementation can be easily extended. The tools, AALPY and TEMPEST, can be used as black boxes. Therefore, there is no need to know the implementation details of these tools. The only caveat is that TEMPEST is easiest to use through a Docker container.

5.1 Case Study Subjects

Gridworlds. We used three types of parameterized gridworlds, the smallest instances are depicted in Fig. 2, Fig. 3 and Fig. 4. Each gridworld has a dedicated *start* tile and a *goal* tile, marked by *Entry* and *Goal* on the left-hand side of the figures. A gridworld might also have *intermediate-goal* tiles. If a tile is marked as *pit*, then this tile marks an unsafe location and the agent is not allowed to visit this tile. Black tiles represent *walls* that restrict movement but are not safety critical. Additionally, each tile has a *terrain*, denoted by lowercase letters on the right-hand side of the figures. If a tile is "slippery", the tile is labeled with an arrow and grey gradients on the left-hand side of the figures. If an agent tries to move from a slippery tile, the intended movement of the agent might be altered into the direction of the arrow with a specific tile-dependent probability. The length of arrows corresponds to the probability of slipping. That is, a long arrow pointing downward left means that the agent is very likely to slip either to the left or downwards. Additionally, every tile has (x, y) coordinates.

Gridworld Shapes. Next, we discuss each of the three gridworld shapes briefly, where Figs. 2, 3 and 4 show the smallest gridworld of each shape. To get insights into how the state space affects learning, we vary each type of gridworld in size by creating eight versions of increasing size.

- *zigzag:* In the *zigzag* gridworlds illustrated in Fig. 2, we have pairs of pit tiles located in alternation at the bottom and the top of the map with a fixed distance between adjacent pit pairs. The goal is placed so that the agent could move along a straight line from left to right, but it would travel across slippery tiles next to the pits. The shield thus helps to avoid these dangerous tiles to perform zigzag walks to the goal.
- *slippery shortcuts:* The *slippery shortcuts* gridworlds illustrated in Fig. 3 are similar to the *zigzag* maps in that the agent could take shortcuts across slippery tiles next to pits. In this case, the probability of unsuccessful moves decreases with increasing distance from the pits. Hence, an optimal policy has to find a balance between taking risks and gaining higher reward due to shorter paths.
- *walls:* In the *walls* gridworlds illustrated in Fig. 4, the agents must find a way from the start to the goal by navigating around walls and pits that block the shortest paths. There are fewer slippery tiles.

Reinforcement Learning. We implemented a tabular Q-learning agent. The agent's task is to navigate from start to goal by moving into one of the four cardinal directions at each time step.

Fig. 2. The smallest of the zigzag gridworlds.

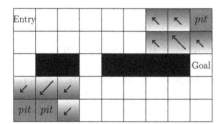

Fig. 3. The smallest of the slippery shortcut gridworlds.

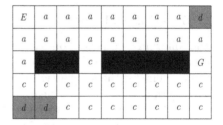

Fig. 4. The smallest of the wall gridworlds.

Every training episode, the agent collects reward traces of the form $\tau = (x_0, y_0), a_1, r_1, (x_1, y_1) \ldots a_n, r_n, (x_n, y_n)$ with x_i and y_i representing the x and y coordinates of the tiles. The set of available *actions* comprises of the four actions {left, right, up, down} to move into the corresponding direction. The *reward function* of the agent is defined as follows:

- If the agent reaches the goal within less than t_{max} steps, it receives a reward of $+100$. Additionally, reaching the goal ends the training episode.
- If the agent reaches a tile with a *pit*, it receives a punishment of -100 and the training episode ends.
- Additionally, the agent receives a reward of -0.5 per step.
- Gridworlds might have intermediate goal states that are rewarded with $+20$ but do not terminate the episode.

We use the following *learning parameters* for all experiments: The tabular Q-learning agent was trained with a learning rate of $\alpha = 0.1$, a discount factor of $\gamma = 0.9$, and an initial exploration rate of $\epsilon = 0.4$ throughout all experiments.

We chose an exponential epsilon decay of $\epsilon' = 0.9999 \cdot \epsilon$ with an update after every learning episode.

MDP Learning. To get the observations for MDP learning, we perform an abstraction over the states via the function Z. Given a concrete state (x, y), the function $Z((x, y))$ maps to a pair $(terr, Pit)$, where $terr$ is the terrain of the tile at (x, y) and Pit is a set of propositions denoting whether a pit is located in the neighboring tiles in each of the four cardinal directions.

For example, if the agent is at the coordinate $(1, 0)$ in Fig. 2, with the origin of coordinates on the bottom left, the abstract observation would be $Z((1, 0)) = (c, \{pit\text{-}right\})$. The terrain is c and there is a pit on the right.

Shield Construction. In all experiments, visiting a pit represents a safety violation. This property can be represented in LTL as follows: $\varphi = \mathbf{G}(\neg pit)$. Using this specification φ and a deterministic labeled MDP $\mathcal{M}_\square$, we compute a shield $\pi_\square$ using a relative threshold $\lambda_{sh} = 0.95$ and a finite horizon of $h = 2$. Thus, for any given state, the resulting shield $\pi_\square$ allows an action a if the probability of not falling into a pit within the next 2 steps is at least $0.95 \cdot \alpha$, with α being the probability of not falling into a pit when taking the optimal action a'.

5.2   Experimental Results

In the following, we report on the performance of RL agents augmented with learned shields compared to the performance of unshielded RL agents.

To account for the stochastic nature of the environment and RL, we repeat every experiment 30 times. For each experiment, the number of iterations is set to $n_{iter} = 30$, the number of training episodes per iteration is $n_{episodes} = 1000$, and the maximal length of a training episode is set to $t_{max} = 200$ steps.

To evaluate the learned policies, we execute the policies at various stages throughout training and compare their performance. For every iteration, i.e., after every 1000th training episode, we evaluate the intermediate policies of the agents by setting the exploration rate ϵ to 0 and performing 1000 episodes. Over these 1000 episodes, we compute the average cumulative reward of the intermediate policy. We refer to this value as *return*. For shielded agents, their corresponding shields are used during the intermediate executions for evaluation.

Figure 5, Fig. 7, and Fig. 9 show plots of the results of this evaluation, where the x-axes display the episodes and the y-axes display the return. The average performance of the *shielded agents* is represented by a thick *green line*, whereas a thick *red* line represents the average performance of *unshielded agents*. The light green and light red areas depict the range between the minimum and maximum performance of the shielded and the unshielded agents, respectively. Figure 6, Fig. 8, and Fig. 10 depict the number of safety violations throughout training, where the x-axes display the episodes and the y-axes display the number of times the agent visited a pit. The average number of safety violations of the *shielded agents* are represented by a thick *green line*, whereas a thick *red* line represents the average number of safety violations of *unshielded agents*. The light green and light red areas depict the range between the minimum and maximum number

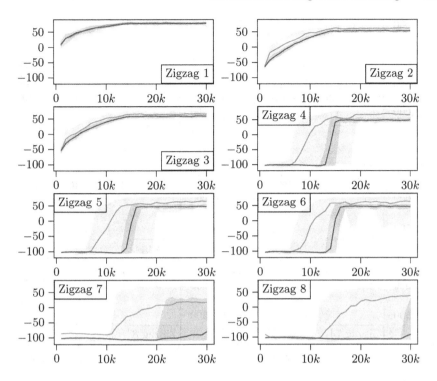

Fig. 5. The return gained by intermediate policies throughout reinforcement learning in the *zigzag* gridworlds. The x-axes display the return and the y-axes display the episodes at which policies are evaluated. The green plots represent shielded performance, whereas the red plots represent unshielded performance.

of safety violations of the shielded and the unshielded agents, respectively. In the following, we discuss the results from the experiments with the different gridworld shapes.

5.3   Zigzag Gridworlds

We start by discussing the performance of the RL agents in the *zigzag* gridworlds; see Fig. 2 for the smallest such environment. Figure 5 shows the return, and Fig. 6 shows the number of safety violations at various stages of RL.

The experiments in Fig. 5 show almost identical returns and number of safety violations for shielded and unshielded agents for the three smallest gridworld instances. Starting with the fourth-smallest gridworld, shielded RL performs better on average. Initially, during the first episodes of both RL configurations, the average return is approximately −100, which is the penalty for falling into a pit. This means that the agent consistently falls into pits in the early stages of learning. After approximately 7 iterations, i.e., at episode 7000, the shielded agents start to reach the goal states, which leads to an increase in the return

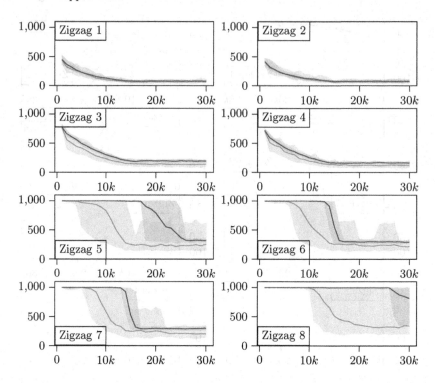

Fig. 6. The number of safety violations throughout RL in the *zigzag* gridworlds. The x-axes display the number of violations and the y-axes display the episodes at which the policies are evaluated. The green plots represent the number of violations under the shielded policies, whereas the red plots represent the same under unshielded policies.

and a decrease in the number of safety violations. Unshielded agents need about twice the time to reach the goal location. Similar observations can be made for the next larger environments *Zigzag 5* and *Zigzag 6*, too. For the two largest *zigzag* gridworlds, unshielded RL fails to consistently reach the goal after 30,000 training episodes. These two environments require relatively long paths to be traversed and the gained rewards are sparse. Hence, learned safety shields may benefit RL in environments with sparse rewards, where safety violations may prevent the agents from visiting states that give a positive reward. The decreases in the number of safety violations, as shown in Fig. 6, match the observations on the performance increases illustrated in Fig. 5.

On the negative side, note that the growth of the return is steeper for unshielded RL. For example, considering the environment *Zigzag 4*, it takes about 10000 episodes to reach an average return greater than 0 in the shielded case and it takes 15000 episodes in the unshielded case. Hence, there are 3000 episodes between first reaching the goal and reaching it more consistently for shielded RL, whereas unshielded RL only requires 1000 episodes to make this jump in performance.

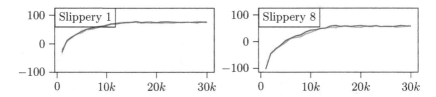

Fig. 7. Return gained by intermediate policies throughout RL in the *slippery shortcuts* gridworlds. The x-axes display the return and the y-axes display the episodes at which policies are evaluated. Green plots: shielded agent, red plots: unshielded agent.

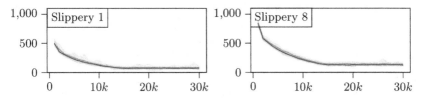

Fig. 8. The number of safety violations throughout RL in the *slippery shortcuts* gridworlds. The x-axes display the number of violations and y-axes display the episodes at which the policies are evaluated. Green plots: shielded agent, red plots: unshielded agent.

Furthermore, consider the range between the minimum and the maximum return that is depicted by the shaded areas in the figures. The minimum return of unshielded RL is often lower than the minimum return of shielded RL even though it performs better on average. There is more variance in the return obtained by shielded RL. Also, the range between the minimum and the maximum number of safety violations is high for *Zigzag 8* until the end of training. This could result from learning of MDPs that do not sufficiently capture safety-relevant information. We leave a closer investigation to future work.

5.4   Slippery Shortcuts Gridworlds

Next, we examine the performance of shielded and unshielded RL in the *slippery shortcuts* gridworlds illustrated in Fig. 3. Figure 7 shows the average returns, and Fig. 8 shows the number of safety violations gained by RL agents throughout learning. In contrast to the *zigzag* gridworlds, there is hardly any difference between the shielded and the unshielded configurations for any size of the environment, neither for the return nor for the number of safety violations. Therefore, we only printed the instances of *slippery 1* and *slippery 8* to safe space. Moreover, there is very little variability, as the minimum and maximum returns (safety violations) are very close to their average. Hence, performance is mostly governed by RL and shielding has little influence. In these environments, the agents succeed in finding safe paths without requiring assistance from a shield. This may result from the pits being farther away from optimal paths, as compared to the *zigzag* gridworlds.

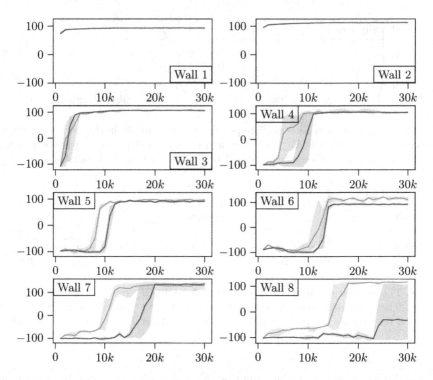

Fig. 9. Return gained by intermediate policies throughout RL in the *walls* gridworlds. The x-axes display the return and the y-axes display the episodes at which policies are evaluated. Green plots: shielded agent, red plots: unshielded agent.

5.5 Wall Gridworlds

In the following, we discuss the experiments performed on the *walls* gridworlds of Fig. 4. Figure 9 shows the returns, and Fig. 10 shows the number of safety violations gained at different stages of learning. As for the *zigzag* gridworlds, we see hardly any difference between shielded and unshielded RL for the three smallest environments, whereas shielded RL performs better in the larger environments. Unlike before, however, there is less variability in the performance and number of safety violations of shielded RL. In Fig. 4, we can see that the slippery tiles are farther away from the optimal route, which is also true for the larger *walls* gridworlds. As a result, learned MDPs do not need to be as accurate with respect to probability estimations for effective shields to be created. Especially for the largest example, *Wall 8*, shielding improves performance and reduces the number of safety violations considerably. It takes about 18000 episodes to learn a policy that consistently reaches the goal in all 30 repetitions of the corresponding experiments. In contrast, unshielded RL fails to consistently find a good policy even after 30000 episodes.

Finally, let us investigate a potential reason for performance improvements resulting from shielding or the absence thereof. In Fig. 11, we show the size of

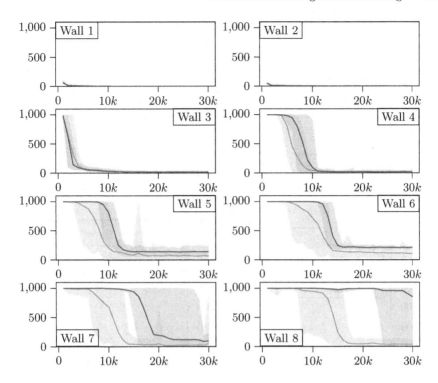

Fig. 10. The number of safety violations throughout RL in the *walls* gridworlds. The x-axes display the number of violations and y-axes display the episodes at which the policies are evaluated. Green plots: shielded agent, red plots: unshielded agent.

learned MDPs compared to the size of the *walls* environments, i.e., the number of tiles in every environment. Since the environment size is constant in an experiment, it is shown as a black straight line. The learned MDP size, measured in the number of states, generally increases throughout the learning due to more information getting available. It can be seen that for the first three environment sizes, the final learned MDPs are slightly larger than the environment. Hence, these MDPs cannot represent the environments and their safety-relevant features more efficiently than a Q-table. The fact that learned MDPs are even larger than the environments from which they are learned results from two properties of our learning setup. First, MDPs learned by IOALERGIA only converge in the large sample limit to the true underlying MDPs [24]. There are no guarantees for MDPs learned from finite amounts of data. Second and more importantly, abstraction introduces non-determinism, while MDP learning basically performs a determinization of the resulting non-deterministic MDP. This determinization causes the number of states to increase, similar to the construction of belief MDPs from partially observable MDPs [9].

When the environment is larger than the learned MDP modeling safety-relevant features of the environment, shielding improves RL performance. This

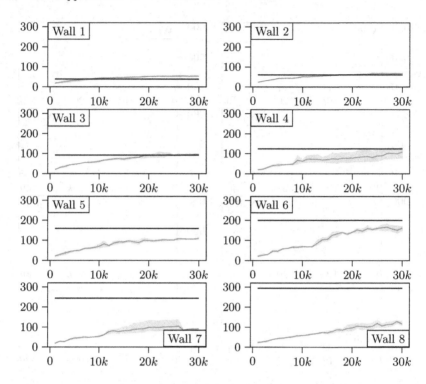

Fig. 11. Average size of learned MDPs for the *walls* gridworlds (x-axes) plotted in green compared to the size of the environment plotted as a black line. The y-axes display the episode at which the MDP size was measured.

holds for all environments from *Wall 4* throughout *Wall 8*. Comparing Fig. 9 or Fig. 10 with Fig. 11, we can see that the larger the size difference between the environment and the learned MDP is, the larger the performance impact or reduction in the number of safety violations.

5.6   Discussion

We conclude this section with a discussion of the main results of our experiments and some insights that we gained. Our results show that learned shields can improve RL performance as illustrated by our first and third set of experiments. In the first case of the *zigzag* gridworlds, the agent has to traverse along tiles located closely to pits in order to reach the goal. Therefore, a shield is able to prevent many safety violations. In the case of the *walls* gridworlds, we observed that learning shields especially pays off when the learned safety MDP is much smaller than the complete environment. We will explore this connection in future work, as it may enable scaling to larger environments. Deep reinforcement learning can efficiently solve tasks in complex environments, such as, computer games [27], while we can abstract away non-safety-relevant details to learn small MDPs for shielding.

In the *slippery shortcut* gridworlds, we observed that shielding does not necessarily improve performance. It seems easier for the agent to infer through RL how to navigate safely than in the other examples.

6   Conclusion

We presented an approach for iterative safe reinforcement learning via learned shields. At runtime, we learn environmental models from collected traces and continuously update shields that prevent safety violations during execution. RL with learned shields comprises three steps: (1) An RL agent exploring the environment, protected by a shield, and collecting abstracted experiences, which represent safety-information about the environment. (2) Learning a deterministic labeled MDP from the collected data of the RL agent. (3) Synthesizing a shield from such an MDP.

In contrast to most previous work on shielding, which commonly requires abstract environment models, the proposed approach is model-free and therefore applicable in black-box environments. We learn environment models solely from experiences of the RL agent. The agent can also infer its policy using a model-free approach, such as, Q-learning [41]. The downside is that we cannot enforce absolute safety. In order to learn safety-relevant information, the agent needs to experience some safety violations. Despite this limitation, our evaluation shows that in most cases, RL with learned shields converges more quickly than unshielded RL. Since optimal policies in our experiments should inflict hardly any safety violations, faster convergence implies that shielded agents run into fewer safety violations.

In future work, we will explore RL with learned shields in environments of larger size, where we aim to combine deep RL with MDP learning. Our intuition is that we can generally represent safety-relevant environmental features concisely with an MDP over abstract observations. We expect this to be true even if, for instance, the agent perceives its environment by processing high-resolution images. In addition to other (deep) RL techniques, we will explore different automata learning techniques. For instance, we could integrate RL more directly into active automata learning of stochastic system models [35, 37]. By learning timed automata [2, 25, 36, 39], we could extend learning-based shielding to systems with time-dependent behaviour.

Acknowledgments. This work has been supported by the "University SAL Labs" initiative of Silicon Austria Labs (SAL) and its Austrian partner universities for applied fundamental research for electronic based systems. Additionally, this project has received funding from the European Union's Horizon 2020 research and innovation programme under grant agreement No 956123 - FOCETA.

References

1. Aichernig, B.K., Mostowski, W., Mousavi, M.R., Tappler, M., Taromirad, M.: Model learning and model-based testing. In: Bennaceur, A., Hähnle, R., Meinke, K. (eds.) Machine Learning for Dynamic Software Analysis: Potentials and Limits. LNCS, vol. 11026, pp. 74–100. Springer, Cham (2018). https://doi.org/10.1007/978-3-319-96562-8_3

2. Aichernig, B.K., Pferscher, A., Tappler, M.: From passive to active: learning timed automata efficiently. In: Lee, R., Jha, S., Mavridou, A., Giannakopoulou, D. (eds.) NFM 2020. LNCS, vol. 12229, pp. 1–19. Springer, Cham (2020). https://doi.org/10.1007/978-3-030-55754-6_1

3. Aichernig, B.K., Tappler, M.: Probabilistic black-box reachability checking (extended version). Formal Methods Syst. Des. **54**(3), 416–448 (2019)

4. Alshiekh, M., Bloem, R., Ehlers, R., Könighofer, B., Niekum, S., Topcu, U.: Safe reinforcement learning via shielding. In: Proceedings of the 32nd International Conference on Artificial Intelligence, AAAI 2018, New Orleans, Louisiana, USA, February 2–7, 2018, vol. 32, pp. 2669–2678. AAAI Press (2018). https://www.aaai.org/ocs/index.php/AAAI/AAAI18/paper/view/17211

5. Baier, C., Katoen, J.: Principles of Model Checking. MIT Press (2008)

6. Bloem, R., Könighofer, B., Könighofer, R., Wang, C.: Shield synthesis: runtime enforcement for reactive systems. In: Baier, C., Tinelli, C. (eds.) TACAS 2015. LNCS, vol. 9035, pp. 533–548. Springer, Heidelberg (2015). https://doi.org/10.1007/978-3-662-46681-0_51

7. Brockman, G., et al.: OpenAI gym. CoRR arXiv:abs/1606.01540 (2016)

8. Carrasco, R.C., Oncina, J.: Learning stochastic regular grammars by means of a state merging method. In: Carrasco, R.C., Oncina, J. (eds.) ICGI 1994. LNCS, vol. 862, pp. 139–152. Springer, Heidelberg (1994). https://doi.org/10.1007/3-540-58473-0_144

9. Cassandra, A.R., Kaelbling, L.P., Littman, M.L.: Acting optimally in partially observable stochastic domains. In: Hayes-Roth, B., Korf, R.E. (eds.) Proceedings of the 12th National Conference on Artificial Intelligence, Seattle, WA, USA, July 31 - August 4, 1994, Volume 2. pp. 1023–1028. AAAI Press/The MIT Press (1994). http://www.aaai.org/Library/AAAI/1994/aaai94-157.php

10. Cobleigh, J.M., Giannakopoulou, D., PĂsĂreanu, C.S.: Learning assumptions for compositional verification. In: Garavel, H., Hatcliff, J. (eds.) TACAS 2003. LNCS, vol. 2619, pp. 331–346. Springer, Heidelberg (2003). https://doi.org/10.1007/3-540-36577-X_24

11. Corsi, D., Marchesini, E., Farinelli, A.: Formal verification of neural networks for safety-critical tasks in deep reinforcement learning. In: de Campos, C.P., Maathuis, M.H., Quaeghebeur, E. (eds.) UAI. Proceedings of Machine Learning Research, vol. 161, pp. 333–343 (2021). https://proceedings.mlr.press/v161/corsi21a.html

12. Fu, J., Topcu, U.: Probably approximately correct MDP learning and control with temporal logic constraints. In: Fox, D., Kavraki, L.E., Kurniawati, H. (eds.) Robotics: Science and Systems X, University of California, Berkeley, USA, 12–16 July 2014 (2014). http://www.roboticsproceedings.org/rss10/p39.html

13. Furelos-Blanco, D., Law, M., Russo, A., Broda, K., Jonsson, A.: Induction of sub-goal automata for reinforcement learning. In: The Thirty-Fourth AAAI Conference on Artificial Intelligence, AAAI 2020, The Thirty-Second Innovative Applications of Artificial Intelligence Conference, IAAI 2020, The Tenth AAAI Symposium on Educational Advances in Artificial Intelligence, EAAI 2020, New York, NY,

USA, February 7–12, 2020, pp. 3890–3897. AAAI Press (2020). https://ojs.aaai. org/index.php/AAAI/article/view/5802

14. Gaon, M., Brafman, R.I.: Reinforcement learning with non-Markovian rewards. In: The Thirty-Fourth AAAI Conference on Artificial Intelligence, AAAI 2020, The Thirty-Second Innovative Applications of Artificial Intelligence Conference, IAAI 2020, The Tenth AAAI Symposium on Educational Advances in Artificial Intelligence, EAAI 2020, New York, NY, USA, February 7–12, 2020, pp. 3980–3987. AAAI Press (2020). https://ojs.aaai.org/index.php/AAAI/article/view/5814

15. Giacobbe, M., Hasanbeig, M., Kroening, D., Wijk, H.: Shielding atari games with bounded prescience. In: Proceedings of the 20th International Conference on Autonomous Agents and Multiagent Systems, AAMAS 2021, Virtual Event, United Kingdom, 3–7 May, 2021, pp. 1507–1509. ACM (2021). https://doi.org/10. 5555/3463952.3464141

16. Hasanbeig, M., Jeppu, N.Y., Abate, A., Melham, T., Kroening, D.: Deepsynth: automata synthesis for automatic task segmentation in deep reinforcement learning. In: Thirty-Fifth AAAI Conference on Artificial Intelligence, AAAI 2021, Thirty-Third Conference on Innovative Applications of Artificial Intelligence, IAAI 2021, The Eleventh Symposium on Educational Advances in Artificial Intelligence, EAAI 2021, Virtual Event, 2–9 February 2021, pp. 7647–7656. AAAI Press (2021). https://ojs.aaai.org/index.php/AAAI/article/view/16935

17. Howar, F., Steffen, B.: Active automata learning in practice. In: Bennaceur, A., Hähnle, R., Meinke, K. (eds.) Machine Learning for Dynamic Software Analysis: Potentials and Limits. LNCS, vol. 11026, pp. 123–148. Springer, Cham (2018). https://doi.org/10.1007/978-3-319-96562-8_5

18. Icarte, R.T., Waldie, E., Klassen, T.Q., Valenzano, R.A., Castro, M.P., McIlraith, S.A.: Learning reward machines for partially observable reinforcement learning. In: Wallach, H.M., Larochelle, H., Beygelzimer, A., d'Alché-Buc, F., Fox, E.B., Garnett, R. (eds.) Advances in Neural Information Processing Systems 32: Annual Conference on Neural Information Processing Systems 2019, NeurIPS 2019, December 8–14, 2019, Vancouver, BC, Canada. pp. 15497–15508 (2019). https://proceedings. neurips.cc/paper/2019/hash/532435c44bec236b471a47a88d63513d-Abstract.html

19. Jansen, N., Könighofer, B., Junges, S., Serban, A., Bloem, R.: Safe reinforcement learning using probabilistic shields (invited paper). In: Konnov, I., Kovács, L. (eds.) 31st International Conference on Concurrency Theory, CONCUR 2020, September 1–4, 2020, Vienna, Austria (Virtual Conference). LIPIcs, vol. 171, pp. 3:1–3:16. Schloss Dagstuhl - Leibniz-Zentrum für Informatik (2020). https://doi.org/ 10.4230/LIPIcs.CONCUR.2020.3

20. Kiran, B.R., et al.: Deep reinforcement learning for autonomous driving: a survey. IEEE Trans. Intell. Transp. Syst. (2021)

21. Könighofer, B., Lorber, F., Jansen, N., Bloem, R.: Shield synthesis for reinforcement learning. In: Margaria, T., Steffen, B. (eds.) ISoLA 2020. LNCS, vol. 12476, pp. 290–306. Springer, Cham (2020). https://doi.org/10.1007/978-3-030-61362-4_16

22. Könighofer, B., Rudolf, J., Palmisano, A., Tappler, M., Bloem, R.: Online shielding for stochastic systems. In: Dutle, A., Moscato, M.M., Titolo, L., Muñoz, C.A., Perez, I. (eds.) NFM 2021. LNCS, vol. 12673, pp. 231–248. Springer, Cham (2021). https://doi.org/10.1007/978-3-030-76384-8_15

23. Mao, H., Chen, Y., Jaeger, M., Nielsen, T.D., Larsen, K.G., Nielsen, B.: Learning Markov decision processes for model checking. In: Fahrenberg, U., Legay, A., Thrane, C.R. (eds.) Proceedings Quantities in Formal Methods, QFM 2012, Paris,

France, 28 August 2012. EPTCS, vol. 103, pp. 49–63 (2012). https://doi.org/10. 4204/EPTCS.103.6

24. Mao, H., et al.: Learning deterministic probabilistic automata from a model checking perspective. Mach. Learn. **105**(2), 255–299 (2016). https://doi.org/10.1007/ s10994-016-5565-9

25. Mediouni, B.L., Nouri, A., Bozga, M., Bensalem, S.: Improved learning for stochastic timed models by state-merging algorithms. In: Barrett, C., Davies, M., Kahsai, T. (eds.) NFM 2017. LNCS, vol. 10227, pp. 178–193. Springer, Cham (2017). https://doi.org/10.1007/978-3-319-57288-8_13

26. Meinke, K., Sindhu, M.A.: Incremental learning-based testing for reactive systems. In: Gogolla, M., Wolff, B. (eds.) TAP 2011. LNCS, vol. 6706, pp. 134–151. Springer, Heidelberg (2011). https://doi.org/10.1007/978-3-642-21768-5_11

27. Mnih, V., et al.: Playing atari with deep reinforcement learning. CoRR arXiv:abs/1312.5602 (2013)

28. Muškardin, E., Aichernig, B.K., Pill, I., Pferscher, A., Tappler, M.: AALpy: an active automata learning library. In: Hou, Z., Ganesh, V. (eds.) ATVA 2021. LNCS, vol. 12971, pp. 67–73. Springer, Cham (2021). https://doi.org/10.1007/978-3-030-88885-5_5

29. Muskardin, E., Tappler, M., Aichernig, B.K., Pill, I.: Reinforcement learning under partial observability guided by learned environment models. CoRR arXiv:abs/2206.11708 (2022)

30. Nouri, A., Raman, B., Bozga, M., Legay, A., Bensalem, S.: Faster statistical model checking by means of abstraction and learning. In: Bonakdarpour, B., Smolka, S.A. (eds.) RV 2014. LNCS, vol. 8734, pp. 340–355. Springer, Cham (2014). https:// doi.org/10.1007/978-3-319-11164-3_28

31. Peled, D.A., Vardi, M.Y., Yannakakis, M.: Black box checking. J. Autom. Lang. Comb. **7**(2), 225–246 (2002). https://doi.org/10.25596/jalc-2002-225

32. Pranger, S., Könighofer, B., Posch, L., Bloem, R.: TEMPEST - synthesis tool for reactive systems and shields in probabilistic environments. In: Hou, Z., Ganesh, V. (eds.) ATVA 2021. LNCS, vol. 12971, pp. 222–228. Springer, Cham (2021). https://doi.org/10.1007/978-3-030-88885-5_15

33. Pranger, S., Könighofer, B., Tappler, M., Deixelberger, M., Jansen, N., Bloem, R.: Adaptive shielding under uncertainty. In: 2021 American Control Conference, ACC 2021, New Orleans, LA, USA, 25–28 May, 2021, pp. 3467–3474. IEEE (2021). https://doi.org/10.23919/ACC50511.2021.9482889

34. Sutton, R.S., Barto, A.G.: Reinforcement learning - an introduction. Adaptive computation and machine learning. MIT Press (1998). https://www.worldcat.org/ oclc/37293240

35. Tappler, M., Aichernig, B.K., Bacci, G., Eichlseder, M., Larsen, K.G.: L^*-based learning of markov decision processes (extended version). Formal Aspects Comput. **33**(4–5), 575–615 (2021). https://doi.org/10.1007/s00165-021-00536-5

36. Tappler, M., Aichernig, B.K., Larsen, K.G., Lorber, F.: Time to learn – learning timed automata from tests. In: André, É., Stoelinga, M. (eds.) FORMATS 2019. LNCS, vol. 11750, pp. 216–235. Springer, Cham (2019). https://doi.org/10.1007/ 978-3-030-29662-9_13

37. Tappler, M., Muškardin, E., Aichernig, B.K., Pill, I.: Active model learning of stochastic reactive systems. In: Calinescu, R., Păsăreanu, C.S. (eds.) SEFM 2021. LNCS, vol. 13085, pp. 481–500. Springer, Cham (2021). https://doi.org/10. 1007/978-3-030-92124-8_27

38. Vaandrager, F.W.: Model learning. Commun. ACM **60**(2), 86–95 (2017). https:// doi.org/10.1145/2967606

39. Verwer, S., de Weerdt, M., Witteveen, C.: A likelihood-ratio test for identifying probabilistic deterministic real-time automata from positive data. In: Sempere, J.M., García, P. (eds.) ICGI 2010. LNCS (LNAI), vol. 6339, pp. 203–216. Springer, Heidelberg (2010). https://doi.org/10.1007/978-3-642-15488-1_17

40. Waga, M., Castellano, E., Pruekprasert, S., Klikovits, S., Takisaka, T., Hasuo, I.: Dynamic shielding for reinforcement learning in black-box environments. CoRR arXiv:abs/2207.13446 (2022)

41. Watkins, C.J.C.H., Dayan, P.: Technical note q-learning. Mach. Learn. **8**, 279–292 (1992). https://doi.org/10.1007/BF00992698

42. Xu, Z., et al.: Joint inference of reward machines and policies for reinforcement learning. In: Beck, J.C., Buffet, O., Hoffmann, J., Karpas, E., Sohrabi, S. (eds.) Proceedings of the Thirtieth International Conference on Automated Planning and Scheduling, Nancy, France, 26–30 October, 2020, pp. 590–598. AAAI Press (2020). https://ojs.aaai.org/index.php/ICAPS/article/view/6756

Safe Policy Improvement in Constrained Markov Decision Processes

Luigi Berducci[✉] and Radu Grosu

CPS Group, TU Wien, Vienna, Austria
luigi.berducci@tuwien.ac.at

Abstract. The automatic synthesis of a policy through reinforcement learning (RL) from a given set of formal requirements depends on the construction of a reward signal and consists of the iterative application of many policy-improvement steps. The synthesis algorithm has to balance target, safety, and comfort requirements in a single objective and to guarantee that the policy improvement does not increase the number of safety-requirements violations, especially for safety-critical applications. In this work, we present a solution to the synthesis problem by solving its two main challenges: reward-shaping from a set of formal requirements and safe policy update. For the first, we propose an automatic reward-shaping procedure, defining a scalar reward signal compliant with the task specification. For the second, we introduce an algorithm ensuring that the policy is improved in a safe fashion, with high-confidence guarantees. We also discuss the adoption of a model-based RL algorithm to efficiently use the collected data and train a model-free agent on the predicted trajectories, where the safety violation does not have the same impact as in the real world. Finally, we demonstrate in standard control benchmarks that the resulting learning procedure is effective and robust even under heavy perturbations of the hyperparameters.

Keywords: Reinforcement learning · Safe policy improvement · Formal specification

1 Introduction

Reinforcement Learning (RL) has become a practical approach for solving complex control tasks in increasingly challenging environments. However, despite the availability of a large set of standard benchmarks with well-defined structure and reward signals, solving new problems remains an art.

There are two major challenges in applying RL to new synthesis problems. The first, arises from the need to define a good reward signal for the problem. We illustrate this challenge with an autonomous-driving (AD) application. In AD, we have numerous requirements that have to be mapped into a single scalar reward signal. In realistic applications, more than 200 requirements need to be considered when assessing the course of action [14]. Moreover, determining the

© The Author(s), under exclusive license to Springer Nature Switzerland AG 2022
T. Margaria and B. Steffen (Eds.): ISoLA 2022, LNCS 13701, pp. 360–381, 2022.
https://doi.org/10.1007/978-3-031-19849-6_21

relative importance of the different requirements is a highly non-trivial task. In this realm, there are a plethora of regulations, ranging from safety and traffic rules to performance, comfort, legal, and ethical requirements.

The second challenge concerns the RL algorithm with whom we intend to search for an optimal policy. Considering most of the modern RL algorithms, especially model-free policy-gradient methods [53], they require an iterative interaction with the environment, from which they collect fresh experiences for further improving the policy. Despite their effectiveness, a slight change in the policy parameters could have unexpected consequences in the resulting performance. This fact often results in learning curves with unstable performances, strongly depending on the tuning of hyperparameters and algorithmic design choices [28]. The lack of guarantees and robustness in the policy improvement still limits the application of RL outside controlled environments or simulators.

In this paper, we tackle the two problems mentioned above by proposing a complete design pipeline for safe policies: from the definition of the problem to the safe optimization of the policy (Fig. 1). We discuss how to structure the problem from a set of formal requirements and enrich the reward signal while keeping a sound formulation. Moreover, we define the conditions which characterize a correct-by-construction algorithm in this context and demonstrate its realizability with high-confidence off-policy evaluation. We propose two algorithms, one model-free and one model-based, respectively. We formally prove that they are correct by construction and evaluate their performance empirically.

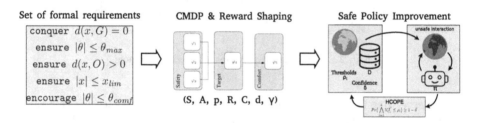

Fig. 1. Overall RL pipeline to solve formally-specified control tasks.

2 Motivating Example

We motivate our work with a *cart-pole example* extended with safety, target, and comfort requirements, as follows: A *pole* is attached to a *cart* that moves between a *left* and a *right limit*, within a flat and frictionless environment. The environment has a *target* area within the limits and a static *obstacle* hanging above the track. We define five requirements for the cart-pole, as shown in Table 1.

We aim to teach the cart-pole to satisfy all requirements. The system is controlled by applying a continuous *force* to the cart, allowing the left and right movements of the cart-pole with different velocities. In order to reach the goal and satisfy the target requirement Req_1, the cart-pole must do an uncomfortable

Table 1. Cart-pole example – informal requirements.

Req ID	Description
Req_1	The cart shall reach the target in bounded time
Req_2	The pole shall never fall from the cart
Req_3	The pole shall never collide with the obstacle
Req_4	The cart shall never leave the left/right limits
Req_5	The cart shall keep the pole balanced within a comfortably small angle as often as possible

and potentially unsafe maneuver: since moving a perfectly balanced pole would result in a collision with the obstacle, thus violating the safety requirement Req_3, the cart-pole must lose balancing and pass below it. Furthermore, if the obstacle is too large, or the cart does not apply enough force once passing the obstacle, it may not be able to reach the target without falling, thus violating the safety requirement Req_2. A sequence of pictures showing the cart-pole successfully overcoming the obstacle in the environment is depicted in Fig. 2.

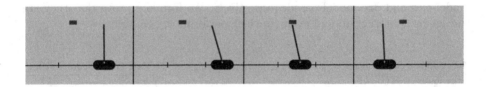

Fig. 2. A cart-pole overcomes a hanging obstacle.

Observe that not all requirements have the same importance for this task. We regard the safety requirements as fundamental constraints on the agent's behavior. A safety violation compromises the validity of the entire episode. The target requirement expresses the main objective, and its completion is the agent's reason to be. Finally, comfort requirements are secondary objectives that should be optimized as long as they do not interfere with the other two classes of requirements. In the remainder of this paper, we will use this motivating example to illustrate the steps that lead to the proposed methodology.

3   Related Work

Safety is a well-known and highly-researched problem in the RL community, and the related literature is wide [11,23]. Many different definitions and approaches have emerged over the years, so we will first clarify the interpretations of safety that we adopt. Much work considers safety as the property of the trained policy, determining whether the agent satisfies a set of constraints. They either try to converge to a safe policy at the end of the training [2,5,10,15], or try to ensure safety during the entire training process [4,16,18,45,51,54,56,64].

Placing ourselves in a design perspective, we consider safety as a property of the RL algorithm instead. By safety, we mean that a safe algorithm will not return a policy with performance below a given threshold, with high probability guarantees. Building on this interpretation, we will later define the conditions for correct-by-construction RL algorithms. In the following, we review the main approaches relevant to our contribution.

Safe Policy Improvement. Early representative of these algorithms are CPI [34,46] that provide monotonically improving updates at the cost of enormous sample complexity. More recently, [52] introduced TRPO, the first policy-gradient algorithm which builds on trust-region methods to guarantee policy improvement. However, its sound formulation must be relaxed in practice for computational tractability. The class of algorithms more relevant for our work is based on off-policy evaluation [47,57]. Seminal works in this field is HCPI [58,59] that use *concentration inequalities* [40] to define high-confidence lower bounds on the *importance sampling* estimates [47] of the policy performance. More recently, this class of algorithms has been shown to be part of the general Seldonian framework [60]. We build on this formalism to define our approach and differ from the existing work by proposing a novel interface with a set of formally specified requirements, and propose Daedalus-style solutions [58] to tackle the problem of iterative improvement in an online setting.

Policy Evaluation with Statistical Model Checking. Statistical guarantees on the policy evaluation for some temporal specification is commonly solved with statistical model checking (SMC) [3,35]. Recent works have proposed SMC for evaluating a NN decision policy operating in an MDP [24]. However, while SMC relies on collecting a large number of executions of the policy in the environment and hypothesis testing for providing performance bounds, our off-policy setting tackles a different problem. In off-policy evaluation, the model of the environment is generally unknown and we cannot deploy the decision policy in the environment because it could be costly or dangerous. Unlike SMC, we cannot directly collect statistics with the decision policy. Conversely, we try to approximate the expected performance using data collected by another policy.

RL with Temporal Logic. Much prior work adopts *temporal logic* (TL) in RL. Some of it focuses on the decomposition of a complex task into many sub tasks [33,61]. Other on formulations tailored to tasks specified in TL [21,29,31,36]. Several works use the quantitative semantics of TL (i.e., STL and its variants) to derive a reward signal [7,32,37]. However, they describe the task as a monolithic TL specification and compute the reward on complete [37] or truncated trajectories [7]. In this work, we use HPRS, introduced in [9] to mitigate the reward sparsity and subsequent credit-assignment problem, which combines the individual evaluation of requirements into a hierarchically-weighted reward, capturing the priority among the various classes of requirements.

Multi-objective RL. Multi-objective RL (MORL) studies the optimization of multiple and often conflicting objectives. MORL algorithms learn single or multiple policies [38,50]. There exist several techniques to combine multiple reward signals into a single scalar value (i.e., scalarization), such as linear or non-linear projections [8,42,62]. Other approaches formulate structured rewards by imposing or assuming a preference ranking on the objectives and finding an equilibrium among them [1,22,55,65]. [13] proposes to decompose the task specification into many requirements. However, they do not consider any structured priority among requirements and rely on the arbitrary choice of weights for each of them. In general, balancing between safety and performance shows connections with MORL. However, we focus on the safety aspects and how to guarantee safety below a certain threshold with high probability. These characteristics are not present in MORL approaches.

Hierarchically Structured Requirements. The use of partially ordered requirements to formalize complex tasks has been proposed in a few works. The *rulebook* formalism [14] represents a set of prioritized requirements, and it has been used for evaluating the behaviors produced with a planner [14], or generating adversarial testing scenarios [63]. In [48], a complementary inverse RL approach proposes learning dependencies for formal requirements starting from existing demonstrations. Conversely, we use the requirements to describe our task and define a Constrained MDP, and then focus on the design of a safe policy-improvement algorithm.

Model-Based Reinforcement Learning. Among the first representatives of model-based RL algorithms is PILCO [19], which learned a Gaussian process for low-dimensional state systems. More recent works showed that it is possible to exploit expressive neural-networks models to learn complex dynamics in robotics systems [41], and use them for planning [17] or policy learning [30]. In the context of control from pixel images, world models [25] proved that it is possible to learn accurate dynamic models for POMDPs by using noisy high-dimensional observations instead of accurate states. Their application in planning [27], and later in policy learning [26], have achieved the new state-of-the-art performance in many benchmarks and were recently applied to real-world robots [12].

4   Preliminaries

4.1   Reinforcement Learning

Reinforcement Learning (RL) aims to infer an intelligent agent's policy that takes actions in an environment in a way that maximizes some notion of expected return. The environment is typically modeled as a Markov decision process (MDP), and the return is defined as the cumulative discounted reward.

Definition 1. *A Markov Decision Process (MDP) is a tuple* $M = (S, A, p, R, \gamma)$, *where S is a set of states; A is a set of possible actions; $p : S \times A \times S \to [0, 1]$ is a transition probability function (where $p(s_{t+1}|a_t, s_t)$ describes the probability of arriving in state s_{t+1} if action a_t was taken at state s_t); $R : S \times A \times S \to \mathbb{R}$ is a deterministic reward function, assigning a scalar value to a transition; $\gamma \in [0, 1]$ is the discount factor that balances the importance of achieving future rewards.*

In RL, one aims to find a policy $\pi : S \times A \to [0, 1]$ which maps states to action probabilities, such that it maximizes the expected sum of rewards collected over episodes (*or trajectories*) τ:

$$\pi^\star = \arg\max_\pi \mathbb{E}_{\tau \sim \mu(\cdot|\pi)} \Big[\sum_{t=0}^\infty \gamma^t R(s_t, a_t, s_{t+1}) \Big],$$

where $\mu(\tau|\pi)$ represents the distribution over episodes observed when sampling actions from some policy π, and $\tau \sim \mu(\cdot|\pi)$ denotes an episode that was sampled from this distribution.

Conventional RL approaches do not explicitly consider safety constraints in MDPs. Constrained MDPs [6] extend the MDP formalism to handle such constraints, resulting in the tuple $M = (S, A, p, R, C, \gamma, d)$, where $C : S \times A \times S \to \mathbb{R}$ is a cost function and $d \in \mathbb{R}$ is a cost threshold. We aim to teach the agent to *safely* interact with the environment. More concretely, considering the episodes $\tau \sim \mu(\cdot|\pi)$, the expected cumulative cost must be below the threshold d; that is, the constraint is $\mathbb{E}_{\tau \sim \mu(\cdot|\pi)} \big[\sum_{t=0}^\infty \gamma^t C(s_t, a_t, s_{t+1},) \big] \leq d$. Formally, the constrained optimization problem consists of finding $\pi^\star$ such that:

$$\pi^\star = \arg\max_\pi \mathbb{E}_{\tau \sim \mu(\cdot|\pi)} \Big[\sum_{t=0}^\infty \gamma^t R(s_t, a_t, s_{t+1},) \Big]$$

$$\text{subject to } \mathbb{E}_{\tau \sim \mu(\cdot|\pi)} \Big[\sum_{t=0}^\infty \gamma^t C(s_t, a_t, s_{t+1},) \Big] \leq d$$

We denote the expected cumulative discounted reward and cost as V^π and V_C^π, respectively. When dealing with multiple constraints, we use C_i, d_i, and $V_{C_i}^\pi$ to denote the i-th cost function, its threshold, and expected cumulative cost.

4.2 Hierarchical Task Specifications

Requirements Specification. In [9], we formally define a set of expressive operators to capture requirements often occurring in control problems. Considering atomic predicates $p \doteq f(s) \geq 0$ over observable states $s \in S$, we extend existing task-specification languages (e.g., SpectRL [33]) and define requirements as:

$$\varphi \doteq \texttt{achieve } p \mid \texttt{conquer } p \mid \texttt{ensure } p \mid \texttt{encourage } p \qquad (1)$$

Commonly, a task can be defined as a set of requirements from three basic classes: *safety*, *target*, and *comfort*. Safety requirements, of the form $\texttt{ensure } p$, are

Table 2. Cart-pole example – formalized requirements.

Req Id	Formula Id	Formula
Req1	φ_1	**conquer** $d(x, G) = 0$
Req2	φ_2	**ensure** $|\theta| \leq \theta_{max}$
Req3	φ_4	**ensure** $d(x, O) > 0$
Req4	φ_3	**ensure** $|x| \leq x_{lim}$
Req5	φ_5	**encourage** $|\theta| \leq \theta_{comf}$

naturally associated to an invariant condition p. Target requirements, of the form `achieve` p or `conquer` p, formalize the one-time or respectively the persistent achievement of a goal within an episode. Finally, comfort requirements, of the form `encourage` p, introduce the soft satisfaction of p, as often as possible, without compromising task satisfaction.

Let $\mathbb{T}$ be the set of all finite episodes of length T. Then, each requirement φ induces a Boolean function $\sigma : \mathbb{T} \to \mathbb{B}$ evaluating whether an episode $\tau \in \mathbb{T}$ satisfies the requirement φ. Formally, given a finite episode τ of length T, we define the requirement-satisfaction function σ as follows:

$$\tau \models \text{achieve } p \qquad\qquad \text{iff } \exists i \leq T, \tau_i \models p$$

$$\tau \models \text{conquer } p \qquad\qquad \text{iff } \exists i \leq T, \forall j \geq i, \tau_j \models p$$

$$\tau \models \text{ensure } p \qquad\qquad \text{iff } \forall i \leq T, \tau_i \models p$$

$$\tau \models \text{encourage } p \qquad\qquad \text{iff true}$$

We explain below the proposed evaluation of comfort requirements. In our interpretation, they represent secondary objectives, and their satisfaction does not alter the truth of the evaluation. In fact, as long as the agent is able to safely achieve the target, we consider the task satisfied. For this reason, the satisfaction of comfort requirement always evaluates to true. To further clarify the proposed specification language, we formalize the requirements for the running example.

Example 1. Consider the motivating cart-pole example. Now let us give the formal specification of its requirements. The state is the tuple $(x, \dot{x}, \theta, \dot{\theta})$, where x is the position of the cart, $\dot{x}$ is its velocity, θ is the angle of the pole to the vertical axis, and $\dot{\theta}$ is its angular velocity. We first define: (1) the angle θ_{max} of the pole at which we consider the pole to fall from the cart; (2) the maximum angle θ_{comf} of the pole that we consider to be comfortable; (3) the world limit x_{lim}; (4) the position G of the goal; (5) the set of points O defining the static obstacle; and (6) a distance function d between locations in the world (e.g., euclidean distance), that, with a slight abuse of notation, we extend to measure the distance between the cart position and a set of points. Then, the task can be formalized with the requirements reported in Table 2.

Task as a Partially-Ordered Set. We formalize a task by a set of formal requirements Φ, assuming that the target is unique and unambiguous. Formally, $\Phi = \Phi_S \uplus \Phi_T \uplus \Phi_C$ such that:

$$\Phi_S := \{\varphi \mid \varphi \doteq \texttt{ensure } p\}$$
$$\Phi_C := \{\varphi \mid \varphi \doteq \texttt{encourage } p\}$$
$$\Phi_T := \{\varphi \mid \varphi \doteq \texttt{achieve } p \vee \varphi \doteq \texttt{conquer } p\}$$

The target requirement is required to be unique ($|\Phi_T| = 1$).

We use a very natural interpretation of importance among the class of requirements, which considers decreasing importance from safety, to target, and to comfort requirements. Formally, this natural interpretation of importance defines a (strict) partial order relation $\prec$ on Φ as follows:

$$\varphi \prec \varphi' \text{ iff } (\varphi \in \Phi_S \wedge \varphi' \notin \Phi_S) \vee (\varphi \in \Phi_T \wedge \varphi' \in \Phi_C)$$

The resulting pair $(\Phi, \prec)$ forms a partially-ordered set of requirements and defines our task. Extending the semantics of satisfaction to a set, we consider a task accomplished when all of its requirements are satisfied:

$$\tau \models \Phi \text{ iff } \forall \varphi \in \Phi, \tau \models \varphi. \tag{2}$$

5   Contribution

In this section, we present the main contribution of this work: a correct-by-construction RL pipeline to solve formally-specified control tasks. First, we formalize a CMDP from the set of requirements, providing the intuition behind its sound formulation. Then, we describe the potential-based reward proposed in [9] that we use to enrich the learning signal and still benefit from correctness guarantees. Finally, we present an online RL algorithm that iteratively updates a policy while maintaining the performance for safety requirements.

5.1   Problem Formulation

The environment is considered a tuple $E = (S, A, p)$, where S is the set of states, A is the set of actions, and $p(s_{t+1}|s_t, a_t)$ is its dynamics, that is, the probability of reaching state s' by performing action a in state s. Given a task specification $(\Phi, \prec)$, where $\Phi = \Phi_S \uplus \Phi_T \uplus \Phi_C$, we define a CMDP $M = (S, A, p, R, C, \gamma, d)$ by formulating its reward R and cost functions C_i to reflect the semantics of $(\Phi, \prec)$.

We consider episodic tasks of length T, where the episode ends when the task satisfaction is decided: either through a safety violation, a timeout, or the goal achievement. When one of these events occurs, we assume that the MDP is entering a *final* absorbing state s_f, where the decidability of the episode cannot be altered anymore. The goal-achievement evaluation depends on the target operator adopted: for $\texttt{achieve } p$ the goal is achieved when visiting at time $t \leq T$ a state s_t such that $s_t \models p$; for $\texttt{conquer } p$ the goal is achieved if there is a time $i \leq T$ such that for all $i \leq t \leq T$, $s_t \models p$.

We adopt a straightforward interface for safety requirements, requiring the cost function $C_i(s, a, s')$ to be a binary indicator of the violation of the i-th safety requirement $\phi_i \in \Phi_S$ when entering s' from s: 0 if the current state satisfies ϕ_i and 1 if the current state violates ϕ_i. We bound the expected cumulative discounted cost by d_i, a user-provided safety threshold that depends on the specific application considered:

$$V_{C_i}^\pi = \mathbb{E}_{\tau \sim \mu(\cdot | \pi)}[\sum_{t=0}^{T} \gamma^t C_i(s_t, a_t, s_{t+1})] \leq d_i$$

The choice of this cost function promotes simplicity, requiring users to only be able to detect safety violations and relieving them from the burden of defining more complex signals. Moreover, the resulting cost metric $V_{C_i}^\pi$ reflects the failure probability discounted over time by the factor γ and makes the choice of the threshold d_i more intuitive by interpreting it in a probabilistic way.

We complete the CMDP formulation by defining a sparse reward, incentivizing goal achievement. Let p be the property of the unique target requirement. Then, for safe transitions $\langle s_t, a_t, s_{t+1} \rangle$, we define the following reward signal:

$$R(s_t, a_t, s_{t+1}) = \begin{cases} 1 & \text{if } s_{t+1} \models p \\ 0 & \text{otherwise} \end{cases}$$

The rationale behind this choice is that the task's satisfaction depends on the satisfaction of safety and target requirements. In the same way, the reward R incentives safe transitions to states that satisfy the target requirement, and the violation of any safety requirements terminates the episode, precluding the agent from collecting any further reward. It follows that R incentives to reach the target and stay there as long as possible, in the limit until T.

5.2   Reward Shaping

We additionally define a shaped reward with HPRS [9] to provide a dense training signal and speed-up the learning process. Since we consider a CMDP and model the safety requirements as constraints, we restrict the HPRS definition to target and comfort requirements.

We consider predicates $p(s) \doteq f(s) \geq 0$, where the value $f(s)$ is bounded in $[m, M]$ for all states s. Let $f_-(s) = min(0, f(s))$ and $\Phi_{tc} = \Phi_T \uplus \Phi_C$. We use the continuous normalized signal $r(\varphi, s) = 1 - \frac{f_-(s)}{m}$ to define the potential shaping function Ψ as follows:

$$\Psi(s) = \sum_{\varphi \in \Phi_{tc}} \left(\prod_{\varphi' \in \Phi_{tc} : \varphi' \prec \varphi} r(\varphi', s) \right) \cdot r(\varphi, s)$$

This potential function is a weighted sum over all scores $r(\varphi, s)$ for target and comfort requirements, where the weights are determined by a product of the scores of all specifications that are strictly more important (hierarchically) than φ. Crucially, these weights adapt dynamically at every step.

Corollary 1. *The optimal policy for the CMDP M', where its reward R' is defined as below:*

$$R'(s_t, a_t, s_{t+1}) = R(s_t, a_t, s_{t+1}) + \gamma \Psi(s_{t+1}) - \Psi(s_t) \tag{3}$$

is also an optimal policy for the CMDP M with reward R.

The corollary stated in [9] follows by the fact that Ψ is a potential function (i.e., depends only on the current state) and by the results in [43]. This result remark that the proposed reward shaping is correct since it preserves the policy optimality of the CMDP M.

The proposed hierarchical-potential signal has a few crucial characteristics. First, it is a potential function and can be used to augment the original reward signal without altering the optimal policy of the resulting CMDP. Second, it is a multivariate signal that combines target and comfort objectives with multiplicative terms. A linear combination of them, as typical in multi-objective scalarization, would assume independence among objectives. Consequently, any linear combination would not be expressive enough to capture the interdependence between requirements. Finally, the weights dynamically adapt at every step according to the satisfaction degree of the requirements.

5.3   Safe Policy Improvement in Online Setting

This section presents an online RL algorithm that uses a correct-by-construction policy-improvement routine. While this approach is general enough to be used on any CMDP, we use it with the shaped reward signal and costs presented in the previous section.

At each iteration, the algorithm performs a correct-by-construction refinement of the current policy π, with high probability. This means that, with high probability, the algorithm returns a policy π' whose safety performance is not worse than that of π. Since we are working in a model-free setting, with access to only a finite amount of off-policy data, we can define correct-by-construction only up to certain confidence δ. Below is the formal definition.

Definition 2. *Let M be a CMDP with cost functions C_i for $i \in [1, k]$, π a policy, and $D_n \sim \mu(\cdot|\pi)$ a finite dataset of experiences collected with π. A policy-improvement routine $\mathcal{A}$ is correct-by-construction if for any δ:*

$$\pi' = \mathcal{A}(\pi, D_n, \delta) \quad s.t. \quad Pr(\bigwedge_{i=1}^{k} V_{C_i}^{\pi'} \leq V_{C_i}^{\pi}) \geq 1 - \delta$$

Having defined what correct-by-construction means, we describe how we can build an update mechanism to prevent the deployment of an unsafe policy.

High-Confidence Off-Policy Policy Evaluation. Before releasing a policy π' for deployment in the environment, we need to estimate its safety performance using a set of trajectories D_n collected with the previous deployed policy π. We assume to know a threshold ρ_+, being either an acceptable upper bound for the cost in our application or an estimate of the performance of the last deployed policy π. We aim to evaluate a candidate policy π' and check if its expected cumulative costs are below the thresholds with a probability of at least $1 - \delta$.

We use *importance sampling* to produce an unbiased estimator of $\rho(\pi')$ over a trajectory τ collected by running π. The estimator is defined as

$$\hat{\rho}(\pi'|\tau, \pi) = \prod_{t=1}^{|\tau|} \frac{\pi'(a_t|s_t)}{\pi(a_t|s_t)} \left(\sum_{t=1}^{|\tau|} \gamma^t C(s_t, a_t, s_{t+1}) \right)$$

Computing the *importance weighted returns* gives us unbiased estimators of the safety performance [47]. The mean over estimators from n trajectories in D_n is also unbiased, $\hat{\rho} = \frac{1}{n} \sum_{i}^{n} \hat{\rho}(\pi'|\tau_i, \pi)$. However, we want to provide statistical guarantees regarding the resulting value. We use the one-sided Student-t test to obtain a $1 - \delta$ confidence upper bound on $\hat{\rho}$.

Let $\hat{\rho}_i$ be the i-th unbiased estimator obtained by importance sampling, the Student-t test defines:

$$\hat{\rho} = \frac{1}{n} \sum_{i}^{n} \hat{\rho}_i,$$

$$\sigma = \sqrt{\frac{1}{n-1} \sum_{i}^{n} (\hat{\rho}_i - \hat{\rho})^2}$$

and proves that with probability $1 - \delta$ that:

$$\rho \leq \hat{\rho} + \frac{\sigma}{\sqrt{m}} t_{1-\delta, n-1}$$

where $t_{1-\delta, n-1}$ is the $(1 - \delta)100$ percentile of the Student's t distribution with $n-1$ degrees of freedom. Under the assumption of normally distributed $\hat{\rho}$, which is a reasonable assumption [57] for large n by *central limit theorem* (CLT), we use the Student's t-test to obtain a guaranteed upper bound on ρ. If the upper bound is below the threshold ρ_+, we can release the current policy π in the environment because we know that its expected cumulative cost is not higher than ρ_+ with probability at least $1 - \delta$.

Safe Model-Free Policy Improvement (SMFPI). Among the most successful approaches in model-free optimization are *policy gradient* methods [53]. They update the policy by estimating the policy gradient over a finite batch of episodes D_n. A typical gradient estimator for a policy π_θ parametrized by θ is

$$\hat{g} = \mathbb{E}_{(s_t, a_t) \in D_n} \left[\nabla_\theta \log \pi_\theta(a_t|s_t) \hat{A}_t \right]$$

where $\hat{A}_t$ is an estimator of the advantage function and, in its simplest form, corresponds to the discounted cumulative return.

The main limitation of these approaches is due to the on-policy nature of policy gradient methods. At each policy update, they must collect new data by interacting with the environment to compute the gradients. Reusing the same trajectories to perform many updates is not theoretically justified and can perform catastrophic policy updates in practice. The first algorithm we propose, SMFPI, directly uses this policy-gradient update and estimates the return as the sum of the shaped rewards, as presented in the previous section. The following subsection discusses a model-based solution to improve data efficiency by learning a dynamics model.

Safe Model-Based Policy Improvement (SMBPI). Model-based algorithms are known to be more sample efficient than model-free ones. The data collected over the training process can be used to fit a dynamics model that serves as a simulator of the real environment.

Despite the variety of model-based approaches, we use the dynamics model for training a model-free agent on predicted trajectories, reducing the required interactions with the real environment. The dynamics model is reusable over many iterations, and for this reason, we consider it a data-efficient alternative.

Learning the Dynamics. We consider the problem of learning an accurate dynamical model. Traditional approaches use Bayesian models (e.g., GPs) [19] for their efficiency in low-data regimes, but training on a large dataset and high-dimensional data is prohibitive. Modern literature in deep RL [17] suggests that using an ensemble of neural networks can produce competitive performance with scarce data and efficiently scale to large-data regimes.

Since we intend to represent a potentially stochastic state-transition function, capturing the noise of observations and process, we train a model to parametrize a probability distribution. We assume a diagonal Gaussian distribution model p_θ and let a neural network predict the mean $\mu_\theta(s,a)$ and the log standard deviation $log\,\sigma_\theta(s,a)$. Instead of learning to predict the following state $s_{t+1} = p_\theta(s_t, a_t)$, we train our dynamics model to predicts the change with respect to the current state $\Delta s_{t+1} = p_\theta(s_t, a_t)$ [20,41].

However, training on scarce data may lead to overfitting and extrapolation errors in the area of the state-action space that are not sufficiently supported by the collected experience. A common solution to prevent the algorithm from exploiting these regions consists of adopting an ensemble of models $\{p_{\theta_i}\}_{i=1}^m$. With this ensemble representing a finite set of plausible dynamics of our system, we predict the state trajectories and propagate the dynamics uncertainty by shooting N particles from the current state s_t. At each timestep, we uniformly sample one of the ensemble's models. The choice of the ensemble size (i.e., the number m of dynamics models) is crucial to capture the uncertainty in the underlying stochastic dynamics adequately. While a small ensemble might introduce a significant model bias in policy optimization, a large ensemble increases the computational and memory cost for learning and storing the models.

Policy Optimization with Learned Dynamics. The dynamical model defines an MDP that approximates the real environment. This provides a simulator from which we can sample plausible trajectories without harmful interaction.

Starting from true states sampled from our buffer of past experiences, we generate predictions using the dynamical model $\hat{s}_{t+1} \sim p_\theta(\hat{s}_t, a_t)$, for action $a_t \sim \pi(\hat{s}_t)$. We assume the reward function $r_t = R(\hat{s}_t, a_t, \hat{s}_{t+1})$ and the cost functions $c_{i,t} = C_i(\hat{s}_t, a_t, \hat{s}_{t+1})$ to be known. In general, the learned model could predict them, so in the following, we refer to the predictive model as able to generate state, reward and costs, i.e., $(s_{t+1}, r_t, c_{i,t}) \sim p_\theta(s_t, a_t)$.

Considering the predicted trajectories over a finite horizon H, we use model-free RL to train the policy. This approach is agnostic to the specific algorithm adopted. We consider two approaches for dealing with safety:

1. *Pessimistic Reward.* We alter the MDP transitions when visiting unsafe states (where the cost exceeds the threshold). In this case, the system enters an absorbing state where it repeatedly collects a high penalty $-C$.
2. *Constrained optimization.* We define the unconstrained Lagrangian objective

$$V(\pi) - \sum_{i=1}^{C} \lambda_i V_{C_i}(\pi)$$

for some multiplier λ_i. Using gradient-based optimization, we iteratively update the policy parameters and the dual variables λ_i.

Correct-by-Construction RL Algorithms. Having introduced various algorithmic solutions to tackle the policy optimization process, we report the pseudocode of the complete algorithm in Algorithm 1.1. Then, we state an important result derived from adopting high-confidence off-policy evaluation.

Theorem 1. *Algorithm 1.2 (SMFPI) and Algorithm 1.3 (SMBPI) are correct-by-construction policy-improvement routines.*

Proof. Using the results from high-confidence off-policy evaluation literature [59], we demonstrate that each policy π' returned by SMFPI or SMBPI has expected cost less than or equal to the expected cost of the initial policy π with probability at least $1 - \delta$. If $\pi' = \pi$, then the condition is trivially satisfied, so let us assume π' to be a different policy. According to the algorithm, π' satisfies:

$$\rho^i \leq \rho^i_+, \ \forall i \in [1, k]$$

By definition of ρ^i using Student-t test and confidence $\frac{\delta}{k}$, and under the assumption of normally-distributed cost sample means, we know that for each i:

$$Pr\big(V_{C_i}^{\pi'} \leq V_{C_i}^{\pi}\big) \geq 1 - \frac{\delta}{k}$$

and equivalently that

$$Pr\big(V_{C_i}^{\pi'} > V_{C_i}^{\pi}\big) < \frac{\delta}{k}$$

Using the Union Bound, we finally show that the probability of the event in which at least one of the costs violates the correctness condition is at most δ.

$$Pr\left(\bigvee_{i=1}^{k} V_{C_i}^{\pi'} > V_{C_i}^{\pi}\right) < \sum_{i=1}^{k} Pr\left(V_{C_i}^{\pi'} > V_{C_i}^{\pi}\right) = \delta$$

This statement is equivalent to the following condition which concludes the proof.

$$Pr\left(\bigwedge_{i=1}^{k} V_{C_i}^{\pi'} \leq V_{C_i}^{\pi}\right) \geq 1 - \delta.$$

Algorithm 1.1. Safe Policy Optimization

Require: Initial policy π, confidence δ for policy improvement
  Initialize prediction model p_θ, empty buffer D and D_{test}
  for N epochs **do**
    Collect data with π in environment:

$$D = D \cup \{(s_t, a_t, s_{t+1}, r_t, c_t^1, ..., c_t^k, \log \pi(a_t|s_t))\}_t$$

   Estimate safety performance of current policy $\rho_+^i(\pi)$, $\forall i \in [1, k]$
    Optimize policy with SPI (Algorithm 1.2 or 1.3):

$$\pi = \mathtt{SPI}(\pi, D, \rho_+, \delta)$$

  end for
  return π

Algorithm 1.2. Safe Model-free Policy Improvement (SMFPI)

Require: Initial policy π, data $D \sim \mu_{(\cdot|\pi)}$, safety thresholds ρ_+^i, confidence δ
  $\pi' = \pi$
  Split D into D_{train} and D_{test}.
  for L epochs **do**
    Perform g policy updates of policy π' with data D_{train}
    Upper bound costs: $\forall i = 1..k$, $\rho^i(\pi') = HCOPE(\pi', D_{test}, \delta/k)$
    if $\forall i \in [1, k] \, \rho^i \leq \rho_+^i$ **then**
      return π'
    end if
  end for
  return π {no better policy found}

---

6 Experiments

In this section, we provide an empirical evaluation of the proposed approach. Since it relies on two distinct contributions, the shaping reward and the

---

Algorithm 1.3. Safe Model-based Policy Improvement (SMBPI)

Require: Initial policy π, data $D \sim \mu_{(\cdot|\pi)}$, safety thresholds ρ_+^i, confidence δ
  Initialize or reuse predictive model p_θ
  Empty model buffer D_{model}
  $\pi' = \pi$
  Split D into D_{train} and D_{test}.
  for L epochs **do**
    Fit dynamics model p_θ on dataset D_{train}

$$\theta \leftarrow \arg\max_\theta \mathbb{E}\left[\log p_\theta(s', r, c|s, a)\right]$$

    Collect h-step predicted trajectories with π' and store in D_{model}
    Perform g policy updates of policy π' with data D_{model}
    Upper bound costs: $\forall i = 1..k$, $\rho^i(\pi') = HCOPE(\pi', D_{test}, \delta/k)$
    if $\forall i = 1..k \, \rho^i \leq \rho_+^i$ **then**
      return π'
    end if
  end for
  return π {no better policy found}

---

correct-by-construction policy improvement, we structure the experiments in two phases to evaluate each component in isolation.

6.1   Automatic Reward Shaping from Task Specification

We evaluate the proposed reward shaping against two standard RL benchmarks: (1) *The cart-pole* environment, which has already been presented as a motivating example; (2) *The bipedal-walker*, whose main objective is to move forward towards the end of the field without falling. We formulate one safety, one target, and four comfort requirements for the bipedal walker.

Aiming to evaluate the automatic reward shaping process from formal task specifications, we benchmark HPRS against two prior approaches using temporal logic. To formalize the task in a single specification, we consider it as the conjunction of safety and target requirements. The baselines methods to shape a reward signal are the following:

- *TLTL* [37] specifies tasks in a bounded (Truncated) LTL variant, equipped with an infinity-norm quantitative semantics [39]. The quantitative evaluation of the episode is used as a reward. We employ the RTAMT monitoring tool to compute the episode robustness [44].
- *BHNR* [7] specifies tasks in a fragment of STL with the filtering semantics of [49]. The reward uses a sliding-window approach to produce more frequent feedback to the agent: at each step, it uses the quantitative semantics to evaluate a sequence of H states.

Since each reward formulation has its scale, comparing the learning curves needs an external, unbiased assessment metric. To this end, we introduce a *policy-assessment metric* (PAM) F, capturing the logical satisfaction of various requirements. We use the PAM to monitor the learning process and compare HPRS to the baseline approaches (Fig. 3).

Let $\Phi = \Phi_S \uplus \Phi_T \uplus \Phi_C$ be the set of requirements defining the task. Then, we define F as follows:

$$F(\Phi, \tau) = \sigma(\Phi_S, \tau) + \tfrac{1}{2}\sigma(\Phi_T, \tau) + \tfrac{1}{4}\sigma_{avg}(\Phi_C, \tau)$$

where $\sigma(\Phi, \tau) \in \{0, 1\}$ is the satisfaction function evaluated over Φ and τ. We also define a time-averaged version for any comfort requirement $\varphi = \texttt{encourage}\ p$, as follows:

$$\sigma_{avg}(\varphi, \tau) = \sum_{i=1}^{|\tau|} \frac{\mathbb{1}(s_i \models p)}{|\tau|}.$$

Its set-wise extension computes the average over the set.

Corollary 2. *Consider a task $(\Phi, \prec)$ and an episode τ. Then, the following relations hold for F:*

$$F(\Phi, \tau) \geq 1.0 \leftrightarrow \tau \models \Phi_S, \quad F(\Phi, \tau) \geq 1.5 \leftrightarrow \tau \models \Phi$$

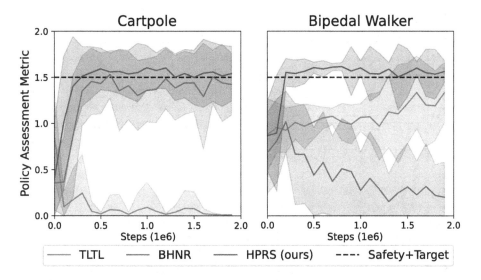

Fig. 3. Performance evaluation with respect to the Policy Assessment Metric (PAM). This external metric is not used in training but to provide a sound evaluation of the requirements and accounting for the different rewards scales. The threshold indicates the task satisfaction (dashed line), as explained in Corollary 2. All the curves report mean and standard deviation over five seeds.

6.2   Safe Policy Improvement in Online Setting

We evaluate the Safe Policy Improvement on a simple cart-pole task, where the agent target is to remain close to the goal location while keeping the pole safely balanced for an episode of 200 steps. We benchmark the proposed algorithm SMFPI with Vanilla Policy Gradient (VPG), which performs unconstrained updates based on the gradient estimates. We consider two scenarios of hyper-parameter configurations, respectively with a favorable and unfavorable value of the *learning rate (LR)*. Figure 4 shows the performance as the mean and

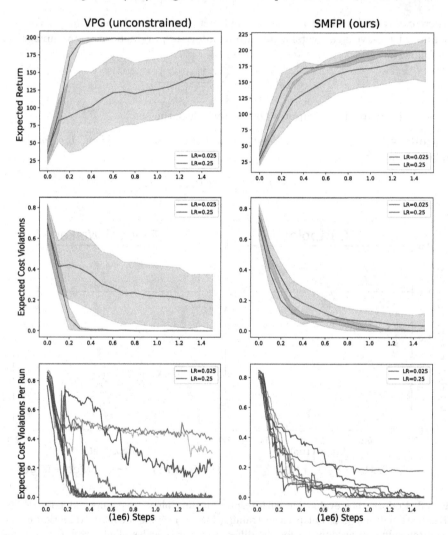

Fig. 4. Performance for cumulative reward and cost violations under different hyper-parameter configurations with learning rate *(LR)* 0.025 and 0.25. The aggregated performance in the first two rows indicates the mean and standard deviation over five runs. The last row shows the running cost estimate on the current batch for each of the five runs.

standard deviation of expected return and cost, aggregated over many runs. We also report a running estimate of the expected cost for each run to compare the oscillation of cost during the iterative policy updates.

Under a favorable hyperparameter setting $LR = 0.025$, we can observe that both algorithms iteratively increase the expected return and decrease the expected cost. As expected, VPG converges faster to the optimal value. However, under the unfavorable hyperparameter setting $LR = 0.25$, the unconstrained policy update of VPG leads to high variance in the statistics and catastrophic oscillation in the cost per run. Conversely, SMFPI shows a good policy improvement and much lower variance in the learning curve due to a more conservative policy update. We also observe a monotonic decrease in expected cost, empirically demonstrating the effectiveness of the proposed approach. We observe small statistical fluctuations in the estimated cost per run, which could depend on two factors: (1) Online estimation of the cost on the current batch of data, (2) Use of $\delta = 0.05$, which guarantees a safe update up to certain confidence. When the current batch contains few samples, the variance of the visualized cost estimate is high. However, SMFPI does not update the policy in small-data regimes because it cannot guarantee the improvement with sufficient confidence.

In this experiment, we show that the proposed algorithm is effective for safely learning a decision policy. Starting from a random policy, SMFPI can iteratively update the policy until it reaches the optimal return value without showing any drop in expected cost. Its performance is robust to different hyperparameters settings, which plays a critical role in modern deep RL algorithms. Compared with unconstrained RL algorithms under optimal hyperparameters, the convergence of SMFPI is slower. However, finding the correct hyperparameters by trial and error is not always an option in critical applications.

7   Conclusion and Future Work

In this work, we presented a policy-synthesis pipeline, showing how to formalize a CMDP, starting from a set of formal requirements describing the task. We further enrich the reward with a potential function that does not alter the policy optimality under the standard potential-based shaping. We further define correct-by-construction policy-improvement routines and propose two online algorithms, one model-free and one model-based, to solve the CMDP starting from an unsafe policy. Using high-confidence off-policy evaluation, we can guarantee that the proposed algorithms will return an equally good or improved policy with respect to the safety constraints. We finally evaluate the overall pipeline, combining reward shaping and correct-by-construction policy improvement, and show empirical evidence of their effectiveness. The proposed algorithm is robust under different hyperparameters tuning, while unconstrained baselines perform updates that deteriorate the safety performance and preclude the algorithm from converging to optimal performances.

Compared with previous approaches that mainly focus on a batch setting, we propose to use high-confidence off-policy evaluation online. In future work, we intend to investigate the proposed model-based approach regarding data efficiency and scalability of off-policy evaluation in an online setting. We plan to extend the benchmarks with more complex tasks, targeting robotics applications and autonomous driving, study the convergence property more in-depth, and characterize the eventual distance to the optimal policy.

Acknowledgement. Luigi Berducci is supported by the Doctoral College Resilient Embedded Systems. This work has received funding from the Austrian FFG-ICT project ADEX.

References

1. Abels, A., Roijers, D., Lenaerts, T., Nowé, A., Steckelmacher, D.: Dynamic weights in multi-objective deep reinforcement learning. In: International Conference on Machine Learning, pp. 11–20. PMLR (2019)
2. Achiam, J., Held, D., Tamar, A., Abbeel, P.: Constrained policy optimization. In: Precup, D., Teh, Y.W. (eds.) Proceedings of the 34th International Conference on Machine Learning, ICML 2017, Sydney, NSW, Australia, 6–11 August 2017. Proceedings of Machine Learning Research, vol. 70, pp. 22–31. PMLR (2017). http://proceedings.mlr.press/v70/achiam17a.html
3. Agha, G., Palmskog, K.: A survey of statistical model checking. ACM Trans. Model. Comput. Simul. (TOMACS) **28**(1), 1–39 (2018)
4. Alshiekh, M., Bloem, R., Ehlers, R., Könighofer, B., Niekum, S., Topcu, U.: Safe reinforcement learning via shielding. CoRR arXiv:1708.08611 (2017)
5. Altman, E.: Constrained markov decision processes with total cost criteria: Lagrangian approach and dual linear program. Math. Methods Oper. Res. **48**(3), 387–417 (1998)
6. Altman, E.: Constrained Markov decision processes, vol. 7. CRC Press (1999)
7. Balakrishnan, A., Deshmukh, J.V.: Structured reward shaping using signal temporal logic specifications. In: 2019 IEEE/RSJ International Conference on Intelligent Robots and Systems (IROS), pp. 3481–3486 (2019). https://doi.org/10.1109/IROS40897.2019.8968254
8. Barrett, L., Narayanan, S.: Learning all optimal policies with multiple criteria. In: Proceedings of the 25th International Conference on Machine Learning, pp. 41–47 (2008)
9. Berducci, L., Aguilar, E.A., Ničković, D., Grosu, R.: Hierarchical potential-based reward shaping from task specifications. arXiv (2021). https://doi.org/10.48550/ARXIV.2110.02792
10. Bertsekas, D.P.: Constrained optimization and Lagrange multiplier methods. Academic press (2014)
11. Brunke, L., et al.: Safe learning in robotics: From learning-based control to safe reinforcement learning. CoRR arXiv:2108.06266 (2021)
12. Brunnbauer, A., et al.: Latent imagination facilitates zero-shot transfer in autonomous racing. arXiv preprint arXiv:2103.04909 (2021)
13. Brys, T., Harutyunyan, A., Vrancx, P., Taylor, M.E., Kudenko, D., Nowé, A.: Multi-objectivization of reinforcement learning problems by reward shaping. In: 2014 International Joint Conference on Neural Networks (IJCNN), pp. 2315–2322. IEEE (2014)
14. Censi, A., et al.: Liability, ethics, and culture-aware behavior specification using rulebooks. In: International Conference on Robotics and Automation, ICRA 2019, Montreal, QC, Canada, May 20–24, 2019, pp. 8536–8542 (2019)

15. Chow, Y., Ghavamzadeh, M., Janson, L., Pavone, M.: Risk-constrained reinforcement learning with percentile risk criteria. CoRR arXiv:1512.01629 (2015)
16. Christiano, P.F., Leike, J., Brown, T.B., Martic, M., Legg, S., Amodei, D.: Deep reinforcement learning from human preferences. In: Guyon, I., von Luxburg, U., Bengio, S., Wallach, H.M., Fergus, R., Vishwanathan, S.V.N., Garnett, R. (eds.) Advances in Neural Information Processing Systems 30: Annual Conference on Neural Information Processing Systems 2017, December 4–9, 2017, Long Beach, CA, USA, pp. 4299–4307 (2017). https://proceedings.neurips.cc/paper/2017/hash/d5e2c0adad503c91f91df240d0cd4e49-Abstract.html
17. Chua, K., Calandra, R., McAllister, R., Levine, S.: Deep reinforcement learning in a handful of trials using probabilistic dynamics models. Advances in neural information processing systems 31 (2018)
18. Dalal, G., Dvijotham, K., Vecerík, M., Hester, T., Paduraru, C., Tassa, Y.: Safe exploration in continuous action spaces. CoRR arXiv:1801.08757 (2018)
19. Deisenroth, M., Rasmussen, C.E.: Pilco: A model-based and data-efficient approach to policy search. In: Proceedings of the 28th International Conference on machine learning (ICML-11), pp. 465–472. Citeseer (2011)
20. Deisenroth, M.P., Fox, D., Rasmussen, C.E.: Gaussian processes for data-efficient learning in robotics and control. IEEE Trans. Pattern Anal. Mach. Intell. **37**(2), 408–423 (2013)
21. Fu, J., Topcu, U.: Probably approximately correct MDP learning and control with temporal logic constraints. In: Fox, D., Kavraki, L.E., Kurniawati, H. (eds.) Robotics: Science and Systems X, University of California, Berkeley, USA, July 12–16, 2014 (2014). https://doi.org/10.15607/RSS.2014.X.039. http://www.roboticsproceedings.org/rss10/p39.html
22. Gábor, Z., Kalmár, Z., Szepesvári, C.: Multi-criteria reinforcement learning. In: Shavlik, J.W. (ed.) Proceedings of the Fifteenth International Conference on Machine Learning (ICML 1998), Madison, Wisconsin, USA, July 24–27, 1998, pp. 197–205. Morgan Kaufmann (1998)
23. García, J., Fernández, F.: A comprehensive survey on safe reinforcement learning. J. Mach. Learn. Res. **16**, 1437–1480 (2015). http://dl.acm.org/citation.cfm?id=2886795
24. Gros, T.P., Hermanns, H., Hoffmann, J., Klauck, M., Steinmetz, M.: Deep Statistical Model Checking. In: Gotsman, A., Sokolova, A. (eds.) FORTE 2020. LNCS, vol. 12136, pp. 96–114. Springer, Cham (2020). https://doi.org/10.1007/978-3-030-50086-3_6
25. Ha, D., Schmidhuber, J.: World models. arXiv preprint arXiv:1803.10122 (2018)
26. Hafner, D., Lillicrap, T., Ba, J., Norouzi, M.: Dream to control: Learning behaviors by latent imagination. arXiv preprint arXiv:1912.01603 (2019)
27. Hafner, D., Lillicrap, T., Fischer, I., Villegas, R., Ha, D., Lee, H., Davidson, J.: Learning latent dynamics for planning from pixels. In: International Conference on Machine Learning, pp. 2555–2565. PMLR (2019)
28. Henderson, P., Islam, R., Bachman, P., Pineau, J., Precup, D., Meger, D.: Deep reinforcement learning that matters. In: Proceedings of the AAAI Conference on Artificial Intelligence, vol. 32 (2018)
29. Icarte, R.T., Klassen, T., Valenzano, R., McIlraith, S.: Using reward machines for high-level task specification and decomposition in reinforcement learning. In: International Conference on Machine Learning, pp. 2107–2116. PMLR (2018)
30. Janner, M., Fu, J., Zhang, M., Levine, S.: When to trust your model: Model-based policy optimization. Advances in Neural Information Processing Systems 32 (2019)

31. Jiang, Y., Bharadwaj, S., Wu, B., Shah, R., Topcu, U., Stone, P.: Temporal-logic-based reward shaping for continuing reinforcement learning tasks. In: Proceedings of the AAAI Conference on Artificial Intelligence 35(9), pp. 7995–8003, May 2021. https://ojs.aaai.org/index.php/AAAI/article/view/16975

32. Jones, A., Aksaray, D., Kong, Z., Schwager, M., Belta, C.: Robust satisfaction of temporal logic specifications via reinforcement learning (2015)

33. Jothimurugan, K., Bansal, S., Bastani, O., Alur, R.: Compositional reinforcement learning from logical specifications. CoRR arXiv:2106.13906 (2021)

34. Kakade, S., Langford, J.: Approximately optimal approximate reinforcement learning. In: Proceedings of 19th International Conference on Machine Learning. Citeseer (2002)

35. Legay, A., Lukina, A., Traonouez, L.M., Yang, J., Smolka, S.A., Grosu, R.: Statistical model checking. In: Steffen, B., Woeginger, G. (eds.) Computing and Software Science. LNCS, vol. 10000, pp. 478–504. Springer, Cham (2019). https://doi.org/10.1007/978-3-319-91908-9_23

36. Li, X., Ma, Y., Belta, C.: A policy search method for temporal logic specified reinforcement learning tasks. In: 2018 Annual American Control Conference (ACC), pp. 240–245 (2018)

37. Li, X., Vasile, C.I., Belta, C.: Reinforcement learning with temporal logic rewards. In: 2017 IEEE/RSJ International Conference on Intelligent Robots and Systems (IROS), pp. 3834–3839 (2017). https://doi.org/10.1109/IROS.2017.8206234

38. Liu, C., Xu, X., Hu, D.: Multiobjective reinforcement learning: a comprehensive overview. IEEE Trans. Syst. Man Cybern. Sys. 45(3), 385–398 (2015). https://doi.org/10.1109/TSMC.2014.2358639

39. Maler, O., Nickovic, D.: Monitoring temporal properties of continuous signals. In: Lakhnech, Y., Yovine, S. (eds.) FORMATS/FTRTFT -2004. LNCS, vol. 3253, pp. 152–166. Springer, Heidelberg (2004). https://doi.org/10.1007/978-3-540-30206-3_12

40. Massart, P.: Concentration inequalities and model selection: Ecole d'Eté de Probabilités de Saint-Flour XXXIII-2003. Springer (2007)

41. Nagabandi, A., Kahn, G., Fearing, R.S., Levine, S.: Neural network dynamics for model-based deep reinforcement learning with model-free fine-tuning. In: 2018 IEEE International Conference on Robotics and Automation (ICRA), pp. 7559–7566. IEEE (2018)

42. Natarajan, S., Tadepalli, P.: Dynamic preferences in multi-criteria reinforcement learning. In: Proceedings of the 22nd International Conference on Machine Learning, pp. 601–608 (2005)

43. Ng, A.Y., Harada, D., Russell, S.: Policy invariance under reward transformations: Theory and application to reward shaping. In: Proceedings of the Sixteenth International Conference on Machine Learning, pp. 278–287. Morgan Kaufmann (1999)

44. Ničković, D., Yamaguchi, T.: RTAMT: online robustness monitors from STL. In: Hung, D.V., Sokolsky, O. (eds.) ATVA 2020. LNCS, vol. 12302, pp. 564–571. Springer, Cham (2020). https://doi.org/10.1007/978-3-030-59152-6_34

45. Phan, D.T., Paoletti, N., Grosu, R., Jansen, N., Smolka, S.A., Stoller, S.D.: Neural simplex architecture. CoRR arXiv:1908.00528 (2019)

46. Pirotta, M., Restelli, M., Pecorino, A., Calandriello, D.: Safe policy iteration. In: International Conference on Machine Learning, pp. 307–315. PMLR (2013)

47. Precup, D.: Eligibility traces for off-policy policy evaluation. Computer Science Department Faculty Publication Series, p. 80 (2000)

48. Puranic, A.G., Deshmukh, J.V., Nikolaidis, S.: Learning from demonstrations using signal temporal logic in stochastic and continuous domains. IEEE Robot. Autom. Lett. 6(4), 6250–6257 (2021). https://doi.org/10.1109/LRA.2021.3092676

49. Rodionova, A., Bartocci, E., Nickovic, D., Grosu, R.: Temporal logic as filtering. In: Proceedings of the 19th International Conference on Hybrid Systems: Computation and Control, pp. 11–20 (2016)
50. Roijers, D.M., Vamplew, P., Whiteson, S., Dazeley, R.: A survey of multi-objective sequential decision-making. J. Artif. Int. Res. **48**(1), 67–113 (2013)
51. Saunders, W., Sastry, G., Stuhlmüller, A., Evans, O.: Trial without error: Towards safe reinforcement learning via human intervention. CoRR arXiv:1707.05173 (2017)
52. Schulman, J., Levine, S., Moritz, P., Jordan, M.I., Abbeel, P.: Trust region policy optimization. CoRR arXiv:1502.05477 (2015)
53. Schulman, J., Wolski, F., Dhariwal, P., Radford, A., Klimov, O.: Proximal policy optimization algorithms. arXiv preprint arXiv:1707.06347 (2017)
54. Shalev-Shwartz, S., Shammah, S., Shashua, A.: Safe, multi-agent, reinforcement learning for autonomous driving. CoRR arXiv:1610.03295 (2016)
55. Shelton, C.: Balancing multiple sources of reward in reinforcement learning. In: Leen, T., Dietterich, T., Tresp, V. (eds.) Advances in Neural Information Processing Systems, vol. 13. MIT Press (2001)
56. Thananjeyan, B., et al.: Recovery RL: safe reinforcement learning with learned recovery zones. IEEE Robotics Autom. Lett. **6**(3), 4915–4922 (2021). https://doi.org/10.1109/LRA.2021.3070252
57. Thomas, P., Theocharous, G., Ghavamzadeh, M.: High-confidence off-policy evaluation. In: Proceedings of the AAAI Conference on Artificial Intelligence, vol. 29 (2015)
58. Thomas, P., Theocharous, G., Ghavamzadeh, M.: High confidence policy improvement. In: Bach, F., Blei, D. (eds.) Proceedings of the 32nd International Conference on Machine Learning. Proceedings of Machine Learning Research, vol. 37, pp. 2380–2388. PMLR, Lille, France, 07–09 Jul 2015. https://proceedings.mlr.press/v37/thomas15.html
59. Thomas, P.S.: Safe reinforcement learning (2015)
60. Thomas, P.S., Castro da Silva, B., Barto, A.G., Giguere, S., Brun, Y., Brunskill, E.: Preventing undesirable behavior of intelligent machines. Science **366**(6468), 999–1004 (2019)
61. Toro Icarte, R., Klassen, T.Q., Valenzano, R., McIlraith, S.A.: Teaching multiple tasks to an rl agent using ltl. In: Proceedings of the 17th International Conference on Autonomous Agents and MultiAgent Systems, pp. 452–461 (2018)
62. Van Moffaert, K., Drugan, M.M., Nowé, A.: Scalarized multi-objective reinforcement learning: novel design techniques. In: 2013 IEEE Symposium on Adaptive Dynamic Programming and Reinforcement Learning (ADPRL), pp. 191–199 (2013). https://doi.org/10.1109/ADPRL.2013.6615007
63. Viswanadha, K., Kim, E., Indaheng, F., Fremont, D.J., Seshia, S.A.: Parallel and multi-objective falsification with SCENIC and VERIFAI. In: Feng, L., Fisman, D. (eds.) RV 2021. LNCS, vol. 12974, pp. 265–276. Springer, Cham (2021). https://doi.org/10.1007/978-3-030-88494-9_15
64. Wilcox, A., Balakrishna, A., Thananjeyan, B., Gonzalez, J.E., Goldberg, K.: LS3: latent space safe sets for long-horizon visuomotor control of iterative tasks. CoRR arXiv:2107.04775 (2021)
65. Zhao, Y., Chen, Q., Hu, W.: Multi-objective reinforcement learning algorithm for mosdmp in unknown environment. In: 2010 8th World Congress on Intelligent Control and Automation, pp. 3190–3194 (2010). https://doi.org/10.1109/WCICA.2010.5553980

Runtime Verification Meets Controller Synthesis

Shaun Azzopardi⑩, Nir Piterman⑩, and Gerardo Schneider(✉)⑩

University of Gothenburg, Gothenburg, Sweden
{shaun.azzopardi,nir.piterman,gerardo.scheider}@gu.se

Abstract. Reactive synthesis guarantees correct-by-construction controllers from logical specifications, but is costly—2EXPTIME-complete in the size of the specification. In a practical setting, the desired controllers need to interact with an environment, but the more precise the model of the environment used for synthesis, the greater the cost of synthesis. This can be avoided by using suitable abstractions of the environment, but this in turn requires appropriate techniques to mediate between controllers and the real environment. Runtime verification can help here, with monitors acting as these mediators, and even as activators or orchestrators of the desired controllers. In this paper we survey literature for combinations of monitors with controller synthesis, and consider other potential combinations as future research directions.

Keywords: Reactive synthesis · Controllers · Runtime verification · Monitors

1 Introduction

Developing programs correctly is difficult, always requiring iteratively finding and repairing bugs. The traditional formal solution is model checking, which can be employed to confirm the correctness of programs with respect to some specification (often in linear temporal logic). Recently, significant effort has instead gone into *reactive synthesis*, the study and development of techniques that automatically produce correct-by-construction programs from LTL specifications [19,25,26]. See, for example, [13] for an introduction to reactive synthesis.

In the setting of an adversarial environment, where certain goals are desired, reactive synthesis techniques can be used to determine if these goals are always achievable and if the answer is positive, to construct a program that achieves these goals. This kind of program is called a *controller*, and both the goals and the environment are usually described in linear temporal logic (LTL).

Unfortunately, practical considerations can make this costly—already for LTL specifications the problem is 2EXPTIME-complete [26]. In what concerns

This research is funded by the ERC consolidator grant D-SynMA under the European Union's Horizon 2020 research and innovation programme (grant agreement No. 772459).

T. Margaria and B. Steffen (Eds.): ISoLA 2022, LNCS 13701, pp. 382–396, 2022.
https://doi.org/10.1007/978-3-031-19849-6_22

cost, on the other hand, formal verification allows one to verify whether an existing system satisfies the desired specification, at a cheaper price (e.g., PSPACE-complete for model checking of LTL [28]). This is even more true for runtime verification on single execution prefixes at runtime [18]. However, reactive synthesis is still more alluring, since it promises to solve the problem of automatically developing a controller for whatever the environment does, when possible, at least in a theoretical setting—the price is worth paying.

Applying reactive synthesis in a practical setting however may not be easy. One problem is that a desired controller may need to interact with systems whose full representation in LTL can be very large, the size of which is a parameter to the 2EXPTIME-complete complexity of reactive synthesis. This problem can be handled by using appropriate abstractions of the environment. For example, if the environment is at times engaged in a process that requires several actions in sequence, but the reactive synthesis problem is only interested in the point this process ends, then we can do with only one proposition that is true when the process ends. This avoids the need to have a proposition for every possible state of the environment. However, applying such high-level controllers in practical settings requires an interface with the real environment that adapts real-world events to the expected higher-level, abstract events. In literature we find *monitors* used in such a manner.

Monitors are objects that observe a system. In runtime verification they are used to output, given a certain execution prefix, whether the system currently satisfies or violates a certain property [18]. Synthesising such monitors is cheap but when combined with reactive synthesis they open up the possibility to solve problems not expressible in LTL (see Sect. 3), or at least to reduce the size (and thus cost) of the reactive synthesis problem. Essentially, their use can be to abstract away parts of specification, to reduce the synthesis problem to a kernel of the original specification.

In literature we find several ways in which monitors are used thusly. In this paper we set out to survey these combinations, mostly based on our own experience and contributions in this line. More concretely, we classify the approaches found in literature as according the following:

i) Monitors to identify what guarantee should start holding and when (Sect. 3);
ii) Monitors for environment assumptions (Sect. 4); and
iii) Monitors as orchestrators between controllers (Sect. 5).

Before presenting these, in the next section we give some brief background to runtime verification and reactive synthesis, and after in Sect. 6 we consider and propose other combinations providing future directions for research, and we give our concluding remarks in Sect. 8.

2 Background

We give a brief background on runtime verification and reactive synthesis, with a running example of a monitor and a reactive synthesis problem.

2.1 Runtime Verification

Runtime verification (RV) is a lightweight verification technique, consolidated in between informal non-exhaustive techniques like testing and formal static verification techniques like model checking, static verification and theorem proving. In a way, RV is understood to be a good complementary approach surmounting the weaknesses of those techniques.

RV techniques allow the construction of monitors for the execution of software systems in order to ensure the validity of a given property, or the detection of its violation, at runtime [15,18]. These monitors can be constructed from higher-level formal specifications, usually LTL, but also from more operational and more expressive symbolic automata.

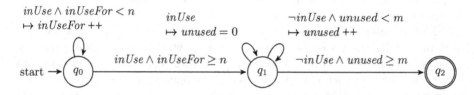

Fig. 1. Monitor that checks that the room has been in use for n time steps, after which when there is a period of m time steps where the room is empty it flags.

Symbolic automata monitors are finite-state automata, with internal variables. Rather than labelling transitions by events, these automata's transitions are labelled by propositional guards over events and internal variables, and actions on the internal variables. This allows succinct program-like specifications, leaving it up to the writer how much information to encode in the control-flow and how much to make symbolic.

An example is the monitor illustrated in Fig. 1. This monitor represents operationally some implementation that, through sensors, detects when people are in the room (*inUse*). Moreover, it deduces that the room needs cleaning depending on how long the room has been in use and after that waits for enough time to pass until the room no longer has any foot traffic (¬*inUse*). Reaching q_2 is the point at which the monitor identifies the room as being dirty, and thus ready to be cleaned.

There are several variations on these monitors that include richer features, like a notion of timers and communication over channels [11]. In runtime verification they have been used to monitor programs written in different programming languages, e.g., Java [11], and Solidity [4].

```
INPUTS { ROOMCLEAN; INROOM; DOORLOCKED; }
OUTPUTS { GOTOROOM; LEAVEROOM; CLEAN; LOCKDOOR; }

ASSUMPTIONS {
    G F (!GOTOROOM || INROOM);
    G F (!LEAVEROOM || !INROOM);
    G F (!(LOCKDOOR && INROOM && CLEAN) || ROOMCLEAN);
    G ((DOORLOCKED && ROOMCLEAN) -> X ROOMCLEAN);
    G ((!ROOMCLEAN && !CLEAN) -> X !ROOMCLEAN);
    G ((!INROOM && !GOTOROOM) -> X !INROOM);
    G ((INROOM && !LEAVEROOM) -> X INROOM);
    G (LOCKDOOR -> X DOORLOCKED);
    G (!LOCKDOOR -> X !DOORLOCKED);
}
GUARANTEES {
    F (ROOMCLEAN && (X F !INROOM) && (X F !DOORLOCKED));
}
```

Fig. 2. Snippet in TLSF [16] format for the reactive synthesis of a cleaning robot.

2.2   Reactive Synthesis

Controllers are programs that control for a certain goal in the context of some environment. Focusing on reactive controllers, the problem of *reactive synthesis* is to construct controllers from *linear temporal logic* (LTL) specifications [26]. We assume familiarty with LTL, but for completeness, LTL is the language over a set of atomic propositions AP, with negation, conjunction, the unary operator next (X), and the binary operator *until* (U). The *eventually* operator (F) is often used, where $F\phi \stackrel{\text{def}}{=} true\,U\phi$ and the *always* (or *globally*) operator: $G\phi \stackrel{\text{def}}{=} \neg F\neg\phi$.

Specifications in reactive synthesis are of the form:

$$\mathcal{A} \to \mathcal{G},$$

where $\mathcal{A}$ is the *assumption* specification, restricting the way variables can be controlled by the environment, and $\mathcal{G}$, the *guarantee* specification, describing behaviour the desired controller should induce. The environment is assumed to be adversarial, and when for every possible environment behaviour the controller can always ensure $\mathcal{G}$ then problem is said to be *realisable*, otherwise it is said to be *unrealisable* and then no controller exists. This problem of LTL realizability is known to be 2EXPTIME-complete [26].

Consider Fig. 2 as an example of a reactive synthesis problem for a robot to clean a room. We have a partition of propositions into *input* (*uncontrollable*) and *output* (*controllable*) propositions. The assumptions are an abstraction of the robot's environment and the effect of the robot's actions (outputs) on the environment. The guarantees require that a robot synthesised using this specification will eventually clean the room, and then leave the room while leaving the room unlocked. This problem is realisable: Fig. 3 shows a controller for it.

3   Monitoring for Guarantees

Monitors can be used to identify the point at which a certain property is satisfied or violated. In reactive synthesis we often want to activate the obligation for the controller to satisfy some guarantee once the environment behaves in some way. In literature we find two ways in which monitors are exploited to aid this. Initially, we look at our own work [5], that consider *a priori* monitors that identify points where we require some guarantees. We also look into an approach by Finkbeiner et al. [14], where guarantees become known only at runtime. In that work monitors are used to ensure outstanding co-safety obligations arising from the initially required guarantees hold even when requirements change at runtime and a new controller needs to be generated and used.

Monitor Triggers. We start with an example, based on the cleaning robot example. Consider we have an *a priori* precise notion of when the room is dirty and needs cleaning, given as a program-like monitor, as illustrated in Fig. 1. Consider the problem of finding a strategy for a cleaning robot to ensure a room is clean. The question then is how to synthesise a strategy for a cleaning robot to ensure the room is eventually cleaned *whenever* this obligation starts holding (at q_2).

In [5] we propose to specify such problems with the combination of symbolic monitors ($\mathcal{M}$) and LTL (assumptions A and guarantees ϕ), in two ways: simple triggering $A \rightarrow \mathcal{M} : \phi$ and triggering with repetition $A \rightarrow (\mathcal{M}; \phi)^*$. The point at which a monitor triggers the obligation to satisfy ϕ is clear, given appropriate final states in $\mathcal{M}$. However, an important aspect, is that it is not obvious at which point a controller for ϕ should return back control to $\mathcal{M}$. For general LTL formulas there is no specific point at which an obligation is satisfied, e.g., an invariant $G\phi'$ would have to continue enforcing ϕ' forever. However, for co-safety formulas there is such a natural point: the end of a tight or *satisfaction-informative* prefix (the dual of the violation-informative prefix of [17]). [5] gives a 2EXPTIME-complete algorithm to construct a controller that finishes executing when such a point has been reached, remaining within the same complexity class as reactive synthesis. Simply plugging in such a controller $\mathcal{C}$ for $A \rightarrow \phi$, with $\mathcal{M}$, results in $(\mathcal{M}; \mathcal{C})^*$, a controller for the original formula.

This approach has limitations. Assumptions about the environment have to be stateless, given the controller synthesis is done for $A \rightarrow \phi$. For stateful

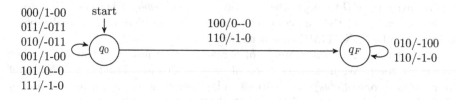

Fig. 3. Cleaning robot controller, as given by Strix [19]—inputs (outputs) on left (right)-hand side of transition labels, with 0 (1) at nth position for input (output) denotes nth proposition in input (output) list (from Fig. 2) being false (true).

assumptions one would have to reason about their state at points where the monitor triggers, and at the point the required controller gives back control to the monitor. Moreover, to have many such trigger constructs running in parallel is problematic, since it does not allow to re-use the compositional synthesis method we described, e.g. the synthesis of a controller for $(\mathcal{M}; \phi) \wedge (\mathcal{M}'; \phi')$ cannot be delegated to just synthesising a controller for ϕ and for ϕ' independently, but requires synthesising both together.

On the other hand, properly abstracting the monitor in LTL (which is possible in this case) results in very large controllers even for small values of n and m in the monitor. For example, setting $n = m = 2$ in $\mathcal{M}$, and combined with $\mathcal{G}$ appropriately, Strix [19], the state-of-art tool in LTL reactive synthesis, produces a controller with around four times the transitions as that of the symbolic monitor and the tight controller for $\mathcal{G}$. Moreover, this continues to increase as n and m increases, while with our approach changing the value of the parameters does not change the size of the final controller.

Obligation Monitors. In our work, there is an *a priori* description on when an obligation is in effect, and of the obligated LTL requirement itself. These may however both be relaxed. In general, reactive synthesis assumes that the guarantees do not change at runtime. However this is not necessarily the case in a practical setting—often requirements change and systems are taken offline. Monitors have been used to aid the process of updating such obligations.

Finkbeiner et al. [14] consider the problem of *live synthesis*, where a system may be replaced by another at runtime. They consider that at the point where the replacement occurs, there may be outstanding obligations from the requirements of the first system that would be violated if it is simply replaced with a synthesised controller for the new requirements. Instead, they require that the new controller also satisfies these outstanding obligations. The problem then is how to identify what the obligations are at the exact point of replacement.

For example, consider a setting where we want to re-assign the cleaning robot to clean other room. If we do the handover between the old and new strategy naïvely, the robot could leave the first room unclean. A more natural requirement on this handover would ensure the robot achieves one last time its co-safety requirements in the first room, before moving to the second room. For example, consider a setting where we want to re-assign the cleaning robot to clean other room. If we do the handover between the old and new strategy naïvely, the robot could leave the first room unclean. A more natural requirement on this handover would ensure the robot achieves one last time its co-safety requirements in the first room, before moving to the second room.

Considering outstanding obligations as co-safety properties, Finkbeiner et al. [14] use monitors to consider any remaining outstanding obligations. They synthesise monitors at the same time as the original controller is synthesised, that monitors for the remaining obligations given any execution prefix of the controller. Then, when a system update must be effected then the new controller is synthesised to also satisfy the obligations the monitor signals as outstanding.

In our example, if the cleaning robot has not yet managed to clean the room, then the new strategy will take this into account and clean the room, unlock the door, and leave the room, before leaving for its new mission. Similarly, if it has cleaned the room but not yet unlocked the door and left the room, it will do so before attempting the next mission.

Compare this also with the approach of [24], where additional specifications are required for the transition between the new and old specifications. This work also assumes additional signals that control the transition process.

4   Monitoring for Assumptions

As mentioned, commonly, a reactive synthesis problem has two parts: *guarantees* (G) we wish a controller to control for in the context of some *assumptions* (A) about the environment, i.e. the specification $A \implies G$. If the assumptions can be invalidated by the controller then the specification becomes true, and the controller has 'won' since the implication then becomes trivially true whatever the controller does after. This is not always ideal. Often, we want to exclude solutions to a reactive synthesis problem where the controller invalidates the assumption, since it is not usually the intention of the designer. Excluding these kinds of solutions usually requires expertise in modelling the environment in the assumptions appropriately. There is however work to exclude these automatically, e.g., for the GR(1) subset of LTL [20].

Moreover, reactive synthesis is adversarial, i.e., the environment is assumed not to invalidate its own assumptions, but in a practical setting the real-world environment may actually violate the constraints that were assumed. This may be due to imprecise modelling or unpredicted changes that occur during the lifetime of the system. Theoretically this is not problematic, since the controller simply wins in this case. Practically this can be a problem—an assumption violation may go unnoticed and lead to a controller working based on information that is not accurate. This can lead it to trying to fulfil a now impossible goal, resulting in a waste of resources at best and at worst interfering with the goals of other agents. In this setting, the controller would ideally halt or change its behaviour once the environment no longer satisfies our original assumptions about it, for which we can exploit monitors. Monitors for environment assumptions can be run concurrently with the controller, stopping the controller (or taking other actions) if an environment assumption is violated. We consider two works along this direction.

Unmodelled Environment Behaviour. In a practical setting, the designer may not give exact or even sound environment assumptions, but instead give a necessary abstraction of the environment assumptions. This measure may be taken to reduce complexity, or in the case that the environment model is not discrete or expressible in LTL. In this case we do not fulfil our goals simply by the environment remaining within the bounds of our necessary version of the assumptions. Here, having an environment assumption monitor running concurrently with the controller also can be useful, to signal possible failure of the controller, due to unmodelled environment behaviour. This setting is considered by Zudaire et.al. in [32], and described further below.

In a hybrid setting, a description of the environment and guarantees are given in a language richer than LTL (e.g., with events carrying real numbers). To use automatic reactive synthesis techniques entails discretising these descriptions, and thus abstracting them. In this case, monitoring the LTL version of the environment assumption may not be enough. For example, instead of describing a sensor's behaviour in detail, its LTL abstraction may simply be abstracted with one boolean variable that is set as true when the sensor's value is above a certain value. However, at runtime a sensor may become miscalibrated due to external factors (e.g., weather), although in the reactive synthesis problem we may choose not to model this (since we may not necessarily be able to control for the non-modelled factors).

In [32], Zudaire et al. handle the above problem by combining temporal task planning with streaming runtime verification. Discrete task specifications are enriched with an explicit representation of the assumptions about the continuous world allowing, in this way, the monitoring of the validity of these assumptions, and thus reacting to it accordingly. See [32] for an application of the technique to three different scenarios in the context of Unmanned Aerial Vehicles.

In this case, instead of monitoring for the complete LTL abstraction, we can monitor for a richer specification of the abstraction that captures the non-modelled behaviour. This monitor can then be used to notify when realisability of the concrete problem is no longer ensured, due to non-modelled factors. It can also be used in a *predictive* manner, where the possibility of failure is detected before it occurs and (continuous) control measures are taken to prevent it (e.g., recalibration of sensor is carried out when accuracy falls beneath a certain level, before a collision occurs).

Unknown Environment. In another case, the environment may not be known. A sound assumption to make here would be simply *true*, but this would make any interesting goal unrealisable, given it puts no limitations on the environment. However, there are techniques to identify environment assumptions for which a goal is realisable (e.g., [7,8]). If these assumptions are reasonably minimal and weak, they can be used to synthesise a controller for the goal that can work in a number of settings. Moreover, in the general case, beliefs about the environment may turn out to be false and at runtime unexpected behaviour may be exhibited.

Environment monitors in these cases can also be used to monitor for the environment assumptions used for synthesis, but moreover they can be used at runtime to adjust these assumptions. In this line of work, Wong et al. [30] propose that when a violation is detected, the environment behaviour at runtime can be used to re-synthesise a new controller that takes this new behaviour into account. Before this, if the assumption violation still allows progress, the controller maintains safety and takes action to allow progress when the environment returns to the expected behaviour.

5   Monitors as Orchestrators in Contextual Missions

In [22] Maoz and Ringert list three main challenges concerning the application of reactive synthesis to the robotics domain. The first challenge concerns the scalability of using high-level declarative specification languages like LTL. Reasoning in LTL is not something developers are used to—they are used to more imperative languages, while LTL specifications can quickly become very complex. Moreover, writing appropriate assumptions (and guarantees) is an art in and of itself, and inadequate assumptions can lead to problematic implementations, as discussed in the previous sections. The second challenge is the need for techniques to abstract from time and complex data, to allow for more tractable synthesis. The final challenge relates to having appropriate support for the development process, e.g., a tool integrating both verification and testing of the controller, to allow the developer to check the controller respects their intentions, or techniques that allow re-using previous synthesis artefacts when the specification evolves (to avoid full re-synthesis).

The use of monitors has been proposed to help tackle these challenges (see an initial proposal by Mallozzi et al. in [21, Chap. 7]). In particular: (1) monitors add a level of imperativeness to a specification (as we also saw in Section. 3); (2) reasoning about time, data, and complex behaviour can be relegated to monitors, while still being represented in a formal structure, amenable to verification; and (3) the use of monitors as orchestrators between different guarantees/controllers can allow different parts of a specification to be synthesised separately (with some caveats). In this section we briefly describe an application of monitors with reactive synthesis as described in [21, Chap. 7]—a framework using monitors as orchestrators in robotic missions with contextual missions/guarantees.

Let us consider a very simple example: an robot (or agent here) needs to clean rooms r_1 and r_2 (task 1) one after the other during the day, and rooms r_3 and r_4 (task 2) during the night (see Fig. 4). Switching between tasks happens when the *context* switches (from day to night and vice-versa).

Synthesising a controller for the above simple example is within reach using existing techniques, however the synthesis needs to be done at a global level and not compositionally, thus a certain context's task changing (e.g., the layout of furniture in one room is changed) requires re-synthesis for the whole mission. Ideally, when possible, one would want to synthesise only for the changed tasks. Moreover, should the context not be expressible in LTL, appropriate abstractions (perhaps of time or complex data) would need to be used, adding to the complexity of the problem.

However, in these kinds of specifications one can attempt to do better. Under different contexts, the robot has different tasks, which suggests that it would be useful if the controller for each tasks could be synthesised separately and then integrated later somehow with appropriate logic for context monitoring. This first solution is not without its problems thought: trying to do a certain task may have an effect on the state of another tasks. In a monolitic reactive synthesis approach this is handled smoothly (the controller is aware of the states of every task), but attempting to do things compositionally requires extra work

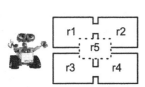

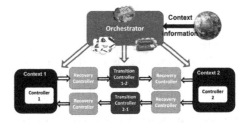

Fig. 4. A robot cleaning 4 regions.

Fig. 5. A high-level representation of contextual robot missions for 2 contexts.

to transition smoothly between tasks. This however may be unavoidable when the specification required goes beyond LTL, or involves large numbers of variables such as to make the synthesis problem intractable.

For that, Mallozzi et al. in [21, Chap. 7] suggest an architecture and development environment composed of the following key components:

1. *Agents:* The agent has tasks (LTL specifications), each associated with a certain context (explained next). These tasks are achievable through appropriately synthesised controllers acting under different contexts[1]. They can be automatically synthesised from LTL specifications, or other specification languages like Spectra [23]. The authors also allow programs in general.
2. *Contexts:* One assumes a set of contexts (in the example here *day* or *night*), and a function that determines the current context from some knowledge about the current state of the world. For example contexts can be geographical, like the neighbourhood of a city the controller is currently in; or something more complex, like being in a certain neighbourhood at a certain time of day. An important aspect is that context can change, i.e. the current context depends on the current point in time, and the previous behaviour of the environment and the system.
3. *Recovery controllers:* Agents have no control on which context they are in at any time-step. Thus, when the context changes, they are expected to transition seamlessly to making progress in the task of the next context. However, the state of the task of this next context may have changed since the last time the agent was in that context (e.g., someone may have moved some things around in a room), and thus the agent might need to do some *recovery* task to either get the agent or the environment in a state where the agent can continue where they left off (e.g., returning the things moved around to their previous position). Similarly, before leaving a context, it is reasonable to prespecify that the agent leaves it in a safe state (e.g., turned off any lights). Recovery controllers serve these purposes.

---

[1] Some of these may be written manually, or provided *a priori*, and appropriately model checked.

4. *Transition controllers:* This is activated after the recovery controller leaves the state in the previous context in a sane state, and activates the recovery controller to prepare the state of the new context for the agent to continue.
5. *Orchestrator:* This is in charge of notifying the controllers of the change in context in the real-world, and triggering of the actual change in context in the system, as illustrated in Fig. 5.

Such a framework integrates the use of reactive synthesis in a much richer setting. Using runtime monitors as orchestrators (or context monitors) in this case adds considerable power: one can easily write simple monitors with the capabilities of counting, accumulating, computing averages, memorising current states, etc., besides the fact of allowing for parameterised specifications. There is then a tradeoff between the strong guarantees about what is synthesised and the expressive power of the orchestration against the requirement to have to specify recovery transitions However, this can be managed in this setting through the use of verification, which is possible for domains beyond synthesis.

Note that [21, Chap. 7] only presents an *ad hoc* solution to the problem given in Fig. 4 when contexts are given by propositional variables ("night" and "day"). A more general solution along the lines of the architecture presented in (Fig. 5) for more general contexts and that can handle dynamic changes, is still missing.

6   Other Potential Combinations

We have seen monitors used effectively alongside controllers in extending the scope of reactive synthesis. In each of these uses of monitors, the interaction between monitors and controllers is, however, very specific and limited. Limiting interaction has its benefits—it preempts the need for reasoning about complex interactive behaviour. However, it also prevents interesting deeper applications. We consider further possible combinations here.

Concurrent Monitors and Controllers. We can imagine discrete environment events that can be controlled by monitors, e.g., a monitor written in a rich language can be used to monitor the continuous world to notify a discrete controller about some event. Some approaches, as we saw in Sect. 4, simply ignore these more complex specifications, and use complete restrictions of them (e.g., that a sensor can never become miscalibrated), with a monitor attempting to take care of their violation at a higher-layer. This approach however trades overall correctness guarantees of the hybrid controller, for easier automatic synthesis, since the monitor's behaviour may be crucial for realisability of the full problem.

As a first step, we are currently exploring the incorporation of more program-like descriptions of the environment (encoded as symbolic monitors) in a reactive synthesis problem. This would allow including complex specifications or implementations of the environment in a reactive synthesis, and through an appropriate (sound) abstraction-refinement loop automatically synthesising a controller. This will reduce the current necessary abstraction decisions the developer would have to do, while it extends the scope of reactive synthesis to richer domains.

We are also considering the use of monitors to abstract away parts of a given LTL formula that are purely about the environment. Such an approach could enable to reduce a synthesis problem by replacing some sub-formula with a new variable, and composing the controller for the abstracted formula with the monitor for the removed sub-formula. The crucial aspect of this problem is that assumptions about the new variable may need to be added to make the abstract problem realisable, and in the worst case full knowledge of the hidden sub-formula may be needed. For example, consider a co-safety formula about the environment ϕ, if we have a guarantee $G(\phi \implies Fc)$, where c is a controller event. If this is all we have, then replacing ϕ in the guarantee by a fresh environment event e suffices, and the controller generated can be composed with a monitor for ϕ (that outputs e at every step ϕ is tightly/informatively satisfied [5]) to create a controller for the original problem.

Monitors for Discretising Data-Carrying Events. Another problem to be tackled is that of controllers for specification that require more than a finite alphabet, but also data-carrying events. Consider a standard arbiter example, where we want every request to eventually be matched by a grant. A standard way of specifying this in LTL is to not allow new requests in between a request and the corresponding grant, given the limitations with regards to counting in LTL. A more general specification would be able to index an incoming request, and check that there is a grant with a matching index. Consider a monitor with a counter, that decorates a given request with the current value of the counter, increases the counter, and then triggers a controller to eventually perform the associated grant. The controller can be parametrised with a number, such that the events it generates are parametrised by this number, and the monitor can then activate such a distinct controller each time a request comes in. Such a system has an infinite alphabet, but re-uses simpler LTL reactive synthesis techniques.

Running controllers in parallel is not simple however. These controllers may be sharing resources, and thus the synthesis from a grant specification needs to be modified such that a controller is aware there may be other controllers working in parallel. A monitor here can also be used to mediate between the controllers. A controller only needs to be aware of its own version of the events (tagged by some number), and that the same events with a different number can occur. A naïve solution would seem to require the controller being aware of the whole infinite alphabet, however a monitor can be used to turn any event labelled by another number into a generic *other* event, that can still be enough for realising a controller.

7   Related Work

Monitors have been used as enforcers of properties at runtime, where if a system, acting as a *shield* [6]. This is done through suppression and/or insertion of system events by the enforcer, ensuring the property holds at runtime. The setting of these approaches is usually that of an existing system and a shield that enforces some (co-)safety or infinite-renewal properties about the system. Reactive synthesis of LTL is more general that LTL runtime enforcement, given the limitations of monitoring with regards to liveness properties.

Runtime verification has been exploited in other contexts to manage the expense or limitations of other techniques, e.g., static verification [1–3,9] and testing [10]. Moreover it has found applications beyond the dynamic analysis of software, see [27] for a survey.

Other work that combines in some way monitors with reactive synthesis is by Maoz and Ringert. In [23] they consider a language that includes a notion of monitors, but these become part of the specification to be controlled, not benefiting from treating monitors separately. Ehlers and Finkbeiner consider a monitoring approach where prefixes are classified into whether the specification remains realisable or not, or has been violated or fulfilled [12]. Chou et al. do something similar, but for linear stochastic systems [31].

An *ad hoc* combination of monitors with reactive synthesis is given in [29]. In that paper, Ulus and Belta use runtime monitors to check and enforce safety properties (e.g., to avoid certain locations or collision for robots), while control techniques enforce the high-level mission. Monitored properties are expressed as regular expressions and past temporal logic formulas. Monitors are also used to discard unsafe trajectories from a proposed set of trajectories.

8   Conclusions

Reactive synthesis provides strong guarantees, but becomes harder the more precise and rich a specification language. In this paper we have seen how runtime monitoring techniques have been used to increase the scope of reactive synthesis without increasing the hardness, by relegating parts of an envisioned system to a monitor. We have surveyed techniques in literature along these lines, including our own previous work, and identified three main kinds of monitor-synthesis synergies: monitors to identify or trigger obligations; monitors that identify assumption violation; and monitors that act as orchestrators between controllers.

We identified some promising possible combinations. One is the use of monitors in parallel with controllers, where monitors can even correspond to some general non-regular property of the environment, or to a sub-formula of the LTL specification we want to synthesise. We have also described how monitors can have more control by dynamically activating copies of the same controller, possibly in parallel, and mediating between these (e.g., to allow use of shared resources), and decorating of their outputs according to some scheme, to ensure, for example, that the nth request is matched by a grant from the nth controller.

We hope the reader may find other novel and interesting ways to combine in a systematic and useful way runtime verification and reactive controller synthesis.

References

1. Ahrendt, W., Chimento, J.M., Pace, G.J., Schneider, G.: A specification language for static and runtime verification of data and control properties. In: Bjørner, N., de Boer, F. (eds.) FM 2015. LNCS, vol. 9109, pp. 108–125. Springer, Cham (2015). https://doi.org/10.1007/978-3-319-19249-9_8
2. Ahrendt, W., Chimento, M., Pace, G., Schneider, G.: Verifying data- and control-oriented properties combining static and runtime verification: theory and tools. Formal Methods Syst. Des. **51**(1), 200–265 (2017). https://doi.org/10.1007/s10703-017-0274-y
3. Azzopardi, S., Colombo, C., Pace, G.J.: A technique for automata-based verification with residual reasoning. In: MODELSWARD 2020, pp. 237–248. SCITEPRESS (2020). https://doi.org/10.5220/0008981902370248
4. Azzopardi, S., Ellul, J., Pace, G.J.: Monitoring smart contracts: ContractLarva and open challenges beyond. In: Colombo, C., Leucker, M. (eds.) RV 2018. LNCS, vol. 11237, pp. 113–137. Springer, Cham (2018). https://doi.org/10.1007/978-3-030-03769-7_8
5. Azzopardi, S., Piterman, N., Schneider, G.: Incorporating monitors in reactive synthesis without paying the price. In: Hou, Z., Ganesh, V. (eds.) ATVA 2021. LNCS, vol. 12971, pp. 337–353. Springer, Cham (2021). https://doi.org/10.1007/978-3-030-88885-5_22
6. Bloem, R., Könighofer, B., Könighofer, R., Wang, C.: Shield synthesis: - runtime enforcement for reactive systems. In: Baier, C., Tinelli, C. (eds.) TACAS 2015. LNCS, vol. 9035, pp. 533–548. Springer, Heidelberg (2015). https://doi.org/10.1007/978-3-662-46681-0_51
7. Cavezza, D.G., Alrajeh, D., György, A.: Minimal assumptions refinement for realizable specifications. In: FormaliSE'20, pp. 66–76. ACM (2020). https://doi.org/10.1145/3372020.3391557
8. Chatterjee, K., Henzinger, T.A., Jobstmann, B.: Environment assumptions for synthesis. In: van Breugel, F., Chechik, M. (eds.) CONCUR 2008. LNCS, vol. 5201, pp. 147–161. Springer, Heidelberg (2008). https://doi.org/10.1007/978-3-540-85361-9_14
9. Chimento, J.M., Ahrendt, W., Pace, G.J., Schneider, G.: StaRVOOrS?: A tool for combined static and runtime verification of Java. In: Bartocci, E., Majumdar, R. (eds.) RV 2015. LNCS, vol. 9333, pp. 297–305. Springer, Cham (2015). https://doi.org/10.1007/978-3-319-23820-3_21
10. Chimento, M., Ahrendt, W., Schneider, G.: Testing meets static and runtime verification. In: FormaliSE@ICSE'18, pp. 30–39. ACM (2018). https://doi.org/10.1145/3193992.3194000
11. Colombo, C., Pace, G.J., Schneider, G.: LARVA – safer monitoring of real-time java programs (tool paper). In: SEFM'09, pp. 33–37. IEEE Computer Society (2009)
12. Ehlers, R., Finkbeiner, B.: Monitoring realizability. In: Khurshid, S., Sen, K. (eds.) RV 2011. LNCS, vol. 7186, pp. 427–441. Springer, Heidelberg (2012). https://doi.org/10.1007/978-3-642-29860-8_34
13. Finkbeiner, B.: Synthesis of reactive systems. In: Esparza, J., Grumberg, O., Sickert, S. (eds.) Dependable Software Systems Engineering, NATO Science for Peace and Security Series - D: Information and Communication Security, vol. 45, pp. 72–98. IOS Press (2016). https://doi.org/10.3233/978-1-61499-627-9-72
14. Finkbeiner, B., Klein, F., Metzger, N.: Live synthesis. In: Hou, Z., Ganesh, V. (eds.) ATVA 2021. LNCS, vol. 12971, pp. 153–169. Springer, Cham (2021). https://doi.org/10.1007/978-3-030-88885-5_11

15. Havelund, K., Goldberg, A.: Verify your runs. In: Meyer, B., Woodcock, J. (eds.) VSTTE 2005. LNCS, vol. 4171, pp. 374–383. Springer, Heidelberg (2008). https://doi.org/10.1007/978-3-540-69149-5_40

16. Jacobs, S., Klein, F., Schirmer, S.: A high-level LTL synthesis format: TLSF v1.1. In: Piskac, R., Dimitrova, R. (eds.) Proceedings Fifth Workshop on Synthesis, SYNT@CAV 2016, Toronto, Canada, 17–18 July, 2016. EPTCS, vol. 229, pp. 112–132 (2016). https://doi.org/10.4204/EPTCS.229.10

17. Kupferman, O., Vardi, M.Y.: Model checking of safety properties. In: Halbwachs, N., Peled, D. (eds.) CAV 1999. LNCS, vol. 1633, pp. 172–183. Springer, Heidelberg (1999). https://doi.org/10.1007/3-540-48683-6_17

18. Leucker, M., Schallhart, C.: A brief account of runtime verification. J. Logic Alg. Prog. **78**(5), 293–303 (2009)

19. Luttenberger, M., Meyer, P.J., Sickert, S.: Practical synthesis of reactive systems from LTL specifications via parity games. Acta Informatica **57**(1–2), 3–36 (2020)

20. Majumdar, R., Piterman, N., Schmuck, A.-K.: Environmentally-friendly GR(1) synthesis. In: Vojnar, T., Zhang, L. (eds.) TACAS 2019. LNCS, vol. 11428, pp. 229–246. Springer, Cham (2019). https://doi.org/10.1007/978-3-030-17465-1_13

21. Mallozzi, P.: Designing Trustworthy Autonomous Systems. Ph.D. thesis, Chalmers, Sweden (2020)

22. Maoz, S., Ringert, J.O.: On the software engineering challenges of applying reactive synthesis to robotics. In: RoSE'18, pp. 17–22 (2018)

23. Maoz, S., Ringert, J.O.: Spectra: a specification language for reactive systems. Softw. Syst. Model. **20**(5), 1553–1586 (2021). https://doi.org/10.1007/s10270-021-00868-z

24. Nahabedian, L., Braberman, V.A., D'Ippolito, N., Honiden, S., Kramer, J., Tei, K., Uchitel, S.: Dynamic update of discrete event controllers. IEEE Trans. Software Eng. **46**(11), 1220–1240 (2020). https://doi.org/10.1109/TSE.2018.2876843

25. Piterman, N., Pnueli, A., Sa'ar, Y.: Synthesis of reactive(1) designs. In: Emerson, E.A., Namjoshi, K.S. (eds.) VMCAI 2006. LNCS, vol. 3855, pp. 364–380. Springer, Heidelberg (2005). https://doi.org/10.1007/11609773_24

26. Pnueli, A., Rosner, R.: On the synthesis of a reactive module. In: POPL'89, pp. 179–190. ACM Press (1989). https://doi.org/10.1145/75277.75293

27. Sánchez, C., et al.: A survey of challenges for runtime verification from advanced application domains (beyond software). Formal Methods in System Design, pp. 1–57, August 2019. https://doi.org/10.1007/s10703-019-00337-w

28. Sistla, A.P., Clarke, E.M.: The complexity of propositional linear temporal logics. J. ACM **32**(3), 733–749 (1985). https://doi.org/10.1145/3828.3837

29. Ulus, D., Belta, C.: Reactive control meets runtime verification: a case study of navigation. In: Finkbeiner, B., Mariani, L. (eds.) RV 2019. LNCS, vol. 11757, pp. 368–374. Springer, Cham (2019). https://doi.org/10.1007/978-3-030-32079-9_21

30. Wong, K.W., Ehlers, R., Kress-Gazit, H.: Correct high-level robot behavior in environments with unexpected events. In: Robotics: Science and Systems X (2014). https://doi.org/10.15607/RSS.2014.X.012

31. Yoon, H., Chou, Y., Chen, X., Frew, E., Sankaranarayanan, S.: Predictive runtime monitoring for linear stochastic systems and applications to geofence enforcement for UAVs. In: Finkbeiner, B., Mariani, L. (eds.) RV 2019. LNCS, vol. 11757, pp. 349–367. Springer, Cham (2019). https://doi.org/10.1007/978-3-030-32079-9_20

32. Zudaire, S., Gorostiaga, F., Sánchez, C., Schneider, G., Uchitel, S.: Assumption monitoring using runtime verification for uav temporal task plan executions. In: ICRA 2021, pp. 6824–6830. IEEE (2021). https://doi.org/10.1109/ICRA48506.2021.9561671

Assumption Monitoring of Temporal Task Planning Using Stream Runtime Verification

Felipe Gorostiaga[1]([⊠])[iD], Sebastián Zudaire[2][iD], César Sánchez[1][iD], Gerardo Schneider[3][iD], and Sebastián Uchitel[4,5][iD]

[1] IMDEA Software Institute, Madrid, Spain
felipe.gorostiaga@imdea.org
[2] Instituto Balseiro - Univ. Nacional de Cuyo, San Carlos de Bariloche, Argentina
[3] University of Gothenburg, Gothenburg, Sweden
[4] Univ. de Buenos Aires, Buenos Aires, Argentina
[5] Imperial College London, London, UK

Abstract. Temporal task planning uses formal techniques such as reactive synthesis to guarantee that a robot will succeed in its mission. This technique requires certain explicit and implicit assumptions and simplifications about the operating environment of the robot, including its sensors and capabilities. A robot executing a plan can produce a *silent mission failure*, where the user may believe that the mission goals were achieved when instead the assumptions were violated at runtime. This entails that mitigation and remediation opportunities are missed.

Monitoring at runtime can detect complex assumption violations and identify silent failures, but such monitoring requires the ability to describe and detect sophisticated temporal properties together with quantitative and complex data. Additional challenges include (1) ensuring the correctness of the monitors and a correct interplay between the planning execution and the monitors, and (2) that monitors run under constrained environments in terms of resources.

In this paper we propose a solution based on stream runtime verification, which offers a high-level declarative language to describe sophisticated monitors together with guarantees on the execution time and memory usage. We show how monitors can be combined with temporal planning not only to monitor assumptions but also to support mitigation and remediation in UAV missions. We demonstrate our approach both in real and simulated flights for some typical mission scenarios.

1 Introduction

Specifying and developing sophisticated behavior of autonomous systems is a notoriously difficult task. Formal methods is a very tempting approach to the

This work was funded in part by the Madrid Regional Government under project "S2018/TCS-4339 (BLOQUES-CM)" and by a research grant from Nomadic Labs and the Tezos Foundation.

T. Margaria and B. Steffen (Eds.): ISoLA 2022, LNCS 13701, pp. 397–414, 2022.
https://doi.org/10.1007/978-3-031-19849-6_23

rigorous development of robots and other autonomous systems. Temporal task planning consists of defining a task specification of complex robot behaviors, for example, using a fragment of the linear temporal logic (LTL), as we do in this paper. The LTL specification is then transformed into a system using controller synthesis, which implements an operational strategy that guarantees to achieve the desired task [7]. The limitations of current synthesis technology require several modeling simplifications to be able to encode the robot, its environment and the mission goals. Consequently, the correctness of the approach depends not only on the correctness of the specification and the synthesis tools used, but also on certain explicit and implicit assumptions about the robot's operating environment, sensors and capabilities. A robot executing a plan can *silently fail* to fulfill the task if the assumptions are violated at runtime, leading the user to mistakenly believe that a mission has been accomplished successfully, which can have significant practical consequences. Sometimes the assumptions can fail due to unforeseen circumstances. Also, the current synthesis technology that is typically used for temporal planning requires a discretization and simplification of the environment that may not always be respected at runtime.

Monitoring assumption violations at runtime can detect silent failures and provide mitigation and remediation opportunities. In this paper we show how temporal task planning can be combined with stream runtime verification (SRV) to monitor both explicit and implicit assumptions on which those plans rely. More concretely, we describe a method to detect and predict assumption violations at runtime to further improve the assurance of robotic behavior.

We use a language and system based on the SRV language LOLA to describe the monitors. LOLA is a good language for this goal because:

- it has clean semantics,
- its expressive yet succinct syntax results in natural specifications,
- the language allows easy extensions (like new datatypes) and I/O of rich events, and
- it allows the creation of predictive functions such as Kalman filters.

Additionally, LOLA allows a theoretical analysis of monitor specifications, which lets us calculate beforehand the constant amount of memory required to run the monitors throughout the entire execution independently of the length of the trace.

We integrate SRV and temporal task planning for two typical mission scenarios of an Unmanned Aerial Vehicle (UAV). We show a simplified architecture of the interplay between the components from temporal task planning and runtime verification in Fig. 1. The mission planning using temporal task problem involves the description of both a temporal task specification and a LOLA specification. From these specifications we synthesize a controller and a monitor which communicate with the motion planner, with the vehicle, and with each other through sensors and actuators. We have implemented the UAV controller using MAVLink [2] and we demonstrate our approach empirically both in real flights using the Parrot AR.Drone 2.0 with an onboard mounted Raspberry Pi Zero W and in flights simulated using the Software in the Loop ArduPilot Simulator [1],

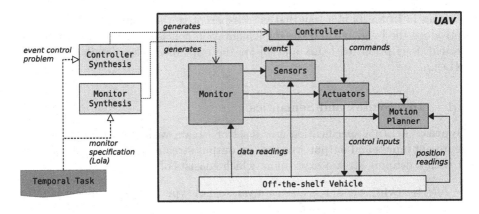

Fig. 1. Architecture for SRV + UAV Temporal Planning.

applying offline and online monitoring. In this paper we focus on the Stream Runtime Verification part of the approach, and we explain the specifications of the properties to monitor. More details on the mission planning stage and the interaction between the UAV controller and the monitors are available in [11].

The rest of the paper is structured as follows. Section 2 revisits stream runtime verification and the language LOLA. Section 3 explains the concept of implicit assumptions and silent mission failures, presenting multiple examples. Section 4 describes an empirical evaluation. Finally, Sect. 5 concludes.

2   The Stream Runtime Verification Language Lola

We briefly revisit stream runtime verification for synchronous streams. A *synchronous stream* is a sequence of values from a data domain. We refer to the value at the n-th position in a sequence z as $z(n)$. For example, the sequence $altitude = [350, 360, 289, 320, 330]$ contains the successive values of the altitude of an unmanned aerial vehicle. In this sequence $altitude(0) = 350$ and $altitude(2) = 289$. This sequence can be obtained, for example, by sampling a sensor of the UAV every five seconds.

Streams are typed using *data theories*, which are essentially sets of values and interpreted function symbols. The function symbols are used to build stream expressions, and are equipped with an associated implementation that allows computing a result value once the values of the arguments are provided.

LOLA is a synchronous SRV language. Specifications (or programs) in LOLA declare the relation between output streams (verdicts) and input streams (observations). In this paper we will use an implementation of LOLA called HLOLA[1] (see [5]) written in the purely functional language Haskell. The distinguishing feature of HLola is that data theories are not decided a-priori and hard-wired in the tool. Instead, HLola borrows (almost) arbitrary Haskell datatypes as data

---

[1] HLola is available at https://github.com/imdea-software/hlola.

theories in LOLA [6] in a way that is transparent to the monitor engine. We will introduce the language and the implementation concisely. See [3, 4] for rigorous formal descriptions of LOLA and [5] for the implementation details of the tool HLOLA.

2.1 LOLA Syntax and Semantics

Syntax. A LOLA specification uses a set of stream variables which are used to represent inputs and output streams. An output stream is defined by associating it with a defining stream expression, which consists of:

- *offsets* $v[k|d]$ where v is a stream variable of type D, k is an integer number and d a value from D, and
- *function applications* $f\ t_1 \dots t_n$ in which f is applied to stream expressions $t_1, \dots, t_n$ of the right types.

Constants are 0-ary function symbols. A stream variable v represents a stream of values of the type of v. If v is an input stream, the values will be provided incrementally, and if v is an output stream the values will be computed by the monitor incrementally. An offset expression $v[-1|d]$ captures the value of sequence v in the previous position. If there is no previous instant, the value d is returned instead. The particular case of an offset with $k = 0$ requires no default value as the index is always guaranteed to be within the range of the sequence, in which case we use $v[\textbf{now}]$. A LOLA specification consists of a set I of typed input stream variables, a set O of typed output stream variables, and a set of defining equations, $y_i = e_i$, one per output variable $y_i \in O$ where e_i is a stream expression of the same type as y_i. Note that expression e_i can use any stream variables from I and O, including y_i. The defining equations describe the relation between input and output streams. Note that functions f used to build expressions do not need to know about time or offsets. Examples of these function include $\wedge$, $\vee$, $+$, vector multiplication, etc. At runtime, the implementation of theses functions will provide values for the temporal engine to evaluate. This is the essence of stream runtime verification where the temporal reasoning and the algorithms to compute values are kept separate.

Example 1. The specification *"the mean altitude in the last 3 instants"* can be expressed in LOLA as follows, where denom calculates the number of instants that are taken into account to compute the average.

```
1 input Double altitude
2 output Double denom = min 2 denom[-1|0] + 1
3 output Double mean =
4      (altitude[-2|0] + altitude[-1|0] + altitude[now]) / denom[now]
5 output Bool ok_altitude = mean[now] < 400
```

In this specification $I = \{\texttt{altitude}\}$ and $O = \{\texttt{denom}, \texttt{mean}, \texttt{ok\_altitude}\}$. Also, altitude, denom and mean are streams of **Double** values, while ok_altitude is a stream of **Bool** values.

Semantics. Semantics of LOLA specifications are given in terms of valuations. A valuation ρ consists of the assignment of one sequence ρ_x for each stream variable x, all of the same length. The semantics of LOLA is defined in terms of valuations of expressions $[\![e_x]\!]$ as follows:

–For offsets:
$$[\![v[i|c]]\!](j) = \begin{cases} \rho_v(j+i) & \text{if } 0 \leq j + i < L \\ c & \text{otherwise} \end{cases}$$

–For functions:
$$[\![f\ e_1 \ldots e_k]\!](j) = f\ [\![e_1]\!](j) \ldots [\![e_k]\!](j)$$

Note that f on the left hand side of the semantic definition of a function represents the syntactic representation of the function (the constructor of expressions) while the f on the right hand side represents the function evaluator.

We say that a valuation ρ satisfies a LOLA specification φ whenever every output variable y satisfies its defining equation e_y, i.e. when $\rho_y = [\![e_y]\!]$. See [4] for a more rigorous explanation of valuations, where a simple graph traversal of the specifications is used to guarantee correct semantics and to statically compute bounds of the resources needed to perform the monitoring.

HLOLA: A Powerful Implementation of LOLA. HLOLA is an implementation of LOLA developed as an embedded language in Haskell with an extra layer of syntactic facilities. This embedding, called lift deep embedding, extends the notion of eDSL and is described in [3]. This implementation strategy allows us to incorporate constructs from the host language Haskell into LOLA, such as let-bindings, where clauses, partial application, list comprehension, etc. We can also use higher order to seamlessly define parametric streams, and we give access to the modules system of Haskell to allow the separation of independent pieces of code. An HLOLA specification can import an arbitrary Haskell module as well as a LOLA *theory* (the implementation of types and functions for a specific domain) or *library* (auxiliary stream definitions of general purpose) with the directive **use** at the beginning of the specification.

The powerful type system of Haskell ensures the type-correctness of a specification as well as its syntactic well-formedness. Extra checks specific to the LOLA language such as the validity of the dependency graph are assessed by a routine in the HLOLA engine prior to the monitor execution.

The main function that implements the monitoring algorithm is *runSpec*, which takes an HLOLA specification and an input trace for every **input** stream and returns the successive events of the **output** streams. As a by-product of developing HLOLA as an eDSL in Haskell, the datatypes that constitute an HLOLA specification and the function *runSpec* are defined in Haskell as well, and as such can be lifted to become a theory ready to be used as a data theory of HLOLA itself. This has enabled the use of HLOLA specifications as a theory from within the language [6].

We describe now this HLOLA feature, that simplifies specifications in many occasions by allowing the evaluation of data as the result of the computation of a monitor, in order to use the results in higher monitoring activities. We call this feature nested monitoring or nested specifications. Nested specifications allow spawning and executing monitors dynamically, collecting the result of a stream in each invocation and using it as a value in the caller monitor. Defining an *inner* specification involves giving it a name and adding an extra clause: **return** x **when** y where x is a stream of any type and y is a **Boolean** stream. The type of the stream x determines the type of the value returned when the specification is invoked dynamically. Optionally, the definition of a nested specification can require parameters, which can be different in each invocation. Once we have defined a nested specification, we can execute it using the function *runSpec* from the theory Lola, importing the theory and providing the necessary parameters and lists of values for the input streams as lists of values of the corresponding types, in the order in which they are defined in the nested specification.

When a nested specification with a return clause **return** x **when** y is executed, the computation will return the value of the stream x at the first time y becomes *True*, or the last value of x if y never holds in the execution. As a consequence, if y becomes *True* in the middle of an execution, the monitor does not have to run until the end to compute a value and can anticipate the result. This opens the door to evaluate the nested specification incrementally and return the outcome as soon as the outcome is definitive. If the specification contains no input stream, then it is executed until the **return** stream becomes *True*.

Example 2. Consider the following specification, which calculates whether input numeric streams p and q have crossed in the last 50 instants. We define a topmost specification as follows:

```
1  use theory Lola
2  use innerspec crossspec
3  input Double p
4  input Double q
5  output [Double] last50 <Stream Double str> = let
6    prev = take 49 (last50 str[-1|[]])
7    in str[now] ++ prev
8  output Bool haveCrossed = let
9    ps = last50 p
10   qs = last50 q
11   in runSpec (crossspec ps[now] qs[now])
```

The output stream haveCrossed invokes the nested specification crossspec with the lists of the last 50 events of p and q as inputs. We use the auxiliary Haskell function **take** to keep the first 49 elements of the previous list in the variable prev, to which we append the corresponding new value.

The inner specification uses the Haskell function **signum** –which returns −1, 0, or 1, indicating the sign of the argument– to check that the sign of the difference is maintained throughout the entire subtrace:

```
1 innerspec Bool crossspec
2 input Double p
3 input Double q
4 output Bool cross =
5   signum (p[now] - q[now]) /== signum (p[-1|p[now]] - q[-1|q[now]])
6 return cross when cross
```

Note that the inner monitor returns as soon as the signals are detected to cross.

3   Implicit Assumptions and Silent Mission Failures

Temporal task planning using reactive synthesis requires a discrete description of the goal (and the world in which the system will operate). Creating discrete domains for complex continuous environments requires introducing assumptions regarding the relation between the discrete abstraction and the intention in the real world that typically includes continuous variables. Thus, the objective in the *real world* can be informally described as "A_{RW} implies G_{RW}" (where A_{RW} represents the assumptions in the real world and G_{RW} represents the mission goal in the real world). Reactive synthesis solves this problem by using *discrete* goals and assumptions $A_D \rightarrow G_D$. The correctness of the solution is based on two additional assumptions: "A_{RW} implies A_D" and "G_D implies G_{RW}", in other words that the discrete assumptions hold in the real world and that accomplishing the discrete goals imply accomplising the mission in the real world.

We refer to A_{RW} and the last two implications as *implicit assumptions*. A *silent mission failure* occurs when a system fails to achieve its goals G_{RW} but A_{RW} does not hold either. As a consequence the implication "A_{RW} implies G_{RW}" is satisfied, making it impossible for the system user to distinguish if G_{RW} holds or if A_{RW} did not hold.

3.1   Handling Assumption Violations

We show two scenarios in which we combine temporal task planning and Stream Runtime Verification

(A) Flagging assumption violations after a mission concludes in order to detect silent failures.

(B) Triggering recovery measures online, such as replanning or mission abortion, immediately upon an assumption violation using quantitative streams in specifications to facilitate plan adjustment[2].

---

[2] The complete discrete event control problems and assumption used to synthesise plans and monitors, and the data obtained from the real and simulated flights discussed in this section is available at http://mtsa.dc.uba.ar.

We now discuss these separately by describing two missions.

SRV for Offline Monitoring. The first mission uses SRV for assumption monitoring and logging. This is a search and rescue mission with a no-fly zone, with the instruction of landing when the target is found. The monitor processes the incoming events and monitors and logs assumption violations alongside the associated relevant information, which can then be used offline for mission post-hoc analysis.

In this mission we monitor two assumptions. The first assumption checks that the UAV never enters the no-fly zone, and, if it does, measures the degree of violation as the distance inside the no-fly zone. The second assumption ensures that the area sensed when entering a zone covers the zone completely.

The first assumption can be easily monitored by calculating for each input position reading, the depth inside the no-fly zone, returning **Nothing** if the UAV is not within a forbidden zone.

There are several ways one could monitor the second assumption. In this specification we monitor a stronger property that requires the attitude and position of the vehicle to be within certain bounds. Since these data measurements may carry noise we include in the monitor specification a filtering phase that implements a first order low-pass filter. Note that most cameras may require several seconds to capture a high resolution image, specially on low-end hardware. For this reason, it is necessary to monitor that the filtered attitude and position is within the required bounds for every instant between the open_capture command and its corresponding response event, which is the time frame in which a picture is being taken. Below we show an HLOLA specification that encodes both assumptions.

```
1 use theory Geometry2D
2 use haskell Data.Maybe
3 use haskell Data.List
4 data Attitude = Attitude {yaw ::Double, roll ::Double, pitch ::Double}
5 data Target   = Target {x :: Double, y :: Double, num_wp :: Double}
6 data Position = Position {x :: Double, y :: Double, alt :: Double}
7 type Vector = (Double, Double)
8 type Position = (Double, Double)
9 type Polygon = [(Double, Double)]
```

```
10 input Attitude   attitude
11 input Vector     velocity
12 input Position   position
13 input Double     altitude
14 input Target     target
15 input [Polygon]  noflypolys
16 input [String]   events_within
17 output Bool all_ok_capturing = capturing[now] `implies`
18   (height_ok[now] && near[now] && roll_ok[now] && pitch_ok[now])
19 output Bool flying_in_safe_zones = flying_in_poly[now] === Nothing
20 output (Maybe Polygon) flying_in_poly = let
21   position_in_poly = pointInPoly filtered_pos[now]
22   in find position_in_poly noflypolys[now]
23 output (Maybe Double) depth_into_poly = let
24   mSides = funmap polygonSides flying_in_poly[now]
25   distance_from_pos = shortestDist filtered_pos[now]
26   in funmap distance_from_pos mSides
27   where
28   shortestDist x = minimum (map distancePointSegment x)
29   funmap f Nothing = Nothing
30   funmap f (Just x) = Just (f x)
31 output Bool capturing = let
32   has_capture = "capture" `belongsto` events_within[now]
33   in has_capture || open_capture [-1|False]
34 output Bool open_capture =
35   lastIsCapture open_capture[-1|False] events_within[now]
36   where
37   lastIsCapture dflt [] = dflt
38   lastIsCapture _ xs = last xs == "capture"
39 output Double f_pos_component <(Position->Double) field> = let
40   tau     = 0.6
41   _this   = f_pos_component field
42   in (field position[now] + tau*(2*_this[-1|0] - _this[-2|0]/2))
43     / (1 + 1.5*tau)
44 output Double filtered_x   = (f_pos_component x)[now]
45 output Double filtered_y   = (f_pos_component y)[now]
46 output Double filtered_alt = (f_pos_component alt)[now]
47 output Position filtered_pos = (filtered_x[now], filtered_y[now])
48 output Bool near = distance filtered_pos[now] target[now] < 1
49 output Bool height_ok = filtered_alt[now] > 0
50 output Bool roll_ok  = abs (roll attitude[now]) < 0.0523
51 output Bool pitch_ok = abs (pitch attitude[now]) < 0.0523
```

The specification imports geometric facilities from **theory** Geometry2D, and Haskell libraries Data.Maybe and Data.List, and defines custom datatypes to interpret the data from the UAV, in lines 1–9. The input streams of this specification, declared in lines 10–16 encompass the state of the UAV, the current target position, the no-fly zones and the onboard camera events to detect when a picture is being captured. The output stream all_ok_capturing declared in line 17 assesses that, whenever the vehicle is taking a picture, the height, roll and pitch are acceptable and the vehicle is near the target location. The output stream flying_in_safe_zones from line 19 reports if the UAV is flying outside the forbidden regions. The stream flying_in_poly in line 20 partially applies the function pointInpoly from the theory Geometry2D to the current position to find and return the forbidden region in which the vehicle is flying, if any, using the Haskell function **find**. The output stream depth_into_poly defined in line 23 takes the minimum of the distances between the vehicle position and every side of the forbidden region inside of which the vehicle is flying, if any.

The intermediate stream capturing from line 31 expresses whether the UAV is taking a picture, using the auxiliary stream open_capture declared in line 34. The streams filtered_alt and filtered_pos from lines 47 and 48 represent the location and altitude of the UAV filtered to reduce noise from the sensors, a procedure that is implemented generically by the parameterized stream filtered_pos_component in line 40. The intermediate stream near declared in line 49 takes the distance from the vehicle location to its target and checks if it is lower than 1. Finally, the streams height_ok, roll_ok, and pitch_ok from lines 49–51 calculate that the corresponding attitude of the vehicle is within certain predefined boundaries.

A logger will store the values of all these streams whenever all_ok_capturing is *False* to detect a silent failure and allow a post-hoc analysis.

SRV for Online Monitoring and Adaptation. In the second mission we demonstrate how SRV can be used, beyond logging, to support remediation actions during the flight by interacting with components of the UAV controller. We ran an ordered patrol mission (as described in [8]) of three locations with no-fly zones.

We built a monitor that uses quantitative data to *predict* the violation of assumptions, enabling the possibility of reacting to anticipate and avoid the faulty behavior *before* it occurs. To achieve this, the HLOLA monitor specification encodes a simplified non-linear 2D model of a fixed-wing UAV and the full extent of the waypoint guidance control algorithm of ArduPilot. Part of the input to this monitor includes the current state of the system (position, attitude, wind) and the list of waypoints for the current trajectory. The monitor uses this input together with the non-linear model of the UAV and the guidance control algorithms to produce, by means of simulation into the future, a prediction of the UAV's flight path.

We add an *Extended Kalman Filter* (EKF) to estimate in-flight a parameter *tau* from the simplified UAV models, helping to diminish the error in the predicted flight path. Other parameter identification techniques could be used instead (e.g., least squares), but we aimed to show HLOLA's ability to implement state-of-the-art estimation algorithms.

The monitor produces an event to indicate that the monitor anticipates an abnormal situation in the future:

- If the UAV is predicted to hit the target zone but far from its center point, then a nearMiss event is produced.
- If the target zone is to be completely missed, an event goFailed is produced. Our monitor is specified to hold its failure prediction for several time instants before producing a goFailed, to allow the controller to attempt to correct the airspeed.
- Finally, the monitor produces an event abnormalDrift when the predicted distance of the UAV to its intended location is beyond a threshold.

To utilize the output of our predictive monitors, the following three requirements are added to the mission plan:

(1) upon a nearMiss the UAV should reattempt to visit the location immediately,
(2) upon a goFailed the UAV should skip the location and move onto the next location to patrol, and
(3) upon an abnormalDrift event, the UAV should abort mission and land.

We monitor two properties. The first property predicts how close to the center of the target zone the UAV will pass, so that the UAV controller can either abort the mission or try to correct the flight path based on the degree of the error predicted.

The second property observes how the UAV is following the planned path by predicting the estimated time of arrival and total flight distance. A significant difference is likely to be due to wind conditions, which is not considered by the plan. The monitor uses this estimated arrival time and distance to compute the speed at which the vehicle is more likely to succeed in closely following the trajectory, and the controller uses this information to change the speed of the UAV accordingly.

Below we show the HLOLA specification that monitors both assumptions.

```
1 use theory Geometry2D
2 use theory SimulatedGuidance
3 use theory GuidanceTheory
4 use haskell Data.Either
5 use theory Lola
6 use innerspec simuguidance
7 type Matrix = [[Double]]
```

```
 8 input NonLinearData navigation_data
 9 input Vector        velocity
10 input Point         position
11 input Point         target
12 input Vector        target_dir
13 output Double intersDistance = let
14   r0 = (position[now], velocity[now])
15   r1 = (target[now], target_dir[now])
16   in intersectionDistance r0 r1
17 output Double pi_controller =
18   saturate (21 + estimated_error[now] * 0.5 + err_int[now])
19   where
20   saturate x = if x<15 then 15 else if x>30 then 30 else x
21 output Double estimated_error =
22   21 - distance estim_data[now] / time estim_data[now]
23 output (Matrix, Double, Double) kfuStream = let
24   inroll     = initial_roll navigation_data[now]
25   prev_iroll = initial_roll navigation_data[-1| navigation_data[now]]
26   dt         = 0.05
27   dfltM      = [[0.01,0],[0,0.01]]
28   kfp        = kalman_filter_predict navigation_data[now] 1 tau[-1|0.5]
29   in
30   kalman_filter_update
31       matrix_kfiltered[-1| dfltM] prev_iroll tau[-1|0.5]
32       inroll kfp dt
33 output Matrix matrix_kfiltered =
34   fst3 kfuStream[now]
35 output Double tau = let
36   thd3 kfuStream [now]
37 output ([Point2], Double, Bool, Double, Double) simulated_guidance =
38   let wp_radius_wp = get_wp_radius_wp navigation_data[now]
39   in
40   runSpec (simuguidance navigation_data[now] tau[now] 200 wp_radius_wp)
41   where
42   get_wp_radius_wp (NLD _ wp_list _ _ n_wp radius_list _ _ _ _ _) =
43     filter farEnoughWP
44       (drop n_wp (zip3 wp_list radius_list (Nothing:map Just wp_list)))
45   farEnoughWP (_, _, Nothing) = True
46   farEnoughWP (nwp, _, Just prev_wp) = norm (nwp 'minus' prev_wp)>0.01
```

```
47 output [Point2] simulated_guidance_wps = let
48    fst5 simulated_guidance[now]
49 output Estimation estim_data =
50    simulate_guidance tau[now] navigation_data[now]
51 output Double err_int = if isSaturated pi_controller[-1|21] then
52    err_int [-1|0] else err_int [-1|0] + estimated_error [now] * 0.03
53    where
54    isSaturated x = x==15 || x==30
```

The input streams are data about the state of the vehicle at every instant (navigation_data, velocity and position) and its current target destination (target and target_dir).

The output stream intersDistance of line 13 estimates how far from the target location the UAV will pass, returning −1 if the UAV is actually moving away from the target location. The output stream pi_controller shown in line 17 is used to control the UAV's airspeed set-point, taking a reference velocity of 21 meters per second and an estimation of the average UAV speed along with the predicted flight path, generated from the predicted arrival time and flight distance, which is calculated by the stream estim_data, declared in line 49. The main idea is that in order to correctly follow the planned path one must satisfy a constant turn radius assumption, which (for the UAV) translates into constant ground-speed. When the UAV has tailwind, for a constant airspeed, it will fly at a faster ground-speed than when it experiences headwind. Controlling the ground-speed around a fixed value (by actuating on the airspeed set-point) helps following the desired path more accurately.

The intermediate stream kfuStream shown in line 23 implements the EKF at every instant, and the intermediate stream simulated_guidance from line 37 simulates the UAV trajectory based on the current navigation_data, the tau (provided by the EKF and extracted in line 35), a maximum flight time of 200 and the target path, given by the list of its waypoints.

The function simulate_guidance from the theory GuidanceTheory uses a nested specification simuguidance to simulate the trajectory of the UAV over the current list of waypoints, which is captured in the input stream route.

```
1 innerspec ([Point2], Double, Bool, Double, Double) simuguidance
2                      <NonLinearData nld><Double tau> <Double maxtime>
3 use theory GuidanceTheory
4 use theory Geometry2D
5 use theory Lola
6 use haskell Data.List.Extra
7 use innerspec simuinner
```

```
 8 type Route = (Point2, Double, Maybe Point2)
 9 input Route route
10 output ReachStateType reaching_state = let
11   roll = reach_roll [-1|initial_roll nld]
12   yaw = reach_yaw [-1|initial_yaw nld]
13   distance = reach_distance [-1|0]
14   time = reach_time [-1|0]
15   pos = reach_pos [-1|initial_pos nld]
16   in
17   runSpec
18     (simuinner nld tau maxtime pos yaw roll time distance route[now])
19 output Bool reached_maxtime = reached_maxtime_field reaching_state[now]
20 output Double reach_time = reach_time_field reaching_state[now]
21 output Double reach_distance = reach_distance_field reaching_state[now]
22 output Double reach_yaw = reach_yaw_field reaching_state[now]
23 output Double reach_roll = reach_roll_field reaching_state[now]
24 output Point2 reach_pos = reach_pos_field reaching_state[now]
25 output [Point2] wps =
26   snoc wps[-1| []] reach_pos[now]
27   where
28   snoc ls x = ls ++ [x]
29 output Bool has_reached = reached_maxtime [-1|False]
30 output ([Point2], Double, Bool, Double, Double) ret =
31   (wps[now], reach_roll[now], reached_maxtime[now],
32     reach_time[now], reach_distance[now])
33 return ret when has_reached
```

The successive values of route are the linear trajectories that the UAV is expected to go through. The monitor simuguidance will run until the route is covered or until the **maxtime** is exceeded. For every part of the route, simuguidance will spin up a second level nested specification simuinner to simulate successive small steps of the flight in a path between two waypoints.

```
1 innerspec ReachStateType simuinner <NonLinearData nld> <Double tau>
2   <Double maxtime> <Point2 dpos> <Double dyaw> <Double droll>
3   <Double dtime> <Double ddistance> <(Point2, Double, Maybe Point2) wps>
4 use theory GuidanceTheory
5 use theory Geometry2D
6 data ReachStateType = RST {
7   reached_maxtime_field :: Bool, reach_time_field :: Double,
8   reach_distance_field :: Double, reach_yaw_field :: Double,
9   reach_roll_field :: Double, reach_pos_field :: Point2 }
```

```
10 const dt = 0.05
11 const g = 9.8
12 const lim_roll_cd = 65 * pi / 180
13 const limit = sin lim_roll_cd
14 const NLD navll_d _ navll_p _ _ _ _ gamma vel_a vel_w _ = nld
15 const (dposx, dposy) = dpos
16 const (next_wp, wp_radius, mprev_wp) = wps
17 output Double time = step_time [-1|dtime]
18 output Double step_time = time[now] + dt
19 output Double yaw = step_yaw [-1|dyaw]
20 output Double step_yaw = let
21   yaw_dot = (g * (sin (roll[now]))) / vel_a
22   in yaw[now] + dt * yaw_dot
23 output Double posx = step_posx [-1|dposx]
24 output Double step_posx =
25   posx[now] + dt * (vel_a * sin yaw[now] + (vel_w * sin gamma))
26 output Double posy = step_posy [-1| dposy]
27 output Double step_posy =
28   posy[now] + dt * (vel_a * cos yaw[now] + (vel_w * cos gamma))
29 output Point2 pos = P posx[now] posy[now]
30 output Double roll = step_roll [-1|droll]
31 output Double step_roll = let
32   vel_g = (fst.get_ground_speed vel_w vel_a gamma) yaw[now]
33   hdg = (snd.get_ground_speed vel_w vel_a gamma) yaw[now]
34   gcp = guidance_control_parameters navll_d navll_p next_wp
35                                    prev_wp[now] vel_g hdg pos[now]
36   ll = fst3 gcp
37   k_ll = snd3 gcp
38   eta = thd3 gcp
39   demanded_roll = (asin.max (-limit).min limit)
40                     ((k_ll * vel_g * vel_g * sin eta) / (ll * g))
41   in
42   (dt * demanded_roll + tau * roll[now]) / (tau + dt)
43 output Double distance = step_distance [-1|ddistance]
44 output Double step_distance = let
45   step_pos = (step_posx[now], step_posy[now])
46   in distance[now] + norm (step_pos 'minus' pos[now])
47 output Point2 prev_wp = maybe pos[now] Leaf mprev_wp
48 output Bool reached_maxtime = time[now] >= maxtime && maxtime > 0
49 output Bool stop_simulation = let
50   vnwp = verify_next_waypoint next_wp wp_radius prev_wp[now] pos[now]
51   in reached_maxtime[now] || vnwp /== INTRAVEL
52 output ReachStateType ret = RST reached_maxtime[now] time[now]
53                                distance[now] yaw[now] roll[now] pos[now]
54 return ret when stop_simulation
```

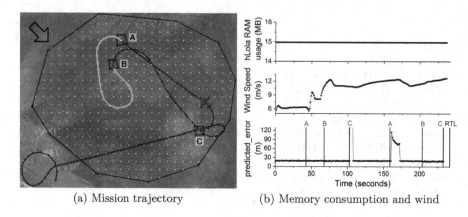

(a) Mission trajectory   (b) Memory consumption and wind

Fig. 2. Mission trajectory and flight data

Every execution of `simuinner` updates the UAV roll, yaw, and position, the time consumed, and the distance reached in the simulation step. The nested monitor `simunner` has no input stream and as a consequence it will execute until `stop_simulation` becomes *True*. The monitor calculates the trajectory of the UAV updating its position, distance traveled, roll, and yaw according to simulation steps of 0.05 time units. The simulation stops when the `maxtime` is reached, or when the UAV is no longer `INTRAVEL` and returns the latest state of the UAV, along with the total time consumed and the information of whether the maximum time was reached.

4   Empirical Evaluation

Our UAV control system (including the HLOLA monitors) was built for MAVLink [2] complying aerial vehicles, and tested extensively on the ArduPilot Software-In-The-Loop (SITL) simulator as in [9]. We have used this simulator (see [10]) to seamlessly transition from simulation to actually flying a fixed-wing vehicle based on a Pixhawk. The controller was run on a single Raspberry Pi.

To evaluate if the UAV entered no-fly zones during its mission using offline monitoring, we have carried out real flights using the Parrot Ar.Drone 2.0 and an onboard mounted Raspberry Pi Zero W, which we have used to log the flight data. The HLOLA monitor used a constant amount of memory of around 13.4 megabytes during the whole post-flight analysis.

The mission that uses online monitoring to predict and correct the behavior of the UAV was simulated on the ArduPlane SITL simulator, with a Raspberry Pi 3B+ as the simulated hardware, just like in [10]. We show the actions taken by the monitor during the patrol mission in Fig. 2(a). We have incremented the simulated wind speed over time to mimic an adverse situation and trigger the monitor, as we show in Fig. 2(b). By doing so, the second time the UAV travels from A to B, the predicted arrival distance error rises over 100 m, triggering the calculation of a new trajectory until one that guarantees the correct arrival of the UAV to the location is found. After the second time C is visited, the wind is too strong and the UAV is commanded to return to the launch point. Figure 2(b) also illustrates the memory consumption of the monitor, which remains practically constant as expected (see [3] for details about the memory consumption of HLOLA).

Our experiments show how we can monitor assumptions for UAV missions using HLOLA with negligible interference with the main navigation system, in particular with constant memory consumption and in constant time per event, providing support for the hypotheses that motivated the use of SRV and HLOLA.

5   Conclusion

We have applied the infrastructure from Runtime Verification to monitor assumptions in the context of temporal task planning, both offline for post-hoc analysis and online to enable remediation actions.

We have been able to describe the assumptions with HLOLA, a very expressive language for Stream Runtime Verification, using multi-level specifications to predict the behavior of the vehicle using complex estimators. We have automatically synthesized the monitors that collect and process sophisticated data, generating rich verdicts while providing strong correctness and resource consumption guarantees.

We are currently working on a deeper interplay of monitoring and planning in an architecture that allows modular and flexible definitions of widely diverse UAV missions, reusing monitors across different tasks, and leveraging on the formal semantics and guarantees from the field of Stream Runtime Verification to further improve the reliability of robots running temporal plans.

References

1. SITL/ardupilot simulator (software in the loop). http://ardupilot.org/. Accessed 20 Oct 2021
2. Atoev, S., Kwon, K., Lee, S., Moon, K.: Data analysis of the mavlink communication protocol. In: ICISCT 2017, pp. 1–3, November 2017
3. Ceresa, M., Gorostiaga, F., Sánchez, C.: Declarative stream runtime verification (hLola). In: Oliveira, B.C.S. (ed.) APLAS 2020. LNCS, vol. 12470, pp. 25–43. Springer, Cham (2020). https://doi.org/10.1007/978-3-030-64437-6_2
4. D'Angelo, B., et al.: LOLA: runtime monitoring of synchronous systems. In: Proceedings of the 12th International Symposium of Temporal Representation and Reasoning (TIME'05), pp. 166–174. IEEE CS Press (2005)
5. Gorostiaga, F., Sánchez, C.: HLola: a very functional tool for extensible stream runtime verification. In: TACAS 2021. LNCS, vol. 12652, pp. 349–356. Springer, Cham (2021). https://doi.org/10.1007/978-3-030-72013-1_18
6. Gorostiaga, F., Sánchez, C.: Nested monitors: monitors as expressions to build monitors. In: Feng, L., Fisman, D. (eds.) RV 2021. LNCS, vol. 12974, pp. 164–183. Springer, Cham (2021). https://doi.org/10.1007/978-3-030-88494-9_9

7. Kress-Gazit, H., Fainekos, G., Pappas, G.: Translating structured english to robot controllers. Advanced Robotics **22**, 1343–1359 (2008)

8. Menghi, C., Tsigkanos, C., Pelliccione, P., Ghezzi, C., Berger, T.: Specification patterns for robotic missions. IEEE Trans. Softw. Eng., 1 (2019)

9. d. S. Barros, J., Oliveira, T., Nigam, V., Brito, A.V.: A framework for the analysis of uav strategies using co-simulation. In: SBESC 2016, pp. 9–15, November 2016

10. Zudaire, S.A., Garrett, M., Uchitel, S.: Iterator-based temporal logic task planning. In: 2020 IEEE International Conference on Robotics and Automation (ICRA), pp. 11472–11478 (2020). https://doi.org/10.1109/ICRA40945.2020.9197274

11. Zudaire, S., Gorostiaga, F., Sánchez, C., Schneider, G., Uchitel, S.: Assumption monitoring using runtime verification for UAV temporal task plan executions. In: Proceedings of IEEE International Conference on Robotics and Automation (ICRA 2021). IEEE (2021)

Verification and Validation
of Concurrent and Distributed
Heterogeneous Systems

Verification and Validation of Concurrent and Distributed Heterogeneous Systems (Track Summary)

Marieke Huisman[1] and Cristina Seceleanu[2(✉)]

[1] University of Twente, Enschede, The Netherlands
m.huisman@utwente.nl
[2] Mälardalen University, Västerås, Sweden
cristina.seceleanu@mdu.se

Abstract. A major trend in computing during the last decade has been the ubiquity of distributed, heterogeneous systems that make use of multi-languages for implementation, or services delivered by IoT devices. Since all distributed systems must, by their very nature, make use of some form of concurrent programming, the latter becomes even more challenging than traditionally, with the increase of hardware concurrency and sources of heterogeneity. In this context, developing reliable, safe and secure distributed systems, without sacrificing performance, is notoriously difficult. This requires novel models, logical notations, and verification techniques, or extensions, improvements and combinations of existing ones, to capture the behavior of such systems and provide guarantees that they meet various specific requirements. The track on Verification and Validation of Concurrent and Distributed Heterogeneous Systems aims to present and discuss advances of formal methods applicable to the assurance of different kinds of heterogeneous systems, as well as new insights provided by validating the methods on real-world case studies.

1 Motivation and Goals

Demands for computing power and better performance are only going to increase. The cloud, mobile and IoT systems are all playing a role in creating big expectations for enterprises, placing tremendous strain on developers that must manage a number of important—often conflicting—system properties, including reliability, predictability, security and others, as well as complex interactions among system components. This justifies the proliferation of frameworks and tools intended to make the design and implementation of such heterogeneous and distributed systems easier (e.g., Hadoop: https://hadoop.apache.org/docs/current/, OpenCL: https://www.khronos.org/opencl/). Nevertheless, ensuring that the latter are safe, and that their behavior remains predictable and correct, lies on the "shoulders" of formal methods, via different tools and techniques to reason about (heterogeneous) distributed systems [4,8,12,17] and concurrent software [2,5,9,11,14,16].

T. Margaria and B. Steffen (Eds.): ISoLA 2022, LNCS 13701, pp. 417–421, 2022.
https://doi.org/10.1007/978-3-031-19849-6_24

Despite many existing results, questions such as: How can formal verification techniques for concurrent systems be extended to ensure properties over distributed objects?, How can one analyze multi-lingual distributed programs efficiently?, How can one ensure properties of complex industrial concurrent software?, or How can we capture, control and verify smart applications formally? are still awaiting answers.

The **Verification and Validation of Concurrent and Distributed Heterogeneous Systems** (VVCDHS) track focuses on tackling the above questions, by presenting invited papers that propose models, techniques, and tools for the rigorous description and analysis of concurrent and distributed systems characterized by heterogeneity stemming from various sources, such as multi-language programming, the need for adaptivity, the use of smart components, or IoT applications, etc. The included contributions give a good overview of the current state-of-the-art in the verification of heterogeneous concurrent and distributed systems, and propose solutions to difficult problems related to logics for distributed objects that evolve over time, modeling and verification of systems that need to perform adaptations, modular verification of concurrent algorithms, applying academic formal verification tools to industrial systems, runtime verification of IoT device security of communication, and formal modeling of systems-of-systems control. The track closes with a discussion on ways in which we can leverage verification and validation techniques for concurrency and distribution to tackle modern topics of heterogeneous and smart systems assurance, including the scalability and industrial applicability of the formal approaches.

Finally, we would like to express our deep gratitude to the ISoLA organizers, in particular Prof. Tiziana Margaria and Prof. Bernhard Steffen, for their tenacious work to provide the infrastructure for our and other tracks, which allows vivid and creative discussions among researchers and practitioners in different communities, leading to new insights and perspectives of the techniques and foundations of formal methods and their application.

2   Overview of Contributions

In *An Efficient VCGen-based Modular Verification of Relational Properties* [1], the authors Lionel Blatter, Nikolai Kosmatov, Virgile Prevosto, and Pascale Le Gall propose a verification conditions generation (VCG) technique to prove relational properties over a language with support for procedure calls and aliasing. The technique enables a modular approach to verification, allowing to use relational properties as hypothesis in proving other relational properties. The language is formalized in COQ, where the authors prove the main result, that is, the verification conditions generated by the proposed VCG can be used to prove relational properties, modularly.

In *On Binding in the Spatial Logic for Closure Spaces* [3], the authors Laura Bussi, Vincenzo Ciancia, Fabio Gadducci, Diego Latella, and Mieke Massink present a logic to express properties over objects distributed over space, and evolving over time. The authors propose two different extensions of the spatial logic for closure spaces, and its spatio-temporal variant, with spatial quantification operators useful for reasoning about the existence of particular spatial objects in a space, and the dynamic evolution of such spatial objects in time and space. The expressiveness of the operators is illustrated via several representative examples, out of which the leader election one shows that such logics could even be useful to specify the correctness of distributed algorithms.

In *An IoT Digital Twin for Cyber-Security Defence based on Runtime Verification* [6], the authors Jorge David de Hoz Diego, Anastasios Temperekidis, Panagiotis Katsaros, and Charalambos Konstantinou propose a security-decoupling solution for IoT networked devices. The proposed solution deploys a security module to the IoT device, and uses a Digital Twin (DT) to detect potentially compromised packets communicated from either a remote device or a local process. The approach provides information that one can use to mitigate potential cyber-security attacks. The rule-based runtime verification implemented under a security context assumption shows that, by isolating local traffic, the DT monitor can detect and track threats occurring by unauthorized communication attempts.

In *A thread-safe Term Library* [7], the authors Jan Friso Groote, Maurice Laveaux, and P.H.M. van Spaendonck present the design, implementation and model checking of a new thread-safe Term library with several novel aspects including the new busy-forbidden protocol, that is, a protocol with functionality similar to the readers-writers lock, but with improvements aiming to make it faster. The authors prove by model checking the key properties of the library, which guarantee thread safety and liveness.

In *ST4MP: A Blueprint of Multiparty Session Typing for Multilingual Programming* [10], the authors Sung-Shik Jongmans and José Proença provide a multiparty session types (MPST) method to simplify the construction and analysis of distributed systems implemented in multiple programming languages. In order to verify processes in such a heterogeneous setting, the authors generate API in multiple languages, by their newly introduced tool called ST4MP "Session Types Fo(u)r Multilingual Programming". The ST4MP approach so far focuses on three languages: Java, Scala and Rust, which are widely used for programming distributed systems.

In *On Deductive Verification of an Industrial Concurrent Software Component with VerCors* [13], the authors Raúl E. Monti, Robert Rubbens, and Marieke Huisman present their experience with verifying memory safety and data race freedom in an industrial case study of a concurrent module of a tunnel control system written in Java. The employed tool is VerCors, a software verification tool that requires annotating the code before carrying out verification. Using VerCors led to discovering two concurrency bugs related to memory access. The findings, as well as the underlying verification paradigm have been presented to the industrial partner, and feedback has been collected. Based on this feedback, the authors gain insight that could guide further improvement of VerCors and the entire verification process also.

In *Exploring a Parallel SCC Algorithm Using TLA+ and the TLC Model Checker* [18], the author Jaco van de Pol describes a case study on using the TLA+ model checker to increase the understanding of Bloemen's parallel SCC decomposition concurrent algorithm. The paper explains how the algorithm and correctness properties can be specified in TLA+ (both a naive version and an improved version), and reports on findings. For ten concrete instances (two workers on ten small graphs), the improved version of the specification satisfies the correctness properties. The paper also explains that various further modifications of the improved specification violate the correctness properties, sometimes unexpectedly.

In *A Formal Model of Metacontrol in Maude* [15], authors Juliane Päßler, Esther Aguado, Gustavo Rezende Silva, Silvia Lizeth Tapia Tarifa, Carlos Hernández Corbato, and Einar Broch Johnsen present an executable formal model of a self-adaptive system based on metacontrol, by formalizing a smart house-heating application in Maude. All the layers of the self-adaptive system of systems have been captured, and the evaluation for different scenarios of environment inputs and system failures has shown an improved performance of the smart house system with respect to its requirements when the Metacontroller performs architectural adaptation, when compared to the situation when the system's behavior is limited to one of the individual controllers.

References

1. Blatter, L., Kosmatov, N., Prevosto, V., Le Gall, P.: An efficient vcgen-based modular verification of relational properties. In: Margaria, T., Steffen, B. (eds.) ISoLA 2022. LNCS, vol. 13701, pp. 498–516. Springer, Cham (2022)
2. Blom, S., Darabi, S., Huisman, M., Oortwijn, W.: The VerCors tool set: verification of parallel and concurrent software. In: Polikarpova, N., Schneider, S. (eds.) IFM 2017. The VerCors Tool Set: Verification of Parallel and Concurrent Software, vol. 10510, pp. 102–110. Springer, Cham (2017). https://doi.org/10.1007/978-3-319-66845-1_7
3. Bussi, L., Ciancia, V., Gadducci, F., Latella, D., Massink, M.: On binding in the spatial logic for closure spaces. In: Margaria, T., Steffen, B. (eds.) ISoLA 2022. LNCS, vol. 13701, pp. 479–497. Springer, Cham (2022)
4. Cai, S., Gallina, B., Nyström, D., Seceleanu, C.: Effective test suite design for detecting concurrency control faults in distributed transaction systems. In: Margaria, T., Steffen, B. (eds.) ISoLA 2018. LNCS, vol. 11246, pp. 355–374. Springer, Cham (2018). https://doi.org/10.1007/978-3-030-03424-5_24
5. da Rocha Pinto, P., Dinsdale-Young, T., Gardner, P.: TaDA: a logic for time and data abstraction. In: Jones, R. (ed.) ECOOP 2014. LNCS, vol. 8586, pp. 207–231. Springer, Heidelberg (2014). https://doi.org/10.1007/978-3-662-44202-9_9
6. de Hoz Diego, J.D., Temperekidis, A., Katsaros, P., Konstantinou, C.: An iot digital twin for cyber-security defence based on runtime verification. In: Margaria, T., Steffen, B. (eds.) ISoLA 2022. LNCS, vol. 13701, pp. 556–574. Springer, Cham (2022)
7. Groote, J.F., Laveaux, M., van Spaendonck, P.H.M.: A thread-safe term library. In: Margaria, T., Steffen, B. (eds.) ISoLA 2022. LNCS, vol. 13701, pp. 422–459. Springer, Cham (2022)

8. Hawblitzel, C., et al.: Ironfleet: proving practical distributed systems correct. In: Proceedings of the 25th Symposium on Operating Systems Principles, SOSP 2015, pp. 1–17. ACM (2015)

9. Jacobs, B., Smans, J., Philippaerts, P., Vogels, F., Penninckx, W., Piessens. , F.: VeriFast: a powerful, sound, predictable, fast verifier for C and Java. In: NFM (2011)

10. Jongmans, S.-S., Proença, J.: St4mp: a blueprint of multiparty session typing for multilingual programming. In: Margaria, T., Steffen, B. (eds.) ISoLA 2022. LNCS, vol. 13701, pp. 460–478. Springer, Cham (2022)

11. Jung, R., et al.: Iris: monoids and invariants as an orthogonal basis for concurrent reasoning. In: POPL, pp. 637–650. ACM (2015)

12. Krogh-Jespersen, M., Timany, A., Ohlenbusch, M.E., Gregersen, S.O., Birkedal, L.: Aneris: a mechanised logic for modular reasoning about distributed systems. In: ESOP 2020. LNCS, vol. 12075, pp. 336–365. Springer, Cham (2020). https://doi.org/10.1007/978-3-030-44914-8_13

13. Monti, R.E., Rubbens, R., Huisman, M.: On deductive verification of an industrial concurrent software component with vercors. In: Margaria, T., Steffen, B. (eds.) ISoLA 2022. LNCS, vol. 13701, pp. 517–534. Springer, Cham (2022)

14. Müller, P., Schwerhoff, M., Summers, A.J.: Viper - a verification infrastructure for permission-based reasoning. In: VMCAI (2016)

15. Päßler, J., Aguado, E., Silva, G.R., Tarifa, S.L.T., Hernández Corbato, C., Johnsen, E.B.: A formal model of metacontrol in maude. In: Margaria, T., Steffen, B. (eds.) ISoLA 2022. LNCS, vol. 13701, pp. 575–596. Springer, Cham (2022)

16. Sergey, I., Nanevski, A., Banerjee, A.: Mechanized verification of fine-grained concurrent programs. In: PLDI, pp. 77–87. ACM (2015)

17. Sharma, R., Bauer, M., Aiken, A.: Verification of producer-consumer synchronization in GPU programs. In: Proceedings of PLDI 2015, pp. 88–98. ACM (2015)

18. van de Pol, J.: Exploring a parallel scc algorithm using tla+ and the tlc model checker. In: Margaria, T., Steffen, B. (eds.) ISoLA 2022. LNCS, vol. 13701, pp. 535–555. Springer, Cham (2022)

A Thread-Safe Term Library
(with a New Fast Mutual Exclusion Protocol)

Jan Friso Groote[(✉)] [ID], Maurice Laveaux[ID], and P. H. M. van Spaendonck[ID]

Department of Mathematics and Computer Science,
Eindhoven University of Technology, Eindhoven, The Netherlands
{J.F.Groote,M.Laveaux,P.H.M.v.Spaendonck}@tue.nl

Abstract. Terms are one of the fundamental mathematical concepts in computing. E.g. every expression characterisable by a context free grammar is a term. We developed a *thread-safe* Term Library. The biggest challenge is to implement hyper-efficient multi-reader/single-writer mutual exclusion for which we designed the new *busy-forbidden protocol*. Model checking is used to show both the correctness of the protocol and the Term Library. Benchmarks show this Term Library has little overhead compared to sequential versions and outperforms them already on two processors. Using the new library in an existing state space generation tool, very substantial speed ups can be obtained.

Keywords: Term library · Mutual exclusion · Thread-safe · Model checking

1 Introduction

A term is a common mathematical structure. Many concepts can be represented as terms, such as programs, specifications and formulas. Many operations in computing are term transformations, such as compilation. In computer science a term is a far more commonly used concept than structures such as arrays, lists or matrices. This makes it remarkable that terms are not a standard data structure in common programming languages such as C++ and Java.

To our knowledge the first term library stems from the realm of program transformations. In [2,4–6,17] an ATerm library of so called *annotated terms* has been proposed, which contains terms with meta information. Stripping away all bells and whistles from this ATerm format, a very plain and elegant term data structure remains.

Our terms are defined in the standard way. We start out with a given set of function symbols F where each function symbol $f \in F$ has an arity ar_f. Each constant function symbol, i.e. with arity 0, is a term. Given a function symbol $f \in F$ with $ar_f > 0$, and terms $t_1, \ldots, t_{ar_f}$, the expression $f(t_1, \ldots, t_{ar_f})$ is also a term. These are the only two ways to construct a term.

Supported by projects 612.001.751 (NWO, AVVA) and 00795160 (TTW, MASCOT).

T. Margaria and B. Steffen (Eds.): ISoLA 2022, LNCS 13701, pp. 422–459, 2022.
https://doi.org/10.1007/978-3-031-19849-6_25

As an example, we provide terms where some constants represent variables. We can have function symbols $\{0, 1, x, y, +\}$ and have terms $0 + 1$, $x + 1$ and $x + y$. The 'constants' x and y allow for different operations than the constants 0 and 1, as it is natural to define a substitution operation for the constant x, whereas that would be less natural for the constant 0. In a similar way, terms with binders can be represented. For instance, in the term $\lambda x.t$ the λ is just a binary function symbol and the first subterm is the variable x.

As in the ATerm library, terms are stored in a maximally shared way. Once created, terms remain as stable structures in memory until they are garbage collected. This leads to a smaller memory footprint, because equal terms are only stored once. Comparing terms is also computationally cheap, as two terms are equal iff they occupy the same address in memory. Also note that handing a term over to another thread is also cheap, as only the address of the term needs to be transferred. This avoids serialising and deserialising terms as done in [3]. A disadvantage is that subterms cannot be replaced. If a subterm needs to be changed, the whole surrounding term must be reconstructed.

With a steadily increasing number of computational cores in computers, it is desirable to have a parallel implementation of a term library. As terms have a tree-like structure, one would expect concurrent tree algorithms, as provided by the EXCESS project [30] or the PAM library [28], to be a useful solution. However, these tree libraries concentrate on manipulating the trees themselves, by adding and removing nodes, and rebalancing when required. This would not allow maximal sharing of terms, which have to be static structures in memory.

Early attempts to create a thread-safe term library led to intriguing wait-free algorithms [9,10,16]. The assumption was that thread synchronisation was the root cause of performance issues, and this is avoided when algorithms are wait-free. But this did not turn out to be entirely true. As the operations to create, inspect and destroy terms occur frequently and are computationally very cheap, a thread-safe implementation allows for hardly any overhead. Wait-free algorithms are intricate and their overhead is deadly for performance in this case. The same applies to the introduction of mutex variables surrounding construction, inspection and deletion of terms.

Although the need and advantages of having terms that can be accessed by multiple threads have already been stressed in the original publications, it turns out to be hard to make a thread-safe term library that is competitive with sequential implementations. This is most likely the reason that no thread-safe term libraries exist, except for a non-published Java implementation [20].

In this article we present a thread-safe term library that is competitive with sequential term libraries. We first observe that with some minor adaptations, *i.e.*, essentially introducing a Treiber stack [29] in a hash table, inspection and construction of terms can happen concurrently. Secondly, we note that garbage collection on the one hand, and construction/moving/copying of terms on the other hand must be mutually exclusive, and construction happens far more often than garbage collection.

Therefore, we require a mutual exclusion algorithm with behaviour of a readers-writer lock [26], where construction of terms can happen simultaneously (=readers), and garbage collection (=writer) must be done in isolation. However, standard readers-writer locks are too expensive. We designed the *busy-forbidden protocol* that employs this asymmetric access pattern as well as the cache structure of modern processors. Obtaining access to construct a term only requires access to two bits, virtually always available in the local cache of the current processor. Besides this, we developed thread-safe term protection mechanisms, either using atomic operations for reference counting, or by employing explicit thread-local protection sets.

Experiments show that the new Term Library scales well and for practical tasks it is already beneficial when only two processors are available. The solution with a standard readers-writer lock and especially the Java implementation are substantially slower than our implementation with the busy-forbidden protocol.

The correctness of thread-safe implementations is subtle. Therefore, we use the mCRL2 model checking toolset [13] to design both the busy-forbidden protocol and the Term Library, and prove their correctness properties, before implementation. This turned out to be very effective, as we did not have to struggle with obscure faults due to parallel behaviour in the algorithm. It is intended that the new thread-safe Term Library will form the heart of the new release of the mCRL2 toolset. The currently existing early prototype already achieves speed ups of a factor 12 on 16 processors for a computationally intensive task, namely state space generation, which is more than just promising.

2   The Term Data Structure

In [4,5] a term library has been proposed. A term is a very frequently used concept within computer science. The original motivation for terms as a basic data structure came from research in software transformation [6,17]. The model checking toolset mCRL2 uses terms to represent all internal concepts, such as modal formulas, transition systems and process specifications [13].

2.1   The External Behaviour of the Term Library

Terms are constructed out of *functions symbols*, or for short *functions*, from some given set F. Each function $f \in F$ has a number of arguments ar_f, generally called the *arity* of f. A function symbol with arity 0 is called a *constant*.

Definition 1. *Let F be a set of function symbols. The set of terms T_F over F is inductively defined as follows:*

if $f \in F, f$ has arity ar_f and $t_1, \ldots, t_{ar_f} \in T_F$, then $f(t_1, \ldots, t_{ar_f}) \in T_F$.

Simple numeric expressions are typical examples of terms. The function symbols are $0, 1, 2, 3, +, *$ where $0, 1, 2, 3$ are constants and $+$ and $*$ have arity 2. An example of a term as a tree structure is given in Fig. 1.

The term library in [4,5] allows to annotate terms, hence the name ATerm, but we do not use this feature. This original ATerm proposal also supported special terms representing numbers, strings, lists and even 'blobs' containing arbitrary data. We made our own implementation of a term library where besides terms as defined in Definition 1, there are also facilities for lists and 64-bit machine numbers. As these are in many respects the same as terms constructed out of function symbols, we ignore lists and numbers in this exposition.

Fig. 1. The tree for $3 + 4 * 2$.

From the perspective of a programmer terms are immutable maximally shared tree structures in memory. This means that if two (sub)terms are the same, they are represented by the same address in memory. The term library provides essentially the following limited set of operations on terms:

Create. Given a function symbol f and terms $t_1, \ldots, t_{ar_f}$ construct a term $f(t_1, \ldots, t_{ar_f})$. This operation can fail when there is not enough memory.
Destroy. Indicate that a term t will not be accessed anymore by this thread. Terms that are not accessed by any thread must ultimately be garbage collected.
Copy/move. Move or copy a term. This essentially means move or copy the address of the term.
Argument. Obtain the i-th subterm t_i of a term $f(t_1, \ldots, t_{ar_f})$.
Function. Obtain the function symbol f of a term $f(t_1, \ldots, t_{ar_f})$.
Equality. For terms t and u determine whether t and u are equal. Note that due to maximal sharing this operation only requires constant time.

Due to the immutable nature of terms in memory it is not possible to simply replace a subterm of a term. If a subterm must be changed, the whole surrounding term must be copied. On the other hand terms are very suitable for parallel programming. Threads can safely traverse protected terms in memory as the treads can be sure that these terms will not change.

By storing terms as maximally shared trees, the only non trivial operations on terms are the creation of a new term and the destruction of an existing term. Given a function symbol f and subterms $t_1, \ldots, t_{ar_f}$ it must be determined whether the term $f(t_1, \ldots, t_{ar_f})$ already exists. This is done using a hash table. If the term already exists, this term is returned. If not, a new term node labelled with f pointing to the subterms $t_1, \ldots, t_{ar_f}$ must be made.

The typical usage pattern of terms is that they are visited very often obtaining arguments or function symbols. Creation of a term is also a very frequent operation, where in the majority of cases a term is created that already occurs in the hash table. Only rarely a garbage collect is taking place.

2.2   Behavioural Properties of the Term Library

The Term Library guarantees the following properties, checked using model checking, see Sect. 4.

1. A term and all its subterms remain in existence at exactly the same address, with unchanged function symbol and arguments, as long as it is not destroyed.
2. Two stored terms t_1 and t_2 always have the same non-null address iff they are equal.
3. Any thread that is not busy creating or destroying a term, can always initiate the construction of a new term or the destruction of an owned term.
4. Any thread that started creating a term or destroying a term, will eventually successfully finish this task provided there is enough memory to store one more term than those that are in use. But it is required that other threads behave fairly, in the sense that they will not continually create and destroy terms or stall other threads by busy waiting.

Note that the properties above imply some notion of garbage collection in the sense that if a thread makes and destroys terms, and these are not garbage collected, at some point no new terms can be created due to a lack of memory and in that case property 4 above would be violated.

2.3   The Implementation of the Thread-Safe Term Library

Terms are implemented in the Term Library by storing them in a hash table. Whenever a term with function symbol f and arguments $t_1, \ldots, t_{ar_f}$ is created, the hash table is used to find out whether $f(t_1, \ldots, t_{ar_f})$ already exists. If yes, its current address is returned. If no, a new term $f(t_1, \ldots, t_{ar_f})$, is inserted in the hash table and its address is returned.

Another possible solution would be to use a CTrie [25] instead of the hash table. However CTries main advantage, memory conservation, over performance, makes it less suitable for our Term Library, which must be suitable to deal with huge numbers of term manipulations in short time spans.

Terms in our Term Library can be constructed and accessed in parallel. When a thread created a term, this term and all its subterms are immutable and stored at fixed addresses in memory, and this means that any term can be accessed safely by all threads that have not destroyed the term.

We have two ways to implement garbage collection in the thread-safe Term Library, namely reference counting and the use of protection sets, which ensure that non-destroyed terms remain in memory. Garbage collection is performed by a single thread. Note that mark-and-sweep algorithms exist where creation and destruction can be done simultaneously [10] but these are very complex. As garbage collection is relatively fast, such advanced algorithms are not necessary.

In reference counting, each term has a reference count that is incremented by one whenever a term is created or copied, and decremented by one if a thread drops a reference to the term. Terms that are not in use anymore have a reference count of zero and can be garbage collected. This can easily be performed by visiting all terms, which are stored in traversable structures.

An alternative is to use term protection sets. Whenever a term is stored at some address, this address is stored in a separate protection set, locally maintained by each thread. When the address is not used anymore for a term, it is removed from the set. As every address can only be stored once, a simple hash table suffices to implement the protection set. Garbage collection consists of marking all terms reachable via some protection set, and removing all others.

In the parallel setting changing reference counts or inserting/deleting addresses in protection sets must be sequentially consistent meaning that they cannot be rearranged in the programs. Changing reference counts must be atomic and can lead to cache contention as the reference counts are accessible by all threads. Operations on the protection sets are far more complex than changing a reference count, but they are always local in a thread, and depending on the style of programming need to be executed far less often than changing a reference count. From the benchmarks we derive that protection sets are preferable.

If we only create terms, this can be done in parallel as well. We use a dedicated hash table with a bucket list in the form of a linked list to check whether a term already exists. If the term does not exist, it is added using a compare and swap operation to the bucket list of the appropriate entry of the hash table. If in the mean time another thread creates the same term, the compare and swap fails, informing the thread that it has to inspect the hash table again to find out whether the term came into existence. This is Treiber's stack, which is sufficient since terms are not simultaneously deleted from the bucket lists. Deletion only occurs during garbage collection, and during garbage collection no new terms are allowed to be constructed.

Accessing terms during garbage collection and rehashing is perfectly safe. But it is not allowed to create or copy terms while garbage collection or rehashing is going on. This requires a mutual exclusion protocol where either multiple threads can create and copy terms simultaneously, which we call the *shared* tasks, or a single thread can be involved in garbage collection or rehashing, which is called the *exclusive* task.

This is the same as a readers-writer lock [26] where multiple readers or at most one writer can access a shared resource. Reading is the shared task, and writing is exclusive. As we observed that creating and copying terms is done very frequently compared to garbage collection, shared access must be cheap and exclusive access can be expensive. Most standard readers-writer locks require at least one access to a common mutex variable for shared access which is so costly that parallel implementations based on the readers-writer lock run on multiple processors failed to outperform the sequential implementation. This observation is supported by the benchmarks. We developed a completely new protocol, called the *busy-forbidden* protocol serving our needs, which is described in the next section.

Using the busy-forbidden protocol, a compare and swap to insert terms in bucket lists for the hash table, the implementation of thread-safe Term Library is pretty straightforward but delicate. Table 1 contains the code for creating and destroying terms. In this code enter_shared, leave_shared, enter_exclusive and leave_exclusive are part of the busy-forbidden protocol described in the next section. The function h is a hash function that takes a function symbol f, and subterms $t_1, \ldots, t_n$, and calculates a possibly non-unique hash. The func-

Table 1. Pseudocode description of the thread-safe Term Library.

```
1   create(thread p, symbol f, subterms t₁,...,tₙ)        destroy(thread p, term t)
2       enter_shared(p);                                       unprotect(p);
3       hash := h(f,t₁,...,tₙ);                                 possibly do GC(p)
4       bucket := buckets[hash];
5       t := insert(bucket, f, t₁,...,tₙ);                 GC(thread p)
6       protect(p,t);                                          enter_exclusive(p);
7       leave_shared(p);                                       forall t ∈ hash_table
8       return t;                                                  if not protected(t)
9                                                                      remove t;
10  insert(bucket b, symbol f, subterms t₁,...,tₙ)          leave_exclusive(p);
11      old_head, node := b.top;
12      do
13          if node.head represents f(t₁,...,tₙ)
14              return node.head;
15          node := node.tail;
16      while (node ≠ NULL);
17      t := construct f(t₁,...,tₙ);
18      if not cmpswap(b.top, old_head, Node(t, old_head))
19          destruct t;
20          return insert(b, f, t₁,...,tₙ);
21      return t;
```

tions **protect**, **unprotect** and **protected** refer to the protection mechanisms described earlier, in which $\texttt{protected}(t)$ will return true if and only if the term t is protected by some thread. Besides this, each bucket b in the hash table contains an atomic pointer $b.top$ that allows atomic loads and an atomic compare-and-swap operation **cmpswap**, which returns true if and only if successful. The call $\text{GC}(p)$ stands for doing a garbage collect by thread p.

Using an mCRL2 model of the behaviour of the Term Library, the behavioural properties mentioned in Sect. 2.2 have been model checked. This is described in Sect. 4.

3   The Busy-Forbidden Protocol

The busy-forbidden protocol is of independent interest. This protocol guarantees that at most one thread can be in state *Exclusive* and if a thread is in state *Exclusive*, no thread is in state *Shared*, and vice versa, if there are threads in state *Shared*, then there is no thread in the state *Exclusive*. It behaves in a similar way as a readers-writer lock [26], called a shared mutex in C++.

The busy-forbidden protocol is designed for the situation where shared access is frequent whereas exclusive access is infrequent.

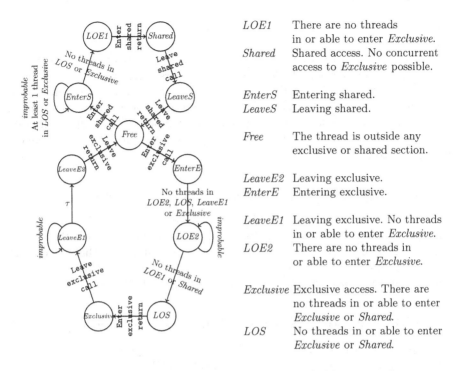

LOE1 There are no threads in or able to enter *Exclusive*.

Shared Shared access. No concurrent access to *Exclusive* possible.

EnterS Entering shared.
LeaveS Leaving shared.

Free The thread is outside any exclusive or shared section.

LeaveE2 Leaving exclusive.
EnterE Entering exclusive.

LeaveE1 Leaving exclusive. No threads in or able to enter *Exclusive*.
LOE2 There are no threads in or able to enter *Exclusive*.

Exclusive Exclusive access. There are no threads in or able to enter *Exclusive* or *Shared*.
LOS No threads in or able to enter *Exclusive* or *Shared*.

Fig. 2. The external behaviour of the busy-forbidden protocol.

3.1 The External Behaviour of the Busy-Forbidden Protocol

We first look at the external behaviour of this protocol. As indicated above, threads can request for shared or exclusive access by calling one of the two functions **enter_shared** and **enter_exclusive**. The functions starting with **leave** are used to indicate that access is no longer required.

We make the external behaviour more precise by modelling it as a state automaton, actually obtained by the specification in mCRL2 used for verification. From the perspective of a single thread, the behaviour is depicted in Fig. 2. The calls are modelled by actions **Enter/Leave shared/exclusive call**. Returning from the function is modelled by actions ending in **return**.

The centre state, marked *Free*, indicates that the thread is not involved in the protocol. It is outside the shared and exclusive sections. Following the arrows in a clockwise fashion, a thread obtains access. In the state *EnterS* the thread requested shared access, and it will get it when there are no threads in the states *LOS* or *Exclusive*. From the figure it is quite easy to see that the protocol indeed satisfies the mutual exclusion constraints mentioned above.

We went to great length to ensure that the behaviour of Fig. 2 for multiple threads is divergence-preserving branching bisimilar to the implementation below [11,12]. This equivalence is equal to branching bisimulation, but it does not remove τ-loops, *i.e.*, loops of internal actions. It preserves not only safety but also liveness properties, and allows us to use this specification to verify the Term Library.

The loop at *EnterS* occurs typically when another thread is in state *Exclusive* for a lengthy period. The loop at *LOE2* occurs when another thread is in *Shared* and refuses to leave. The loop in *LeaveE1* is required to obtain a concise equivalent external behaviour. When the busy protocol is used as intended, *i.e.*, threads only use common accesses for a short time, and the implementation uses the right internal scheduling, these loops rarely occur. They are therefore marked *improbable*.

3.2   The Implementation of the Busy-Forbidden Protocol

The code for entering and leaving the exclusive sections is described in Table 2. The busy-forbidden protocol is implemented by assigning to each thread two atomic flags, called *busy* and *forbidden*. The flag *busy* indicates that the current thread is in its shared section and can only be written to by this thread. The flag *forbidden* indicates that some thread is having exclusive access.

Table 2. Pseudocode description of the busy-forbidden protocol.

1	**enter_shared**(*thread p*)	1	**enter_exclusive**(*thread p*)
2	*p.busy* := *true*;	2	*mutex.lock*();
3	**while** *p.forbidden*	3	**while exists** *thread q* **with**
4	*p.busy* := *false*;	4	¬*q.forbidden*
5	**if** *mutex.timed_lock*()	5	**select** *thread r*
6	*mutex.unlock*();	6	*r.forbidden* := *true*;
7	*p.busy* := *true*;	7	**if** *r.busy* **or sometimes**
8		8	*r.forbidden* := *false*;
1	**leave_shared**(*thread p*)	1	**leave_exclusive**(*thread p*)
2	*p.busy* := *false*;	2	**while exists** *thread q* **with**
3		3	*q.forbidden*
4		4	**select** *thread r*
5		5	**usually do**
6		6	*r.forbidden* := *false*;
7		7	**sometimes do**
8		8	*r.forbidden* := *true*
9		9	*mutex.unlock*();

Besides the flags there is one generic mutual exclusion variable, called *mutex*. The variable *mutex* can not only be locked and unlocked, but also provides a timed lock operation *timed_lock*(). It tries to lock the mutex, and if that fails after a certain time, it returns false without locking it. The timed lock is only important for performance, and can be replaced by a wait instruction or even be omitted altogether.

When entering the shared section, a thread generally only accesses its own *busy* and *forbidden* flags as *forbidden* is almost always false. These flags are only rarely accessed by other threads and therefore virtually always available in the local cache of the processor executing the thread. In the rare case when the *forbidden* flag is set, this thread backs off using *mutex* to try again later. In principle the while-loop can be iterated indefinitely, giving rise to the internal loop in state *EnterS* in the specification. Leaving the shared section consists of only setting the *busy* flag of the thread to false.

Accessing the exclusive section is far more expensive. By using *mutex*, mutual access to the exclusive section is obtained. Subsequently, the *forbidden* flag for each thread p is set to true, unless the *busy* flag of thread p is set, as in this case the *forbidden* flag must be set to false again.

There is a non immediately obvious scenario where one thread refuses to leave the shared section, and two other threads p_2 and p_3 want to access the shared and exclusive section, respectively. Thread p_3 cannot obtain exclusive access, but hence should not indefinitely block shared access for p_2. Hence, p_3 must set the *forbidden* flag of p_2 to false if *busy* of p_1 is true.

Without the **sometimes** part, which represents an arbitrary heuristic which only rarely holds, the implementation is not divergence-preserving bisimilar to the specification, as reading $r.busy = false$ in line 9, once all other forbidden flags have been set, leads to a state without an internal loop, which does not occur in the specification. Without the **sometimes** part, a matching specification would become substantially more complex exhibiting exactly when each *forbidden* flag is set, rendering the specification far less abstract and hence making it less useful.

When leaving the exclusive section a thread resets all *forbidden* flags of the other threads. If this is done in a predetermined sequence the divergence-preserving branching bisimilar external behaviour becomes very complex, as this sequence has an influence on the precise sequence other threads can enter the shared section. By resetting and sometimes even setting the *forbidden* flag, a comprehensible provably equal external behaviour is obtained, although it leads to another τ-loop in the specification. Practically, re-resetting the flag is hardly ever needed, certainly not for the Term Library. However, it is interesting to further investigate the optimal use of the timing of *mutex* in `enter_shared`, as well as the optimal rate of occurrence of the **sometimes** instructions for generic uses of the busy-forbidden protocol.

We modelled the specification and implementation of the busy-forbidden protocol in mCRL2 (see Sect. 4) and proved them divergence-preserving branching bisimilar.

3.3   Behavioural Properties of the Busy-Forbidden Protocol

As an extra check we also formulate a number of natural requirements that should hold for this protocol. These requirements have been verified by formulating them as modal properties.

1. There should never be more than one thread present in the exclusive section.
2. There should never be a thread present in the exclusive section while one or more threads are present in the shared section.

3. When a thread requests to enter the shared section, it will be granted access within a bounded number of steps, unless there is another thread in the exclusive section.
4. When a thread requests to enter the exclusive section, it will be granted access within a bounded number of steps, unless there is another thread in the shared or in the exclusive section.
5. When a thread requests to leave the exclusive/shared section, it will leave it within a bounded number of steps.
6. A thread not in the exclusive or shared section can instantly start to enter the exclusive or shared section.

For properties 3, 4, and 5 granting access and leaving can be indefinitely postponed if other threads are entering and leaving exclusive and shared sections, or when other threads are in the while loops, continuously writing forbidden and busy flags. This means that the algorithm relies on fair scheduling of threads.

3.4   Existing Readers-Writer Locks

Common readers-writer locks, such as `std::shared_mutex` in C++17 in MSVC, use a mutual exclusion variable when entering and leaving the shared/reader section. This leads to poor scalability and is one of the reasons why the usage of readers-writer locks is often discouraged [7].

The readers-writer lock by Mellor-Crumney and Scott [23] reduces resource contention by using a counter to keep track of the amount of current readers and introducing a queue system in which threads only have to notify the thread next in line when they leave the lock. This lock is further improved by Krieger et al. [19] by reducing the amount of shared variables to a single pointer and using a double-linked list instead of a queue such that reader threads can leave the lock without having to wait for neighbouring readers to also be done reading. However, the single shared pointer needs to be updated using a costly compare-and-swap operation every time a thread enters the lock, which becomes a bottleneck when multiple threads try to enter at the same time.

Lev et al. [21] provide several readers-writer lock algorithms aimed at improving scalability by significantly reducing resource contention through the use of a tree-like data structure called C-SNZI. Lev et al. show that their algorithms outperform other readers-writer locks when the majority of accesses, $i.e.$, $\geq 80\%$, are read accesses. Concurrent read-accesses however still have resource contention with a 100% read workload, whereas the busy-forbidden protocol has none. Thus, this implies that the busy-forbidden protocol outperforms the C-SNZI based algorithms for our use case.

3.5   Performance of the Busy-Forbidden Protocol

We have implemented the busy-forbidden protocol in C++ and assess its scalability compared to that of the `std::shared_mutex` by having threads repeatedly enter and leave the shared/reader section or the exclusive/writer section. Each thread uses a random number generator to decide on which section to enter and then leave, with a preset probability of 99.99% of a thread deciding to enter and leave the shared/reader section. This probability was chosen as it corresponds to that of a typical use case such as state space generation.

Figure 3 shows the wall clock time of #*threads* threads entering and then leaving a random section 10^9 times per thread. The values displayed are the averages of 5 different runs. The measurements were taken on an Intel i7-7700HQ processor and the C++ code was compiled using the MSVC19 compiler with the -O2 flag enabled. The wall clock time of std::shared_mutex for more than 4 threads is omitted from the graph as it is too large to nicely display.

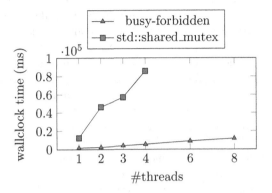

Fig. 3. Readers-writer lock benchmarks.

We observe in Fig. 3 that the busy-forbidden protocol performs significantly better than the std::shared_mutex and costs only a minimal amount of overhead. This can also be seen in Fig. 5 (a), discussed in Sect. 5, in which the busy-forbidden protocol and std::shared_mutex are used in combination with our implementation of the parallel Term Library.

4 Modelling and Verifying the Algorithms

As parallel algorithms are hard to get correct, we made models of the busy-forbidden protocol, of both specification and implementation, and the thread-safe Term Library in the process modelling language mCRL2 and verified the properties by formulating them in the modal mu-calculus [13]. The specification model is a direct reflection of the external behaviour shown in Fig. 2. The resulting implementation models are a direct reflection of the pseudocode in Table 1 and 2. The formulas are a one to one translation of the requirements listed in this article. For this reason, and for the reason of space, the models and formulas, are not included in this article[1].

Due to the nature of model checking, we only verify the models for finite instances. We repeatedly found that when protocols or distributed systems are erroneous, the problems already reveal themselves in small instances [14]. Used in this way, model checking is so efficient that it can effectively be used within the workflow of constructing software. The busy-forbidden protocol was modelled and proven, before implementation commenced, and we did not run into any problem with it during implementation.

---

[1] All models and formulas can be found in Appendices B and C, respectively.

A general equivalence proof has since been given for the specification and implementation of the busy-forbidden protocol [27], using an extension of the Cones and Foci method [8, 15].

The correctness of the protocol and library have not been proven in general for any number of threads and terms. Unfortunately, we do not know of any effective method to prove modal formulas on models with a complexity such as ours, either automatically or manually, for any number of threads and terms, and consider this an important direction of research.

The model of the busy-forbidden protocol does not include the *mutex.timed_-lock()* statement as it is only important for performance. The **sometimes** keywords are modelled as non-deterministic choices. The specification and implementation are proven to be divergence preserving branching bisimulation equivalent, for up to 7 concurrent threads.

We transformed the six requirements discussed in Sect. 3.3 into modal logic formulas, and verified them both on the specification and the implementation, although the latter was not really necessary due to their equivalency. The equivalence and properties were verified, both on the specification as well as on the implementation model, for up to 7 threads. We uncovered a number of issues and obtained various insights while doing the verification for 2 and 3 threads. The verification with more threads, although increasingly time consuming, did not lead to any additional insight.

The model is primarily concerned with the thread-safe creation and garbage collection of terms, and therefore the typical term structure, where terms contain subterms, is also not part of the model, and as such only uses terms with arity 0. We use the equivalent specification model of the busy-forbidden protocol instead of its implementation model, as it is significantly smaller. Furthermore, the model of the Term Library does not include buckets or a hashing function. Instead the hash table is modelled as a simple associative array, with atomic *contains* and *insert* operations.

The four properties discussed in Sect. 2.2 are also translated into modal logic and verified for finite instances. We have verified these properties for up to 3 threads, using 3 different terms and 4 possible addresses, giving us reasonable certainty that the thread-safe Term Library works as intended. We were unable to verify our properties on larger state spaces as they became too big to verify automatically. For example the state space of the aforementioned setup with 4 threads instead of 3 has 129 billion states.

5 Performance Evaluation

We have implemented a sequential and a thread-safe version of the Term Library. Both of these implementations are almost identical except for the synchronisation primitives added to the thread-safe version where necessary, including the busy-forbidden protocol. Furthermore, we have implemented both reference counting and address protection sets as garbage collection strategies in both implementations for comparison. We compare these with the sequential ATerm library as used in the mCRL2 toolset [13] and with a thread-safe Java implementation [20] of the Term Library used in tools such as Spoofax [18], which was the only other thread-safe term library that we could find. All reported measurements are the average of five runs with an AMD EPYC 7452 32-Core processor, unless stated otherwise.

The results are listed in the plots in Figs. 4 and 5. In these plots the y-axis indicates the wall clock time in seconds and the x-axis the number of threads (#threads). The triangles are the thread-safe reference count implementation and the squares the thread-safe set protection implementation. For the sequential versions we have circles for the reference count version, diamonds for the protection set version and plusses for the original implementation. The results for the sequential implementations are extended horizontally for easier comparison. Finally, the dashed line indicates the thread-safe Java implementation and the dotted line is our thread-safe implementation where the busy-forbidden protocol has been replaced by a std::shared_mutex. This last implementation uses protection sets.

In Fig. 4 we report three experiments, one per row, designed to obtain insight in how the new thread-safe library performs for specific tasks. In the left column all threads access the same shared term, whereas in the right column each thread operates on its own term, but these distinct terms are stored in common data structures and accessed via the hash table common for all threads.

In Fig. 4 (a) we measure how expensive it is to create a term in parallel. The threads create a term $t_{400\,000}$ defined as follows. The term t_0 is equal to a constant c and t_i is $f(t_{i-1}, t_{i-1})$ for a function symbol f of arity two, which is the most common arity used in practice. Note that due to sharing, this term consists of $400\,001$ term nodes. In (b) each thread creates the term $t_{400\,000/\#threads}$ instead. With each term starting with a unique constant per thread, creating a total of $400\,000 + \#threads$ term nodes.

In Figs. 4 (c) and (d) we measure the time it takes to create $1000/\#threads$ instances of the terms used in respectively (a) and (b). This measures the time to create terms that are already present in the term library, and this essentially boils down to a hash table lookup. In diagram (d) the Java results are left out as Java consistently requires more than 100 s. In the lower diagram, i.e.(e), we measure the time to perform $1000/\#threads$ breadth-first traversals on a term t_{20}.

The traversals do not employ the shared structure, hence $2^{21} - 1$ terms are visited per traversal. We observe that for this benchmark there is no difference in timings between traversing the term t_{20} and traversing a unique term per thread.

We conclude that our term library completely outperforms the Java implementation. For creating terms, the std::shared_mutex is slower. For traversing terms no locking is required, and therefore, no difference is observed. The dotted line is hidden under the line with the boxes[2]. Except for creating new terms, the term library clearly benefits from the extra processors, outperforming the

---

[2] All benchmark results are listed in Appendix C.

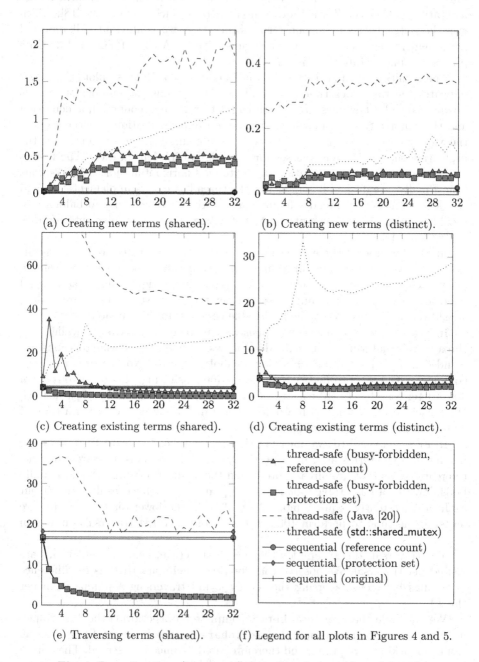

(a) Creating new terms (shared).

(b) Creating new terms (distinct).

(c) Creating existing terms (shared).

(d) Creating existing terms (distinct).

(e) Traversing terms (shared).

(f) Legend for all plots in Figures 4 and 5.

Fig. 4. Execution time (in seconds) plotted against number of threads.

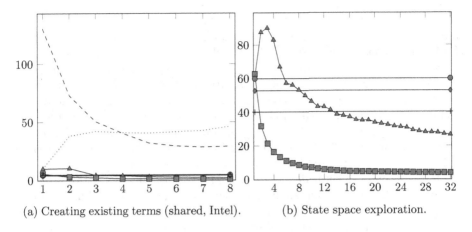

(a) Creating existing terms (shared, Intel).   (b) State space exploration.

Fig. 5. Additional experiments comparing execution times versus threads.

sequential libraries with two processors using protection sets. When creating new terms, scaling goes reasonably well when beyond 12 processors. We observe in Fig. 4 (c) that the reference counting implementation for a few threads is unexpectedly inefficient. In order to understand this, we retried the experiments on an Intel i7-7700HQ processor, reported in Fig. 5 (a). Here, none of the anomalies occur, and notably, Java even outperforms the `std::shared_mutex` implementation with more than four threads. This is in line with our many other experiments that compiler and processor have a large influence on such benchmarks.

The dedicated benchmarks are promising, but in order to get insight in the behaviour of the Term Library in practical situations, we incorporated the Term Library in the mCRL2 toolset and used it to generate the state space of the 1394 firewire protocol [22]. Essentially each thread picks an unexplored state from a common state buffer, and using term rewriting, generates all states reachable from this state, putting them back in the buffer. With protection sets, two threads are already sufficient to outperform all sequential implementations, and scaling is very good, where with 16 threads, the state space is generated more than 12 times faster. Reference counting is clearly a less viable option, which is most likely due to the fact that often the same terms, such as *true* and *false*, are accessed when calculating next states, leading to atomically changing the same reference count often. Note that in this prototype, nothing has been done yet to optimise thread access to the common state buffer, being simply protected by a mutex.

A   The mCRL2 Language and Modal Formulas

The models are written in mCRL2. This is a modelling language based on CCS (Calculus of Communicating Processes) [24] and ACP (Algebra of Communicating Processes) [1]. It is based on atomic actions. Every occurrence of an atomic action causes a state change. Typically, calling a function, or returning from a function, setting or reading a global variable are modelled by atomic actions. Each action consists of a label and a possible set of data parameters, *e.g.*, the *lock*(p) action has p as a data parameter. The tau or hidden action τ has a special status, as it is an action of which the occurrence cannot be observed directly.

Actions can be sequentially composed using the dot ('·') operator. Alternative composition, where nondeterministically one of the options can be chosen, is denoted using a plus ('+'). The $\sum_{e:S}$ operator denotes the application of the ('+') operator over all elements of some set S. The if-then-else is written as $c{\rightarrow}p{\diamond}q$ where p is executed if c is true, otherwise the process q takes place.

Parallel composition is denoted by $\|$ and allows the actions of two processes to both interleave and occur simultaneously. Using the **comm** and **allow** operators, we can enforce that only specific actions can and must occur simultaneously. For example, **comm**($\{a, b\}{\rightarrow}c$), **allow**($\{c, d, e\}, (d \cdot a)\|(b \cdot e))$) enforces that the actions d and e can not occur simultaneously, while a and b must occur simultaneously with any other action, signified with c. As a result, $d \cdot c \cdot e$ is the only possible sequence of actions that can occur.

Recursive behaviour is denoted using equations, typically of the form $X = p$, *e.g.*, $X = a{\cdot}X$ is the process that can perform an infinite number of a's. Similar to actions, the process variables X can contain data parameters. A counter can thus be described as $C(n{:}\mathbb{N}) = up{\cdot}X(n{+}1)$. An important type of data parameter that we use is a function. For example, the process variable $Y(m : \mathbb{N} \rightarrow \mathbb{B})$ uses a mapping m from natural numbers to booleans. The function update $m[n \mapsto b]$ specifies that $m[n \mapsto b](k)$ equals b if $k = n$, and otherwise, it equals $m(k)$.

The safety and liveness properties that we verify, are written in the modal mu-calculus. These consist of conjunctions ($\wedge$), disjunctions ($\vee$), implications ($\rightarrow$), negations ($\neg$), quantification ($\exists, \forall$) and *true* and *false*, each with their usual meaning. Besides this there is a modality $\langle a\rangle\phi$ that is valid if we can take an action a after which ϕ holds. Similarly, the modality $[a]\phi$ holds iff after every possible a action ϕ holds. The action a inside these modalities can also consist of possibly multiple actions. This can be done through sequential composition ($\cdot$), choice ($\cup$), intersection ($\cap$) and complement ($\overline{a}$). For example, the formula $\langle\overline{a} \cup \overline{b}\rangle true$ only holds if we can do some action that is neither a or b. The expression *true* in a modality represents the set of all actions. Using Kleene's star on a set of actions, all sequences over the action in this set are expressed. An often occurring pattern is $[true^*]\phi$ expressing that ϕ must hold in all states reachable via a sequence of actions.

We can also write recursive formulas using the minimal fixed point operator $\mu X.\phi$ and the maximal fixed point operator $\nu X.\phi$. For example, the formula $\nu X.\langle a\rangle X$ expresses that we must be able to perform action a after which the same formula still holds. Thus this formula only holds if we can perform an infinite amount of a actions. The difference between a minimal and a maximal fixed point is that iteration through the fixed point variable must be bounded in a minimal fixed point.

A fixed point construction used in several properties is

$$\nu X.\mu Y.([\overline{succes \cup interrupt}]Y \wedge [interrupt]X \wedge \langle true^*.succes \rangle true)$$

This says that an action *succes* will always occur within a finite amount of steps, unless an action *interrupt* continuously occurs. But even in that case *succes* must remain possible. This construction is useful for properties in which we state that something must eventually happen given fair scheduling.

The fixed point operators also allow us to pass on parameters in the same way we can do for process variables. This allows us, for example, to keep track of the number of times that a given action has occurred. We discuss one such fixed point operator in Appendix B.

B   mCRL2 Specifications for the Busy-Forbidden Protocol

In this section we give the formal mCRL2 specifications of the implementation and the external behaviour, *i.e.*, the specification, of the busy-forbidden protocol that are used to perform the model and equivalence checking. The process specification given in Table 3 exactly matches the external behaviour shown in Fig. 2. We define P to be the (finite) set of threads and we define S to be a data set representing the set of states:

$$S = \{ Free,\ EnterS,\ LOE1,\ Shared,\ LeaveS,$$
$$EnterE,\ LOE2,\ LOS,\ Exclusive,\ LeaveE1,\ LeaveE2 \}$$

The mapping s maps each thread to their current state. Initially, $s(p) = Free$ for all $p \in P$. The conditions for performing transitions are the same as the conditions in the diagram of the external behaviour.

Observe that we use a typewriter font (for example `enter_shared_call`) to indicate visible actions and an italics font (for example *store$_p$*) to indicate internal actions that will be hidden for divergence-preserving branching bisimulation reductions.

The mCRL2 specification of the implementation is separated per function. Entering the shared section is specified in Table 4 and leaving it in Table 5. Entering the exclusive section is specified in Table 6 and leaving it in Table 7.

Note that we use actions to model the assignments to variables. For example *store$_p$*(*Busy(p), true, p*) corresponds to the assignment of *true* to *p.busy* in the implementation pseudocode. The process algebra has no global variables and we use an additional process and actions to read from and write to these variables. For the atomic flags we introduce a struct F that is defined below to declare a busy and a forbidden flag per thread.

$$\texttt{sort}\ F = \texttt{struct}\ Busy(P)\ |\ Forbidden(P)$$

Table 3. Specification of the busy-forbidden protocol corresponding to Fig. 2.

$$
\begin{aligned}
BF(s : P \to S) = \ & \textstyle\sum_{p:P} \cdot (\\
& (s(p) \approx \mathit{Free}) \\
& \to \texttt{enter\_shared\_call}(p).BF(s[p \mapsto \mathit{EnterS}]) \\
+ \ & (s(p) \approx \mathit{EnterS}) \\
& \to ((\neg \exists_{p':P}. \ s(p') \in \{LOS, \mathit{Exclusive}\}) \to \tau.BF(s[p \mapsto LOE1]) \\
& \diamond \ \mathit{improbable}.BF(s)) \\
+ \ & (s(p) \approx LOE1) \\
& \to \texttt{enter\_shared\_return}(p).BF(s[p \mapsto \mathit{Shared}]) \\
+ \ & (s(p) \approx \mathit{Shared}) \\
& \to \texttt{leave\_shared\_call}(p).BF(s[p \mapsto \mathit{LeaveS}]) \\
+ \ & (s(p) \approx \mathit{LeaveS}) \\
& \to \texttt{leave\_shared\_return}(p).BF(s[p \mapsto \mathit{Free}]) \\
+ \ & (s(p) \approx \mathit{Free}) \\
& \to \texttt{enter\_exclusive\_call}(p).BF(s[p \mapsto \mathit{EnterE}]) \\
+ \ & (s(p) \approx \mathit{EnterE} \wedge \neg \exists_{p':P}. \ s(p') \in \{LOE2, LOS, \mathit{Exclusive}\}) \\
& \to \tau.BF(s[p \mapsto LOE2]) \\
+ \ & (s(p) \approx LOE2) \\
& \to \mathit{improbable}.BF(s) \\
+ \ & (s(p) \approx LOE2 \wedge \neg \exists_{p':P}. \ s(p') \in \{LOE1, \mathit{Shared}\}) \\
& \to \tau.BF(s[p \mapsto LOS]) \\
+ \ & (s(p) \approx LOS) \\
& \to \texttt{enter\_exclusive\_return}(p).BF(s[p \mapsto \mathit{Exclusive}]) \\
+ \ & (s(p) \approx \mathit{Exclusive}) \\
& \to \texttt{leave\_exclusive\_call}(p).BF(s[p \mapsto \mathit{LeaveE1}]) \\
+ \ & (s(p) \approx \mathit{LeaveE1}) \\
& \to \mathit{improbable}.BF(s) \\
+ \ & (s(p) \approx \mathit{LeaveE1}) \\
& \to \tau.BF(s[p \mapsto \mathit{LeaveE2}]) \\
+ \ & (s(p) \approx \mathit{LeaveE2}) \\
& \to \texttt{leave\_exclusive\_return}(p).BF(s[p \mapsto \mathit{Free}]) \ )
\end{aligned}
$$

Table 8 shows the behaviour of the *Busy* and *Forbidden* flags for every thread and the *mutex* variable. We model the 'while' construction in the pseudocode by recursion and have added the *improbable* action to ensure equivalence modulo divergence-preserving branching bisimulation. When entering the exclusive section, we use a set *forbidden* (and for leaving *allowed*) to keep track of the threads whose forbidden flag have already been set to *true* (*false* when leaving).

Table 9 shows the specification for the behaviour of a thread. Each thread repeatedly chooses (non-deterministically) to enter and leave either the shared or exclusive section. Finally, Table 10 contains the complete mCRL2 specification of the various processes in a parallel composition and the necessary communication to deal with the atomic flags and mutex.

As the next step, we transformed the six requirements discussed in Sect. 3.3 into modal logic formulas, and verified them on the specification. Note that these properties are preserved by divergence-preserving branching bisimulation, so verifying the implementation is not necessary. We discuss property 2 in detail as an illustration of what such formulas look like. The informal description of the property reads:

2. There should never be a thread present in the exclusive section while one or more threads are present in the shared section.

The corresponding modal formula is shown in Table 12. We use a maximal fixpoint with two data parameters, namely n_{shared} and $n_{exclusive}$, both initially 0. The argument n_{shared} indicates the number of threads present in the shared section, and $n_{exclusive}$ the number in the exclusive section. At lines 2 through 5, we keep track of the amount of threads present in each section, updating the variables after each respective action. At lines 6 through 11, we state that our variables stay the same, after any action that is not one of the four aforementioned actions. Finally, at line 12, we state that threads are only allowed to be either present in exclusive or are present in shared.

The formula for property 1 is shown in Table 11 and states that when a thread enters the exclusive section, no other thread may enter that section till it leaves the section. The formulas for properties 3 and 4 are presented in Tables 13 and 15 and use data parameters to count the number of threads in the exclusive section or in any section respectively. Note that these are two subformulas with identical structure for shared and exclusive sections respectively. Finally, properties 4 and 6 presented in Tables 14 and 16 use boolean parameters to keep track of whether any thread is in the shared or exclusive sections, respectively. This is more efficient than keeping track of the exact amount of threads.

The properties were verified for up to 7 threads. The specification model has about three million states and the implementation model about 11 billion states.

Table 4. mCRL2 specification for the implementation of `enter_shared`.

$EnterShared(p : P) =$
    `enter_shared_call`(p) .
    $TryBothFlags(p)$.
    `enter_shared_return`(p)

$TryBothFlags(p : P) =$
    $store_p(Busy(p), true, p).($
        $load_p(Forbidden(p), \ true, \ p)$.
        $store_p(Busy(p), false, p).improbable. TryBothFlags(p)$
    $+ \ load_p(Forbidden(p), false, p) \ )$

Table 5. mCRL2 specification for the implementation of `leave_shared`.

$LeaveShared(p : P) =$
    `leave_shared_call`(p) .
    $store_p(Busy(p), false, p)$.
    `leave_shared_return`(p)

Table 6. mCRL2 specification for the `enter_exclusive` function in Table 2.

$EnterExclusive(p : P) =$
    `enter_exclusive_call`(p)
    $lock_p(p)$.
    $SetAllForbiddenFlags(p, \ \emptyset)$.
    `enter_exclusive_return`(p)

$SetAllForbiddenFlags(p : P, \ forbidden : Set(P)) =$
    $(\forall_{p':P}.p \in forbidden)$
    $\rightarrow internal$
    $\diamond \ \sum_{p':P} .store_p(Forbidden(p'), true, p).($
        $load_p(Busy(p'), false, p)$.
        $SetAllForbiddenFlags(p, \ forbidden \cup \{p'\})$
    $+ \ load_p(Busy(p'), true, p)$.
        $store_p(Forbidden(p'), false, p).improbable$.
        $SetAllForbiddenFlags(p, \ forbidden \setminus \{p'\})$
    $+ \ store_p(Forbidden(p'), false, p).improbable$.
        $SetAllForbiddenFlags(p, \ forbidden \setminus \{p'\}) \ )$

Table 7. mCRL2 specification for the `leave_exclusive` function in Table 2.

$LeaveExclusive(p : P) =$
  `leave_exclusive_call`(p) .
  $AllowAllThreads(p, \emptyset)$.
  $unlock_p(p)$.
  `leave_exclusive_return`(p)

$AllowAllThreads(p : P, \ allowed : Set(P)) =$
  $(\forall_{q:P}.q \in allowed)$
  $\rightarrow internal$
  $\diamond\ \sum_{p':P} \cdot ($
   $store_p(Forbidden(p'), false, p)$.
   $AllowAllThreads(p, \ allowed \cup \{p'\})$
  $+\ store_p(Forbidden(p'), true, p).improbable$
   $AllowAllThreads(p, \ allowed \setminus \{p'\}\ ))$

Table 8. mCRL2 specifications for the atomic flags and the mutex.

$Flags(flags : F \rightarrow Bool) =$
$\sum_{f:F,p:P} \cdot ($
  $\sum_{b:Bool} \cdot store_f(f, b, p).Flag(flags[f \mapsto b])$
 $+\ load_f(f, flags(f), p).Flag(flags)$
  $)$

$Mutex(locked : Bool) =$
$\sum_{p:P} \cdot ($
  $locked$
  $\rightarrow lock_m(p).Mutex(true)$
  $\diamond\ unlock_m(p).Mutex(false)\ )$

Table 9. mCRl2 specification for a thread p interacting with the protocol.

$Thread(p : P) =$
  $EnterShared(p)$.
  $LeaveShared(p)$.
  $Thread(p)$
 $+\ EnterExclusive(p)$.
  $LeaveExclusive(p)$.
  $Thread(p)$

Table 10. mCRL2 specification for the busy-forbidden protocol.

allow({
    store, load,
    lock, unlock,
    internal, improbable,
    enter_shared_call, enter_shared_return,
    leave_shared_call, leave_shared_return,
    enter_exclusive_call, enter_exclusive_return,
    leave_exclusive_call, leave_exclusive_return
    }, comm({
        $store_f | store_p \rightarrow store,$
        $load_f | load_p \rightarrow load,$
        $lock_m | lock_p \rightarrow lock,$
        $unlock_m | unlock_p \rightarrow unlock$
        },
        $Thread(p_1) \;||$
        $\vdots$
        $Thread(p_{|P|}) \;||$
        $Flags(\lambda f{:}F.false) \;||$
        $Mutex(false)$))

Table 11. Modal formula for property 1: "There should never be more than one thread present in the exclusive section".

$[true^*]$
$[\exists_{p \in P} : \texttt{enter\_exclusive\_return}(p)]$
$[\exists_{p \in P} : \texttt{leave\_exclusive\_call}(p)^*]$
$[\exists_{p \in P} : \texttt{enter\_exclusive\_return}(p)]$
$false$

Table 12. The modal formula for property 2: "There should never be a thread present in the exclusive section while one or more threads are present in the shared section".

$\nu X(n_{shared} : Nat = 0,\; n_{exclusive} : Nat = 0).$
    $(\forall_{p:P}.[\texttt{enter\_shared\_return}(p)]X(n_{shared} + 1, n_{exclusive}))$
$\wedge\;\; (\forall_{p:P}.[\texttt{enter\_exclusive\_return}(p)]X(n_{shared}, n_{exclusive} + 1))$
$\wedge\;\; (\forall_{p:P}.[\texttt{leave\_shared\_call}(p)]X(n_{shared} - 1, n_{exclusive}))$
$\wedge\;\; (\forall_{p:P}.[\texttt{leave\_exclusive\_call}(p)]X(n_{shared}, n_{exclusive} - 1))$
$\wedge\;\; [\;\; \overline{(\exists_{p:P}.\texttt{enter\_shared\_return}(p)\;)}$
$\cap\;\; \overline{(\exists_{p:P}.\texttt{enter\_exclusive\_return}(p)\;)}$
$\cap\;\; \overline{(\exists_{p:P}.\texttt{leave\_shared\_call}(p)\;)}$
$\cap\;\; \overline{(\exists_{p:P}.\texttt{leave\_exclusive\_call}(p)\;)}$
$\;\;]X(n_{shared}, n_{exclusive}).$
$\wedge\;\; \neg(n_{exclusive} > 0 \wedge n_{shared} > 0)$

Table 13. Modal formula for property 3: "When a thread requests to enter the shared section, it will be granted access within a bounded number of steps, unless there is another thread in the exclusive section".

$\nu X(n_{exclusive} : Nat = 0).$
$\quad [\exists_{p:P}. \; \texttt{enter\_exclusive\_call}(p)]X(n_{exclusive} + 1)$
$\wedge \; [\exists_{p:P}. \; \texttt{leave\_exclusive\_return}(p)]X(n_{exclusive} - 1)$
$\wedge \; [\; \overline{(\exists_{p:P}. \; \texttt{enter\_exclusive\_call}(p))}$
$\qquad \cap \; \overline{(\exists_{p:P}. \; \texttt{leave\_exclusive\_return}(p))}$
$\quad] \; X(n_{exclusive})$
$\wedge \; \forall_{p:P}.[\texttt{enter\_shared\_call}(p)]$
$\quad \nu Y(n'_{exclusive} : Nat = n_{exclusive}).\mu Z(n''_{exclusive} : Nat = n'_{exclusive}). \; ($
$\qquad [\; \overline{\texttt{enter\_shared\_return}(p)}$
$\qquad \cap \; \overline{(\exists_{p':P}. \; \texttt{enter\_shared\_call}(p'))}$
$\qquad \cap \; \overline{(\exists_{p':P}. \; \texttt{enter\_exclusive\_call}(p'))}$
$\qquad \cap \; \overline{(\exists_{p':P}. \; \texttt{leave\_exclusive\_return}(p'))}$
$\qquad \cap \; \overline{improbable}$
$\qquad] \; (\; ((n''_{exclusive} \approx 0) \implies Z(n''_{exclusive}))$
$\qquad \wedge \; ((n''_{exclusive} > 0) \implies Y(n''_{exclusive})) \;)$
$\quad \wedge \; [\exists_{p':P}. \; \texttt{enter\_shared\_call}(p')]Y(n''_{exclusive})$
$\quad \wedge \; [\exists_{p':P}. \; \texttt{enter\_exclusive\_call}(p')]Y(n''_{exclusive} + 1)$
$\quad \wedge \; [\exists_{p':P}. \; \texttt{leave\_exclusive\_return}(p')]Y(n''_{exclusive} - 1)$
$\quad \wedge \; [improbable]Y(n''_{exclusive})$
$\quad \wedge \; \langle true^*.\texttt{enter\_shared\_return}(p)\rangle true \;)$

Table 14. Modal formula for property 5: "When a thread requests to leave the exclusive/shared section, it will leave it within a bounded number of steps".

$[true^*] \; \forall_{p:P}.($
$\quad [\texttt{leave\_shared\_call}(p)]\nu X.\mu Y.($
$\qquad [\; \overline{\texttt{leave\_shared\_return}(p)}$
$\qquad \cap \; \overline{(\exists_{p':P}. \; \texttt{enter\_exclusive\_call}(p'))}$
$\qquad \cap \; \overline{(\exists_{p':P}. \; \texttt{enter\_shared\_call}(p'))}$
$\qquad \cap \; \overline{improbable} \;] \; Y$
$\quad \wedge \; [\; (\exists_{p':P}. \; \texttt{enter\_exclusive\_call}(p'))$
$\qquad \cup \; (\exists_{p':P}. \; \texttt{enter\_shared\_call}(p'))$
$\qquad \cup \; (improbable) \;] \; X$
$\quad \wedge \; \langle true^*.\texttt{leave\_shared\_return}(p)\rangle true \;)$
$\wedge \; [\texttt{leave\_exclusive\_call}(p)]\nu X.\mu Y.($
$\qquad [\; \overline{\texttt{leave\_exclusive\_return}(p)}$
$\qquad \cap \; \overline{(\exists_{p':P}. \; \texttt{enter\_exclusive\_call}(p'))}$
$\qquad \cap \; \overline{(\exists_{p':P}. \; \texttt{enter\_shared\_call}(p'))}$
$\qquad \cap \; \overline{improbable} \;] \; Y$
$\quad \wedge \; [\; (\exists_{p':P}. \; \texttt{enter\_exclusive\_call}(p'))$
$\qquad \cup \; (\exists_{p':P}. \; \texttt{enter\_shared\_call}(p'))$
$\qquad \cup \; (improbable) \;] \; X$
$\quad \wedge \; \langle true^*.\texttt{leave\_exclusive\_return}(p)\rangle true \;) \;)$

Table 15. Modal formula for property 4: "When a thread requests to enter the exclusive section, it will be granted access within a bounded number of steps, unless there is another thread in the shared or in the exclusive section".

$\nu X(n_{blocking} : Nat = 0).$

$\quad [\exists_{p:P}. \texttt{ enter\_exclusive\_call}(p)]X(n_{blocking} + 1)$

$\quad \wedge \;[\exists_{p:P}. \texttt{ enter\_shared\_call}(p)]X(n_{blocking} + 1)$

$\quad \wedge \;[\exists_{p:P}. \texttt{ leave\_shared\_return}(p)]X(n_{blocking} - 1)$

$\quad \wedge \;[\exists_{p:P}. \texttt{ leave\_exclusive\_return}(p)]X(n_{blocking} - 1)$

$\quad \wedge \;[\quad \overline{(\exists_{p:P}. \texttt{ enter\_exclusive\_call}(p))}$

$\qquad \cap \;\overline{(\exists_{p:P}. \texttt{ leave\_exclusive\_return}(p))}$

$\qquad \cap \;\overline{(\exists_{p:P}. \texttt{ enter\_shared\_call}(p))}$

$\qquad \cap \;\overline{(\exists_{p:P}. \texttt{ leave\_shared\_return}(p))}$

$\qquad]\, X(n_{exclusive})$

$\quad \wedge \;\forall_{p:P}.[\texttt{enter\_exclusive\_call}(p)]$

$\qquad \nu Y(n'_{blocking} : Nat = n_{blocking}).\mu Z(n''_{blocking} : Nat = n'_{blocking}).\;($

$\qquad\quad [\quad \overline{\texttt{enter\_exclusive\_return}(p)}$

$\qquad\quad \cap \;\overline{(\exists_{p':P}. \texttt{ enter\_shared\_call}(p))}$

$\qquad\quad \cap \;\overline{(\exists_{p':P}. \texttt{ leave\_shared\_return}(p))}$

$\qquad\quad \cap \;\overline{(\exists_{p':P}. \texttt{ enter\_exclusive\_call}(p'))}$

$\qquad\quad \cap \;\overline{(\exists_{p':P}. \texttt{ leave\_exclusive\_return}(p'))}$

$\qquad\quad \cap \;\overline{improbable}$

$\qquad\quad]\,(\;((n''_{blocking} \approx 0) \implies Z(n''_{blocking}))$

$\qquad\qquad \wedge \;((n''_{blocking} > 0) \implies Y(n''_{blocking}))\;)$

$\qquad \wedge \;[\exists_{p':P}. \texttt{ enter\_shared\_call}(p')]Y(n''_{blocking} + 1)$

$\qquad \wedge \;[\exists_{p':P}. \texttt{ leave\_shared\_return}(p')]Y(n''_{blocking} - 1)$

$\qquad \wedge \;[\exists_{p':P}. \texttt{ enter\_exclusive\_call}(p')]Y(n''_{blocking} + 1)$

$\qquad \wedge \;[\exists_{p':P}.\;(p' \not\approx p) \;\wedge\; \texttt{enter\_exclusive\_return}(p')]Y(n''_{blocking} - 1)$

$\qquad \wedge \;[improbable]Y(n''_{exclusive})$

$\qquad \wedge \;\langle true^* . \texttt{enter\_exclusive\_return}(p)\rangle true\;)$

Table 16. Modal formula for property 6: "A thread not in the exclusive or shared section can instantly start to enter the exclusive or shared section".

$\forall_{p:P}.\nu X(b_{shared} : Bool = false,\; b_{exclusive} : Bool = false).$

$\quad [\texttt{enter\_shared\_call}(p)]X(true, b_{exclusive})$

$\quad \wedge \;[\texttt{leave\_shared\_return}(p)]X(false, b_{exclusive})$

$\quad \wedge \;[\texttt{enter\_exclusive\_call}(p)]X(b_{shared}, true)$

$\quad \wedge \;[\texttt{leave\_exclusive\_return}(p)]X(b_{shared}, false)$

$\quad \wedge \;[\quad \overline{\texttt{enter\_shared\_call}(p)}$

$\qquad \cap \;\overline{\texttt{leave\_shared\_return}(p)}$

$\qquad \cap \;\overline{\texttt{enter\_exclusive\_call}(p)}$

$\qquad \cap \;\overline{\texttt{leave\_exclusive\_return}(p)}$

$\qquad]\, X(n_{shared}, n_{exclusive})$

$\quad \wedge \;((\neg n_{shared} \wedge \neg n_{exclusive}) \implies (\;$

$\qquad \langle \texttt{enter\_exclusive\_call(p)}\rangle true$

$\qquad \wedge \;\langle \texttt{enter\_shared\_call(p)}\rangle true)\;)$

C   mCRL2 Specifications for the Term Library

In this section we give the formal mCRL2 specifications of the implementation of the term library that is used to perform model checking. Creating a term is specified in Table 17 and destroying a term in Table 18. In this model, the set P corresponds to the set containing all threads, T to the set containing all terms and A to the set containing all memory addresses. The set $A_\perp = A \cup \{\perp\}$ with $\perp \notin A$ contains the extra element $\perp$ meaning no address or a NULL pointer. To ensure finiteness and reduce the complexity of the model, the set T only contains a finite amount of constants, $i.e.$, terms of arity zero.

Table 17. mCRL2 specification for the create function shown in Table 1.

$Create(p : P,\ t : T,\ lm : T \to A_\perp) =$
    $\texttt{create\_call}(p,\ t)$.
    $EnterShared(p)$.
    $Create_2(p,\ t,\ lm)$

$Create_2(p : P,\ t : T,\ lm : T \to A_\perp) =$
$\sum_{a:A_\perp}\ \cdot($
    $contains_p(t, a, p)$.
    $(a \approx \perp)$
    $\to \sum_{a':A} \cdot ($
        $construct\_term_p(t, a', p).($
            $insert_p(t, a', true, p)$.
            $Create_3(p,\ t,\ lm,\ a')$
           $+\ insert_p(t,\ a',\ false,\ p)$.
            $destruct\_term_p(t,\ a',\ p)$.
            $Create_2(p,\ t,\ lm)$))
    $\diamond\ Create_3(p,\ t,\ lm,\ a)$)

$Create_3(p : P, t : T,\ lm : T \to A_\perp,\ a : A) =$
    $protect_p(t,\ a,\ p)$.
    $LeaveShared(p)$.
    $\texttt{create\_return}(p,\ t,\ a)$.
    $Thread(p,\ lm[t \mapsto a])$

First of all, we introduce processes *EnterShared*, *LeaveShared*, *EnterExclusive* and *LeaveExclusive* to interact with the busy-forbidden specification *BF* specified in Table 3. To distinguish between the term library and the protocol all actions such as $\texttt{enter\_shared\_call}$ are split into action $\texttt{enter\_shared\_call}_{bf}$

for the protocol and **enter_shared_call**$_p$ for the term library. Finally, we have the process *MainMemory* to model the main memory by keeping track of *used* memory addresses, the process *HashTable* to model a hash table as an associative array, and process *ReferenceCounter* to track a reference counter for every address (or term). Destroying a term is specified in Table 18, which uses the same other processes as the creation function. Again, there are two separate processes to model the behaviour of the while loop. In Table 19 the behaviour of the main memory, the hash table and the reference counter are specified.

The specification in Table 20 models the behaviour of each thread. Each thread repeatedly tries to either creates a term it does not yet know, or it destroys a known term. Finally, Table 21 shows the complete specification including the communication between various processes used to model the thread-safe term library.

Table 18. mCRL2 specification for the destroy function shown in Table 1.

$Destroy(p : P, \ t : T, \ lm : T \rightarrow A_\perp) =$
    destroy_call$(p, \ t)$.
    $unprotect_p(t, \ lm(t), \ p).($
       $skip$
    $+ \ skip.GC(p) \ )$.
    destroy_return(p) .
    $Thread(p, \ lm[t \mapsto \perp])$

$GC(p : P) =$
    $EnterExclusive(p)$.
    $GC_2(p, \ \emptyset)$

$GC_2(p : P, \ checked : FSet(T)) =$
    $(\forall_{t:T}.t \in checked)$
    $\rightarrow LeaveExclusive(p)$
    $\diamond \ \sum_{t:T} .(t \notin checked) \rightarrow ($
       $contains_p(t, \ \perp, \ p)$.
       $GC_2(p, \ checked \cup \{t\}$
     $+ \ \sum_{a:A} .contains_p(t, \ a, \ p).($
       $protected_p(a, \ true, \ p)$.
       $GC_2(p, \ checked \cup \{t\})$
      $+ \ protected_p(a, \ false, \ p)$.
       $destruct\_term_p(t, \ a, \ p)$.
       $delete_p(t, \ p)$.
       $GC_2(p, \ checked \cup \{t\}) \ ) \ )$

To verify the model of the thread-safe term library we again specify a number of modal formulas for the properties described in Sect. 2.2. The modal formula for property 1 specified in Table 22 uses a mapping a from addresses to terms and the finite set *owners* containing all threads that own/protect term t as data parameters. If at any point in time a `create(t)` returns a different address than the current address, then the term must not be owned by any thread. The modal formula in Table 23 for property 2 uses the same constructs to check whether terms on the same address are also equivalent.

The formula for property 3 shown in Table 24 uses a boolean parameter *busy* to keep track of whether the thread p is creating (or destroying) a term. Furthermore, the parameter *known* is a finite set containing all terms that thread p knows. If at any point in time *busy* is false, then the process must be able to start destroying any term in *known* and start creating any term not currently in *known*. Finally, for property 4 the formula shown in Table 25 uses again the construction which (under fairness) indicates that term creation and destruction will finish within a finite number of steps. Note that the subformulas for creation and destruction have an identical structure.

Table 19. mCRL2 specifications of the main memory, hash table and reference counters used in the term library specification.

$MainMemory(used : FSet(A)) =$

$\sum_{p:P,t:T,a:A} \cdot ((a \notin used)$

$\quad \rightarrow construct\_term_{mm}(t,a,p).MainMemory(used \cup \{a\})$

$\quad \diamond \ destruct\_term_{mm}(t,a,p).MainMemory(used \setminus \{a\}) \ )$

$HashTable(m : T \rightarrow A_\perp) =$

$\sum_{t:T,p:P} \cdot ($

$\quad contains_{ht}(t,m(e),p).HashTable(m)$

$\quad + \sum_{a:A} \cdot (m(e) \approx \perp)$

$\quad \rightarrow insert_{ht}(t,a,true,p).HashTable(m[e \mapsto a]$

$\quad \diamond \ insert_{ht}(t,a,false,p).HashTable(m)$

$\quad + delete_{ht}(t,p).HashTable(m[e \mapsto \perp]) \ )$

$ReferenceCounter(counter : A \rightarrow Nat) =$

$\quad \sum_{t:T,p:P} \cdot protect_{rc}(t,a,p) \ .$

$\quad ReferenceCounter(counter[a \mapsto counter(a) + 1]$

$\quad + \sum_{t:T,p:P} \cdot unprotect_{rc}(t,a,p) \ .$

$\quad ReferenceCounter(counter[a \mapsto counter(a) - 1]$

$\quad + \sum_{t:T,p:P} \cdot protected_{rc}(t,a,counter(a) \not\approx 0,p) \ .$

$\quad ReferenceCounter(counter)$

Table 20. mCRL2 specification of a thread p interacting with the term library.

$$Thread(p : P,\ lm : T \to A_\perp) =$$
$$\left(\sum_{t:T} \cdot (lm(t) \approx \perp) \to Create(p, t, lm)\right)$$
$$+\ \left(\sum_{t:T} \cdot (lm(t) \not\approx \perp) \to Destroy(p, t, lm)\right)$$

Table 21. mCRL2 specification for the thread-safe term library.

$$\mathbf{allow}(\{$$

$construct\_term,\ destruct\_term,$

$contains,\ insert,\ delete,$

$protect,\ unprotect,\ protected,$

$skip,\ improbable,$

$enter\_shared\_call,\ enter\_shared\_return,$

$leave\_shared\_call,\ leave\_shared\_return,$

$enter\_exclusive\_call,\ enter\_exclusive\_return,$

$leave\_exclusive\_call,\ leave\_exclusive\_return,$

$\mathtt{create\_call},\ \mathtt{create\_return},$

$\mathtt{destroy\_call},\ \mathtt{destroy\_return}$

$\},\ \mathbf{comm}(\{$

$construct\_term_{mm}\,|\,construct\_term_p \to construct\_term,$

$destruct\_term_{mm}\,|\,destruct\_term_p \to destruct\_term,$

$contains_{ht}\,|\,contains_p \to contains,$

$insert_{ht}\,|\,insert_p \to insert,$

$delete_{ht}\,|\,delete_p \to delete,$

$protect_{rc}\,|\,protect_p \to protect,$

$unprotect_{rc}\,|\,unprotect_p \to unprotect,$

$protected_{rc}\,|\,protected_p \to protected,$

$enter\_shared\_call_{bf}\,|\,enter\_shared\_call_p \to enter\_shared\_call,$

$enter\_shared\_return_{bf}\,|\,enter\_shared\_return_p \to enter\_shared\_return,$

$leave\_shared\_call_{bf}\,|\,leave\_shared\_call_p \to leave\_shared\_call,$

$leave\_shared\_return_{bf}\,|\,leave\_shared\_return_p \to leave\_shared\_return,$

$enter\_exclusive\_call_{bf}\,|\,enter\_exclusive\_call_p \to enter\_exclusive\_call,$

$enter\_exclusive\_return_{bf}\,|\,enter\_exclusive\_return_p \to enter\_exclusive\_return,$

$leave\_exclusive\_call_{bf}\,|\,leave\_exclusive\_call_p \to leave\_exclusive\_call,$

$leave\_exclusive\_return_{bf}\,|\,leave\_exclusive\_return_p \to leave\_exclusive\_return\ \},$

$Thread(p_1)\ ||$

$\vdots$

$Thread(p_{|P|})\ ||$

$MainMemory(\emptyset)\ ||$

$HashTable(\lambda t{:}T.\perp)\ ||$

$ReferenceCounter(\lambda a{:}A.\ 0)\ ||$

$BF(\lambda p{:}P.Free)\ )\ )$

Table 22. Formulation of property 1: "A term and all its subterms remain in existence at exactly the same address, with unchanged function symbol and arguments, as long as it is not destroyed".

$\forall_{t:T}.\nu X(a : A_\perp = \perp, \ owners : FSet(P) = \emptyset).$
　　$(\forall_{p:P,a':A}.$
　　　　$[\texttt{create\_return}(p,t,a')] \ ($
　　　　　　$X(a', owners \cup \{p\})$
　　　　　$\wedge \ (a \not\approx a' \implies owners \approx \emptyset) \ ) \ )$
　$\wedge \ (\forall p : P. \ [\texttt{destroy\_call}(p,t)]X(a, owners \setminus \{p\}))$
　$\wedge \ [\quad \overline{\exists_{p:P,a':A}.\texttt{create\_return}(p,t,a')}$
　　$\cap \ \overline{\exists_{p:P}.\texttt{destroy\_call}(p,t)}$
　　$] \ X(a, owners)$

Table 23. Modal formula for property 2: "Two stored terms t_1 and t_2 always have the same non-null address iff they are equal".

$\forall_{a:A,t_1:T}.\nu X(t : T = t_1, \ owners : FSet(P) = \emptyset).$
　　$(\forall_{p:P,t_2:T}.$
　　　　$[\texttt{create\_return}(p,t_2,a)] \ ($
　　　　　　$X(t_2, owners \cup \{p\})$
　　　　　$\wedge \ (t \not\approx t_2 \implies owners \approx \emptyset) \ ) \ )$
　$\wedge \ (\forall_{p:P}. \ [\texttt{destroy\_call}(p,t)]X(t, owners \setminus \{p\}))$
　$\wedge \ [\quad \overline{\exists_{p:P,t':T}.\texttt{create\_return}(p,t',a)}$
　　$\cap \ \overline{\exists_{p:P}.\texttt{destroy\_call}(p,t)}$
　　$] \ X(t, owners)$

Table 24. Modal formula for property 3: "Any thread that is not busy creating or destroying a term, can always initiate the construction of a new term or the destruction of an owned term, *i.e.*, a term that this thread has exclusive access to".

$\forall_{p:P}. \ \nu X(busy : Bool = false, known : FSet(T) = \emptyset).$
　　$(\neg busy) \to ($
　　　　$(\forall_{t:T}.(t \notin known) \implies [\tau^*]\langle\tau^*.\texttt{create\_call}(p,t)\rangle true)$
　　　$\wedge \ (\forall_{t:T}.(t \in known) \implies [\tau^*]\langle\tau^*.\texttt{destroy\_call}(p,t)\rangle true) \ )$
　$\wedge \ [\quad (\exists_{t:T}.\texttt{create\_call}(p,t))$
　　$\cup \ (\exists_{t:T}.\texttt{destroy\_call}(p,t))$
　　$] \ X(true, owned)$
　$\wedge \ (\forall_{t:T}. \ [\exists_{a:A}.\texttt{create\_return}(p,t,a)]X(false, owned \cup \{t\}))$
　$\wedge \ (\forall_{t:T}. \ [\texttt{destroy\_return}(p,t)]X(false, owned \setminus \{t\}))$
　$\wedge \ [\quad \overline{(\exists_{t:T}.\texttt{create\_call}(p,t))}$
　　$\cap \ \overline{(\exists_{t:T}.\texttt{destroy\_call}(p,t))}$
　　$\cap \ \overline{(\exists_{t:T,a:A}.\texttt{create\_return}(p,t,a))}$
　　$\cap \ \overline{(\exists_{t:T}.\texttt{destroy\_return}(p,t))}$
　　$] \ X(busy, owned)$

Table 25. Modal formula(s) for property 4: "Any thread that started creating a term or destroying a term, will eventually successfully finish this task provided there is enough memory to store one more term than those that are in use. But it is required that other threads behave fairly, in the sense that they will not continually create and destroy terms or stall other threads by busy waiting".

$$([\mathit{true}^*]\forall_{p:P,t:T}.[\mathbf{create\_call}(p,t)]\ \nu X_c.\ \mu Y_c.(\\
\quad \forall_{p':P}.(p \not\approx p') \implies\\
\qquad [\ (\exists_{t':T}.\ \mathbf{create\_call}(p',t'))\\
\qquad \cup\ (\exists_{t':T}.\ \mathbf{destroy\_call}(p',t'))\\
\qquad \cup\ \mathit{improbable}\,]\ X_c\\
\quad \wedge\ [\ \overline{(\exists_{a:A}.\ \mathbf{create\_return}(p,t,a))}\\
\qquad \cap\ \overline{(\exists_{p':P}.(p \not\approx p') \cap (\exists_{t':T}.\ \mathbf{create\_call}(p',t')))}\\
\qquad \cap\ \overline{(\exists_{p':P}.(p \not\approx p') \cap (\exists_{t':T}.\ \mathbf{destroy\_call}(p',t')))}\\
\qquad \cap\ \overline{\mathit{improbable}}\,]\ Y_c\\
\quad \wedge\ \langle \mathit{true}^*.\exists_{a:A}.\ \mathbf{create\_return}(p,t,a)\rangle\, \mathit{true}\ )\ )\\
\wedge\\
([\mathit{true}^*]\forall_{p:P,t:T}.[\mathbf{destroy\_call}(p,t)]\ \nu X_d.\ \mu Y_d.(\\
\quad \forall_{p':P}.(p \not\approx p') \implies\\
\qquad [\ (\exists_{t':T}.\ \mathbf{create\_call}(p',t'))\\
\qquad \cup\ (\exists_{t':T}.\ \mathbf{destroy\_call}(p',t'))\\
\qquad \cup\ \mathit{improbable}\,]\ X_d\\
\quad \wedge\ [\ \overline{\mathbf{destroy\_return}(p,t)}\\
\qquad \cap\ \overline{(\exists_{p':P}.(p \not\approx p') \cap (\exists_{t':T}.\ \mathbf{create\_call}(p',t')))}\\
\qquad \cap\ \overline{(\exists_{p':P}.(p \not\approx p') \cap (\exists_{t':T}.\ \mathbf{destroy\_call}(p',t')))}\\
\qquad \cap\ \overline{\mathit{improbable}}\,]\ Y_d\\
\quad \wedge\ \langle \mathit{true}^*.\mathbf{destroy\_return}(p,t)\rangle\, \mathit{true}\ )\ )$$

D   Benchmark Data

The benchmark tests and information shown in Figs. 4 and 5 are hard to read exactly. Therefore, we repeat the corresponding precise benchmark numbers in Table 28 up to and including Table 26. Each wall-clock time is measured in seconds.

The measurements in Table 27 came from benchmarking performed on an Intel i7-7700HQ processor. All other measurements were obtained through benchmarking on an AMD EPYC 7452 32-Core processor.

The benchmark results in Table 28 were obtained by having each thread create a term $t_{400\,000}$, with t_0 being a constant, and t_{i+1} equal to $f(t_i, t_i)$. No garbage collection was performed during the benchmark. Note that only one copy of the term is actually stored in memory. So, most threads wanting to construct some term $f(t_i, t_i)$ detect that the term already exists, and only need to return its address, without actually creating it.

The benchmark results in Table 29 were obtained by having each thread create its own copy of the term $t_{400\ 000/\#threads}$, and measuring the wall-clock time. Note that although each thread creates its own term, all terms are stored in the data structures in an intermixed way. Note that as there is no sharing here, each thread stores a full copy of the term in memory.

The benchmark results in Table 30 and 31 were obtained by measuring the wall-clock time of creating $1000/\#threads$ instances of the terms used in Table 28 and 29. Before we start measuring the wall-clock times, the terms and subterms have already been inserted into the hash table, thus we are only measuring the cost of performing repeated lookups in our hash table. The experiment reported in Table 30 is the same as the one in Table 27, but the former is run on an AMD EPYC 7452 processor whereas the latter uses an Intel i7-7700HQ processor.

The benchmark results in Table 32 were obtained by having each thread perform $1000/\#threads$ breadth-first traversals of the term t_{20} and measuring the wall-clock time. The traversal does not make use of the shared structure of terms, meaning that approximately 10^9 term nodes are visited. Similarly, the benchmark results in Table 33 were obtained by having each thread perform $1000/\#threads$ breadth-first traversals of a term t_{20} that is unique for each thread.

We also measured the wall-clock time of the state space generation of the 1394 firewire protocol using a parallel prototype of the mCRL2 toolset. The results are listed in Table 26.

Table 26. Wall-clock time for state space exploration.

#Threads	1	2	3	4	5	6	7	8	9	10	11
parallel reference counter	61.0	87.6	90.1	83.1	67.0	57.4	56.2	53.3	50.0	46.5	43.4
parallel protection set	62.8	31.7	21.5	16.5	13.4	11.2	9.79	8.67	7.78	7.15	6.54
sequential reference counter	60.0										
sequential protection set	52.9										
original aterm library	40.2										
#Threads	12	13	14	15	16	17	18	19	20	21	22
parallel reference counter	43.3	41.4	38.8	38.1	37.3	35.5	35.2	35.2	33.9	33.2	32.5
parallel protection set	6.07	5.68	5.37	5.06	4.85	4.83	4.72	4.67	4.60	4.56	4.49
#Threads	23	24	25	26	27	28	29	30	31	32	
parallel reference counter	31.7	31.3	30.8	29.4	28.7	28.1	28.0	27.9	27.0	26.6	
parallel protection set	4.44	4.37	4.32	4.23	4.17	4.15	4.11	4.07	4.02	3.99	

Table 27. Wall-clock time for creating existing terms (shared, Intel).

# Threads	1	2	3	4	5	6	7	8
parallel reference counter	10.0	10.4	4.42	4.08	3.22	2.74	2.38	2.22
parallel protection set	5.68	3.09	2.36	1.60	1.52	1.30	1.14	1.02
sequential reference counter	4.61							
sequential protection set	4.20							
original aterm library	4.83							
parallel java	130	73.0	50.4	40.5	32.1	29.5	28.5	29.2
std::shared_mutex	10.3	38.1	42.1	41.0	40.7	41.7	42.7	46.2

Table 28. Wall-clock time for creating new terms (shared).

# Threads	1	2	3	4	5	6	7	8	9	10	11
parallel reference counter	0.03	0.11	0.22	0.14	0.26	0.34	0.28	0.29	0.39	0.51	0.53
parallel protection set	0.03	0.07	0.07	0.20	0.15	0.28	0.20	0.17	0.32	0.34	0.32
sequential reference counter	0.02										
sequential protection set	0.02										
original aterm library	0.01										
parallel java	0.26	0.46	0.68	1.32	1.25	1.20	1.51	1.41	1.36	1.48	1.51
std::shared_mutex	0.03	0.12	0.18	0.32	0.24	0.22	0.38	0.47	0.47	0.55	0.50
# Threads	12	13	14	15	16	17	18	19	20	21	22
parallel reference counter	0.51	0.59	0.50	0.54	0.49	0.53	0.54	0.48	0.5	0.48	0.52
parallel protection set	0.35	0.39	0.32	0.39	0.33	0.41	0.39	0.38	0.38	0.37	0.39
parallel java	1.40	1.51	1.44	1.43	1.38	1.67	1.77	1.87	1.77	1.78	1.85
std::shared_mutex	0.58	0.62	0.63	0.67	0.72	0.74	0.76	0.79	0.83	0.83	0.88
# Threads	23	24	25	26	27	28	29	30	31	32	
parallel reference counter	0.50	0.53	0.50	0.49	0.53	0.51	0.51	0.49	0.48	0.48	
parallel protection set	0.43	0.37	0.39	0.41	0.39	0.39	0.42	0.44	0.39	0.41	
parallel java	1.68	1.95	1.68	1.82	1.81	1.65	1.94	1.94	2.09	1.86	
std::shared_mutex	0.91	0.95	0.96	0.99	0.98	1.04	1.02	1.10	1.11	1.16	

Table 29. Wall-clock time for creating new terms (distinct).

#Threads	1	2	3	4	5	6	7	8	9	10	11
parallel reference counter	0.03	0.03	0.03	0.04	0.03	0.04	0.05	0.07	0.06	0.06	0.06
parallel protection set	0.03	0.05	0.03	0.04	0.03	0.03	0.04	0.05	0.05	0.05	0.06
sequential reference counter	0.02										
sequential protection set	0.02										
original aterm library	0.01										
parallel java	0.26	0.25	0.28	0.26	0.28	0.28	0.28	0.35	0.33	0.35	0.32
std::shared_mutex	0.03	0.04	0.04	0.05	0.10	0.04	0.04	0.09	0.09	0.09	0.09
#Threads	12	13	14	15	16	17	18	19	20	21	22
parallel reference counter	0.06	0.05	0.05	0.07	0.06	0.06	0.05	0.06	0.07	0.06	0.06
parallel protection set	0.05	0.06	0.06	0.05	0.06	0.07	0.06	0.05	0.06	0.06	0.06
parallel java	0.33	0.35	0.32	0.34	0.33	0.34	0.33	0.35	0.33	0.34	0.34
std::shared_mutex	0.09	0.10	0.10	0.10	0.10	0.09	0.11	0.09	0.12	0.11	0.13
#Threads	23	24	25	26	27	28	29	30	31	32	
parallel reference counter	0.07	0.06	0.05	0.06	0.06	0.07	0.07	0.07	0.06	0.06	
parallel protection set	0.06	0.06	0.05	0.07	0.06	0.06	0.05	0.05	0.05	0.06	
parallel java	0.37	0.34	0.35	0.35	0.37	0.35	0.34	0.34	0.35	0.34	
std::shared_mutex	0.13	0.11	0.14	0.09	0.15	0.18	0.15	0.13	0.16	0.13	

Table 30. Wall-clock time for creating existing terms (shared).

#Threads	1	2	3	4	5	6	7	8	9	10	11
parallel reference counter	9.01	35.1	11.5	19.0	9.81	10.6	6.40	6.00	4.90	4.85	3.88
parallel protection set	4.07	2.51	1.66	1.39	1.07	0.96	0.81	0.75	0.67	0.59	0.53
sequential reference counter	4.01										
sequential protection set	3.65										
original aterm library	4.57										
parallel java	104	136	106	103	91.7	84.2	75.5	71.1	64.5	61.6	57.5
std::shared_mutex	6.51	14.2	15.1	15.1	18.7	20.7	22.0	33.3	28.1	25.4	24.5
#Threads	12	13	14	15	16	17	18	19	20	21	22
parallel reference counter	3.51	3.10	2.86	2.77	2.66	2.45	2.61	2.43	2.33	2.27	2.17
parallel protection set	0.49	0.46	0.43	0.41	0.40	0.39	0.37	0.36	0.35	0.32	0.31
parallel java	54.3	51.9	49.4	48.7	46.5	47.7	47.9	48.1	48.6	47.7	46.6
std::shared_mutex	22.8	22.7	23.1	22.6	22.5	22.9	23.2	23.7	24.7	24.1	24.3
#Threads	23	24	25	26	27	28	29	30	31	32	
parallel reference counter	2.16	2.10	2.08	2.04	2.03	1.97	1.82	1.87	1.81	1.81	
parallel protection set	0.32	0.31	0.29	0.3	0.28	0.27	0.29	0.28	0.28	0.29	
parallel java	45.9	45.4	45.8	44.9	44.8	42.4	42.4	42.9	42.1	42.1	
std::shared_mutex	24.7	24.4	25.0	25.1	25.4	25.5	26.0	26.7	27.5	28.3	

Table 31. Wall-clock time for creating existing terms (distinct).

#Threads	1	2	3	4	5	6	7	8	9	10	11
parallel reference counter	9.02	5.15	3.95	3.05	2.64	2.25	2.38	2.41	2.42	2.49	2.24
parallel protection set	3.96	2.66	2.58	2.44	2.27	1.76	1.92	1.86	1.95	1.91	1.79
sequential reference counter	4.02										
sequential protection set	3.71										
original aterm library	4.58										
parallel java	106	212	218	227	260	266	274	276	295	272	287
std::shared_mutex	6.46	13.8	15.5	15.7	18.3	18.5	24.6	33.2	26.9	25.0	23.7
#Threads	12	13	14	15	16	17	18	19	20	21	22
parallel reference counter	2.22	2.27	2.26	2.20	2.39	2.55	2.63	2.58	2.72	2.67	2.67
parallel protection set	1.78	1.76	1.77	1.75	1.81	1.82	1.97	2.05	2.04	2.07	2.07
parallel java	275	287	296	2912	281	286	280	284	294	292	314
std::shared_mutex	22.7	22.4	22.9	22.6	22.2	22.7	23.2	23.8	24.7	24.1	24.1
#Threads	23	24	25	26	27	28	29	30	31	32	
parallel reference counter	2.69	2.69	2.77	2.76	2.8	2.77	2.82	2.84	2.86	2.92	
parallel protection set	2.07	2.10	2.15	2.05	2.12	2.11	2.17	2.22	2.27	2.22	
parallel java	311	308	315	316	324	330	339	332	343	352	
std::shared_mutex	24.4	24.4	25.3	25.3	25.9	25.7	26.3	27.1	27.8	28.7	

Table 32. Wall-clock time for traversing terms (shared).

#Threads	1	2	3	4	5	6	7	8	9	10	11
parallel reference counter	15.7	8.63	5.93	4.60	3.87	3.41	3.00	2.79	2.50	2.45	2.21
parallel protection set	16.7	8.90	6.07	4.66	3.93	3.37	3.01	2.80	2.55	2.41	2.34
sequential reference counter	16.8										
sequential protection set	18.2										
original aterm library	16.4										
parallel java	34.6	34.5	36.0	36.7	36.1	33.6	30.9	28.4	26.4	25.0	22.9
std::shared_mutex	16.2	8.71	5.95	4.54	3.86	3.34	3.01	2.74	2.53	2.40	2.29
#Threads	12	13	14	15	16	17	18	19	20	21	22
parallel reference counter	2.17	2.21	2.23	2.32	2.24	2.14	2.30	2.21	2.11	2.21	2.09
parallel protection set	2.28	2.21	2.30	2.35	2.21	2.26	2.35	2.25	2.33	2.28	2.21
parallel java	17.8	20.6	17.7	19.1	22.3	19.5	19.6	20.4	21.9	21.6	21.5
std::shared_mutex	2.25	2.33	2.28	2.24	2.21	2.22	2.29	2.15	2.24	2.04	2.24
#Threads	23	24	25	26	27	28	29	30	31	32	
parallel reference counter	2.17	2.18	2.13	2.07	2.06	2.09	2.06	2.05	2.13	2.10	
parallel protection set	2.26	2.15	2.12	2.16	2.13	2.07	2.09	2.16	2.03	2.03	
parallel java	17.6	19.2	18.4	20.6	22.7	20.8	18.5	22.5	23.6	19.4	
std::shared_mutex	2.24	2.12	2.18	2.05	2.05	2.2	2.16	2.17	2.02	2.07	

Table 33. Wall-clock time for traversing terms (distinct).

#Threads	1	2	3	4	5	6	7	8	9	10	11
parallel reference counter	18.4	9.61	6.41	4.93	4.10	3.56	3.14	2.88	2.63	2.51	2.34
parallel protection set	17.0	8.80	6.03	4.59	3.85	3.39	3.00	2.78	2.56	2.40	2.28
sequential reference counter	15.9										
sequential protection set	18.3										
original aterm library	17.4										
parallel java	34.5	34.2	35.8	37.0	35.5	33.8	30.1	28.3	27.1	23.4	21.9
std::shared_mutex	16.5	8.59	5.98	4.63	3.99	3.47	3.07	2.88	2.60	2.49	2.43
#Threads	12	13	14	15	16	17	18	19	20	21	22
parallel reference counter	2.36	2.33	2.33	2.28	2.24	2.19	2.26	2.22	2.16	2.20	2.11
parallel protection set	2.31	2.38	2.28	2.31	2.20	2.21	2.21	2.13	2.21	2.16	2.18
parallel java	21.1	17.5	20.9	17.3	18.7	20.8	23.0	18.4	21.6	23.0	22.8
std::shared_mutex	2.56	2.52	2.50	2.41	2.32	2.25	2.4	2.37	2.25	2.34	2.39
#Threads	23	24	25	26	27	28	29	30	31	32	
parallel reference counter	2.27	2.16	2.16	2.13	2.10	2.34	2.13	2.06	2.16	2.05	
parallel protection set	2.27	2.15	2.16	2.17	2.12	2.08	2.11	2.10	2.06	2.04	
parallel java	18.3	22.2	22.3	22.5	18.7	21.7	22.2	19.3	22.8	19.5	
std::shared_mutex	2.18	2.30	2.27	2.34	2.14	2.28	2.08	2.10	2.38	2.26	

References

1. Baeten, J.C.M., Weijland, W.P.: Process Algebra, Cambridge Tracts in Theoretical Computer Science, vol. 18. Cambridge University Press, Cambridge (1990)
2. Bergstra, J.A., Klint, P.: The ToolBus coordination architecture. In: Ciancarini, P., Hankin, C. (eds.) COORDINATION 1996. LNCS, vol. 1061, pp. 75–88. Springer, Heidelberg (1996). https://doi.org/10.1007/3-540-61052-9_40
3. Blom, S., Lisser, B., van de Pol, J., Weber, M.: A database approach to distributed state-space generation. J. Log. Comput. 21(1), 45–62 (2011). https://doi.org/10.1093/logcom/exp004
4. van den Brand, M., de Jong, H.A., Klint, P., Olivier, P.A.: Efficient annotated terms. Softw. Pract. Exp. 30(3), 259–291 (2000)
5. van den Brand, M., Klint, P.: ATerms for manipulation and exchange of structured data: it's all about sharing. Inf. Softw. Technol. 49(1), 55–64 (2007). https://doi.org/10.1016/j.infsof.2006.08.009
6. van den Brand, M., Moreau, P.E., Vinju, J.: Generator of efficient strongly typed abstract syntax trees in Java. IEE Proceedings - Software, vol. 152, pp. 70–78(8), April 2005
7. Cantrill, B., Bonwick, J.: Real-world concurrency. Commun. ACM 51(11), 34–39 (2008). https://doi.org/10.1145/1400214.1400227
8. Fokkink, W., Pang, J., van de Pol, J.: Cones and foci: a mechanical framework for protocol verification. Formal Methods Syst. Des. 29(1), 1–31 (2006). https://doi.org/10.1007/s10703-006-0004-3

9. Gao, H., Groote, J.F., Hesselink, W.: Lock-free dynamic hash tables with open addressing. Distrib. Comput. **18**(1), 21–42 (2005). https://doi.org/10.1007/s00446-004-0115-2

10. Gao, H., Groote, J.F., Hesselink, W.: Lock-free parallel and concurrent garbage collection by mark&sweep. Sci. Comput. Program. **64**(3), 341–374 (2007). https://doi.org/10.1016/j.scico.2006.10.001

11. van Glabbeek, R.J., Luttik, S.P., Trcka, N.: Branching bisimilarity with explicit divergence. Fundam. Informaticae **93**(4), 371–392 (2009). https://doi.org/10.3233/FI-2009-109

12. van Glabbeek, R.J., Weijland, W.P.: Branching time and abstraction in bisimulation semantics. J. ACM **43**(3), 555–600 (1996). https://doi.org/10.1145/233551.233556

13. Groote, J.F., Mousavi, M.R.: Modeling and Analysis of Communicating Systems. MIT Press, Cambridge (2014). https://mitpress.mit.edu/books/modeling-and-analysis-communicating-systems

14. Groote, J.F., Keiren, J.J.A.: Tutorial: designing distributed software in mCRL2. In: Peters, K., Willemse, T.A.C. (eds.) FORTE 2021. LNCS, vol. 12719, pp. 226–243. Springer, Cham (2021). https://doi.org/10.1007/978-3-030-78089-0_15

15. Groote, J.F., Springintveld, J.: Focus points and convergent process operators: a proof strategy for protocol verification. J. Log. Algebr. Methods Program. **49**(1–2), 31–60 (2001). https://doi.org/10.1016/S1567-8326(01)00010-8

16. Hesselink, W., Groote, J.F.: Wait-free concurrent memory management by create and read until deletion (CaRuD). Distrib. Comput. **14**(1), 31–39 (2001). https://doi.org/10.1007/PL00008924

17. de Jong, H.A., Olivier, P.: Generation of abstract programming interfaces from syntax definitions. J. Logic Algebr. Program. **59**(1), 35–61 (2004). https://doi.org/10.1016/j.jlap.2003.12.002

18. Kats, L.C., Visser, E.: The spoofax language workbench: rules for declarative specification of languages and ides. SIGPLAN Not. **45**(10), 444–463 (2010). https://doi.org/10.1145/1932682.1869497

19. Krieger, O., Stumm, M., Unrau, R., Hanna, J.: A fair fast scalable rea, der-writer lock. In: 1993 International Conference on Parallel Processing - ICPP 1993, vol. 2, pp. 201–204 (1993). https://doi.org/10.1109/ICPP.1993.21

20. Lankamp, A.: https://github.com/cwi-swat/aterms/blob/master/shared-objects/src/shared/SharedObjectFactory.java. Accessed 2021; Last Changed 16 Dec 2009

21. Lev, Y., Luchangco, V., Olszewski, M.: Scalable reader-writer locks. In: Proceedings of the Twenty-First Annual Symposium on Parallelism in Algorithms and Architectures. SPAA 2009, pp. 101–110. Association for Computing Machinery, New York (2009). https://doi.org/10.1145/1583991.1584020

22. Luttik, S.P.: Description and formal specification of the link layer of P1394. In: Lovrek, I. (ed.) Proceedings of the 2nd International Workshop on Applied Formal Methods in System Design, pp. 43–56. University of Zagreb, Croatia (1997)

23. Mellor-Crummey, J.M., Scott, M.L.: Synchronization without contention. In: Proceedings of the Fourth International Conference on Architectural Support for Programming Languages and Operating Systems. ASPLOS IV, pp. 269–278. Association for Computing Machinery, New York (1991). https://doi.org/10.1145/106972.106999

24. Milner, R. (ed.): A Calculus of Communicating Systems. LNCS, vol. 92. Springer, Heidelberg (1980). https://doi.org/10.1007/3-540-10235-3

25. Prokopec, A., Bronson, N., Bagwell, P., Odersky, M.: Concurrent tries with efficient non-blocking snapshots. ACM SIGPLAN Not. **47**, 151–160 (2012). https://doi.org/10.1145/2145816.2145836

26. Raynal, M.: Concurrent Programming - Algorithms, Principles, and Foundations. Springer, Cham (2013). https://doi.org/10.1007/978-3-642-32027-9

27. van Spaendonck, P.H.M.: Verification of the busy-forbidden protocol (using an extension of the cones and foci framework) (2022). https://doi.org/10.48550/ARXIV.2208.05334

28. Sun, Y., Blelloch, G.: Implementing parallel and concurrent tree structures. In: Proceedings of the 24th Symposium on Principles and Practice of Parallel Programming. PPoPP 2019, pp. 447–450. Association for Computing Machinery, New York (2019). https://doi.org/10.1145/3293883.3302576

29. Treiber, R.: Systems Programming: Coping with Parallelism. International Business Machines Incorporated, Thomas J. Watson Research (1986)

30. Umar, I., Anshus, O., Ha, P.: GreenBST: energy-efficient concurrent search tree. In: Dutot, P.-F., Trystram, D. (eds.) Euro-Par 2016. LNCS, vol. 9833, pp. 502–517. Springer, Cham (2016). https://doi.org/10.1007/978-3-319-43659-3_37

ST4MP: A Blueprint of Multiparty Session Typing for Multilingual Programming

Sung-Shik Jongmans[1,2] and José Proença[3(✉)]

[1] Open University of the Netherlands, Heerlen, Netherlands
`ssj@ou.nl`
[2] Centrum Wiskunde & Informatica (CWI), NWO-I, Amsterdam, Netherlands
[3] CISTER, ISEP, Polytechnic Institute of Porto, Porto, Portugal
`jose@proenca.org`

Abstract. Multiparty session types (MPST) constitute a method to simplify construction and analysis of distributed systems. The idea is that well-typedness of processes at compile-time (statically) entails deadlock freedom and protocol compliance of their sessions of communications at execution-time (dynamically).

In practice, the premier approach to apply the MPST method in combination with mainstream programming languages has been based on API generation. However, existing MPST tools support only unilingual programming (homogeneity), while many real-world distributed systems are engineered using multilingual programming (heterogeneity).

In this paper, we present a blueprint of ST4MP: a tool to apply the MPST method in multilingual programming, based on API generation.

1 Introduction

Construction and analysis of distributed systems is difficult. Challenges include:

- To implement protocols among roles/participants, by programming *multiparty sessions* of *communicating processes*.
- To verify absence of communication errors, by proving *deadlock freedom* (i.e., the processes can always terminate or reduce) and *protocol compliance* (i.e., if the processes can terminate or reduce, then the protocol allows it).

Multiparty session types (MPST) [17,18] constitute a method to overcome these challenges. The idea is visualised in Fig. 1:

1. First, a protocol among roles $r_1, \ldots, r_n$ is implemented as a session of processes $P_1, \ldots, P_n$ (concrete), while it is specified as a *global type* G (abstract). The global type models the behaviour of all processes together, collectively, from their shared perspective (e.g., "first, a number from Alice to Bob; second, a boolean from Bob to Carol").
2. Next, G is decomposed into local types $L_1, \ldots, L_n$ by *projecting* G onto every role. Every local type models the behaviour of one process alone, individually, from its own perspective (e.g., for Bob, "first, he receives a number from Alice; second, he sends a boolean to Carol).

T. Margaria and B. Steffen (Eds.): ISoLA 2022, LNCS 13701, pp. 460–478, 2022.
https://doi.org/10.1007/978-3-031-19849-6_26

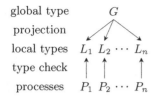

Fig. 1. MPST method.

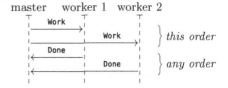

Fig. 2. Master–workers protocol (Example 1).

3. Last, absence of communication errors is verified by *type-checking* every process P_i against local type L_i. MPST theory guarantees that well-typedness at compile-time (statically) implies deadlock freedom and protocol compliance at execution-time (dynamically).

The following example demonstrates the MPST method.

Example 1. In the master–workers protocol, visualised in Fig. 2, first, the *master* ($\mathbf{m}$) tells n *workers* ($\mathbf{w}_1, \ldots, \mathbf{w}_n$) to perform work ($\mathtt{Work}$), in that order; second, the workers tell the master that they are done ($\mathtt{Done}$), in any order.

The following global type specifies the protocol ($n = 2$):

$$G = \mathbf{m} \twoheadrightarrow \mathbf{w}_1{:}\mathtt{Work} \,.\, \mathbf{m} \twoheadrightarrow \mathbf{w}_2{:}\mathtt{Work} \,.\, (\mathbf{w}_1 \twoheadrightarrow \mathbf{m}{:}\mathtt{Done} \,.\, \mathbf{end} \,\|\!|\, \mathbf{w}_2 \twoheadrightarrow \mathbf{m}{:}\mathtt{Done} \,.\, \mathbf{end})$$

Global type $p \twoheadrightarrow q{:}t.G$ specifies the communication of a value of type t_i through the channel from role p to role q, followed by G. Global type $G_1 \| G_2$ specifies the free interleaving of G_1 and G_2. Global type $\mathbf{end}$ specifies termination.

The following local types specify the master ($n = 2$) and a worker (any n):

$$L_{\mathbf{m}} = \mathbf{mw}_1!\mathtt{Work} \,.\, \mathbf{mw}_2!\mathtt{Work} \,.\, (\mathbf{w}_1\mathbf{m}?\mathtt{Done} \,.\, \mathbf{end} \,\|\!|\, \mathbf{w}_2\mathbf{m}?\mathtt{Done} \,.\, \mathbf{end})$$
$$L_{\mathbf{w}_i} = \mathbf{mw}_i?\mathtt{Work} \,.\, \mathbf{w}_i\mathbf{m}!\mathtt{Done} \,.\, \mathbf{end}$$

Local types $pq!t.L$ and $pq?t.L$ specify the send and receive of a value of type t through the channel from role p to role q, followed by L. Local types $L_1 \| L_2$ and $\mathbf{end}$ are similar to the corresponding forms of global types. In general, a local type L_r for role r is mechanically constructed by projecting a global type G onto r, using a recursive function that traverses G's structure. Roughly: every communication in which r participates as sender is preserved as a send in L_r; every communication in which r participates as receiver is preserved as a receive in L_r; every communication in which r does not participate is omitted from L_r.

The following processes implement the master ($n = 2$) and a worker (any n):

$$P_{\mathbf{m}} = \mathbf{mw}_1!\mathtt{work}(\texttt{"grep -o -i foo file.txt | wc -1"}) \,. \qquad P_{\mathbf{w}_i} = \mathbf{mw}_i?x{:}\mathtt{Work} \,.$$
$$\mathbf{mw}_2!\mathtt{work}(\texttt{"grep -o -i bar file.txt | wc -1"}) \,. \qquad\qquad \mathbf{w}_i\mathbf{m}!\mathtt{do}(x) \,.\, \mathbf{end}$$
$$(\mathbf{w}_1\mathbf{m}?\_{:}\mathtt{Done} \,.\, \mathbf{end} \,\|\!|\, \mathbf{w}_2\mathbf{m}?\_{:}\mathtt{Done} \,.\, \mathbf{end})$$

Processes $pq!e.P$ and $pq?x{:}t.P$ implement the send and receive of the value of expression e (evaluated at the sender) through the channel from role p to role q

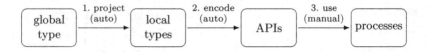

Fig. 3. Workflow of API generation (arrows 1–2 are performed automatically by the tool; arrow 3 is performed manually by the programmer).

into variable x of type t (stored at the receiver), followed by P. Processes $P_1 ||| P_2$ and **end** are similar to the corresponding forms of global/local types.

$L_{\tt m}$ and $L_{{\tt w}_i}$ are projections of G. Furthermore, assuming that the return types of **work** and **do** are Work and Done, $P_{\tt m}$ and $P_{{\tt w}_i}$ are well-typed by $L_{\tt m}$ and $L_{{\tt w}_i}$: roughly, the processes and the local types implement (in terms of concrete values of data) and specify (in terms of abstract types of data) the same behaviour. □

In practice, the premier approach to apply the MPST method in combination with mainstream programming languages has been based on *API generation*. The idea, conceived by Hu and Yoshida [19], is based on the insight that local types can be encoded as *application programming interfaces* (API), such that well-typed usage of the APIs at compile-time implies deadlock freedom and protocol compliance at execution-time (cf. step 3 of the MPST method). The corresponding workflow is visualised in Fig. 3. API generation has been influential: it is used in the majority of tools that support the MPST method, including Scribble [19,20], its many dialects/extensions [7,23,25,28,30,32,39], νScr [38], mpstpp [22], and Pompset [8]. The curious reader can glimpse at Fig. 12 for an excerpt of the generated Scala API (following [8,19]) for the master–workers protocol from Example 1.

Open Problem

So far, MPST tools based on API generation have been developed for a wide range of languages, imperative and functional alike, including (in alphabetic order): F# [30], F* [39], Go [7], Java [19,20,22], OCaml [38], PureScript [23], Rust [25], Scala [8,32], and TypeScript [28]. However, none of the existing tools is capable of generating APIs in multiple languages; they support only *unilingual programming* (homogeneity), often leveraging special features of the host's type system to encode advanced MPST concepts (e.g., type providers in F# to encode MPST-based refinement types [30]). In contrast, many real-world distributed systems are engineered using *multilingual programming* (heterogeneity), where some processes are implemented in one language, but others in another. This open problem has not received due attention.

Figure 4a visualises a naive, seemingly simple/low-effort, solution: reuse an existing MPST tool that can generate APIs in a single language $\mathcal{L}_1$, in combination with language bindings for languages $\mathcal{L}_2, \ldots, \mathcal{L}_n$ using *wrapper libraries* as foreign function interfaces, to write processes in $\mathcal{L}_1, \mathcal{L}_2, \ldots, \mathcal{L}_n$. Whereas executing processes in this way is well-understood, verifying processes in this way—the whole point of using API generation—is not. The key issue is that, to enjoy deadlock freedom and protocol compliance as usual, the language bindings should guarantee that well-typed usage of the wrappers in $\mathcal{L}_2, \ldots, \mathcal{L}_n$ implies well-typed usage of the APIs in $\mathcal{L}_1$. Figure 4b visualises an alternative solution that avoids this issue: use a new tool that can generate APIs in multiple languages $\mathcal{L}_1, \ldots, \mathcal{L}_n$.

Contribution

In this paper, we present the *ST4MP* project. ST4MP is an acronym for "Session Types Fo(u)r Multilingual Programming" and pronounced as "stamp". The aim of ST4MP is to develop a tool to apply the MPST method in multilingual programming, based on API generation, according to the workflow in Fig. 4b.

Existing work focusses on the discovery/invention of new techniques for a single language (e.g., by leveraging special features of the language's type system in generated APIs). In contrast, ST4MP focusses on the combination/integration of existing techniques for multiple languages. That is, in ST4MP, we prioritise "the (re)engineering of existing techniques" over "the science of new ones".

In Sect. 2, we briefly summarise a basic version of MPST theory; it serves as the foundation of ST4MP. In Sect. 3, we present a blueprint of the ST4MP tool, including an overview of the ST4MP language. In Sect. 4, we discuss related work. We emphasise that this paper focusses on the design of ST4MP; the implementation is work-in-progress, part of ongoing efforts, and presented in more detail in a future paper. Moreover, in alignment with the "engineering first, science second"-attitude behind ST4MP, we note that we do not present new techniques in this paper: the blueprint of ST4MP is based on the combination/integration of existing techniques. As a result, this paper can also be read as an introductory article on API generation.

2 MPST Theory in a Nutshell

In this section, we summarise a basic version of MPST theory, based on the more advanced version by Deniélou and Yoshida [10]; given the aim of this

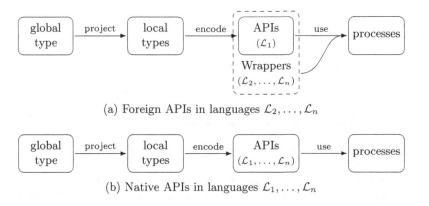

(a) Foreign APIs in languages $\mathcal{L}_2, \ldots, \mathcal{L}_n$

(b) Native APIs in languages $\mathcal{L}_1, \ldots, \mathcal{L}_n$

Fig. 4. Workflows of API generation for multilingual programming.

paper, we omit orthogonal and/or more complicated features from this section (e.g., dynamic channel creation, dynamic process creation, and delegation). Our presentation in this section follows the top-down visualisation in Fig. 1.

2.1 Global Types

Let $\mathbb{R} = \{\texttt{alice}, \texttt{bob}, \texttt{carol}, \texttt{m}, \texttt{w}, \ldots\}$ denote the set of all *roles*, ranged over by p, q, r. Let $\mathbb{T} = \{\texttt{Unit}, \texttt{Bool}, \texttt{Nat}, \texttt{Work}, \texttt{Done}, \ldots\}$ denote the set of all *data types*, ranged over by t. Let $\mathbb{G}$ denote the set of all *global types*, ranged over by G:

$$G ::= p \rightarrow q{:}\{t_i.G_i\}_{1 \leq i \leq n} \mid G_1 \oplus G_2 \mid \mu X.G \mid X \mid \textbf{end} \qquad \oplus ::= \; ||| \; \mid \; \cdot$$

Informally, these forms of global types have the following meaning:

- Global type $p \rightarrow q{:}\{t_i.G_i\}_{1 \leq i \leq n}$ specifies the **asynchronous communication** of a value of type t_i through the channel from role p to role q, followed by G_i, for some $1 \leq i \leq n$. As additional well-formedness requirements, we stipulate: **(1)** $p \neq q$ (i.e., no self-communication); **(2)** $t_i \neq t_j$, for every $1 \leq i < j \leq n$ (i.e., deterministic continuations). We omit the curly brackets when $n = 1$.
- Global type $G_1|||G_2$ specifies the **parallel composition** of G_1 and G_2 that freely interleaves their communications. As an additional well-formedness requirement [10], we stipulate $\mathsf{comm}(G_1) \cap \mathsf{comm}(G_2) = \emptyset$ (i.e., distinct communications in distinct subprotocols), where $\mathsf{comm} : \mathbb{G} \rightarrow 2^{\mathbb{R} \times \mathbb{R} \times \mathbb{T}}$ is a function that maps every global type to the communications that occur in it, represented as triples of the form (p, q, t).
- Global type $G_1 \cdot G_2$ specifies the **sequential composition** of G_1 and G_2.
- Global types $\mu X.G$ and X specify a **recursive protocol**.
- Global type **end** specifies the **empty protocol**.

Example 2. The following global type specifies the master–workers protocol (Example 1) with two extensions (worker i can tell worker $i + 1$ to perform some or none of the work on its behalf; the protocol is repeated):

$$G = \mu X . ((\texttt{m} \rightarrow [\texttt{w}_1, \texttt{w}_2]{:}\texttt{Work} . \texttt{w}_1 \rightarrow \texttt{w}_2{:}\{\texttt{Work} . \texttt{w}_2 \rightarrow \texttt{w}_1{:}\texttt{Done} . G' , \texttt{None} . G'\}) \cdot X)$$

$$G' = \texttt{w}_1 \rightarrow \texttt{m}{:}\texttt{Done} . \textbf{end}|||\texttt{w}_2 \rightarrow \texttt{m}{:}\texttt{Done} . \textbf{end}$$

We write "$\texttt{m} \rightarrow [\texttt{w}_1, \texttt{w}_2]{:}\texttt{Work}$" as a shorthand for "$\texttt{m} \rightarrow \texttt{w}_1{:}\texttt{Work} . \texttt{m} \rightarrow \texttt{w}_2{:}\texttt{Work}$". □

2.2 Local Types and Projection

Let $\dagger \in \{!, ?\}$. Let $\mathbb{L}$ denote the set of all *local types*, ranged over by L:

$$L ::= \underbrace{pq!\{t_i.L_i\}_{1 \leq i \leq n}}_{\text{send}} \mid \underbrace{pq?\{t_i.L_i\}_{1 \leq i \leq n}}_{\text{receive}} \mid L_1 \oplus L_2 \mid \mu X.L \mid X \mid \textbf{end}$$

These forms of local types are similar to the corresponding forms of global types.

Let $G \restriction r$ denote the *projection* of G onto r. Formally, $\restriction$ is the smallest function induced by the equations in Fig. 5. The projection of $p \rightarrow q{:}\{t_i.G_i\}_{1 \leq i \leq n}$ onto r depends on the contribution of r to the communication: if r is sender (resp. receiver), then the projection specifies a send (resp. receive); if r does not

$$p{\to}q{:}\{t_i.G_i\}_{1\le i\le n} \restriction r = \begin{cases} pq!\{t_i.(G_i \restriction r)\}_{1\le i\le n} & \text{if } p = r \neq q \\ pq?\{t_i.(G_i \restriction r)\}_{1\le i\le n} & \text{if } p \neq r = q \\ G_1 \restriction r & \text{if } p \neq r \neq q \text{ and} \\ & \quad G_1 \restriction r = \cdots = G_n \restriction r \end{cases}$$

$$(G_1 \oplus G_2) \restriction r = \begin{cases} \textbf{end} & \text{if: } G_1 \restriction r = \textbf{end} = G_2 \restriction r \\ G_2 \restriction r & \text{if: } G_1 \restriction r = \textbf{end} \neq G_2 \restriction r \\ G_1 \restriction r & \text{if: } G_1 \restriction r \neq \textbf{end} = G_2 \restriction r \\ (G_1 \restriction r) \oplus (G_2 \restriction r) & \text{if: } G_1 \restriction r \neq \textbf{end} \neq G_2 \restriction r \end{cases}$$

$$\mu X.G \restriction r = \mu X.(G \restriction r) \qquad X \restriction r = X \qquad \textbf{end} \restriction r = \textbf{end}$$

Fig. 5. Projection of global types.

contribute to the communication, and if r has a unique continuation, then the projection is that continuation. The latter means that r is insensitive to which type was communicated (which, as a non-contributor to the communication, r does not know). We note that projection is partial: if the projection of a global type onto one of its roles is undefined, then the global type is unsupported. We also note that, for simplicity and because it does not affect this paper, we use the "plain merge" instead of the "full merge" [33].

Example 3. The following local types specify the master and the workers in the extended master–workers protocol (Example 2):

$L'_{\mathtt{w}_1} = \mathtt{mw}_1?\mathtt{Work}.\mathtt{w}_1\mathtt{w}_2!\{\mathtt{Work}.\mathtt{w}_2\mathtt{w}_1?\mathtt{Done}.\mathtt{w}_1\mathtt{m}!\mathtt{Done}.\mathtt{end}, \mathtt{None}.\mathtt{w}_1\mathtt{m}!\mathtt{Done}.\mathtt{end}\}$

$L'_{\mathtt{w}_2} = \mathtt{mw}_2?\mathtt{Work}.\mathtt{w}_1\mathtt{w}_2?\{\mathtt{Work}.\mathtt{w}_2\mathtt{w}_1!\mathtt{Done}.\mathtt{w}_2\mathtt{m}!\mathtt{Done}.\mathtt{end}, \mathtt{None}.\mathtt{w}_2\mathtt{m}!\mathtt{Done}.\mathtt{end}\}$

$L_{\mathtt{m}} = \mu X.(L_{\mathtt{m}}^{\mathrm{Ex.1}} \cdot X) \qquad L_{\mathtt{w}_1} = \mu X.(L'_{\mathtt{w}_1} \cdot X) \qquad L_{\mathtt{w}_2} = \mu X.(L'_{\mathtt{w}_2} \cdot X) \qquad \square$

2.3 Processes and Typing Rules

Let $\mathbb{V}$ denote the set of all *values*, ranged over by v. Let $\mathbb{X}$ denote the set of all *variables*, ranged over by x. Let $\mathbb{E} = \mathbb{V} \cup \mathbb{X} \cup \cdots$ denote the set of all *expressions*, ranged over by e. Let $\mathbb{P}$ denote the set of all *processes*, ranged over by P:

$$P ::= \textbf{if } e\, P_1\, P_2 \mid pq!e.P \mid pq?\{x_i{:}t_i.P_i\}_{1\le i\le n} \mid P_1 \oplus P_2 \mid \mu X.P \mid X \mid \textbf{end}$$

Informally, these forms of processes have the following meaning:

- Process **if** $e\, P_1\, P_2$ implements the **conditional choice** between P_1 and P_2.
- Process $pq!e.P$ implements the **send** of the value of expression e through the channel from role p to role q, followed by P. Asynchronous sends can be combined with conditional choices to implement *internal choices*.
- Process $pq?\{x_i{:}t_i.P_i\}_{1\le i\le n}$ implements the **receive** of a value into variable x_i of type t_i through the channel from role p to role q, followed by P_i (i.e., type switch on the received value), for some $1 \le i \le n$. Asynchronous receives can be used to implement *external choices*. Thus, through an internal choice and a reciprocal external choice, the sender can "select" a value of a particular type to control whereto the receiver "branches off".

$$\frac{\Gamma \vdash e : \mathsf{Bool} \quad \Gamma \vdash P_1 : L \quad \Gamma \vdash P_2 : L}{\Gamma \vdash \mathsf{if}\ e\ P_1\ P_2 : L}\ [\text{IF}] \qquad\qquad \frac{\Gamma \vdash P : L}{\Gamma \vdash \mu X.P : \mu X.L}\ [\text{MU}]$$

$$\frac{\Gamma \vdash e : t_i \quad \Gamma \vdash P : L_i \quad 1 \le i \le n}{\Gamma \vdash pq!e.P : pq!\{t_i.L_i\}_{1 \le i \le n}}\ [\text{SEND}] \qquad\qquad \frac{}{\Gamma \vdash X : X}\ [\text{VAR}]$$

$$\frac{\Gamma, x_i : t_i \vdash P_i : L_i\ \text{for every}\ 1 \le i \le n}{\Gamma \vdash pq?\{x_i{:}t_i.P_i\}_{1 \le i \le n} : pq?\{t_i.L_i\}_{1 \le i \le n}}\ [\text{RECV}] \qquad\qquad \frac{}{\Gamma \vdash \mathbf{end} : \mathsf{end}}\ [\text{END}]$$

$$\frac{\Gamma \vdash P_1 : L_1 \quad \Gamma \vdash P_2 : L_2}{\Gamma \vdash P_1 \,|\!|\!|\, P_2 : L_1 \,|\!|\!|\, L_2}\ [\text{PAR}] \qquad\qquad \frac{\Gamma \vdash P_1 : L_1 \quad \Gamma \vdash P_2 : L_2}{\Gamma \vdash P_1 \cdot P_2 : L_1 \cdot L_2}\ [\text{SEQ}]$$

Fig. 6. Well-typedness of processes.

- Process $P_1 |\!|\!| P_2$ implements the **parallel composition** of P_1 and P_2. We note that $P_1 |\!|\!| P_2$ is intended to implement *one* role (i.e., there is no communication between P_1 and P_2); the only purpose of parallel composition is to allow the sends and receives of P_1 and P_2 to be ordered dynamically at execution-time.
- Process $P_1 \cdot P_2$ implements the **sequential composition** of P_1 and P_2.
- Processes $\mu X.G$ and X implement a **recursive role**.
- Process **end** implements the **empty role**.

Let $\Gamma \vdash e{:}t$ denote *well-typedness* of expression e by data type t in environment Γ. Let $\Gamma \vdash P{:}L$ denote *well-typedness* of process P by local type L in environment Γ. Formally, $\vdash$ is the smallest relation induced by the rules in Fig. 6. Rule [SEND] states that a send is well-typed by $pq!\{t_i.L_i\}_{1 \le i \le n}$ if, for some $1 \le k \le n$, the value to send is well-typed by t_k and the continuation is well-typed by L_k. Dually, rule [RECV] states that a receive is well-typed by $pq?\{t_i.L_i\}_{1 \le i \le n}$ if, for every $1 \le i \le n$, the continuation is well-typed by L_i under the additional assumption that the received value is well-typed by t_i. Thus, a well-typed process needs to be able to consume all specified inputs, but produce only one specified output.

Theorem 1. (Deniélou and Yoshida [10]**).** *If G is a well-formed global type in which roles $r_1, \ldots, r_n$ occur, and if $\vdash P_i{:}(G \restriction r_i)$ for every $1 \le i \le n$, then the session of $P_1, \ldots, P_n$ is deadlock-free and protocol-compliant with respect to G.*

Example 4. The following processes implement the master and the workers in the extended master–workers protocol (Example 2):

$$P'_{\mathtt{w}_1} = \mathtt{mw}_1?x{:}\mathsf{Work}\,.\,\mathtt{if}\ \mathtt{delegate\_work}(x) \begin{cases} \mathtt{w}_1\mathtt{w}_2!\mathtt{x}\,.\,\mathtt{w}_2\mathtt{w}_1?\mathtt{y}{:}\mathsf{Done}\,.\,\mathtt{w}_1\mathtt{m}!\mathtt{y}\,.\,\mathbf{end} \\ \mathtt{w}_1\mathtt{w}_2!\mathtt{none}()\,.\,\mathtt{w}_1\mathtt{m}!\mathtt{do}(x)\,.\,\mathbf{end} \end{cases}$$

$$P'_{\mathtt{w}_2} = \mathtt{mw}_1?x{:}\mathsf{Work}\,.\,\mathtt{w}_1\mathtt{w}_2? \begin{cases} \mathtt{y}{:}\mathsf{Work}\,.\,\mathtt{w}_2\mathtt{w}_1!\mathtt{do}(\mathtt{y})\,.\,\mathtt{w}_2\mathtt{m}!\mathtt{do}(x)\,.\,\mathbf{end} \\ \_{:}\mathsf{None}\,.\,\mathtt{w}_2\mathtt{m}!\mathtt{do}(x)\,.\,\mathbf{end} \end{cases}$$

$$P_{\mathtt{m}} = \mu X\,.\,(P_{\mathtt{m}}^{\text{Ex.1}} \cdot X) \qquad P_{\mathtt{w}_1} = \mu X\,.\,(P'_{\mathtt{w}_1} \cdot X) \qquad P_{\mathtt{w}_2} = \mu X\,.\,(P'_{\mathtt{w}_2} \cdot X) \qquad \square$$

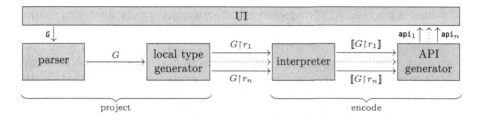

Fig. 7. Architecture of the ST4MP tool.

3   Blueprint of ST4MP

In this section, we present the blueprint of the *ST4MP tool* (henceforth simply called "ST4MP"). ST4MP is a tool to apply the MPST method in multilingual programming, based on API generation, according to the workflow in Fig. 4b. This section focusses on the design; the implementation is work-in-progress, part of ongoing efforts, and presented in more detail in a future paper.

Figure 7 visualises the architecture of ST4MP: boxes represent components; arrows represent data flow between them. The parser and the local type generator correspond to arrow "project" in Fig. 4b, while the interpreter and the API generator correspond with arrow "encode". Next, we discuss the purpose of every component in more detail, along with the main design decisions.

3.1   UI

As ST4MP aims to support multilingual programming, the purpose of the UI is to offer a language-independent and cross-platform user interface.

The main design decision related to the UI has been to make it accessible and usable through any contemporary browser, instead of through a separate plug-in for a particular IDE/editor (to avoid the situation in which programmers are forced to install software only to be able to use ST4MP). As a result, while ST4MP is implemented in Scala, it is compiled to HTML-JavaScript-CSS. A live snapshot is available at https://arca.di.uminho.pt/st4mp/, which is based on our previous Pompset tool [8].

3.2   Parser

The purpose of the parser is to consume a global type in concrete syntax G as input, written in the *ST4MP language* (henceforth simply called "ST4MP"), and produce a global type in abstract syntax G as output (Sect. 2.1). The parser also checks additional well-formedness requirements.

The main design decisions related to the parser have been:

- Use a language-independent notation for data types based on *JSON* ("Java-Script Object Notation") [6]. JSON is a domain-specific language for typed

values; it has been widely adopted as a "text syntax that facilitates structured data interchange between all programming languages" [6]. We use JSON also to auto-serialise (i.e., convert binary data in one language into a common textual exchange format) and auto-deserialise (i.e., convert back to binary data, possibly in another language) inside generated APIs, as clarified shortly.
- Use a language-independent notation for global types based on *Featherweight Scribble* [31]. Featherweight Scribble is a domain-specific language for global types; it was chosen because it is a core fragment of Scribble [19,20] (and its extensions [7,23,25,28,30,32,39]), which has been the premier language to apply the MPST method in combination with mainstream programming languages.

Let ℓ range over *identifiers* in ST4MP (i.e., strings consisting of alphanumericals). Let T and G range over *data types* and *global types* in ST4MP:

$$T ::= \ell(\ell_1 : T_1, \ldots, \ell_n : T_n) \mid \text{[}T\text{]} \mid \text{Number} \mid \text{String} \mid \text{Boolean}$$

$$G ::= T \text{ from } p \text{ to } q; \mid \text{choice at } p \text{ \{ } G_1 \text{ \} or } \cdots \text{ or \{ } G_n \text{ \}} \mid$$

$$\text{par \{ } G_1 \text{ \} and } \cdots \text{ and \{ } G_n \text{ \} } \mid G_1 \ G_2 \mid \text{rec } \ell \text{ \{ } G \text{ \}} \mid \text{continue } \ell;$$

Informally, these forms have the following meaning:

- Data type $\ell(\ell_1 : T_1, \ldots, \ell_n : T_n)$ specifies an *object*, where ℓ identifies the class of the object, while $\ell_1 : T_1, \ldots, \ell_n : T_n$ identify n typed attributes of the object; parentheses can be omitted when $n = 0$. Data type $\text{[}T\text{]}$ specifies an *array*. The remaining data types are self-explanatory.
- Global types in ST4MP follow closely our formalisation of global types in Sect. 2.1; e.g., $T \text{ from } p \text{ to } q; G$ denotes $p \to q : \{T.G\}$. As additional well-formedness conditions, we require: **(1)** every branch of **choice at** p start with a communication in which p is the sender and the receiver is the same; **(2)** if both $\ell(\ell_1 : T_1, \ldots, \ell_n : T_n)$ and $\ell(\ell_{n+1} : T_{n+1}, \ldots, \ell_{n+m} : T_{n+m})$ are in a global type, then $\ell_1 : T_1, \ldots, \ell_n : T_n = \ell_{n+1} : T_{n+1}, \ldots, \ell_{n+m} : T_{n+m}$ (i.e., if ℓ identifies a class, then it must do so unambiguously).

Example 5. The ST4MP code in Fig. 8 specifies the extended master–workers protocol (Example 2). □

3.3   Local Type Generator

The purpose of the local type generator is to consume a global type G as input and produce local types $G \restriction r_1, \ldots, G \restriction r_n$ as output, by projecting G onto every role $r_1, \ldots, r_n$ that occurs in it (Sect. 2.2).

3.4   Interpreter

The purpose of the interpreter is to consume local types $G \restriction r_1, \ldots, G \restriction r_n$ as input and produce transition-based models of their operational behaviour

```
rec Loop {
  Work(cmd:String) from Master to Worker1;
  Work(cmd:String) from Master to Worker2;
  choice at Worker1 {
    Work(cmd:String) from Worker1 to Worker2;
    Done(res:Number) from Worker2 to Worker1;
  } or {
    None() from Worker1 to Worker2;
  }
  par {
    Done(res:Number) from Worker1 to Master;
  } and {
    Done(res:Number) from Worker2 to Master;
  }
  continue Loop; }
```

Fig. 8. Extended master–workers protocol in ST4MP (Example 5).

$[\![G \restriction r_1]\!], \ldots, [\![G \restriction r_n]\!]$ as output; APIs can subsequently be generated for such models.

The main design decision related to the interpreter has been to support two kinds of transition-based models—*automata* and *pomsets*—based on existing interpretation functions on local types [11,13]. To illustrate the idea, the automaton interpretation of local types is summarised in Fig. 9, including an example; the pomset interpretation is more complicated and explained in detail elsewhere [8]. The reason to support two different models is that they have different advantages and, as such, can serve different purposes:

- The advantage of the automaton interpretation of local types is that it is "total": it is defined for all non-recursive local types and for all tail-recursive local types. Another advantage is that the requirements to generate APIs for automata are relatively low (i.e., no advanced type system features needed and can be implemented, e.g., in Java [19]). The disadvantage is that the automaton interpretation suffers from state explosion in the presence of parallel composition.
- The advantage of the pomset interpretation of local types is that it does not suffer from state explosion (i.e., pomsets offer a more concise representation of concurrency than automata). The disadvantage is that the pomset interpretation is "partial": it is defined only for non-recursive local types and top-level tail-recursive local types (i.e., of the form $\mu X.(L \cdot X)$, where L is non-recursive) that are, moreover, choice-free. Another disadvantage is that the requirements to generate APIs for pomsets are relatively high (i.e., advanced type system features are needed; e.g., match types in Scala [1,8]).

Example 7. L_m in Example 3 is both top-level tail-recursive and choice-free, so it can be interpreted not only as an automaton (Example 6 in Fig. 9) but also as a pomset (Cledou et al. [8]). In this way, state explosion can be avoided (i.e.,

Let $\Sigma = \{pq!t \mid p \neq q\} \cup \{pq?t \mid p \neq q\}$ denote the set of all *type-level actions* ("the alphabet"), ranged over by σ. Let $\mathbb{A}$ denote the set of all *automata* over Σ, ranged over by A. Formally, an automaton is a tuple (S, s_i, s_f, δ), where S denotes a set of *states*, $s_i, s_f \in S$ denote the *initial state* and the *final state*, and $\delta : S \times \Sigma \rightharpoonup S$ denotes a *transition function*.

Let $\llbracket L \rrbracket_{\text{aut}}$ denote the *interpretation* of local type L as an automaton. Formally, $\llbracket - \rrbracket_{\text{aut}}$ is the smallest function induced by the following equations:

$$\llbracket \mathbf{end} \rrbracket_{\text{aut}} = \rightarrow\bigcirc\!\!\!\!\bigcirc$$

$$\llbracket pq\dagger\{t_i.L_i\}_{1\leq i\leq n} \rrbracket_{\text{aut}} = \;\rightarrow\bigcirc\cdots$$

$$\text{s.t., for every } 1 \leq i \leq n, \; \llbracket L_i \rrbracket_{\text{aut}} = \rightarrow\; A_i$$

$$\llbracket L_1 \;|||\; L_2 \rrbracket_{\text{aut}} = (S_1 \times S_2, (s_{1i}, s_{2i}), (s_{1f}, s_{2f}), \delta)$$

$$\text{s.t. } \delta((s_1, s_2), \sigma) = \begin{cases} (s_1', s_2) & \text{if } \delta_1(s_1, \sigma) = s_1' \\ (s_1, s_2') & \text{if } \delta_2(s_2, \sigma) = s_2' \end{cases}$$

$$\llbracket L_1 \cdot L_2 \rrbracket_{\text{aut}} = (S_1 \cup S_2, s_{1i}, s_{2f}, \hat{\delta}_1 \cup \delta_2)$$

$$\text{s.t. } \hat{\delta}_1(s_1, \sigma) = \begin{cases} s_1' & \text{if } \delta_1(s_1, \sigma) = s_1' \neq s_{1f} \\ s_{2i} & \text{if } \delta_1(s_1, \sigma) = s_1' = s_{1f} \end{cases}$$

$$\llbracket \mu X.(L_1 \cdot X) \rrbracket_{\text{aut}} = (S_1, s_{1i}, s_{1f}, \hat{\delta}_1) \quad \text{s.t. } \hat{\delta}_1(s_1, \sigma) = \begin{cases} s_1' & \text{if } \delta_1(s_1, \sigma) = s_1' \neq s_{1f} \\ s_{1i} & \text{if } \delta_1(s_1, \sigma) = s_1' = s_{1f} \end{cases}$$

The interpretation of **end** is the automaton that accepts the empty language. The interpretation of $pq\dagger\{t_i.L_i\}_{1\leq i\leq n}$ is the automaton that accepts the language of words that begin with $pq\dagger t_i$ and continue with a word accepted by the interpretation of L_i; the visualisation is intended to convey that the final states of the interpretations of $L_1, \ldots, L_n$ are "superimposed" to form a single new final state. The interpretations of $L_1 \;|||\; L_2$ and $L_1 \cdot L_2$ are the automata that accept the shuffle and the concatenation of the languages accepted by the interpretations of L_1 and L_2.

Example 6. The following automata are the interpretations of $L_\blacksquare$ (left) and $L_{\mathbf{w}_1}$ (right) in the extended master-workers protocol (Example 3):

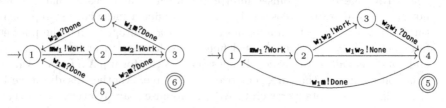

We note that state 6 (left) and state 5 (right) are unreachable. $\qquad\square$

Fig. 9. Interpreting local types as automata [11].

the automaton has $O(2^n)$ states in general, where n is the number of workers) to reduce both the time to generate an API and the space to store it.   □

3.5 API Generator

The purpose of the API generator is to consume operational models $[\![G \restriction r_1]\!], \ldots, [\![G \restriction r_n]\!]$ as input and produce APIs $api_1, \ldots, api_n$ as output.

The underlying principle is that a process P_i is well-typed by local type $G \restriction r_i$ (Sect. 2) if, and only if, every possible sequence of sends and receives by P_i can be simulated by a sequence of transitions of $[\![G \restriction r_i]\!]$. The "trick" is to structure the API in such a way that when the compiler successfully type-checks the API's usage, it has effectively computed a sequence of transitions of $[\![G \restriction r_i]\!]$ for every possible sequence of sends and receives by P_i. The main technique to achieve this is to represent every state of $[\![G \restriction r_i]\!]$ as an object (broadly construed), and every transition as a method (broadly construed), such that every call of method t on object s is well-typed if, and only if, the transition represented by t is allowed in the state represented by s.

From the programmer's perspective, to use the API, a function f needs to be defined that consumes an "initial state object" s0 as input and produces a "final state object" as output. Inside of f, initially, the only actions that can be performed, are those for which a well-typed method call on s0 exists. When such a method is called, an action is performed and a fresh "successor state object" s1 is returned. Subsequently, the only actions that can be performed, are those for which a well-typed method call on s1 exists. When such a method is called, another action is performed, and another fresh "successor successor state object" s2 is returned. This goes on until the final state object is returned (if any).

When a method call is *not* well-typed, it means that: **(1)** the transition is not allowed in the state; **(2)** hence, the local type does not specify the action; **(3)** hence, the action is not allowed in the protocol. As successor state objects become available only after predecessor state objects are used, *and assuming that every state object is used exactly once*, well-typed usage of the API implies protocol compliance. Moreover, as a final state object must have been provided upon termination, *and assuming that there are no other sources of non-terminating or exceptional behaviour*, well-typed usage of the API also implies deadlock freedom. We note that these two additional assumptions cannot be statically enforced in many languages [7,19,22,28,30,32,38]: checking the first assumption requires a form of substructural types, while checking the second assumption is generally undecidable. However, the first assumption can be dynamically monitored using lightweight checks at execution-time.[1]

The main design decisions related to the API generator have been to:

---

[1] Thus, typically, the application of the MPST method using API generation is not absolutely zero-cost in terms of overhead: while the vast majority of the work is done statically, a bit of work is done dynamically. Previous experiments indicate that this overhead is negligible in practice, though (e.g., [7]).

	JSON	Scala
object	$\ell(\ell_1\colon T_1, \ldots, \ell_n\colon T_n)$	class $\ell(\ell_1\colon T_1, \ldots, \ell_n\colon T_n)$ (generated)
array	`[T]`	`Array[T]`
number	`Number`	`Int	Double` (union type)
string	`String`	`String`
boolean	`Boolean`	`Boolean`

Fig. 10. Mapping between types in JSON and Scala.

- Support three languages initially: Java, Scala, and Rust. We selected Java because it is one of the most-used languages today.[2] We selected Scala and Rust because their type systems have special features (match types in Scala and ownership types in Rust) that can be leveraged in generated APIs.
  We note that the combination of Java and Scala also presents original research opportunities: as both languages are executed by the JVM, it is interesting to investigate if special API generation techniques can be developed to leverage the common runtime environment (e.g., to reduce communication latency relative to TCP connections).
- Use TCP and JSON as language-independent mechanisms to transport and represent data. That is, ST4MP will include code in every API to create/configure the underlying TCP connections, plus code to (de)serialise data to JSON values. To illustrate the idea, for Scala, the JSON mapping is summarised in Fig. 10.
- Use existing techniques to generate APIs for transition-based models of local types, namely those conceived by Hu and Yoshida [19] for automata (in Java, Scala, and Rust) and Cledou et al. [8] for pomsets (in Scala). To illustrate the idea, for automata in Scala, the former technique is summarised in Fig. 11, including an example illustrated in Fig. 12; the latter technique is more complicated and explained elsewhere [8].

Example 9. In the extended master-workers protocol, the master can be implemented using the Scala API based on pomsets (to avoid state explosion); the workers can be implemented in Java, Scala, and/or Rust based on automata. □

4   Related Work

The idea to interpret local types as automata was conceived by Deniélou and Yoshida [11,12], within the framework of *communicating finite state machines* (CFSM) [5]. A central notion in this work is *multiparty compatibility*: it is used to provide a sound and complete characterisation between global types and *systems* (i.e., parallel compositions of automata that communicate through asynchronous

---

[2] https://www.tiobe.com/tiobe-index/.

Suppose that (S, s_i, s_f, δ) is the automaton interpretation of the local type for role r:

- Every state $s \in S$ is represented as class $\langle r \rangle \$ \langle s \rangle$ in the API, where $\langle r \rangle$ and $\langle s \rangle$ are identifiers for r and s (and $\$$ is a meaningless separator).
- Every transition $\delta(s, \sigma)$ is represented as a method of class $\langle r \rangle \$ \langle s \rangle$ to perform action σ and return an instance of class $\langle r \rangle \$ \langle \delta(s, \sigma) \rangle$.

If s has only !-transitions of the form $\delta(s, rq_1!t_1), \ldots, \delta(s, rq_n!t_n)$, then:

```
class ⟨r⟩$⟨s⟩(net: Network):
    def send(q: ⟨q₁⟩, e: ⟨t₁⟩): ⟨r⟩$⟨δ(s,pq₁!t₁)⟩ = ...
    ...
    def send(q: ⟨qₙ⟩, e: ⟨tₙ⟩): ⟨r⟩$⟨δ(s,pqₙ!tₙ)⟩ = ...
```

Parameter net of class $\langle r \rangle \$ \langle s \rangle$ encapsulates the underlying communication infrastructure; it is used inside of every send method to perform the "real send". Parameter q of every send method is the identifier of the receiver, parameter e is the value to send, and the return value is a successor state object. These methods mimic $pq!e.P$ (Section 2.3). If s has only ?-transitions of the form $\delta(s, p_1r?t_1), \ldots, \delta(s, p_nr?t_n)$, then:

```
class ⟨r⟩$⟨s⟩(net: Network):
    def recv(f1: (⟨p₁⟩, ⟨t₁⟩, ⟨r⟩$⟨δ(s,p₁q?t₁)⟩) => ⟨r⟩$⟨s_f⟩,
        ...,
        fn: (⟨pₙ⟩, ⟨tₙ⟩, ⟨r⟩$⟨δ(s,pₙq?tₙ)⟩) => ⟨r⟩$⟨s_f⟩) = ...
```

Parameter fi of method recv is the i-th *continuation*; it is called with the identifier of the sender, the value to receive, and a successor state object after the "real receive". This method mimics $pq?\{x_i:t_i.P_i\}_{1 \leq i \leq n}$ (Section 2.3). If s has both !-transitions and ?-transitions, an error is reported.

Example 8. The APIs in Figure 12 are generated for $[\![L_\blacksquare]\!]_{\text{aut}}$ and $[\![L_{w_1}]\!]_{\text{aut}}$ in the extended master–workers protocol (Example 6 in Figure 9). We note that classes M\$6 and W1\$5 represent unreachable final states.
Furthermore, functions m and w1 in Figure 12. which use the generated APIs, are Scala versions of $P_\blacksquare$ and P_{w_1} (Example 4). We note that the two sends in the implementation of the master cannot be swapped (i.e., first to worker 2, second to worker 1): the resulting code would not be well-typed, indicating that the protocol is violated. We also note that we omitted all type annotations for parameters in continuations; they can be inferred by the compiler.   □

Fig. 11. Generating Scala APIs for automata.

---

channels). Multiparty compatibility was further studied and generalised in subsequent work, to cover timed behaviour [4], more flexible choice [26], and nonsynchronisability [27].

The idea to represent automata as APIs was conceived by Hu and Yoshida [19, 20], for Java. The approach has subsequently been used in combination with numerous other programming languages as well, including F# [30], F* [39], Go [7], OCaml [38], PureScript [23], Rust [25], Scala [32], and TypeScript [28]. In many of these works, special features of the type system of "the host" are leveraged to offer additional compile-time guarantees and/or support

```
// generated API (excerpt)
class M$1(net: Network):
  def send(q: W1, e: Work): M$2 = ...
class M$2(net: Network):
  def send(q: W2, e: Work): M$3 = ...
class M$3(net: Network):
  def recv(f1: (W1, Done, M$4) => M$6,
           f2: (W2, Done, M$5) => M$6): M$6 = ...
class M$4(net: Network):
  def recv(f2: (W2, Done, M$1) => M$6): M$6 = ...
class M$5(net: Network):
  def recv(f1: (W1, Done, M$1) => M$6): M$6 = ...
class M$6(net: Network)
type M$Initial = M$1
type M$Final   = M$6

// process
def m(s: M$Initial): M$Final = s.
  send(W1, new Work("grep -o -i foo file.txt | wc -l")).
  send(W2, new Work("grep -o -i bar file.txt | wc -l"))).
  recv((_, x, s) => s.recv(
       (_, y, s) => { println(x.res + y.res); m(s) }),
    (_, x, s) => s.recv(
       (_, y, s) => { println(x.res + y.res); m(s) }))
```

(a) Master

```
// generated API (excerpt)
class W1$1(net: Network):
  def recv(f: (M, Work, W1$2) => W1$5): W1$5 = ...
class W1$2(net: Network):
  def send(q: W2, e: Work): W1$3 = ...
  def send(q: W2, e: None): W1$4 = ...
class W1$3(net: Network):
  def recv(f: (W2, Done, W1$4) => W1$5): W1$5 = ...
class W1$4(net: Network):
  def send(q: M, e: Done): W1$1 = ...
class W1$5(net: Network):
type W1$Initial = W1$1
type W1$Final   = W1$5

// process
def w1(s: W1$Initial): W1$Final = s.
  recv((_, x, s) => if delegateWork(x) then
    s.send(W2, x).recv((_, y, s) => w1(s.send(M, y))) else
    w1(s.send(W2, new None()).send(M, doWork(x))))
```

(b) Worker 1

Fig. 12. Generated Scala APIs and processes for the extended master–workers protocol (Example 8 in Fig. 11).

MPST extensions. For instance, Neykova et al. and Zhou et al. use type providers in F# and refinement types in F* to generate APIs that support MPST-based refinement [30,39], while King et al. and Lagaillardie et al. use indexed monads in PureScript and ownership types in Rust to support static linearity [23,25].

Alternative approaches (i.e., not based on API generation) to apply the MPST method in combination with mainstream programming languages include the work of Imai et al. [21] (for OCaml), the work of Harvey et al., Kouzapas et al., and Voinea et al. [16,24,37] (for Java, using a typestate extension), and the work of Scalas et al. [34,35] (for Scala, using an external model checker). Furthermore, there exist approaches to apply the MPST method that rely on *monitoring* and/or *assertion checking* at execution-time [2,3,9,15,29,30]. The motivation is that in practice, some distributed components of a system might not be amenable to static type-checking (e.g., the source code is unavailable), but they can be dynamically monitored for compliance.

The idea to represent local types as pomsets was conceived by Guanciale and Tuosto [13], in a continuation of earlier work on pomset-based semantics of global types [36]. A key contribution of Guanciale and Tuosto is a sound procedure to determine if a pomset interpretation of a global type is *realisable* as a collection of pomset interpretations of the global type's projections. The PomCho tool [14] supports analysis (including counterexample generation), visualisation, and projection of pomsets. However, PomCho cannot generate APIs.

5   Conclusion

Multiparty session types (MPST) constitute a method to simplify construction and analysis of distributed systems. In practice, the premier approach to apply the MPST method in combination with mainstream programming languages has been based on API generation. However, existing tools support only unilingual programming (homogeneity), while many real-world distributed systems are engineered using multilingual programming (heterogeneity). In this paper, we presented a blueprint of ST4MP: a tool to apply the MPST method in multilingual programming, based on API generation.

Acknowledgements. *Sung-Shik Jongmans:* Netherlands Organisation of Scientific Research (NWO): 016.Veni.192.103.

José Proença: This work was partially supported by National Funds through FCT/MCTES (Portuguese Foundation for Science and Technology), within the CISTER Unit (UIDP/UIDB/04234/2020) and the IBEX project (PTDC/CCI-COM/4280/2021); also by national funds through FCT and European funds through EU ECSEL JU, within project VALU3S (ECSEL/0016/2019 - JU grant nr. 876852) – The JU receives support from the European Union's Horizon 2020 research and innovation programme and Austria, Czech Republic, Germany, Ireland, Italy, Portugal, Spain, Sweden, Turkey. Disclaimer: This document reflects only the author's view and the Commission is not responsible for any use that may be made of the information it contains.

References

1. Blanvillain, O., Brachthäuser, J.I., Kjaer, M., Odersky, M.: Type-level programming with match types. Proc. ACM Program. Lang. **6**(POPL), 1–24 (2022)
2. Bocchi, L., Chen, T., Demangeon, R., Honda, K., Yoshida, N.: Monitoring networks through multiparty session types. Theor. Comput. Sci. **669**, 33–58 (2017)
3. Bocchi, L., Honda, K., Tuosto, E., Yoshida, N.: A theory of design-by-contract for distributed multiparty interactions. In: Gastin, P., Laroussinie, F. (eds.) CONCUR 2010. LNCS, vol. 6269, pp. 162–176. Springer, Heidelberg (2010). https://doi.org/10.1007/978-3-642-15375-4_12
4. Bocchi, L., Lange, J., Yoshida, N.: Meeting deadlines together. In: CONCUR. LIPIcs, vol. 42, pp. 283–296. Schloss Dagstuhl - Leibniz-Zentrum für Informatik (2015)
5. Brand, D., Zafiropulo, P.: On communicating finite-state machines. J. ACM **30**(2), 323–342 (1983)
6. Bray, T.: The JavaScript Object Notation (JSON) Data Interchange Format. RFC 7159, March 2014. https://doi.org/10.17487/RFC7159, https://www.rfc-editor.org/info/rfc7159
7. Castro-Perez, D., Hu, R., Jongmans, S., Ng, N., Yoshida, N.: Distributed programming using role-parametric session types in Go: statically-typed endpoint APIs for dynamically-instantiated communication structures. Proc. ACM Program. Lang. **3**(POPL), 29:1–29:30 (2019)
8. Cledou, G., Edixhoven, L., Jongmans, S.S., Proença, J.: API generation for multiparty session types, revisited and revised using Scala 3. In: ECOOP. LIPIcs, vol. 222, pp. 27:1–27:28. Schloss Dagstuhl - Leibniz-Zentrum für Informatik (2022)
9. Demangeon, R., Honda, K., Hu, R., Neykova, R., Yoshida, N.: Practical interruptible conversations: distributed dynamic verification with multiparty session types and Python. Formal Methods Syst. Des. **46**(3), 197–225 (2015)
10. Deniélou, P., Yoshida, N.: Dynamic multirole session types. In: POPL, pp. 435–446. ACM (2011)
11. Deniélou, P.-M., Yoshida, N.: Multiparty session types meet communicating automata. In: Seidl, H. (ed.) ESOP 2012. LNCS, vol. 7211, pp. 194–213. Springer, Heidelberg (2012). https://doi.org/10.1007/978-3-642-28869-2_10
12. Deniélou, P.-M., Yoshida, N.: Multiparty compatibility in communicating automata: characterisation and synthesis of global session types. In: Fomin, F.V., Freivalds, R., Kwiatkowska, M., Peleg, D. (eds.) ICALP 2013. LNCS, vol. 7966, pp. 174–186. Springer, Heidelberg (2013). https://doi.org/10.1007/978-3-642-39212-2_18
13. Guanciale, R., Tuosto, E.: Realisability of pomsets. J. Log. Algebraic Methods Program. **108**, 69–89 (2019)
14. Guanciale, R., Tuosto, E.: Pomcho: a tool chain for choreographic design. Sci. Comput. Program. **202**, 102535 (2021)
15. Hamers, R., Jongmans, S.-S.: Discourje: runtime verification of communication protocols in clojure. In: Biere, A., Parker, D. (eds.) TACAS 2020. LNCS, vol. 12078, pp. 266–284. Springer, Cham (2020). https://doi.org/10.1007/978-3-030-45190-5_15
16. Harvey, P., Fowler, S., Dardha, O., Gay, S.J.: Multiparty session types for safe runtime adaptation in an actor language. In: ECOOP. LIPIcs, vol. 194, pp. 10:1–10:30. Schloss Dagstuhl - Leibniz-Zentrum für Informatik (2021)

17. Honda, K., Yoshida, N., Carbone, M.: Multiparty asynchronous session types. In: POPL, pp. 273–284. ACM (2008)
18. Honda, K., Yoshida, N., Carbone, M.: Multiparty asynchronous session types. J. ACM **63**(1), 9:1–9:67 (2016)
19. Hu, R., Yoshida, N.: Hybrid session verification through endpoint API generation. In: Stevens, P., Wąsowski, A. (eds.) FASE 2016. LNCS, vol. 9633, pp. 401–418. Springer, Heidelberg (2016). https://doi.org/10.1007/978-3-662-49665-7_24
20. Hu, R., Yoshida, N.: Explicit connection actions in multiparty session types. In: Huisman, M., Rubin, J. (eds.) FASE 2017. LNCS, vol. 10202, pp. 116–133. Springer, Heidelberg (2017). https://doi.org/10.1007/978-3-662-54494-5_7
21. Imai, K., Neykova, R., Yoshida, N., Yuen, S.: Multiparty session programming with global protocol combinators. In: ECOOP. LIPIcs, vol. 166, pp. 9:1–9:30. Schloss Dagstuhl - Leibniz-Zentrum für Informatik (2020)
22. Jongmans, S.-S., Yoshida, N.: Exploring type-level bisimilarity towards more expressive multiparty session types. In: Müller, P. (ed.) ESOP 2020. LNCS, vol. 12075, pp. 251–279. Springer, Cham (2020). https://doi.org/10.1007/978-3-030-44914-8_10
23. King, J., Ng, N., Yoshida, N.: Multiparty session type-safe web development with static linearity. In: PLACES@ETAPS. EPTCS, vol. 291, pp. 35–46 (2019)
24. Kouzapas, D., Dardha, O., Perera, R., Gay, S.J.: Typechecking protocols with Mungo and StMungo: a session type toolchain for Java. Sci. Comput. Program. **155**, 52–75 (2018)
25. Lagaillardie, N., Neykova, R., Yoshida, N.: Implementing multiparty session types in rust. In: Bliudze, S., Bocchi, L. (eds.) COORDINATION 2020. LNCS, vol. 12134, pp. 127–136. Springer, Cham (2020). https://doi.org/10.1007/978-3-030-50029-0_8
26. Lange, J., Tuosto, E., Yoshida, N.: From communicating machines to graphical choreographies. In: POPL, pp. 221–232. ACM (2015)
27. Lange, J., Yoshida, N.: Verifying asynchronous interactions via communicating session automata. In: Dillig, I., Tasiran, S. (eds.) CAV 2019. LNCS, vol. 11561, pp. 97–117. Springer, Cham (2019). https://doi.org/10.1007/978-3-030-25540-4_6
28. Miu, A., Ferreira, F., Yoshida, N., Zhou, F.: Communication-safe web programming in typescript with routed multiparty session types. In: CC, pp. 94–106. ACM (2021)
29. Neykova, R., Bocchi, L., Yoshida, N.: Timed runtime monitoring for multiparty conversations. Formal Asp. Comput. **29**(5), 877–910 (2017)
30. Neykova, R., Hu, R., Yoshida, N., Abdeljallal, F.: A session type provider: compile-time API generation of distributed protocols with refinements in F#. In: CC, pp. 128–138. ACM (2018)
31. Neykova, R., Yoshida, N.: Featherweight scribble. In: Boreale, M., Corradini, F., Loreti, M., Pugliese, R. (eds.) Models, Languages, and Tools for Concurrent and Distributed Programming. LNCS, vol. 11665, pp. 236–259. Springer, Cham (2019). https://doi.org/10.1007/978-3-030-21485-2_14
32. Scalas, A., Dardha, O., Hu, R., Yoshida, N.: A linear decomposition of multiparty sessions for safe distributed programming. In: ECOOP. LIPIcs, vol. 74, pp. 24:1–24:31. Schloss Dagstuhl - Leibniz-Zentrum für Informatik (2017)
33. Scalas, A., Yoshida, N.: Less is more: multiparty session types revisited. Proc. ACM Program. Lang. **3**(POPL), 30:1–30:29 (2019)
34. Scalas, A., Yoshida, N., Benussi, E.: EFFPI: verified message-passing programs in dotty. In: SCALA@ECOOP, pp. 27–31. ACM (2019)
35. Scalas, A., Yoshida, N., Benussi, E.: Verifying message-passing programs with dependent behavioural types. In: PLDI, pp. 502–516. ACM (2019)

36. Tuosto, E., Guanciale, R.: Semantics of global view of choreographies. J. Log. Algebr. Methods Program. **95**, 17–40 (2018)
37. Voinea, A.L., Dardha, O., Gay, S.J.: Typechecking Java protocols with [St]Mungo. In: Gotsman, A., Sokolova, A. (eds.) FORTE 2020. LNCS, vol. 12136, pp. 208–224. Springer, Cham (2020). https://doi.org/10.1007/978-3-030-50086-3_12
38. Yoshida, N., Zhou, F., Ferreira, F.: Communicating finite state machines and an extensible toolchain for multiparty session types. In: Bampis, E., Pagourtzis, A. (eds.) FCT 2021. LNCS, vol. 12867, pp. 18–35. Springer, Cham (2021). https://doi.org/10.1007/978-3-030-86593-1_2
39. Zhou, F., Ferreira, F., Hu, R., Neykova, R., Yoshida, N.: Statically verified refinements for multiparty protocols. Proc. ACM Program. Lang. **4**(OOPSLA), 148:1–148:30 (2020)

On Binding in the Spatial Logics for Closure Spaces

Laura Bussi[1,2], Vincenzo Ciancia[1], Fabio Gadducci[2], Diego Latella[1], and Mieke Massink[1(✉)]

[1] CNR-ISTI, Pisa, Italy
{l.bussi,v.ciancia,d.latella,m.massink}@isti.cnr.it
[2] Dipartimento di Informatica, Università di Pisa, Pisa, Italy
fabio.gadducci@unipi.it

Abstract. We present two different extensions of the spatial logic for closure spaces (**SLCS**), and its spatio-temporal variant (τ**SLCS**), with spatial quantification operators. The first concerns the existential quantification on *individual points* of a space. The second concerns the quantification on *sets* of points. The latter amounts to a form of quantification over atomic propositions, thus without the full power of second order logic. The spatial quantification operators are useful for reasoning about the existence of particular spatial objects in a space, their spatial relation with respect to other spatial objects, and, in the spatio-temporal setting, to reason about the dynamic evolution of such spatial objects in time and space, including reasoning about newly introduced items. In this preliminary study we illustrate the expressiveness of the operators by means of several small, but representative, examples.

Keywords: Closure spaces · Spatial logics · Spatio-temporal logics · Binding · Propositional quantifiers

1 Introduction

The notion of *space* plays a crucial role in the heterogeneous design, implementation and use of distributed (computer) systems. Debates on the nature of space date back to the ancient times of—and involve—Greek philosophers like Plato and Aristotle. In modern mathematics, spaces are typically defined as sets (of points) with some additional structure. This is the case, for instance, for *topological spaces*, where such additional structure captures a notion of "nearness".

Modal logics have been used since a long time as a means for reasoning about necessity and possibility, but also about (continuous) space. In fact, a topological interpretation of the ◇ modality was proposed already in the thirties by Tarski who later proved, together with McKinsey, that the simple modal logic **S4** is

Research partially supported by the MIUR PRIN 2017FTXR7S IT-MaTTerS. The authors are listed in alphabetical order; they contributed to this work equally.

complete for interpreting $\Diamond$ as *topological closure* on Euclidean spaces, specifically the reals (see e.g. [6] for a detailed account).

Unfortunately, topological spaces turn out to be rather restrictive since there are structures that are useful to represent certain kinds of space but that are not topologies, like, for instance, general graphs or heterogeneous structures including both continuous and discrete notions of space. Consequently, in our work, we consider a larger class of models, namely that of Čech closure spaces, a generalisation of topological spaces [20,33]. The relevant logics have been extended accordingly. In [14,15] the *Spatial Logic for Closure Spaces* (SLCS) has been proposed that has the same operators as **S4**—where the closure operator is denoted by $\mathcal{N}$, standing for "near", instead of by $\Diamond$—plus a *surrounded* operator such that a point satisfies $\Phi_1 \mathcal{S} \Phi_2$ if it lays in a region that (i) consists of points all satisfying Φ_1 and (ii) is surrounded by points satisfying Φ_2.

SLCS has been extended with temporal modalities in [12,13], giving rise to a spatio-temporal logic to reason also on heterogeneous properties concerning dynamic aspects of systems physically distributed in space. Spatial and spatio-temporal *model checking/monitoring* algorithms have been proposed in [12–15,28] and associated tools, among which VoxLogicA [5] and topochecker [9,16], have been developed [5,12,13,21,22]. These, in turn, have been used in various applications, such as bike-sharing [16], Turing patterns [28] and medical image analysis [3–5,9]—where a digital image is interpreted as a regular grid, i.e. a graph with an edge relation that models 2D pixel, or 3D voxel, *adjacency* (also called an *adjacency space*). Recently, the approach has also been extended to *polyhedral models* and polyhedral model checking [7,27], leading to the polyhedral model checker PolyLogicA [7]. Notions of spatial bisimilarity have been proposed as well, and their potential for model minimisation plays an important role in the context of model-checking optimisation [17].

Despite their expressiveness, SLCS and its temporal extension are not suitable for the expression of properties involving dynamic entities that may *appear* or *disappear* over time. In order to reason about such entities, quantification has been introduced in well-known temporal logics such as LTL [25] and CTL [29]. Furthermore, in order to reason about graphs whose topology may change over time, combinations of temporal and graph logics have been proposed [1,19].

A different perspective on quantification is given by *propositional quantification*, introduced in modal logics by Kripke [24] and thoroughly investigated in, for instance, [8,23]. In the latter work, the object of quantification are propositions, and this allows one to reason about possible changes of properties holding in a certain region. In the case of spatial model checking for medical image analysis we mentioned before, this kind of quantification can be useful, for instance, to verify the occurrence of a new lesion in human organ tissue such as in the brain. Introducing quantification may introduce complexity issues [2] and may require the development of novel model checking tools and algorithms [30].

In the present paper, we present a preliminary investigation (ultimately aimed at model checking applications in medical image analysis, such as in [5]), by means of examples, on suitable extensions of SLCS, and its spatio-temporal variant, with quantification operators and with a notion of fresh point creation. We consider both *quantification on points* in the relevant space and *quantification on atomic propositions*. The latter allows for the characterisation of properties of *sets* of points, yet without involving the full power of second order logic.

The paper is organised as follows: Sect. 2 recalls some preliminary definitions, including the "kernel logic" SLCS and its temporal extension τSLCS. Sect. 3 presents ∃xSLCS, the point quantification extension of SLCS, whereas the temporal variant thereof is presented in Sect. 4. The introduction of new points during the evolution of a system is briefly discussed in Sect. 5. Section 6 shows an extension of SLCS with atomic predicate quantification. Finally, Sect. 7 presents a brief discussion on this work and some lines of future work.

2 Preliminaries

Given a set X, we let $\mathcal{P}(X)$ denote the powerset of X. For function $f : A \to B$, $a \in A$, and $b \in B$, we let $f[a \mapsto b]$ be defined as follows: $f[a \mapsto b](x) \triangleq b$, if $x = a$, and $f[a \mapsto b](x) \triangleq f(x)$ otherwise.

The main notion which our framework for modelling space is based on is that of Čech Closure Spaces [33] that provide a convenient common framework for the study of several different kinds of spatial models, including models of discrete and continuous space [31]. More recently the notion of closure space has been used in the context of Artificial Intelligence (see for example [20]). We briefly recall several definitions and results on closure spaces, most of them from [20].

Definition 1 (Closure Space – CS). *A closure space, CS for short, is a pair* $(X, \mathcal{C})$ *where* X *is a non-empty set (of points) and* $\mathcal{C} : \mathcal{P}(X) \to \mathcal{P}(X)$ *is a function satisfying the following axioms: (i)* $\mathcal{C}(\emptyset) = \emptyset$*; (ii)* $A \subseteq \mathcal{C}(A)$ *for all* $A \subseteq X$*; and (iii)* $\mathcal{C}(A_1 \cup A_2) = \mathcal{C}(A_1) \cup \mathcal{C}(A_2)$ *for all* $A_1, A_2 \subseteq X$*.*   •

In the remainder of the paper, we consider only closure spaces $(X, \mathcal{C})$ where X is equipped with equality and $x = x'$ is decidable, for all $x, x' \in X$. It is worth pointing out that topological spaces coincide with the sub-class of CSs where $\mathcal{C}$ satisfies the *idempotence* axiom $\mathcal{C}(\mathcal{C}(A)) = \mathcal{C}(A)$ (see [20,33] for details).

Definition 2 (Quasi-discrete CS – QdCS). *A quasi-discrete closure space is a CS* $(X, \mathcal{C})$ *such that for all* $A \subseteq X$ *it holds that* $\mathcal{C}(A) = \bigcup_{x \in A} \mathcal{C}(\{x\})$*.*   •

Given any relation $R \subseteq X \times X$, define the function $\mathcal{C}_R : \mathcal{P}(X) \to \mathcal{P}(X)$ as follows: for all $A \subseteq X$, $\mathcal{C}_R(A) \triangleq A \cup \{x \in X \mid a \in A$ exists s.t. $(a, x) \in R\}$. It is easy to see that, for any R, $\mathcal{C}_R$ satisfies the axioms of Definition 1 and so $(X, \mathcal{C}_R)$ is a CS. The following theorem is a standard result in the theory of CSs [20].

Theorem 1. *A CS* $(X, \mathcal{C})$ *is quasi-discrete if and only if there is a relation* $R \subseteq X \times X$ *such that* $\mathcal{C} = \mathcal{C}_R$*.*   □

A notable example of quasi-discrete closure spaces that are not necessarily topological spaces is that of general graphs, i.e. graphs where no restriction is imposed on the edge relation. There are also closure spaces that are neither quasi-discrete nor topological. An example of such spaces is a heterogeneous space like the disjoint union of an Euclidean space—a topological space which is clearly not quasi-discrete—with a quasi-discrete, but not topological, closure space[1]. In the sequel, whenever a CS $(X, \mathcal{C})$ is quasi-discrete, we use $\vec{\mathcal{C}}$ to denote $\mathcal{C}_R$, and, consequently, $(X, \vec{\mathcal{C}})$ to denote the closure space, abstracting from the specification of R, when the latter is not necessary. We let $\breve{\mathcal{C}}$ denote $\mathcal{C}_{R^{-1}}$.

We use *paths* over QdCSs; we follow the tradition of topology and define them based on the notion of *continuous function*.

Definition 3 (Continuous function). *A* continuous *function from* $(X_1, \mathcal{C}_1)$ *to* $(X_2, \mathcal{C}_2)$ *is a function* $f : X_1 \to X_2$ *such that* $f^*(\mathcal{C}_1(A)) \subseteq \mathcal{C}_2(f^*(A))$ *for all sets* $A \subseteq X_1$, *where we let* $f^*(B) = \bigcup_{x \in B} f(x)$. •

Should $(X_1, \mathcal{C}_1)$ be a QdCS, continuity coincides with just requiring that $f^*(\mathcal{C}_1(\{x\})) \subseteq \mathcal{C}_2(\{f(x)\})$ for all $x \in X_1$. So, let $(\mathbb{N}, \mathcal{C}_{\text{succ}})$ be the QdCS of natural numbers, where succ is the *successor* relation, i.e. $\text{succ} \triangleq \{(m, n) \mid n = m + 1\}$.

Definition 4 (Quasi-discrete path in). *A* quasi-discrete path in $(X, \vec{\mathcal{C}})$ *is a continuous function from* $(\mathbb{N}, \mathcal{C}_{\text{succ}})$ *to* $(X, \vec{\mathcal{C}})$. •

In the sequel we will consider only quasi-discrete paths. Below, we introduce the notion of closure *model*. To that purpose, we assume that a set AP of *atomic propositions* is given. In addition, the points of the model are often enriched with suitable *attributes*, that can facilitate the definition of appropriate propositions, as briefly described below. Obvious examples of attributes are the *red*, *green* and *blue* components of pixels, seen as RGB vectors—recording the colour intensities—in digital images, when the latter are seen as adjacency spaces.

Definition 5 (Closure model – CM). *Given a set of* atomic propositions AP, *a set of* attribute names A, *and a set of* attribute values AV, *a closure model, CM for short, is a tuple* $(X, \mathcal{C}, A, \mathcal{V})$ *consisting of a closure space* $(X, \mathcal{C})$, *a valuation* $\mathcal{A} : X \times A \to AV$, *assigning to each point and attribute the value of the attribute at that point, and a valuation* $\mathcal{V} : \text{AP} \to \mathcal{P}(X)$ *assigning to each atomic predicate the set of points where it holds.* •

All the definitions for CSs apply to CMs as well; thus, a *quasi-discrete closure model* (QdCM for short) is a CM $\mathcal{M} = (X, \vec{\mathcal{C}}, \mathcal{A}, \mathcal{V})$ where $(X, \vec{\mathcal{C}})$ is a QdCS.

2.1   SLCS: The Spatial Logic for Closure Spaces

We recall the kernel logic SLCS; in the present paper, we interpret it on QdCMs.

---

[1] The disjoint union $(X_1, \mathcal{C}_1) + (X_2, \mathcal{C}_2)$ of closure spaces $(X_1, \mathcal{C}_1)$ and $(X_2, \mathcal{C}_2)$ is the closure space $(X, \mathcal{C})$ whose set of points X is the disjoint union $X_1 + X_2 \triangleq \{(x, 1) \mid x \in X_1\} \cup \{(x, 2) \mid x \in X_2\}$ while, for $A \subseteq X_1 + X_2$ we define $\mathcal{C}(A) \triangleq \{(x, 1) \mid x \in A_1\} \cup \{(x, 2) \mid x \in A_2\}$ with $A_j \triangleq \{x \mid (x, j) \in A\}$ for $j = 1, 2$.

Definition 6 (Spatial Logic for Closure Spaces – SLCS). *For $p \in$ AP the syntax of the logic is the following*

$$\Phi ::= p \mid \neg \Phi \mid \Phi \wedge \Phi \mid \vec{\rho}\,\Phi[\Phi] \mid \bar{\rho}\,\Phi[\Phi]$$

Satisfaction $\mathcal{M}, x \models \Phi$ of an SLCS formula Φ at point $x \in X$ in QdCM $\mathcal{M} = (X, \vec{\mathcal{C}}, \mathcal{A}, \mathcal{V})$ is defined by induction on the structure of formulas

$$
\begin{aligned}
\mathcal{M}, x &\models p & &\Leftrightarrow x \in \mathcal{V}(p) \\
\mathcal{M}, x &\models \neg \Phi & &\Leftrightarrow \mathcal{M}, x \models \Phi \text{ does not hold} \\
\mathcal{M}, x &\models \Phi_1 \wedge \Phi_2 & &\Leftrightarrow \mathcal{M}, x \models \Phi_1 \text{ and } \mathcal{M}, x \models \Phi_2 \\
\mathcal{M}, x &\models \vec{\rho}\,\Phi_1[\Phi_2] & &\Leftrightarrow \text{path } \pi \text{ and index } \ell \text{ exist s.t. } \pi(0) = x \text{ and } \mathcal{M}, \pi(\ell) \models \Phi_1 \\
& & &\quad \text{and for all indexes } j : 0 < j < \ell \text{ implies } \mathcal{M}, \pi(j) \models \Phi_2 \\
\mathcal{M}, x &\models \bar{\rho}\,\Phi_1[\Phi_2] & &\Leftrightarrow \text{path } \pi \text{ and index } \ell \text{ exist s.t. } \pi(\ell) = x \text{ and } \mathcal{M}, \pi(0) \models \Phi_1 \\
& & &\quad \text{and for all indexes } j : 0 < j < \ell \text{ implies } \mathcal{M}, \pi(j) \models \Phi_2
\end{aligned}
$$

A point x satisfies formula $\vec{\rho}\,\Phi_1[\Phi_2]$ if a point that satisfies Φ_1 can be reached from x, via a path whose internal points, if any, all satisfy Φ_2. Conversely, x satisfies formula $\bar{\rho}\,\Phi_1[\Phi_2]$ if it can be reached from a point that satisfies Φ_1, via a path whose internal points, if any, all satisfy Φ_2.

Note that, in the context of space, and in particular when dealing with notions of directionality (e.g. one-way roads, public area gates), it is essential to be able to distinguish between the concept of "reaching" and that of "being reached". A formula like $\vec{\rho}(\texttt{rescue-area} \wedge \neg(\bar{\rho}\,\texttt{danger-area})[\texttt{true}])[\texttt{safe-corridor}]$, given a suitable interpretation of the atomic propositions, expresses the fact that, via a safe corridor, a rescue area can be reached that cannot be reached from a dangerous area. Such situations have no obvious counterpart in the temporal domain, where there can be more than one future, like in the case of branching time logics, but there is typically only one, fixed, past, i.e. the one that occurred[2].

It is also worth noting that it is not always possible to define the reversed path in CSs: indeed, while this is immediate in the case, for instance, of graphs, the same idea is not applicable in continuous spaces, as, e.g., used in [7,27]. Thus, for the sake of generality, the semantics for the "reach" and "being reached" operators is given explicitly.

The standard derived operators $\vee$ and $\implies$ will be used in the sequel: $\Phi_1 \vee \Phi_2 \equiv \neg(\neg \Phi_1 \wedge \neg \Phi_2)$ and $\Phi_1 \implies \Phi_2 \equiv \neg \Phi_1 \vee \Phi_2$. We recall here that the proximity operator $\vec{\mathcal{N}}$ defined as $\mathcal{M}, x \models \vec{\mathcal{N}} \Phi \Leftrightarrow x \in \vec{\mathcal{C}}(\{x' \in X \mid \mathcal{M}, x' \models \Phi\})$, for QdCMs can be derived from the *reachability* one, namely $\vec{\mathcal{N}} \Phi \equiv \bar{\rho}\,\Phi[\texttt{false}]$; similarly $\bar{\mathcal{N}} \Phi \equiv \vec{\rho}\,\Phi[\texttt{false}]$, with $\mathcal{M}, x \models \bar{\mathcal{N}} \Phi \Leftrightarrow x \in \bar{\mathcal{C}}(\{x' \in X \mid \mathcal{M}, x' \models \Phi\})$. In particular, $\vec{\mathcal{N}}$ coincides with the classical $\Diamond$ closure modality.

Finally, we recall that in [14,15] a *surrounded* operator $\mathcal{S}$ was introduced such that a point x satisfies $\Phi_1 \mathcal{S} \Phi_2$ if and only if it belongs to a set of mutually connected points all satisfying Φ_1 and this set is directly surrounded by points all satisfying Φ_2. In other words, no path rooted in x can leave the Φ_1 area without

---

[2] There are a few exceptions to this view of past-tense operators, e.g. [26,32].

passing by a point satisfying Φ_2. It is worth noting that the surrounded operator can be expressed using $\vec{\rho}$ as follows: $\Phi_1 \, \mathcal{S} \, \Phi_2 \equiv \Phi_1 \wedge \neg\vec{\rho}(\neg(\Phi_1 \vee \Phi_2))[\neg\Phi_2]$.

2.2 τSLCS: The Temporal Extension of SLCS

We recall here a temporal extension of SLCS, similar to the one presented in [12,13], that provides a formal, unified framework for reasoning about both spatial and temporal features of systems and their behaviour. The version of SLCS defined in [12,13] is based on the proximity and surrounded operators, both expressible in terms of reachability operators, as we have seen in Sect. 2.1.

For what concerns the satisfaction relation, now a *spatio-temporal* model $\mathcal{M}$ (more simply, just a *temporal* model) is composed of a Kripke structure and a family of closure models, one for each world of the Kripke structure.

Definition 7 (Temporal closure model - TCM). *Given a set of atomic propositions* AP, *a temporal* closure model, *TCM for short, is composed of a Kripke structure* $\mathcal{K} = (S, T)$—*with set of states (worlds)* S *and transition (accessibility) relation* $T \subseteq S \times S$—*and of a family* $\{(X, \mathcal{C})_s, \mathcal{V}_s, \mathcal{A}_s\}_{s \in S}$ *of closure models. We say that TCM* $\mathcal{M} = ((S, T), \{(X, \mathcal{C})_s, \mathcal{V}_s, \mathcal{A}_s\}_{s \in S})$ *is conservative if, for all* $s, s' \in S$, *it holds* $X_s \subseteq X_{s'}$ *whenever* $(s, s') \in T$.   •

All definitions for CMs extend also to TCMs; so, for instance, a quasi-discrete temporal closure model, QdTCM for short, is a temporal closure model where all closure models (i.e., one for each state $s \in S$) are quasi-discrete. Here, we consider only conservative QdTCM[3]. This means that space can only *grow* when time advances: i.e., the points of space *can never be lost*. This condition simplifies the definition of spatio-temporal logics; we leave the investigation of non-conservative models to future work. We recall the definition of temporal paths.

Definition 8. *Given Kripke structure* $\mathcal{K} = (S, T)$ *and* $s \in S$, *a temporal path rooted in* s *is a function* $\tau : \mathbb{N} \to S$ *such that* $\tau(0) = s$ *and* $(\tau(i), \tau(i+1)) \in T$ *for all* $i \in \mathbb{N}$. *For* $s \in S$, T_s *denotes the set of all temporal paths* τ *rooted in* s. •

Note that the above definition implies that the relation T is total, which is readily obtained by adding self-loops (s, s) whenever there is no s' s.t. $(s, s') \in T$.

Definition 9 (Spatio-Temporal Logic for Closure Spaces – τSLCS). *For* $p \in$ AP *the syntax of the logic is the following*

$$\Phi ::= p \mid \neg\Phi \mid \Phi \wedge \Phi \mid \vec{\rho}\,\Phi[\Phi] \mid \bar{\rho}\,\Phi[\Phi] \mid \mathsf{A}\varphi \mid \mathsf{E}\varphi$$

$$\varphi ::= \mathcal{X}\Phi \mid \Phi\,\mathcal{U}\,\Phi$$

Given QdTCM $\mathcal{M} = (\mathcal{K}, \{(X, \vec{\mathcal{C}})_s, \mathcal{V}_s, \mathcal{A}_s\}_{s \in S})$, *with* $\mathcal{K} = (S, T)$, *satisfaction* $\mathcal{M}, s, x \models \Phi$ *of a formula* Φ *in state* $s \in S$ *and at point* $x \in X_s$ *is defined by*

---

[3] In [12,13], the stronger condition $X_s = X_{s'}$ for all $s, s' \in S$ was required.

induction on the structure of formulas as given below

$$\mathcal{M}, s, x \models p \qquad \Leftrightarrow x \in \mathcal{V}_s(p)$$
$$\mathcal{M}, s, x \models \neg \Phi \qquad \Leftrightarrow \mathcal{M}, s, x \models \Phi \text{ does not hold}$$
$$\mathcal{M}, s, x \models \Phi_1 \wedge \Phi_2 \Leftrightarrow \mathcal{M}, s, x \models \Phi_1 \text{ and } \mathcal{M}, s, x \models \Phi_2$$
$$\mathcal{M}, s, x \models \vec{\rho}\, \Phi_1[\Phi_2] \Leftrightarrow \text{path } \pi \text{ in } (X, \vec{\mathcal{C}})_s \text{ and index } \ell \text{ exist s.t.}$$
$$\pi(0) = x \text{ and } \mathcal{M}, s, \pi(\ell) \models \Phi_1$$
$$\text{and for all indexes } j : 0 < j < \ell \text{ implies } \mathcal{M}, s, \pi(j) \models \Phi_2$$
$$\mathcal{M}, s, x \models \bar{\rho}\, \Phi_1[\Phi_2] \Leftrightarrow \text{path } \pi \text{ in } (X, \vec{\mathcal{C}})_s \text{ and index } \ell \text{ exist s.t.}$$
$$\pi(\ell) = x \text{ and } \mathcal{M}, s, \pi(0) \models \Phi_1$$
$$\text{and for all indexes } j : 0 < j < \ell \text{ implies } \mathcal{M}, s, \pi(j) \models \Phi_2$$
$$\mathcal{M}, s, x \models \mathsf{A}\,\varphi \qquad \Leftrightarrow \text{for all } \tau \in \mathcal{T}_s \text{ it holds } \mathcal{M}, \tau, x \models \varphi$$
$$\mathcal{M}, s, x \models \mathsf{E}\,\varphi \qquad \Leftrightarrow \tau \text{ exists s.t. } \tau \in \mathcal{T}_s \text{ and } \mathcal{M}, \tau, x \models \varphi$$

$$\mathcal{M}, \tau, x \models \mathcal{X}\, \Phi \qquad \Leftrightarrow \mathcal{M}, \tau(1), x \models \Phi$$
$$\mathcal{M}, \tau, x \models \Phi_1 \mathcal{U} \Phi_2 \Leftrightarrow n \text{ exists s.t. } n \in \mathbb{N} \text{ and } \mathcal{M}, \tau(n), x \models \Phi_2$$
$$\text{and for all } n' \in \mathbb{N} \text{ s.t. } 0 \leq n' < n \text{ it holds}$$
$$\mathcal{M}, \tau(n'), x \models \Phi_1$$

In the sequel we will often use the *eventually* operator F, that is derived from $\mathcal{U}$ in the standard way: $\mathsf{F}\,\Phi \equiv \mathsf{true}\,\mathcal{U}\,\Phi$. In addition, we define the following operator ag as derived from E and F as follows: $\mathsf{ag}\,\Phi \equiv \neg\,\mathsf{E}\,\mathsf{F}\neg\,\Phi$. Similarly, we define eg as follows: $\mathsf{eg}\,\Phi \equiv \neg\,\mathsf{A}\,\mathsf{F}\neg\,\Phi$.

3   ∃xSLCS: Point Existential Extension of SLCS

We extend the logic presented in Sect. 2.1 with a *point existential quantification* operator $\exists\gamma.\_$. To that purpose, we assume a denumerable set Γ of *point variables*, ranged over by $\gamma, \gamma', \gamma_1 \ldots$ Furthermore, we use the standard notion of free occurrence of a (point) variable in a formula, with respect to quantifiers. We also refine the syntax of the logic, by introducing a syntactic category E of *expressions* on the attributes of points, and point equality, as specified below.

For set A of attribute names, set AC of attribute constants—which is assumed to include boolean values, true and false, for which the usual boolean operators are assumed defined— and set Γ of point variables, with a distinguished item this $\notin \Gamma$, the abstract syntax for expressions E follows

$$E ::= c \mid a \mid \gamma = \gamma \mid \gamma = \mathsf{this} \mid \gamma.a \mid \mathsf{this}.a \mid f(E, \ldots, E) \qquad (1)$$

where $c \in AC$, $a \in A$, $\gamma \in \Gamma$ and f is the name of an n-ary function; f can denote any standard function of attribute values, e.g., equality, for which a standard semantics $\mathcal{I}_F$ is assumed given. Similarly, we assume an interpretation function $\mathcal{I}_C$ for attribute constants that maps every attribute constant c to a value $\mathcal{I}_C(c) \in AV$. The special item this will be used for referring to the point on which the formula at hand—which the expression where this occurs is a component of—is interpreted, as shown in Example 1 below.

Assertions are the subclass of expressions that evaluate to boolean values[4]. In order to compute assertions we define below the valuation function $\mathcal{E}$ of expressions E that extends function $\mathcal{A}$ in the expected way. Function $\mathcal{E}$ is defined using an auxiliary variable assignment (partial) function $\mu : (\Gamma \cup \{\texttt{this}\}) \to X$. We let μ_0 denote the assignment that is undefined for all elements of $\Gamma \cup \{\texttt{this}\}$. For all $x \in X$, $c \in AC$, $a \in A$, $\gamma, \gamma_1, \gamma_2 \in \Gamma$ and $\mu : (\Gamma \cup \{\texttt{this}\}) \to X$

$$
\begin{aligned}
\mathcal{E}_\mu(x, c) &\triangleq \mathcal{I}_C(c) \\
\mathcal{E}_\mu(x, a) &\triangleq \mathcal{A}(x, a) \\
\mathcal{E}_\mu(x, \gamma_1 = \gamma_2) &\triangleq \mu(\gamma_1) = \mu(\gamma_2) \\
\mathcal{E}_\mu(x, \gamma = \texttt{this}) &\triangleq \mu(\gamma) = \mu(\texttt{this}) \\
\mathcal{E}_\mu(x, \gamma.a) &\triangleq \mathcal{A}(\mu(\gamma), a) \\
\mathcal{E}_\mu(x, \texttt{this}.a) &\triangleq \mathcal{A}(\mu(\texttt{this}), a) \\
\mathcal{E}_\mu(x, f(E_1, \ldots, E_n)) &\triangleq \mathcal{I}_F(f)(\mathcal{E}_\mu(x, E_1), \ldots, \mathcal{E}_\mu(x, E_n)).
\end{aligned}
$$

Definition 10 ($\exists x$SLCS). *The syntax of $\exists x$SLCS is the same as in Definition 6 with the addition of the following productions*

$$\Phi ::= E \mid \exists \gamma . \Phi$$

The scope of γ in $\exists \gamma . \Phi$ is Φ. For every $\exists x$SLCS formula Φ, where no point variable occurs free, satisfaction $\mathcal{M}, x \models \Phi$ of Φ at point $x \in X$ in QdCM $\mathcal{M} = (X, \vec{\mathcal{C}}, \mathcal{A}, \mathcal{V})$ is defined as follows

$$\mathcal{M}, x \models \Phi \Leftrightarrow \mathcal{M}, \mu_0[\texttt{this} \mapsto x], x \models\mid \Phi$$

where relation $\models\mid$ is defined below, by induction on the structure of the formulas

$$
\begin{aligned}
\mathcal{M}, \mu, x \models\mid p \quad &\Leftrightarrow x \in \mathcal{V}(p) \\
\mathcal{M}, \mu, x \models\mid \neg\Phi \quad &\Leftrightarrow \mathcal{M}, \mu, x \models\mid \Phi \text{ does not hold} \\
\mathcal{M}, \mu, x \models\mid \Phi_1 \wedge \Phi_2 \quad &\Leftrightarrow \mathcal{M}, \mu, x \models\mid \Phi_1 \text{ and } \mathcal{M}, \mu, x \models\mid \Phi_2 \\
\mathcal{M}, \mu, x \models\mid \vec{\rho}\,\Phi_1[\Phi_2] \quad &\Leftrightarrow \text{path } \pi \text{ and index } \ell \text{ exist s.t. } \pi(0) = x \text{ and } \mathcal{M}, \mu, \pi(\ell) \models\mid \Phi_1 \\
& \qquad \text{and for all indexes } j : 0 < j < \ell \text{ implies } \mathcal{M}, \mu, \pi(j) \models\mid \Phi_2 \\
\mathcal{M}, \mu, x \models\mid \bar{\rho}\,\Phi_1[\Phi_2] \quad &\Leftrightarrow \text{path } \pi \text{ and index } \ell \text{ exist s.t. } \pi(\ell) = x \text{ and } \mathcal{M}, \mu, \pi(0) \models\mid \Phi_1 \\
& \qquad \text{and for all indexes } j : 0 < j < \ell \text{ implies } \mathcal{M}, \mu, \pi(j) \models\mid \Phi_2 \\
\mathcal{M}, \mu, x \models\mid E \quad &\Leftrightarrow \mathcal{E}_\mu(x, E) \text{ is true} \\
\mathcal{M}, \mu, x \models\mid \exists \gamma . \Phi \quad &\Leftrightarrow \text{there is } x' \in X \text{ s.t. } \mathcal{M}, \mu[\gamma \mapsto x'], x \models\mid \Phi.
\end{aligned}
$$

The universal quantifier operator is derived from the existential one, in the usual way: $\forall \gamma . \Phi \equiv \neg \exists \gamma . \neg \Phi$.

Example 1. Suppose we are interested in the safety condition of a building where (adjacent) rooms, corridors and stairs—collectively called "premises"—are connected by means of doors that can be locked or unlocked. In particular, we

---

[4] For the sake of notational simplicity, we refrain from giving an explicit syntactic characterisation of assertions here.

consider a critical safety hazard the fact that there are premises with a concentration of a certain substance in the air higher than a given threshold `threshold` that are reachable from other premises, via unlocked doors, i.e. doors that can accidentally be opened by unauthorized people. We can model the building as a QdCM $\mathcal{M} = ((X, \vec{\mathcal{C}}), \mathcal{V}, \mathcal{A})$ where each element $x \in X$ has an attribute, `sort`, that can take as values those represented by the following constants: `room, corridor, stair, door` $\in AC$. The topological requirement that premises are connected one another via doors can be enforced by a requirement on $\vec{\mathcal{C}}$ and $\mathcal{A}$, namely, that for all $x, y \in X$

- if $\mathcal{A}(x, \mathtt{sort}) \neq \mathcal{I}_C(\mathtt{door})$ and $y \in \vec{\mathcal{C}}(\{x\}) \setminus \{x\}$, then $\mathcal{A}(y, \mathtt{sort}) = \mathcal{I}_C(\mathtt{door})$;
- if $\mathcal{A}(y, \mathtt{sort}) = \mathcal{I}_C(\mathtt{door})$ and $x \in \vec{\mathcal{C}}(\{y\}) \setminus \{y\}$, then $\mathcal{A}(x, \mathtt{sort}) \neq \mathcal{I}_C(\mathtt{door})$.

Moreover, every $x \in X$ has an attribute `concentration` that can take natural numbers as values and is relevant only for elements representing rooms, corridors and stairs. Finally, attribute `status` takes as values those represented by `locked, unlocked` $\in AC$ and is relevant only for doors. The hazardous situation can then be formalised by formula ϕ_1, defined below, that states that there is a location (i.e., room, corridor or stairs) from which premises can be reached, via locations and unlocked doors, in which the substance concentration is higher than the threshold

$$\phi_1 \equiv \exists \gamma.(\neg(\gamma.\mathtt{sort} = \mathtt{door}) \wedge \vec{\rho} \, \phi_2 \, [\phi_3])$$

where

$$\phi_2 \equiv \neg(\mathtt{sort} = \mathtt{door}) \wedge \mathtt{concentration} > \mathtt{threshold}$$

$$\phi_3 \equiv (\mathtt{sort} = \mathtt{door}) \Rightarrow (\mathtt{status} = \mathtt{unlocked}).$$

Note the *global* nature of the formula: either all points in X satisfy it or none does. In contrast, if we replace ϕ_2 with ϕ_2' defined below, we get a formula that is satisfied by $x \in X$ only if the unsafe location has the same sort as x

$$\phi_2' \equiv \mathtt{sort} = \mathtt{this.sort} \wedge \mathtt{concentration} > \mathtt{threshold}$$

•

Example 2. We consider the example proposed in [19] that falls in the category of circle elimination games and is a sort of distributed leader survivor game. The choice of the example is motivated by the large use of leader election protocols in the area of distributed systems design and applications[5].

A finite set of entities is given; the entities are connected through communication channels in such a way that a ring topology is formed. The game evolves

---

[5] In line with [19], we are not interested in the algorithm(s) used for deciding the winner of the game. We are only interested in providing a representation for the configurations of the game and investigating properties of any such configuration, as well as of the whole game, that can be expressed using the extensions of SLCS we discuss in the present paper.

performing a series of elimination rounds. After each round the loser is eliminated from the game: his neighbours should be connected in such a way that the ring is closed and no longer includes the loser. The game ends when there is only one entity left: the leader, that is, the winner of the game.

A session of the game can be represented as a sequence of graphs, each graph modelling the situation at a given step of the game. For instance, the graph $\mathbf{G_0}$ of Fig. 1a represents a configuration in which there are three agents—the nodes n_0, n_1, n_2—and three channels—the edges e_0, e_1, e_2, with source and target functions, s and t, defined as follows: $s^{\mathbf{G_0}} = \{e_0 \mapsto n_0, e_1 \mapsto n_2, e_2 \mapsto n_1\}$ and $t^{\mathbf{G_0}} = \{e_0 \mapsto n_1, e_1 \mapsto n_0, e_2 \mapsto n_2\}$. A final (correct) configuration is represented by a graph with a single node, say n_1—the (unique) winner—and a single edge, say e, the source and target of which coincide with this node—i.e. $s(e) = t(e) = n_1$, namely a self-loop in n_1 (Fig. 1c).

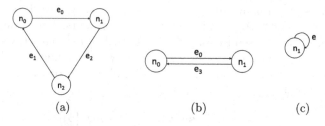

(a)   (b)   (c)

Fig. 1. (a) A configuration with three agents and three communication channels; (b) an intermediate configuration in which n_2 has been eliminated; (c) a configuration where the leader (n_1, in this case) has emerged.

We can represent a configuration in the game using a QdCM $(X, \vec{\mathcal{C}}, \mathcal{A}, \mathcal{V})$, the underlying binary relation of which is the empty relation (so that $\vec{\mathcal{C}}(A) = A$ for all $A \subseteq X$) and where each $x \in X$ can represent either an agent of the game or a communication channel. To that purpose, we use again a **sort** attribute, that takes as values those represented by **node, edge** $\in AC$. Finally, attributes **source** and **target**—relevant only for elements of sort **edge**—yield the (unique identifier of the) source and target node of an edge. Under the above assumptions, a leader can be specified as follows

$$\mathbf{leader}(\gamma) \equiv (\gamma.\mathbf{sort} = \mathbf{edge}) \wedge (\gamma.\mathbf{source} = \gamma.\mathbf{target}).$$

The game terminates correctly only if there is a *unique* leader. Unicity can be specified as follows

$$\mathbf{correctNLeader}(\gamma_1, \gamma_2) \equiv (\mathbf{leader}(\gamma_1) \wedge \mathbf{leader}(\gamma_2)) \Rightarrow (\gamma_1 = \gamma_2).$$

Thus a correct final configuration is one in which there is a unique leader, as specified by the formula $(\exists \gamma.\mathbf{leader}(\gamma)) \wedge (\forall \gamma_1. \forall \gamma_2.\mathbf{correctNLeader}(\gamma_1, \gamma_2))$.

The two requirements on the leader can obviously be expressed in a combined way by the following formula: $\exists \gamma_1.(\mathbf{leader}(\gamma_1) \wedge (\forall \gamma_2.\mathbf{leader}(\gamma_2) \implies \gamma_1 = \gamma_2))$.

We close the example noting that the same technique based on unique identifiers can be used for expressing properties about the size of a system (see page 191 of [19]). For instance a bound of two is expressed as follows

$$\mathbf{at-most-two} \equiv \forall \gamma_1.\forall \gamma_2.\forall \gamma_3.\{\gamma_1 = \gamma_2 \vee \gamma_2 = \gamma_3 \vee \gamma_3 = \gamma_1\}.$$

4 $\exists x \tau$SLCS: Point Existential Temporal Extension of SLCS

We extend the spatio-temporal logic presented in Sect. 2.2 with the *point existential quantification* operator $\exists \gamma.\_$ introduced in Sect. 3. To that purpose, we need to extend the valuation function $\mathcal{E}$ with an additional parameter for the state where the evaluation has to be performed

$$\mathcal{E}_\mu(x, c, s) \triangleq \mathcal{I}_C(c)$$
$$\mathcal{E}_\mu(x, a, s) \triangleq \mathcal{A}_s(x, a)$$
$$\mathcal{E}_\mu(x, \gamma_1 = \gamma_2, s) \triangleq \mu(\gamma_1) = \mu(\gamma_2)$$
$$\mathcal{E}_\mu(x, \gamma = \mathbf{this}, s) \triangleq \mu(\gamma) = \mu(\mathbf{this})$$
$$\mathcal{E}_\mu(x, \gamma.a, s) \triangleq \mathcal{A}_s(\mu(\gamma), a)$$
$$\mathcal{E}_\mu(x, \mathbf{this}.a, s) \triangleq \mathcal{A}_s(\mu(\mathbf{this}), a)$$
$$\mathcal{E}_\mu(x, f(E_1, \ldots, E_n), s) \triangleq \mathcal{I}_F(f)(\mathcal{E}_\mu(x, E_1, s), \ldots, \mathcal{E}_\mu(x, E_n, s)).$$

Definition 11 ($\exists x \tau$SLCS). *The syntax of $\exists x \tau$SLCS is the same as in Definition 9 with the addition of the following productions*

$$\Phi ::= E \mid \exists \gamma.\Phi$$

The scope of γ in $\exists \gamma.\Phi$ is Φ. For every $\exists x \tau$SLCS formula Φ, where no point variable occurs free, satisfaction $\mathcal{M}, s, x \models \Phi$ of Φ in state $s \in S$ and at point $x \in X_s$ in QdTCM $\mathcal{M} = (\mathcal{K}, \{(X, \vec{\mathcal{C}})_s, \mathcal{V}_s, \mathcal{A}_s\}_{s \in S})$, with $\mathcal{K} = (S, T)$, is defined as follows

$$\mathcal{M}, s, x \models \Phi \Leftrightarrow \mathcal{M}, \mu_0[\mathbf{this} \mapsto x], s, x \models\!\mid \Phi$$

where relation $\models$ is defined below, by induction on the structure of the formulas

$$\mathcal{M}, \mu, s, x \models p \quad\quad\quad \Leftrightarrow x \in \mathcal{V}_s(p)$$
$$\mathcal{M}, \mu, s, x \models \neg\Phi \quad\quad\quad \Leftrightarrow \mathcal{M}, \mu, s, x \models \Phi \text{ does not hold}$$
$$\mathcal{M}, \mu, s, x \models \Phi_1 \wedge \Phi_2 \Leftrightarrow \mathcal{M}, \mu, s, x \models \Phi_1 \text{ and } \mathcal{M}, \mu, s, x \models \Phi_2$$
$$\mathcal{M}, \mu, s, x \models \vec{\rho}\, \Phi_1[\Phi_2] \Leftrightarrow \text{path } \pi \text{ in } (X, \vec{\mathcal{C}})_s \text{ and index } \ell \text{ exist s.t.}$$
$$\pi(0) = x \text{ and } \mathcal{M}, \mu, s, \pi(\ell) \models \Phi_1$$
$$\text{and for all indexes } j:$$
$$0 < j < \ell \text{ implies } \mathcal{M}, \mu, s, \pi(j) \models \Phi_2$$
$$\mathcal{M}, \mu, s, x \models \overset{\scriptscriptstyle\leftarrow}{\rho}\, \Phi_1[\Phi_2] \Leftrightarrow \text{path } \pi \text{ in } (X, \vec{\mathcal{C}})_s \text{ and index } \ell \text{ exist s.t.}$$
$$\pi(\ell) = x \text{ and } \mathcal{M}, \mu, s, \pi(0) \models \Phi_1$$
$$\text{and for all indexes } j:$$
$$0 < j < \ell \text{ implies } \mathcal{M}, \mu, s, \pi(j) \models \Phi_2$$
$$\mathcal{M}, \mu, s, x \models E \quad\quad\quad \Leftrightarrow \mathcal{E}_\mu(x, E, s) \text{ is true}$$
$$\mathcal{M}, \mu, s, x \models \exists \gamma.\Phi \quad\quad \Leftrightarrow \text{there is } x' \in X_s \text{ s.t. } \mathcal{M}, \mu[\gamma \mapsto x'], s, x \models \Phi$$
$$\mathcal{M}, \mu, s, x \models \mathbf{A}\varphi \quad\quad\quad \Leftrightarrow \text{for all } \tau \in \mathcal{T}_s \text{ it holds } \mathcal{M}, \mu, \tau, x \models \varphi$$
$$\mathcal{M}, \mu, s, x \models \mathbf{E}\varphi \quad\quad\quad \Leftrightarrow \tau \text{ exists s.t. } \tau \in \mathcal{T}_s \text{ and } \mathcal{M}, \mu, \tau, x \models \varphi$$

$$\mathcal{M}, \mu, \tau, x \models \mathcal{X}\,\Phi \quad\quad\quad \Leftrightarrow \mathcal{M}, \mu, \tau(1), x \models \Phi$$
$$\mathcal{M}, \mu, \tau, x \models \Phi_1 \mathcal{U} \Phi_2 \Leftrightarrow n \text{ exists s.t. } n \in \mathbb{N} \text{ and } \mathcal{M}, \mu, \tau(n), x \models \Phi_2$$
$$\text{and for all } n' \in \mathbb{N} \text{ s.t. } 0 \leq n' < n \text{ it holds}$$
$$\mathcal{M}, \mu, \tau(n'), x \models \Phi_1.$$

●

Example 3. Let us consider again the building of Example 1. We want to formalise the fact that whenever the building is in a hazardous situation, as specified by formula ϕ_1, it will recover from it. This is the same to say that there is no evolution in the behaviour of the building where a situation is reached in which ϕ_1—expressing the hazardous situation—holds and in no future configuration $\neg\phi_1$ holds. This is formalised by ϕ_4 as follows

$$\phi_4 \equiv \neg\mathbf{EF}(\phi_1 \wedge \neg\mathbf{AF}\neg\phi_1)$$

or equivalently, using the **eg** derived operator

$$\phi_4 : \neg\mathbf{E}\,\mathbf{F}\,\mathbf{eg}\,\Phi_1$$

A stronger property is expressed by ϕ_5 below where we also require that eventually nowhere the concentration is above the threshold

$$\phi_5 \equiv \neg\mathbf{EF}(\phi_1 \wedge \neg\mathbf{AF}(\neg\phi_1 \wedge \mathbf{AF}\,\phi_6))$$

where $\phi_6 \equiv \forall\gamma.\mathbf{safe}(\gamma)$ and predicate **safe** is defined as follows

$$\mathbf{safe}(\gamma) \equiv (\neg(\gamma.\mathbf{sort} = \mathbf{door})) \Rightarrow \gamma.\mathtt{concentration} \leq \mathtt{threshold}.$$

●

Example 4. With reference to Example 2, now we consider a QdTCM $\mathcal{M} = ((S,T), \{(X, \vec{\mathcal{C}})_s, \mathcal{V}_s, \mathcal{A}_s\}_{s \in S})$. In [19] the following properties are introduced

ψ_1: *for all departing paths, eventually there will be a leader* (Example 4.2 on page 185, property ψ_1);

ψ_2: *there is an entity that, for all departing paths, will eventually become the leader* (Example 4.2 on page 185, property ψ_2);

ψ_3: *for any evolution of the game, eventually there will be a state containing an entity that will become the leader* (Example 4.2 on page 185, property ψ_3);

ψ_4: *any evolution, starting from any state, will lead to a state with (at least) a leader* (property **p1** on pages 181 and 193).

In $\exists x \tau$SLCS property ψ_1 can be expressed as $\psi_1 \equiv \mathsf{AF}\, \exists \gamma.\mathbf{leader}(\gamma)$. Property ψ_2 is expressed by formula $\psi_2 \equiv \exists \gamma.\mathsf{AF}\,\mathbf{leader}(\gamma)$, while property ψ_3 is expressed by $\psi_3 \equiv \mathsf{AF}\,\psi_2$. Property ψ_4 is expressed as

$$\psi_4 \equiv \mathbf{ag}\, \mathsf{A}\, \mathsf{F}(\exists \gamma.\mathbf{leader}(\gamma)).$$

In Example 2 we have shown a formula expressing existence and uniqueness of the leader. The following formula enforces the property at the global level

$$\mathsf{AF}(\exists \gamma_1.(\mathbf{leader}(\gamma_1) \wedge (\forall \gamma_2.\mathbf{leader}(\gamma_2) \implies \gamma_1 = \gamma_2))).$$

•

5 $\exists \tau \nu$xSLCS: Dealing with Fresh Point Names

In situations where the space can change (e.g., grow) during the computation, it can be useful to quantify *only* over those paths where such a change takes place. For instance, with reference to the leader election example (Example 2), one might want to express that existence and unicity of the leader are preserved whenever new entities enter the game (see Example 5 below). Similarly, it can be useful to quantify *only* over those paths where no such changes take place. In addition, in the first case, one might be interested requiring that *all* newly introduced points satisfy a certain property or that such a property is indeed satisfied by *some* of such new points. Therefore, we extend the spatio-temporal logics presented in Sect. 2.2 with modalities A_ν and E_ν, quantifying over paths where new points are introduced; in contrast, modalities $\mathsf{A}_{\bar{\nu}}$ and $\mathsf{E}_{\bar{\nu}}$ quantify over paths where *no* new points are introduced.

In addition, we introduce the *point quantified* next unary operators $\mathcal{X}_{\forall \gamma_-}$ and $\mathcal{X}_{\exists \gamma_-}$; the former universally quantifies over all *new* points whereas the latter quantifies existentially over *new* points.

Definition 12 ($\exists \tau \nu$xSLCS)**.** *The syntax of* $\exists \tau \nu$xSLCS *is the same as in Definition 11 with the addition of the following productions*

$$\Phi ::= \mathsf{A}_\nu\, \varphi \mid \mathsf{A}_{\bar{\nu}}\, \varphi \mid \mathsf{E}_\nu\, \varphi \mid \mathsf{E}_{\bar{\nu}}\, \varphi$$

$$\varphi ::= \mathcal{X}_{\forall \gamma} \Phi \mid \mathcal{X}_{\exists \gamma} \Phi$$

The scope of γ in $\mathcal{X}_{\forall \gamma} \Phi$ and in $\mathcal{X}_{\exists \gamma} \Phi$ is Φ. For every $\exists \tau \nu x$SLCS formula Φ, where no point variable occurs free, satisfaction $\mathcal{M}, s, x \models \Phi$ of Φ in state $s \in S$ and at point $x \in X_s$ in QdTCM $\mathcal{M} = (\mathcal{K}, \{(X, \vec{C})_s, \mathcal{V}_s, \mathcal{A}_s\}_{s \in S})$, with $\mathcal{K} = (S, T)$, is defined as follows

$$\mathcal{M}, s, x \models \Phi \Leftrightarrow \mathcal{M}, \mu_0[\text{this} \mapsto x], s, x \Vmodels \Phi$$

where relation $\Vmodels$ is defined by induction on the structure of the formulas as in Definition 11, with the addition of the following equalities

$$\mathcal{M}, \mu, s, x \Vmodels \mathsf{A}_\nu \varphi \quad \Leftrightarrow \text{ for all } \tau \in \mathcal{T}_s \text{ s.t. } X_{\tau(0)} \subset X_{\tau(1)} \text{ it holds } \mathcal{M}, \mu, \tau, x \Vmodels \varphi$$
$$\mathcal{M}, \mu, s, x \Vmodels \mathsf{A}_{\bar{\nu}} \varphi \quad \Leftrightarrow \text{ for all } \tau \in \mathcal{T}_s \text{ s.t. } X_{\tau(0)} = X_{\tau(1)} \text{ it holds } \mathcal{M}, \mu, \tau, x \Vmodels \varphi$$
$$\mathcal{M}, \mu, s, x \Vmodels \mathsf{E}_\nu \varphi \quad \Leftrightarrow \text{ there is } \tau \in \mathcal{T}_s \text{ s.t. } X_{\tau(0)} \subset X_{\tau(1)} \text{ and } \mathcal{M}, \mu, \tau, x \Vmodels \varphi$$
$$\mathcal{M}, \mu, s, x \Vmodels \mathsf{E}_{\bar{\nu}} \varphi \quad \Leftrightarrow \text{ there is } \tau \in \mathcal{T}_s \text{ s.t. } X_{\tau(0)} = X_{\tau(1)} \text{ and } \mathcal{M}, \mu, \tau, x \Vmodels \varphi$$

$$\mathcal{M}, \mu, \tau, x \Vmodels \mathcal{X}_{\forall \gamma} \Phi \Leftrightarrow \text{ for all } x' \in X_{\tau(1)} \setminus X_{\tau(0)} \text{ it holds } \mathcal{M}, \mu[\gamma \mapsto x'], \tau(1), x' \Vmodels \Phi$$
$$\mathcal{M}, \mu, \tau, x \Vmodels \mathcal{X}_{\exists \gamma} \Phi \Leftrightarrow \text{ there is } x' \in X_{\tau(1)} \setminus X_{\tau(0)} \text{ s.t. } \mathcal{M}, \mu[\gamma \mapsto x'], \tau(1), x' \Vmodels \Phi.$$

With reference to the above definition, recall that for temporal path τ, $X_{\tau(0)}$ is the current space and $X_{\tau(1)}$ is the space at the next step of the computation.

Example 5. With reference to Example 2, the fact that the existence and unicity of the leader is preserved in the next time instant if a new element is added to the game can be expressed now by the following formula

$$\xi \equiv \mathsf{A}_\nu \mathcal{X}((\exists \gamma . \mathbf{leader}(\gamma)) \wedge (\forall \gamma_1 . \forall \gamma_2 . \mathbf{correctNLeader}(\gamma_1, \gamma_2))).$$

The requirement can be turned into an invariant in the expected way: $\mathsf{ag}\, \xi$. The following formula is true only if the number of entities keeps growing forever during the evolution of the game: $\neg \mathsf{EF}\, \mathsf{E}_{\bar{\nu}} \, \mathsf{F}\, \mathsf{true}$.

Example 6. Again with reference to Example 1, suppose that, due to new safety & security rules, additional premises have to be added eventually. Obviously, authorities will require that these new rooms, corridors or stairs have a concentration of the dangerous material that is less than the given threshold, as formalised by the following formula: $\mathsf{AF}((\mathsf{E}_\nu \mathcal{X}_{\exists \gamma} \mathbf{safe}(\gamma)) \wedge (\mathsf{A}_\nu \mathcal{X}_{\forall \gamma} \mathbf{safe}(\gamma)))$, with $\mathbf{safe}(\gamma)$ defined as in Example 3.

6   ∃pSLCS: Predicate Existential Extension of SLCS

In this section, we extend the logic presented in Sect. 2.1 with an *atomic proposition existential quantification* operator $\exists v.\_$. The operator we introduce quantifies over atomic propositions in a rather syntactic way, since two different atomic proposition symbols are not considered equal (not even if they denote the same subset of points of the space). In this variant of SLCS, atomic propositions play the role of *labels* or *identities* that can be associated to sets of points.

Although quantification operators have a wide applicability, we are particularly interested in applications in the field of medical imaging, and especially embedding known *lesion tracking* methods in the logical framework of VoxLogicA. Lesion tracking is the labelling of different lesions of a patient along the temporal axis (e.g., in *longitudinal studies*). In that context, it is required that the same label is assigned to the same lesion in different temporal snapshots. Several lesion tracking algorithms exist, aimed at different kinds of lesions. Since the number of lesions found in a patient is unknown *a priori*, in order to model the situation in our logical language, we intend to use atomic propositions to denote such lesions by internal labels, so that one can express formulas such as "there is a lesion x that outgrows all the other ones after one month", and then use x in other formulas, to better qualify the lesion x. We note in passing that the identification of the motion of discrete regions alongside the temporal axis is also the main topic of [20], where, notably, closure spaces are used as models.

Further examples include the analysis of video streams [11], in which different entities may be labelled by non-logical primitives, ranging from simple connected components labelling operations to machine-learning based methods. Similarly to the lesion tracking example, it is not known at formula design time how many entities exist in the analysed stream, and the identity of each entity is meant to be denoted by (internal) atomic propositions.

To that purpose, we assume a denumerable set *var* of *proposition variables*, ranged over by $v, v', v_1 \dots$ For formula Φ, $p \in$ AP and variable v we let $\Phi[p/v]$ denote, as usual, the formula obtained by substituting all *free occurrences* of v in Φ with p, where the notion of free occurrence is the standard one, with respect to quantifiers. The substitution is performed syntactically: a variable occurrence is thus replaced by a *proposition name*. This kind of syntactic quantification is inspired by the work of Demri et al. on LTL with the freeze quantifier [18].

We refine the syntax of the logic by introducing a syntactic category of *proposition expressions P* and an equality operator on proposition letters.

Definition 13 ($\exists$pSLCS). *For $p \in$ AP and $v \in Var$ the syntax of $\exists$pSLCS is the same as in Definition 6 with the addition of the following productions*

$$\Phi ::= v \mid \exists v.\Phi \mid P = P$$

$$P ::= p \mid v.$$

The scope of v in $\exists v.\Phi$ is Φ. For every $\exists$pSLCS formula Φ, where no proposition variable occurs free, satisfaction $\mathcal{M}, x \models \Phi$ of Φ at point $x \in X$ in QdCM $\mathcal{M} = (X, \vec{\mathcal{C}}, \mathcal{A}, \mathcal{V})$ is defined by induction on the structure of formulas as in Definition 6, with the addition of the following equalities

$$\mathcal{M}, x \models \exists v.\Phi \quad \Leftrightarrow \text{ there is atomic proposition } p \in \text{AP s.t. } \mathcal{M}, x \models \Phi[p/v]$$
$$\mathcal{M}, x \models P_1 = P_2 \Leftrightarrow P_1 \text{ and } P_2 \text{ are the same atomic proposition.}$$

Example 7. Consider model $\mathcal{M} = (X, \vec{\mathcal{C}}, \mathcal{A}, \mathcal{V})$, where $X = \{x_1, x_2, x_3, x_4, x_5\}$, $\mathcal{V}(p) = \{x_1, x_2, x_3\}$ and $\mathcal{V}(q) = \{x_3, x_4, x_5\}$, for $p \neq q$. We can use the following formula for overlap detection

$$\eta_1 \equiv \exists v_1. \exists v_2. v_1 \wedge v_2 \wedge \neg(v_1 = v_2).$$

Clearly, the formula η_1 holds only in point x_3, as $\mathcal{V}(q) \cap \mathcal{V}(p) = \{x_3\}$, assigning p and q to v_1 and v_2, respectively. Thus we have that $\mathcal{M}, x_3 \models \eta_1$ whereas $\mathcal{M}, x_j \not\models \eta_1$ for $j \in \{1, 2, 4, 5\}$.

Example 8. In this example we show how $\exists$pSLCS formulas can be used to distinguish regions in a digital image based on their identity (which is not possible in "classic" SLCS). Let us consider the image of Fig. 2a and let us assume that all the points (pixels) belonging to a *connected region* of the same colour have been labelled with the same label—this can easily be achieved by running a standard algorithm for computing the connected components on the image. In terms of logics, we can assume that such labels are elements of AP; without loss of generality, let us call them $1, 2, 3, 4, 5, 6, 7$, identifying each of the yellow, red and blue areas in the image. In addition, we assume that all yellow pixels satisfy atomic proposition yellow, and similarly for red and blue pixels and atomic propositions red and blue, respectively. So, we assume $\{1, 2, 3, 4, 5, 6, 7, \texttt{yellow}, \texttt{red}, \texttt{blue}\} \subseteq$ AP; we also assume that atomic propositions $1, 2, 3, 4, 5, 6$ and 7 are unknown to users—for instance they are the result of the algorithm for computing connected components mentioned above—so that they cannot use them explicitly in the formulas. Under these assumptions, formula η_2 below can be used to distinguish the top-left yellow region from the bottom-left one

$$\eta_2 \equiv \texttt{yellow} \wedge \vec{\rho}\, \eta_3[\texttt{yellow}]$$

where

$$\eta_3 \equiv \texttt{yellow} \wedge \forall v_1. \forall v_2. ((\vec{\rho}\, (v_1 \wedge \neg \texttt{blue})[\texttt{blue}] \wedge \vec{\rho}\, (v_2 \wedge \neg \texttt{blue})[\texttt{blue}]) \implies v_1 = v_2)$$

In fact, any point of the top-left yellow region satisfies η_2, having v_1 and v_2 assigned to the label 3, which identifies the top red area, whereas no point of the bottom-left yellow one satisfies it. Note also that there is no need to explicitly mention red in the formula, as it is the only possible area satisfying $\neg\texttt{blue}$ which is reachable via a blue path. Finally, we can find the unique label identifying the yellow top circle by mean of the formula

$$\exists v. v \wedge \eta_2$$

Example 9. With reference to Fig. 2b, let us assume a similar labelling schema as for Example 8, with $\{1, 2, 3, 4, 5, 6, \texttt{red}, \texttt{blue}\} \subseteq$ AP. It is easy to see that formula η_4 below distinguishes the points of any of the two red regions in the top from those of the red one in the bottom of the image

$$\eta_4 \equiv \texttt{red} \wedge \vec{\rho}\, \eta_5[\texttt{red}]$$

(a)   (b)

Fig. 2. Two example images: interesting areas can be identified by means of atomic propositions and the existential quantifier over propositions. Note that areas are not treated as nodes and edges, rather as regions of adjacent pixels having colors red, yellow and blue. (Color figure online)

where

$$\eta_5 \equiv \forall v_1.\forall v_2.v_1 \wedge \vec{\rho}\, v_2[\texttt{blue}] \wedge \neg(v_1 = \texttt{blue} \vee v_2 = \texttt{blue} \vee v_1 = v_2)$$

Any point of any of the two red regions in the top satisfies η_4, whereas no point of the red region in the bottom satisfies it.

7   Conclusions and Future Work

In this work we presented a preliminary investigation on binding in the setting of spatial and spatio-temporal logic. Our aim was to provide an intuition of how we can deal with identity of (groups of) points in a space by means of quantifiers. We provided illustrative examples of how these can be used to express interesting properties in different settings, i.e., when dealing with images and graphs, and introduced a point quantified spatio-temporal logic for closure spaces. The extension of τSLCS with predicate binding is as expected, and is not introduced here for reasons of space. Furthermore, while this preliminary investigation focuses on conservative spatio-temporal models, in future work we plan to consider also non-conservative ones, thus widening the set of possible application domains. We note in passing that it is very likely that some of the presented logical constructs can be expressed in more general formalisms such as first or second order logic, or the modal μ-calculus. Although this may be the subject of future investigation, we remark that our main aim is to investigate model checking algorithms for the newly introduced extensions. Therefore, the study of fragments that admit an efficient model checking algorithm is more immediate to our research line. In particular, a major objective is to extend the tool VoxLogicA [5] with a suitable implementation of the binding operator, in order to apply spatial model checking to a larger set of case studies. In particular, we plan to exploit the computational power of GPUs in order to achieve high efficiency via parallelisation, in a similar way as done for standard operators in its variant VoxLogicA-GPU [10].

References

1. Baldan, P., Corradini, A., König, B., Lluch Lafuente, A.: A temporal graph logic for verification of graph transformation systems. In: Fiadeiro, J.L., Schobbens, P.-Y. (eds.) WADT 2006. LNCS, vol. 4409, pp. 1–20. Springer, Heidelberg (2007). https://doi.org/10.1007/978-3-540-71998-4_1

2. Bednarczyk, B., Demri, S.: Why propositional quantification makes modal logics on trees robustly hard? In: LICS 2019, pp. 1–13. IEEE (2019)

3. Belmonte, G., Broccia, G., Ciancia, V., Latella, D., Massink, M.: Feasibility of spatial model checking for nevus segmentation. In: Bliudze, S., Gnesi, S., Plat, N., Semini, L. (eds.) FormaliSE@ICSE 2021, pp. 1–12. IEEE (2021)

4. Belmonte, G., Ciancia, V., Latella, D., Massink, M.: Innovating medical image analysis via spatial logics. In: ter Beek, M.H., Fantechi, A., Semini, L. (eds.) From Software Engineering to Formal Methods and Tools, and Back. LNCS, vol. 11865, pp. 85–109. Springer, Cham (2019). https://doi.org/10.1007/978-3-030-30985-5_7

5. Belmonte, G., Ciancia, V., Latella, D., Massink, M.: VoxLogicA: a spatial model checker for declarative image analysis. In: Vojnar, T., Zhang, L. (eds.) TACAS 2019. LNCS, vol. 11427, pp. 281–298. Springer, Cham (2019). https://doi.org/10.1007/978-3-030-17462-0_16

6. van Benthem, J., Bezhanishvili, G.: Modal logics of space. In: Aiello, M., Pratt-Hartmann, I., van Benthem, J. (eds.) Handbook of Spatial Logics, pp. 217–298. Springer, Dordrecht (2007). https://doi.org/10.1007/978-1-4020-5587-4_5

7. Bezhanishvili, N., Ciancia, V., Gabelaia, D., Grilletti, G., Latella, D., Massink, M.: Geometric model checking of continuous space. CoRR arXiv:abs/2105.06194 (2021)

8. Bull, R.A.: On modal logic with propositional quantifiers. J. Symb. Log. 34(2), 257–263 (1969)

9. Buonamici, F.B., Belmonte, G., Ciancia, V., Latella, D., Massink, M.: Spatial logics and model checking for medical imaging. Int. J. Softw. Tools Technol. Transf. 22(2), 195–217 (2020)

10. Bussi, L., Ciancia, V., Gadducci, F.: Towards a spatial model checker on GPU. In: Peters, K., Willemse, T.A.C. (eds.) FORTE 2021. LNCS, vol. 12719, pp. 188–196. Springer, Cham (2021). https://doi.org/10.1007/978-3-030-78089-0_12

11. Bussi, L., Ciancia, V., Gadducci, F., Latella, D., Massink, M.: Towards model checking video streams using VoxLogicA on GPU's. In: DataMod 2021. LNCS, Springer, Cham (2022, to appear)

12. Ciancia, V., Gilmore, S., Grilletti, G., Latella, D., Loreti, M., Massink, M.: Spatio-temporal model checking of vehicular movement in public transport systems. Int. J. Softw. Tools Technol. Transf. 20(3), 289–311 (2018)

13. Ciancia, V., Grilletti, G., Latella, D., Loreti, M., Massink, M.: An experimental spatio-temporal model checker. In: Bianculli, D., Calinescu, R., Rumpe, B. (eds.) SEFM 2015. LNCS, vol. 9509, pp. 297–311. Springer, Heidelberg (2015). https://doi.org/10.1007/978-3-662-49224-6_24

14. Ciancia, V., Latella, D., Loreti, M., Massink, M.: Specifying and verifying properties of space. In: Diaz, J., Lanese, I., Sangiorgi, D. (eds.) TCS 2014. LNCS, vol. 8705, pp. 222–235. Springer, Heidelberg (2014). https://doi.org/10.1007/978-3-662-44602-7_18

15. Ciancia, V., Latella, D., Loreti, M., Massink, M.: Model checking spatial logics for closure spaces. J. Log. Methods Comput. Sci. 12(4) (2016)

16. Ciancia, V., Latella, D., Massink, M., Paškauskas, R., Vandin, A.: A tool-chain for statistical spatio-temporal model checking of bike sharing systems. In: Margaria, T., Steffen, B. (eds.) ISoLA 2016. LNCS, vol. 9952, pp. 657–673. Springer, Cham (2016). https://doi.org/10.1007/978-3-319-47166-2_46

17. Ciancia, V., Latella, D., Massink, M., de Vink, E.P.: On bisimilarities for closure spaces - preliminary version. CoRR arXiv:abs/2105.06690 (2021)

18. Demri, S., Lazić, R.: LTL with the freeze quantifier and register automata. ACM Trans. Comput. Log. **10**(3) (2009)

19. Gadducci, F., Lluch-Lafuente, A., Vandin, A.: Counterpart semantics for a second-order μ-calculus. Fund. Inform. **118**(1–2), 177–205 (2012)

20. Galton, A.: A generalized topological view of motion in discrete space. Theoret. Comput. Sci. **305**(1–3), 111–134 (2003)

21. Grosu, R., Smolka, S.A., Corradini, F., Wasilewska, A., Entcheva, E., Bartocci, E.: Learning and detecting emergent behavior in networks of cardiac myocytes. Commun. ACM **52**(3), 97–105 (2009)

22. Haghighi, I., Jones, A., Kong, Z., Bartocci, E., Grosu, R., Belta, C.: Spatel: a novel spatial-temporal logic and its applications to networked systems. In: Girard, A., Sankaranarayanan, S. (eds.) HSCC 2015, pp. 189–198. ACM (2015)

23. Holliday, W.H.: A note on algebraic semantics for S5 with propositional quantifiers. Notre Dame J. Formal Log. **60**(2), 321–332 (2017)

24. Kripke, S.A.: A completeness theorem in modal logic. J. Symb. Log. **24**(1), 1–14 (1959)

25. Kröger, F., Merz, S.: First-order linear temporal logic. In: Kröger, F., Merz, S. (eds.) Temporal Logic and State Systems, pp. 153–179. Springer, Heidelberg (2008). https://doi.org/10.1007/978-3-540-68635-4_5

26. Kurtonina, N., de Rijke, M.: Bisimulations for temporal logic. J. Logic Lang. Inform. **6**(4), 403–425 (1997)

27. Loreti, M., Quadrini, M.: A spatial logic for a simplicial complex model. CoRR arXiv:abs/2105.08708 (2021)

28. Nenzi, L., Bortolussi, L., Ciancia, V., Loreti, M., Massink, M.: Qualitative and quantitative monitoring of spatio-temporal properties with SSTL. J. Log. Methods Comput. Sci. **14**(4) (2018)

29. Patthak, A., Bhattacharya, I., Dasgupta, A., Dasgupta, P., Chakrabarti, P.: Quantified computation tree logic. Inf. Process. Lett. **82**(3), 123–129 (2002)

30. Rensink, A.: Model checking quantified computation tree logic. In: Baier, C., Hermanns, H. (eds.) CONCUR 2006. LNCS, vol. 4137, pp. 110–125. Springer, Heidelberg (2006). https://doi.org/10.1007/11817949_8

31. Smyth, M.B., Webster, J.: Discrete spatial models. In: Aiello, M., Pratt-Hartmann, I., van Benthem, J. (eds.) Handbook of Spatial Logics, pp. 713–798. Springer, Dordrecht (2007). https://doi.org/10.1007/978-1-4020-5587-4_12

32. Stirling, C.: Modal and temporal logics. In: Abramsky, S., Gabbay, D., Maibaum, T. (eds.) Handbook of Logic in Computer Science, pp. 477–563. Oxford University Press, Oxford (1993)

33. Čech, E.: Topological spaces. In: Pták, V. (ed.) Topological Spaces, chap. III, pp. 233–394. Publishing House of the Czechoslovak Academy of Sciences/Interscience Publishers, Wiley, Prague/London-New York-Sydney (1966). Revised edition by Z. Frolíc, M. Katětov. Scientific editor, V. Pták. Editor of the English translation, C.O. Junge. MR0211373

An Efficient VCGen-Based Modular Verification of Relational Properties

Lionel Blatter[1,2] , Nikolai Kosmatov[3,4(✉)] , Virgile Prevosto[3] ,
and Pascale Le Gall[5]

[1] Karlsruhe Institute of Technology, 76131 Karlsruhe, Germany
lionel.blatter@mpi-sp.org
[2] Max Planck Institute for Security and Privacy, 44799 Bochum, Germany
[3] Université Paris-Saclay, CEA, List, 91120 Palaiseau, France
{nikolai.kosmatov,virgile.prevosto}@cea.fr
[4] Thales Research and Technology, 91120 Palaiseau, France
[5] CentraleSupélec, Université Paris-Saclay, 91190 Gif-sur-Yvette, France
pascale.legall@centralesupelec.fr

Abstract. Deductive verification typically relies on function contracts that specify the behavior of each function for a single function call. *Relational properties* link several function calls together within a single specification. They can express more advanced properties of a given function or relate calls to different functions, possibly run in parallel. However, relational properties cannot be expressed and verified directly in the traditional setting of modular deductive verification. Recent work proposed a new technique for relational property verification that relies on a verification condition generator to produce logical formulas that must be verified to ensure a given relational property. This paper presents an overview of this approach and proposes important enhancements. We integrate an optimized verification condition generator and extend the underlying theory to show how relational properties can be proved in a modular way, where one relational property can be used to prove another one, like in modular verification of function contracts. Our results have been fully formalized and proved sound in the CoQ proof assistant.

1 Introduction

Modular deductive verification [19] is used to prove that every function f of a given program respects its *contract*. Such a contract is, basically, an implication: if the given *precondition* is true before a call to f and the call terminates[1], the given *postcondition* is true when f returns control to the caller. However, some kinds of properties are not easily reducible to a single function call. Indeed, it is often necessary to express a property that involves several functions, possibly executed in parallel, or relates the results of several calls to the same function for different arguments. Such properties are known as *relational properties* [6].

---

[1] Termination can be either assumed (partial correctness) or proved separately (full correctness) in a classical way [16]; for the purpose of this paper we can assume it.

T. Margaria and B. Steffen (Eds.): ISoLA 2022, LNCS 13701, pp. 498–516, 2022.
https://doi.org/10.1007/978-3-031-19849-6_28

```
//Command c_sum:
if x_1 < x_2 then {
    x_3 := x_3 + x_1;
    x_1 := x_1 + 1;
    call(y_sum)
} else { skip }
```

Relational property $\mathcal{R}_1$ between commands c_ω^1 and c_ω^2:

$$\{\, x_2\langle 1\rangle = x_2\langle 2\rangle \,\} \begin{array}{l} // \ c_\omega^1: \\ x_1 := 1; \\ x_3 := 0; \\ \mathbf{call}(y_{sum}) \end{array} \ \langle 1\rangle \sim \begin{array}{l} // \ c_\omega^2: \\ x_1 := 0; \\ x_3 := 0; \\ \mathbf{call}(y_{sum}) \end{array} \ \langle 2\rangle \ \{\, x_3\langle 1\rangle = x_3\langle 2\rangle \,\}$$

Fig. 1. Recursive command c_{sum}, associated as a body with procedure name y_{sum}, and relational property $\mathcal{R}_1$ between two commands, denoted c_ω^1 and c_ω^2, involving a call to this procedure.

Examples of such relational properties include monotonicity (i.e. $x \leq y \Rightarrow f(x) \leq f(y)$), involving 2 calls, or transitivity $(\mathrm{cmp}(x, y) \geq 0 \wedge \mathrm{cmp}(y, z) \geq 0 \Rightarrow \mathrm{cmp}(x, z) \geq 0)$, involving 3 calls. In secure information flow [3], *non-interference* is also a relational property. Namely, given a partition of program variables between high-security variables and low-security variables, a program is said to be non-interferent if any two executions starting from states in which the low-security variables have the same initial values will end up in a final state where the low-security variables have the same values. In other words, high-security variables cannot interfere with low-security ones.

Motivation. Lack of support for relational properties in verification tools was already faced by industrial users (e.g. in [8] for C programs). The usual way to deal with this limitation is to use *self-composition* [3,9,30], product programs [2] or other self-composition variants [31]. Those techniques are based on code transformations that are relatively tedious and error-prone. Moreover, they are hardly applicable in practice to real-life programs with pointers like in C. Namely, self-composition requires that the compared executions operate on completely separated (i.e. disjoint) memory areas, which might be extremely difficult to ensure for complex programs with pointers. Modular verification of relational properties is another important feature: the user may want to rely on some relational properties in order to verify some other ones.

Example 1 (relational property). Figure 1 shows an example of a recursive command (that is, program) c_{sum}. We clearly distinguish the name and the body of a procedure. The procedure named y_{sum} is assumed to have command c_{sum} as its body, so that c_{sum} recursively calls itself. Given three global integer variables x_1, x_2 and x_3, command c_{sum} adds to x_3 (used as an accumulator) the sum $x_1 + (x_1 + 1) + \cdots + (x_2 - 1)$ if $x_1 < x_2$, and has no effect otherwise.

Figure 1 also shows an example of a relational property $\mathcal{R}_1$ (inspired by [2]) stating the equivalence of two commands c_ω^1 and c_ω^2 (assumed to be run on separate memory states), which assign x_1 and x_3 before calling y_{sum}. The relational property is written here in Benton's notation [6]: tags $\langle 1\rangle$ and $\langle 2\rangle$ are used to distinguish the programs linked by the property. When variables of the linked programs have the same names, such a tag after a variable name also helps to distinguish the instance of the variable used in the relational precondition and postcondition (written in curly braces, resp., on the left and on the right).

Property $\mathcal{R}_1$ states that if x_2 has the same value before the execution of c_ω^1 and before the execution of c_ω^2, then x_3 will have the same value after their executions. Indeed, c_ω^1 will compute in x_3 the sum $1 + 2 + \cdots + (x_2 - 1)$, while c_ω^2 will compute in x_3 the sum $0 + 1 + 2 + \cdots + (x_2 - 1)$.

In this paper, we show how relational property $\mathcal{R}_1$ can be verified using another relational property $\mathcal{R}_3$ linking two runs of c_{sum} rather than using a full functional contract of c_{sum}. More precisely, $\mathcal{R}_3$ (that will be formally defined below in Fig. 5) generalizes the situation of $\mathcal{R}_1$ and states that the resulting value of x_3 after two runs of c_{sum} will be the same if the initial state of the second run is exactly one iteration of c_{sum} behind that of the first run.   □

Approach. Our recent work [11] proposed an alternative to self-composition that is not based on code transformation or relational rules. It directly relies on a standard verification condition generator (VCGen) to produce logical formulas to be verified (typically, with an automated prover) to ensure a given relational property. This approach requires no extra code processing (such as sequential composition of programs or variable renaming). Moreover, no additional separation hypotheses are required. The locations of each program are separated by construction: each program has its own memory state. This approach has been formalized on a minimal language L, representative of the main issues relevant for relational property verification. L is a standard WHILE language extended with annotations, procedures and pointers. Notably, the presence of dereferences and address-of operations makes it representative of various aliasing problems with (possibly, multiple) pointer dereferences of a real-life language like C. An example of a relational property for programs with pointers was given in [11]. We formalize the proposed approach and prove its soundness in the COQ proof assistant [33]. Our COQ development[2] contains about 3700 lines.

Contributions. We give an overview of the VCGen-based approach for relational property verification (presented in [11]) and enhance the underlying theory with several new features. The new technical contributions of this paper include:

– a COQ formalization and proof of soundness of an optimized VCGen for language L, and its extension to the verification of relational properties;
– an extension of the framework allowing not only to *prove* relational properties, but also to *use* them as hypotheses in the following proofs;
– a COQ formalization of the extended theory.

We also provide an illustrative example and, as another minor extension, add the capacity to refer to old values of variables in postconditions.

Outline. Section 2 introduces the imperative language L used in this work. Functional correctness is defined in Sect. 3. The extension of functional correctness to relational properties is presented in Sect. 4. Then, we prove the soundness of an optimized VCGen in Sect. 5, and show how it can be soundly extended to verify relational properties in Sect. 6. Finally, we present related work in Sect. 7 and concluding remarks in Sect. 8.

---

[2] Available at https://github.com/lyonel2017/Relational-Spec/.

2 Syntax and Semantics of the Considered Language L

2.1 Locations, States, and Procedure Contracts

We denote by $\mathbb{N} = \{0, 1, 2, \dots\}$ the set of natural numbers, by $\mathbb{N}^* = \{1, 2, \dots\}$ the set of nonzero natural numbers, and by $\mathbb{B} = \{\text{True}, \text{False}\}$ the set of Boolean values. Let $\mathbb{X}$ be the set of program *locations* and $\mathbb{Y}$ the set of *program (procedure) names*, and let $x, x', x_1, \dots$ and $y, y', y_1, \dots$ denote metavariables ranging over those respective sets. We assume that there exists a bijective function $\mathbb{N} \to \mathbb{X}$, so that $\mathbb{X} = \{x_i \mid i \in \mathbb{N}\}$. Intuitively, we can see i as the *address* of location x_i.

Let Σ be the set of functions $\sigma : \mathbb{N} \to \mathbb{N}$, called *memory states*, and let $\sigma, \sigma', \sigma_1, \dots$ denote metavariables ranging over Σ. A state σ maps a location to a value using its address: location x_i has value $\sigma(i)$.

We define the *update* operation of a memory state $set(\sigma, i, n)$, also denoted by $\sigma[i/n]$, as the memory state σ' mapping each address to the same value as σ, except for i, bound to n. Formally, $set(\sigma, i, n)$ is defined by the following rules:

$$\forall \sigma \in \Sigma, x_i \in \mathbb{X}, n \in \mathbb{N}, x_j \in \mathbb{X}. \; i = j \Rightarrow \sigma[i/n](j) = n, \tag{1}$$

$$\forall \sigma \in \Sigma, x_i \in \mathbb{X}, n \in \mathbb{N}, x_j \in \mathbb{X}. \; i \neq j \Rightarrow \sigma[i/n](j) = \sigma(j). \tag{2}$$

Let Ψ be the set of functions $\psi : \mathbb{Y} \to \mathbb{C}$, called *procedure environments*, mapping program names to commands (defined below), and let $\psi, \psi_1, \dots$ denote metavariables ranging over Ψ. We write $\text{body}_\psi(y)$ to refer to $\psi(y)$, the commands (or *body*) of procedure y in a given procedure environment ψ. An example of a procedure environment ψ_{sum} is given in Fig. 5, where $\text{body}_{\psi_{\text{sum}}}(y_{\text{sum}}) = c_{\text{sum}}$.

Preconditions (or *assertions*) are predicates of arity one, taking as parameter a memory state and returning an equational first-order logic formula. Let metavariables $P, P_1, \dots$ range over the set $\mathbb{P}$ of preconditions. For instance, using λ-notation, precondition P assessing that location x_3 is bound to 2 can be defined by $P \triangleq \lambda\sigma.\sigma(3) = 2$. This form will be more convenient for relational properties (than e.g. $x_3 = 2$) as it makes explicit the memory states on which a property is evaluated.

Postconditions are predicates of arity two, taking as parameters two memory states and returning an equational first-order logic formula. Its two arguments refer to the initial and the final state. For instance, postcondition Q assessing that location x_1 was incremented (that is, $x_1 = \text{old}(x_1) + 1$) can be defined in λ-notation by $Q \triangleq \lambda\sigma\sigma'. \sigma'(1) = \sigma(1) + 1$. Let metavariables $Q, Q_2, \dots$ range over the set $\mathbb{Q}$ of postconditions.

Finally, we define the set Φ of *contract environments* $\phi : \mathbb{Y} \to \mathbb{P} \times \mathbb{Q}$, and metavariables $\phi, \phi_1, \dots$ to range over Φ. More precisely, ϕ maps a procedure name y to the associated (procedure) *contract* $\phi(y) = (\text{pre}_\phi(y), \text{post}_\phi(y))$, composed of a pre- and a postcondition for procedure y. As usual, a procedure contract will allow us to specify the behavior of a single call to the corresponding procedure, that is, if we start executing y in a memory state satisfying $\text{pre}_\phi(y)$, and the evaluation terminates, the pair composed of the initial and final states will satisfy $\text{post}_\phi(y)$.

$$a ::= n \qquad\qquad \text{natural const.}$$
$$| \ x \qquad\qquad\qquad \text{location}$$
$$| * x \qquad\qquad\quad \text{dereference}$$
$$| \&x \qquad\qquad\quad\ \text{address}$$
$$| \ a_1 \ op_a \ a_2 \quad \text{arithm. oper.}$$

$$b ::= true \ | \ false \quad \text{Boolean const.}$$
$$| \ a_1 \ op_b \ a_2 \qquad\quad \text{comparison}$$
$$| \ b_1 \ op_l \ b_2 \ | \ \neg b_1 \qquad \text{logic oper.}$$

$$c ::= \mathbf{skip} \qquad\qquad\qquad\qquad \text{do nothing}$$
$$| \ x := a \qquad\qquad\quad \text{direct assignment}$$
$$| * x := a \qquad\qquad \text{indirect assignment}$$
$$| \ c_1; c_2 \qquad\qquad\qquad\qquad \text{sequence}$$
$$| \ \mathbf{assert}(P) \qquad\qquad\qquad \text{assertion}$$
$$| \ \mathbf{if} \ b \ \mathbf{then} \ \{c_1\} \ \mathbf{else} \ \{c_2\} \qquad \text{condition}$$
$$| \ \mathbf{while} \ b \ \mathbf{inv} \ P \ \mathbf{do} \ \{c_1\} \qquad\quad \text{loop}$$
$$| \ \mathbf{call}(y) \qquad\qquad\qquad \text{procedure call}$$

Fig. 2. Syntax of arithmetic and Boolean expressions and commands in L.

$$\xi_a[\![n]\!]\sigma \triangleq n \qquad \xi_a[\![x_i]\!]\sigma \triangleq \sigma(i) \qquad \xi_a[\![*x_i]\!]\sigma \triangleq \sigma(\sigma(i)) \qquad \xi_a[\![\&x_i]\!]\sigma \triangleq i$$

Fig. 3. Evaluation of expressions in L (selected rules).

2.2   Syntax for Expressions and Commands

Let $\mathbb{E}_a$, $\mathbb{E}_b$ and $\mathbb{C}$ denote respectively the sets of arithmetic expressions, Boolean expressions and commands. We denote by $a, a_1, \ldots$; $b, b_1, \ldots$ and $c, c_1, \ldots$ metavariables ranging, respectively, over those sets. Syntax of arithmetic and Boolean expressions is given in Fig. 2. Constants are natural numbers or Boolean values. Expressions use standard arithmetic, comparison and logic binary operators, denoted respectively $op_a ::= \{+, \times, -\}$, $op_b ::= \{\leqslant, =, \ldots\}$, $op_l ::= \{\vee, \wedge\}$. Since we use natural values, the subtraction is bounded by 0, as in COQ: if $n' > n$, the result of $n - n'$ is considered to be 0. Expressions also include locations, possibly with a dereference or an address operator.

Figure 2 also presents the syntax of commands in L. Sequences, skip and conditions are standard. An assignment can be done to a location directly or after a dereference. Recall that a location x_i contains as a value a natural number, say v, that can be seen in turn as the address of a location, namely x_v, so the assignment $*x_i := a$ writes the value of expression a to the location x_v, while the address operation $\&x_i$ computes the address i of x_i. An assertion command $\mathbf{assert}(P)$ indicates that an assertion P should be valid at the point where the command occurs. The loop command $\mathbf{while} \ b \ \mathbf{inv} \ P \ \mathbf{do} \ c_1$ is always annotated with an invariant P. As usual, this invariant should hold when we reach the command and be preserved by each loop step. Command $\mathbf{call}(y)$ is a procedure call. All annotations (assertions, loop invariants and procedure contracts) will be ignored during the program execution and will be relevant only for program verification in Sect. 5. Procedures do not have explicit parameters and return values (hence we use the term *procedure call* rather than *function call*). Instead, as in assembly code [23], parameters and return value(s) are shared implicitly between the caller and the callee through memory locations: the caller must

$$\langle \mathbf{assert}(P), \sigma \rangle \overset{\psi}{\to} \sigma \qquad \frac{\xi_a[\![a]\!]\sigma = n}{\langle x_i := a, \sigma \rangle \overset{\psi}{\to} \sigma[i/n]} \qquad \frac{\xi_a[\![a]\!]\sigma = n}{\langle *x_i := a, \sigma \rangle \overset{\psi}{\to} \sigma[\sigma(i)/n]} \qquad \frac{\langle \mathrm{body}_\psi(y), \sigma_1 \rangle \overset{\psi}{\to} \sigma_2}{\langle \mathbf{call}(y), \sigma_1 \rangle \overset{\psi}{\to} \sigma_2}$$

Fig. 4. Operational semantics of commands in L (selected rules).

Procedure environment: $\qquad\qquad\qquad \psi_{\mathsf{sum}} \triangleq \{ y_{\mathsf{sum}} \to c_{\mathsf{sum}} \}$

Hoare triple $\mathcal{R}_2$: $\qquad\qquad \psi_{\mathsf{sum}} : \{ \mathrm{True} \}\, c_{\mathsf{sum}}\, \{ \mathrm{old}(x_1) \geqslant \mathrm{old}(x_2) \Rightarrow \mathrm{old}(x_3) = x_3 \}$

Relational property $\mathcal{R}_3$:
$$\psi_{\mathsf{sum}} : \left\{ \begin{array}{l} x_1\langle 2 \rangle < x_2\langle 2 \rangle\ \wedge \\ x_2\langle 1 \rangle = x_2\langle 2 \rangle\ \wedge \\ x_1\langle 1 \rangle = x_1\langle 2 \rangle + 1\ \wedge \\ x_3\langle 1 \rangle = x_3\langle 2 \rangle + x_1\langle 2 \rangle \end{array} \right\} c_{\mathsf{sum}}\langle 1 \rangle \sim c_{\mathsf{sum}}\langle 2 \rangle \left\{ x_3\langle 1 \rangle = x_3\langle 2 \rangle \right\}$$

Fig. 5. A procedure environment ψ_{sum} associating procedure name y_{sum} with its body c_{sum} (see Fig. 1), a Hoare triple $\mathcal{R}_2$ for command c_{sum}, and a relational property $\mathcal{R}_3$ linking two runs of c_{sum}.

put/read the right values at the right locations before/after the call. Finally, to avoid ambiguity, we group sequences of commands with { }.

2.3 Operational Semantics

Evaluation of arithmetic and Boolean expressions in L is defined by functions ξ_a and ξ_b. Selected evaluation rules for arithmetic expressions are shown in Fig. 3. Operations $*x_i$ and $\&x_i$ have a semantics similar to the C language, i.e. dereferencing and address-of. Semantics of Boolean expressions is standard [36].

Based on these evaluation functions, we can define the operational semantics of commands in a given procedure environment ψ. Selected evaluation rules are shown in Fig. 4. As said above, both assertions and loop invariants can be seen as program annotations that do not influence the execution of the program itself. Hence, command $\mathbf{assert}(P)$ is equivalent to a skip. Likewise, loop invariant P has no influence on the semantics of **while** b **inv** P **do** $\{c\}$.

We write $\Vdash \langle c, \sigma \rangle \overset{\psi}{\to} \sigma'$ to denote that $\langle c, \sigma \rangle \overset{\psi}{\to} \sigma'$ can be derived from the rules of Fig. 4. Our CoQ formalization, inspired by [29], provides a deep embedding of L, with an associated parser, in files `Aexp.v`, `Bexp.v` and `Com.v`.

3 Functional Correctness

We define functional correctness in a similar way to the original *Hoare triple* definition [19], except that we also need a procedure environment ψ, leading to a quadruple denoted $\psi : \{P\}c\{Q\}$. We will however still refer by the term "Hoare triple" to the corresponding program property, formally defined as follows.

Definition 1 (Hoare triple). *Let c be a command, ψ a procedure environment, and P and Q two assertions. We define a Hoare triple $\psi : \{P\}c\{Q\}$ as follows:*

$$\psi : \{P\}c\{Q\} \triangleq \forall \sigma, \sigma' \in \Sigma.\ P(\sigma) \wedge (\Vdash \langle c, \sigma \rangle \overset{\psi}{\to} \sigma') \Rightarrow Q(\sigma, \sigma').$$

Informally, our definition states that, for a given ψ, if a state σ satisfies P and the execution of c on σ terminates in a state σ', then (σ, σ') satisfies Q.

Example 2. Figure 5 gives an example of a Hoare triple denoted $\mathcal{R}_2$.   □

Next, we introduce notation $CV(\psi, \phi)$ to denote the fact that, for the given ψ and ϕ every procedure satisfies its contract.

Definition 2 (Contract Validity). *Let ψ be a procedure environment and ϕ a contract environment. We define contract validity $CV(\psi, \phi)$ as follows:*

$$CV(\psi, \phi) \triangleq \forall y \in \mathbb{Y}. \ \psi : \{\text{pre}_\phi(y)\}\textbf{\textit{call}}(y)\{\text{post}_\phi(y)\}).$$

The notion of contract validity is at the heart of modular verification, since it allows assuming that the contracts of the callees are satisfied during the verification of a Hoare triple. More precisely, to state the validity of procedure contracts without assuming anything about their bodies in our formalization, we will consider an arbitrary choice of implementations ψ' of procedures that satisfy the contracts, like in the first assumption of Theorem 1 below. This theorem, taken from [1, Th. 4.2] and reformulated for L in [11], states that $\psi : \{P\}c\{Q\}$ holds if we can prove the contract of (the bodies in ψ of) all procedures in an arbitrary environment ψ' respecting the contracts, and if the validity of contracts of ϕ for ψ implies the Hoare triple itself. This theorem is the basis for modular verification of Hoare Triples, as done for instance in Hoare Logic [19,36] or verification condition generation.

Theorem 1 (Recursion). *Given a procedure environment ψ and a contract environment ϕ such that the following two assumptions hold:*

$$\forall \psi' \in \Psi. \ CV(\psi', \phi) \Rightarrow \forall y \in \mathbb{Y}, \psi' : \{\text{pre}_\phi(y)\}\text{body}_\psi(y)\{\text{post}_\phi(y)\},$$
$$CV(\psi, \phi) \Rightarrow \psi : \{P\}c\{Q\},$$

we have $\psi : \{P\}c\{Q\}$.

We refer the reader to the CoQ development, more precisely the results `recursive_proc` and `recursive_hoare_triple` in file `Hoare_Triple.v` for a complete proof of Theorem 1.

4   Relational Functional Correctness

Relational properties can be seen as an extension of Hoare triples. But, instead of linking one program with two properties, the pre- and postconditions, relational properties link n programs to two properties, called *relational precondition* and *relational postcondition*. A *relational precondition* or *assertion* (resp., *relational postcondition*) for n programs is a predicate taking a sequence of n (resp., $2n$) memory states and returning a first-order logic formula. Metavariables $\widehat{P}, \widehat{P'}, \ldots$ (resp., $\widehat{Q}, \widehat{Q'}, \ldots$) range over the corresponding sets. As a simple example, the relational postcondition of $\mathcal{R}_1$ (written in Fig. 1 in Benton's notation) can be stated in λ-notation as follows: $\lambda \sigma_1, \sigma_2, \sigma_1', \sigma_2' \cdot \sigma_1'(3) = \sigma_2'(3)$.

A *relational property* is a property about n programs $c_1, \ldots, c_n$, stating that if each program c_i starts in a state σ_i and ends in a state σ_i' such that $\widehat{P}(\sigma_1, \ldots, \sigma_n)$ holds, then $\widehat{Q}(\sigma_1, \ldots, \sigma_n, \sigma_1', \ldots, \sigma_n')$ holds, where $\widehat{P}$ is a relational precondition and $\widehat{Q}$ is a relational postcondition. We formally define relational correctness similarly to functional correctness (cf. Definition 1), except that we now use sequences of commands and memory states. We abbreviate by $(u_k)^n$ a sequence of elements $(u_k)_{k=1}^n = (u_1, \ldots, u_n)$, where k ranges from 1 to n. If $n \le 0$, $(u_k)^n$ is the empty sequence denoted [ ]. If $n = 1$, $(u)^1$ is the singleton sequence (u).

Definition 3 (Relational Hoare Triple). *Let ψ be a procedure environment, $(c_k)^n$ a sequence of n commands ($n \in \mathbb{N}^*$), $\widehat{P}$ and $\widehat{Q}$ relational pre- and postcondition for n commands. The relational correctness of $(c_k)^n$ with respect to $\widehat{P}$ and $\widehat{Q}$, denoted $\psi : \{\widehat{P}\}(c_k)^n\{\widehat{Q}\}$, is defined as follows:*

$$\psi : \{\widehat{P}\}(c_k)^n\{\widehat{Q}\} \triangleq$$

$$\forall (\sigma_k)^n, (\sigma_k')^n. \ \widehat{P}((\sigma_k)^n) \wedge (\bigwedge_{i=1}^n \Vdash \langle c_i, \sigma_i \rangle \xrightarrow{\psi} \sigma'_i) \Rightarrow \widehat{Q}((\sigma_k)^n, (\sigma_k')^n).$$

For $n = 1$, this notion defines a Hoare triple. It also generalizes Benton's notation [6] for two commands: $\psi : \{\widehat{P}\}c_1 \sim c_2\{\widehat{Q}\}$. As Benton's work mostly focused on comparing equivalent programs, using symbol $\sim$ was quite natural.

Example 3. Relational property $\mathcal{R}_3$ introduced in Example 1 is formalized (in Benton's notation) in Fig. 5. Below, we will illustrate modular verification of relational properties by deducing $\mathcal{R}_1$ from $\mathcal{R}_3$ and partial contract $\mathcal{R}_2$ of c_{sum}. □

We will now extend Theorem 1 to relational contract environments. A *relational contract environment* $\widehat{\phi}$ maps a sequence of program names $(y_k)^n$ to a *relational contract*, composed of a relational pre- and postcondition, denoted $\widehat{\phi}((y_k)^n) = (\widehat{\text{pre}}_{\widehat{\phi}}((y_k)^n), \widehat{\text{post}}_{\widehat{\phi}}((y_k)^n))$. Practical applications require only a finite number of properties, so the relational contract can be assumed trivial for all except a finite number of sequences. A relational contract environment generalizes a contract environment, since a standard procedure contract is a relational contract (for a sequence of exactly one element). Notice that $\widehat{\phi}$ considers only one relational property for a given sequence $(y_k)^n$: this is not a limitation since several properties can be encoded in one contract. We define the set of relational contract environments $\widehat{\Phi}$, and metavariables $\widehat{\phi}, \widehat{\phi}_0, \widehat{\phi}_1, \ldots$ will range over $\widehat{\Phi}$.

We introduce notation $CV_r(\psi, \widehat{\phi})$ to denote the fact that all procedures defined in ψ satisfy the relational contracts in which they are involved in $\widehat{\phi}$.

Definition 4 (Relational Contract Validity). *Let ψ be a procedure environment and $\widehat{\phi}$ a relational contract environment. We define $CV_r(\psi, \widehat{\phi})$ as follows:*

$$CV_r(\psi, \widehat{\phi}) \triangleq \forall (y_k)^n \in \text{dom}(\widehat{\phi}), \ n > 0 \Rightarrow \psi : \{\widehat{\text{pre}}_{\widehat{\phi}}((y_k)^n)\}(\mathit{call}(y_k))_{k=1}^n\{\widehat{\text{post}}_{\widehat{\phi}}((y_k)^n)\}.$$

Theorem 2 (Relational Recursion). *Given a procedure environment ψ and a relational contract environment $\widehat{\phi}$ such that the following two assumptions hold:*

$$\forall \psi' \in \Psi.CV_r(\psi', \widehat{\phi}) \Rightarrow$$
$$\forall (y_k)^n \in \mathrm{dom}(\widehat{\phi}), \psi' : \{\widehat{\mathrm{pre}}_{\widehat{\phi}}((y_k)^n)\}(\mathrm{body}_\psi(y_k))_{k=1}^n\{\widehat{\mathrm{post}}_{\widehat{\phi}}((y_k)^n)\},$$

$$CV_r(\psi, \widehat{\phi}) \Rightarrow \psi : \{\widehat{P}\}(c_k)^n\{\widehat{Q}\}$$

then we have $\psi : \{\widehat{P}\}(c_k)^n\{\widehat{Q}\}$.

The Coq proof (which is a straightforward extension of the proof of Theorem 1) is available in `Rela.v`, Theorem `recursion_relational`.

5   Optimized Verification Condition Generator

A standard way [16] for verifying that a Hoare triple holds is to use a verification condition generator (VCGen). In this section, we formalize a VCGen for Hoare triples such that if all verification conditions that it generates are valid, then the Hoare triple is valid according to Definition 1. The VCGen described in this section is based on optimizations introduced in [15]. Such optimizations allow the VCGen to return formulas whose size is linear with respect to the size of the program itself, and are now part of any state-of-the-art deductive verification tool. The key idea is to avoid splitting verification condition generation into two separated sub-generation at each conditional. The definition is formalized in Coq in the file `Vcg_Opt.v`, where we also prove that the verification conditions of this optimized VCGen imply those of the naive VCGen presented in [11]. This will allow us to use the optimized VCGen (or more generally any VCGen satisfying the properties stated in Theorem 3 below) for the verification of relational properties as well (see Sect. 6).

5.1   Verification Condition Generator

When defining the naive VCGen in [11], we proposed a modular definition. Namely, we divided it into three functions T_c, T_a and T_f. Here, we follow the same approach for the optimized VCGen, using three new functions $T_c^{\triangleright}$, $T_a^{\triangleright}$, and $T_f^{\triangleright}$:

- function $T_c^{\triangleright}$ generates the main verification condition, expressing that the postcondition holds in the final state, assuming auxiliary annotations hold;
- function $T_a^{\triangleright}$ generates auxiliary verification conditions stemming from assertions, loop invariants, and preconditions of called procedures;
- finally, function $T_f^{\triangleright}$ generates verification conditions for the auxiliary procedures that are called by the main program, to ensure that their bodies respect their contracts.

$$\mathcal{T}_c^{\triangleright}[\![\mathbf{skip}]\!](\sigma, \sigma', \phi, f) \triangleq f(\sigma = \sigma')$$

$$\mathcal{T}_c^{\triangleright}[\![x_i := a]\!](\sigma, \sigma', \phi, f) \triangleq f(\sigma' = set(\sigma, i, \xi_a[\![a]\!]\sigma))$$

$$\mathcal{T}_c^{\triangleright}[\![*x_i := a]\!](\sigma, \sigma', \phi, f) \triangleq f(\sigma' = set(\sigma, \sigma(i), \xi_a[\![a]\!]\sigma))$$

$$\mathcal{T}_c^{\triangleright}[\![\mathbf{assert}(P)]\!](\sigma, \sigma', \phi, f) \triangleq f(P(\sigma) \wedge \sigma = \sigma')$$

$$\mathcal{T}_c^{\triangleright}[\![c_0; c_1]\!](\sigma, \sigma', \phi, f) \triangleq \forall \sigma''. \mathcal{T}_c^{\triangleright}[\![c_0]\!](\sigma, \sigma'', \phi, \lambda p_1.$$
$$\mathcal{T}_c^{\triangleright}[\![c_1]\!](\sigma'', \sigma', \phi, \lambda p_2. f(p_1 \wedge p_2)))$$

$$\mathcal{T}_c^{\triangleright}[\![\mathbf{if}\ b\ \mathbf{then}\ \{c_0\}\ \mathbf{else}\ \{c_1\}]\!](\sigma, \sigma', \phi, f) \triangleq \mathcal{T}_c^{\triangleright}[\![c_0]\!](\sigma, \sigma', \phi, \lambda p_1.$$
$$\mathcal{T}_c^{\triangleright}[\![c_1]\!](\sigma, \sigma', \phi, \lambda p_2.$$
$$f((b \equiv \mathrm{True} \Rightarrow p_1) \wedge (b \equiv \mathrm{False} \Rightarrow p_2))))$$

$$\mathcal{T}_c^{\triangleright}[\![\mathbf{call}(y)]\!](\sigma, \sigma', \phi, f) \triangleq f(\mathrm{pre}_\phi(y)(\sigma) \wedge \mathrm{post}_\phi(y)(\sigma, \sigma'))$$

$$\mathcal{T}_c^{\triangleright}[\![\mathbf{while}\ b\ \mathbf{inv}\ inv\ \mathbf{do}\ \{c\}]\!](\sigma, \sigma', \phi, f) \triangleq f(inv\ \sigma \wedge inv\ \sigma' \wedge \neg(\xi_b[\![b]\!]\sigma'))$$

Fig. 6. Definition of function $\mathcal{T}_c^{\triangleright}$ generating the main verification condition.

Definition 5 (Function $\mathcal{T}_c^{\triangleright}$ generating the main verification condition).
Given a command c, two memory states σ and σ', a contract environment ϕ, and a function f taking a formula as argument and returning a formula, function $\mathcal{T}_c^{\triangleright}$ returns a formula defined by case analysis on c as shown in Fig. 6.

State σ represents the state before executing the command, while σ' represents the state after it. Intuitively, the argument that gets passed to f is the formula that relates σ and σ' according to c itself. Thus, if f is of the form $\lambda p. p \Rightarrow Q(\sigma, \sigma')$, as in Theorem 3 below, the resulting formula is a verification condition for post-condition Q to hold.

For **skip**, which does nothing, both states are identical. For assignments, σ' is simply the update of σ. An assertion introduces a hypothesis over σ but leaves it unchanged. For a sequence, a fresh memory state σ'' is introduced, and we compose the VCGen. For a conditional, if the condition evaluates to True, we select the condition from the *then* branch, and otherwise from the *else* branch. Note that, contrary to the naive VCGen, we perform a single call to f, ensuring the linearity of the formula.

The rule for calls simply assumes that before the call σ satisfies $\mathrm{pre}_\phi(y)$ and after the call σ and σ' satisfy $\mathrm{post}_\phi(y)$. Finally, $\mathcal{T}_c^{\triangleright}$ assumes that, for a loop, both the initial state σ and the final one σ' satisfy the loop invariant. Additionally, in σ' the loop condition evaluates to False. As for an assertion, the callee's precondition and the loop invariant are just assumed to be true; function $\mathcal{T}_a^{\triangleright}$, defined below, generates the corresponding proof obligations.

Example 4. For $c \triangleq \mathbf{if}\ \mathrm{False}\ \mathbf{then}\ \{\mathbf{skip}\}\ \mathbf{else}\ \{x_1 := 2\}$ we have:

$$\mathcal{T}_c^{\triangleright}[\![c]\!](\sigma, \sigma', \phi, \lambda p.\ p \Rightarrow \sigma'(1) = 2) \equiv$$
$$(\mathrm{False} \equiv \mathrm{True} \Rightarrow \sigma = \sigma') \wedge (\mathrm{False} \equiv \mathrm{False} \Rightarrow \sigma' = set(\sigma, 1, 2)) \Rightarrow \sigma'(1) = 2.$$

$\square$

Lemma 1 establishes a relation between functions $T_c^\triangleright$ and T_c: the formulas generated by $T_c^\triangleright$ imply the formulas generated by T_c.

Lemma 1. *Given a program c, a procedure contract environment ϕ, a memory state σ and an assertion P, if we have $\forall \sigma' \in \Sigma,\ T_c^\triangleright[\![c]\!](\sigma, \sigma', \phi, \lambda p.\, p \Rightarrow P(\sigma'))$, then we have $T_c[\![c]\!](\sigma, \phi, P)$.*

Proof. By structural induction over c.   □

$$T_a^\triangleright[\![\mathbf{skip}]\!](\sigma, \phi) \triangleq \text{True}$$

$$T_a^\triangleright[\![x := a]\!](\sigma, \phi) \triangleq \text{True}$$

$$T_a^\triangleright[\![*x := a]\!](\sigma, \phi) \triangleq \text{True}$$

$$T_a^\triangleright[\![\mathbf{assert}(P)]\!](\sigma, \phi) \triangleq P(\sigma)$$

$$T_a^\triangleright[\![c_0; c_1]\!](\sigma, \phi) \triangleq T_a^\triangleright[\![c_0]\!](\sigma, \phi) \wedge$$
$$\forall \sigma',\ T_c^\triangleright[\![c_0]\!](\sigma, \sigma', \phi, \lambda p.\, p \Rightarrow T_a^\triangleright[\![c_1]\!](\sigma', \phi))$$

$$T_a^\triangleright[\![\mathbf{if}\ b\ \mathbf{then}\ \{c_0\}\ \mathbf{else}\ \{c_1\}]\!](\sigma, \phi) \triangleq (\xi_b[\![b]\!]\sigma' \Rightarrow T_a^\triangleright[\![c_0]\!](\sigma, \phi)) \wedge$$
$$(\neg(\xi_b[\![b]\!]\sigma') \Rightarrow T_a^\triangleright[\![c_1]\!](\sigma, \phi))$$

$$T_a^\triangleright[\![\mathbf{call}(y)]\!](\sigma, \phi) \triangleq \mathrm{pre}_\phi(y)(\sigma)$$

$$T_a^\triangleright[\![\mathbf{while}\ b\ \mathbf{inv}\ inv\ \mathbf{do}\ \{c\}]\!](\sigma, \phi) \triangleq inv(\sigma) \wedge$$
$$(\forall \sigma',\ inv(\sigma') \Rightarrow \xi_b[\![b]\!]\sigma' \Rightarrow T_a^\triangleright[\![c]\!](\sigma', \phi)) \wedge$$
$$(\forall \sigma'\sigma'',\ inv(\sigma') \Rightarrow T_c^\triangleright[\![c]\!](\sigma', \sigma'', \phi, \lambda p.\, p \Rightarrow inv(\sigma'')))$$

Fig. 7. Definition of function $T_a^\triangleright$ generating auxiliary verification conditions.

Definition 6 (Function $T_a^\triangleright$ generating the auxiliary verification condition). *Given a command c, a memory state σ representing the state before the command, and a contract environment ϕ, function $T_a^\triangleright$ returns a formula defined by case analysis on c as shown in Fig. 7.*

Basically, $T_a^\triangleright$ collects all assertions, preconditions of called procedures, as well as invariant establishment and preservation, and lifts the corresponding formulas to constraints on the initial state σ through the use of $T_c^\triangleright$.

As for $T_c^\triangleright$, the formulas generated by $T_a^\triangleright$ imply those generated by T_a.

Lemma 2. *For a given program c, a procedure contract environment ϕ, and a memory state σ, if we have $T_a^\triangleright[\![c]\!](\sigma, \phi)$, then we have $T_a[\![c]\!](\sigma, \phi)$.*

Proof. By structural induction over c.   □

Finally, we define the function that generates the conditions for verifying that the body of each procedure defined in ψ respects its contract defined in ϕ.

Definition 7 (Function $\mathcal{T}_f^{\triangleright}$ generating the procedure verification condition). $\mathcal{T}_f^{\triangleright}$ *takes as argument two environments ψ and ϕ and returns a formula:*

$$\mathcal{T}_f^{\triangleright}(\phi, \psi) \triangleq \forall y, \sigma, \sigma'. \ \mathrm{pre}_\phi(y)(\sigma) \Rightarrow$$
$$\mathcal{T}_a^{\triangleright}[\![\mathrm{body}_\psi(y)]\!](\sigma, \phi) \wedge \mathcal{T}_c^{\triangleright}[\![\mathrm{body}_\psi(y)]\!](\sigma, \sigma', \phi, \lambda p.p \Rightarrow \mathrm{post}_\phi(y)(\sigma, \sigma')).$$

Finally, the formulas generated by $\mathcal{T}_f^{\triangleright}$ imply those generated by $\mathcal{T}_f$.

Lemma 3. *For a given procedure environment ψ, and a procedure contract environment ϕ, if we have $\mathcal{T}_f^{\triangleright}(\phi, \psi)$, then we have $\mathcal{T}_f(\phi, \psi)$.*

Proof. Using Lemmas 1 and 2. □

The definition of the optimized VCGen and its link to the naive version can be found in file Vcg_Opt.v of the COQ development.

5.2 Hoare Triple Verification

Using the VCGen defined in Sect. 5.1, we can state the theorem establishing how a Hoare Triple can be verified. The proof can be found in file Correct.v of the COQ development.

Theorem 3 (Soundness of VCGen). *Assume that we have $\mathcal{T}_f^{\triangleright}(\phi, \psi)$ and*

$$\forall \sigma. \ P(\sigma) \Rightarrow \mathcal{T}_a^{\triangleright}[\![c]\!](\sigma, \phi),$$
$$\forall \sigma, \sigma'. \ P(\sigma) \Rightarrow \mathcal{T}_c^{\triangleright}[\![c]\!](\sigma, \sigma', \phi, \lambda p.p \Rightarrow Q(\sigma, \sigma')).$$

Then we have $\psi : \{P\}c\{Q\}$.

Proof. By soundness of the naive VCGen [11, Th. 3] and Lemmas 1, 2, 3. □

6 Modular Verification of Relational Properties

In this section, we propose a modular verification method for relational properties (defined in Sect. 4) using the optimized VCGen defined in Sect. 5 (or, more generally, any VCGen respecting Theorem 3). First, we define the function $\mathcal{T}_{cr}^{\triangleright}$ for the recursive call of $\mathcal{T}_c^{\triangleright}$ on a sequence of commands and memory states.

Definition 8 (Function $\mathcal{T}_{cr}^{\triangleright}$). *Given a sequence of commands $(c_k)^n$ and a sequence of memory states $(\sigma_k)^n$, a contract environment ϕ and a function f taking as argument a formula and returning a formula, function $\mathcal{T}_{cr}^{\triangleright}$ is defined by induction on n for the basis ($n = 0$) and inductive case ($n \in \mathbb{N}^*$) as follows:*

$$\mathcal{T}_{cr}^{\triangleright}([\,], [\,], [\,], \phi, f) \triangleq f(True),$$
$$\mathcal{T}_{cr}^{\triangleright}((c_k)^n, (\sigma_k)^n, (\sigma_k')^n, \phi, f) \triangleq$$
$$\mathcal{T}_c^{\triangleright}[\![c_n]\!](\sigma_n, \sigma_n', \phi, \ \lambda p_n. \ \mathcal{T}_{cr}^{\triangleright}((c_k)^{n-1}, (\sigma_k)^{n-1}, (\sigma_k')^{n-1}, \phi, \lambda p_{n-1}. \ f(p_n \wedge p_{n-1}))).$$

Intuitively, like in Definition 5, the argument that gets passed to f is the formula that relates the n pre-states $(\sigma_k)^n$ to the n post-states $(\sigma'_k)^n$ when all $(c_k)^n$ are executed. Again, if f is of the form $\lambda p.p \Rightarrow \widehat{Q}((\sigma_k)^n, (\sigma'_k)^n)$, the resulting formula is a verification condition for the relational postcondition $\widehat{Q}$ to hold. More concretely, for $n = 2$, and f as above, we obtain:

$$\mathcal{T}^{\triangleright}_{cr}((c_1, c_2), (\sigma_1, \sigma_2), (\sigma'_1, \sigma'_2), \phi, \lambda p.p \Rightarrow \widehat{Q}((\sigma_1, \sigma_2), (\sigma'_1, \sigma'_2))) \equiv$$
$$\mathcal{T}^{\triangleright}_c[\![c_2]\!](\sigma_2, \sigma'_2, \phi, \lambda p_2.\mathcal{T}^{\triangleright}_c[\![c_1]\!](\sigma_1, \sigma'_1, \phi, \lambda p_1.p_2 \wedge p_1 \Rightarrow \widehat{Q}((\sigma_1, \sigma_2), (\sigma'_1, \sigma'_2)))).$$

We similarly define a notation for the auxiliary verification conditions for a sequence of n commands. Basically, this is the conjunction of the auxiliary verification conditions generated by $\mathcal{T}^{\triangleright}_a$ on each individual command.

Definition 9 (Function $\mathcal{T}^{\triangleright}_{ar}$). *Given a sequence of commands $(c_k)^n$ and a sequence of memory states $(\sigma_k)^n$, we define function $\mathcal{T}^{\triangleright}_{ar}$ as follows:*

$$\mathcal{T}^{\triangleright}_{ar}((c_k)^n, (\sigma_k)^n, \phi) \triangleq \bigwedge_{i=1}^{n} \mathcal{T}^{\triangleright}_a[\![c_i]\!](\sigma_i, \phi).$$

A standard contract over a single procedure y can be used directly whenever there is a call to y. For a relational contract over $(y_k)^n$, things are more complicated: there is not a single program point where we can apply the relational contract. Instead, we have to somehow track in the generated formulas all the calls that have been made, and to guard the application of the relational contract by a constraint stating that all the appropriate calls have indeed taken place. In order to achieve that, we start by defining a notation for the conjunction of a sequence of procedure calls and associated memory states:

Definition 10 (Functions $\mathcal{P}_{call}$ and $\mathcal{P}_{pred}$).

$$\mathcal{P}_{call}(y, \sigma, \sigma', \psi) \triangleq \Vdash \langle \mathbf{call}(y), \sigma \rangle \xrightarrow{\psi} \sigma',$$

$$\mathcal{P}_{pred}((y_k)^n, (\sigma_k)^n, (\sigma'_k)^n, \psi) \triangleq \bigwedge_{i=1}^{n} \mathcal{P}_{call}(y_i, \sigma_i, \sigma'_i, \psi).$$

Then, we can define function $\mathcal{T}_{pr}$ translating relational contracts into a logical formula, using $\mathcal{P}_{pred}$ to guard its application with tracked calls.

Definition 11 (Function $\mathcal{T}_{pr}$).

$$\mathcal{T}_{pr}(\widehat{\phi}, \psi) \triangleq$$
$$\forall (y_k)^n, (\sigma_k)^n, (\sigma'_k)^n, \; n > 0 \;\Rightarrow\; \mathcal{P}_{pred}((y_k)^n, (\sigma_k)^n, (\sigma'_k)^n, \psi) \;\Rightarrow$$
$$\widehat{\mathrm{pre}}_{\widehat{\phi}}((y_k)^n)(\sigma_k)^n \;\Rightarrow\; \widehat{\mathrm{post}}_{\widehat{\phi}}((y_k)^n)(\sigma_k)^n(\sigma'_k)^n.$$

We now define function $\mathcal{L}$ to lift a relational procedure contract with an associated tracked call predicate and reduce it to a standard contract.

$$\mathcal{L}(\widehat{\phi}, \psi) \triangleq \lambda y.(\lambda\sigma.\widehat{\mathrm{pre}}_{\widehat{\phi}}((y)^1)(\sigma)^1, \lambda\sigma\sigma'.\widehat{\mathrm{post}}_{\widehat{\phi}}((y)^1)(\sigma)^1(\sigma')^1 \wedge \mathcal{P}_{call}(y, \sigma, \sigma', \psi)).$$

Finally, using function $\mathcal{T}_{pr}$ and $\mathcal{L}$, we can define function $\mathcal{T}_{fr}^{\triangleright}$ for generating the verification condition for verifying that the bodies of each sequence of procedures respect the relational contract defined in $\widehat{\phi}$: thanks to $\mathcal{L}$, each call instruction will result in a corresponding $\mathcal{P}_{call}$ occurrence in the generated formula, so that it will be possible to make use of the relational contracts hypotheses in $\mathcal{T}_{pr}$ when the appropriate sequences of calls occur.

Definition 12 (Function $\mathcal{T}_{fr}^{\triangleright}$).

$$\mathcal{T}_{fr}^{\triangleright}(\widehat{\phi}, \psi) \triangleq$$

$$\forall (y_k)^n, (\sigma_k)^n, (\sigma_k')^n, \psi', \ \widehat{\mathrm{pre}_{\widehat{\phi}}}((y_k)^n) \ \Rightarrow \ \mathcal{T}_{pr}(\widehat{\phi}, \psi') \ \Rightarrow$$

$$\mathcal{T}_{ar}^{\triangleright}((\mathrm{body}_{\psi}(y_k))_{k=1}^n, (\sigma_k)^n, \mathcal{L}(\widehat{\phi}, \psi')) \land$$

$$\mathcal{T}_{cr}^{\triangleright}((\mathrm{body}_{\psi}(y_k))_{k=1}^n, (\sigma_k)^n, (\sigma_k')^n, \mathcal{L}(\widehat{\phi}, \psi'), \lambda p.p \Rightarrow \widehat{\mathrm{post}_{\widehat{\phi}}}((y_k)^n))).$$

Using functions $\mathcal{T}_{cr}^{\triangleright}$, $\mathcal{T}_{ar}^{\triangleright}$ and $\mathcal{T}_{fr}^{\triangleright}$, we can now give the main result of this paper, i.e. that the verification of relational properties with the VCGen is correct.

Theorem 4 (Soundness of relational VCGen). *For any sequence of commands* $(c_k)^n$, *contract environment* $\widehat{\phi}$, *procedure environment* ψ, *and relational pre- and postcondition* $\widehat{P}$ *and* $\widehat{Q}$, *if the following three properties hold:*

$$\mathcal{T}_{fr}^{\triangleright}(\widehat{\phi}, \psi), \tag{3}$$

$$\forall (\sigma_k)^n, \psi', \ \widehat{P}((\sigma_k)^n) \land \mathcal{T}_{pr}(\widehat{\phi}, \psi) \ \Rightarrow \ \mathcal{T}_{ar}^{\triangleright}((c_k)^n, (\sigma_k)^n, \mathcal{L}(\widehat{\phi}, \psi')), \tag{4}$$

$$\forall (\sigma_k)^n, (\sigma_k')^n, \psi', \ \widehat{P}((\sigma_k)^n) \land \mathcal{T}_{pr}(\widehat{\phi}, \psi) \ \Rightarrow$$

$$\mathcal{T}_{cr}^{\triangleright}((c_k)^n, (\sigma_k)^n, (\sigma_k')^n, \mathcal{L}(\widehat{\phi}, \psi'), \lambda p.p \Rightarrow \widehat{Q}((\sigma_k)^n, (\sigma_k')^n)), \tag{5}$$

then we have $\psi : \{\widehat{P}\}(c_k)^n\{\widehat{Q}\}$.

In other words, a relational property is valid if all relational procedure contracts are valid, and, assuming the relational precondition holds, both the auxiliary verification conditions and the main relational verification condition hold. The corresponding CoQ formalization is available in file `Rela.v`, and the CoQ proof of Theorem 4 is in file `Correct_Rela.v`.

Example 5. Consider $\psi = \psi_{\mathrm{sum}}$ and $\widehat{\phi}$ which encodes $\mathcal{R}_2$ and $\mathcal{R}_3$. The relational property $\mathcal{R}_1$ of Fig. 1 can now be proven valid in a modular way, using $\mathcal{R}_2$ and $\mathcal{R}_3$, by the proposed technique based on Theorem 4 (see file `Examples.v` of the CoQ development). For instance, (5) becomes the formula of Fig. 8. There, the relational precondition is given by (6), while the simplified (instantiated for sequence $(y_{\mathrm{sum}}, y_{\mathrm{sum}})$) translation of the relational contracts $\mathcal{T}_{pr}(\widehat{\phi}, \psi)$ is given by (7). Finally, (8) gives the main verification condition:

$$\mathcal{T}_{cr}^{\triangleright}((c_{\omega}^1, c_{\omega}^2), (\sigma_1, \sigma_2), (\sigma_1', \sigma_2'), \mathcal{L}(\widehat{\phi}, \psi'), \lambda p.p \Rightarrow \sigma_1'[3] = \sigma_2'[3]), \text{ where } \mathcal{L}(\widehat{\phi}, \psi') =$$

$$\{y_{\mathrm{sum}} \to (\lambda\sigma.\, \mathrm{True}, \lambda\sigma, \sigma'.\, \sigma[1] \geqslant \sigma[2] \Rightarrow \sigma[3] = \sigma'[3] \land \mathcal{P}_{call}(y_{\mathrm{sum}}, \sigma, \sigma', \psi'))\}.$$

Long for a manual proof, such formulas are well-treated by solvers.   □

$$\forall \sigma_1, \sigma_2, \sigma_1', \sigma_2', \psi.$$

$$\boxed{\sigma_1(1) = \sigma_2(1)} \tag{6}$$

$$\wedge$$

$$
\begin{array}{|c|}
\hline
(\forall \sigma_1, \sigma_2, \sigma_1', \sigma_2'. \\
\mathcal{P}_{call}(y_{\mathrm{sum}}, \sigma_1, \sigma_1', \psi) \wedge \mathcal{P}_{call}(y_{\mathrm{sum}}, \sigma_2, \sigma_2', \psi) \wedge \\
\sigma_2(1) < \sigma_2(2) \wedge \sigma_1(2) = \sigma_2(2) \wedge \\
\sigma_1(1) = \sigma_2(1) + 1 \wedge \sigma_1(3) = \sigma_2(3) + \sigma_2(1) \\
\Rightarrow \\
\sigma_1'(3) = \sigma_2'(3)) \\
\hline
\end{array}
\tag{7}
$$

$$\Rightarrow$$

$$
\begin{array}{|c|}
\hline
\forall \sigma_1'', \sigma_1''', \sigma_2'', \sigma_2'''. \\
\sigma_1'' = set(\sigma_1, 1, 1) \wedge \sigma_1''' = set(\sigma_1'', 3, 0) \wedge \\
((\sigma_1'''(1) \geqslant \sigma_1'''(2) \Rightarrow \sigma_1'''(3) = \sigma_1'(3)) \wedge \mathcal{P}_{call}(y_{\mathrm{sum}}, \sigma_1''', \sigma_1', \psi)) \wedge \\
\sigma_2'' = set(\sigma_2, 1, 0) \wedge \sigma_2''' = set(\sigma_2'', 3, 0) \wedge \\
((\sigma_2'''(1) \geqslant \sigma_2'''(2) \Rightarrow \sigma_2'''(3) = \sigma_2'(3)) \wedge \mathcal{P}_{call}(y_{\mathrm{sum}}, \sigma_2''', \sigma_2', \psi)) \\
\Rightarrow \\
\sigma_1'(3) = \sigma_2'(3) \\
\hline
\end{array}
\tag{8}
$$

Fig. 8. Assumption (5) of Theorem 4 illustrated for property $\mathcal{R}_1$ of Fig. 1.

7   Related Work

Relational Property Verification. Significant work has been done on relational program verification (see [26,27] for a detailed state of the art). We discuss below some of the efforts the most closely related to our work.

Various relational logics have been designed as extensions to Hoare Logic, such as Relational Hoare Logic [6] and Cartesian Hoare Logic [32]. As our approach, those logics consider for each command a set of associated memory states in the very rules of the system, thus avoiding additional separation assumptions. Limitations of these logics are often the absence of support for aliasing or a limited form of relational properties. For instance, Relational Hoare Logic supports only relational properties with two commands and Cartesian Hoare Logic supports only k-safety properties (relational properties on the same command). Our method has an advanced support of aliasing and supports a very general definition of relational properties, possibly between several dissimilar commands.

Self-composition [3,9,30] and its derivations [2,14,31] are well-known approaches to deal with relational properties. This is in particular due to their flexibility: self-composition methods can be applied as a preprocessing step to different verification approaches. For example, self-composition is used in combination with symbolic execution and model checking for verification of voting functions [5]. Other examples are the use of self-composition in combination with verification condition generation in the context of the Java language [13] or the C language [9,10]. In general, the support of aliasing of C programs in these last efforts is very limited due the problems mentioned earlier. Compared to these techniques, where self-composition is applied before the generation of verification conditions (and therefore requires taking care about separation of memory states of the considered programs), our method can be seen as relating the considered programs' semantics directly at the level of the verification conditions, where separation of their memory states is already ensured, thus avoiding the need to take care of this separation explicitly.

Finally, another advanced approach for relational verification is the translation of the relational problem into Horn clauses and their proof using constraint solving [22,34]. The benefit of constraint solving lies in the ability to automatically find relational invariants and complex self-composition derivations. Moreover, the translation of programs into Horn clauses, done by tools like REVE[3], results in formulas similar to those generated by our VCGen. Therefore, like our approach, relational verification with constraint solving requires no additional separation hypothesis in presence of aliasing.

Certified Verification Condition Generation. In a broad sense, this work continues previous efforts in formalization and mechanized proof of program language semantics, analyzers and compilers, such as [7,12,18,20,21,24,25,28,29,35]. Generation of certificates (in Isabelle) for the BOOGIE verifier is presented in [28]. The certified deductive verification tool WhyCert [18] comes with a similar soundness result for its verification condition generator. Its formalization follows an alternative proof approach, based on co-induction, while our proof relies on induction. WhyCert is syntactically closer to the C language and the ACSL specification language [4], while our proof uses a simplified language, but with a richer aliasing model. Furthermore, we provide a formalization and a soundness proof for relational verification, which was not considered in WhyCert or in [28].

Our previous work [11] presented a method for relational property verification based on a naive VCGen. To the best of our knowledge, the present work is the first proposal of *modular* relational property verification based on an *optimized* VCGen for a representative language with procedure calls and aliases with a full mechanized formalization and proof of soundness in COQ.

8   Conclusion

We have presented in this paper an overview of a method for modular verification of relational properties using an optimized verification condition generator, without relying on code transformations (such as self-composition) or making additional separation hypotheses in case of aliasing. This method has been fully formalized in COQ, and the soundness of recursive relational verification using

---

[3] https://formal.kastel.kit.edu/projects/improve/reve/.

a verification condition generator (itself formally proved correct) for a simple language with procedure calls and aliasing has been formally established.

This work opens the door for interesting future work. Currently, for relational properties, product programs [2] or other self-composition optimizations [31] are the standard approach to deal with complex loop constructions. We expect that user-provided coupling invariants and loop properties can avoid having to rely on code transformation methods. Showing this in our framework is the next step, before the investigation of termination and co-termination [17,34] for extending the modularity of relational contracts.

References

1. Apt, K., de Boer, F., Olderog, E.: Verification of Sequential and Concurrent Programs. Texts in Computer Science, Springer, London (2009). https://doi.org/10.1007/978-1-84882-745-5
2. Barthe, G., Crespo, J.M., Kunz, C.: Relational verification using product programs. In: Butler, M., Schulte, W. (eds.) FM 2011. LNCS, vol. 6664, pp. 200–214. Springer, Heidelberg (2011). https://doi.org/10.1007/978-3-642-21437-0_17
3. Barthe, G., D'Argenio, P.R., Rezk, T.: Secure information flow by self-composition. J. Math. Struct. Comput. Sci. **21**(6), 1207–1252 (2011). https://doi.org/10.1017/S0960129511000193
4. Baudin, P., et al.: ACSL: ANSI/ISO C Specification Language (2021). https://frama-c.com/html/acsl.html
5. Beckert, B., Bormer, T., Kirsten, M., Neuber, T., Ulbrich, M.: Automated verification for functional and relational properties of voting rules. In: Proceedings of the 6th International Workshop on Computational Social Choice (COMSOC 2016) (2016)
6. Benton, N.: Simple relational correctness proofs for static analyses and program transformations. In: Proceedings of the 31st ACM SIGPLAN-SIGACT Symposium on of Programming Languages (POPL 2004), pp. 14–25. ACM (2004). https://doi.org/10.1145/964001.964003
7. Beringer, L., Appel, A.W.: Abstraction and subsumption in modular verification of C programs. In: ter Beek, M.H., McIver, A., Oliveira, J.N. (eds.) FM 2019. LNCS, vol. 11800, pp. 573–590. Springer, Cham (2019). https://doi.org/10.1007/978-3-030-30942-8_34
8. Bishop, P.G., Bloomfield, R.E., Cyra, L.: Combining testing and proof to gain high assurance in software: a case study. In: Proc. of the 24th International Symposium on Software Reliability Engineering (ISSRE 2013), pp. 248–257. IEEE (2013). https://doi.org/10.1109/ISSRE.2013.6698924
9. Blatter, L., Kosmatov, N., Le Gall, P., Prevosto, V.: RPP: automatic proof of relational properties by self-composition. In: Legay, A., Margaria, T. (eds.) TACAS 2017. LNCS, vol. 10205, pp. 391–397. Springer, Heidelberg (2017). https://doi.org/10.1007/978-3-662-54577-5_22
10. Blatter, L., Kosmatov, N., Le Gall, P., Prevosto, V., Petiot, G.: Static and dynamic verification of relational properties on self-composed C code. In: Dubois, C., Wolff, B. (eds.) TAP 2018. LNCS, vol. 10889, pp. 44–62. Springer, Cham (2018). https://doi.org/10.1007/978-3-319-92994-1_3

11. Blatter, L., Kosmatov, N., Prevosto, V., Le Gall, P.: Certified verification of relational properties. In: ter Beek, M.H., Monahan, R. (eds.) iFM 2022. LNCS, vol. 13274, pp. 86–105. Springer, Cham (2022). https://doi.org/10.1007/978-3-031-07727-2_6

12. Blazy, S., Maroneze, A., Pichardie, D.: Verified validation of program slicing. In: Proceedings of the 2015 Conference on Certified Programs and Proofs (CPP 2015), pp. 109–117. ACM (2015). https://doi.org/10.1145/2676724.2693169

13. Dufay, G., Felty, A., Matwin, S.: Privacy-sensitive information flow with JML. In: Nieuwenhuis, R. (ed.) CADE 2005. LNCS (LNAI), vol. 3632, pp. 116–130. Springer, Heidelberg (2005). https://doi.org/10.1007/11532231_9

14. Eilers, M., Müller, P., Hitz, S.: Modular product programs. In: Ahmed, A. (ed.) ESOP 2018. LNCS, vol. 10801, pp. 502–529. Springer, Cham (2018). https://doi.org/10.1007/978-3-319-89884-1_18

15. Flanagan, C., Saxe, J.B.: Avoiding exponential explosion: generating compact verification conditions. In: Proceedings of the 28th ACM SIGPLAN Symposium on Principles of Programming Languages (POPL 2001), pp. 193–205. ACM (2001). https://doi.org/10.1145/360204.360220

16. Floyd, R.W.: Assigning meanings to programs. In: Proceedings of Symposia in Applied Mathematics. Mathematical Aspects of Computer Science, vol. 19, p. 19–32 (1967). https://doi.org/10.1090/psapm/019/0235771

17. Hawblitzel, C., Kawaguchi, M., Lahiri, S.K., Rebêlo, H.: Towards modularly comparing programs using automated theorem provers. In: Bonacina, M.P. (ed.) CADE 2013. LNCS (LNAI), vol. 7898, pp. 282–299. Springer, Heidelberg (2013). https://doi.org/10.1007/978-3-642-38574-2_20

18. Herms, P.: Certification of a tool chain for deductive program verification. Ph.D thesis, Université Paris Sud - Paris XI, January 2013. https://tel.archives-ouvertes.fr/tel-00789543

19. Hoare, C.A.R.: An axiomatic basis for computer programming. Commun. ACM 12(10), 576–580 (1969). https://doi.org/10.1145/363235.363259

20. Jourdan, J., Laporte, V., Blazy, S., Leroy, X., Pichardie, D.: A formally-verified C static analyzer. In: Proceedings of the 42nd Annual ACM SIGPLAN-SIGACT Symposium on Principles of Programming Languages (POPL 2015), pp. 247–259. ACM (2015). https://doi.org/10.1145/2676726.2676966

21. Jung, R., Krebbers, R., Jourdan, J., Bizjak, A., Birkedal, L., Dreyer, D.: Iris from the ground up: a modular foundation for higher-order concurrent separation logic. J. Funct. Program. 28, e20 (2018). https://doi.org/10.1017/S0956796818000151

22. Kiefer, M., Klebanov, V., Ulbrich, M.: Relational program reasoning using compiler IR - combining static verification and dynamic analysis. J. Autom. Reason. 60(3), 337–363 (2018). https://doi.org/10.1007/s10817-017-9433-5

23. Kip, I.: Assembly Language for x86 Processors, 7th edn. Prentice Hall Press, Hoboken (2014)

24. Krebbers, R., Leroy, X., Wiedijk, F.: Formal C semantics: CompCert and the C standard. In: Klein, G., Gamboa, R. (eds.) ITP 2014. LNCS, vol. 8558, pp. 543–548. Springer, Cham (2014). https://doi.org/10.1007/978-3-319-08970-6_36

25. Leroy, X., Blazy, S.: Formal verification of a C-like memory model and its uses for verifying program transformations. J. Autom. Reason. 41(1), 1–31 (2008)

26. Maillard, K., Hritcu, C., Rivas, E., Van Muylder, A.: The next 700 relational program logics. In: Proc. of the 47th ACM SIGPLAN Symposium on Principles of Programming Languages (POPL 2020), vol. 4, pp. 4:1–4:33 (2020). https://doi.org/10.1145/3371072

27. Naumann, D.A.: Thirty-seven years of relational Hoare logic: remarks on its principles and history. In: Margaria, T., Steffen, B. (eds.) ISoLA 2020. LNCS, vol. 12477, pp. 93–116. Springer, Cham (2020). https://doi.org/10.1007/978-3-030-61470-6_7

28. Parthasarathy, G., Müller, P., Summers, A.J.: Formally validating a practical verification condition generator. In: Silva, A., Leino, K.R.M. (eds.) CAV 2021. LNCS, vol. 12760, pp. 704–727. Springer, Cham (2021). https://doi.org/10.1007/978-3-030-81688-9_33

29. Pierce, B.C., et al.: Logical Foundations. Software Foundations Series, vol. 1, Electronic Textbook (2018). http://www.cis.upenn.edu/~bcpierce/sf

30. Scheben, C., Schmitt, P.H.: Efficient self-composition for weakest precondition calculi. In: Jones, C., Pihlajasaari, P., Sun, J. (eds.) FM 2014. LNCS, vol. 8442, pp. 579–594. Springer, Cham (2014). https://doi.org/10.1007/978-3-319-06410-9_39

31. Shemer, R., Gurfinkel, A., Shoham, S., Vizel, Y.: Property directed self composition. In: Dillig, I., Tasiran, S. (eds.) CAV 2019. LNCS, vol. 11561, pp. 161–179. Springer, Cham (2019). https://doi.org/10.1007/978-3-030-25540-4_9

32. Sousa, M., Dillig, I.: Cartesian Hoare logic for verifying k-safety properties. In: Proceedings of the 37th Conference on Programming Language Design and Implementation (PLDI 2016), pp. 57–69. ACM (2016). https://doi.org/10.1145/2908080.2908092

33. The Coq Development Team: The Coq Proof Assistant (2021). https://coq.inria.fr/

34. Unno, H., Terauchi, T., Koskinen, E.: Constraint-based relational verification. In: Silva, A., Leino, K.R.M. (eds.) CAV 2021. LNCS, vol. 12759, pp. 742–766. Springer, Cham (2021). https://doi.org/10.1007/978-3-030-81685-8_35

35. Wils, S., Jacobs, B.: Certifying C program correctness with respect to compcert with verifast. CoRR arXiv:abs/2110.11034 (2021)

36. Winskel, G.: The Formal Semantics of Programming Languages - An Introduction. Foundation of Computing Series. MIT Press, Cambridge (1993)

On Deductive Verification of an Industrial Concurrent Software Component with VerCors

Raúl E. Monti[✉][iD], Robert Rubbens[✉][iD], and Marieke Huisman[iD]

Formal Methods and Tools, University of Twente, Enschede, The Netherlands
{r.e.monti,r.b.rubbens,m.huisman}@utwente.nl

Abstract. This paper presents a case study where a concurrent module of a tunnel control system written in Java is verified for memory safety and data race freedom using VerCors, a software verification tool. This case study was carried out in close collaboration with our industrial partner Technolution, which is in charge of developing the tunnel control software. First, we describe the process of preparing the code for verification, and how we make use of the different capabilities of VerCors to successfully verify the module. The concurrent module has gone through a rigorous process of design, code reviewing and unit and integration testing. Despite this careful approach, VerCors found two memory related bugs. We describe these bugs, and show how VerCors could have found them during the development process. Second, we wanted to communicate back our results and verification process to the engineers of Technolution. We discuss how we prepared our presentation, and the explanation we settled on. Third, we present interesting feedback points from this presentation. We use this feedback to determine future work directions with the goal to improve our tool support, and to bridge the gap between formal methods and industry.

Keywords: Case study · Verification · Concurrency

1 Introduction

Software components for critical infrastructure should be kept to the highest standards of safety and correctness. Traditional methods for acquiring high safety standards include code reviewing and testing. These improve the reliability of software, but do not and cannot guarantee the absence of bugs. Software is also becoming more concurrent every year. The number of execution scenarios in concurrent software is even greater than in classical sequential software, due to interleaving and timing aspects. This makes code reviewing and testing even less effective. Specifically, there are too many interleavings of multiple threads, causing problematic interleavings to easily be missed during code reviewing and testing. Furthermore, concurrency related bugs such as data races and race conditions are intrinsically difficult to analyse with testing, since their effects are

© The Author(s) 2022
T. Margaria and B. Steffen (Eds.): ISoLA 2022, LNCS 13701, pp. 517–534, 2022.
https://doi.org/10.1007/978-3-031-19849-6_29

platform dependent. For example, changing the OS of the system could cause previously passing tests to fail, due to different scheduling policies. It is also hard to test for specific interleavings. Hence, methods besides testing and code reviewing are needed to achieve the highest standards of safety and correctness in concurrent software.

To complement classical methods in the context of concurrent and critical infrastructure software, we believe formal methods must be considered. In particular, formal methods that can deal with the concurrent context must be used. In contrast to code review and testing, formal verification is exhaustive and can formally guarantee the absence of bugs in different stages of the software development cycle. Moreover, formal verification uses a standard semantics of the language in question, which guarantees consistent behaviour across platforms. Whenever platforms disagree, formal verification ensures that this difference is accounted for in the code. These properties of formal verification makes software more predictable, and hence safer.

Despite recent advances in software verification capabilities, the use of formal methods in industry is still limited. We think that case studies that show the successful application of formal methods will greatly contribute towards further adoption of formal methods in industry in two ways. First, it showcases the advances and capabilities of software verification tools to our industrial partners. Second, it generates valuable feedback, with which we can improve our tools and further adapt them to the software production cycle. This work discusses such a case study, where we verify a safety critical software for tunnel traffic control using our software verification tool VerCors.

VerCors is a deductive verifier, specialised in the verification of *concurrent* software [4]. It supports Java, C, OpenCL, and a custom input language called PVL. VerCors can prove several useful generic properties about programs, such as memory safety and absence of data races. Additionally, VerCors can prove functional correctness properties, such as "the sum of all integers in the array is computed". To verify programs with VerCors, the programs must be annotated by the user, following a Design by Contract like approach. Annotations are pre- and post-conditions of methods, specifying permissions to access memory locations and functional properties about the program state. VerCors processes the program and the annotations, and verifies if the program adheres to the annotations by applying a deductive program logic optimised for reasoning about concurrent programs. VerCors has been applied to concurrent algorithms [19, 21, 22], and also to industrial code in earlier case studies [11, 18].

This paper is the result of a close collaboration with Technolution [25], a Dutch software and hardware development company located in Gouda, the Netherlands, with a recorded experience in developing safety-critical industrial software. It is also the next part in a series of papers to investigate the feasibility of applying formal methods within the design and production process of Technolution. For more information on the earlier parts, we refer the reader to [11, 18]. Finally, this paper is also an attempt to approach industrial partners to collaborate on the broader goal of making deductive verification, and specifically VerCors, available for industrial practitioners. This collaboration is carried out in the context of the *VerCors Industrial Advisory Board*, with the goal to learn how to introduce deductive verification into the production cycle of software, and to improve the tool and make it easier to use. Another important goal of the VerCors Industrial Advisory Board is to make industrial partners aware of the guarantees of formal verification, in contrast to the weaker guarantees of testing based quality assurance. This paper discusses our efforts to communicate our results and explain the verification process to the engineers at Technolution, as well as their feedback on our approach.

In particular, we discuss the verification of software for a tunnel on a road called the Blankenburgverbinding [3]. This tunnel and the hard- and software supporting it will be responsible for funnelling thousands of cars every day. The control software of this tunnel monitors and controls almost every aspect of the tunnel, in both normal and calamity situations. Thus, in order to give some safety guarantees to its daily users, it is highly important that the software conforms to the requirements of the national regulations and to the specifications provided by the engineers who design and develop it. To demonstrate how formal methods can help here, we applied our software verification tool VerCors to a submodule of the control software of the tunnel, in particular to analyse concurrency related issues such as data races and memory safety.

To develop the tunnel software, Technolution followed an iterative V-model approach. The customer handed in the requirements in form of a BSTTI document [16] and LTS specifications. These were used to derive actual software requirements via system decomposition and design. In addition to the custom validation flow of the V-model, the customer also imposed requirements on the development process. These included, but were not limited to, units being inspected to verify that they implement their requirements via Fagan inspection performed by a developer not involved in creation and review of the code, requirements-based testing at software module level (i.e. higher integration level than units) using the MC/DC coverage approach, and UI-design based testing at a software chain level (i.e. integration of multiple systems) with a process flow approach.

This rigorous approach to software development resulted in them spotting some unexpected behaviour in their tunnel software, where a certain condition over the state snapshot of a component was evaluated differently at two spots throughout which the snapshot should remain unchanged. Nevertheless, later they could not reproduce this behaviour and, by the time we were given the code to analyse, they had not been able to spot a bug that might explain this behaviour. The code we received was already in testing phase. As can be seen in this paper, we discovered concurrency related bugs in this code, which we think were likely the cause of the unexpected behaviour. We show that VerCors can effectively catch this kind of bugs, in production phase, by using simple code annotations in the form of methods pre and post-conditions specifying the memory access pattern of such methods.

The goal of this particular study is three-fold. First we want to investigate how much we can support the verification of industrial Java software with Ver-Cors. Second, we want to focus this time on a *concurrent* piece of software and on concurrency issues such as data races, for which our tool is specialised. Notice that to exploit modern architectures, modern software is often concurrent, and not many deductive verification tools can deal with this. Third, we want to investigate how our verification procedure can be improved for industrial adoption. For this, we are particularly interested in the feedback from the Technolution team with respect to the verification procedure we followed.

Contributions. In this paper we discuss the following:

- Details of the tunnel verification case study, such as the analysis workflow and the problems we discovered.
- The process of communicating our results to Technolution.
- The feedback from Technolution and its engineers regarding our analysis and our presentation of it.
- Future plans for VerCors and the analysis of concurrent industrial software.

Outline. Section 2 presents the background for this research, i.e., we describe the tunnel software and architecture. We also explain how to use VerCors for concurrent software verification. In Sect. 3 we discuss our process of verification of the concurrent data manager module, we explain the bugs we spotted, and we show how applying VerCors would have avoided these bugs. Section 4 describes the experience of explaining our procedure and reporting our results to the engineers at Technolution, and their feedback. Section 5 describes our own reflection and future directions towards our goal of improving VerCors for industrial application. Additionally, we mention some broader goals for the formal methods community. Finally, Sect. 6 summarises and concludes.

2   Background

In this section we describe the two technologies relevant to this paper. First, we describe the system architecture of the tunnel software. Then, we describe VerCors, the tool used for verification of Java code.

2.1   Tunnel System Architecture

In the Netherlands, the architecture of software for tunnels is regulated by the Basic Specification of Technical Installations for Tunnels (BSTTI[1]). The BSTTI [16] specifies that the architecture for tunnel software is strictly hierarchical. The system is summarised in Fig. 1.

At the top layer of this hierarchy are the human operators that operate the system. These operators give commands to the system, and inspect the values

---

[1] *In Dutch:* BasisSpecificatie Tunnel-Technische Installatie.

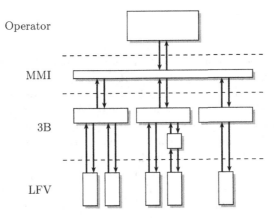

Fig. 1. Informal overview of the architecture specified by the BSTTI.

of various sensors in the system, using the Human-Machine Interface (MMI[2]) layer. The MMI processes these commands and forwards these to components of the Control, Instruct, Guard (3B[3]) layer. The 3B layer and its components are responsible for the high-level control of the physical subsystems of the tunnel. Examples of 3B components are water drainage, lighting, and electricity systems. As 3B components can be responsible for controlling entire subsystems, they also have a degree of autonomy. The individual 3B elements communicate with components in the Logical Function Fulfiller (LFV[4]) layer. Components in the LFV layer abstract the communication with the sensors and actuators of the tunnel to check and control them. Examples of these sensors and actuators are the smoke sensors and fans, the lights, or the entrance barriers. They can be located at various places in the tunnel and are connected to their LFV counterparts over various kinds of network connections following different protocols.

According to the BSTTI [16], the system must follow these general principles:

- Control must flow from the human operator level to the LFV level.
- Communication must take place along the parent-child hierarchy outlined in Fig. 1. Specifically, sideways communication between neighbouring 3B/LFV components, or between 3B components and LFV components that have no parent-child relation, must not take place.

These principles were prescribed because they make actions taken by the system traceable. If the physical system takes a certain action, the strict hierarchy allows tracing back to which component or decision caused the action. Note that it might not always be a human who caused the action. Since 3B components can have a degree of autonomy, it is possible that an autonomous action causes a physical action to take place.

---

[2] Man-Machine Interface.
[3] Besturing, Bediening, Bewaking.
[4] Logische Functie Vervuller.

2.2   VerCors

VerCors [4] is a deductive verifier for concurrent programs. It supports Java, C, OpenCL, and the Prototypal Verification Language (PVL). To make verification of concurrent programs tractable, VerCors uses permission-based separation logic [10]. This version of separation logic uses permissions to decide whether threads can read or write shared data. A complete permission allows a thread to write, but does not obligate it to. A fraction of a permission only allows a thread to read. This ensures that at any given moment, there can only be one writer, or many readers, but not both at the same time. We refer to a write permission as "write" while we refer to a fractional read permission as "read". Fractions of permissions can be distributed between threads. When a thread no longer needs a permission, fractions of a permission can be recombined into a complete permission. In particular, permissions are never duplicated, ensuring that there can only be at most one write permission.

Alternatively, permission fractions can also be represented as concrete numbers. In this case, a "write" permissions corresponds to a fraction of **1**. A "read" permission corresponds to any fraction between **0** and **1**, such as $\frac{1}{2}$ or $\frac{3}{4}$. Operationally, having a permission fraction bigger than **0** and smaller than **1** allows a thread to read a memory location, but not write to it. In this work, we mostly use the terms read and write, but in more complicated contracts, sometimes the numerical form is required. For a more thorough introduction to permission-based separation logic, we refer the reader to "Specification and Verification of Multithreaded Object-Oriented Programs with Separation Logic" by Clément Hurlin [12].

To prepare methods for analysis with VerCors, they need to be annotated with pre- and post-conditions. Pre- and post-conditions are sometimes also referred to as the contract of a method. Pre-conditions describe the permissions a method needs from the caller, as well as any functional properties that must hold when the method is called. Post-conditions indicate the permissions that a method returns to the caller, as well as any functional properties that may be assumed. For example, when an object is constructed, permissions to access the fields of the object are returned by the constructor of the object. As a functional property, the constructor can guarantee that all fields are zero-initialized.

In Listing 1 an example is shown of such permission annotations in Java. The annotations are placed in comments and are highlighted. In the annotations, the expression after the requires keyword specifies the pre-condition of the method. In this case, permission is required for the total field of class C. The ensures keyword indicates the postcondition. In this case, the permissions from the precondition are returned to the caller of the add method, as well as the functional property that total is incremented by x.

When verifying an individual method, methods that are called are not re-verified, instead their pre-condition is established and their post-condition assumed. This is called modular verification, and it ensures that the correctness of a method does not depend on the implementation of other methods. This means that it is easy to update method implementations without break-

```
1  class C {
2    int total;
3
4    //@ requires Perm(total, write);
5    //@ ensures Perm(total, write) ** total == \old(total) + x;
6    void add(int x) {
7      total += x;
8    }
9  }
```

Listing 1. Example usage of permissions in Java. Write permission is required in the pre-condition of method **add**. Because of this, **add** can only be called when the caller has write permission for **total**. Then, the field **total** is incremented by the value **x**. Finally, the **write** permissions are returned via the post-condition, as well as the functional property that **total** is incremented by **x**.

ing the correctness of other methods. If necessary, implementations of methods can also temporarily be omitted, which can be useful for describing and enforcing interfaces between independent teams, or when implementations are not yet available.

3 Verification of the Concurrent Data Manager Module

When discussing our plans for collaboration with Technolution, the engineers suggested as a case study their new control software for the Baak tunnel. For this tunnel, they have developed a system that is responsible for controlling and reporting on all critical and non-critical components, such as escape doors, fire-prevention measures, water drainage systems, lighting, ventilation, etcetera. In order to reduce the time spent in spotting a concurrent candidate module to analyse, we agreed to meet a first time with an engineer, experienced with the tunnel software, who could guide us through it.

In this first meeting the engineers from Technolution not only suggested a set of modules to verify, but also pointed out a problem that they would like us to consider, since it was most likely a concurrency issue. The system they had built at that point was functional, behaved properly, and passed all tests. However, sometimes, according to their data logs, certain status data would unexpectedly change during execution of the system. These unexpected changes were never problematic in realistic scenarios, so therefore they considered it benign. However, it was still unexpected, and they would like to understand why this happens.

As a first step, we decided to go through the code base and try to understand the structure. We used a couple of meetings with the Technolution team to get some guidance around the code. Also, several times we asked for further code to inspect, such as supporting libraries of the system.

We found that the components of a tunnel can be quite diverse, and to cope with that diversity, several layers of abstraction and interfacing code had been built into the tunnel software, which made it non-trivial to understand for us. Nevertheless this was not a problem for our verification approach, as it is modular at the level of methods, and annotating the code was straightforward. We ran VerCors on the fly, while annotating the code, and even mocked some library calls, by means of abstract methods and ghost code. We did have problems with VerCors lacking support for some frequently used Java features, such as inheritance and generics. Once we decided on the module to verify, the effort to abstract from unsupported Java features and annotate the code was very little; the annotations were trivial to us, and it took just an afternoon to reach the conclusions. Moreover, due to the simplicity of the specification, VerCors was able to verify the code in just a couple of seconds.

3.1   Event Loop Analysis

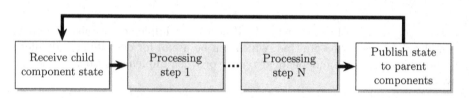

Fig. 2. The 3B function processing event loop.

We inspected the event loop of the main module, because most of the concurrent behaviour happens there. This involved peeling off the abstraction layers of the event loop framework, which is responsible for receiving and dispatching messages and executing each step of the processing loop of 3B components. This process repeats until the main module is shut down. An illustration of the typical processing loop of a 3B function can be found in Fig. 2. A processing loop starts by obtaining the state of all the child components for this 3B function (first rectangle in the figure). This state is then used to take control decisions along several processing steps inside the loop (shaded rectangles in the figure). It is here that the Technolution engineers where suspecting that something is wrong. In particular, during this control decision period, this state *must not change*. The suspicion was that somehow the state *was being changed*.

Continuing the explanation of Fig. 2, at the end of the loop our own state is prepared and made available to the upper 3B functions in the hierarchy (see Fig. 1 for clarification). In general, 3B functions and LFV components work asynchronously. The communication of the state between LFVs and 3B functions is managed by specialised data managers which need to synchronise the state of these asynchronous elements at the start and end of the 3B function processing loop. In a generic *data manager* of the event loop framework, we were able to spot two problems through manual inspection of the source code.

Problem 1: Forbidden Data Sharing. The first problem was related to aliasing between references to data structures representing the status of the child components of a 3B function. To better understand this, let us look at

Fig. 3: each 3B function uses two copies of the data structure representing the status of its child LFVs and 3B functions. One of these copies, the "internal" copy, represents the internal knowledge that a 3B function has of its children. It is used by the 3B function processor to make control decisions and should remain unchanged during the time of a processing loop iteration, this is, along the shaded steps in Fig. 2. On the other hand, the "dynamic" copy is updated each time a status update message from a child component is received. These messages arrive at any point during a processing loop iteration and the updates are asynchronously applied. At the end of an event iteration, the dynamic copy is used by the *data manager* to update the internal copy.

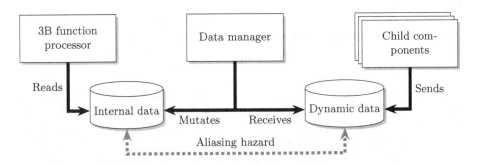

Fig. 3. Shared data snapshots.

It turns out that the data manager accidentally aliased both the internal and the dynamic copies. This is a simple but common mistake, and in line with the expectations of the Technolution engineers. The internal copy would then change midway through a processing loop iteration whenever the dynamic copy would receive an update.

As a verification exercise, we decided to annotate the data manager module in order to demonstrate how we could have avoided this mistake by using VerCors. Actually, we simplified the module for the sake of focusing on the interesting aspects, and to avoid incompatibilities with our current support of the Java language. We further discuss this in Sect. 5. As we expected, it turned out to be straightforward to rule out this mistake. List. 2 shows a simplification of the actual aliasing bug and the annotations we used. Lines 9 and 10 are the preconditions specifying that we need permissions to *write* on `internal` and its field `value` while we need to be able to read `dynamic` and its field `value`. Our postconditions, at lines 11 and 12, specify that these permissions should also be returned to the caller. We specify permissions to each of them separately, using the separation conjunction (**), since they should correspond to two different data structures.

At line 16, `dynamic` is assigned to `internal`. Therefore, `internal.value` and `dynamic.value` represent the same memory location. At this point VerCors complains about our postcondition. List. 3 shows the VerCors output for this

```
1    class Data{
2      int value;
3    }
4
5    class Manager{
6      Data internal;
7      Data dynamic;
8
9      //@ requires Perm(internal, write) ** Perm(dynamic, read);
10     //@ requires Perm(internal.value, write) ** Perm(dynamic.value, write);
11     //@ ensures Perm(internal, write) ** Perm(dynamic, read);
12     //@ ensures Perm(internal.value, write) ** Perm(dynamic.value, write);
13     void sync() {
14       internal.value = dynamic.value;
15       ...
16       internal = dynamic;
17     }
18   }
```

Listing 2. Ruling out aliasing with VerCors

faulty case. The error message "PostConditionFailed:InsufficientPermission" at line 11 indicates that we are missing permissions to access a memory location. The brackets and dashes at lines 5 and 7 indicate where the problem lies: we do not posses the amount of permission we want to ensure in the second half of line 12 of our code. In fact, we already gave up all the permission we had on this memory location through its alias, in the first half of the same postcondition line. After VerCors indicates something is wrong, the user must find out why this is the case and spot the undesired aliasing.

After analysing this bug with the engineers involved in our case study, we concluded that this aliasing would likely have been the reason of the unexpected behaviour they had detected. It apparently had not affected the overall behaviour of the system, but the reason why such a bug did not extend into a serious fault was not clear. The enormous amount of execution scenarios due to interleaving and timing aspects also makes it difficult to reproduce the immediate effects of this bug. The bug should be fixed since we cannot exclude that it may, under certain circumstances, trigger a major fault in the tunnel control system.

Problem 2: Internal Data Leakage. A second bug was spotted while annotating this module for verification with VerCors. Another method of the module was leaking a reference to a private field of the class. List. 4 illustrates this case. This is not harmful on its own, but it is usually considered bad practice. This may unintentionally allow a user of this class to concurrently access the field without following its synchronisation regime, which may result in a data race. Permission annotations in VerCors will not disallow acquiring the reference, but the annotations will ensure that there is no way to access any fields of this reference without holding the necessary permissions. This restriction rules out any data races.

```
1   Errors! (1)
2   === Manager.java                    ===
3      //@ requires Perm(internal.value, write) ** Perm(dynamic.value, write);
4      //@ ensures Perm(internal, write) ** Perm(dynamic, read);
5                                        [--------------------------
6      //@ ensures Perm(internal.value, write) ** Perm(dynamic.value, read);
7                                        ------------------------]
8      void sync() {
9         internal.value = dynamic.value;
10  ----------------------------------------
11     PostConditionFailed:InsufficientPermission
12  ========================================
13  === Manager.java                    ===
14     //@ requires Perm(internal.value, write) ** Perm(dynamic.value, write);
15     //@ ensures Perm(internal, write) ** Perm(dynamic, read);
16                                       [-------------
17     //@ ensures Perm(internal.value, write) ** Perm(dynamic.value, read);
18                                       -------------]
19     void sync() {
20        internal.value = dynamic.value;
21  ----------------------------------------
22     caused by
23  ========================================
24  The final verdict is Fail
```

Listing 3. VerCors output for alias spotting

```
1   class Manager{
2     private Data internal; // protected_by(this)
3
4     synchronized Data get_internal() {
5       return internal;
6     }
7   }
```

Listing 4. Reference to private data leakage

3.2 Discussion on the Discovered Bugs

The two bugs we found are typically overlooked by testing and manual inspection: their effects are triggered by very specific combinations of timings and interleaving that are too complicated to cover by test cases. A manual inspection may mistakenly consider these usages to be safe, or overlook them while searching for functional behaviour bugs instead of memory safety.

The effects of these bugs in a deployed system might be dangerous as it is hard to claim they do not cause incorrect behaviour. To prove that they do not cause incorrect behaviour, one would have to consider all possible interleavings of the processes of the system. The difficulty of this inspection increases exponentially when the number of concurrent processes and timing factors increases. In other words, proving that the system is not affected by the bugs by manual inspection is untractable.

Fortunately, the memory bugs we found are detectable with VerCors, by annotating methods in a straightforward manner with the permissions they require/ensure for the fields that they read/modify. An example of this can be found in the the pre- and post-conditions of List. 2. These annotations are made compulsory by the tool, meaning that if they are not there the tool will terminate with an error. If verification succeeds, then VerCors guarantees that there is no data race in the code.

4   Results Presentation

In this section we describe our preparation process and presentation of the results to the bigger team of engineers at Technolution, which included a broader group than just those involved in the case study. We also describe our impressions of the final presentation and discuss the most interesting feedback points from the audience.

4.1   Presentation Design Process

After the case study was analysed by hand and translated to VerCors, we wanted to present our findings to a bigger audience of engineers at Technolution. However, we had experienced in former meetings with the Technolution team that we had not been able to effectively explain what VerCors checks, and how to annotate programs for VerCors. Therefore, we agreed to be careful and first present the results only to the Technolution team involved in the case study.

It turned out the initial presentation had several shortcomings, which we discuss here, because we think they provide important general insights.

First, the initial presentation tried to explain several useful verification concepts. For example, it discussed the benefits of fractional permissions, compared to non-splittable ownership tickets. It also discussed the difference between annotating only for memory safety, and annotating for functional properties as well. This was done to show how we use VerCors. However, without a formal methods background, the explanation of these tradeoffs is hard to follow. Additionally, most of these concepts are not necessary in order to explain the basis of our approach to verification of memory safety. The solution was to *only* focus on this basis, which is: annotating code with permissions.

Second, the examples used in the initial presentation combined orthogonal concepts to make the examples non-trivial. While engaging for experts, we found out that this is bad for teaching how an approach works. This is especially relevant in the context of a presentation, where the audience needs to understand the slides quickly and explanations need to be short. The solution is to make the examples more targeted. Even when discussing the fundamental basis of our verification approach, each example should only highlight the one relevant aspect of it. For instance, our final presentation contained a code example that had exactly *one* error. The code example on the next slide added exactly *one* annotation, consisting of only one permission, to resolve the error. Additionally, examples from the initial presentation were split up such that each sub-example fit on one screen with a large font. With each example presented in isolation and using as few lines of code as possible, they were also easier to understand.

Third, some of the examples in the initial presentation contained concerns unrelated to verifying concurrency, such as division by zero and rounding. The solution was to ensure that no concerns appear in the example that are unrelated to concurrency or memory safety, since we experienced that this would deviate the attention of the audience to topics we are not interested in discussing.

For the particular case of Technolution, we found out that it was useful to compare our approach with the Rust language, which was familiar to them [17]. This was actually suggested by the Technolution side during our presentation preparation meetings. We also took care with how we phrased certain concepts. Since there might be a difference between what we regard as a permission and what an engineer regards as a permission, we had to ensure this was not a problem from the beginning.

Finally, we made sure to clarify that we do not execute the code, but logically analyse it. For this, we compared it to making a pen and paper proof. This is needed to step away from the usual runtime verification approach of unit and integration testing.

To summarise, we learned that a "good" formal methods presentation to a non-formal audience should have at least the following properties:

- Introduce only key concepts of the formalism in question that are actually needed to understanding the basic idea of the formalism.
- Examples should present only one new concept at a time. Combining orthogonal concepts into one example is not helpful.
- Examples must be short, to ensure they fit on one slide, can be interpreted quickly by the audience, and also be explained quickly by the presenters.
- Examples must not contain unrelated concerns. The domain of the audience might introduce concerns the presenters are not aware of. Therefore, experts in the domain of the audience should be asked beforehand.
- Determine concepts the audience is already familiar with, and draw parallels between those and the concepts in the presentation. However: take care that the audience does not take this analogy too far, to avoid misunderstanding. Avoiding reuse of terms from the audience domain can help.

Additionally, our overall approach consisted of several iterations of refining the presentation using feedback of the smaller group. We think this helped us to narrow down what the Technolution engineers would most likely be interested in, what information would benefit them, and what information could be safely discarded from the presentation. It also helped us to agree on the proper language to transfer this knowledge. The drawback of this approach is that it is time consuming, because the presentation had to be presented twice before the final presentation. Furthermore, the feedback had to be documented by Technolution, and also had to be processed by us. Nevertheless, we think that this process will be quicker next time, due to reusing lessons learned in this case study.

4.2   Presentation Conclusions

During and after the final presentation, several questions were asked and comments were made, both by the presenters and the audience. We have collected the most insightful and applicable ones below.

Testing Exceeds Verification in Short term Gains. During the presentation it was mentioned that some teams do not even use testing to its fullest. We agree with the observation that it is more beneficial for most projects to first test 80% of their code base, before starting to consider formal verification. Additionally, there are formal methods to enhance and/or multiply the testing effort. Some examples are generation of test cases, mutation testing and QuickCheck-like testing [6,13,26].

Annotation & Specification Culture. Speaking from the experience of the Technolution engineers, it is impossible to ask engineers to write the annotations needed to use VerCors, or formal verification tools in general. Engineers do not even write comments that you would like to have in the general case. Therefore, there is a big gap between the annotations engineers are willing to write, and what verification tools require. This can be improved upon by the formal verification tools, by having smarter tools, generating some annotations, having design shorthands, and setting effective defaults. But, the difference is so big, that to adopt formal verification tools widely, there also needs to be a culture shift about commenting and annotating code.

Similarities to Rust. Most engineers have heard of or worked with Rust. Verification tools can exploit this to lower the barrier for using verification tools, and make them more easily understandable and adoptable.

Optimise for the Common Case. Related to Rust, an approach that the engineers thought could be useful to verification tools is the "optimise for the common case" approach. In this approach, tools optimise for the use case that is most common in practice. For exceptional or unsafe use cases, alternative syntaxes and escape hatches are added. Usually, these alternative syntaxes are also more verbose, making non-standard code also visually distinct. Furthermore, the general case should be safe and hard to get wrong. If applied successfully, we expect that the usage of this approach could reduce the amount of annotation needed for verification, improve the readability and decrease the unwillingness of the programmer to follow the verification path.

Library Calls. Some engineers expressed concerns about not having contracts for libraries that a team uses. It is true that if a library has no contracts, someone needs to write them. However, it is not a problem that the source of the library is not available due to modular verification (explained in Sect. 2.2). Additionally, there are ways to reduce friction caused by these missing contracts. For example, it is possible to create a central database of library contracts. For cases where the specification for a library is not in the database, the specification language could offer syntax for defining contracts for a library separately.

Why not Use Automatic Static Analysis Tools Instead? An engineer pointed out that he had some experience with various static and automatic analysis tools. They raised the valid question of why code should be annotated for VerCors, when there are tools that can spot memory bugs without annotations. Some examples of such tools are Klocwork [14], FindBugs [9], Coverity [8] and SonarQube [24]. Our answer to this question is that these kind of static analysis tools are not verification tools. Instead, they do a "best effort" analysis to find patterns that *may* relate to bugs. This means such tools are not exhaustive, and can report false positives and warnings which have to be manually inspected. Verification tools, in contrast, give strong formal guarantees on the validity of the queried property over the analysed system. In other words, given a specification that faithfully models the desired behaviour, false positives are rare.

Additionally, code analysis tools often can be used in tandem. Therefore, we think it can be beneficial for teams to use tools with different purposes at different stages of development, or even simultaneously. This way the quality of the final product can be maximised.

5   Future Research

Future research for the VerCors team will go in several directions.

One direction of research is to reduce the number of annotations required before VerCors can be used. Currently, if there are no annotations in the code, VerCors cannot make any assumptions about the code. However, for industrial code, simple assumptions are often correct. For example, two fields on one object usually do not contain the same reference. We expect that it will cost less effort to annotate for the exceptions of the previous rule, than to annotate wherever it applies. Additionally, research is already being done to see if some of the required annotations can be generated instead.

Another direction of research is to improve the support of VerCors for Java features such as inheritance and generics. Currently a manual translation to a subset of Java is necessary to verify industrial Java code with VerCors, however efforts are being made to improve the support [20,23].

Finally, we think future research of the formal methods community as a whole should be about designing simpler specification languages which are closer to the concepts and models of software development teams. We found that the semantics of our specification terminology is distant from the intuition of the engineers. The understandability of specification languages is a common problem in the formal verification community. For example, consider Linear or Branching time logics [15], μ-calculus [5] and other algebras commonly used to specify designs in model checking. The learning curve of these languages is too steep and they become impractical for the daily use of a software engineer. Therefore the next step has to be one of effective reduction: reducing the expressive power of these languages down to a level where they can be easily understood, while retaining enough power to check properties that are of interest to the engineers. Progress is already being made on this with languages such as SALT [1] and Sugar [2], and all the work surrounding the Bandera Specification Language (BSL) [7].

6 Conclusion

We have applied VerCors to a submodule of tunnel control software. This software contained a known benign but unexpected runtime behaviour, which lacked an explanation. Through manual analysis, a bug and a weakness were found, one of which is a possible explanation of the unexpected runtime behaviour. We have communicated our results to the Technolution team and the Technolution engineers through a carefully prepared presentation that underwent multiple feedback rounds from the Technolution team. This allowed us to focus on the information that is most useful to the engineers, and leave out the information that is not directly necessary.

The results of this presentation are suggestions and insights from the engineers of Technolution. For example, it was suggested that there are similarities between Rust and our annotations which VerCors can exploit. It was also suggested that there should be support for easily modelling contracts of software libraries. Another observation we have made is that there is a large gap between the annotations that must be written to apply VerCors, and the maximum amount of annotations engineers are typically willing to write. There was also an observation from an engineer that, in the short term, proper testing practices yield more benefits than formal verification does in the short term.

Finally, we have discussed future directions for our work, such as implementing assumptions about the typical structure of industrial Java code in VerCors, as well as adding more extensive support for the Java language in VerCors.

Acknowledgements. We thank Technolution for the opportunity to analyse their code, their guidance and support.

References

1. Bauer, A., Leucker, M., Streit, J.: SALT—structured assertion language for temporal logic. In: Liu, Z., He, J. (eds.) ICFEM 2006. LNCS, vol. 4260, pp. 757–775. Springer, Heidelberg (2006). https://doi.org/10.1007/11901433_41
2. Beer, I., Ben-David, S., Eisner, C., Fisman, D., Gringauze, A., Rodeh, Y.: The temporal logic sugar. In: Berry, G., Comon, H., Finkel, A. (eds.) CAV 2001. LNCS, vol. 2102, pp. 363–367. Springer, Heidelberg (2001). https://doi.org/10.1007/3-540-44585-4_33
3. Welkom bij de Blankenburgverbinding. https://www.blankenburgverbinding.nl/. Accessed 21 Jan 2022

4. Blom, S., Darabi, S., Huisman, M., Oortwijn, W.: The VerCors tool set: verification of parallel and concurrent software. In: Polikarpova, N., Schneider, S. (eds.) IFM 2017. LNCS, vol. 10510, pp. 102–110. Springer, Cham (2017). https://doi.org/10.1007/978-3-319-66845-1_7

5. Bradfield, J., Walukiewicz, I.: The mu-calculus and model checking. In: Handbook of Model Checking, pp. 871–919. Springer, Cham (2018). https://doi.org/10.1007/978-3-319-10575-8_26

6. Claessen, K., Hughes, J.: QuickCheck: a lightweight tool for random testing of Haskell programs. SIGPLAN Not. **35**(9), 268–279 (2000). https://doi.org/10.1145/357766.351266

7. Corbett, J.C., Dwyer, M.B., Hatcliff, J., Robby: a language framework for expressing checkable properties of dynamic software. In: Havelund, K., Penix, J., Visser, W. (eds.) SPIN Model Checking and Software Verification, 7th International SPIN Workshop, Stanford, CA, USA, August 30–September 1, 2000, Proceedings. LNCS, vol. 1885, pp. 205–223. Springer, Cham (2000). https://doi.org/10.1007/10722468_13

8. Coverity. https://www.synopsys.com/software-integrity/security-testing/static-analysis-sast.html. Accessed 18 May 2022

9. Findbugs. https://findbugs.sourceforge.net/. Accessed 18 May 2022

10. Haack, C., Huisman, M., Hurlin, C., Amighi, A.: Permission-based separation logic for multithreaded java programs. Log. Methods Comput. Sci. **11**(1) (2015). https://doi.org/10.2168/LMCS-11(1:2)2015, https://lmcs.episciences.org/998

11. Huisman, M., Monti, R.E.: On the industrial application of critical software verification with VerCors. In: Margaria, T., Steffen, B. (eds.) ISoLA 2020. LNCS, vol. 12478, pp. 273–292. Springer, Cham (2020). https://doi.org/10.1007/978-3-030-61467-6_18

12. Hurlin, C.: Specification and Verification of Multithreaded Object-Oriented Programs with Separation Logic. Ph.D. thesis, Université Nice Sophia Antipolis (09 2009)

13. Jia, Y., Harman, M.: An analysis and survey of the development of mutation testing. IEEE Trans. Softw. Eng. **37**(5), 649–678 (2011). https://doi.org/10.1109/TSE.2010.62

14. Klocwork. https://www.perforce.com/products/klocwork. Accessed 18 May 2022

15. Kropf, T.: Introduction to Formal Hardware Verification, 1st edn. Springer, Heidelberg (1999). https://doi.org/10.1007/978-3-662-03809-3

16. Landelijke Tunnelstandaard (National Tunnel Standard). http://publicaties.minienm.nl/documenten/landelijke-tunnelstandaard. Accessed Apr 2022

17. Matsakis, N.D., Klock II, F.S.: The rust language. In: ACM SIGAda Ada Letters, vol. 34, pp. 103–104. ACM (2014)

18. Oortwijn, W., Huisman, M.: Formal verification of an industrial safety-critical traffic tunnel control system. In: Ahrendt, W., Tapia Tarifa, S.L. (eds.) IFM 2019. LNCS, vol. 11918, pp. 418–436. Springer, Cham (2019). https://doi.org/10.1007/978-3-030-34968-4_23

19. Oortwijn, W., Huisman, M., Joosten, S.J.C., van de Pol, J.: Automated verification of parallel nested DFS. In: Biere, A., Parker, D. (eds.) TACAS 2020. LNCS, vol. 12078, pp. 247–265. Springer, Cham (2020). https://doi.org/10.1007/978-3-030-45190-5_14

20. Rubbens, R.: Improving Support for Java Exceptions and Inheritance in VerCors, May 2020. http://essay.utwente.nl/81338/

21. Safari, M., Huisman, M.: Formal verification of parallel prefix sum and stream compaction algorithms in CUDA. Theoret. Comput. Sci. (2022). https://doi.org/10.1016/j.tcs.2022.02.027
22. Safari, M., Oortwijn, W., Joosten, S., Huisman, M.: Formal verification of parallel prefix sum. In: Lee, R., Jha, S., Mavridou, A., Giannakopoulou, D. (eds.) NFM 2020. LNCS, vol. 12229, pp. 170–186. Springer, Cham (2020). https://doi.org/10.1007/978-3-030-55754-6_10
23. Şakar, O.: Extending support for Axiomatic Data Types in VerCors, April 2020. https://essay.utwente.nl/80892/
24. Sonarqube. https://www.sonarqube.org/. Accessed 18 May 2022
25. Technolution. https://www.technolution.eu. Accessed Apr 2022
26. Timmer, M., Brinksma, H., Stoelinga, M.: Model-based testing, NATO science for peace and security series D: Information and Communication Security, vol. 30, pp. 1–32. IOS Press (2011). https://doi.org/10.3233/978-1-60750-711-6-1

Exploring a Parallel SCC Algorithm
Using TLA$^+$and the TLC Model Checker

Jaco van de Pol$^{1,2(\boxtimes)}$ (iD)

^{1} Department of Computer Science, Aarhus University,
Åbogade 34, 8200 Aarhus, Denmark
jaco@cs.au.dk
^{2} University of Twente, DSI, Formal Methods and Tools,
P.O.-Box 217, 7500 AE Enschede, The Netherlands

Abstract. We explore a parallel SCC-decomposition algorithm based on a concurrent Union-Find data structure. In order to increase confidence in the algorithm, it is modelled in TLA$^+$. The TLC model checker is used to demonstrate that it works correctly for all possible interleavings of two workers on a number of small input graphs.

To increase the understanding of the algorithm, we investigate some potential invariants. Some of these are refuted, revealing that the algorithm allows suboptimal (but still correct) executions. Finally, we investigate some modifications of the algorithm. It turns out that most modifications lead to an incorrect algorithm, as revealed by the TLC model checker.

We view this exploration as a first step to a full understanding and a rigorous correctness proof based on invariants or step-wise refinement.

Keywords: Parallel SCC algorithm · Concurrent Union-Find data structure · PlusCal/TLA$^+$ specification · TLC model checker

1 Introduction

This paper studies a parallel algorithm for the detection of Strongly Connected Components (SCCs), which proceeds by sharing and merging partial SCCs that are maintained in a concurrent Union-Find data structure [2,3]. Previous work provided an informal correctness proof of the algorithm, and demonstrated a good experimental parallel speedup, even for graphs with a few large SCCs.

In order to increase confidence in the correctness of the algorithm, and to facilitate a detailed understanding, this paper presents a TLA$^+$specification of the algorithm. This is analysed in the TLA$^+$-toolbox [7], mainly by means of the TLC model checker [17]. The specification allows to check that for a limited number of workers and a couple of small graphs, all fair executions terminate, and all possible interleavings yield the correct SCC-decomposition.

In addition, to increase detailed understanding of the algorithm, we postulated a number of additional assertions and invariants, several of which were refuted by the model checker. The counter examples revealed some weird and

© The Author(s), under exclusive license to Springer Nature Switzerland AG 2022
T. Margaria and B. Steffen (Eds.): ISoLA 2022, LNCS 13701, pp. 535–555, 2022.
https://doi.org/10.1007/978-3-031-19849-6_30

suboptimal (but still correct) executions, in which work is being duplicated. Finally, efforts to improve the algorithm failed, because the model checker discovered that several subtle modifications to the algorithm lead to errors.

Context. SCC decomposition has numerous applications as a fundamental building block in graph algorithms. We are mostly interested in applications in formal methods, such as model checking LTL properties, preprocessing for weak bisimulation reduction, and analysis of Markov chains. Since these methods are used for the verification of safety-critical systems, they must themselves be guaranteed correct. At the same time, intricate parallel algorithms have been designed, to scale the methods to realistic systems. To maximize parallel speed up, locking mechanisms are avoided where possible. This makes the correctness argumentation quite hard. This has led to the formal verification of several model checking algorithms, like a full LTL model checker [6], a model checker for Timed Automata [16], a sequential [12] and parallel algorithm [11] for Nested Depth-First Search, and sequential SCC-decomposition algorithms [4,8]. We are not aware of a formal verification of a parallel SCC algorithm.

There are many SCC decomposition algorithms. Tarjan provided the first sequential linear-time algorithm [14]. The algorithm analysed in this paper is closer to Dijkstra's sequential SCC algorithm [5]. Since then, several distributed SCC algorithms have been developed [1,10]. These algorithms apply to graphs that are partitioned among several workers. This paper is concerned with parallel SCC algorithms (multi-core parallelism), where the graph is in global, shared memory so all workers have access to it. Typically, the workers share some information on explored SCCs. Examples are the algorithm by Gavin Lowe [9] and the algorithm by Étienne Renault [13]. These algorithms make different trade-offs when two workers start working on the same SCC. For instance, one could suspend one of the workers, or one could redo the whole SCC with a single worker. This paper studies the algorithm from Vincent Bloemen, following the presentation of his thesis [2], first published in [3]. The special feature of this algorithm is that multiple workers can work on the same SCC, sharing partial SCCs with each other. This is relevant for graphs with a few large SCCs.

2   Preliminaries

The SCC algorithm takes as input a rooted directed graph $G = (V, E, v_0)$, where V is a finite set of nodes (states), $E \subseteq V \times V$ is the set of directed edges (transitions), and v_0 is the root (initial state). The algorithm works on-the-fly (useful for model checking). It starts at v_0 and discovers new E-successors through a function $next : V \to 2^V$. We write $v \to^* w$ if (v, w) is in the transitive-reflexive closure of E. A subset $S \subseteq V$ is strongly connected if for all $v, w \in S$, $v \to^* w$. We call such S a *partial* SCC. A *strongly connected component* (SCC) of G is a *maximal* subset that is strongly connected.

Partitions of a set can be maintained in the Union-Find data structure, which is a forest where every element has a pointer to its parent in the same equivalence class. The elements that point to themselves are the roots. One finds the representative of an element by following the parent pointers to the root. Two elements can be united by assigning the parent pointer of the root of one to the root of the other. These operations run in amortized (near)-constant time [15].

2.1 A Parallel SCC Algorithm Based on Concurrent Union-Find

We first provide an informal explanation of the parallel SCC decomposition algorithm based on concurrent Union-Find, following the presentation in the PhD thesis of Vincent Bloemen [2], originally published in [3]. We present the algorithm in a top-down fashion. The full original algorithm is included in Appendix A for easy reference. We refer to the thesis for more detailed explanations.

Main Procedure. The main procedure UFSCC (Algorithm 1) runs an independent Depth-First-Search (DFS) for each worker p. A newly visited node v is pushed on a worker-local stack R_p (line 7), which will contain states to be merged in partial SCCs. There are two globally shared data-structures:

- A Union-Find forest, storing the current partitioning in partial SCCs
- A Cyclic List, enabling an enumeration over all nodes in a partial SCC

The DFS proceeds per partial SCC, rather than per node: From node v, UFSCC is recursively called (line 12) for each "new" successor w of each node v' that is in the same partial SCC as v. The nodes v' are picked from the Cyclic List (line 8, 18). The calls to successors w are performed in random order (line 10), to encourage workers to operate on different parts of the graph.

If a worker has already visited some node in the partial SCC of w (but it is not yet fully explored), a loop has been detected: In this case, v and w and all intermediate nodes on the local stack R_p definitely belong to the same SCC, so they can be united in the UF-forest (line 14–16). Note that this partial SCC is not necessarily complete.

To find out if the partial SCC of successor w is either completely "explored", or if it was already "found" by worker p, or else if it is entirely "new" for worker p, we maintain two more pieces of globally shared information. This information applies to partial SCCs, so it is stored at the roots of the Union-Find forest.

- A UF-status, indicating if this partial SCC is completely explored,
- A bit set UF-workers, storing all workers that have found this partial SCC.

Based on the UF-status and the Worker set, the function MakeClaim (Algorithm 2) can easily determine the status of a newly visited node. To establish the status of a node a, it must first find the root of a (line 2), to obtain the information on the partial SCC. MakeClaim has a side-effect: If a is newly visited, the worker set of the root is updated (line 8).[1] This is a bit complicated, since in the mean-time, other workers may have extended this partial SCC, so the UF-root of a may have advanced. This is solved by the while loop (line 7–9), after which p must be in the worker set of the UF-root of a.

---

[1] Although not stated explicitly, this assignment is taken to be atomic.

Concurrent Union-Find Forest. We proceed to the explanation of the implementation of the UF-forest (Algorithms 3 and 4). The Find procedure (Algorithm 3) simply follows the parent-pointers, until a self-loop is found, indicating that we reached the root of this equivalence class. The path is shortened for future calls.

To determine if a and b belong to the SameSet (Algorithm 3), we find their roots and check if they are equal; if so, they definitely belong to the same SCC (line 16). Since SameSet is a non-atomic operation, it can happen that the (common) root of a and b has advanced in between. If so, we repeat the whole procedure in the new situation (line 18). If not, we return False, since (at least at some point during SameSet) a and b were in a different partial SCC.

The concurrent Unite function (Algorithm 4) is the most complicated. Given the nodes a and b to unite, it will find their minimal root q and maximal root r (line 11–15). The unite function has three tasks:

- The parent of q shall be r (the direction is fixed to avoid cycles);
- The union of the worker sets of q and r shall be stored at r;
- The cyclic lists of q and r shall be combined into a single cyclic list.

The main complication is that concurrent unites may happen. We avoid intermediate updates to q by locking its root. The lock is implemented in the UF-status (with values "Live", "Lock" and "Explored"). LockRoot uses an atomic Compare-And-Swap (CAS) to ensure that only one worker can hold the lock on q. It also checks that the root of q has not been advanced in the meantime. If we cannot lock q, the whole Unite-procedure is restarted (line 16). After obtaining the lock on q, its parent pointer can be safely updated to r (line 20). Note that q can never become a root, so there is no need to ever unlock its UF-status.

The cyclic lists must be merged as well. This is explained in the next subsection. Finally, we must store the union of the worker sets of r and q at the new root. Another complication arises: In the meantime, the root of r may have advanced! This is solved by the loop on line 21–24: We keep copying and uniting the worker set of the most recent root of r and q, until r is its own root.

Cyclic List. We now explain the Cyclic List, which is used to enumerate all nodes in a partial SCC. The cyclic list is implemented by a simple next-pointer. Each node also has a list-status, which can be "Busy", "Lock", or "Done". The main operations are to *enumerate* the "Busy" elements of the list (PickFromList, Algorithm 5), to *remove* elements from the list (RemoveFromList, Algorithm 5), and to *merge* two cyclic lists (integrated in Unite, Algorithm 4, line 17–19). Two auxiliary operations are to *lock* (LockList, Algorithm 4), and to *unlock* (integrated in Unite, Algorithm 4, line 25–26) elements in the list.

Merging two cyclic lists (Algorithm 4) proceeds by locking a "Busy" element from each list (line 17, 18), then swapping their two next-pointers (line 19), and finally unlocking them (line 25–26). LockList traverses the cyclic list (line 6, 9) and tries to "Lock" elements by a CAS-operation. If this succeeds, we return the locked element. Otherwise, we simply give up and try the next element in the list. Unlocking (line 25, 26) proceeds by assigning the list-status to "Busy" again.

The RemoveFromList function (Algorithm 5) updates the list-status from "Busy" to "Done" in a CAS operation (line 19). Note that "Locked" elements cannot be removed, but are retried (line 18) as long they are locked. Removed ("Done") nodes are still part of the cyclic list. We keep them, since other workers might still point to them, and they should be able to pick the next "Busy" node.

Finally, PickFromList (Algorithm 5) picks the next "Busy" node from the cyclic list. Starting at node a, it waits until a is unlocked (busy waiting, line 2,4). If a is "Busy", it can be returned (line 3). If a is "Done", we proceed to the next node, b (line 5). If $a = b$, the cyclic list must be empty, so the partial SCC is completely explored. This is properly stored in the UF-status field of the UF-root of a (line 8). A CAS operation is used, to ensure that only one worker reports a newly discovered SCC (line 9). In this case, we return NULL, since this SCC doesn't contain a "Busy" node. Otherwise, we wait until b is unlocked (busy-wait loop line 11–13). If b is "Busy", we return it. If b is also "Done", we need to proceed with the next state in the cyclic list, c (line 14, 16). Finally, we shorten the path $a \rightarrow b \rightarrow c$ (skipping b, line 15) to avoid long chains of removed nodes in the next call to PickFromList.

2.2 TLA$^+$ and TLC

The underlying logic of TLA$^+$ is simple, but powerful. The formalism is first-order predicate logic, where (untyped) variables range over sets (in the sense of ZF). TLA$^+$ comes with a library of predefined sets and standard operators on them, including natural numbers, functions, sequences, and the definitions of (linear time) temporal logic.

A system specification consists of a collection of state variables, and the definition of an initial predicate (on state variables) and a next-state predicate (on state variables and their primed variants). A TLA$^+$ specification is completed by weak (or strong) fairness assumptions, to ensure that there is some progress.

The PlusCal language allows the specification of algorithms using a simple programming language with assignments, if-then-else statements, while-loops, recursive procedures, and (fair) parallel composition. Atomicity is specified by adding program labels that serve as interleaving points. As a result, the PlusCal specification of the UFSCC algorithm follows the original pseudocode rather closely. Specifications in PlusCal are automatically translated to TLA$^+$.

Given the specification, one creates a finite model by fixing the number of workers, and fixing a particular input graph. We used the TLC model checker to prove that all interleavings allowed by the algorithm terminate and lead to a correct SCC decomposition. The TLC model checker supports parallel computation, symmetry reduction, and stores visited states on disk. TLC produces a counter example trace when a property is violated. We used the Visual Studio Code plug-in for TLA, for its great support to filter and navigate huge counter examples. Also, managing multiple specifications and models is well-supported.

Proving correctness for all number of workers, or for each input graph, is beyond the scope of model checking. We have not yet used the TLA proof checker, which would require to specify inductive invariants for the UFSCC algorithm.

3 Modeling and Analysis Process

We constructed an initial specification (Sect. 3.1) of the UFSCC algorithm in Plus-Cal, following the pseudocode (Appendix A) closely. We extended the specification with properties to express its functional correctness, i.e. the detection of the correct SCCs (Sect. 3.3). We added additional assertions to test some intuitions about the algorithm. Since the state space was large, we started with random simulation runs to test these assertions for small graphs and a few workers. Later we realized that the state space was actually infinite, due to recursive calls in busy-waiting loops. We then made a second specification (Sect. 3.2), avoiding recursive busy waiting. This allowed us to investigate the full state space.

We detected that some of the conjectured invariants did not hold (Sect. 4). The counter-examples to these invariants show some suboptimal traces, that we had not anticipated. However, we have not found traces that violate the overall correctness of the algorithm. It is of course possible that errors would occur on larger graphs, or with more workers. We also analysed some modifications of the algorithm, most of which were incorrect, as detected by the model checker.

3.1 Initial Specification – Good for Simulation

The initial specification follows the pseudocode in a rather straightforward manner. All in all, building the first executable model that covered the whole algorithm only took around one full day. Since TLA$^+$ is a rich specification language, the global data structures UF (Union-Find forest) and CL (cyclic list) can be modelled directly as mathematical functions. These globally shared variables are declared and initialized as follows. Here *init* is the initial state of the graph, and *Workers* is the set of worker identities, both specified in a separate model.

```
variables
  UF = [ n\in Nodes |-> [
            parent        |-> n,
            workers       |-> IF n=init THEN Workers ELSE {},
            uf_status     |-> "live"                            ]];
  CL = [ n\in Nodes |-> [
            next          |-> n,
            list_status   |-> "busy"                            ]];
```

All procedures in Appendix A could be easily formalised as PlusCal procedures. As an example, we provide the Find-operation (Algorithm 3, line 1–4) in PlusCal, below on the left. On the right, we show the procedure RemoveFromList (Algorithm 5, line 17–18) in PlusCal, using a busy-wait loop and the macro CAS. In PlusCal, a procedure cannot return a result. Instead, we declared thread-local variables for the return value of each procedure (like returnFind below). In an attempt to reduce the state space, we reset these global variables at the call site, as soon as we have read the result (not shown here). Note that the labels indicate interleaving points: All statements between two labels occur atomically.

```
procedure Find(a)
    variable p;
    {
f1: p := UF[a].p;
f2: if (p /= a)
    { call Find(p);
f3:    UF[a].p := returnFind };
    else
    { returnFind := p };
f4: return
    }
```

```
procedure RemoveFromList(a) {
r1: while
        (CL[a].stat/= "done")
    {
    CAS(CL[a].stat,"busy","done")
    };
return
}
```

Main Procedure and Parallel Processes. The main procedure is UFSCC. We use the "with"-construct from PlusCal to select an arbitrary successor w_1 non-deterministically from the successors of v_1, which is the element picked from the cyclic list of v. Here *next* refers to the transitions in the input graph, which is modeled in a separate model.

The whole system consists of a weakly-fair parallel composition over all *Workers* (a constant set defined in a separate model), where each process executes UFSCC from the *initial* state. Each worker maintains its Roots stack as a thread-local variable, initialized as the empty sequence. We use weak fairness to avoid that processes stutter for ever, violating termination of the algorithm.

```
procedure UFSCC(v)
    variables v1, w, succ, ...
{
m1: Roots := <<v>> \o Roots;
    call PickFromList(v);
m2: v1 := returnPick;
m3: while (v1 /= null) {
        succ := next[v1];
m4:     while (succ /= {}) {
            with (w1 \in succ) {
            w := w1;
            succ := succ \ {w1} };
... } ... } ... }
```

```
fair process (W \in Workers)
    variables
    Roots = << >>,
    returnFind, returnPick ;
{ main: call UFSCC(init); }
```

Atomicity. PlusCal uses program labels to specify atomicity: code between two program labels is executed atomically; interleaving (and branching) can only happen at program labels. We took the following modeling decision: To ensure that every "atomic" block performs at most one global memory access, we introduce a label (like f1) for each program statement with a global memory access. PlusCal also requires labels for loops, procedure calls and returns, etc.

There are two exceptions to the rule: The first exception is when the pseudocode insisted on atomic updates. For instance, line 23 in Algorithm 4 (Unite) states that theworker set must be updated atomically. So, despite three global memory accesses, we model this line with only one label in the TLA$^+$ specification:

```
u11: UF[r].workers := UF[r].workers \union UF[q].workers;
```

In contrast, line 19 of the same algorithm tells that the pointer Swap happens non-atomically. So this we modelled using multiple labels (i.e., breaking it in two atomic pointer assignments), as shown on the left below.

The other exception is where the pseudocode uses CAS statements, which we modeled by a macro, shown below on the right. Note that macros cannot contain labels, so they are treated as atomic blocks by definition.

```
u8: tmp := CL[a].next;
    CL[a].next := CL[b].next;
u9: CL[b].next := tmp;
```

```
macro CAS(x,old,new) {
  returnCAS := (x=old);
  if (returnCAS) { x:=new }
}
```

Deviations from the Original Algorithm. We made the following deviations from the pseudocode when interpreting it in the specification:

- We slightly rearranged the code for esthetic reasons. For instance, we split UF and CL in two data-structures. We also inlined the LockRoot procedure, which was only called from one place in Unite.
- To simplify the main process, we did not model the initial assignment to the worker set (Algorithms 1, line 3, 4), but instead, we did this in the initialisation of the UF data structure (as shown in the code above).
- Although not indicated explicitly, we took the worker set update in Make-Claim (Algorithm 2) as an atomic update, similar to the update in Unite.
- Note that PickFromList returns NULL if the cyclic list is empty. This procedure is called: (i) From the main procedure UFSCC (Algorithm 1, line 8, 18); the while loop terminates when PickFromList returns NULL. (ii) From LockList, but now the case that NULL is returned is not handled. To make this an explicit assumption, we replaced line 7 in LockList (Algorithm 4) by an assertion checking for NULL. We have not detected a violation of this assertion.

3.2   Improved Specification – Good for Model Checking

The initial specification led to very large state spaces, even when run with only 2 workers on a graph with only 3 nodes. As a consequence, initially we could not apply complete model checking, but only run simulations.

Busy Waiting in Recursion. Later, we realized that the state space was actually infinite. The reason is that the pseudocode models busy-waiting loops with recursion. For instance, the procedure LockList (Algorithm 4, l. 5–9) was initially modeled as shown below (left). Note that if the CAS fails, we retry locking the list by the recursive call at line 9. Recall that PlusCal is translated to TLA⁺; the translation involves the introduction of a stack to model procedure calls and recursion. Although the LockList procedure terminates (after the other worker releases the lock), an unbounded number of executions of the loop can happen in between, leading to an unbounded stack.[2]

Our remedy was to replace tail-recursive calls by goto-statements. Note that the re-specification of LockList on the right below leads to a finite state space. We replaced all tail-recursion by goto-statements, to reduce the state space.

```
procedure LockList(a)              procedure LockList(a)
  variable s                         variable s
  {                                  {
11: call PickFromList(a);         11: call PickFromList(a);
12: s := returnPick;              12: s := returnPick;
    assert s /= null;                 assert s /= null;
    CAS(CL[s].stat,                   CAS(CL[s].stat,
           "busy", "lock");                  "busy", "lock");
13: if (returnCAS) {              13: if (returnCAS) {
        returnLock := s;                  returnLock := s;
        return                            return
    } else {                          } else {
        call LockList(s);                 a := s;
14:     return                            goto 11;
    }                                 }
} \* 1st model: tail recursion    } \* 2nd model: goto-loop
```

Replace Busy-Wait by Await. In a final attempt to reduce the state space, we tried to avoid busy-wait loops at all, by using the *await* statement of PlusCal. As an example, we show the start of the procedure PickFromList (Algorithm 5, line 1–3). On the left we show the initial specification in PlusCal (we modelled the do-while by a goto statement). On the right, we show the improved version, where the busy-waiting loop with goto is replaced by the await-statement.

```
procedure PickFromList(a)          procedure PickFromList(a)
  variable status, b, c, root;       variable b, c, root ;
  {                                  {
pX: status := CL[a].stat;         pX: await CL[a_P].stat /= "lock";
    if (status = "lock")              if (CL[a].stat = "busy") {
    { goto pX } else                      returnPick := a;
    if (status = "busy") {         p1:     return
        returnPick := a;               };
p1:     return                    ...}
    };  ... }
```

We have no formal justification for these modifications, but now at least the state space of the algorithm for a fixed graph and set of workers is finite. For 2 workers and graphs of 4 nodes (like those in Appendix B), the state space is around 2–15 Million nodes. For state spaces of this size, model checking is feasible on a consumer-laptop and runs within a couple of minutes. For 3 workers on a graph of only 3 nodes, the state space grew already to 67 Million nodes. This becomes painful for larger graphs, but one could still fall back on simulation.

3.3   Specifying the Correctness Property and Other Assertions

Next to the specification of the system, we need to specify the correctness criterion. The main claim is that UFSCC terminates, and upon termination the Union-Find forest contains the graph partitioning in the correct SCCs. We specified and checked the expected SCCs for each model instance separately.

Model Instances. A model instance is specified in a separate configuration file. The example below (left) shows a fragment of a model instance. It specifies a graph of 4 nodes and 5 edges. Note that the sequence of edges can be interpreted as a function from nodes to set of nodes. It can be easily checked that this graph has two SCCs. Since our Union-Find structure always takes the largest node as representative, we can specify the expected root for each node. These expected SCCs will be used to express the correctness claim.

The model instance also provides a value to the set of workers. In the example below (right), we introduce two workers w_1 and w_2 as distinct model constants.

```
Nodes == { 1,2,3,4 }
next == << {2}, {1,3}, {4}, {3} >>
init == 1
expected == << 2, 2, 4, 4 >>
```

```
CONSTANTS
    w1 = w1
    w2 = w2
    Workers = {w1, w2}
```

Main Correctness Claim. For the main correctness claim, we define an operator (logical function) that computes the root of a node in the UF-forest *in a single snapshot*. Note that this is quite different from the Find-procedure, which does not work atomically (the UF forest can be modified by concurrent workers) and has a side effect (path shortening). The ideal find operator is defined recursively. Note that TLA$^+$ allows that recursive operators are only partially specified. In this case, if the UF-structure contained loops, the value of "find" would not be defined everywhere.

```
RECURSIVE find(_)
    find(n) == IF UF[n].parent=n THEN n ELSE find(UF[n].parent)
Correct == (\A w\in Workers : pc[w] = "Done") =>
                        (\A x\in Nodes : find(x) = expected[x])
Termination == <>(\A w \in Workers: pc[w] = "Done")
```

Given the logical find-operator and the expected SCCs, partial correctness can be stated easily. In *Correct* above, we state that when all workers are done, the root of every node in the graph is as expected. Note that this is an invariant that trivially holds for all states, except those where all processes have finished. The LTL property *Termination* indicates that all fair runs lead to a state where all processes have returned from the initial UFSCC call. Together, *Correct* and *Termination* (and the fact that the program doesn't crash halfway due to a type/value error) specify total correctness under weak fairness.

4   Findings from Model Checking Experiments

The specification in the previous section has a finite state space, given a fixed input graph and a fixed number of workers. So in principle, the TLC model checker can generate the full state space and explore if the algorithm works correctly for all possible interleavings, and all possible graph traversals (recall that the next successor is selected non-deterministically). The *bad news* is that the state space could only be computed for rather small graphs and a few workers. The *good news* is that the algorithm was correct for all instances that we tried. We tried 2 workers on 10 graphs of 3–4 nodes, from various initial positions. See Appendix B for an impression of a few input graphs.

This is insufficient information to conclude that the algorithm is also correct for more workers on larger input graphs. The royal road to increase the confidence in the algorithm would be to identify and prove a number of inductive invariants that imply correctness. At the moment we don't know the proper invariants of the algorithm. The intermediate contribution of this work is to investigate a number of potential invariants. It appears that several conjectured invariants actually don't hold, as revealed by some weird (but not wrong) executions (Sects. 4.2, 4.3). This might diminish the confidence in the algorithm.

We also studied a number of modifications of the algorithm. These are partly inspired by efforts to "restore" some conjectured invariants and avoid weird executions, and partly by a wish to simplify or restructure the specification in clear layers. In particular, we would wish to separate code at the UF level from code at the CL level. We believe that this would facilitate a proof by step-wise refinement. Currently, it is mainly the Unite-procedure that mixes the two levels.

Our findings indicate that most modifications made the algorithm wrong (Sects. 4.1, 4.4). We don't know if this should increase or decrease the confidence in the algorithm: On the one hand, it shows that the correctness of the algorithm is rather fragile, and one could imagine that the original algorithm fails on a slightly different input graph. On the other hand, it shows that wrong algorithms can be caught by model checking, even with 2 workers running on the 10 small input graphs that we constructed. We will now discuss these findings in more detail.

4.1   Simplifying the Equivalence Check (SameSet)

Consider the procedure SameSet (Algorithm 3, l. 13–18). It finds the roots of a and b. If the roots are equal, a and b clearly belong to the same set. The reverse is actually not true in a concurrent setting! First of all, SameSet could return False, even though a and b have been united in between by another worker. One could argue that this result is correct, since SameSet should have returned False if it had just been a bit faster. Still, at line 17, we only return False if the root of a has not changed in the meantime. Otherwise, we start all over (l. 18).

The problem with this approach is that it seems complicated, it looks a-symmetric (we don't check if the root of b has changed), and it seems to relieve the symptom rather than the cause of the problem: what if the root of a is updated right after we check that it wasn't updated in line 17?

For these reasons, we tried a simplification, replacing line 17 and 18 by just returning "False". However, this simple change leads to serious consequences:

- On some graphs, the modified UFSCC gave wrong answers, by merging different SCCs into a single one.
- On some graphs, the modified UFSCC crashed, by attempting to pop an element from the empty Roots-stack.

The TLC model checker produces counter-examples, i.e. concrete runs of the modified algorithm that lead to the problematic behaviour. Although these traces get long, after some analysis they explained why these problems occur.

The disturbing situation in SameSet occurs when a and b are initially in the same partition, but the root of this partition is updated in between finding the root of a and b. In that case, the roots seems different, and a wrong result is reported. In this sense, returning False directly after line 16 would result in a SameSet procedure that is not even reflexive.

Now why is this problematic? The procedure SameSet is called by the main procedure UFSCC while popping roots from the stack *as long as the source and target of the current transition $v \to w$ are not in the same set!* (Algorithm 1, l. 14–16). The effect of the erroneous version of SameSet is that we keep popping and uniting states from the Roots stack. This means that an SCC is either merged with the previous SCC on the stack, or if there is no such SCC on the stack, we try to pop from the empty stack!

We conclude that the complication in SameSet is necessary. As already explained in [2], it guarantees to return True if and only if a and b are in the same set at some point during the execution of SameSet. We believe that this requirement can be formalized using the logical (ideal) find-operator as follows:

$$\left(\mathit{find}_{pre}(a) = \mathit{find}_{pre}(b)\right) \Rightarrow \left(\mathit{returnSame} = \mathit{True}\right) \Rightarrow \left(\mathit{find}_{post}(a) = \mathit{find}_{post}(b)\right)$$

4.2   Monotonicity of Worker Sets and Atomic Updates

The worker set is used to detect cycles in the graph: In UFSCC (Algorithm 1) and MakeClaim (Algorithm 2), if a worker p explores an edge (v, w) and p already occurs in the worker set of the root of w, then it ran into a cycle, and it can be concluded that v and w are in the same SCC. Recall that the worker sets are updated atomically in Unite (Algorithm 4, l. 23) and MakeClaim (Algorithm 2, l. 8).

A reasonable conjecture is that these atomic updates ensure that the worker sets are monotonically increasing. To challenge the specification, we check that this property holds for atomic worker updates, but is violated if we update the worker set in a non-atomic manner. The property is easily formalized as a TLA property on all reachable transitions, as *Monotonic1* below.

```
Monotonic1 == [][\A y\in Nodes :
                 UF[y].workers \subseteq UF[y].workers']_<<UF>>
Monotonic2 == [][\A y\in Nodes :
        UF[find(y)].workers \subseteq UF[find(y)].workers']_<<UF>>
```

Indeed, this property holds with atomic updates, but it is violated by a version of the specification with non-atomic updates. The model checker returns an execution which boils down to the following well-known scenario: Assume the worker set is X and it is extended concurrently by Y_1 and Y_2. With atomic updates, the end result is $(X \cup Y_1) \cup Y_2$ or $(X \cup Y_2) \cup Y_1$, which denotes the same set. With non-atomic updates, the workers can first both read X, and then one writes $X \cup Y_1$ and subsequently the other writes $X \cup Y_2$. The second update violates monotonicity, since the update from Y_1 is lost.

Note that property *Monotonic1* only looks at the worker set *per node*, while the relevant information would check the worker set *per partial SCC*. We challenged the specification further with property *Monotonic2*, which states that for every node, the worker set of its *root node* is increasing. Surprisingly, the model checker returned an execution where this property is failing, even in the model with atomic updates! After analysing the execution, the following scenario is possible due to the order of steps in Unite (Algorithm 4, l. 20–23).

Assume worker w_1 unites roots r and q, with worker set W_r and W_q. It first updates the parent pointer of q to r. In a second step, it adds W_q to W_r. But *in between these steps the invariant is violated*, since the worker set of q's root r is still W_r, suddenly missing elements from W_q. Assume that in between these two steps, another worker w_2 checks the worker set of a node v whose parent points to q (in MakeClaim). Even though w_2 might be in the worker set of q, it is *not yet* in the worker set of r, the new root of v! The situation will be restored soon by w_1, but it is too late: w_2 has already decided that its node v is "new", instead of recognizing that its partial SCC was already "found".

Is this bad? Apparently, the violation of *Monotonic2* doesn't lead to a wrong result. Still, it can lead to extra computations. If worker w_2 doesn't find itself in the worker set of the root of node v, it will continue the search, potentially revisiting a part of the graph unnecessarily. We tried to construct examples where this behaviour could lead to wrong answers, but we didn't succeed. Also, the computation always terminated (there are only finitely many unites). However, these examples led to discovery of violations of other expected properties, as reported in Subsect. 4.3. Our attempts to improve the algorithm so that property *Monotonic2* holds failed, as reported in Subsect. 4.4.

4.3   Duplication on the Stack

Related to non-monotonicity of the worker sets, we investigated another property that indicates duplication of work: this time, we check an assertion at the beginning of the UFSCC loop that the node v that is pushed on the Roots-stack R is not already on the stack. Indeed, this property was violated on the same graphs that violated the *Monotonicity2* property.

Two BSc students at AU, Jesper Steensgaard and Jonathan Starup, discovered another reason that some nodes occur multiple times on the Roots stack: UFSCC traverses all nodes v' in the same partial SCC, and recurses on all their successors w. This causes double work, since some of these successors belong to the same SCC, and will only be removed from the cyclic list when we backtrack from them. One could skip those successors w that belong to the current SCC.

4.4   Changing the Order of Updates During Unite

Finally, we tried some variants of the algorithm, changing the order of the steps in the Unite procedure. After initialisation, Unite performs the following 5 steps:

1. It locks two elements in the cyclic lists (l. 17, 18)
2. It merges the cyclic lists (l. 19)
3. It updates the parent pointer (l. 20)
4. It updates the worker set of the root in a loop (l. 21–24)
5. It releases the list locks (l. 25–26)

Note that, since these steps don't happen atomically, other workers might see inconsistent states, where for instance the cyclic lists of two nodes are already merged, but the two nodes are not yet the same according to the UF-forest. Similarly, they could be the same, but the worker set has not yet been updated. The "Locked" value of the UF-status and the CL-status are the only warning signs for other workers that something might be wrong.

We tried several modifications of the order of these 5 steps. TLC discovered problems for several reorderings, in particular it revealed concrete counter examples for $(1, 2, 4, 3, 5)$, where the worker set is updated before the parent pointer. We had hoped that this order would restore the monotonicity property.

TLC also reported concrete counter-examples to $(3, 4, 1, 2, 5)$ and $(1, 2, 5, 3, 4)$, where updating the UF-parent happens outside the region between locking and unlocking the CL-nodes. We had hoped to minimize the locked region, to potentially increase performance, and also to separate the CL-related code from the UF-related code. Also, one would think that the CL-list locks only need to protect updates to the CL-list, but this is apparently not true.

On the other hand, we found no concrete counter-examples to the modification $(1, 2, 3, 5, 4)$, so it seems that the update of the worker set can happen outside the locked region. Moving the loop of lines 21–24 outside the locked region could potentially give a performance speedup. Also, the order of updating the parent pointer and the cyclic list doesn't seem to matter: We found no counter-examples to $(1, 3, 2, 4, 5)$ and $(1, 3, 2, 5, 4)$. From our experiments, we conclude that:

– The parent pointer must be updated *before* the worker set is updated.
– The update of the UF parent-pointer must happen inside the CL lock region.

If one violates the first requirement, as in (1, 2, 4, 3, 5), the following can happen: Assume worker w_1 starts at some node n_1 and worker w_2 finds out that nodes n_1 and n_2 can be united. The new root will be n_2, so worker w_2 updates the worker set at n_2 to $\{w_1, w_2\}$ *before it updates the parent pointer*. In the meantime, worker w_1 now explores the edge from n_1 to n_2. It notices that it already found (the SCC of) node n_2 (since w_1 is now in n_2's worker set). However, n_1 and n_2 are not yet the same (since the parent pointer has not yet been updated by w_2). Hence, w_1 starts popping the Roots stack, possibly leading to spurious unites, or even to a crash due to popping from the empty stack (TLC found both scenarios).

If one violates the second requirement by updating the parent pointer *before* locking the list elements, as in (3, 4, 1, 2, 5), another worker might already remove the elements that still must be locked in the cyclic list. In this case, Lock-List (Algorithm 4) crashes due to the assertion triggered because PickFromList (Algorithm 5) returns NULL.

If one violates the second requirement by updating the parent pointer *after* unlocking the list elements, as in (1, 2, 5, 3, 4), it can happen that the *last node* returned by PickFromList (Algorithm 5) has already an unlocked CL-status, but its UF-status is still "Locked" instead of "Live". But then the CAS-operation on line 8 fails, so the UF-status of this node is never updated to "Explored". When backtracking in UFSCC and visiting the same node again through another path, it is not "Explored" so it will be considered "Found" and UFSCC erroneously starts popping from the Roots stack (Algorithm 1, l. 14–16).

This subtle error shows that the proper invariants of the algorithm should somehow relate the UF-status and the CL-status, to avoid that UF-locked states are returned by PickFromList.

5   Conclusion

In an attempt to understand a parallel SCC-detection algorithm based on a concurrent Union-Find forest, and to increase the trust in its correctness, we modeled the algorithm in TLA$^+$ and analysed it for a number of small graphs with the TLC model checker. The analysis revealed that the algorithm behaves correctly for 2 workers on a couple of small graphs. This does not prove its correctness, but it may increase confidence in its correctness.

We also showed that some natural invariants can be violated, leading to suboptimal runs of the algorithm with some work duplication. This may reduce the trust in the correctness, since such behaviour might violate the correctness on larger graphs or with more workers (beyond the horizon of the model checker). We did not find such examples, though. The original author was aware of possible work duplication. It should not affect correctness and it occurs only with a small probability. Avoiding it with extra locks could be even more costly. Experimental evaluation has demonstrated good speedups of the current strategy [2,3].

Finally, we tried to increase our understanding and confidence by slight modifications to the algorithm. The results are mixed. Some small modifications seem to be possible without violating correctness. One of the suggested modifications might even increase parallel speedup, by moving the loop to update the worker set outside the locked region. We tried some other small modifications to maintain interesting invariants that could avoid duplicate work and keep worker-set information monotonic. However, these modifications were erroneous and could be refuted by small graphs. Apparently, larger modifications would be required to maintain these invariants.

These experiments also reveal that the invariants needed for a full understanding and correctness proof of the algorithm will be quite complicated. We hope that the scenarios revealed by model checking and reported in this work will contribute to the discovery of the proper invariants and potentially to simplifications of the algorithm. Of course, these simplifications should not decrease the parallel performance of the algorithm. For instance, adding extra locks would ease correctness reasoning, but at the expense of decreased parallel performance.

Acknowledgements. The author acknowledges the investigation by Jesper Steensgaard and Jonathan Starup, who found some suboptimal behaviours in the cyclic list during their BSc talent-track project. The author is grateful to Stephan Merz for introducing him to TLA$^+$ during an extended research visit at Nancy (France). The author acknowledges useful discussions with Simon Thrane Hansen (AU) on simplifying the model and help with the TLC model checker. Finally, he is grateful to Stephan Merz, Vincent Bloemen, and the anonymous reviewers for useful feedback on a draft of the paper.

A   The Original Concurrent Union-Find SCC Algorithm

Here we present the original algorithm UFSCC, taken from the thesis of Vincent Bloemen [2]. The pseudo-code is copied with consent of the author. We present the algorithm top-down, in Algorithm 1–6.

Algorithm 1 Implementation of the UFSCC algorithm ([2], Alg. 9)

```
 1  ∀p ∈ [1...P] : R_p := ∅ // local stack for each worker
 2  function UFSCC_main(v_θ, P)
 3      forall p ∈ [1...P] do
 4          └ MakeClaim(v_θ, p) // set worker IDs for state v_θ
 5      └ UFSCC_1(v_θ)‖...‖UFSCC_P(v_θ) // run in parallel

 6  function UFSCC_p(v)
 7      R_p.Push(v)
 8      v' := PickFromList(v) // pick a Busy state from S(v)
 9      while v' ≠ NULL do
10          forall w ∈ Random(Succ(v')) do
11              claim := MakeClaim(w, p) // (ignore claim_explored)
12              if claim = claim_new then UFSCC_p(w) // (locally) new
13              else if claim = claim_found then // cycle detected
14                  while ¬SameSet(v, w) do
15                      r := R_p.Pop()
16                      └ Unite(r, R_p.Top()) // merge top two stack states
17          RemoveFromList(v') // fully handled all states from Succ(v')
18          └ v' := PickFromList(v') // pick next state
19      └ if v = R_p.Top() then R_p.Pop() // remove completed SCC
```

Algorithm 2 Determining the status of a state with the worker set ([2], Alg. 6)

```
 1  function MakeClaim(a, p)
 2      root_a := Find(a)
 3      if UF[root_a].uf_status = Explored then
 4          └ return claim_explored // completely explored SCC
 5      if p ∈ UF[root_a].workers then
 6          └ return claim_found // set already contains worker ID
 7      while p ∉ UF[root_a].workers do
 8          UF[root_a].workers := UF[root_a].workers ∪ {p} // add worker ID
 9          └ root_a := Find(root_a) // ensure that the worker ID is added
10      return claim_new
```

Algorithm 3 Find and SameSet functions ([2], Alg. 5)

```
 1  function Find(a)
 2  │  if UF[a].parent ≠ a then
 3  │  │  └ UF[a].parent := Find(UF[a].parent) // path compression
 4  │  └ return UF[a].parent // return the root

13  function SameSet(a, b)
14  │  rootₐ := Find(a)
15  │  root_b := Find(b)
16  │  if rootₐ = root_b then return True
17  │  if UF[rootₐ].parent = rootₐ then return False
18  │  └ return SameSet(rootₐ, root_b)
```

(we removed the Unite-function from Alg. 3, since it will be refined by Alg. 4)

Algorithm 4 The Unite procedure of the iterable union-find ([2], Alg. 8)

```
 1  function LockRoot(a)
 2  │  if CAS(UF[a].uf_status, Live, Lock) then
 3  │  │  └ if UF[a].parent = a then return True
 4  │  └ return False // unable to lock root (unnecessary to unlock)

 5  function LockList(a)
 6  │  s := PickFromList(a) // pick a Busy state
 7  │  if s = NULL then return NULL // cannot lock an explored SCC
 8  │  if CAS(UF[s].list_status, Busy, Lock) then return s
 9  │  └ return LockList(s) // locked by another worker, try again

10  function Unite(a, b)
11  │  rootₐ := Find(a)
12  │  root_b := Find(b)
13  │  if rootₐ = root_b then return // already united
14  │  r := max(rootₐ, root_b) // largest index is the new root
15  │  q := min(rootₐ, root_b)
16  │  if ¬LockRoot(q) then return Unite(rootₐ, root_b) // try again
17  │  a_List := LockList(a) // lock the list states
18  │  b_List := LockList(b)
19  │  Swap(UF[a_List].next, UF[b_List].next) // non-atomic instruction
20  │  UF[q].parent := r // update parent (to some state in S(r))
21  │  do // update the worker set for the root
22  │  │  r := Find(r)
23  │  │  UF[r].workers := UF[r].workers ∪ UF[q].workers // atomic
24  │  while UF[r].parent ≠ r // ensure that we update the root
25  │  UF[a_List].list_status := Busy // unlock the locked list states
26  │  └ UF[b_List].list_status := Busy
```

Algorithm 5 The cyclic-list part of the iterable union-find ([2], Alg. 7)

```
 1 function PickFromList(a)
 2    do // wait until a is not locked (another worker may be uniting)
 3    |  if UF[a].list_status = Busy then return a
 4    while UF[a].list_status ≠ Done
 5    b := UF[a].next // a.list_status = Done (exit from do-while)
 6    if a = b then // self-loop of a Done state ⇒ all states are Done
 7    |  root_a := Find(a) // mark the SCC Explored, if not already done
 8    |  if CAS(UF[root_a].uf_status, Live, Explored) then
 9    |  |  report SCC root_a // optionally, report the SCC root
10    |  return NULL // no state to pick from an Explored SCC
11    do // also make sure that b is not locked, return b if it's Busy
12    |  if UF[b].list_status = Busy then return b
13    while UF[b].list_status ≠ Done // exit if status = Done
14    c := UF[b].next // we have a → b → c via next pointers
15    UF[a].next := c // a and b are Done ⇒ shrink the list: a → c
16    return PickFromList(c) // recursively traverse the cyclic list

17 function RemoveFromList(a)
18    while UF[a].list_status ≠ Done do // try again if a is locked
19    |  CAS(UF[a].list_status, Busy, Done) // only remove Busy state
```

Algorithm 6 Atomic Compare and Swap instruction ([2], Alg. 4)

```
 1 function CAS(x, a, b)
 2    if x = a then
 3    |  x := b
 4    |  return True
 5    else return False
```

This algorithm is supposed to run in one atomic step.

B Example Input Graphs for SCC Algorithm

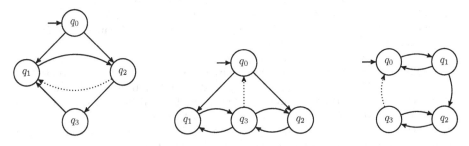

Above we show six small example input graphs on which we tested the TLA+ specification of the pseudocode in Appendix A. (The dotted lines are optional).

References

1. Barnat, J., Chaloupka, J., van de Pol, J.: Distributed algorithms for SCC decomposition. J. Log. Comput. **21**(1), 23–44 (2011). https://doi.org/10.1093/logcom/exp003
2. Bloemen, V.: Strong connectivity and shortest paths for checking models. Ph.D. thesis, University of Twente, July 2019. https://doi.org/10.3990/1.9789036547864
3. Bloemen, V., Laarman, A., van de Pol, J.: Multi-core on-the-fly SCC decompositiona. In: PPOPP, pp. 8:1–8:12. ACM (2016). https://doi.org/10.1145/2851141.2851161
4. Chen, R., Cohen, C., Lévy, J., Merz, S., Théry, L.: Formal proofs of Tarjan's strongly connected components algorithm in Why3, Coq and Isabelle. In: ITP, LIPIcs, vol. 141, pp. 13:1–13:19. Schloss Dagstuhl - Leibniz-Zentrum für Informatik (2019). https://doi.org/10.4230/LIPIcs.ITP.201a9.13
5. Dijkstra, E.W.: Finding the maximum strong components in a directed graph. In: Selected Writings on Computing: A Personal Perspective. Texts and Monographs in Computer Science, Springer, New York (1982). https://doi.org/10.1007/978-1-4612-5695-3
6. Esparza, J., Lammich, P., Neumann, R., Nipkow, T., Schimpf, A., Smaus, J.-G.: A Fully verified executable LTL model checker. In: Sharygina, N., Veith, H. (eds.) CAV 2013. LNCS, vol. 8044, pp. 463–478. Springer, Heidelberg (2013). https://doi.org/10.1007/978-3-642-39799-8_31
7. Kuppe, M.A., Lamport, L., Ricketts, D.: The TLA+ toolbox. In: F-IDE@FM. EPTCS, vol. 310, pp. 50–62 (2019). https://doi.org/10.4204/EPTCS.310.6
8. Lammich, P.: Verified efficient implementation of Gabow's strongly connected component algorithm. In: Klein, G., Gamboa, R. (eds.) Interactive Theorem Proving. ITP 2014, LNCS, vol. 8558. pp. 325–340. Springer, Cham (2014). https://doi.org/10.1007/978-3-319-08970-6_21
9. Lowe, G.: Concurrent depth-first search algorithms based on Tarjan's algorithm. Int. J. Softw. Tools Technol. Transf. **18**(2), 129–147 (2016). https://doi.org/10.1007/s10009-015-0382-1
10. McLendon-III, W., Hendrickson, B., Plimpton, S.J., Rauchwerger, L.: Finding strongly connected components in distributed graphs. J. Parallel Distrib. Comput. **65**(8), 901–910 (2005). https://doi.org/10.1016/j.jpdc.2005.03.007
11. Oortwijn, W., Huisman, M., Joosten, S.J.C., van de Pol, J.: Automated verification of parallel nested DFS. In: TACAS 2020. LNCS, vol. 12078, pp. 247–265. Springer, Cham (2020). https://doi.org/10.1007/978-3-030-45190-5_14
12. Pol, J.C.: Automated verification of nested DFS. In: Núñez, M., Güdemann, M. (eds.) FMICS 2015. LNCS, vol. 9128, pp. 181–197. Springer, Cham (2015). https://doi.org/10.1007/978-3-319-19458-5_12
13. Renault, E., Duret-Lutz, A., Kordon, F., Poitrenaud, D.: Variations on parallel explicit emptiness checks for generalized Büchi automata. Int. J. Softw. Tools Technol. Transf. **19**(6), 653–673 (2017). https://doi.org/10.1007/s10009-016-0422-5
14. Tarjan, R.E.: Depth-first search and linear graph algorithms. SIAM J. Comput. **1**(2), 146–160 (1972). https://doi.org/10.1137/0201010
15. Tarjan, R.E., van Leeuwen, J.: Worst-case analysis of set union algorithms. J. ACM **31**(2), 245–281 (1984). https://doi.org/10.1145/62.2160

16. Wimmer, S., Lammich, P.: Verified model checking of timed automata. In: Beyer, D., Huisman, M. (eds.) TACAS 2018. LNCS, vol. 10805, pp. 61–78. Springer, Cham (2018). https://doi.org/10.1007/978-3-319-89960-2_4

17. Yu, Y., Manolios, P., Lamport, L.: Model checking TLA$^+$ specifications. In: Pierre, L., Kropf, T. (eds.) CHARME 1999. LNCS, vol. 1703, pp. 54–66. Springer, Heidelberg (1999). https://doi.org/10.1007/3-540-48153-2_6

An IoT Digital Twin for Cyber-Security Defence Based on Runtime Verification

Jorge David de Hoz Diego[1], Anastasios Temperekidis[2],
Panagiotis Katsaros[1,2(✉)], and Charalambos Konstantinou[1]

[1] CEMSE Division, King Abdullah University of Science and Technology (KAUST),
Thuwal, Saudi Arabia
{jorge.diego,charalambos.konstantinou}@kaust.edu.sa
[2] Department of Informatics, Aristotle University of Thessaloniki,
Thessaloniki, Greece
{anastemp,katsaros}@csd.auth.gr

Abstract. A security decoupling approach for IoT device communications is presented, based on a Digital Twin with runtime verification capabilities. The solution proposed assumes that a local agent (security module) can be deployed to the IoT device by the IoT server. The runtime verification approach implemented in the Digital Twin detects possible violations of protected communications from either a remote device or a local compromised process and provides timely and valuable information for countering a potential cyber-security attack. Moreover, only a subset of the observed traffic needs to be monitored, which induces negligible overhead and allows deploying the Digital Twin in IoT devices with limited computational resources. Runtime verification was implemented by adopting a rule-based approach for monitoring parametric events, i.e. the packets that carry data.

Keywords: Security-by-design · IoT · Digital twin · Runtime verification

1 Introduction

Security needs to be a top priority in the design of Internet-of-Things (IoT) systems [1]. However, in IoT application development we are witnessing lately a pervasive trend towards using third-party components [2], which complicates the enforcement of security guarantees on IoT device communications and their preservation after software updates to counter new cybersecurity threats [3,4].

This work was supported in part by King Abdullah University of Science and Technology (Research Translation Funding REI/1/4851-01-01).

This research has been co-funded by the European Union and Greek national funds through the Operational Program Competitiveness, Entrepreneurship and Innovation, under the call RESEARCH - CREATE - INNOVATE II (project code: T2EDK-02617).

T. Margaria and B. Steffen (Eds.): ISoLA 2022, LNCS 13701, pp. 556–574, 2022.
https://doi.org/10.1007/978-3-031-19849-6_31

A promising perspective is a secure-by-design approach for IoT systems development [5]. Such an approach builds security into the system by relying on security modules to provide certain guarantees [6], while allowing the application modules to interact transparently. Via proper security decoupling, the developer does not need to know the inner mechanisms of the security modules used.

However, the aforementioned challenge cannot be tackled in a straightforward manner, whereas functionality and reduced time to market are urgent priorities to which manufacturers pay preference attention when designing software [7]. IoT verticals are usually devised as a specific solution for a problem in response to a detected market niche [8], while features of major importance, such as security or interoperability, are not taken into due consideration. When new cybersecurity threats arise, fast-devised patches may eventually break interoperability with third-party components [9] or applications. In other cases, the vulnerability mitigation is delayed, due to the application dependence on unpatched or legacy application programming interfaces (APIs) [10].

Secure (local or remote) communications usually rely on an API or framework to provide necessary guarantees to application functions. Though the API is intended to be stable in time, it may be subject to changes that trigger additional application updates. Instead of this, we advocate an application-agnostic modularity paradigm through securing communications. According to the IoTsafe security architecture [11,12] (Fig. 1), the security decoupled communication for IoT devices can be achieved through a transparent proxification relying exclusively on the network sockets API (see the socket proxy in the IoT device of Fig. 1) that is very unlikely to change in the foreseeable future [13].

In this paper, we leverage this security decoupling concept and propose deploying into the security architecture of the IoT device a *digital twin (DT) for the runtime verification* of the IoT device communication. DTs are virtual models used to analyse and diagnose a system's operation in real-time [14]. The role of the DT in our case is to replicate the device communication and any changes of it over time by keeping track of the security status of used sockets to detect possible interference of communications from external devices/internal processes that should not be allowed by the socket used. Unlike a Digital Shadow [15], the DT can take immediate action when a situation is detected to update the physical system accordingly. It relies on runtime verification of a small subset of the traffic (packets rejected by the secure socket), which induces negligible monitoring overhead, and makes the approach applicable to IoT devices that are characterized by limited computational resources. This also contributes to reducing the workload of any other DT in the server monitoring the status of the network, as the DTs on the devices will induce only limited overhead in the server, when a potentially harmful situation is detected.

The solution proposed supports an *holistic evaluation of communication protocols in diverse deployments*, as opposed to DTs in related literature [16–19]. Due to the security decoupling, the IoT device communications are securely end-to-end forwarded by a local proxy through a virtual network space in the server (shown as a dotted line rectangle in Fig. 1). Thus, the isolated communica-

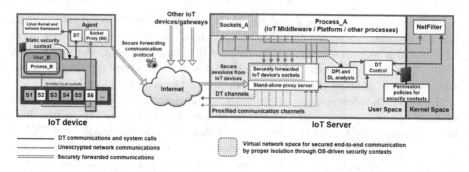

Fig. 1. Security decoupled communications to allow digital twin (DT) monitoring and control in IoT devices [12].

tions can use non-secure protocols, such as the constrained application protocol (CoAP) instead of CoAP secure (CoAPs). Furthermore, it is easy to support the transparent deployment of other DTs, specific to various IoT device types, due to the safe use of unencrypted payloads by properly isolated communications. This eliminates the need to deal with the protocol encryption mechanisms, separately for each different IoT device and simplifies any required real-time operation involving deep packet inspection [20].

Formal verification through runtime monitoring ensures the isolation required for the communications to run securely, as per the operating system (OS)-driven security context (SC) provided by IoTsafe. More concretely, we focus in this work on a careful review of the workings of the static SCs in the IoT device, since the operation in a dynamic server environment is based on these fundamental concepts as well. The runtime monitoring actions of the DT occur in the agent deployed for security decoupled communications (Fig. 1), providing major advantages in terms of limiting the monitoring overhead. The agent sets the SCs locally in the device, and monitors any attempt of violating the isolation by any remote machine or local process. The DT only has to process the rejected packets derived from unauthorised traffic, therefore minimising the monitoring overhead. Furthermore, this local computation alleviates the computing load of the DT in the server, as the agent efficiently notifies only of the events subject to further investigation. This agent can also take early mitigation actions, contributing to considerably reducing the risks derived from a potential attack escalation.

The rest of the paper is structured as follows. Section 2 reviews related initiatives, research works, and discusses how our proposed solution compares with them. In Sect. 3, we describe the security decoupling architecture and the role of the DT for IoT device communications. Section 4 introduces our run-time verification approach, for the communications in the IoT devices and presents preliminary experimental results for a log obtained from a prototype implementation of the IoTsafe architecture. Finally, in Sect. 5, the paper concludes with a critical overview of the current developments toward the operational deployment of the solution proposed and its future research prospects.

2   Related Work

Most of the current cybersecurity issues are related to deficiencies in the application programming and the lack of modularity. These defects, connected to software architecture flaws, are prone to persist in the system for significant periods of time, increasing the maintenance costs [21]. Software using low cohesion and highly coupled modules is usually correlated with common bugs difficult to eradicate. Likewise, poorly coded modifications or work-around measures generate patches, but without consideration of the software architecture's original flaws, those patches end up incurring technical debt [22]. This can lead to unstable interfaces between modules, difficult to support in the mid-long term [23].

The relevance of adequate software design methodologies raises when considering the cost of addressing bugs at a post-product release stage. This may account on average for more than 30x of the original cost of resolving the same issue in design stages [24]. Furthermore, in security-related concerns, this cost may rise up to 100× [25]. These figures could justify that outdated devices should be decommissioned with new versions with better functionalities. However, the European Union (EU) regulatory bodies, in pursuit of the recent Circular Economy Action Plan, have focused on *"electronics, information and communication technologies (ICT) as a priority for implementing the right to repair, including the right to update obsolete software."* [26]. Thus, the manufacturers will have to provide full support for their devices and promote a longer lifespan of the products, or in case they become discontinued, such products should become open-source [27].

One feasible strategy proposed to increase the lifetime of products in the Circular Economy refers to the Servitization concept [28]. With this approach, businesses are encouraged to provide services derived from their products. This should contribute to prolonging their lifespan thanks to a renovated interest in extending the support by leveraging software modularity. As an example, captured from the EU RECLAIM project [29], complementary services can be provided from legacy products after including new software modules: *"software modules can be installed in the machine itself, as a DT, and predictive models about maintenance, degradation and quality can be built based on collected data, and afterwards resold to the new customer"* [30].

The EU Commission is aware of these challenges and fosters the modularity of software to simplify the security certification of composited products [8,31]. The software composability will depend on how these modules are interconnected [32] while taking into account the context of use in force by regulations, such as the Cybersecurity Act assurance levels [33]. This will allow an IoT device to be composed of different (hardware and software) modules with a high degree of independence from each other. If one module becomes insecure, it can be replaced without affecting the others and the security of the entire device can be re-certified with just a new certification of the new module. This has been put into practice with Payment-Card-Industry [34] compliant payment methods, e.g., a payment kiosk is composed of different hardware and software. In this case, the payment module is hardware and software independent from the rest of the device, allowing a more inexpensive way of devising and maintaining payment kiosks in hotels, rentals, grocery stores, etc., by reusing security modules.

Devices running DT for runtime verification are considered resilient systems that can self-monitor, self-diagnose and, ultimately, self-heal [35]. In [36], the authors apply this to satellites, to improve their protection against cyber attacks. However, a DT of the complete system has to be operated on the ground and requires a special security protocol for synchronization with the satellite. Extrapolation of this scheme to IoT environments may not be feasible because of the associated costs. However, if modularity is applied, this would allow deploying only the DTs of critical assets of the device for runtime verification.

Recent works in IoT security decoupling [11,12], demonstrate that it is feasible to develop independent security modules able to operate transparently to the core IoT device applications. This allows these applications, even legacy ones no longer maintained and insecure, to delegate transparently major security concerns into the security modules. Thus, the operation of the IoT device application is facilitated in terms of communication and security, as the security module can be managed independently from the application. This simplifies distributed architectures through scalability and resilience. New functionalities can be added to the IoT device application without redesigning security modules. Likewise, in the event of a failure or a new vulnerability, the security module can be upgraded independently from the IoT device application, so that the system continues to function as intended [37].

To improve cyber-resilience, these security modules can be supported by reduced DTs specifically devised to provide runtime verification of the relevant device communications. Conversely, despite applying DTs in diverse industrial systems, only a few are destined for networking purposes. In [38], a holistic DT architecture for the industrial IoT (IIoT) is presented, where the network component is considered through the adoption of the concept of a network digital twin (NDT). The main purpose of the NDT is to enable quick validation of networking solutions in an industrial environment, since it is continuously linked to the physical world from the early design stage to the production phase. The NDT enables performing the what-if analysis. This allows operators to detect network misconfigurations, bottleneck links, observe network performance in case of disasters or predict future network behaviors under different events without impact in the real world [39]. However, end-to-end holistic modeling of communication is lacking, i.e., a deterministic model of the communications socket-to-socket. This would facilitate further detailed analysis of situations in which the compromised device attempts a local attack inside the device on other services. This would contribute to early detection to prevent its spreading to other devices.

The scalability and modularity of a DT refer to twins of individual machines or parts that can be combined to form a twin of a larger system, but there are no works related to this [40]. This is in part due to the different formats, protocols, and standards that prevent current DT tools to be integrated and used simultaneously for a particular objective [41]. However, if the modularity of the physical system is preserved in DTs, then standardization and software independence should become feasible also in the DTs. This could allow the DT of a particular infrastructure or device to be "shareable" with different infrastructures or devices. Thus, DTs should become affordable to IoT deployments that currently operate without them and could benefit from their advantages. In order to achieve this, we propose leveraging on security decoupling of the IoT device application at a communication level [42], to allow a DT to monitor and control its communications transparently through the agent devised for security decoupling.

3 Digital Twin and Application-Agnostic Security Modules for IoT Communication

3.1 IoTsafe Security Architecture

In Fig. 1, we present the IoT device in which the security decoupling is applied for a communication of the IoT application (*Process_B*) addressed to the *agent*. *Process_B* has delegated the security concerns of the communication protocol to a *security module* featured by an *agent* of the server. This *agent* forwards securely and transparently the communication to the server, while the local communications between *Process_B* and the *agent* are isolated by an OS-driven static *security context* (SC) configured by the *agent* through the network framework.

This approach embodies the modularity and independence features required to allow portability and interoperability of the DT with other devices/systems. To allow for a straightforward application-agnostic implementation, five conditions are necessary, so that the kernel and its modules need no customization:

a. the *agent* must be application-agnostic and operate transparently to *Process_B*;
b. the kernel must provide privilege separation, to allow *Process_B* to run in a different account to the rest of the processes;
c. the kernel will include a network framework with privilege separation;
d. the network framework must be capable to apply filtering and marking traffic rules, following a stateful policy (responses are forwarded back), and
e. the marking rules must be applied to the traffic in the same order as entered into the system and before the filtering rules.

These conditions are usually met by default in standard implementations of the Linux kernel. In this scheme, the *agent* together with the network framework can collect and process raw data of the ongoing communications. Later on, this information can be exploited by other DTs on the server (Fig. 2). The predictability of IoT devices behaviour is leveraged by the security decoupling module (*agent*) and the network framework to limit the possible communications to only those expected to occur under normal operation. Any unauthorised communication is detected and rejected by the network framework and monitored and logged by the DT in the *agent*.

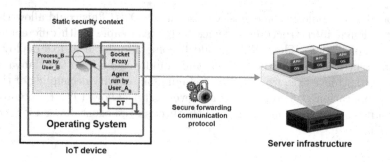

Fig. 2. IoT device with security decoupling including a portable application-agnostic DT agent for network security runtime verification.

3.2   Transparent Secure Communication with Security Decoupling

As it was previously explained, the security decoupling scheme of Fig. 2 does not require any modification in the IoT application or custom kernel modules. It exploits common functionalities available in POSIX-like systems, such as Linux and some RTOS systems like FreeRTOS.

The setup of the SC by the *agent* to allow isolation in the IoT device communication (Fig. 3) comprises the following steps [11,42]:

- The IoT device kernel boots and the first process to run is a super server such as *inetd* [43] which will manage all privileged ports including the *socket proxy*.
- The super server has a configuration that binds the *socket proxy* to prevent any process but the *agent* to bind it.
- Once the *agent* is executed, it takes control of the socket and deploys through it a *socket proxy* that securely forwards traffic back and forth to a particular service of the IoT platform in the *server infrastructure*.
- During the booting process, the *agent* deploys some filtering and marking rules to isolate the traffic between the *Process_B* and the *Socket_Proxy* by protecting the local IP addresses to be used:
  - (F1) Any traffic between a protected and a non-protected IP address is discarded.
  - (F2) Any traffic from inside the device to a local protected IP address with TOS = 0 is discarded (TOS is the IP field Type-Of-Service).
  - (M1) Any local traffic with destination a protected IP address is marked with TOS = 0.

With these rules, any port using a protected IP, either privileged or ephemeral, is virtually isolated. A process cannot send/receive packets in any port of the protected local address, since those packets will contain a TOS!=0. This implies:

- An external device may mark its packets and send them to a local protected socket, but F1 will discard them as protected addresses only can communicate with a local protected address in the same device.

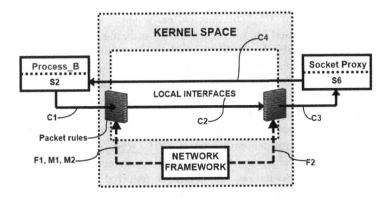

Fig. 3. Isolated communication between an IoT device user process (*Process_B*) and a local internal socket (*Socket_Proxy*). The communication between *Process_B* and the IoT platform in the server is addressed transparently through the *Socket_Proxy*, due to a static SC that allows local communication inside the IoT device, while preserving the isolation [11].

- An internal process may send packets to a local protected socket, but F2 will discard them, since the default marking is TOS=0.
- An internal process may mark its packets with TOS!=0 and address them to a local protected socket, but M1 will mark them with TOS=0 when they leave the user space and enter the kernel space, and then discarded by F2.

An SC is defined (source of a traffic communication request, and destination socket of such a traffic request) by the Linux account running the application. This SC allows communication from any process from the user account to proceed to the protected destination socket. In Fig. 2, the SC is configured as *ConnIDUser_B (Process_B), Direct Proxy*. This SC is referred to as *ConnID* and implies that any traffic from any application ran by *User_B* to the *Direct Proxy* will be marked with TOS=ConnID (M2). *Process_B* and *Direct Proxy* use a protected local IP to communicate as follows (Fig. 3): *Process_B* sends packets to *Socket_Proxy* (C1). These packets, even if marked, are set with TOS=ConnID upon entering the kernel space through the ephemeral socket S2 (socket numbers used are those shown in Fig. 1). Such packets proceed (C2) through the local interfaces to the *socket proxy* S6, and as they have a TOS=!0 they are successfully addressed (C3) to their destination. Any response of the socket proxy is allowed to be forwarded back, as the behaviour of the filtering and marking rules of the network framework follow a state-full firewall policy. If *Process_B* uses a local IP not protected by the F1 rule, the traffic will be discarded upon entering the kernel space.

The SC set by the *agent* through the network framework will allow only the authorised traffic. All rejected packets by the kernel due to any unauthorised communication can be monitored by the DT through the kernel log. This will allow the DT to detect misconfigurations or attacks addressed to isolated sockets, without a valid SC previously established to allow such communication.

The performance of this communication scheme and its overhead have been thoroughly discussed for various scenarios utilizing SSH-based proxy techniques [11]. The attainable bandwidth and the time required to complete diverse load tests favor our scheme, when compared to the standard TLS/DTLS security in scenarios with a realistic (not too small) communication payload. The results also apply to constrained IoT devices communicating in environments with high interference [12]. Regarding the latency, it is not significantly increased in high-delay channels [44]. However, in low-delay environments, further elaboration is required. The various implementations of SSH server/client provide different results based on the technology they are built upon and their default parameters. For low latency scenarios, fine-tuning is required in aspects such as the sliding window communication protocol implemented in SSH. Another possible avenue of research is the latest transport protocol QUIC [45] over UDP and its implementation in SSH [46], which can provide the improved performance features we require.

3.3   Monitoring Testbed

In order to validate the correct isolation of the local communications, we designed a monitoring testbed (Fig. 4) that consists of the following:

- *Process_B* (IoT device application) will be featured by a program (Telnet client) sending a random word every second to a mock local proxy of the IoT platform service.
- The local mock *socket proxy* is featured with an echo server that mimics a simple IoT platform by replying with the same word that *Process_B* sends.
- This communication occurs in an SC {User2, Proxy, ConnID}
- *User2* runs a *Process_B* and has a user identifier (UID) of 102 that for simplicity will match ConnID.
- The echo server runs at the local socket 127.0.0.1:7777.
- The only local IP address protected and reserved for communication through security contexts is 127.0.0.1.

The testbed was conducted in a virtual machine running Centos 7 with a Linux kernel 3.10.0. No modifications were applied to the system, kernel, or any of its modules. The testbed starts with the *agent* protecting the local IP address 127.0.0.1 by complete isolation according to the rules F1, F2, and M1. Then, the *agent* sets up the SC by including rule M2. The DT will monitor any rejected packet by the kernel and this will allow determining the proper actions to address the detected situation. The considered tests are the following:

- Test 1: A connection attempt from User1 to 127.0.0.1:7777 (S6) without a valid SC.
- Test 2: A connection attempt from User1 to 127.0.0.1:ephemeral_socket (S2) without a valid SC. The ephemeral_socket includes the port in use by the client of the User2 account sending random payload to the echo server.

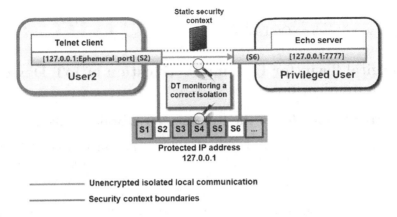

Fig. 4. Proposed testbed to monitor the isolation of the security context under different scenarios.

- Test 3: A connection attempt from User2 to 127.0.0.1:7778 without a valid SC.
- Test 4: A connection attempt from User2 to 127.0.0.1:ephemeral_socket (S2) without a valid SC. Even when User2 has an SC to communicate towards 127.0.0.1:7777, communicating to a socket opened by a process owned by the same User2 is not allowed without the appropriate SC.
- Test 5: A connection attempt from User2 to 127.0.0.1:7777 from the unprotected local IP address 127.0.0.2. Even when User2 has an SC to communicate towards 127.0.0.1:7777, communicating from an unprotected socket (unprotected IP address) is not allowed.
- Test 6: A connection attempt to 127.0.0.1:7777 from a public address 69.197.185.94. Public addresses are unprotected and the related traffic addressed to/from a protected IP address is always discarded.

The tests ran in a loop with a pause every 5 s. The DT was monitoring the rejected packets that may represent possible misconfiguration or attack attempts. In the device, a set of other Linux services exist [47], and some of them make use of the local IP address periodically. These programs were considered as possible threats in the tests and the system had to monitor their activity.

In a real scenario in which the DT operates in an IoT device, the DT could leverage the information inferred by the monitor to deploy timely countermeasures. The server side can further improve this initial response thanks to the aggregated information of all DTs of the different IoT devices. Thus, the servers could reliably support threat models such as STRIDE [48]. Likewise, implementing this type of security-decoupled communication scheme may be considered a special type of middleboxes [49], in which it is possible to leverage further information derived from the unencrypted payload of the packets. Thus, the server-side DT could also support a complementary threat-driven approach beyond the network scope, such as OCTAVE [50].

4 Digital Twin for Runtime Verification of IoT Device Communications

4.1 Formal Definition of the Runtime Verification Problem

We denote by $ip_{add} \in \mathcal{D}_{IP}$, a variable with values from the domain of IP addresses $\mathcal{D}_{IP} = \{127.0.0.1, 127.0.0.2, 69.197.185.94, \ldots\}$ from/to which the packets are communicated. Also, with $p \in \mathcal{D}_{ports}$ we denote a variable representing a port from the domain of ports $\mathcal{D}_{ports} = \{7777, 7778, \ldots\}$ and with $u \in \mathcal{D}_{uids}$ a user, when $\mathcal{D}_{uids} \cup \{u_{pr}\}$ denotes the domain of users, including the privileged user u_{pr}.

A socket $s \in \mathcal{D}_{IP} \times \mathcal{D}_{ports}$ is defined as the pair (ip_{add}, p) of the IP address ip_{add} and port p for which s has been created.

The following predicates (facts) are used:

- $protected(ip_{add})$ is **true** if ip_{add} is protected
- $remote(ip_{add})$ is **true** if ip_{add} is a remote IP address
- $isolated(s)$ is **true** if s is isolated
- $sc(ip_{add}, p, u)$ is **true** if a SC has been configured for the socket (ip_{add}, p) and the user $u \in \mathcal{D}_{uids} \cup \{u_{pr}\}$
- $tainted(s)$ is **true** if s is tainted

The DT implements the following axioms, for all $ip_{add} \in \mathcal{D}_{IP}$ and $p \in \mathcal{D}_{ports}$:

- $protected(ip_{add}) \rightarrow isolated((ip_{add}, p))$
- $\forall u, u' \in \mathcal{D}_{uids} \cup \{u_{pr}\}: sc(ip_{add}, p, u) \wedge sc(ip_{add}, p, u') \rightarrow (u = u') \vee ((u = u_{pr}) \vee (u' = u_{pr}))$

The DT runtime monitor is formalized as a *data automaton* [51], a suitable formalism for specifying runtime monitors for *traces* of *data-carrying events*. Such events are given as tuples $id(v_1, \ldots, v_n)$ that consist of an event name id and a list of values $v_1, \ldots v_n$. If $e \in Event$ is a data-carrying event, of the form mentioned previously, then a trace $\sigma \in Trace = Event^*$ is a list of events.

The events monitored by the DT are:

- `rejected(src, dst, spt, dpt, uid)`
  refers to a rejected packet originated from IP address `src` and source port `spt` and sent to IP address `dst` and destination port `dpt` by the user `uid`
- `SC(ip, port, uid)`
  refers to configuring a SC for the socket at the IP address `ip` and port `port`, for the user `uid`
- `protect(ip)`
  refers to configuring the IP address `ip` as protected
- `socket(ip, port)`
  refers to configuring a socket at the IP address `ip` and port `port`

The states $st \in State$ of a data automaton are parameterized with arbitrary values given by expressions in an expression language, i.e. $st = id(v_1, \ldots, v_n)$. Thus, the set of possible states may be infinite, depending on the value domains.

The states of our DT are parameterized by the socket identifiers, i.e. $q_0(s)$ means that the socket $s = (ip_{add}, p)$ is in q_0. For any socket s, we can have one of the following:

q_0: $\neg$ $isolated(s)$, which denotes the fact that s is initialized

q_1: $isolated(s)$ and $\forall u \in \mathcal{D}_{uids} \cup \{u_{pr}\} : \neg sc(ip_{add}, p, u)$, which denotes the fact that s is initialized but no SC is enforced

q_2: $isolated(s)$ and $\exists u \in \mathcal{D}_{uids} \cup \{u_{pr}\} : sc(ip_{add}, p, u)$, which denotes the fact that s is initialized and a SC is enforced

The behaviour of a data automaton is defined by *transitions*. Every such transition is specified as a *pattern* followed by :: to introduce a *condition* and then by $\rightarrow$ to define one or more *actions*. When the pattern matches an event or a state of the data automaton, all its formal parameters match the parameters of the event/state. If the pattern matches and the condition evaluates to true, the action(s) is/are executed, leaving the current state, unless it is an *always* state. In the latter case, whenever a transition is executed out of the state, an implicit self-loop keeps the state in memory to monitor further events.

When the **error** action happens, an error is reported that refers to the violation of the monitored property. For the DT, the **error** action happens, when for some socket s:

$$tainted(s)$$

i.e. s becomes tainted. In this case, the DT deactivates s, enforces action A_2 and notifies the IoT server by sending the error trace. This includes only the events (rejected packets) that contributed to the error, which is useful information to potentially apply additional countermeasures and investigate the cyber-security threat encountered.

The data automaton for the DT is formally represented by a labelled transition system $(S, Event, \rightarrow, i, F)$, where $S \subseteq State$ is the set of all possible states, $Event$ is the set of parameterized events mentioned previously, $\rightarrow \subseteq S \times (Event \times \mathbb{B}) \times S$ is a transition relation, which defines transitions from a state to another, as a result of an observed event, $i \subseteq S$ is the set of initial states (noted as *init*) and $F \subseteq S$ the set of final states.

Hereafter, we specify the transitions of the DT data automaton, as it was implemented using the rule-based runtime verification system LogFire [52]. Isolated sockets of the device are represented as blocking sockets, i.e., sending and receiving are mutually exclusive actions and only one communication per socket is allowed [53, 54].

monitor DTMonitor {

    protect(ip) $\rightarrow$ *protected*(ip)

    socket(ip, port) $\rightarrow$ $q_0(ip, port)$

$q_0(ip, port) :: protected(ip) \rightarrow q_1(ip, port), \mathbf{A_0}$

SC(ip,port,uid) $\rightarrow sc(ip, port, uid)$

$q_1(ip, port) :: sc(ip, port, \_) \rightarrow q_2(ip, port), \mathbf{A_1}$

rejected(src,dst,spt,dpt,uid) $:: protected(src) \land \_(src, spt)$
$\rightarrow \mathbf{A_2}$, error

rejected(src,dst,spt,dpt,uid) $:: \neg protected(src) \land \_(dst, dpt)$
$\rightarrow$ if $remote(src)$ then
    if $sc(dst, dpt, \_)$
        $\mathbf{A_3}, q_2(dst, dpt)$
    else
        $\mathbf{A_3}, q_1(dst, dpt)$
  else
    if $sc(dst, dpt, \_)$
        $\mathbf{A_4}, q_2(dst, dpt)$
    else
        $\mathbf{A_4}, q_1(dst, dpt)$

$q_0(ip, port)\{$
   $protected(ip) \rightarrow$ **ok**
$\}$

$q_1(ip, port)\{$
   $sc(ip, port, \_) \rightarrow$ **ok**
$\}$
$\}$

To easily follow the rules of the DTMonitor, we depict in Fig. 5 the *parameterized socket states* in the example of Fig. 2, when a single SC is established[1]. The actions A_0 - A_4 enforced by the DT are also explained, along with the inferred information (S_1 - S_3) when a rejected packet is processed.

The behaviour of the DTMonitor includes a number of transitions for its initial states that are by default considered as **always** states. It also includes two transitions that are enabled only in the $q_0(ip, port)$ and $q_1(ip, port)$ states. These transitions are used to update the parameterized state of a socket, i.e. to leave from its current state.

4.2 Runtime Verification for the Monitoring Testbed

We present the results obtained by the DTMonitor, for the tests described in Sect. 3.3. In all cases, the DTMonitor reports the event (rejected packet) monitored and when a socket becomes tainted (error) it also reports the monitor transitions that have lead to the error.

---

[1] In case of a non-blocking isolated socket, in (1) and (2) the socket could send or receive a packet independently of its current state.

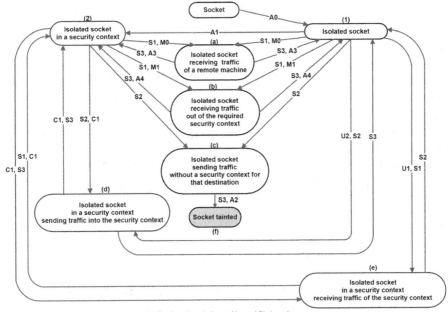

MO: Remote machine
M1: Local machine

S1: Socket receives communication
S2: Socket sends the communication
S3: Socket terminates communication

C0: SC not in force for the socket operation
C1: SC in force for the socket operation

A0: The Agent inserts the marking and filtering rules
A1: The Agent inserts the marking SC rule
A2: The DT taints the socket, terminates all processes from the user using the socket and bans the local user
A3: The DT taints the remote machine
A4: The DT terminates the local socket source of the transmission, all processes from the user using the socket (not the socket of the diagram that receives the communication) and bans the local user
U1: Communication received by a user's process as a response to a valid communication under a security context applied to the user. This occurs thanks to the stateful behavior of the network framework.
U2: Communication sent by a user's process through this socket according to a valid security context applying to the user

Fig. 5. State diagram of the isolated sockets in the IoT device, for the case where only a static SC is applied and the isolated sockets are set as blocking.

Test 1:
```
'reject("127.0.0.1","127.0.0.1","0x00","0x00","37700","7777","101")
rejected_package_prot_ip
execute S3 & A2 ->uid:101 src:127.0.0.1 spt:37700 socketState:1
------------------------
*** ERROR SOCKET TAINTED
------------------------
[1] 'protect("127.0.0.1") --> 'Protected("127.0.0.1")
[3] 'socket("127.0.0.1","37700") --> 'Socket(0,"127.0.0.1","37700")
[3] 'socket("127.0.0.1","37700") --> 'Socket(1,"127.0.0.1","37700")
[12]'reject("127.0.0.1","127.0.0.1","0x00","0x00","37700","7777","101")
--> 'Fail("ERROR SOCKET TAINTED")
```

Test 2:
```
'reject("127.0.0.1","127.0.0.1","0x00","0x00","45492","46846","101")
rejected_package_prot_ip
execute S3 & A2 ->uid:101 src:127.0.0.1 spt:45492 socketState:1
```

The monitor transitions to the error are omitted due to space limitations.

Test 3:
```
'reject("127.0.0.1","127.0.0.1","0x00","0x00","37704","7778","102")
rejected_package_prot_ip
execute S3 & A2 ->uid:102 src:127.0.0.1 spt:37704 socketState:1
```

The monitor transitions to the error are omitted due to space limitations.

Test 4:
```
'reject("127.0.0.1","127.0.0.1","0x00","0x00","45496","46846","102")
rejected_package_prot_ip
execute S3 & A2 ->uid:102 src:127.0.0.1 spt:45496 socketState:1
```

The monitor transitions to the error are omitted due to space limitations.

Test 5:
```
'reject("127.0.0.2","127.0.0.1","0x00","0x00","33637","7777","102")
rejected_package_prot_ip
execute S3 & A4 -> uid:102 dst:127.0.0.1, dpt:7777 socketState:2
```

Test 6:
```
'reject("69.197.185.94","127.0.0.1","0x00","0x00","45575","7777","101")
rejected_package_prot_ip
(execute S3 & A3 -> uid:101 dst:127.0.0.1, dpt:7777 socketState:2)
```

The DT operates successfully by monitoring only the rejected packets. Under normal operation (with no rejected packets), this would imply that the overhead is negligible. To validate this assumption, we ran the described tests for one hour. A DT applied to all packets would have to monitor 26451 communication events. The proposed DT implementation requires monitoring only 1689 events, accounting for a reduction of 93% of the original overhead.

5   Conclusions and Future Work

IoT environments demand technical solutions to tackle security threats, but without the detriment of any of the stakeholders involved. DT technology provides the means to monitor and control a distributed system, such as most IoT deployments, but the particulars of each of the verticals involved, render the adoption of DTs difficult, due to the inherent cost. Modularity applied to DTs can provide portability and application-agnostic implementations that could fulfill the constraints of IoT deployments. To address this priority, we explore in this paper the advantages of security decoupling approaches. In particular, we focus on an application level to leverage the independence of the security modules (Agents) towards incorporating a DT there. A monitoring DT in an IoT device with security-decoupled applications and modularity preserved, provides multiple benefits when compared with standard DT implementations:

- A single DT for network runtime monitoring can fit multiple IoT devices and applications implementing security decoupled strategies in communications.

- Monitoring of the entire network can be achieved in a distributed fashion across the IoT ecosystem.
- Each device contributes to the network monitoring by detecting early any unexpected situation or threat related to network communications or local compromised applications behaving awkwardly.
- The overhead is dramatically reduced in the server thanks to this distributed architecture based on *agents*. Ideally, the DTs of the *agents* only communicate to the server the traffic related to unexpected situations preventing the server from analysing all IoT devices' activity logs in real-time.

To validate the correct isolation of communications in the IoT device's security-decoupled architecture, we have presented a DT for the runtime verification of sockets operating under a security context and a testbed considering various scenarios. We concluded that the isolation of the local traffic is successful and the DT monitor was able to detect and track the threats derived from unauthorised communication attempts to the local protected IP or any of the isolated sockets in the device. In a real scenario, this allows the DT to take countermeasures autonomously to prevent a rapid escalation of the threat to other devices/systems.

In future work, we will study the server counterpart of the security decoupling architecture. The analysis of the sockets operating in a system with a static security context will be further elaborated to support the behaviour of multiple dynamic security contexts. We will evaluate potential latency increments related to proxied communications and feasible mitigating actions by tuning the proxy parameters and transport protocols. We also expect substantial performance improvements in the server-side DT, allowing real-time monitoring of any possible attack in the IoT network thanks to the achieved reduced overhead of this work.

References

1. Arora, A., Kaur, A., Bhushan, B., Saini, H.: Security concerns and future trends of internet of things. In: 2019 2nd International Conference on Intelligent Computing, Instrumentation and Control Technologies (ICICICT), vol. 1, pp. 891–896, July 2019
2. Mikkonen, T., Taivalsaari, A.: Software reuse in the era of opportunistic design. IEEE Softw. **36**(3), 105–111 (2019)
3. Thung, F., et al.: Automated deprecated-api usage update for android apps: how far are we? In: 2020 IEEE 27th International Conference on Software Analysis, Evolution and Reengineering (SANER), pp. 602–611 (2020)
4. Xenofontos, C., Zografopoulos, I., Konstantinou, C., Jolfaei, A., Khan, M.K., Choo, K.-K.R.: Consumer, commercial, and industrial IOT (in)security: attack taxonomy and case studies. IEEE Internet Things J. **9**(1), 199–221 (2022)
5. Corser, G.: Internet of things (IoT) security best practices. IEEE Internet Initiative, Tech. Rep., 2017. https://standards.ieee.org/wp-content/uploads/import/documents/other/whitepaper-internet-of-things-2017-dh-v1.pdf. Accessed 25 Apr 2022

6. Maroof, U., Shaghaghi, A., Michelin, R., Jha, S.: iRECOVer: patch your IoT on-the-fly. Futu. Gene. Comput. Syst. **132**, 178–193 (2022) [Online]. https://www.sciencedirect.com/science/article/pii/S0167739X22000589

7. Cheruvu, S., Kumar, A., Smith, N., Wheeler, D.M.: Conceptualizing the Secure Internet of Things, pp. 1–21. Apress, Berkeley (2020), [Online]. https://doi.org/10.1007/978-1-4842-2896-8_1

8. E. U. A. for Network and I. Security: IoT security standards gap analysis. mapping of existing standards against requirements on security and privacy in the area of IoT (v1.0). ENISA, Tech. Rep. (2018). https://www.enisa.europa.eu/publications/cybersecurity-certification-eucc-candidate-scheme-v1-1.1. Accessed 25 Apr 2022

9. Mohd Aman, A.H., Yadegaridehkordi, E., Attarbashi, Z.S., Hassan, R., Park, Y.-J.: A survey on trend and classification of internet of things reviews. IEEE Access **8**, 111 763–111 782 (2020)

10. Anand, P., Singh, Y., Selwal, A., Singh, P.K., Felseghi, R.A., Raboaca, M.S.: IoVT: Internet of vulnerable things? Threat architecture, attack surfaces, and vulnerabilities in internet of things and its applications towards smart grids. Energies **13**(18) (2020). https://www.mdpi.com/1996-1073/13/18/4813

11. De Hoz Diego, J.D., Saldana, J., Fernández-Navajas, J., Ruiz-Mas, J.: IOTsafe, decoupling security from applications for a safer IoT. IEEE Access **7**, 29 942–29 962 (2019)

12. de Hoz Diego, J.D., Saldana, J., Fernández-Navajas, J., Ruiz-Mas, J.: Decoupling security from applications in COAP-based IoT devices. IEEE Internet of Things J. **7**(1), 467–476 (2020)

13. Papastergiou, G., et al.: De-ossifying the internet transport layer: a survey and future perspectives. IEEE Commun. Surveys Tutor. **19**(1), 619–639, Firstquarter (2017)

14. Grieves, M.: Digital twin: manufacturing excellence through virtual factory replication. Digital Twin Inst. Tech. Rep., March 2015

15. Bergs, T., Gierlings, S., Auerbach, T., Klink, A., Schraknepper, D., Augspurger, T.: The concept of digital twin and digital shadow in manufacturing. Procedia CIRP **101**, 81–84 (2021), 9th CIRP Conference on High Performance Cutting. [Online]. https://www.sciencedirect.com/science/article/pii/S2212827121006612

16. Eckhart, M., Ekelhart, A.: Towards security-aware virtual environments for digital twins. In: Proceedings of the 4th ACM Workshop on Cyber-Physical System Security, series. CPSS 2018, pp. 61–72. Association for Computing Machinery, New York (2018) [Online]. https://doi.org/10.1145/3198458.3198464

17. G.A. for Connected Industries and Automation. Using digital twins to integrate 5g into production networks. Tech. Rep. (2021). https://www.enisa.europa.eu/publications/cybersecurity-certification-eucc-candidate-scheme-v1-1.1. Accessed 25 Apr 2022

18. Khan, L.U., Saad, W., Niyato, D., Han, Z., Hong, C.S.: Digital-twin-enabled 6g: Vision, architectural trends, and future directions. IEEE Commun. Mag. **60**(1), 74–80 (2022)

19. Zhao, L., Han, G., Li, Z., Shu, L.: Intelligent digital twin-based software-defined vehicular networks. IEEE Netw. **34**(5), 178–184 (2020)

20. Yuan, X., Wang, X., Lin, J., Wang, C.: Privacy-preserving deep packet inspection in outsourced middleboxes. In: IEEE INFOCOM 2016 - The 35th Annual IEEE International Conference on Computer Communications, pp. 1–9 (2016)

21. Cai, Y., Xiao, L., Kazman, R., Mo, R., Feng, Q.: Design rule spaces: a new model for representing and analyzing software architecture. IEEE Trans. Softw. Eng. **45**(7), 657–682 (2019)

22. Fairbanks, G.: Ur-technical debt. IEEE Softw. **37**(4), 95–98 (2020)
23. Feng, Q., Kazman, R., Cai, Y., Mo, R., Xiao, L.: Towards an architecture-centric approach to security analysis. In: 2016 13th Working IEEE/IFIP Conference on Software Architecture (WICSA), pp. 221–30, April 2016
24. Tassey, G.: The economic impacts of inadequate infrastructure for software tesing. Tech. Rep. (2002). https://www.nist.gov/system/files/documents/director/planning/report02-3.pdf, National Institute of Standards and Technology. Accessed 25 Apr 2022
25. Kumar, S., Kaur, A., Jolly, A., Baz, M., Cheikhrouhou, O.: Cost benefit analysis of incorporating security and evaluation of its effects on various phases of agile software development. Math. Probl. Eng. **2021**, 7837153, August 2021. [Online]. https://doi.org/10.1155/2021/7837153
26. D.-G. for Communication: Circular economy action plan. for a cleaner and more competitive Europe. European Commission, Tech. Rep. (2019)
27. Calisto Friant, M., Vermeulen, W.J., Salomone, R.: Analysing European Union circular economy policies: words versus actions. Sustain. Prod. Consump, **27**, 337–353 (2021). [Online]. https://www.sciencedirect.com/science/article/pii/S2352550920313750
28. Mastrogiacomo, L., Barravecchia, F., Franceschini, F.:Definition of a conceptual scale of servitization: proposal and preliminary results. CIRP J. Manuf. Sci. Technol. **29**, 141–156 (2020), New Research Advances on Product Service System along the Lifecycle [Online]. https://www.sciencedirect.com/science/article/pii/S1755581718300610
29. RE-manufaCturing and Refurbishment LArge Industrial equipMent: extending the life of large industrial equipment. H2020 EU Grant agreement ID: 869884. 2019–2023. https://cordis.europa.eu/project/id/869884 Accessed 25 Apr 2022
30. Alessandro Fontana, L.R., Leone, D., Barni, A.: Reclaim project D4.1: circular economy driven lifetime extension strategies. EU Horizon 2020 grant 869884, Tech. Rep. (2020). https://ec.europa.eu/research/participants/documents/downloadPublic?documentIds=080166e5db5b6032&appId=PPGMS. Accessed 25 Apr 2022
31. E. U. A. for Network and I. Security: EUCC, a candidate cybersecurity certification scheme to serve as a successor to the existing sog-is (v1.1.1). Tech. Rep. (2021). https://www.enisa.europa.eu/publications/cybersecurity-certification-eucc-candidate-scheme-v1-1.1. Accessed 25 Apr 2022
32. Hernandez-Ramos, J.L., Matheu, S.N., Skarmeta, A.: The challenges of software cybersecurity certification [building security in]. IEEE Secur. Privacy **19**(1), 99–102 (2021)
33. ENISA: Regulation (eu) 2019/881 of the european parliament and of the council of 17 April 2019 on ENISA (the European Union agency for cybersecurity) and on information and communications technology cybersecurity certification (cybersecurity act). , Tech. Rep. (2019). https://eur-lex.europa.eu/eli/reg/2019/881/oj. Accessed 25 Apr 2022
34. PCI Security Standards Council (2022). https://www.pcisecuritystandards.org/. Accessed 26 May 2022
35. Francesco, F.: Digital twins as run-time predictive models for the resilience of cyber-physical systems: a conceptual framework. Phil. Trans. R. Soc. A. **379**, 2207 (2021)

36. Hou, Z., Li, Q., Foo, E., Dong, J.S., de Souza, P.: A digital twin runtime verification framework for protecting satellites systems from cyber attacks. In: 2022 26th International Conference on Engineering of Complex Computer Systems (ICECCS), pp. 117–122 (2022)
37. Mosleh, M., Dalili, K., Heydari, B.: Distributed or monolithic? A computational architecture decision framework. IEEE Syst. J. **12**(1), 125–136 (2018)
38. Kherbache, M., Maimour, M., Rondeau, E.: When digital twin meets network softwarization in the industrial IoT: real-time requirements case study. Sensors **21**,24 (2021). https://www.mdpi.com/1424-8220/21/24/8194
39. Almasan, P., et al.: Digital twin network: opportunities and challenges. (2022) [Online]. arXiv:2201.01144
40. Liu, Y.K., Ong, S.K., Nee, A.Y.C.: State-of-the-art survey on digital twin implementations. Adv. Manuf. **10**(1), 1–23 (2022). https://doi.org/10.1007/s40436-021-00375-w
41. Qi, Q., et al.: Enabling technologies and tools for digital twin. Digital twin towards smart manufacturing and Industry 4.0. J. Manuf. Syst. **58**, 3–21. (2021) [Online]. https://www.sciencedirect.com/science/article/pii/S027861251930086X
42. de Hoz Diego, J.D.: Secure communication method and system using network socket proxying. U.S. patent 11 050. Tech. Rep. (2021). https://patentscope.wipo.int/search/en/detail.jsf?docId=US328388155. Accessed 25 Apr 2022
43. Inetd - the super server. Tech. Rep. (2020). BSD System Manager's Manual. https://www.freebsd.org/cgi/man.cgi?query=inetd. Accessed 25 Apr 2022
44. de Hoz, J.D., et al.: Leveraging on digital signage networks to bring connectivity IOT devices. Tecnia **26**(1), 89–100 (2016). [Online]. https://zaguan.unizar.es/record/95466?ln=en
45. Iyengar, M.T.J.: [RFC 9000] QUIC: A UDP-based multiplexed and secure transport. Internet Engineering Task Force, Tech. Rep., May 2021. [Online]. https://datatracker.ietf.org/doc/rfc9000/
46. Bider, D.: QUIC-based UDP transport for secure shell. Internet Engineering Task Force, Tech. Rep., December 2020. [Online]. https://datatracker.ietf.org/doc/html/draft-bider-ssh-quic-09
47. The cPanel & WHM Service Daemons (2021): https://docs.cpanel.net/knowledge-base/cpanel-product/the-cpanel-service-daemons/. Accessed 26 May 2022
48. Praerit Garg, L.K.: The stride threat model. Microsoft, Tech. Rep., 12 2009. [Online]. https://docs.microsoft.com/en-us/previous-versions/commerce-server/ee823878(v=cs.20)
49. Carpenter, S.B.B.: [RFC 3234] middleboxes: taxonomy and issues. Internet Engineering Task Force, Tech. Rep., 02 2002. [Online]. https://www.rfc-editor.org/rfc/rfc3234
50. Octave forte: establish a more adaptable and robust risk program. The Software Engineering Institute, Tech. Rep., June 2020. [Online]. https://resources.sei.cmu.edu/library/asset-view.cfm?assetid=643959
51. Havelund, K.: Monitoring with data automata. In: Margaria, T., Steffen, B. (eds.) ISoLA 2014. LNCS, vol. 8803, pp. 254–273. Springer, Heidelberg (2014). https://doi.org/10.1007/978-3-662-45231-8_18
52. Havelund, K.: Rule-based runtime verification revisited. Int. J. Softw. Tools Technol. Transfer **17**(2), 143–170 (2015)
53. accept(2). Linux Programmer's Manual, Tech. Rep. (2021). https://man7.org/linux/man-pages/man2/accept.2.html. Accessed: 25 Apr 2022
54. connect(2). Linux Programmer's Manual, Tech. Rep. (2021). https://man7.org/linux/man-pages/man2/connect.2.html. Accessed 25 Apr 2022

A Formal Model of Metacontrol in Maude

Juliane Päßler[1] , Esther Aguado[2] , Gustavo Rezende Silva[3] ,
Silvia Lizeth Tapia Tarifa[1(✉)] , Carlos Hernández Corbato[3] ,
and Einar Broch Johnsen[1]

[1] University of Oslo, Oslo, Norway
{julipas,sltarifa,einarj}@ifi.uio.no
[2] Universidad Politécnica de Madrid, Madrid, Spainpg
e.aguado@upm.es
[3] Technical University of Delft, Delft, The Netherlands
{g.rezendesilva,c.h.corbato}@tudelft.nl

Abstract. Nowadays smart applications appear in domains span-
ning from commodity household applications to advanced underwater
robotics. These smart applications require adaptation to dynamic environments, changing requirements and internal system errors Metacontrol
takes a systems of systems view on autonomous control systems and self-
adaptation, by means of an additional layer of control that manipulates
and combines the regular controllers. This paper develops a formal model
of a Metacontrol architecture. We formalise this Metacontrol architecture
in the context of an autonomous house heating application, enabling
different controllers to be dynamically combined in order to meet user
requirements to a better extent than the individual controllers in isolation. The formal model is developed in the Maude rewriting system,
where we show results comparing different scenarios.

1 Introduction

There is an emerging development of "smart" applications in an increasing number of domains, ranging from commonplace IoT-based household applications to
advanced underwater robotics. A key to this smartness is the applications' ability to flexibly adapt to variability in their operational conditions. Control theory
and recent AI-based methods enable the development of different domain controllers that adapt to variability in the physical environment by combining sensor
data and a diversity of models to determine the output of the system actuators,
achieving great performance and a degree of system-level autonomy for different
requirements. This is called first-order self-adaptation [15]. However, varying user
requirements and internal system variability due to faults or emergent behaviour
in systems that comprise multiple controllers pose additional second-order adaptation challenges [15]. Self-adaptive systems with multiple points of view and
methodologies have been proposed from the software community to develop

This work was supported by the European Union's Horizon 2020 Framework Programme through the MSCA network REMARO (Grant Agreement No. 956200) and
the ROBOMINERS project (Grant Agreement No. 820971).

T. Margaria and B. Steffen (Eds.): ISoLA 2022, LNCS 13701, pp. 575–596, 2022.
https://doi.org/10.1007/978-3-031-19849-6_32

software systems that meet the previous adaptation requirements. These systems have been commonly conceptualised following the MAPE-K schema [6,18] that stands for Monitor, Analyse, Plan, and Execute based on Knowledge.

Metacontrol is a layered framework for achieving autonomy, independently of the application and the system; i.e., it takes a very structured system of systems view on the self-adaptation problem. It adds an additional layer of control that manipulates and combines the domain controllers to fulfil different combinations of requirements or to ensure resilience by enabling the overall application to adapt to changes in the underlying system such as, e.g., broken devices. Thus, Metacontrol enables extensible self-adaptation for autonomous systems that can accommodate new user requirements or new functionality to an application, by addressing only second-order adaptation based on application-independent reasoning. For this purpose, its MAPE-K loop is driven by knowledge that adheres to TOMASys [13] (the *Teleological and Ontological Model of Autonomous Systems* metamodel), which aims to provide the necessary concepts for modelling the functional knowledge of autonomous systems [16].

In this paper, we formalise a Metacontrol architecture for a smart house, detailing an autonomous house heating application. This use case is inspired by the work of Arcaini et al. [2] on a model of concurrent MAPE-K controllers (but not of Metacontrol), using abstract state machines [5]. Our main focus here is on the logical structure of architectures based on Metacontrol; i.e., the model captures the input assumed to be available to the different layers of the control structure and the control decisions that the different layers make. We develop models of independent controllers for the house heating application and show that each of these is able to maintain some of the given user requirements, but not the overall combined requirements. These models are then extended with a Metacontrol layer that, by dynamically combining the different existing controllers, is able to meet the requirements to a greater extent.

The formalisation is realised in Maude [12], a tool to develop and analyse executable models in rewriting logic. Rewriting Logic is a flexible framework combining computation and logic in which systems can be modelled with low representational distance [19]. In this paper, we use simulations in Maude to analyse the performance of the controllers with respect to the user requirements in fairly predictable environments; in future work, we plan to expand our model to analyse the additional responsiveness that seems achievable by exploiting a Metacontrol layer in less predictable environments by means of model checking techniques.

The main contributions in this paper are:

- an executable formal model of a system of systems Metacontrol architecture developed in the Maude rewrite tool;
- a use case of autonomous layered control for a smart house heating application, which we use to explain and illustrate the formal model; and
- we show how the formal model can be used to analyse the developed metacontrol designs with respect to user requirements.

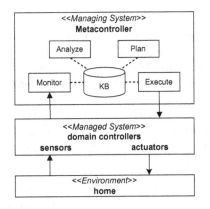

Fig. 1. The metacontrol framework.

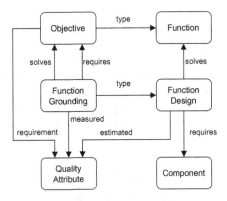

Fig. 2. Elements of TOMASys.

2 Background

2.1 Metacontrol

Metacontrol [13] gives systems the capability to perform self-adaptation in order to maintain their functionalities at an expected performance, in the presence of external disturbances, faults, and unexpected behaviour. Thus, Metacontrol enables an increased level of autonomy and reliability in a system.

Metacontrol is realised by adding an extra control layer that closes a feedback loop with the original system, monitoring, and adapting the original system through architectural reconfiguration when necessary. According to the MAPE-K model for self-adaptive systems, this results in the separation of the system into two distinct layers or subsystems: the *managing system*, whose main element is a reusable metacontroller, and the *managed system*, which is the original system.

For the metacontroller to be application independent, it exploits engineering knowledge at runtime. System engineers model relevant information about how the system works following the TOMASys metamodel [13], and this model forms the basis for the knowledge base (KB), which drives the Metacontrol MAPE-K adaptation loop. All steps interact with the KB, storing additional information, and retrieving system knowledge to facilitate decision making (see Fig. 1).

The *monitor* step is responsible for measuring so-called *quality attributes* (discussed below) for the functionalities of the system. The *analyse* step is responsible for deciding whether the managed system needs to reconfigure. For this, it needs to decide whether the measured quality attributes meet the requirements of the current configuration of the managed system. When reconfiguration is needed, the *plan* step is responsible for selecting a new configuration for the managed system that potentially satisfies its requirements. The *execute* step is responsible for carrying out the reconfiguration of the managed system.

Figure 2 shows a high-level representation of the TOMASys metamodel for the Metacontrol functional layer, which is our focus in this paper. A *function* represents an abstract functionality of the system, e.g., controlling the temperature. A *function design* is an engineering design solution that solves a specific function, e.g., a specific controller to control the temperature. An *objective* is a concrete instance of a function that the system desires to achieve at runtime, e.g., maintaining the room temperature in the range 18–22 °C. A *function grounding* is the runtime instantiation of a function design that is selected to solve a specific objective. A quality attribute (QA) is a measurable property of a system that is used to indicate how well the system satisfies its requirements, e.g., the amount of energy that the temperature control system consumes. In TOMASys there are *required*, *expected*, and *measured* QAs:

- *required QAs* capture quantitative requirements that a function should meet;
- *estimated QAs* are assumed for each function design as expected performance values with respect to the corresponding quantitative requirements; and
- *measured QAs* are associated to function groundings to capture the current performance with respect to the corresponding quantitative requirements.

2.2 Maude

Maude [12,22] is a specification and analysis system based on rewriting logic (RL) [19]. While algebraic specification techniques [25] can be used to specify the static structure of the system and the relations between the data, RL extends an algebraic specification with transitions rules which capture the dynamic behaviour of a system. In a rewrite theory (Σ, E, R), Σ defines the (ground) terms tr as operators over sorts (which can be understood as types), E is a set of equations that define equivalences between terms in Σ, and R is a set of labelled rewrite rules.

Equational theories (Σ, E) are developed by first defining *sorts st* and *functions* from a (possibly empty) list *stlist* of sorts to a given sort *st*:

sort *st* .
op *f* : *stlist* $\longrightarrow$ *st* .

Terms tr are then built from functions in a sort-correct manner, and *patterns t* are terms in which some functions are replaced by variables. *Conditional equations* in E, which express the equality of any terms that match given patterns if a given condition holds, are specified by

ceq *t* = *t′* **if** *cond*

where the matching substitution additionally applies to the condition. The condition can be a conjunction of equalities between patterns. Maude assumes that the equations form a terminating and confluent reduction system which is used to represent equivalence classes by canonical terms (i.e., all terms can be reduced to unique normal forms).

Rewrite theories (Σ, E, R) additionally specify *conditional rewrite rules* in R, which express that a term matching a given pattern can transition into another term if a condition holds, as follows:

Req.	Name	Description
R_1	*Morning water heating*	The water heater should be turned on in the morning.
R_2	*Minimise dispersion*	The system should avoid high dispersion states, i.e., window wide open and strong heating together.
R_3	*Comfortable temperature*	The smart house temperature shall always be between a range of comfortable temperatures.
R_4	*Air purity*	The heating system shall maintain a good air quality level.

Fig. 3. Requirements of the heating system. Here, the requirements R_3 and R_4 are quantitative system properties which are monitored by the quality attributes.

crl [*label*]: $t \Rightarrow t'$ **if** *cond* .

Here, the condition is a conjunction of rewrites and equalities that must hold for the rule to apply to a given term which matches t. Rewrite rules apply to equivalence classes of terms; i.e., Maude uses the equations to reduce terms to normal form in between rule applications. Therefore, when auxiliary functions are needed, these can be defined in equational logic and thus evaluated in between the state transitions [19].

When modelling executable systems, system components are typically modelled by terms of suitable sorts, organised hierarchically in modules, and the global state configuration is represented as a multiset of these terms [22]. An object in a given state can have the form < Oid : Class | a_1 : $v_1, \ldots, a_n$: v_n >, where Class is the class name, Oid the object identifier, and a_i are attributes with corresponding values v_i. Given an initial configuration, the Maude tool supports simulation and breadth-first search through reachable states, and model checking of systems with a finite number of reachable states [12,22].

3   The Smart House Use Case

Let us consider a smart house with an automatic heating system. This use case was originally presented in [2]. Here, we present a variation of the use case to motivate a self-adaptive heating system that includes various controllers that partially fulfil the requirements and a metacontroller that turns the different controllers on and off with the aim of improving the system behaviour. The house consists of a room with one window, one heater and one water heater. Its intended behaviour is specified through a set of requirements defined in Fig. 3. The smart house system has various controllers that control

Act.	Stat.	Temp.	Air Qu.
Heater	*VH*	1.23	-0.9
	FH	0.615	-0.45
	OFF	0	0
Water heater	*ON*	0,3	-0,125
	OFF	0	0
Window	*O*	-2.0	2.0
	HO	-1.0	1.0
	C	0	-0.125

Fig. 4. Assumed actuator effects on temperature and air quality.

three actuators, the heater, the water heater, and the window, and it has a temperature sensor (a thermometer), an air quality sensor, and a global clock to keep track of time.

The heater can be set to very hot *VH*, fairly hot *FH* or *OFF*, the water heater to *ON* or *OFF*, and the window to open *O*, half open *HO*, or closed *C*. A thermometer measures the temperature as a float value, where a comfortable temperature ranges over values between (and including) 18 and 22 °C. An air quality sensor measures the air quality as a float value, where a good level is represented by a value ≥ 0. The clock ranges over integer values from 1 to 24, and changes in a round-robin manner to represent discrete time units as time advances during a 24-hour day. We define all time units between, and including, 6 and 12 to be *MORNING* and all other time units as *NOT MORNING*.

In Fig. 4 we model the impact that the state of the actuators has on the temperature and air quality. For every time step, the total impact on the temperature and air quality is calculated as the sum of the effects of each actuator. The temperature of the smart house is also affected by the environment, e.g., the outside temperature, which varies depending on the time of the day. We further consider additional variability of the environment (see the online material).

3.1   The Controller Layer

The operation of the smart house system is based on controllers that receive readings from the temperature and air quality sensors as well as the clock value as input. Depending on the sensor readings and whether it is morning or not, the active controller selects a status for each actuator. The controller's goal is to fulfil some of the requirements displayed in Fig. 3 by changing the state of the actuators. The smart house heating system has four controllers: a controller that prioritises temperature (comfort controller), a controller that prioritises air quality (eco controller), and two degraded controllers, which only act upon one of the heaters, using only two of the three actuators in the smart house.

The controllers have policies based on rules to decide upon the state of the actuators, depending on the inputs (temperature, air quality, and clock), and assuming that the actuators' effect on the temperature and air quality in the room are as the presented in Fig. 4.

The comfort controller uses all actuators and has a strong preference for *comfort temperature*. Its control policy is defined to meet to a certain degree the requirements in Fig. 3: (1) a policy stricter than R_3: reach and maintain the desired comfort temperature measurements as a priority, even if that means slightly worse air purity measurements, and (2) R_1: the water heater is always on in the morning.

The controller policy is depicted as a decision diagram in Fig. 5. The nodes represent the temperature T, clock CLK, air quality AQ, and window W. The edges represent the status of each node. The leaves represent the desired state of the actuators, as described in Fig. 4, in the order: heater, water heater, and window. Note that the controllers check whether the temperature is within 19.0 °C

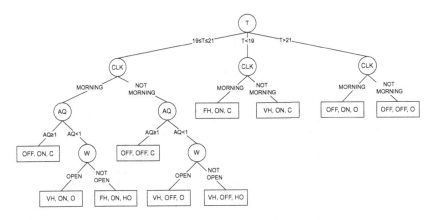

Fig. 5. Decision diagram for the comfort controller, where the leaf nodes indicate the controller's decision for the state of the heater, water heater and window.

and 21.0 °C and whether the air quality is above 1, so they use different values than the ones defined in the system requirements. This was done to create some buffer during which the controllers can react before the temperature and air quality pass the thresholds of 18.0 °C and 22.0 °C, respectively 0. Based on the decision tree, we can already observe that some requirements of Fig. 3 are not met, as the controller prioritises a comfortable temperature. In particular, some rules violate R_2 since the controller uses the very hot heater state VH and the open window state O together.

The eco controller uses all actuators and has a strong preference for *air purity*. Its control policy is defined to meet to a certain degree the requirements in Fig. 3: (1) a policy stricter than R_4: reach and maintain the desired air purity measurements as a priority, even if it means a slightly worse comfortable temperature measurements, (2) R_1: the water heater is always on in the morning, (3) an extension of R_2: if the temperature is high and it is morning, only reduce the temperature with the window half open to avoid losing heat too quickly.

Degraded controllers are defined for each heater that may break, so the degraded controllers can be used when that happens. *Degraded controller A* assumes that the heater is broken and therefore always *OFF*. *Degraded controller B* assumes that the water heater is broken and therefore always *OFF*.

Decision diagrams, similar to the one showed in Fig. 5, are included for the remaining controllers in the online repository[1].

---

[1] The full model of the smart house Metacontrol architecture, including all scenarios and results, is available at https://github.com/remaro-network/Maude_Metacontrol.

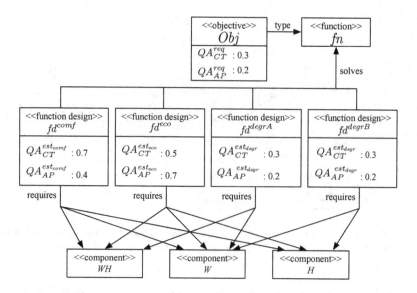

Fig. 6. Elements of the smart house TOMASys metamodel.

4   The Metacontrol Layer for the Smart House Use Case

In this section we present the Metacontrol layer for the smart house use case, modelling R_3 and R_4 in Fig. 3 as an abstract functionality of the system that the metacontroller aims to maintain. The overall system includes all the controllers presented in Sect. 3.1. The comfort controller prioritises R_3 over R_4, while the policy of the eco controller does the opposite. In case a heater breaks, the degraded controllers can be used. The adaptation problem that the metacontroller solves is configuring the smart house application by selecting at each instant the best controller to perform both R_3 and R_4.

4.1   The TOMASys Metamodel

The quantitative requirements R_3 and R_4 are captured in the TOMASys metamodel, as explained in Sect. 2.1. Figure 6 provides an overview of the TOMASys model for this use case.

Function. Requirements R_3 and R_4 can be represented as a *function fn*: use a controller to keep the smart house temperature and air quality at a desired level. Observe that in the general case, the metacontroller can operate based on different functions that depend on different quality attributes at the same time.

Quality Attributes. To quantify the extent to which the system satisfies the requirements R_3 and R_4, we use the *quality attributes* QA_{CT} (comfortable temperature) and QA_{AP} (air purity). These quality attributes occur as *required* quality attributes in the objective, as *estimated* quality attributes in the function designs, and as *measured* quality attributes in the function grounding, and will be further discussed in the respective paragraphs.

Objective. An objective is a concrete instance of the function fn. A desired range for the temperature and a good level for the air quality are given by the *objective Obj*: keep the smart house temperature between (and including) 18 and 22 °C and the air quality ≥ 0. To evaluate whether an objective has been fulfilled, the metacontroller uses minimum thresholds for each quality attribute, such thresholds are denoted as *required quality attributes* QA_{CT}^{req} and QA_{AP}^{req}. These values also reflect the priorities that are set in the system. The higher the value, the higher the priority. For the smart house use case, we want to prioritise comfortable temperature; therefore $QA_{CT}^{req} > QA_{AP}^{req}$, see Fig. 6. We denote this objective as $Obj(QA_{CT}^{req}, QA_{AP}^{req})$. Observe that, in general, there is one objective for each function since the objective is an instance of a function.

Function Design. We denote each function design in Fig. 6 as

$$fd^{id}(QA_{CT}^{est_{id}}, QA_{AP}^{est_{id}}, Cmp_{id}) ,$$

where

- id is one of the identifiers of the controllers,
- QA_{CT}^{est} and QA_{AP}^{est} are *estimated* quality attribute values for comfortable temperature and air purity, and
- $Cmp \subseteq \{heater, waterheater, window\}$ are *required* components.

Function Grounding. If a controller is selected, we *ground* its function design. This instance is then called *function grounding*. In the function grounding, we store the *measured* quality attributes QA_{CT}^{meas} and QA_{AP}^{meas} that reflect the degree to which the quality attributes are fulfilled at the moment.

If one of the actuators fails or the measured quality attribute values are lower than the required ones, then the function grounding will be marked as in error, which will trigger reconfiguration in the metacontroller. This includes grounding a (new) function design.

Quality Attribute Values. Figure 6 includes the required and estimated values for the quality attributes used in the use case. The function design fd^{comf} captures the goal of the comfort controller: to prioritise a comfortable temperature in the room and then, if the temperature is good enough, try to maintain a reasonable air quality, thus $QA_{CT}^{est_{comf}} > QA_{AP}^{est_{comf}}$. The function design fd^{eco} focuses on a good air quality, therefore $QA_{CT}^{est_{eco}} < QA_{AP}^{est_{eco}}$.

For simplicity all degraded controllers have the same estimated values in our model, which are assumed to be lower than the estimated values for the other controllers, and prioritise room temperature.

All the above elements are used by the metacontroller to decide when to switch between the different controllers, so that the system does its best to meet both requirements R_3 and R_4.

4.2   Metacontrol Operation

We now detail the operation of the metacontroller, following the MAPE-K loop, where the knowledge base of the MAPE-K loop includes all the elements and relationships among the elements defined in Sect. 4.1.

Monitor. During the monitor step, the metacontroller uses some collected logs in the system to calculate the current measured values of the quality attributes. In particular, we assume that the heating system has a log for the temperature values in the room $T = t_0, t_1, \ldots, t_n$ and a log for the air quality values in the room $A = a_0, a_1, \ldots, a_n$, where $t_i, a_i \in \mathbb{Q}$ for all $i = 0, \ldots, n$. They were retrieved from the sensors every time step $0, \ldots, n$, where n is the current time step. Let $N \in \mathbb{N}$ be the size of the time window that we want to consider for the computation of the current values of the quality attributes. We now decide whether a temperature t_i is considered to be a comfortable temperature. Let $CT : \mathbb{Q} \longrightarrow \{0,1\}$ be defined as

$$CT(t_i) = \begin{cases} 1 & \text{if } 19.1 \le t_i \le 21.5, \\ 0 & \text{otherwise.} \end{cases} \tag{1}$$

The measured quality attribute QA_{CT}^{meas} for comfortable temperature is then given by the function $QA_{CT}^{meas} : \mathbb{N} \times \mathbb{Q}^n \longrightarrow [0,1]$, defined as follows:

$$QA_{CT}^{meas}(N, T) = \frac{\sum_{i=(n-N)}^{n} CT(t_i)}{N}. \tag{2}$$

We compute the measured air purity as a function $AP : \mathbb{Q} \longrightarrow \{0,1\}$, defined as:

$$AP(a_i) = \begin{cases} 1 & \text{if } a_i \ge 0.7, \\ 0 & \text{otherwise.} \end{cases} \tag{3}$$

The measured quality attribute QA_{AP}^{meas} for air purity is then given by a function $QA_{AP}^{meas} : \mathbb{N} \times \mathbb{Q}^n \longrightarrow [0,1]$, defined as follows:

$$QA_{AP}^{meas}(N, A) = \frac{\sum_{i=(n-N)}^{n} AP(a_i)}{N}. \tag{4}$$

Observe that the thresholds for comfortable temperature and air purity in CT and AP differ from the system requirements in Sect. 3. This difference anticipates the adaptation that will be done the metacontroller. Finally, if $n < N$, we only consider the first n time steps in both QA_{CT}^{meas} and QA_{AP}^{meas}.

Analyse. During the analysis step, the metacontroller first checks whether one of the actuators is in error. If yes, then the current function grounding is marked to be in error. If all actuators work, the metacontroller compares the measured quality attribute values QA_{CT}^{meas} and QA_{AP}^{meas} with the required QA values in the objective $Obj(QA_{CT}^{req}, QA_{AP}^{req})$. If at least one measured QA value is lower than the respective required QA value, then the current function grounding is marked to be in error. The QAs that have a lower than required value are marked as underachieved. For example, if $QA_{CT}^{meas} = 0.2$, then QA_{CT} is marked as underachieving since $QA_{CT}^{req} = 0.3$, see Fig. 6.

Plan. If the metacontroller marked the function grounding to be in error, then during the planning step the metacontroller needs to select a new function design to ground. In the case where both quality attributes are underachieved, the objective $Obj(QA_{CT}^{req}, QA_{AP}^{req})$ prioritises the QA for comfortable temperature since $QA_{CT}^{req} > QA_{AP}^{req}$.

Assuming that the system is at time step n, we define $available_n$ as the set of function designs that are available at time step n, i.e., the set of function designs whose required components only contain components that are not broken. Furthermore, we define $poorQA_n$ as the set of QAs that are underachieved at time step n. The planning step in the metacontroller acts slightly different depending on two cases:

Case 1: *The metacontroller only needs to look at the required components to choose a function design.* In our particular scenario, this is the case in which either the heater or the water heater is failing.
In this case $available_n \subseteq \{fd^{degrA}, fd^{degrB}\}$. Since in our scenario only one of the heaters can be broken, $available_n$ will have exactly one element, which the metacontroller chooses to be grounded in the execute step.

Case 2: *The metacontroller needs to look into the QAs that are marked as underachieved.* In our particular scenario, this is the case in which all the actuators are working normally. Thus, $available_n$ consists of all function designs. In this case $poorQA_n \subseteq \{QA_{CT}, QA_{AP}\}$. Observe that $poorQA_n$ contains at least one element. Let $QA_x \in poorQA_n$ be the QA with the highest priority in $poorQA_n$. The metacontroller searches for the function design in $available_n$ with the highest estimated value for QA_x, i.e., the function design with identifier i such that for all function designs in $available_n$ with identifier j it holds that $QA_x^{est_i} \geq QA_x^{est_j}$.

Execute. During the execute step, the chosen function design is grounded and the controller associated with this function design is activated, triggering execution in the controller layer as described in Sect. 3.1.

```
1    op ⟨Scheduler | Status:  _ , RuleApplied:  _ ⟩ : ScheduleComp Bool ⟶ Scheduler .
2    op ⟨ _ : Clock | Timesteps:  _, Time:  _, TempLog:  _, AqLog:  _ ⟩
3         : Oid Timesteps Time TVPList TVPList ⟶ Clock .
4    op ⟨ _ : Thermometer | Degrees:  _ ⟩ : Oid Temperature ⟶ Thermometer .
5    op ⟨ _ : Airquality | Value:  _ ⟩ : Oid AirqualityStatus ⟶ Airquality .
6    op ⟨ _ : Heater | _ ⟩ : Oid Attribute ⟶ Heater .
7    op ⟨ _ : Waterheater | _ ⟩ : Oid Attribute ⟶ Waterheater .
8    op ⟨ _ : Window | _ ⟩ : Oid Attribute ⟶ Window .
9    op ⟨ _ : ComfortController | Selected:  _ ⟩ : Oid Selected ⟶ ComfortController .
10   op ⟨ _ : EcoController | Selected:  _ ⟩ : Oid Selected ⟶ EcoController .
11   op ⟨ _ : DegradedContrA | Selected:  _ ⟩ : Oid Selected ⟶ DegradedContrA .
12   op ⟨ _ : DegradedContrB | Selected:  _ ⟩ : Oid Selected ⟶ DegradedContrB .
13   op ⟨Environment | Version:  _ ⟩ : Nat ⟶ Environment .
```

Fig. 7. Selected objects of the smart house heating system, modelled in Maude.

5   Modelling the Smart House Use Case in Maude

We now describe the Maude model of the metacontrolled smart house application, including all elements described in Sects. 3 and 4. A multiset Configuration is used to represent the components of the Metacontrol ecosystem, as suggested in Sect. 2.2. A Configuration contains all objects that are crucial for the model of the smart house, detailed in the sequel. Figures 7 and 11 give the syntax of a selection of these objects. The full model can be found in the online repository.

5.1   Model Dynamics

The following elements model the execution of the entire self-adaptive system, as described in Fig. 1.

Scheduler is an object of sort Scheduler (see Fig. 7, Line 1) that captures the MAPE-K loop and ensures that rules are applied in the correct order, according to Fig. 8. It keeps track of which sets of rules can be applied, using the attribute Status, and schedules which components can apply rules. The attribute RuleApplied indicates whether one of the rules in the active set has already been applied. The scheduler object is present in all rules. A rule can only be applied if the scheduler object has the right value in the attribute Status, and if the attribute RuleApplied is false, e.g., see the rule in Fig. 9. The scheduler makes the model deterministic. However, different configurations will trigger different rules inside the sets.

Time is modelled with an object of sort Clock (see Fig. 7, Line 2) that captures the passage of time in the system, which works together with a rule for modelling how time advances. It has attributes

- Timesteps: a natural number representing the current time step in the system,
- Time: the current time, and
- TVPList: a list of (Timestep, Float)-pairs.

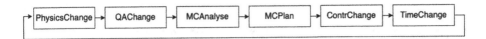

Fig. 8. The order in which the different set of rules are applied.

After each time step, a pair representing the current time step and temperature (air quality) is added to the temperature log TempLog (respectively to the air quality log AqLog). As described in Sect. 3, we assume that one time step is one hour, so the time is computed as the current time steps modulo 24. Furthermore, a sort TimedConfiguration is introduced. It is used in certain rules to ensure that rules are applied to the full global state configuration and not only to subsets. If the scheduler indicates that the time should advance, then a rule that increases the Timesteps by one, computes the new Time and adds new pairs to TempLog and AqLog is applied.

5.2 The Smart House Model

In this section, we present the model of the managed system, as displayed in Fig. 1 and described in Sect. 3.

Thermometer models the measurement of the current temperature in the room. An object of sort Thermometer (see Fig. 7, Line 4) has the attribute Temperature that is a float value that reflects the current temperature in the smart house.

Air quality sensor models the measurement of the current air quality value in the room. An object of sort Airquality (see Fig. 7, Line 5) has the attribute AirqualityStatus that is a float value that reflects the current air quality value in the smart house.

Actuators have an object identifier Oid and a multiset of Attributes (see Fig. 7, Lines 6–8). Thus, the attributes that are necessary for an actuator are not explicitly specified. However, each actuator should have exactly one instance of the following attributes:

- Status: can be of sort HeaterStatus, WaterheaterStatus or WindowStatus, depending on the actuator, and represents the current status of the actuator;
- EffectTemp: the effect of the actuator on the temperature, specified as a float value;
- EffectAQ: the effect of the actuator on the air quality, specified as a float value; and
- Broken: indicates whether the actuator is broken or not.

See Fig. 4 for further details about the effect of the actuators on the temperature and air quality.

```
1   crl [CContrTempOkAqOk] :
2      ⟨H : Heater | A ⟩ ⟨WH : Waterheater | A1 ⟩ ⟨W : Window | A2 ⟩
3      ⟨T : Thermometer | Degrees: DG ⟩ ⟨AQ : Airquality | Value: AQS ⟩
4      ⟨C : Clock | Timesteps: TS, Time: TI, TempLog: TL, AqLog: AL ⟩
5      ⟨CC : ComfortController | Selected: true ⟩
6      ⟨Scheduler | Status: ContrChange, RuleApplied: false ⟩
7      ⇒
8      (msg hOff from CC to H)(msg whOff from CC to WH)(msg closed from CC to W)
9      ⟨H : Heater | A ⟩ ⟨WH : Waterheater | A1 ⟩ ⟨W : Window | A2 ⟩
10     ⟨T : Thermometer | Degrees: DG ⟩ ⟨AQ : Airquality | Value: AQS ⟩
11     ⟨C : Clock | Timesteps: TS, Time: TI, TempLog: TL, AqLog: AL ⟩
12     ⟨CC : ComfortController | Selected: true ⟩
13     ⟨Scheduler | Status: ContrChange, RuleApplied: true ⟩
14     if morning(TI) ==false /\ hot(DG) ==false /\ cold(DG) ==false
15     /\ aqok(AQS) ==true .
```

Fig. 9. A rule for the comfort controller in Maude (coloured text highlights changed or new elements).

Physics. If the scheduler indicates that the temperature and air quality should be changed, then a rule is applied to change them according to the status of the actuators and the time, as specified in Sect. 3. We also implemented three different ways the environment can influence the temperature and air quality in the room, where two of them do not only depend on the time of the day, but also on the time step. The environment behaviour can be selected via the attribute Value of the object Environment (see Fig. 7, Line 13).

5.3   The Controller Layer

The controllers, defined in Sect. 3.1, are modelled as objects; the attribute Selected indicates if a controller is currently active (see Fig. 7, Lines 9–12).

The policies of the controllers are captured as rules. If a controller is active and the scheduler indicates that the controller should apply a rule, then the appropriate rule, which aims to change the status of the actuators, is applied. However, if an actuator is broken, its status should not be changed. We use a sort Msg for passing messages from a controller to an actuator, defined as **op** msg_from_to_ : ActuatorStatus Oid Oid → Msg . A broken actuator will not change its status when consuming the message. Otherwise it will change its status to the desired one.

The Maude model has rules that cover all the cases of the decision diagrams of the controllers. A sample rule for the comfort controller, given in Fig. 9, captures a path in the decision diagram of Fig. 5. This rule is applied when it is not morning and the temperature and air quality are OK. The pattern on the left hand side of the rule describes a configuration with the involved actuators, sensors, controllers. The scheduler has status ContrChange and a RuleApplied attribute with value false. The rule creates three messages and changes the attribute RuleApplied to true, which ensures that the controller only applies one

```
1   rl [AnalyseDegA] :
2       {⟨ H : Heater | Broken: yes, A ⟩
3       ⟨ MC : Metacontroller | MetaLog: ML ⟩
4       ⟨ Scheduler | Status: MCAnalyse, RuleApplied: false ⟩
5       ⟨ ErrorPropagation | FgError: false, QaCtError: B, QaApError: B1,
6           ActError: AIE ⟩
7       CONF}
8   ⇒
9       {⟨ H : Heater | Broken: yes, A ⟩
10      ⟨ MC : Metacontroller | MetaLog: ML ⟩
11      ⟨ Scheduler | Status: MCAnalyse, RuleApplied: true ⟩
12      ⟨ ErrorPropagation | FgError: true, QaCtError: false, QaApError: false,
13          ActError: heater ⟩
14      deselect(CONF)} .
```

Fig. 10. A rule for the metacontroller in Maude. The rule is applied when the heater is broken (coloured text highlights changed or new elements).

rule per time step. The rule uses auxiliary functions; e.g., the function morning determines whether the current time is between 6 and 12 o'clock, cold, the functions cold and hot whether it is cold (i.e., less than 19.0 °C) or hot (i.e., more than 21.0 °C), and the function aqok whether the current air quality is above 1.0.

5.4   The Metacontrol Layer

We now present the model of the managing system, as shown in Fig. 1 and described in Sect. 4.

Metacontroller is captured by an object of sort Metacontroller (see Fig. 11, Line 1). The attribute MetaLog contains a list of pairs (Timestep, Value), where Value can be Eco, Comf, DegA, or DegB. At a time step i, the metacontroller might switch between controllers. If so, it adds a pair (i, C_i) to the MetaLog, where C_i represents the controller which has been activated.

A sample rule of the metacontroller in Maude is displayed in Fig. 10. This rule is part of the set of rules for the analysis step. The rule is applied when the heater is broken to propagate the error and to signal in the Metacontrol layer that the system needs reconfiguration. Note that the curly brackets around the configuration enforce that this rule can only be applied to the configuration as a whole. The pattern on the left hand side of the rule describes a configuration with a broken heater, all the necessary components used by the metacontroller, as well as the whole configuration CONF which is not further specified. The scheduler has status MCAnalyse and a RuleApplied attribute with value false. The ErrorPropagation object has a FgError attribute with value false, QaCtError and QaApError attributes with arbitrary boolean values, and an attribute ActError with an arbitrary list of actuators as value. The rule changes the RuleApplied

```
1  op ⟨ _ : Metacontroller | MetaLog: _ ⟩ : Oid MetaLog ⟶ Metacontroller .
2  op ⟨ RequiredQAs | requQaCT: _, requQaAP: _ ⟩ : Rat Rat ⟶ Objective .
3  op ⟨ _ : QaComfTemp | _ ⟩ : Oid QaAttributes ⟶ QaComfTemp .
4  op ⟨ _ : QaAirPurity | _ ⟩ : Oid QaAttributes ⟶ QaAirPurity .
5  op ⟨ _ : FDContr | _ ⟩ : Oid FDAttributes ⟶ FunctionDesign .
6  op ⟨ ErrorPropagation | FgError: _, QaCtError: _, QaApError: _, ActError: _ ⟩
7     : Bool Bool Bool ActuatorList ⟶ InError .
```

Fig. 11. Selected objects used by the metacontroller in Maude.

attribute to true, which ensures that only one analyse rule can be applied every time step. Furthermore, it changes the attribute FgError to true because the function grounding is in error, the attributes QaCtError and QaApError to false, and the attribute ActError to heater because the heater is broken. Lastly, it uses the auxiliary function deselect to deselect the currently active controller.

Quality Attributes can be *required, expected* and *measured* QAs, see Sect. 4.1. They occur in different parts of the model in Maude. The *required* QA values are captured in an object of sort Objective (see Fig. 11, Line 2), where requQaCT and requQaAP are the required QA values for comfortable temperature and air purity, respectively. The *expected* QA values are captured in the function designs (described later). The *measured* QA values are captured in objects of sort QaComfTemp and QaAirPurity (see Fig. 11, Lines 3–4), where QaAttributes is a multiset sort of attributes. Each quality attribute should include each of the following attributes exactly once:

– Consider: a natural number that reflects how many time steps should be considered for the computation of the quality attribute;
– Past: a list of Boolean values recording $CT(t_i)$ in QaComfTemp and $AP(a_i)$ in QaAirPurity, defined in Eqs. 1 and 3, for each time step i;
– Status: the current value of the quality attribute, computed according to Eq. 2 for QaComfTemp and according to Eq. 4 for QaAirPurity;
– QaComputed: a Boolean value that indicates whether the QA was computed in the current time step.

The rules that update the attribute Past and compute the new measured QA values are applied. when enabled by the scheduler.

Function design objects of sort FunctionDesign are defined for every controller Contr, where FDAttributes is a multiset sort of attributes (see Fig. 11, Line 5). Function design objects include the following attributes:

– ConContr: the Oid of the controller connected to this function design;
– ExpQaCT: the expected QA value for comfortable temperature;
– ExpQaAP: the expected air purity QA value; and
– RequActuators: a list of required actuators.

Controllers	NoViol			IntViol		
	Tmp.	AirQu.	Total	Tmp.	AirQu.	Total
Comfort	0	48	48	0.00	16.45	16.45
Eco	29	0	29	15.19	0.00	15.19
Metacontroller	10	14	24	4.815	4.65	9.465

Fig. 12. Collected metrics from running Scenario 1 in Maude.

Function grounding is represented implicitly. Error propagation happens when certain actuators are in error and when quality attributes are under-achieved. This is captured with an object of sort InError (see Fig. 11, Lines 6 and 7), where the Boolean values indicate whether the function grounding, the QA comfortable temperature, or the QA air purity are in error, and ActError is a (possibly empty) list of actuators that are in error.

An Analyse rule is applied before a Plan rule, when enabled by the scheduler. The rules follow the procedure described in Sect. 4.2.

6   Evaluating the Executable Model of the Smart House

This section reports on simulation experiments to evaluate the performance of the controllers and the impact of adding the Metacontrol framework to the system using the developed Maude model. The experiments consist of running the Maude model of the smart house for 200 time steps, measuring relevant metrics, and comparing how the system behaves with the comfort and eco controllers, and with the Metacontrol layer. The experiments were done for the following scenarios: (1) all actuators are working, (2) the heater breaks at time step 75, and (3) the water heater breaks at time step 75. The experiments were also repeated for two other variations of the environment, which gave similar results to the ones reported in the paper. Note that given an initial configuration, the model is deterministic due to the round-robin scheduling policy and the simplification of the variability in the environment. Therefore, one simulation is enough to capture the behaviour of the system in the different scenarios.

The requirements R_3 and R_4 reported in Fig. 3 are instantiated as follows: We assume that a comfortable temperature is between 18 and 22 °C and a good air quality level is above 0. The results obtained for Scenario 1 are summarised in Figs. 12, 13, and 14, respectively, where we considered an initial temperature of 19 °C and an initial air quality of 1.3. We collect metrics that measure the following: *NoViol* counts how many time steps the requirements R_3 and R_4 presented in Fig. 3 are violated. If, for example, the air quality drops below 0 for 2 time steps, *NoViol* will be equal to 2. *IntViol* sums up the severity of the violation with respect to the thresholds. If for example the air quality is –0.5 in time step 1, –1 in time step 2, and 0 in time step 3, it would result in an intensity of violation of –1.5. The collected metrics are shown in Fig. 12.

Figures 13 and 14 show that the comfort controller does not violate R_3, but violates R_4, and the eco controller violates R_3, but not R_4. When Metacontrol is

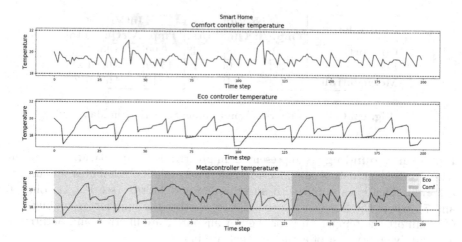

Fig. 13. The evolution of temperature for Scenario 1.

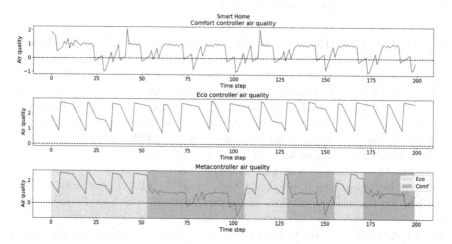

Fig. 14. The evolution of air quality for Scenario 1.

used, both requirements are violated, but the number of times and the intensity of the violations are lower than when the comfort or eco controllers are used in isolation. Similar results were also obtained with the Metacontrol layer for Scenarios 2 and 3. Further experiments injected variability in the environment, where the metacontroller still performed better than the comfort and eco controller in Scenario 1 and at least as good as the comfort controller in Scenarios 2 and 3. All the experiments can be reproduced following the instructions in the online repository.

The results show that for the smart house use case, the additional Metacontrol layer, as modelled in this work, allowed the smart house system to adapt and improve its performance in all the experiments reported in this section.

7   Related Work

Multiple works have addressed formal models of self-adaptive systems in the context of providing assurances [24]. ActivFORMS [17] is a self-adaptation approach that explicitly uses formal models at runtime in the form of timed automata to promote adaptation, thus ensuring that the properties verified at design time are guaranteed at runtime. Compared with Metacontrol, ActivFORMS requires to develop the entire system, i.e. first and second order self-adaptation, using formal methods, while Metacontrol allows to leverage existing domain controllers. ENTRUST [9] is a generic methodology to design reliable self-adaptive software and its associated assurance cases, based on developing verifiable models, such as the automata in ActivFORMS, to check if they satisfy certain properties, such as that the controllers are deadlock free. Our work relates to ActivFORMS and ENTRUST regarding the development and verification of the self-adaptive system models. Our aim is to use Maude to formally model Metacontrol architectures and use it to analyse their properties.

The analysis of self-adaptive systems has been addressed using various formal methods. For example, an abstract modelling framework based on automata is introduced in [3], several papers [10,14,21] use (a subclass of) Petri nets to model self-adaptive systems, and a domain specific language has been proposed to support compositional verification of self-adaptive cyber-physical systems [4].

In our work, we took inspiration from the work of Arcaina et al. [2] on modelling MAPE-K feedback loops with Abstract State Machines, which introduced the Smart House Case Study that we adapted in our paper. However, the controllers they considered in their work correspond to the managed system in our paper; i.e., they model the control level rather than the Metacontrol level considered in our work. Furthermore, they consider a scenario in which multiple controllers can be active at the same time, which differs from our work which only considered the Metacontrol level activating and deactivating different controllers. Thus, they considered a different form of adaptation than in our work. Their work is further developed, for example, in [1].

Maude has previously been used to formalise and study reflection. In particular, rewriting logic allows a universal theory of reflection [11], which is also supported by Maude. Maude has also been used to formalise and study reflection in actor models using a "Russian dolls" architecture [20], especially in the context of reflective middleware [23]. Bruni et. al. [7] proposed a conceptual framework for self-adaptation that they realised in Maude [8]. Their work resembles ours in using a layered model of self-adaptation by means of MAPE-K feedback loops, but differs from ours in that they use a white box approach for implementing self-adaptation, whereas Metacontrol uses a black box approach.

8   Conclusion and Future Work

In this paper, we present the first executable formal model of a self-adaptive system based on Metacontrol. The use of Maude has allowed us to model a use case based on the smart house use case by Arcani et al. [2], including all the layers in such a self-adaptive system of systems, from the physics of the environment, via the first-order adaptation layer formed by the sensors, actuators and controllers, to the second-order adaptation layer defined by the Metacontrol architecture. The results presented in Sect. 6 for different scenarios of environment inputs and system failures validate our model of second-order self-adaptation with Metacontrol. They show an improved performance of the smart house system with respect to its requirements when the metacontroller performs architectural adaptation using the alternative controllers, compared to when the system's behaviour is limited to one of the individual controllers.

We highlight that the goal of this work is not to model the best controllers in the market, but to demonstrate that for scenarios where there are different controllers with specific advantages and limitations, Metacontrol can be used to capture and exploit this knowledge in order to improve the overall system performance. However, the potential to improve performance is deeply dependent on how well-designed the TOMASys metamodel is, especially the QAs.

In this paper, we have used simulations to analyse the benefits of Metacontrol in scenarios with fairly deterministic environments. In future work, we plan to use stronger analysis techniques, such as model checking and the exploration of what-if scenarios, to verify safety as well as liveness properties of the Metacontrol layer's abilities for self-adaptation in more unpredictable environments. For example, it would be interesting to verify properties related to the responsiveness and coverage; e.g., the Metacontrol layer's ability to always eventually regain correct behaviour, the maximal delay in this process, and whether the choice of active controllers will always fluctuate or eventually stabilise. Our long term goal is to analyse Metacontrol under assumptions about the managed system, and identify minimal requirements to the managed system such that the Metacontrol layer can guarantee desired overall correctness properties. A first step in this direction will be to generalise the formal model of the Metacontrol framework by replacing the executable models of the managed system and its environment by declarative specifications of their behaviour.

From the perspective of the design of the Metacontrol framework, our work on the Maude model has already provided insights into the current limitations of both the Metacontrol self-adaptation reasoning based on the TOMASys conceptual model and its execution model. In future work, we plan to extend the TOMASys metamodel to evaluate and prioritise conflicting requirements. Furthermore, we plan to explore the use of behavioural specifications of system components, as discussed above, to enrich the knowledge base of the Metacontrol architecture and integrate predictive analyses by means of formal models in the Metacontrol's self-adaptation layer.

References

1. Arcaini, P., Mirandola, R., Riccobene, E., Scandurra, P.: MSL: a pattern language for engineering self-adaptive systems. J. Syst. Softw. **164**, 110558 (2020). https://doi.org/10.1016/j.jss.2020.110558
2. Arcaini, P., Riccobene, E., Scandurra, P.: Formal design and verification of self-adaptive systems with decentralized control. ACM Trans. Auton. Adapt. Syst. **11**, 1–35 (2016)
3. Borda, A., Koutavas, V.: Self-adaptive automata. In: Proceedings of the 6th Conference on Formal Methods in Software Engineering (FormaliSE 2018), pp. 64–73. ACM, June 2018. https://doi.org/10.1145/3193992.3194001
4. Borda, A., Pasquale, L., Koutavas, V., Nuseibeh, B.: Compositional Verification of self-adaptive cyber-physical systems. In: Proceedings of the 13th International Symposium on Software Engineering for Adaptive and Self-Managing Systems (SEAMS 2018), pp. 1–11, May 2018
5. Börger, E., Stärk, R.F.: Abstract state machines. A method for high-level system design and analysis. In: Boca, P., Bowen, J., Siddiqi, J. (eds.) Formal Methods: State of the Art and New Directions. Springer, London (2003). https://doi.org/10.1007/978-1-84882-736-3_3
6. Brun, Y., et al.: engineering self-adaptive systems through feedback loops. In: Cheng, Betty H. C.., de Lemos, Rogério, Giese, Holger, Inverardi, Paola, Magee, Jeff (eds.) Software Engineering for Self-Adaptive Systems. LNCS, vol. 5525, pp. 48–70. Springer, Heidelberg (2009). https://doi.org/10.1007/978-3-642-02161-9_3
7. Bruni, Roberto, Corradini, Andrea, Gadducci, Fabio, Lluch Lafuente, Alberto, Vandin, Andrea: A conceptual framework for adaptation. In: de Lara, Juan, Zisman, Andrea (eds.) FASE 2012. LNCS, vol. 7212, pp. 240–254. Springer, Heidelberg (2012). https://doi.org/10.1007/978-3-642-28872-2_17
8. Bruni, R., Corradini, A., Gadducci, F., Lluch Lafuente, A., Vandin, A.: Modelling and analyzing adaptive self-assembly strategies with Maude. Sci. Comput. Program. **99**, 75–94 (2015). https://doi.org/10.1016/j.scico.2013.11.043
9. Calinescu, R., Weyns, D., Gerasimou, S., Iftikhar, M.U., Habli, I., Kelly, T.: Engineering trustworthy self-adaptive software with dynamic assurance cases. IEEE Trans. Softw. Eng. **44**(11), 1039–1069 (2017)
10. Camilli, M., Capra, L.: Formal specification and verification of decentralized self-adaptive systems using symmetric nets. Discrete Event Dyn. Syst. **31**(4), 609–657 (2021). https://doi.org/10.1007/s10626-021-00343-3
11. Clavel, M.: Reflection in Rewriting Logic: Metalogical Foundations and Metaprogramming Applications. CSLI Publications, Stanford (2000)
12. Clavel, M., et al. (eds.): All About Maude - A High-Performance Logical Framework, How to Specify, Program and Verify Systems in Rewriting Logic, LNCS, vol. 4350. Springer, Heidelberg (2007). https://doi.org/10.1007/978-3-540-71999-1
13. Corbato, C.H.: Model-based self-awareness patterns for autonomy. Ph.D. thesis, Universidad Politécnica de Madrid (2013)
14. Fakhir, M.I., Kazmi, S.A.R.: Formal specification and verification of self-adaptive concurrent systems. IEEE Access **6**, 34790–34803 (2018). https://doi.org/10.1109/ACCESS.2018.2849821
15. Garlan, D.: The unknown unknowns are not totally unknown. In: Proceedings of the International Symposium on Software Engineering for Adaptive and Self-Managing Systems (SEAMS 2021), pp. 264–265. IEEE, May 2021. https://doi.org/10.1109/SEAMS51251.2021.00047

16. Hernández, C., Bermejo-Alonso, J., Sanz, R.: A self-adaptation framework based on functional knowledge for augmented autonomy in robots. Integr. Comput. Aided Eng. **25**(2), 157–172 (2018)
17. Iftikhar, M.U., Weyns, D.: ActivFORMS: active formal models for self-adaptation. In: Proceedings of the 9th International Symposium on Software Engineering for Adaptive and Self-Managing Systems (SEAMS 2014), pp. 125–134. ACM (2014)
18. Kephart, J.O., Chess, D.M.: The vision of autonomic computing. Computer **36**(1), 41–50 (2003)
19. Meseguer, J.: Twenty years of rewriting logic. J. Log. Algebraic Methods Program. **81**(7–8), 721–781 (2012). https://doi.org/10.1016/j.jlap.2012.06.003
20. Meseguer, José, Talcott, Carolyn: Semantic models for distributed object reflection. In: Magnusson, Boris (ed.) ECOOP 2002. LNCS, vol. 2374, pp. 1–36. Springer, Heidelberg (2002). https://doi.org/10.1007/3-540-47993-7_1
21. Mian, N.A., Ahmad, F.: Modeling and analysis of MAPE-K loop in Self Adaptive Systems using Petri Nets. Int. J. Comput. Sci. Netw. Secur (IJCSNS) **17**, 6 (2017)
22. Ölveczky, P.C.: Designing Reliable Distributed Systems - A Formal Methods Approach Based on Executable Modeling in Maude. Springer London (2017). https://doi.org/10.1007/978-1-4471-6687-0
23. Venkatasubramanian, N., Talcott, C., Agha, G.A.: A formal model for reasoning about adaptive QoS-enabled middleware. ACM Trans. Softw. Eng. Methodol. **13**(1), 86–147 (2004)
24. Weyns, D., et al.: Perpetual assurances for self-adaptive systems. In: de Lemos, Rogério, Garlan, David, Ghezzi, Carlo, Giese, Holger (eds.) Software Engineering for Self-Adaptive Systems III. Assurances. LNCS, vol. 9640, pp. 31–63. Springer, Cham (2017). https://doi.org/10.1007/978-3-319-74183-3_2
25. Wirsing, M.: Algebraic specification. In: Handbook of Theoretical Computer Science, vol. B: Formal Models and Sematics, pp. 675–788. Elsevier and MIT Pres, London (1990)